THE SOHO MINT

THE SOHO MINT

& the Industrialization of Money

Richard Doty

National Museum of American History
Smithsonian Institution

in association with

SPINK

and

The British Numismatic Society

British Numismatic Society Special Publication No. 2

LONDON
1998

© Smithsonian Institution 1998

Published by National Museum of American History
Smithsonian Institution

in association with

Spink & Son Ltd, 5, 6 & 7 King Street, St. James's,
London SW1Y 6QS
and
The British Numismatic Society

ISBN 1 902040 03 1

British Library Cataloguing in Publication data
A CIP catalogue record is available from the
British Library

Set by Columns Design Ltd, Reading
Printed in Great Britain at The University Press, Cambridge

CONTENTS

ACKNOWLEDGEMENTS

I began this book in the autumn of 1983; I finished it on the first day of spring 1996. There have been many individuals and institutions which helped me along the way, without whom the book you now hold would not exist. It is now my pleasant obligation to thank them.

In the book's final stages, I must of course mention Douglas Saville of Spink and Graham Dyer of the British Numismatic Society. Mr Dyer's assistance and counsel were also of the highest importance during the research phase of the book.

Most of that research was done in Great Britain during parts of the years 1983, 1985, 1986, 1988, 1989, and 1993. My travel and living expenses were met through the help of several institutions, including the National Endowment for the Humanities, the National Endowment for the Arts, and the American Philosophical Society, as well as the Smithsonian's Research Opportunities Program. In addition, two individuals, Harry W. Bass, Jr. and Joseph R. Lasser generously assisted with financial help for the last, most critical stage of the British research. I am also most grateful for the understanding and financial underpinning of my two employers over the years, the American Numismatic Society and the Smithsonian Institution, for continuing my salary during my frequent-if-necessary absences.

I owe deep debts to past and present archivists and staff at the Birmingham Central Library, among them Philippa Bassett, John Davies, Judy Dennison, Nicholas Kingsley, Rachel Strain, Fiona Tait, and Christopher Upton. They went far beyond the call of duty, and this book is as much their accomplishment as it is mine. Two individuals at Soho House, Rita McLean and Valerie Loggie, were also most helpful on many occasions, especially in securing illustrations for the book. On balance, those curators of Birmingham's story during the Industrial Revolution are among the finest people with whom it has ever been my privilege to work.

I must thank others still. David Symons of the Department of Archaeology and Ethnography, Birmingham Museum and Art Gallery, offered much good advice and substantive help in the selection of illustrations of Soho coinage; so did Virginia Hewitt and Joe Cribb of the Department of Coins and Medals, British Museum. David Vice, of Format of Birmingham Ltd., was most helpful in the early stages of my research, and Professor Eric Robinson of the University of Massachusetts, Boston, offered crucial insight towards the end. Randolph Zander of Alexandria, Virginia was of assistance in many phases of the research, especially in that for the Russian chapter, while Raymond

Williamson of Lynchburg, Virginia offered valuable advice on the chapter on the United States. F. Carl Braun of Port-au-Prince provided welcome insight into Soho's brief connection with the coinage of Haiti. Harrington Manville also deserves my thanks, for his copy of Soho's auction in 1850 made informative if sad reading.

The illustrations for this book came from several sources, and it is my pleasure to acknowledge them now. Many of the coins are reproduced by kind permission of the Trustees of the British Museum. Others are published by permission of the Birmingham Museums and Art Gallery – as are the portraits of Matthew and Matthew Robinson Boulton. Several of the illustrations of early Birmingham are shown by permission of the Birmingham City Archives, Birmingham Central Library; they include the hand-drawn plan of Soho from 1793, which comes from one of Matthew Boulton's notebooks. One of the numismatic illustrations comes from the American Numismatic Society, more come from the Smithsonian Institution Numismatic Collection. Richard A. Margolis, Richard A. Ponterio, Bowers and Merena Galleries, and Craig A. Whitford supplied others still, while some of the materials you see illustrated are my own – for my work on Soho inspired me to collect a few pieces of its past.

I have quoted extensively from the Matthew Boulton Papers, for they give the flavour of that man, his associates, and their era; permission to do so has been graciously granted to me by the Birmingham Assay Office Charitable Trust.

All of the above individuals and groups made possible the completion of this book. But I cheerfully absolve them of all errors, which are my own; and there will certainly be errors in a study such as this, so much of which consists of material never before published, or even examined. But I shall take my chances with the mistakes, in the hope that they will stimulate further discussion and lead to a better truth.

In the final analysis, I wrote this book because of my feeling that the people of 'the Soho' deserved more recognition than they had hitherto received. So I dedicate this work to them, colleagues of the past, and to a colleague and comrade of the present – my wife, Margaret D'Ambrosio. Her counsel and support have enabled me to keep faith with them. FLOREANT URSAE ET FLOREAT SOHO!

Washington, 20 March 1996

NOTE

The alert reader will notice that I only include a footnote citation when I quote directly. This somewhat unorthodox approach was inspired by the nature of the Matthew Boulton Papers (hereafter MBP), and the nature of their use by previous scholars. When writing the first draft of the first chapters, I came to the unwelcome conclusion that, since virtually nothing had previously appeared in print (at least, nothing other than general accounts or minutely detailed ones on specific coinages), I must provide documentation for virtually every sentence on every page, were I to be true to the strictures of correct documentation. This would have resulted in a work several times as extensive as the one you now hold – and it would have resulted in a work which was virtually unreadable. After consultation with Graham Dyer, I decided to limit the footnotes to directly-quoted material. But I shall cheerfully provide detailed documentation to those interested in it; they may write to me in care of the publishers.

INTRODUCTION

Of Matthew Boulton, his Family, and his World

The life of Matthew Boulton … was bound up with the town of Birmingham and in turn influenced greatly its growth and development during the eighteenth century. He was among the earliest of its townsmen to achieve a more than local reputation, and in doing so helped the name and products of the town to become known to the ends of the earth.

H. W. Dickinson, 1936

Birmingham is my native town; I am interested in its manufactures both as a Merchant, & a Manufacturer[.] Few men have endeavoured more than I have to improve those arts on which it depends, and few Men have more at Stake in it than I have. Surely then, no man can doubt of my sincerity or Zeal for its Honour and prosperity—

M. Boulton, 1783

In the nineteenth century, years of the 'Great Man' school of historic interpretation, it was believed that the individual was supreme, shaping the time and place where he lived. In the twentieth century, historic interpretation swung in the opposite direction: now, time and place were considered dominant, the developmental autonomy of the individual secondary, even non-existent.

The relationship between Matthew Boulton and the eighteenth-century town of Birmingham suggests a different and subtler historical model, one in which a man and his world could meet, influence, and alter each other with a unique degree of reciprocity. If Birmingham made Matthew Boulton, it may be truly said that he in turn made it, moulding it, increasing its significance, and ultimately bettering it.

This reciprocity sprang from the fact that the man and the city where he was born, worked, lived, and died were very much alike. Both were enterprising, deeply patriotic, likely to be narrow-minded in some ways, broad-minded in others, but on balance more receptive than hostile to new individuals and ideas; this receptivity would be an essential ingredient in the success of both. I do not suggest that Matthew Boulton could have come from nowhere *but* this Midlands town: there were many other places which produced enterprising spirits during the British Age of Reason – London, Sheffield, Macclesfield, Leeds and Liverpool, Edinburgh and Glasgow come to mind, while even the hamlet of Llanidan in North Wales could produce a Thomas Williams. But there *was* something about Birmingham that brought out the genius in Matthew Boulton; and he in turn brought out the genius in Birmingham.

In the context of total British history, Birmingham was a latecomer, its career fairly brief. Unlike many other places, there was no Roman settlement on the site of the future city, nor does there appear to have been a consistent habitation here through most of the Middle Ages. It never had a mint – which is a fair indicator of a town's importance through most of Britain's history. Considering what Matthew Boulton was about to attempt and achieve, this fact is ironic.

The area's fortunes began to wax with the waning of the Middle Ages. The sparsely inhabited West Midlands, meeting place of the three counties of Warwickshire, Worcestershire, and Staffordshire, began luring immigrants from all three shires, who were attracted there by the iron of the nearby Black Country. A market town known as 'Bermingham' was alive and flourishing by the 1530s. Powered by the establishment of workshops which made cutlery, iron implements, and especially nails, the settlement prospered and its population grew at a satisfying rate.

It added other trades as the years went by. The importation and spread of the screw press in the seventeenth century, as well as the increased availability of copper and brass (from Cheadle in north Staffordshire and other places), opened up an entire new line of products for the enterprising Midlands town, a line centring on buttons. Matthew Boulton would have much experience with the screw press and its products in times to come.

By the latter years of the seventeenth century, various branches of the 'toy' trade were coming to Birmingham, lured there by the enterprise and reputation of its inhabitants and its enviable location relative to raw materials and the rest of the country. The era used the word 'toy' in a much wider sense than we do today: it was then applied to any metallic commodity whose ratio of value to weight was extremely high, a reflection of the amount of work which had gone into its manufacture. So buttons were toys, as were sugar tongs, tweezers, watch chains, buckles, earrings, and other commodities of adornment – goods of fashion without which an increasingly monied public could not be seen. The town got a 'Jewellery Quarter' three hundred years ago; it has since been relocated, but to this day Birmingham is the centre of the British jewelry industry.

As the eighteenth century opened, two new developments were about to be added to those advantages which the town already enjoyed over less favoured localities. One reason why Birmingham had been able to flourish as a centre of production even at a time of meagre communications was that the types of commodities it made were of high value in proportion to their weight. In this circumstance, pack trains (the most common mode of conveyance) could be used to bring the town's products to the national market, and a tidy profit could still be made. This reinforced the advantage of Birmingham's location in an area of few natural obstacles to movement of goods – other than the abysmal roads, left over from medieval times.

When the building of canals began (cautiously in the late seventeenth century, more confidently in the eighteenth) the range of goods which could be easily conveyed in and out of the town expanded dramatically. Iron was one such commodity, and developments in this line gave Birmingham a second, major, advantage over its rivals.

In the first years of the eighteenth century, Abraham Darby of Coalbrookdale, a Shropshire town some twenty miles northwest of Birmingham, succeeded in smelting iron with coke rather than charcoal. Coke was made from coal. Suddenly the two natural resources with which the nearby Black Country was most abundantly endowed, iron and coal, could receive their full utilization in adjacent Birmingham, and the possibilities for prosperity increased. Birmingham was never to be a centre of heavy industry – with one exception, to be examined later. But its hold on the production of ironware was secured early in the eighteenth century and jealously guarded until well into the twentieth.

A final advantage would play a role in the rise of this Midlands town. Because of Birmingham's obscurity through most of the medieval period, it had never attained borough status, did not enjoy actual representation in Parliament, lacked most elements of civil administration. But this also meant that it had no trade guilds or corporations, for these organizations were inextricably linked to the medieval town. So Birmingham's rise, which came so much later than that of many of its neighbours, would prove a positive advantage: there was no watchdog organization to regulate or restrict human enterprise or methods of production. This made for hardships in the case of the individual worker; but it also provided a powerful allure to the enterprising, and a major benefit to the town.

By the 1720s, Birmingham had around twenty thousand inhabitants. One of the newest of them was Matthew Boulton, born there in September of 1728. By the time he departed some eight decades later, his birthplace's population had increased more than fivefold; the new arrival of 1728 would bear responsibility for much of the increase.

Matthew Boulton was born on the third of the month (the fourteenth, according to modern reckoning). He spent his first years in Snow Hill, then located on the outskirts of town, the last child of Matthew and Christiana Bolton, or Boulton. Of his siblings, one brother died in infancy; a second brother survived into the 1770s, but left no mark of his passage. There was also a sister named Anne, who married Zacchaeus Walker and eventually gave birth to a son of the same name. Both father and son will eventually come into our story.

The origins of the Boulton family are obscure, and we can only trace them as far as John Bolton, who married well and carried his new bride from Litchfield to the greener pastures of Birmingham in the first years of the eighteenth century. John had a son named Matthew, and Matthew had four children, as mentioned above. The early fortunes of the Boulton family paralleled those of their adopted town: like it, they were latecomers. The younger Matthew Boulton was keenly aware of his family's recent rise: he procured arms for himself and his descendants and was always deeply concerned that he, and his family, be taken seriously by the class-conscious shire and country in which they resided. He also adopted his grandfather's expedient of marrying well.[1]

Assisted by his wife's inheritance, John Bolton set himself up as a 'toy' maker, eventually leaving his business to his son Matthew. While toys could be made in a variety of metals, it is probable that John concentrated on articles made of steel, for his son would gain a local renown in that material. This would not have greatly limited John's repertoire: deemed a somewhat exotic commodity in the early eighteenth century, steel was employed in company with gold and silver for seals, tweezers, watch chains, snuffboxes, and a multitude of other items. The younger Matthew Boulton would add many products to the metal's portfolio, ranging from coin dies to faceted jewelry.

We know very little about his childhood. What formal schooling he received was obtained in the academy of Reverend John Hausted, who served as chaplain of St John's Chapel in nearby Deritend. We do not know how long he studied under the Reverend, and his education at the academy must have been patchy. To the end of his life, his spelling remained insecure, even as his grammar gradually became that of an eighteenth-century gentleman. His grasp on science and mathematics was firm, and he had some knowledge of French (although not enough to compose his own letters in that language). His knowledge of human nature was profound, and his social graces were notable even in an age which particularly prized such virtues. Most of these attainments were achieved beyond the walls of the Hausted academy, in the world of manufacturing and commerce, a world which Matthew Boulton entered when very young.

There was never any doubt that he would join his father's business. Elder and younger Boulton entered into a formal partnership in 1749, the year the latter attained his majority. The firm he joined would not have impressed us, and it is unlikely to have impressed him. By the middle years of the eighteenth century, Birmingham already counted such giants in the toy trade as John Taylor, against whose flourishing business the Boulton operation was puny indeed. The younger Boulton always called Taylor 'the Esquire', a term of great respect; but he set out to overtake him all the same.

The fledgling entrepreneur decided that a new way of doing business must be devised, one in which 'control could be exercised over the entire industrial process, from the preparation of raw materials to the manufacture and marketing of the widest possible variety of finished articles'.[2] This emphasis on control over all aspects of the process of production would be of benefit to Boulton, and to posterity. It would someday give the products he made a cachet not enjoyed by his competitors. And slightly modified, it would someday lead him to his two most lasting contributions to human history: the unforgeable coin, and the invention of the progressive manufacturing process.

The young man's energy and aspirations soon convinced him that his father's shop in Snow Hill was too small and poorly arranged. Acting on his son's urging, the elder Boulton began looking for a better site, and a candidate soon presented itself. This was Sarehole Mill, in the manor of Yardley. The Boultons bought the mill in 1755, and they added adjacent Sarehole Farm to the holding the following year. But the enlarged site proved unsatisfactory, for reasons we do not know; while the younger Boulton probably rolled sheet metal on the premises for a few years, he continued to look for a better prospect.

He soon found one:

> in 1761–2 Boulton made a second move, this time to Handsworth Heath, where at a place already called Soho, on the Hockley Brook, he was able to acquire

another small mill, similar to Sarehole, with a substantial piece of recently enclosed heathland attached. An additional advantage of this site was that it was served by the turnpike road from Wednesbury, along which coal and other supplies could be brought quickly and cheaply.[3]

This site would someday stand as one of the points of power of the industrial eighteenth century, and it would someday give the world the most famous minting signature in the story of the modern coin. But its origins were modest, its eminence distant.

Matthew Boulton Senior would not be associated with the new enterprise; he died in 1759. In the same year or the one following, his son had to bear a second loss, that of his young wife Mary, whom he had wedded only a few years before. She may have died in childbirth along with the baby, a common enough domestic tragedy in those years; we cannot be certain. But we know that Boulton mourned her deeply.

While personally devastating, the deaths of his father and his first wife helped make Soho possible. His father had left the toy business to him, while the estate of his wife, who was a daughter and co-heiress of the wealthy Luke Robinson of Litchfield, added to his growing resources. Boulton would eventually marry Robinson's surviving daughter and co-heiress, Anne – but not before overcoming the reservations of the other members of the Robinson family.[4] This second marriage took place in the mid-1760s (the exact date has been lost) and produced two children. The daughter was named Anne, after her mother; as a young adult she became an invalid and played no part in the larger story of Soho. The other child was a son, named Matthew Robinson Boulton. Born in 1770, 'Matt' would indeed play a role in the story to come – but it would not be the one that his father might have wished.

In time, his second wife's dowry would infuse the Soho operation with much-needed cash. But at the beginning of the 1760s, the bridegroom must scramble to get his operation running and to keep it so. At first, he seems merely to have pulled down the small mill on the premises (which was about the same size as the one he had left at Sarehole) and erect a new one of the same size in its place. His resources were simply not enough to do more. He must find a monied partner, were he to further the project. He found one, in the person of John Fothergill. Fothergill would one day prove a great disappointment and be bought out; but for now, his money was more important than any other consideration, and he was welcomed. Soho Manufactory began, its foundation taking place in 1764.

It stood on Hockley Brook, which provided water-power. As it expanded over the years, it became one of the marvels of the district. A plan from one of Boulton's notebooks (for the year 1793) is reproduced elsewhere, as are several views of the buildings themselves. More important than the exterior façade was what went on inside. At Soho, Boulton began developing those ideas on manufacturing which he had acquired during the 1750s. Ten years after its foundation, Soho was described as consisting

of four Squares, with Shops, Warehouses, &c. for a Thousand Workmen, who, in a great variety of Branches, excel in their several Departments; not only in the fabrication of Buttons, Buckles, Boxes, Trinkets, &c. in Gold, Silver, and a variety of Compositions; but in many other Arts, long predominant in France, which lose their Reputation on a Comparison with the product of this Place:

And it is by the Natives hereof, or of the parts adjacent, (whose emulation and taste the Proprietors have spared no Care or Expence to excite and improve) that it is brought to its present flourishing State. The number of ingenious mechanical Contrivances they avail themselves of, by the means of Water Mills, much facilitates their Work, and saves a great portion of Time and Labour.

The Manufactory produced outstanding work in several areas:

The Plated-Work has an appearance of solid Silver, more especially when compared with that of any other Manufactory. Their excellent, ornamented Pieces, in Or-Moulu [ormoulu, gilt work featuring ground gold], have been admired by the Nobility and Gentry, not only of this Kingdom, but of all Europe; and are allowed to surpass any thing of the Kind made abroad: And some Articles lately executed in Silver-Plate, shew that Taste and Elegance of Design prevail here in a Superior Degree, and are, with Mechanism and Chymistry, happily united. The environs of this Building was Seven Years ago a barren, uncultivated Heath; tho' it now contains many Houses, and wears the appearance of a populous Country ... [5]

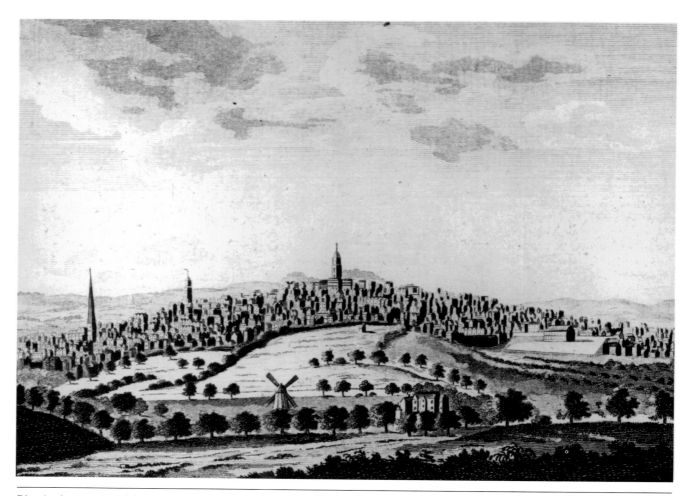

Birmingham in the 1770s. (Courtesy Birmingham City Archives, Birmingham Central Library)

We may pardon this observer for his enthusiasm; he was, after all, Myles Swinney, compiler of a guidebook intended to foment business in the town of Birmingham.

This and later guidebooks give us some of our best data on the growth of Birmingham in the early years of the Industrial Revolution. And it is no coincidence that Soho Manufactory received grateful mention in most of such publications: intimately connected with the town, Boulton's works were one of the sources of its prosperity. Swinney and those who came after chronicled the rise of both.

By 1777, Pearson and Rollason's *Birmingham Directory* was painting the picture of a town in transition, a place of traditional specialties and ones whose introduction was more recent. The authors accorded pride of place to the venerable button industry, but they also described newer crafts, including the manufacture of cast iron goods, papier-mâché, and steam engines. In connection with the latter enterprise, Boulton and Soho received their due, for

> the mechanical genius of this place gave existence to an improvement in the construction of the common Steam Engine [by which the authors probably meant James Watt's separate condenser], which promised to exceed, in private benefit and public utility, every other part of the trade in which the proprietors hereof were engaged.

Boulton's works at Soho currently occupied between four and five thousand square yards, 'and can employ upwards of 700 people within its walls'.[6] This choice of wording suggests that it usually got by with fewer hands, something borne out by Boulton's correspondence – and by the fortunes of the future Soho Mint, which would be rather more seasonable than its proprietor and his artisans might have wished.

Pearson and Rollason put Birmingham's population at around forty thousand, dwelling in seven thousand houses. These figures suggest a satisfying increase over those which we have for the 1720s; they also suggest that the Industrial Revolution had not as yet begun in a significant way.

By the middle of the 1780s, the city's growth was becoming more dramatic, and we may cautiously guess that the 'take-off' point in Birmingham's development occurred sometime around 1780 or slightly before. One contemporary source put its population at 55,750 in 1779 (including adjacent Deritend), and, while it was listed as 52,250 by another writer in 1785 (presumably excluding Deritend), it is evident that something important was now taking place. We lack accurate population data for the next dozen years; but by the end of the eighteenth century, one source was estimating a figure of sixty thousand, while another, working at the beginning of the nineteenth century, put it at nearly seventy thousand, including Deritend. By the year of Matthew Boulton's death, the city contained around eighty thousand inhabitants; and by the year of the death of the firm he founded, the figure stood near a quarter of a million.

What was Birmingham like, two hundred years ago? It is the nature of any locality to be alternately praised and maligned, depending on the view and agenda of the observer, and Birmingham was, and is, no exception. While everyone would agree that the place was a hub of activity, unanimity ended there. Some praised its salubrity, a gentleman named Richard Jabet speaking for all of them:

Matthew Boulton in the 1770s, by J. S. C. Schaak. (Courtesy Birmingham Museums and Art Gallery)

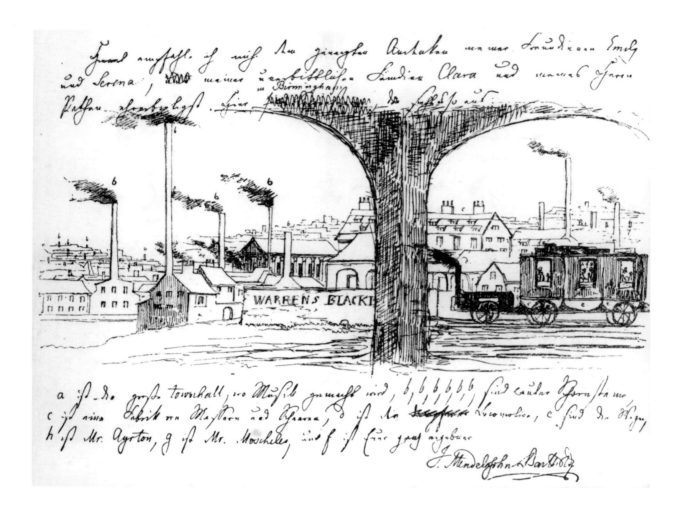

Birmingham in the 1840s, from a drawing by Felix Mendelssohn. (Courtesy Birmingham City Archives, Birmingham Central Library)

> As no part of the town lies flat, the showers promote both cleanliness and health, by removing obstructions … in fact, no place can be more highly favoured with four of the greatest benefits attending human existence: water, air, the sun, and a situation free from damps.[7]

Others were less lavish in their praises, rather more concerned with the town's human element than with its geographic setting. Publishing in 1797, Grafton and Reddell bluntly observed that

> Birmingham is not a place a gentleman would chuse to make a residence. Its continual noise and smoke prevent it from being desirable in that respect. Mr Hutton observes, that gentlemen as well as buttons have been stamped here, but like them, when finished, are moved off.

But the town had an allure all the same, one unrelated to its physical characteristics. The authors had known

> the man of opulence [to] direct his gilt chariot out of Birmingham, who first approached her an helpless orphan in rags. Many estates have been struck out of the anvil, valuable possessions raised by the tongs, and superb houses, in a two-fold sense, erected by the trowel.[8]

Birmingham had the rough edges common to towns on the move from the dawn of urbanization to the present day. But the late eighteenth and early nineteenth centuries witnessed intellectual and social amelioration as well as business growth, and the spiritual dimensions of Birmingham began to catch up with its economic attainments. In 1800, two newspapers were published there, the venerable *Aris's Birmingham Gazette* and the more recent *Chronicle, and Warwickshire and Staffordshire Advertiser*, whose publisher was Myles Swinney, whom we have already met. Two other journals would follow over the next two decades.

Libraries provided other sources of the printed word. The town's first public library was instituted in 1779; thirty years later, it boasted more than fourteen thousand titles, to which some five hundred dues-paying members had access. A second facility was set up in 1796, and there were also medical and law libraries, as well as purely private collections.

After two false starts, an elegant theatre was erected in New Street in 1774. One of its ardent supporters was Samuel Aris, who received a silver theatre pass in recognition of his largesse. The building cost nearly six thousand pounds to erect, and, when it was burned down in 1791, it was promptly rebuilt on a yet more opulent scale.

So the life of the mind was beginning to match pace with the life of the pocketbook. Yet much remained to be done. At the turn of the nineteenth century, there was still no central, all-embracing public market, although there was currently talk of pulling down a slum called the Shambles and putting one there. And the prison situation was a scandal, even by the easygoing standards of the day:

> There are two prisons, one at the bottom of Peck-lane, dark, narrow, and unwholesome within, crowded with dwellings, filth and distress without, by which means the circulation of air is prevented. It is kept by Mr. John Summer. The other [prison] is in Deritend, and is very little better than the former, kept by Mr. William Tart.—*Both are licensed public houses.*— … no [other] town so populous is so wretchedly provided with this necessary evil … [9]

Some of Birmingham's problems originated in its lack of a charter and its correspondingly weak government, signally lacking in coercive powers. There was recognition at the time that the absence of a written constitution was one of the keys to Birmingham's economic success, Ward considering it among the site's most favourable attributes, 'as thereby the attention of the industrious manufacturer can seldom be called off by the interference of party interest'.[10] But rudimentary government could also prove a liability in times of social, political, or economic distress. As early as 1789, Matthew Boulton was concerned about the large number of prostitutes and petty criminals on the streets of the city and the small number of police available to deal with them. Worse, the police were available only during the hours of daylight: night constables were an impossibility because the town lacked the authority to raise funds to hire them. In response, the busy industrialist and his partner Watt served on an *ad hoc* committee set up to deal with the situation; by the end of the year, a subscription had been devised and circulated to set up a *private* night police. Two years later, destructive riots would underscore the need for setting up a real, effective public authority.[11] But little was done, or yet could be done.

Local government approached the farcical. As late as 1830, the town's officers were chosen, not by its inhabitants but by a 'Court Leet' held by the Lord of the Manor of Birmingham. These functionaries consisted of a High Bailiff, a Low Bailiff, two Constables, a Headborough, two High Tasters and two Low Tasters, two Affeesors, and two Leather Sealers. By custom, the High Bailiff had to be a member of the Church of England, while the office of Low Bailiff was reserved to religious dissenters, of which there were a large number within the confines of the town. The High Bailiff convened and conducted the public meetings of the town. The Affeesors assessed and ratified penalties and fines due to the Lord of the Manor, while the High and Low Tasters and the Leather Sealer oversaw quality control over victuals and, of course, leather. What policing got done was the responsibility of the Constables and their assistant, the Headborough, assisted by magistrates who sat twice weekly to hear cases. All of this had been inherited from the Middle Ages, and the best that can be said for it is that it had little noticeable effect on the daily lives of the inhabitants.

By the turn of the nineteenth century, Matthew Boulton was among the best-known of the city's residents – industrialist, reformer, sometime sheriff of the County of Warwickshire (in which guise he once raided a nest of counterfeiters, who had had the effrontery to forge *his coinage*), and keeper of the world-famous Soho Manufactory. The latter may have been even better-known than its creator, appearing in more than a dozen prints, gracing at least two trade tokens, and forming the central design on a number of other products, ranging from snuffboxes to plates. But it reached an apotheosis of sorts in a poem reproduced in the second edition of Grafton and Reddell's guide to the city. This work was the product of J. Morfitt, Esq., and it was written in 1794. A few lines will do:

> Behold yon MANSION flank'd by crouding trees,
> Grace the green slope, and court the southern breeze.
> Genius and Worth with BOULTON there reside,
> BOULTON, of arts the patron and the pride!
> Commerce with rev'rence at thy name shall bow,
> Thou fam'd creator of the fam'd SOHO!

Morfitt later decided to abandon poetry for the law.[12] The Muse thanks him.

Morfitt's lines described the way the eighteenth century remembered Matthew Boulton, as the creator of a famous artistic and industrial landmark; when the twentieth century remembers him at all, it is as a shadowy figure who had something to do with a much more famous man – James Watt, inventor of the steam engine. This picture is incorrect on two points. First, James Watt did not 'invent' the steam engine; he radically improved its ratio of fuel consumption to power. And he did not outshine Matthew Boulton at the time; were it not for the financial and moral support of the latter man, James Watt and not Matthew Boulton would have merited the footnote. Simply put, Watt could not have succeeded without Boulton, whereas Boulton had been doing quite well without Watt. But the two men met, became friends and partners, and changed history. And it may say something about the nature of Matthew Boulton to observe that, even when Watt began receiving accolades which rightfully

Soho in 1798. (Courtesy Birmingham Museums and Art Gallery)

belonged to both men or to Boulton alone, he remained supportive, enthusiastic, and honestly delighted with his associate's good fortune and fame. One could ask no better partner than that.

The connection between Matthew Boulton and James Watt has been related many times by many people – including Watt himself, in a brief 'Memoir' written less than a month after Boulton's death. It began in part as a response to the needs of Soho Manufactory. Much of Soho's activity was powered by water. Boulton's sole source of water-power was Hockley Brook, whose flow was unreliable during much of the year. Around the beginning of 1766, the industrialist thought of introducing a steam engine to lift water from the tail race of his mill back up to Hockley Pool, thereby ensuring a regular source of power regardless of season.[13] But he must decide what type of steam engine would be wanted for the project, for there were two in current use – the Savery engine, which raised water by direct steam pressure on the water, and the Newcomen engine, which raised water by means of a vacuum pump. Boulton leaned toward the Savery engine, and he sent a model of the proposed mechanism to Benjamin Franklin (then resident in London, representing several North American colonies), soliciting the great man's comments. Franklin was supportive but could offer little practical advice; Boulton tinkered with his model through the remainder of the year, but to no great satisfaction. Then a colleague named John Roebuck made a suggestion and opened a door.

Roebuck was one of the early captains of Scottish industry. He brought sulphuric acid from a laboratory curiosity to a viable industrial medium, and he was very active in gold and silver refining (in partnership with Samuel Garbett) and ironworking (also with Garbett: Roebuck was one of the founders of the Carron Works, the first of its kind in Scotland). He turned his gaze to coal, leased mines at Bo'ness, Linlithgowshire, and then attempted to interest his friend Boulton in becoming a partner. The latter demurred – wisely, as it happened, for Roebuck was over-extending his resources and would soon see his business empire come crashing down. But in the midst of the correspondence, Roebuck mentioned that he had met a young maker of mathematical instruments in Glasgow, who, in addition to his chosen profession, had suggested some useful improvements to the Newcomen engine. The young man's name was James Watt.

Watt had just turned thirty, and his career thus far had been promising rather than solidly successful. Always in poor health, he was currently supporting his sizable family as an instrument-maker, investing what energy he had left into the problem of extracting more power from the Newcomen engine. He hit upon the idea of a separate condenser somewhat by accident, but this apparatus (which got around the alternate heating and cooling of the cylinder and thus saved between two-thirds and three-quarters of the coal required by the simple Newcomen machine) would one day render steam engines cheap enough to compete with water, animal, and manual power, would underpin the Industrial Revolution.[14]

Watt explained his invention to Dr Roebuck, who immediately saw its possibilities for his water-filled coal mines at Bo'ness. He invited Watt into a limited partnership to exploit the idea; he also cleared the inventor's considerable debts. Under Roebuck's encouragement, the diffident Watt continued to improve and refine his invention, and Roebuck eventually helped him secure a patent for it (in exchange for which support Watt accorded Roebuck a two-thirds share of future profits).

The patent was granted in January 1769, but the process of securing it had begun the previous summer, when Roebuck had sent Watt to London to guide the idea through the bureaucratic maze. During his return north, Watt detoured to Soho. He had visited the Manufactory some fifteen months previously, but Matthew Boulton had then been absent. Now, at the end of August 1768, the two men met for the first time.

They formed an instant bond. Each supplied what the other lacked. Boulton's natural ebullience made up for Watt's pessimism and diffidence. Watt's brilliance augmented Boulton's competence, and the possibility of assisting this shy genius, of bringing him beyond himself for his own and the common good, appears to have spoken to a deeply-rooted need, a need which also goes far toward explaining Boulton's later and far less successful association with another diffident genius, Jean-Pierre Droz. In sum, the two men became partners on the day they met; it only remained for them to do so in a legal sense.

That occurrence was helped along by John Roebuck, who had overextended himself in many directions, including largesse to an impecunious

Messrs Boulton and Watt, from a medal of 1871. (Author's collection)

Scottish inventor. The year 1772 was one of widespread business panic, and Roebuck found himself in extreme difficulties by that summer. He owed everyone – including Matthew Boulton, to whom he was indebted for £1,200. Rather than asking for the money (which he knew Roebuck was in no condition to pay), Boulton offered to cancel the debt in exchange for Roebuck's interest in James Watt's patent. Since Watt's engine was currently failing to live up to its earlier hopes (and since he lacked the wherewithal to advance its fortunes in any case), Roebuck agreed to the transfer. The deal was concluded in May 1773.

Watt and Boulton were now partners of sorts; but it remained for Boulton to get his new associate from Scotland to the Midlands, and to work at Soho. The way was paved by a tragedy: on 24 September 1773, Watt's first wife Margaret died in childbirth. He was away from home at the time of her death, surveying the route of the future Caledonian Canal. When he learned of the event, the distracted husband was ready to abandon the survey, to abandon Scotland as well. He was ready to make a fresh start, at Soho.

He arrived there on the last day of May 1774. He was given rooms by Boulton in the latter's old quarters in Newhall Walk – not far from today's Birmingham Science Museum, where one of his engines reposes. His first task was to carry his improvements from the experimental to the practical stage. His partner's first task was to get the patent (which had already run through more than a third of its allotted term) extended. Boulton foresaw much additional time and money spent on preliminary work, and there would simply not be enough years left to make expenses, let alone turn a profit. Despite the opposition of men like Edmund Burke (who was opposed to all monopolies, including this one), the two associates managed to secure passage of an Act of Parliament (15 Geo. 3, Cap. 61) which prolonged the patent until 1800 and extended its coverage to Scotland, which had been exempt from the original document of 1769. The King assented to the extension on 22 May 1775; ten days later, Matthew Boulton and James Watt entered into a formal partnership which Dickinson called 'perhaps the most momentous in industrial history'.[15]

It was drawn up on the first of June, would run conterminously with the Act of Parliament. Watt assigned Boulton a two-thirds share of the patent, while Boulton agreed to pay the expenses already incurred (including legal fees), underwrite Watt's continuing experiments, and give him £300 annually for his drawings, directions, and surveys. Any profits were to be divided between the two partners, Boulton receiving two-thirds and Watt one-third. Thus was born Boulton & Watt, the direct ancestor of Boulton, Watt & Company, manufacturer of steam engines, mints – and an industrial coinage to fuel an Industrial Revolution.

Historians have often overlooked the connection between coinage and industrialization, while numismatists have generally been unaware of it. But there was such a link, and it posed one of the greatest early challenges faced by the makers of the Industrial Revolution. Put most simply, the heart of the new economic ways involved *factories* of one sort or another – groupings of people performing a strictly limited number of productive tasks in buildings specifically constructed to or renovated for the purpose. These factories would be located in consideration of availability of water, fuel, and access to markets, not in recognition of earlier determinants of population settlement.

In other words, a factory certainly could go up in an already-populated centre; but if the new requirements were lacking there, it would go up somewhere else. That is why the eighteenth and nineteenth centuries saw a shift of population from older, southern places without new prospects, such as Bristol, to newer, northern ones with new prospects, such as Hull and Manchester.

From the beginning, the aspiring millowner discovered that he could only attract workers in a particular way, and with a particular commodity. And the aspiring millhand found that he could only survive in a new area full of strangers if he received a particular commodity. The commodity in both cases was *coin*: the Industrial Revolution was based on the payment of regular wages, in the form of coinage. And since wages were uniformly low (the millhand might expect to receive six or seven shillings per week, if he were lucky), what the Industrial Revolution initially and most urgently required was *a large number of low-denomination coins*. Without that money, wages could not be paid. And without monetary wages, only a fool would leave the clear air of Norfolk for the sooty air of Leeds, or Manchester, or Hull – or Birmingham.

The dimensions of the problem: a genuine copper halfpenny (1770, top) and a typical Birmingham counterfeit (1775, bottom); the fake weighs precisely half as much as the genuine coin – the difference representing profit to the forger. (National Numismatic Collection, Smithsonian Institution)

As matters stood, there was little small change in circulation, the Royal Mint having ceased copper coinage just as the Industrial Revolution was getting under way, while the last silver struck in quantity dated back to the 1750s. What predominated on the lowest end of the monetary scale, and what our worker might expect to find in his pay packet, was a motley assemblage of counterfeit halfpence and farthings (Boulton estimated that two out of every three coppers were suspect; a slightly later observer put the figure at an astounding ninety-eight percent), augmented in and after 1787 by private copper tokens – the more successful of which were also counterfeited. The centre of counterfeit production lay in Birmingham, just a mile or so from Soho – to the continued annoyance of Matthew Boulton.

We shall see how he addressed the problem, created the first industrial money. But I would suggest a few preliminary observations, for they say a good deal about Matthew Boulton, and something about his world. The first is that, while we see the connection between industrialization and the mandatory expansion of the coinage supply, it is by no means certain that Matthew Boulton saw it. He wanted to create more coinage, to be sure, and he extolled the virtues of his new machinery for that very purpose. But he saw an expansion of output always and only in conjunction with an improvement in quality. When more and better coins were created, they would inevitably drive poorer ones out of commerce – a classic reversal of Gresham's Law, which says that bad money drives out good.

Steam power could create more and better coins, but it could also create them more cheaply. The argument of lower cost bulked quite as large with him as the attraction of greater numbers. And to these still-abstract considerations were added others, more concrete, more personal. The same social conscience which found Boulton serving on a committee on crime and social problems late in 1789 (wherein he recommended putting prisoners in individual cells rather than the pestiferous common cells then universal) saw him recommending a better coinage to a friend early in 1787 on the basis that it might be 'the means of saving many [an] unfortunate Man from an ignominious death'.[16] And the same civic pride which led him to serve his town in a number of offices over the years led him to an interesting idea. If Birmingham were rightly regarded as the home of counterfeit coins (and even Boulton would admit that that was so), let him lead the way in proving what the ingenuity of one Midlands inhabitant could do to eradicate the problem. Let him create a new, more beautiful coin which could not be forged; and the bad repute in which his town now stood would disappear overnight. It would then be seen in its true light, as he had always seen it. Lives would be spared, reputations salvaged; and an Industrial Revolution would proceed.

The pursuit of this dream, for Britain and then for the world, would occupy the final decades of Matthew Boulton's life, and it stands at the heart of this book. But it would be deferred: during the first ten years of the partnership, Matthew Boulton had other, far more pressing considerations in mind. He must keep his associate at work until the new steam engine had been perfected. Then he must interest others in it, defend its secrets from others still.

The first engine built by the firm went into service at Bloomfield Colliery, in Staffordshire, on 8 March 1776. Typically, Watt had counselled caution, more experimentation, while his partner wanted the biggest engine possible, for purposes of show. To Watt's immense relief, the Bloomfield engine was successful, and orders began coming in.

The activities of these first Boulton & Watt engines were highly restricted. They were put to work as replacements for the Newcomen machine, and they did what it had previously done, only more cheaply. They caught the popular imagination – nowhere more than in Cornwall, which had particular problems (deep mines and an absence of nearby coal) which taxed the Newcomen engine to the limits of its abilities and beyond. Watt's engine had greater pumping force, which meant that it could work more deeply, while its miserly consumption of coal was more appealing still. The Duchy's first Boulton & Watt engine went to work at Wheal Busy, in September 1777, James Watt officiating. The popularity of the new power source in Cornwall would eventually lead Matthew Boulton into a financial interest in the copper mines it served, and that, in turn, would help turn him in the direction of a copper coinage for Britain.

Success in Cornwall should not obscure the fact that, well into the 1780s, Boulton & Watt remained on somewhat shaky ground. The uses of Watt's improved engine were limited, for the vertical motion of the piston lent itself to pumping water but little else. And Matthew Boulton's resources were hardly unlimited (especially as he dabbled in such expensive failures as Francis Eginton's 'mechanical paintings'). But Watt continued to tinker, and he eventually devised two improvements, one of which allowed the creation of rotary motion (by means of the famous 'Sun-and-Planet' wheel, patented in 1781) and parallel motion (patented three years later). With these improvements, the utility of the steam engine broadened from the specialized to the universal, and the Industrial Revolution received its primary source of power. On a more immediate level, Boulton & Watt moved out of the red and into the black; and there it remained, through the remainder of the partnership.

By the middle 1790s, James Watt had amassed a fortune and had therefore withdrawn from most aspects of the business. By that time, too, the sons of the two partners were being introduced into it, an event marked by the organization of Soho Foundry. Matthew Boulton and James Watt extended the capital for this new enterprise, which was intended to put an end to the earlier necessity of subcontracting for engine parts: henceforth, all elements would be manufactured under close control in one place. The site in question covered more than eighteen acres of land in Smethwick, about a mile from Soho Manufactory; its purchase was completed on 27 August 1795. Building was undertaken almost immediately and carried out very rapidly, the new enterprise being formally dedicated at a lavish banquet held on 30 January 1796, with Matthew Boulton presiding.

Soho Foundry was a subsidiary of a new organization set up in 1794, called Boulton, Watt & Sons. It initially consisted of five people – Matthew Boulton, James Watt, Matthew Robinson Boulton, James Watt, Jr., and Gregory Watt. The partnership called Boulton & Watt was allowed to run its full term, but any new business was henceforth shunted to the new organization, and to Soho Foundry. In 1800, James Watt's share of the business was divided between his two sons and the main organization became known as Boulton, Watt & Company – which is the name I have generally used for purposes of clarity. Gregory Watt died of tuberculosis in October 1804, his share reverting to his brother. And after the elder Boulton passed on in August 1809, there remained only two parties with interests in Boulton, Watt & Company and Soho Foundry: Matthew Robinson Boulton and James Watt, Jr. It is time briefly to examine these men.

St Mary's Church, Handsworth, where Matthew Boulton and James Watt lie buried.

Of the two, James Watt, Jr. was the more enterprising and in some ways the more interesting. Born of his father's second marriage in 1769, he happened to be studying in Paris at the time of the outbreak of the French Revolution. The young man sympathized with that upheaval in its early stages (to the great anxiety of his father), but denounced its later course and was in turn denounced by Robespierre, obliged to flee the country. He returned to England via a roundabout route in 1794. And later that year, he was given his partnership, in part to settle him down.

He did settle down. By the time of Matthew Boulton's death, young Watt was becoming passionately interested in a new application of his father's motive force, the steamboat. He gave much assistance to Robert Fulton, including the steam engine by which Fulton's *Clermont* was able to make the first successful steam-powered ascent and descent of the Hudson River in 1807. A decade later, Watt bought the *Caledonia*, fitted her with new engines, and sailed her to Holland and up the Rhine, the first man to do so by steam. He remained deeply involved in the problems and prospects of steam navigation through the 1820s and 1830s, and when his partnership with Matthew Robinson Boulton was dissolved in 1840, James Watt, Jr. assumed sole responsibility for Soho Foundry. He died, unmarried, on 2 June 1848.

His partner is the less interesting but more important of the two successors: Matthew Robinson Boulton inherited Soho Manufactory, as well as primary responsibility for his father's coinage enterprises, including Soho Mint. But he always manifested a curious lack of enterprise: James Watt. Jr. was the prime mover in securing work for Soho Foundry, and he functioned in the same capacity for enterprises which were more strictly the affair of his partner. The younger Boulton's business posture was essentially passive, a stance adopted in reaction or response to opportunities which others had suggested. This attitude extended well beyond commerce. On 13 November 1809, a former Soho employee now resident at the Royal Mint wrote him that a seat in Parliament was his for the asking. But Boulton could not be bothered to reply (even though he had no particular business then at hand); and the opportunity slipped away.

I find Matthew Robinson Boulton unappealing – especially in comparison with his father. His lack of enterprise, lack of social conscience, lack of vision, and insistence on personal comfort all contrasted with the characteristics of his father. But I can also see the origins of some of the younger Boulton's flaws. Matthew Boulton was an altogether admirable man – and neither he nor others ever let Matthew Robinson Boulton forget it.

The earliest suggestions of a problem date from the late 1780s, when Matt was in Paris. His father sent him well-meaning letters full of good advice: clean up your penmanship; apply yourself to your studies, and to my business; don't go promenading about Paris except in the company of your tutor; clean up your grammar: your last letter had a number of errors. The elder Boulton knew he was being harsh, and explained his reasons:

> '*Whom the Lord Loveth he chastiseth* and on this principle only, I speak *truth*, although it may not be pleasant to you nor me in y*e* present case[.] Yet I must do my duty towards you, or I shall not do it to my own conscience. I therefore hope you'l do your duty to your self or you cannot do it to me. There is nothing on Earth I so much wish for, as to make you a *Man*, a good Man, a Usefull Man, & consequently a happy Man[.][17]

Matthew Robinson
Boulton in the 1820s, by
Sir Thomas Lawrence and
Martin Archer Shee.
(Courtesy Birmingham
Museums and Art Gallery)

We may imagine things from the perspective of both men. The son was scarcely seventeen years of age: the unsolicited advice may have been sound, but it remained a heavy burden for young shoulders to bear. And the father had concerns of his own. Matt's mother had died some four years previously, in an accident never fully explained. Matthew Boulton must now act as father *and* mother to two adolescents, and his concerns over his business enterprises increased the natural unease of a single parent. As he observed to the young man's tutor in Paris, Matt *had* to be kept busy:

> Youl perhaps say I have given him too much to do but I say it is better that he had too much than too little to do for it is a settled Maxim with me that to prevent a Young Man from doing what he ought not to do He should be constantly employd in the persuit of knowledge or something that is laudable & above all things pray endeavour on all occasions to cultivate in his Heart & Mind principles of honour without which he neither can be a good Man[,] a happy man or a brave one[.] But I must & do object against his going to the Comedy or any other places of publick dissipation unless you are with him. He is virtuous & good at present, & I wish to preserve him so, untill his reason is more mature & thereby he becomes more powerfully shielded[.][18]

All of this advice went for naught. The harder Matthew Boulton pushed, the more he advised, the less his son moved. The more he complained about his son's handwriting, the less readable it became. Stubbornness and its twin, passivity, formed parts of Matthew Robinson Boulton's character from early times; to them were added, must have been added, resentment. And Matthew Boulton would one day sum up the whole of his son's attitude in one word: ingratitude.

That would come at the beginning of 1805. Boulton's health was failing, and his solicitor Ambrose Weston was gently attempting to persuade him to incorporate Matt in his plans for the upcoming British coinage. Boulton replied to Weston's letter (which Weston had suggested should be burned once read), with a cry from the heart:

> In regard to a delicate point you mentioned I assure you upon my honor & Conscience that I woud *now* make him a free Gift of all my Trades, my lands & all I possess in the World, minus a mere pittance such only as is necessary to purchase the necessaries of Life, provided he could be induced to accept it with a *real grateful heart* but the Ethiopians Skin, or Leopards Spots, are not to be changed as I am convinced by every days experience[.][19]

By the spring of the following year, Boulton was changing his will, ensuring that his daughter would be handsomely supported, regardless of his son's disposition toward her, or indeed toward him. The breach between father and son never healed.[20]

Mistrust and ingratitude notwithstanding, the elder man's grip on Soho's affairs grew increasingly slack in the years before his death. When the latter occurred in August 1809, the younger man accorded him the dignity of an elegant funeral, commemorated on copper medals struck for the occasion and given to all who had worked at Soho.

Their designs were simple, even spare, and one might see this as a reflection of the son's parsimony, his continuing rancour. But it is more probable that the designs were simple because there was so little time to prepare them,

A funeral medal given to each Soho employee, 1809. (Author's collection)

in the wake of larger concerns. And in any case, a plain statement, in copper, summed up Matthew Boulton's work in a manner which would have satisfied him, and which pleases us. Let us turn to that work, and to the source of the medal: it is time to visit Soho Mint.

NOTES

1 For Matthew Boulton's antecedents and early career, I am following the account given by Dickinson in *Matthew Boulton* [1936]. The reader is warned, however, that Samuel Smiles (*Lives of Boulton and Watt* [1865]) gave a different version of the early history of the Boulton family. He had John Bolton coming from Northamptonshire and settling at Litchfield, marrying his heiress there, losing most of her money, then sending Matthew Boulton the Elder on to Birmingham to retrieve the family fortunes. I favour Dickinson's version of the story; significantly, while both biographers examined the Matthew Boulton Papers, neither emerged with a remotely accurate conception of Boulton's impact on the main subject of *this* book, the industrialization of money.

2 Victor Skipp, *A History of Greater Birmingham – down to 1830* (Birmingham, 1987), pp. 56–7.

3 Skipp, p. 57.

4 H. W. Dickinson opined that the family was against the match not because they feared that Boulton was a fortune-hunter (and there is no real evidence that he was), 'but because marriage with a deceased wife's sister was contrary to the Table of Kindred and Affinity in our Prayer Book [Book of Common Prayer], and was considered morally wrong in the eyes of ninety-nine persons out of a hundred at that date' (Dickinson, *Matthew Boulton*, p. 35).

5 [Myles Swinney], *The New Birmingham Directory, and Gentleman and Tradesman's Compleat Memorandum Book … Embellished with a North East View of the Soho, Neatly Engraved on Copper* (Birmingham [1774]), unnumbered pp. 8–9. In passing, the frontispiece may contain the earliest surviving view of Soho Manufactory. I have not reproduced it here because the Birmingham Reference Library's copy of the book was inexpertly bound long ago, and the engraving was damaged at that time.

6 [Ann Pearson and James Rollason], *The Birmingham Directory; or, Merchant and Tradesman's Useful Companion …* (Birmingham, 1777), pp. xxxiii–xxxv. The fact that one of the partners in the compilation and dissemination of this guide was a woman is worth noting.

7 [Richard Jabet], *A Concise History of Birmingham …* , 4th edition (Birmingham, 1808), pp. 2–3. This opinion had first been advanced by the eminent Mr Hutton in his *History of Birmingham* (1781), and it was regularly, and enthusiastically, repeated by the town's adherents over the next half century.

8 [Grafton and Reddell], *A Brief History of Birmingham* (London, 1797), p. 4.

9 [Grafton and Reddell], *A Brief History of Birmingham, and Guide to Strangers …* , 2nd edition (Birmingham [1802]), pp. 44–6; emphasis mine.

10 [J. Ward], *The New Birmingham Directory, for the Year 1798 …* (Birmingham, 1798), p. 6.

11 Occurring between 14 and 17 July 1791, the riots destroyed much of the city and adjacent areas, at a cost in excess of £60,000. They also scarred its mentality (and shook its self-esteem) well into the 1830s, if not later.

12 [Grafton and Reddell], 2nd edition, p. xx.

13 While it was first discussed in 1766, the steam-assisted water mill would languish on the drawing board for another twenty years, Boulton meanwhile coping as best he could. His completion of the pumping engine from Hockley Brook to Hockley Pool was probably related to his first coining order for the East India Company – for he would now need to

roll a good deal of copper in a fairly short time, and he must be able to work his rolling mill consistently, regardless of the vagaries of Hockley Brook.

14 It must again be stressed that what Watt had invented represented a potential rather than an actual power source. Nothing could come of it until a way were found of widely producing and marketing the improvement. And that was where Matthew Boulton would enter the picture.

15 Dickinson, p. 86.

16 MBP148, [Private] Letter Book O: Matthew Boulton to Samuel Garbett, 21 April 1787.

17 MBP148, Matthew Boulton to Matthew Robinson Boulton, 19 December 1787; spellings and emphasis in original.

18 MBP148, Matthew Boulton to M. Manuel, undated but likely mid-December 1787; spellings and punctuation in original. The letter was inspired by fears that the tender-hearted tutor would not force his charge to learn French with sufficient zeal. No reply has survived.

19 MBP363, Weston, Ambrose, post-1799 (box 2): Matthew Boulton to Ambrose Weston, 27 January 1805; emphasis and punctuation in original.

20 A small point, but a telling one: Matthew Boulton called his son Matt. *He* called himself Robinson, and virtually all of his correspondence bore the signature 'M. Robinson Boulton'.

CHAPTER 1

Soho's Story

There were three Soho Mints. Two were created by the genius and persistence of Matthew Boulton. The third was created by his son, but it grew directly out of the earlier two.

The first Soho Mint was largely constructed during 1788 and 1789; when numismatists speak of Matthew Boulton's contributions to the history of coinage, they are usually thinking of this facility. But its creator was never totally satisfied with it, because it never worked as he desired (or as he claimed); under the strains of his first British copper coinage, he would pull it down and build anew.

Work on its successor began in the spring of 1798 and was completed a year later. For the next decade, this second facility would dominate minting in the Midlands, and indeed the world. It would be responsible for Boulton's later British copper coinages and his 'resurrected' dollars for the Banks of England and Ireland. Built on a new principle of progressive manufacturing, Soho II was on the cutting edge of current production technology and would serve as the model for the mints Boulton, Watt & Company created and sent around the world. But its glory days scarcely extended beyond the life of its creator: moneying ceased after mid-1813 and was not resumed for nearly a decade. Meanwhile, Matthew Robinson Boulton searched for a buyer. He finally succeeded, and the second Soho Mint was dismantled, crated, and shipped halfway around the globe, to Bombay; its resurrection there is told elsewhere.

That left Soho without a Soho Mint. We can only imagine the younger Boulton's annoyance upon concluding, even before his father's mint was safely out the door, that he would apparently do well to reconstruct what he had finally succeeded in dismantling. And we have no way of imagining his anger when the lucrative business possibilities which had tempted him to rebuild suddenly turned sour. But by then, he had a mint of sorts, the third and final one to be erected on the Soho site.

It remains the least-known of the three. While the actual machinery had been constructed by early 1826, its owner reacted to his economic reversal by refusing to finish it for some years. It would not be fully operable until the summer of 1831. Moreover, it was a much smaller establishment than either of its predecessors. While Matthew Boulton had prided himself on eight coining presses, his son would get by with four, with the other machinery reduced in proportion. But while it may have been modest, this third Soho Mint made money (in both senses of the word) for a quarter of a century, striking coins and tokens for places scattered from Quebec to Singapore. And when it had finally ceased to work for the Boultons, it too was dismantled, removed, and set up elsewhere. But the final venue of this final Soho Mint was much closer to home than Bombay. It was purchased at auction in the spring of 1850 by an enterprising firm named Ralph Heaton & Sons, moved a few hundred yards from Soho to Birmingham proper – and resurrected as the Heaton Mint. Another circle had been closed: among the activities of the first Ralph Heaton had been the supply of dies to Matthew Boulton back in the 1790s.

Anyone who came to Soho during its palmy days realized that he was seeing something important, something epochal; a measure of this feeling was captured in the descriptive accounts left by travellers of the day. In this, the first and second Soho Mints followed in the wake of the original Soho Manufactory, which had been inspiring fulsome accounts (some of them helped along by the proprietor) since the mid-1760s. But the Soho Mint *was* special, and while outsiders may have felt something of its aura, those on the inside felt it far more.

Their awareness took various forms. One of those who worked at the mint in its earliest days simply called it 'the Soho', underscoring its uniqueness. Others vied for credit for inventing the special processes and parts which made the mint the world's first industrial coiner. Indeed, much of what we know today about who invented what has only survived because one of Matthew Boulton's engineers proposed to claim undue portions of the credit for himself in the *Monthly Magazine*, and his erstwhile shop-mates demanded a meeting to discuss what he wrote before he published it. A lengthy memorandum of the discussions (which took place at Soho House on 7 January 1810) has survived; it sheds welcome light on the first trying times of the first Soho Mint. The claims of John Southern were pared down, and his intended article never saw print; but even at his most boastful, Southern would scarcely have disputed the words of James Lawson, another of the participants in those earliest days:

> God only knows the anxiety & unremitted perseverance of your Father to accomplish the end & we all aided & assisted to the best of our powers without ever considering by whose contrivance anything was brought *to bear*— for indeed the bringing of everything to *bear* was by your Fathers perseverance & often by His Hints & personal attendance— for often He attended & persevered in the experiments 'till we were all tired—[1]

Let us heed Lawson's words and assign greatest credit where it is due: if there were ever a man responsible for a new way of seeing the world, then fashioning something to fit his new vision, that man was Matthew Boulton.

* * *

Every story has a beginning; when did Boulton first think of coining by steam? I cannot determine the precise answer. At the 1810 meeting, James Watt claimed that Boulton had had the idea as early as 1774. That date seems much too early to me. Watt and Boulton would not even enter into partnership until the following year, and their first efforts in connection with steam would be firmly restricted to the mining industry through the remainder of the decade. Watt was also vague about dates on many other occasions, and his 'Memorandum concerning Mr Boulton', prepared shortly after the latter's death in 1809, ascribed to the mid-1780s one concept which we know was only being worked on in and after 1791.[2] Watt may have indeed recalled an enthusiastic, early prediction by his new friend that someday steam would create all sorts of things, including money; but I doubt that it went beyond that burst of optimism for many years.

I cannot trace Boulton's connection between steam power and moneying farther back than the early 1780s. He was supplying Samuel Garbett with arguments at the time of the latter's report on the Royal Mint (1782), and in these writings (which have been lost), he suggested introducing 'other Modes of Manufacturing'.[3] The most logical meaning I can take from these words is that Boulton had suggested applying steam power to coining – but my deduction is obviously grounded on the fact that that was what he eventually achieved!

But there are other, slightly later pointers toward the future. In 1810, William Murdock observed that

> he had several conversations with Mr Boulton in Cornwall about 1784 or 1785 upon different modes of working Eight Coining-Presses by means of a sliding-rod connected with the [steam] Engine by a Crank. Among other modes it was proposed to place an Air-pump at the end of the Rod to pull it back. This Air-pump was to communicate with the Condenser of the Engine in order to have the Vacuum formed, & the Area of it was to be half that of the Engine Cylinder. A Drawing of this mode was made by Mr Murdock, … [but it] was not carried into effect, or tried in any way.[4]

By the middle of the 1780s, the marriage of steam to coining had become taken for granted in the mind of Matthew Boulton and the engineers in his employ. That the precise nature of the marriage remained unclear was still unimportant, for the industrialist was not ready to commit himself fully to its pursuit. That indecision would soon disappear, as three events took place in rapid succession. Boulton received his first coining order, which he had to fill in the old way; he witnessed a dramatic demonstration of what coinage might become; and he received a broad invitation to take part in the journey from the old to the new.

Boulton's trials with the 1786–7 Sumatran coinage are related elsewhere – difficulties with timely delivery, inconveniences of creating blanks at Soho, then striking them in London. But he (and we) might have drawn two conclusions from this first attempt: any future coinage must be *completely* effected in one place, and that place must be under the immediate control of Matthew Boulton; and better processes must be employed to create better money. The fledgling coiner had seen what could be produced in the traditional way (and his people in London had even managed modest improvements in that methodology). But the coins which resulted were still disappointing, inartistic, subject to fraud.

As we know, the first of them were struck in the autumn of 1786. As they were exiting his makeshift mint in London, Matthew Boulton was about to be introduced to the second part of the equation. He and Watt were invited to France, to consult with engineers there about the ailing water works at Marly. The two Britons were in Paris by the middle of November, and they remained in France through the rest of 1786, only returning to England in January 1787. They poked and prodded at the steam pumps at Marly; but they also had time for other projects, and for other meetings. It is uncertain who introduced Matthew Boulton to Jean-Pierre Droz. Some years later, Boulton hinted that Droz introduced himself – which certainly seems possible, given the two men's community of interest. Matthew Boulton was striking coins, but was unhappy with the results. Jean-Pierre Droz suggested an improvement which he had devised.

Matthew Boulton, James Watt, and the ingenious Swiss engineer met at the Monnaie de Paris in December 1786, in the presence of the American Minister, Thomas Jefferson. Droz proudly demonstrated his new invention (and he later brought it to Matthew Boulton's rooms for a closer look). What Droz had devised was a 'plateau' – a segmented collar which enveloped a blank as it was struck and automatically split open once striking was finished, releasing the finished coin. The advantage of Droz's plateau was that it allowed *raised* lettering – or anything else, rendered in relief or intaglio – to be applied to a coin within the tightly confined space of a restraining collar. Any piece so treated would therefore display the consistency of diameter which we associate with the one-piece collar, along with a most important deterrent to forgers, the ornamented edge. Droz was attempting to sell the idea to the French Government (and had made a lovely pattern *écu* with a lettered edge by way of enticement; one is illustrated). He told Boulton that he also had an improved coining press to which to fit the plateau, and that he had also discovered a new and better way of multiplying dies. Boulton came away from the encounter suitably impressed. If the coinage of Britain were ever reformed, and were he ever given a hand in its renovation, Monsieur Droz would be an invaluable ally.

And now the final part of the puzzle fell into place: by the beginning of 1787, the Ministry of William Pitt appeared about to order a reform of the nation's copper coinage. The lengthy agitations of Samuel Garbett and others seemed about to bear fruit; and the earlier musings of Matthew Boulton now took a concrete form.

What were Boulton's objectives as the new year opened? He knew that he wanted a coin which was inexpensive to produce – cheaper than the products of the Royal Mint which he and his friend Garbett had been deprecating for years. He wanted something difficult if not impossible to counterfeit, which suggested new methodology, better artistry.[5] He wanted a copper coinage produced and circulated prior to those in other metals, for the need was greatest here, and silver and gold would take care of themselves, the right to strike them inevitably going to he who struck plentiful and unforgeable pieces in the humbler reddish metal. And he wanted this copper coinage for himself, and for Soho.

Boulton's objectives combined private profit with public weal. He would gain from every ton of copper coin he struck. And his reputation and that of Soho would rise in the eyes of Everyman – here was an entrepreneur so successful that he was providing the very coins used by all! Of these two personal considerations, the latter was stronger than the former. From surviving documents, it does not appear likely that Soho cleared more than fifteen pounds or so for each ton coined – which even multiplied by the vast number of tons which Boulton hoped to strike would not mean that much money. Now and

Jean-Pierre Droz's pattern écu for France, 1786. (Courtesy American Numismatic Society, New York)

later, this coiner seems to have been inspired by laudable motives: Matthew Boulton really *was* concerned about the incidence of forgery, which gave his city a bad name, which defrauded the poor of the miserable wages they received, which led many of them to a premature end on the gallows. If he could secure the right to coin British copper, he could rectify many things at once.

Such were Matthew Boulton's thoughts at the beginning of 1787. They easily led to two corollaries: steam power must figure in any new coinage, and so must Jean-Pierre Droz. Matthew Boulton would supply the one and employ the other.

Steam power was already being incorporated in one aspect of future importance to coining at Soho: the rolling of metal. Experiments began in May 1786, an employee named Peter Ewart assisting Boulton in computations about friction, engaging and disengaging mechanisms, and the potential horsepower to be gained from various arrangements. Messrs Boulton and Ewart were not thinking of a steam-powered rolling mill at this point, simply of a mill powered by water in an improved fashion. But steam would enter the equation, for the rolling mill would be moved by water falling from Hockley Pool, *returned to it by a steam engine*. Boulton had definitely constructed such an arrangement by September 1786 and was attempting to sell the idea to an Irish correspondent by the middle of that month, noting that it would provide 'uniform Power for 24 hours p*r* Day the Year round, & that too on the most corr*t* [correct] & precise spot for y*e* Manufacture'.[6] A precedent had been established: when Matthew Boulton introduced a steam engine into any part of any manufacturing process remotely connected with the making of coin, he was preparing for a time when steam would be involved in *all*.

Steam would solve many of the difficulties he had encountered in his first coinage and must encounter in any future ones. It would provide the motive force for striking large coins. It would strike them consistently, for it never tired, never varied. It would make coins more cheaply than other sources of power – and it would make more of them, in part because it could always be at work. With the new motive force allied to new processes, the coins steam-struck could be rendered invulnerable to the forger. But in pursuit of all of this, Boulton would need help. He would need the finest steam engineers of the day. And he would particularly need Jean-Pierre Droz: from the beginning of 1787, the necessity of getting Droz to Soho (and then getting work out of him once he had arrived) loomed ever larger in Matthew Boulton's mind.

Much of the insistence originated in the fact that Boulton was not the only person with his eye on a British copper coinage. He had an extremely enterprising competitor, one who was also gaining moneying experience (and whose products were altogether more impressive than the crude coins Boulton was striking for Sumatra). This competitor was Thomas Williams, a canny North Wales lawyer and the moving spirit behind the Anglesey mines. And to a personal rivalry there was added a competition between the two premier copper producers of the day, Cornwall, in whose success Matthew Boulton had more than a passing interest, and Anglesey, where Thomas Williams was king.

As the two magnates fought for dominance in the copper trade and the copper coinage, so also did they compete for the soul of Jean-Pierre Droz.

Boulton at fifty-eight.
(Courtesy Birmingham
Museums and Art Gallery)

Matt^{w} Boulton

24th June 1787

*From a Wax Medallion modelled from life in the possession of
Mr JOHN RABONE*

The latter was visited by the Copper King himself in the first days of June 1787, and Williams bluntly asked Droz whether he and Boulton were in treaty, and if so, whether he would break that treaty and come to work for the Anglesey group. Boulton (who by this time was convinced that he absolutely *must* have Droz's services, were the British coining contract to be his) fretted at Soho for some days, but finally received assurances that the artist had steadfastly refused Welsh enticements, had remained loyal to Soho. In time, Boulton would wish he had done otherwise.

The attempted seduction of Jean-Pierre Droz was a sideshow to larger events. The first half of 1787 saw much thought but very little concrete accomplishment in the matter of the British coinage. In London, Samuel Garbett attempted to secure a commitment from the busy Prime Minister, only to find that Mr Pitt had more central matters on his mind than a copper coinage produced by Messrs Garbett and Boulton. Also in London, Garbett's son Francis did his best to scotch the plans of Thomas Williams, presumably with the idea that no copper coinage at all was preferable to one produced by the wrong man. At Soho, Matthew Boulton was thinking about the minting process as never before, and he was making some basic decisions. Most significantly, he had definitely opted for steam power in the coining process, married to a particular arrangement of his presses:

> I also intend working the great Presses by a Steam Engine which I have erected in such a manner as to drive or work Ten presses at one time, if it should be necessary and in such a manner that any one of the presses may be stopped without interrupting the others.[7]

He returned to this theme a fortnight later. By then, he had

> contrived & executed in model the means of working 6, 8, 10, or any number of presses without the application of human labour and so that any one press can be stopped in a moment without impeding any of the other machines. The machine that my model represents is besides so constructed that I can work it at any speed I please from 30 to 60 blows pr minute.[8]

We should take these claims with a grain of salt. A perennial optimist, Boulton tended to see solutions before he had securely grasped all aspects of the problem, and he always made greater claims for his machinery and the ideas behind it than it, or they, could support. And in the case of his words just cited, their primary purpose was to persuade Droz to come to Soho and share in the work before it had all been accomplished by others. The tactic failed, and the Swiss remained where he was. And while Boulton had indeed glimpsed one way of moving several presses together or separately, much remained undone in the spring of 1787, including the minor problem of precisely *how* the engine was to connect with the presses. But the idea held promise: worked on through 1787 and 1788, it would finally result in the overhead wheel-and-escapement arrangement of the world's first steam-powered mint. And while most other aspects of that pioneering facility were the products of other minds, the arrangement for powering the presses did originate with Matthew Boulton.

His optimism in the face of adversity has been noted elsewhere. He now became convinced that a British copper coinage was imminent, and that he was all-but-certain to receive the right to strike it. Boulton was mistaken on both counts, but his anticipation gave him a particular insistence when dealing with his Paris correspondent, Monsieur Droz. The latter simply *must* drop everything in France unrelated to Boulton's British project (including Droz's cherished plans for a *French* recoinage, one of the things which had drawn him and Boulton to each other in the first instance); and make dies for Mr Boulton, strike patterns for Mr Boulton, and devise coining presses for Mr

Boulton in France – or better yet, come to Britain and do all those things there.

All of this was contained in a series of increasingly importunate letters from Soho, interleaved with a series of increasingly beleaguered responses from Paris. Boulton opened the correspondence on 7 March 1787, and this salvo might stand for all. He was sanguine about the prospects of the coining project (while admitting that he had not actually got anything from anyone in writing). But the possibilities nonetheless looked solid enough so that Droz must immediately set to work on a die with the head of George III (Boulton was sending along several representations of the monarch, to ease Droz's task). When the die was completed, Droz must strike shilling-size silver pieces from it and send them to Britain with all dispatch. After enquiring about the state of Droz's negotiations for a French coinage (and cheerily offering his assistance, if required), Boulton closed by promising to send along steel for dies; throughout the letter, the need for haste was underscored.

Droz's first response was also typical of his end of the correspondence. He did not bother to reply until 13 April, some five weeks after Boulton had written his first letter (joined by others on the fourteenth of March and the second and fifth of April). Droz complained about the quality of the royal portraits which he had been sent, requesting a life-size plaster bust instead. He was doing his best under difficult circumstances, but worried that the likeness he was creating might not be perfect. More importantly, he had just devised a brilliant new way of marking his coins' edges as he was striking them – a method which was slow, but gave beautiful results. His prospects for a French coinage diminishing after the fall of his sponsor, Finance Minister De Calonne, Droz pledged himself ready to make Boulton's dies, to let Boulton copy his coining press – and even to come to England, if that were Boulton's wish. And money was secondary: Droz would leave the details of remuneration to the well-known generosity of Mr Boulton. Throughout the letter, there shone forth good cheer and charm; and yet, somehow, very little was being accomplished.

A pattern was being established. All through the spring and summer of 1787, Boulton continued to entreat, to wheedle Droz for technical and artistic help from France, for attendance in England. By late April, the requests for dies for a silver sixpence or shilling were beginning to yield to an insistence that Droz instead concentrate his efforts on dies for a copper halfpenny. This, after all, was the primary target of Boulton's hopes, and he urged his correspondent to engrave dies quickly and strike specimen coins with the fancy edges which only he could create. Mr Pitt might still be too busy to consider the copper coinage, but he was bound to send it in the right direction once he saw what Messrs Boulton and Droz could do!

By now, an informal agreement had been reached between the two men, centring on Droz's improved coining press. Boulton had offered to pay Droz £100 for the requisite drawings, plus £100 for every press which was built on Droz's model. Droz agreed – but pleading dire need (his finances having been neglected in pursuit of coining reform), asked for £200 for the first press as a special favour. That was on the last day of April. Ten days later, Boulton acceded, remitting the first of the money the following day. Another pattern was being set: asked to perform, Droz responded by raising his own demands.

Through that summer, Samuel Garbett continued to put pressure on Matthew Boulton for coinage specimens to lay before those in high places.[9] Boulton responded by putting pressure on Droz. Above all else the Swiss must come to Soho, for he and Boulton could get more done in an hour's worth of face-to-face meeting than in a month's worth of correspondence. Droz acknowledged the validity of the point but still demurred, citing the press of business, Soho's dies included. But he finally ran out of excuses at the end of the summer (or, as Brian Gould once observed, simply could not endure any further billets-doux from Mr Boulton). He agreed to make the journey to Soho, to see the aspiring coiner who sat at its centre.

Droz came to Britain at the beginning of September 1787. He first went to Soho, where he and Boulton talked far into the night, plotting what must be done about the nature of British coinage, about who should do it, and when. No formal agreement was concluded between them, but Boulton's faith in the sincerity of his gifted friend was restored, his resolve to retain him on a lengthy basis reinforced. Droz and Boulton travelled to London at the end of the month, and the artist left the country on the sixth (Boulton meanwhile repairing to Cornwall, a journey he had deferred in favour of seeing Droz). As the latter reported, he arrived at Paris on 11 October, full of fire for work, full of gratitude for the man for whom and with whom that work would be done. There was the trifling matter of some small debts incurred in London: surely Mr Boulton wouldn't mind taking care of them …

The latter might have reflected that he had got little of a concrete nature thus far. Droz had said that drawings for the new coining press were forthcoming – but he had not brought them with him to Britain, and Boulton had no idea when they would be ready. But having a general picture of what would be required, Boulton placed an order with Hodgells, Harrison, and Greenbaugh (one of whose members, Joseph Harrison, had been instrumental in setting up the Sumatran mint a year before):

> I am under the necessity of getting two large Coining Presses of the new construction made as soon as possible. But I think it may not be amiss to get one of the small Cutting out Presses made first, & therefore I beg Mr Joseph Harrison would get the Pattern made for the small Press directly, and the Pattern for the large one as soon after as convenient, so that they may be in such forwardness that I may get them finished by Christmas if possible.[10]

With this order, Soho Mint began its transition from the speculative to the actual.

Its proprietor now moved rapidly. November saw him constructing a 'Hotel de Monnoye'; a letter to Droz on 19 November 1787 proudly informed him that work on the structure had been completed;[11] how was Droz getting on?

Droz was not getting on all that well. He was experiencing difficulties with his edge-marking device, taking consolation in the preparation of a medal commissioned by an English grandee whom he had met in London. In any case, he had not realized that Mr Boulton had wanted the pattern halfpence all that quickly: hadn't somebody mentioned next April?

Matthew Boulton certainly had not. A note of anxiety again crept into his portion of the correspondence. The mint room was done; Droz's house was ready; as soon as the dies for the halfpenny were completed and a few specimens struck, the artist simply *must* abandon all other commitments and hurry back to Soho. For the Lords of the Committee on Coin had finally heard the petitions of Samuel Garbett, Matthew Boulton, and their friends: they were now ready for serious discussions about a new copper coinage.

In fact, Boulton had had to put them off. They had summoned him to London about the tenth of December, but he had been laid low by a second major attack of the stone (he had suffered the first late the previous October; the ailment would eventually kill him). He had asked for a postponement of his testimony until the first week in January (and would have to postpone it again, due to his health); in the few weeks of grace, could Droz get something, *anything*, to him in concrete form? All of the good arguments in the world would carry far less weight than one perfectly-struck pattern with a fancy edge which no one else knew how to apply. Boulton had told the Lords that Droz had started to engrave the dies; would Droz make him a liar?

Pleading for understanding, the Swiss would do just that. It was all well and good to urge celerity; but Droz was already working at top speed, could work no harder. And in any case, he had lost Boulton's computations on the size and weight of the proposed halfpence: he obviously must have this information before he could proceed.

With additional requests for halfpenny patterns, Matthew Boulton ended his first year as an industrial coiner. It had not been a particularly successful time, and the man who might make it so was less than fully co-operative. But Boulton hoped for greater success in the new year to come; for a brief period, his hopes seemed to be coming true.

He had his twice-deferred meeting with the Lords of the Committee on Coin. Even without Droz's patterns, the magnates proved sympathetic to the project, happy to oblige in any way. Boulton emerged from his meeting convinced that Soho would indeed receive an order to coin, especially as Thomas Williams' bid for the contract had been defeated. The order to begin might come as early as the Lords' next meeting. It only remained for Jean-Pierre Droz to settle his affairs in Paris, step into the next convenient conveyance, and come to Soho. Meanwhile, he must send along anything he had completed in the way of halfpenny patterns; Boulton would put them to good use in London.

The artist would indeed set out from Paris for Soho; but he would only do so nine months later. And between the time when Boulton invited him and the time when he finally honoured the invitation, what had once appeared a dead certainty fell apart before his employer's horrified eyes.

With the hindsight of two centuries, we can say that events were still moving in Boulton's favour. He was totally unprepared to coin at the beginning of 1788; had he then received orders to do so, he would have been exposed to official and popular ridicule. Matthew Boulton had no idea what he was doing in January 1788 and would only learn his chosen craft the hard way, through time, until he would finally be ready to back his claims with solid evidence. When that day arrived, he would have found a number of elements which must be incorporated in his coining venture – low relief, single-piece collars, and steam. And he would have rejected another element which he had learned he neither needed nor wanted. That ingredient was his best hope of 1787–8, Jean-Pierre Droz. Boulton would pay two thousand pounds for the lesson; and we may conclude that he got off cheaply.

Of course, Boulton lacked our hindsight. From *his* point of view, a year which had begun well had ended poorly. For his efforts had now given him the worst of both worlds: he had finally enticed Droz to Soho and must pay him well for his attendance there; but he had no work for him. Surmounting everything was his dawning realization that Droz was unlikely to be any more enterprising in the Midlands than he had been in France. The coiner's response to the disappointments of a disastrous year gives us his true measure, as it gave the world its first industrialized mint.

His attendance at the Privy Council in fact marked the high point of the year 1788. Upon his return home, he got word from Droz that everything done thus far on Soho's first coining press was wrong; nonetheless, his people could go ahead and finish it, while Droz would prepare a model of the *correct* moneying press – something which Boulton had been attempting to finesse from him over the past several months without success.

Boulton continued to plead for pattern halfpennies to clinch the coining contract through that winter and the following spring. In every case, he was put off or received less than he desired. Droz complained that the perfection demanded on the engraving was ruining his eyes. (Were that the case, one might wonder why he had gone into his profession, or remained in it.) While expressing concern over Droz's ailments (and prescribing a number of nostrums to cure them) Boulton nonetheless urged him to work ever-harder. The Lords, he said, had only given him until the first of June to have his mint up and running: he must create no fewer than eight cutting out presses and six coining presses within five months, in addition to constructing several buildings and a steam engine to power the apparatus!

Boulton would have none of this machinery in working order by 1 June. But the early months of 1788 did see determined efforts, and some progress. Timber was purchased, some of the small presses were cast, and hands were desperately sought – clever, lively young men to erect the new facility and someday set it into motion. But while work went ahead on one side of the Channel, very little was taking place on the other.

Droz continued to dither over details. He finally got the model and drawings for the moneying press finished and sent at the end of March, and Soho began work on six presses on 14 April, hoping to complete them within three months. But Boulton's primary concern now centred on pattern halfpennies to show to the mighty; and here, Droz proved disappointing.

The artist now had two witnesses to his work – a Boulton business associate named Andrew Collins, and the coiner's seventeen-year-old son, Matthew Robinson, or Matt. Their presence may have inspired Droz: he reported that he would finish the halfpenny dies by about the twentieth of February, would be able to strike the first trials by the end of the month. Collins wrote home that Droz really was trying to please, and that the first of his halfpence should indeed be ready early in March. Then came news of a disappointment. Droz's reverse die had failed during tempering, and the artist was only able to send a dozen or so specimens. He must begin again.

He abandoned his engraving for the time being, turning to the press model. He had finished and sent it by the final days of March; meanwhile, the testimonies of Matt and Andrew Collins had persuaded Boulton that Droz had changed his ways and now saw the coining project in the same light as he himself. It was therefore time to offer him a contract.

Jean-Pierre Droz's first attempt: a pattern halfpenny of 1788. (Reproduced by kind permission of the Trustees of the British Museum)

Boulton's initial terms went out on 15 March. They proposed a payment of £500 for the six presses which Boulton proposed to build on Droz's pattern – this in addition to the £200 the artist had already received. Droz would also be engaged to come to England and work there for two years, at an annual salary of £500. He fretted over the two-year stipulation, and that detail remained unsettled for many months – as, in fact, did the other elements of the contract, becoming sources of future dispute.[12] But each man knew (or thought he knew) where the other stood by mid-April; Droz then wrote of coming over and starting work as early as the beginning of May – providing he received another advance of £200 or £300 to settle his affairs in France. Boulton sent the money, and Droz postponed the appearance.

He had still not appeared at the end of May, and Boulton sent off an anxious appeal for his presence and the pattern halfpennies which he had again promised to deliver. This brought a qualified response: early in June, Droz conveyed a box of fifty-four halfpence to Matthew Robinson Boulton, who immediately posted them on to his father. They had been struck from a new reverse die on gilt blanks which the elder Boulton had supplied. While they bore fancy ornamented edges, Droz apologized for the fact that he had had to strike them by hand – which should have suggested to his Soho correspondent that all was not well with the intricate mechanism which was intended to be his contribution to British copper coinage. And Droz did not follow up his patterns with his own appearance: pleading the press of his affairs, he lingered on in Paris.

The hand which Matthew Boulton now held might have been stronger. But he did have several decent cards. His mint was now building; and his designer was now co-operating: Boulton now had a few dozen halfpenny patterns by way of proof. The aspiring moneyer wanted to bring the coinage question to an early resolution, and he realized his hand was probably as strong as it was likely to be for some time. Gathering his resolve, he went to Town to see those who could make all of this effort worthwhile.

Boulton remained in London during most of June, receiving news from his people at Soho (four cutting out presses done and the engine to power them proceeding nicely, three coining press frames cast on Monsieur Droz's model); urging Droz to redouble his efforts (the fifty-four patterns did *not* do him justice; could he send a few more 'struck up perfectly on your great Press'?[13]); and speaking with anyone from the Prime Minister down who might forward the coining business. Several weeks of activity were capped by a meeting with Lord Liverpool at the end of June. Boulton employed every argument at his command, urging a new copper coinage 'to appease the Voice of the Publick & the distresses of Cornwall', but it was not enough: Hawkesbury 'gave me sundry Reasons why the Copper Coinage had been delay'd, & why it must be delay'd, untill he had made some regulations in the Gold Coin'.[14]

This magnate was withholding a portion of the truth. While I know of no contemporary written testimony (this would not have been the sort of thing consigned to paper), one of the reasons why Boulton's proposal had not been acted on favourably in January and was going nowhere in June was the opposition of Britain's traditional coiner, the Royal Mint. Officials at the Tower realized that their antiquated machinery could not possibly coin in the way Mr Boulton claimed (and seemed to be demonstrating by the gilt patterns which he was pressing on all who would accept them). Since they could not coin in his fashion, they determined that he should not do so either.

Official competition: the Royal Mint's pattern halfpenny, by Lewis Pingo, 1788. (Courtesy Birmingham Museums and Art Gallery)

Failure in June put Boulton's project at risk; an event in early autumn would reduce its chances still more. The King fell gravely ill (modern historians believe he suffered from porphyria; his contemporaries believed him mad). Whatever its cause, the illness of George III put a stop to any movement for monetary reform: no one would ask for new copper coins while they were uncertain whose visage should adorn them.

If no coinage were in contemplation, Mr Boulton would not require the services of Monsieur Droz. Unfortunately, no one told the latter; and Soho's repeated entreaties finally bore fruit at the wrong moment. Droz came to England.

His employer was in a distinctly unenviable position. He had already invested £2,000 in the mint project, would obviously spend much more before he was finished. By Midsummer, he was cutting corners wherever possible: discussions about a steam-powered rolling mill were shelved in favour of inexpensive alternatives (and that portion of the mint would remain unmechanized until the rebuilding of 1798–9). But Soho continued to haemorrhage money while still unable to strike it: Boulton must pay for the expensive overhead wheel for the press room, which would be made by John Wilkinson in Bradley, more presses must be cast and fitted up, etc. He could not afford to pursue the project; yet he could not afford to abandon it. And here, too late to be of any immediate use, came Monsieur Droz.

Several people came with him. There was his *perruquier*; the hairdresser's importation raised no problems, and Boulton gave him work at Soho and recommended him to friends. There was an artisan named Duret. Boulton worried that his importation might indeed raise problems (it was illegal to export English mechanics; might not France have a similar law on its books?). But Duret cleared immigration without incident, settled in at Soho, and worked so assiduously on Droz's plateaus that Boulton eventually wrote him a letter of recommendation. Finally, there was Droz's mistress, a Mademoiselle Labonne. She would share the refurbished house with her artist-paramour, and we hear no more of her – until the point when Droz wished to leave Soho for the greener pastures of France '& to dispel all my doubts he [offered] to pledge his Honour or leave his Mistress as an Hostage'.[15]

The company arrived in England during the first week of October, entering the country without incident. Droz's luggage was another matter: it was seized by agents at Dover, and there ensued several anxious weeks, as suspicious Customs officials (abetted by people from the Tower, who were aware of Droz's identity if ignorant of the workings of his precious machinery) poked, pried, and prodded. Boulton sent William Matthews to the King's Warehouse to liberate the luggage; when that proved unsuccessful, he wrote Lord Hawkesbury and William Fawkener. Mint officials must *not* be allowed to examine Droz's models and tools, because they might acquire his secrets for free. Droz was hysterical, Boulton deeply disturbed. But they worried needlessly: the Mint agents overlooked the most important piece of the mechanism (Droz's edge-marking device), and his effects were turned over to the Swiss about a month after they had been taken from him.

Droz's arrival inspired Boulton to make another effort to find employment for him, and for Soho Mint. He candidly described his situation and plans to Thomas Williams on 8 October:

The Copper Coinage hath long been festering in my mind, & I have often wished I had never taken up the subject.

Long looked for is come at last. Mons*r* Droz is arived: & I must now fullfill my engagement with him, or abandon the plan altogether, which I cannot do without the loss of a couple of Thousands. I therefore propose, so soon as I have set him to work, to go to London, & try to bring the [coinage] matter to a crisis.[16]

This would indeed be the policy adopted. Droz would be settled in place, bringing his precious expertise to a mint project already well along. Meanwhile, Boulton would once more go to London, once more begin knocking on doors. Neither approach bore fruit.

Boulton opened this latest campaign with a long letter to Lord Hawkesbury on 12 January 1789, followed by a visit to London later that month. His arguments were familiar: he was losing a great deal of money in pursuit of something the Government had once thought it must have, and which all still agreed it ought to have. The new mint he was currently building would create the finest money in the history of the world – so much more so, now that the greatest artist in Europe was working there. And so on; but Boulton was preaching to the converted, and he was not advancing his fortunes.

They were a hostage to larger events, most notably the health of the King and the uncertainty of his Ministers. But the ailing monarch began recovering early in 1789, and Boulton instantly thought of striking a medal to celebrate the fact. Such a creation might achieve several goals at once. It would give Droz work. It would impress those in high places with his artistry and mechanical genius. It would demonstrate the excellence of his employer's new mint, which could strike coins quite as lovely and artistic as the medal. And sales of the medal would provide ready money, which was currently in rather short supply.

Dies were prepared and pieces struck in gold, silver, copper (both gilt and ungilt), and 'Barton's metal' – a multilayer composition featuring silver rolled onto a copper core. Mintage figures have not survived, but the numbers struck probably amounted to a few thousand. The first of the medals were being distributed by the end of April 1789. All who saw them were impressed with Droz's artistry and Boulton's patriotism. But they failed in their larger objective: they forwarded neither the fortunes of Soho Mint nor those of the copper coinage. Boulton would be still more disappointed when he learned that the King's recovery medal would very nearly represent the sum of Jean-Pierre Droz's useful labour at Soho.

He proved an annoyance and an impediment. He would not work with the other artisans now attempting to breath life into a still-dead mint. He would not teach them how to multiply dies. He would not share his secrets of engraving. Packed off to Windsor to create an accurate likeness of George III, Droz's diffidence prevented him from getting anywhere near the monarch. He seemed to be taking forever to create the master dies and punches which must be in place before a British copper coinage could be begun. And from the non-performance of this expensive foreigner, Boulton's eyes were unavoidably drawn to the accomplishments of the humbler Britons drawn into Soho's employ. Against all odds, and somewhat to their own astonishment, they were succeeding in creating the world's first industrialized mint!

Jean-Pierre Droz's medal for the King's recovery, 1789 – virtually the only work Matthew Boulton ever got out of him. (Author's collection)

Scattered references in the Matthew Boulton Papers indicate that serious work on the mint machinery began in the autumn of 1788. The number of presses to be powered by the overhead wheel now rose from six to eight, and drawings were commissioned and parts devised for connecting the driving wheel to the individual presses. At James Watt's instance, the curved engagement device was taken off the presses (where John Southern had suggested it be placed) and fitted on the overhead wheel instead, a position it would retain. Drawings for the cutting out presses occupied much of that same month (November 1788), and castings for these machines and other portions of the apparatus were done on Boulton's orders at the end of the old year and the beginning of the new.

All of this cost a great deal of money, and the amount invested in the first Soho Mint rapidly mounted. By late January, Boulton's estimate of what it was likely to take to finish the project 'will exceed my expectations upwards of 2000L. & I am perswaded that if I dont put an end to these expences the loss will be doubled'.[17] And the financial picture looked even gloomier a few months later: by mid-April, he was more than five thousand pounds out of pocket, still with nothing to show for it!

Monsieur Droz symbolized all of Boulton's difficulties. He was being paid a handsome salary (which represented a dead loss for the time being); and he was not even performing the labour for which he had been engaged. He complained about everything, and James Lawson, at least, appears to have been terrified of his displeasure. Droz was striking a few patterns by late January but was relying on an old press for the purpose – another indication that all was not well with his own mechanism. And there was little indication that he was performing his other duties, including the preparation of master dies and punches, the instruction of his shop-mates in die multiplication, and the other skilled work for which his employer had hired him. Meanwhile, an ominous development had taken place. Lawson, Southern, Busch, Peploe, and all the other home-grown personnel had decided that no work could be got or expected out of Monsieur Droz – and they were creating the mint in spite of him.

Few traces remain of what happened over the next few months, but we can see hints here and there. The medal for the King's recovery gave the tyro coiners some experience; its production lasted until the beginning of June. By then, Boulton was speaking of a coinage for John Westwood; this work would have involved halfpenny tokens for Macclesfield or Cronebane. And it is here, I think, that we must look for the first money struck by steam in the history of the world.

News of the event was contained in a note from James Lawson to Matthew Boulton in late June. Boulton had gone to London to launch yet another appeal on behalf of work for his mint. Lawson and the others had remained behind, and this mechanic wrote a progress report to his absent superior. It is worth quoting in detail:

> Sir
>
> I am happy to inform you that at present we seem in so fair a way of getting forward— The press has gone for some time past very well, at the rate of nearly 40 pr Min*t* [minute]— It could work much faster if it would return in time. The smallest difference in the height of the dies makes 2 or 3 strokes difference p*r* minute, as the present press has no adjustments, which in the new one will be

easily regulated— We have this week struck about 24 cwt, with many little hindrances, but hope that we shall be able to increase the quantity much next week.

The men were inventing as they went along:

> The principle improvement is in the brushing the blanks [a necessary step: the hot-rolled and cut-out blanks had scale on their surfaces, which would mar them unless removed]. Peter [Ewart] has the merit of it. It is by putting them between two brushes lying at a small angle, so that the pieces, sand and water being put in at one end, as into a mill happer [hopper], come out at the [other] perfectly well brushed both sides and edges at once ... I think that by Monday we may be able to be putting some of the things for the new press in their places— I should be glad to know the quantity you would wish struck pr week, as with one set of hands at the press we can not continue so many hours as might be done ...
>
> Sunday Morning— Mr Southern coming last night in making some experiments with a water damper, prevented my sending this last night as I intended. Today we are examining the engine valves, rotative wheels, &c., and one of the millwrights is dressing the pinion. Bush is working at the new layer in and *Webb* is arranging and cleaning every thing about the press so that I hope every will go on in the morning (my fingers received some small damage, which almost prevents my writing).[18]

From the proceeding, we learn that a single press had been set into motion, and that it was definitely worked by steam. We learn that from the outset its rate of production was somewhat superior to that commonly achieved on a traditional coining apparatus. We learn that some sort of laying on mechanism was in active contemplation but had not yet been perfected. *And we learn that those mechanical contrivances being tested and perfected were not the products of Jean-Pierre Droz.*

They were not Droz's creations because his mechanism worked in a different way. Since it gripped the edges of the piece tightly enough to allow a design to be imprinted there, James Lawson would not have been able to catch his fingers during the coining process. His testimony instead suggests a temporary situation, wherein *no* collar was employed, segmented or plain, the hapless moneyer having at least to flick the struck piece out of the way so that a layer on might put a planchet in its place. None of the Soho-made Roe or Cronebane pieces (or indeed the Parys Mine halfpence minted there in 1789) bear any signs of having been struck in a collar – and from other evidence we know that Soho, and Boulton, were experiencing difficulties with the layer on, ejection, and collar aspects of the coining press until the autumn of 1790. In sum, whatever else we might say about the state of the infant Soho Mint, we are surely justified in asserting that Jean-Pierre Droz's mechanical improvements played no role in it.

As an industrial event was taking place at Soho, that artist was some eighty-five miles away at Windsor, seeking (but failing to obtain) permission to take the King's likeness, first step in another assault on the master die for a British halfpenny. And his employer was in London, where he heard that while such a coinage might indeed take place, it was not likely to happen for some months.

Boulton returned to Soho, purchased Thomas Williams' old presses for several hundred pounds (an expenditure he could ill afford, but a wise one all the same), and solicited and found more work for the mint. Droz returned to Soho and created more halfpenny patterns, which Boulton sent to William Pitt, his new friend Sir Joseph Banks, and other persons of importance. James Lawson, John Southern, Peter Ewart and the others continued to tinker with Boulton's mint.

They adjusted the engaging curves of the wheel and the fly arms of the press, and they were striking fifty-five blows per minute by the sixth of July, averaging six hundredweight of tokens per day later that month. They readied a second press to go into service beside the first. They improved the life of their dies. The problem of recoil was gradually solved, as air pumps were substituted for the earlier counterweights on James Lawson's suggestion. Profiting from his bruised fingers, Lawson would also devise the one-piece, rising collar; once he had done so, a most important consideration for the engagement and retention of Jean-Pierre Droz would disappear. But by that time, Droz would already be on his way out the door.

From the late summer of 1789, a noticeable chill crept into the dealings between this artist and his patron, and it is obvious that the latter was becoming increasingly disenchanted with the former. Previously, Boulton had largely kept his disappointments to himself; now, he began to share them.

One of the first to learn his feelings was his brother-in-law and longtime business associate, Zacchaeus Walker, Sr.:

> You intimate that Mr Droz hath already had £500— from you but I am apprehensive it must be a far larger Sum, as £450— was paid him in Paris, previous to his coming to reside at Soho, besides some Buttons sword Hilts &.c. that he took from Soho on his first visit— …
>
> From your description I can not conceive Mr Droz either honest in Principal, or good in disposition— Honesty in Principal will not warrant one man in taking another's Money without performing what he promises and rendering the agreed value of the money – and a good disposition could not suffer a friend to be injured by such neglect— Indolence, idleness, or any such excuse is too barefaced—
>
> Is there not a man in England to be found, (if not so well as Mr Droz) capable of making you original Punches sufficient for halfpence and upon whom you could depend for making them?[19]

Monsieur Droz honestly doubted the fact, which explains a good deal of his inactivity. But Mr Boulton was about to examine that very question. He was increasingly prone to do so because the prospects of a British coinage (offering the only possible justification for Droz's retention) again appeared to be receding. But before he parted company with him, he would give the man a final chance, sit down with him, discuss what he wanted, *and then draw up a formal agreement.* Each party would then know exactly where he stood. And if a rupture still took place, Boulton's case would be strengthened.

It is almost inconceivable that a formal written contract had yet to be created; but it is nonetheless true. Boulton's commercial acumen was surely keener than that – had it not been, we should never have heard of him. But a curious diffidence took hold whenever he had to deal with Monsieur Droz. He was immensely impressed with the latter's genius, appears to have seen his agreement to come and work for him as a distinct personal favour rather than a simple business agreement. Boulton's eventual disenchantment and resulting bitterness have a deep note of rejection and self-pity about them: he very much wanted to be admired and respected by this man, was deeply hurt and furious when the truth was revealed. Despite this experience, Boulton was never cured of his preference for foreign artists over British ones.

A draft of the agreement between Jean-Pierre Droz and Matthew Boulton has survived; it bears a date of November 1789, and there is solid evidence that it was drawn up about the middle of that month. On his part, Droz agreed to engrave the master dies and create the punches for the intended copper coinage, and to ready a press for die multiplication according to his method. He also agreed to teach Soho how to make his improved coining press with its plateau. On his part, Boulton agreed to pay Droz £1000 in two instalments of £500 each (a portion of which had already been paid). He also agreed to give Droz £200 for the first coining press made on his improved plan and £100 'for every succeeding Press which [Boulton] shall make or cause to be made ... either for His own use or for the use of the Brittish Mint in the Tower of London or elsewhere in Great Britain or Ireland'.[20] Boulton pledged himself to find all the tools and materials which Droz would require, as well as provide lodging. Droz need not stay in England beyond the time required to make his master dies, punches, and one or more presses on his improved model; once these responsibilities were met, the rest of his time was to be his own, available for study and for outside work. Boulton would provide presses for Droz's extracurricular activities, as well as giving the artist a generous portion of the halfpenny patterns which he would create. Any dispute arising from the contract would be referred to a mutual friend of both parties, Charles Dumergue of New Bond Street, London; Dumergue's judgement would be final.

It may be thought that Jean-Pierre Droz was getting the better end of the bargain. And so he was – but *only* if he kept his portion of the agreement. By the time it was drawn up, Matthew Boulton was reasonably certain that he would not. Indeed, he was already looking ahead, and beyond, and was actually doing so *prior* to his contract with Droz.

On 9 November, he wrote to Paris in search of a new artist:

> if it would not give you too much trouble I should be obliged to you if you would ask Le jeune homme, Le Guillocheur, whether he is provided with tools & is capable of turning in a *Lathe* (*tour*) a Steel *Die* (*Coin*) from a Modell of a medal or a piece of Money provided I was to furnish him with a good impression Cast in hardend Steel or in any other hard Metal, or Suppose I was to send him one of my new halfpence (such as I gave to you) in hardend Steel instead of Copper. I ask if he could turn from it a Steel Die in a Lathe & if he can I will send the impression & the Die necessary— from which I shall be better able to judge whether I can be usefull to him or him to me.[21]

The person in question was Jean Baptiste Barthélemy Dupeyrat, who eventually concluded an agreement with Boulton (4 March 1790) to provide assistance in turning portraits on a lathe, such portraits to be used in die multiplication. He sent his transfer machine to Soho the following September but did not accompany it. Dupeyrat's skills were not those of an artist but of a clever craftsman; nonetheless, the fact that Boulton was looking for someone else to do a portion of Droz's work even before he had achieved a written agreement with that artist suggests that he doubted his good faith, contract or no contract.

As the months went by, Boulton's distrust and discontent deepened. They were abetted by continuing ministerial inaction concerning the coinage. In early November, a coining patent once again appeared within reach – another possible reason for the decision to draw up a formal contract with Droz later that month. But the possibility went glimmering again: on 25 December, William Matthews sent a most unwelcome holiday present, news that the Government had decided to postpone the coinage until at least the following February.

Boulton's associates at Soho fuelled his disenchantment with Droz. On 4 January 1790, John Southern observed that Droz's experiments were unlikely to yield practical results but nonetheless cost much time and money. Since Southern was one of those who had contributed most to the actual, functioning mint, his words carried weight with his employer. A week later, James Watt offered his advice: Boulton ought not to pay Droz any additional money 'unless compelled by Law, and if he has no money to feed his lawyers, their zeal will soon ease'.[22] Watt's counsel suggests how far matters had then deteriorated between the entrepreneur and his artist.

The estrangement deepened still more. On 17 March 1790, Boulton took the next logical step: he wrote Droz a letter, suggesting that their differences be settled by arbitration. The process would not take place for several months, and it is quite apparent that the man who suggested it pinned little faith on its efficacy: just one day after giving formal notice to Monsieur Droz, he gave informal notice to Monsieur Dupeyrat that he was now in the market for Droz's successor.

> The Great Artist you saw & who can do every thing with his Tongue (except speak in English) hath induced me by his present conduct to surmise that his intentions are not perfectly honorable. I therefore wish to look out for another good Artist in his line in case I should stand in need of one[.] Hence I am induced to beg the favr of you
> 1st to tell me the name & address of the Engraver you mentiond
> 2d to send me a Medal or other specimen of his work
> 3 d to Enquire if he is willing to come to England & if so
> 4{to let me know at one Word what would be the lowest Sum he would work for Pr Week, or Pr Month or Pr Year upon condition that I pay the Expences of his Journey to this place[.][23]

The person Boulton had in mind was Rambert Dumarest, who would indeed become Droz's successor at Soho.

During the next three months, the relationship between Boulton and Droz grew still colder. The two men named their referees in late March. Boulton now had no faith that anything could be salvaged and candidly told a correspondent that Droz would be returning to Paris that summer. Not having secured an instant response from Dumarest (and having just received yet another suggestion that the Government had finally made up its mind to have him do its copper coinage), Boulton panicked at the end of March: he asked his London agent Richard Chippindall to solicit the help of W. Wilson. Wilson was one of the most inept die-sinkers then working in the Metropolis, which suggests the depths of Boulton's desperation.

He was indeed in a most difficult position. The new mint was still something very close to a dead loss. Yet he must retain all of its personnel and

Jean-Pierre Droz's
halfpenny pattern of 1790.
(Author's collection)

continue to invest money in it, on the chance that its services would be unexpectedly and massively required by the Government. By spring, Boulton's investment in Soho Mint had approached £9,000, excluding the money wasted on Monsieur Droz. He wished he had never heard of the mint, or of this man.

The latter continued to act in character. As Boulton was making a climactic effort to impress the Government, writing a moving appeal to the Lords of Privy Council on 28 May, sending a model of the new mint and more specimens to the Prime Minister a few days later, Jean-Pierre Droz promised swiftly to complete a dozen new master dies, ready for multiplication – and then went off on a two-day holiday which stretched into nearly two weeks.

That marked a new low, and Boulton could only contrast Droz's shoddy behaviour with that of his other personnel, who had by now created improved cutting out presses, were finishing another two coining presses for a total of four, had devised a new and improved milling machine. It was now apparent that Boulton would have a functional mint of some kind with or without Droz's services. And so he reminded the artist of his earlier request for arbitration. Having grown as tired of Boulton as Boulton had of him, Droz agreed. The two submitted their dispute to binding arbitration on 18 June 1790.

Between that day and the time of the award, Boulton solicited information on Droz's conduct from those who had worked with him or had attempted to do so. What he learned of the artist's indolence and arrogance came as no surprise, but it did deepen his anger – and it raised new apprehensions. For James Lawson informed him that, thanks to Droz's conduct, Soho could not currently coin improved regal copper on his pattern even if it won the right to do so. Droz had not finished his master dies, and he had not shown anyone how to multiply those dies required to strike the actual coinage. Nor had he shown anyone how to engrave the pieces of the segmented collar. Nor had he made a die-turning lathe, which he had also promised to do. In fact, Monsieur Droz hadn't done much of anything. While this would provide Mr Boulton with a strong case at arbitration, it would leave him with a rather weaker one if the Government were suddenly to favour his proposal to coin.

The arbitration process began on 10 July, and it lasted for three weeks. Three arbitrators were chosen, John Motteux by Matthew Boulton, a watchmaker named Justin Vuilliamy by Jean-Pierre Droz, and Sir Joseph Banks by the other two. Since Vuilliamy withdrew around the twenty-fifth of the month, the terms of the award came as no surprise.

Handed down on the final day of July 1790, the judgement was distinctly favourable to Matthew Boulton. Droz was ordered to deliver up his models, dies, and puncheons. He must teach Boulton or those chosen by the entrepreneur how to complete one coining press capable of striking pieces as perfect as the patterns seen by Messrs Motteux and Banks; and he must personally strike a ton of the new coins on the new press. He must teach Soho everything he knew about diemaking, including die multiplication. Finally, he must deliver up perfect master punches and dies for the obverse and reverse of the new halfpenny.

On his part, Boulton agreed to pay Droz the sum of £819.17.8 as soon as he had fulfilled his part of the bargain – which, added to the £1,087.5.4 already paid, would mean a total outlay of £1,907.3.0. He would also pay Droz one hundred pounds for each and every coining press constructed to his designs. Droz could remain in his quarters until he had carried out his several tasks. The date by which everything must be done was put at 30 September 1790; but Droz would receive up to six months more to complete the work.

This judgement should have brought a calming of tempers, a successful conclusion to the difficulty; but it did not. The Matthew Boulton Papers contain hundreds of pages of correspondence, beginning in the late summer of 1790 and ending in the early spring of 1791, and an entire book could be written about the convoluted squabble,[24] which brought no credit to either man. In essence, Matthew Boulton finally paid out a few hundred pounds more to Monsieur Droz (and about eighty pounds to a lawyer named Thomas Loggen), and Monsieur Droz did very little but finally went away. But the entire affair did lead to one permanent, and to us beneficial, result: worried that Droz would claim its invention for his own,[25] Boulton took out a patent on the steam-powered press.

He did so on 8 July, just as his dispute with Droz was about to go to arbitration. Patent No. 1757 ('Application of Motive Power to Stamping & Coining, &c.') exists in a printed form, complete with drawings, published in 1855. The Matthew Boulton Papers also have an undated draft in James Watt's hand, suggesting that he and not Boulton drew up the actual document.

Boulton claimed three methods of applying power to coining presses. The first was the one with which we are most familiar, wherein an overhead wheel communicated motion to the presses by means of pinions, curves, and air pumps. A complete description, along with a useful if somewhat confusing drawing, will be found in H. W. Dickinson's *Matthew Boulton* (Cambridge, 1936), pp. 140–2. Boulton added that he used a similar arrangement for creating planchets, the only material difference being that cutting out tools were substituted for the upper and lower dies of the coining process.

No mention of Droz's contributions made their way into this Patent: in the next breath, Matthew Boulton served notice that Droz's essential contribution, the plateau with its segmented collar, had been dropped from any current coining plans:

> (During the raising of the screw or recoil of the bar P. the blank which was coined is pushed out & another is laid in between the dies either by the person who attends it as usual in coining money or other wise by some proper contrivance which does not relate to the present purpose.)[26]

Had Boulton been using Droz's invention, the wording would have been very different, for it is impossible to think of a working segmented collar without some means of ejecting the coin once it had been struck on its faces and edge. The vague wording of this clause suggests to me that Matthew Boulton was still relying on the nimble fingers of James Lawson to remove coins once they were struck; I very much doubt whether he currently had a viable way of striking coinage in *any* sort of collar, segmented or otherwise. In sum, Droz's idea had definitely been abandoned, and Boulton would eventually complain that his people must rework each of the presses built to Droz's plans, *dismantling* the plateau mechanism in order to coin in quantity.

Boulton's Patent mentioned two alternative ideas for powered coinage, both of which he claimed to have invented. The first featured a reciprocating motion centering on a crank. It had actually been brought to his attention by

William Murdock in the mid-eighties, but it was no more workable now than it had been then and was never adopted. The second idea (which John Southern later claimed to have invented, an assertion vigorously disputed by his old shop-mates) featured motion communicated from the engine to the press by an evacuating cylinder. This method would indeed be adopted – at the second Soho Mint and its industrial descendants in Russia, Brazil, Denmark, India, and on Little Tower Hill. It would give far better (and much quieter) service than the method employed at the first Soho Mint; but James Lawson later observed that his master had sunk so much money in the wheel-and-escapement method that he dared not abandon it without extraordinary cause. It served well enough for the coinages which Soho would produce over the next few years; indeed, it would be used for planchet-cutting to the end of Soho's days.

Meanwhile, Boulton's mint continued to limp along. Droz was shoved out of the way and his replacement enticed to the Midlands. Rambert Dumarest had originally intended to come over with Dupeyrat (the two men probably desiring each other's company in the likelihood of encountering Jean-Pierre Droz at Soho). But Dupeyrat declined to come, and a nervous Dumarest made the journey by himself at the end of the summer. He remained at Soho for less than a year, but he nonetheless produced dies for a number of coins and tokens.[27]

Boulton gave him and the mint such work and attention as he could. But the continuing struggle with Droz overshadowed everything else during the final months of 1790 and the first months of 1791. Droz was not performing according to the terms of the agreement. He was excessively secretive. He appeared to be ready to bolt for France as soon as he had learned the secrets of the mint which had been built without his help. His employer's anxiety probably inspired an 'Inventory of Property belonging to Coinage-account', done on the last day of 1790. For Boulton, the document represented an insurance policy, should Droz attempt to abscond with any of the mint's machinery or other effects; for us, it affords a valuable snapshot in time.

Boulton's Patent described a circular arrangement of eight coining presses connected to an engine. At the end of 1790, he had four presses on line – plus a fifth, upon which 'to make experiments'. The mint also boasted a 'shaking machine', employed to feed the tubes which in turn fed planchets to the presses; five layers in (finger devices for positioning planchets and removing the struck coins); and eight cutting out presses (two complete, the other six nearly so), located at Soho Manufactory, adjacent to the rolling mill. (This was the logical place for them, and we see here an early example of Boulton's tendency to see manufacturing as a linear process.) One of the most intriguing elements of the mint was the '*Multiplication Shop, ou la Bastile*', featuring a large press for multiplying dies and 'Cast-Iron Balls 2 Air-pumps & other apparatus compleat in order to multiply y*e* Dies': it is evident that this process, too, was to be accomplished by steam. Annealing shops, a melting shop, a smith's shop, shops for Peploe and Busch, and two steam engines, one for the coining and the other for the blanking, rounded out the Soho inventory – except for a curious entry near the end: 'About 300 Oak Bludgeons to defend Soho with'.[28] The lot of an industrial pioneer and that of his creation were not always safe, and the coiner was preparing for trouble from *all* quarters, foreign artists and fellow inhabitants included.

The early months of 1791 brought mixed fortunes. Boulton obtained a large coining order for Bombay (so large, in fact, that he had to strike the pieces without using restraining collars, in order to get the order filled on time). He finished a halfpenny token order for John Wilkinson. He looked forward to other orders for Glasgow, Southampton, and Anglesey. And Jean-Pierre Droz finally decamped in March. The fortunes of the Soho enterprise were looking up. Or were they?

There was, in fact, a negative side, and the coiner and his creation reached the lowest point in their collective stories during these same months. A regal minting contract was as distant a possibility as it had ever been. Jean-Pierre Droz's preparations to depart and his actual exit in March did not relieve Boulton's anxiety: the Swiss had hopes of being appointed engraver at the Paris mint, and there was no guarantee that he would not tell all that he had learned at Soho to his new employers. Indeed, the acrimony of the previous two years almost assured that he would do so. If Droz found the right set of ears, any hopes that Boulton had for securing an official coining contract for France would disappear – as would his reputation as an inventor. That was probably why he agreed to pay Droz a few hundred pounds more than he was strictly obligated to under the terms of the award: it would be best for Droz to leave in a mollified mood.

Just as Droz was in London, receiving Boulton's drafts from William Matthews, one of the major props to his reputation abruptly ceased to exist. On 3 March, the Albion Mill burned to the water's edge. A showpiece of his new steam technology, its presence in London, grinding plentiful and cheap grain for the poor, had been said by some to have prevented an outbreak similar to that taking place in France. The disaster cost Boulton not less than £6,000, and it took place at a time when he could least afford it.

All of this tension and sense of loss communicated itself to those working at the Soho Mint. Presses broke. Dies cracked almost as soon as they were fitted to the presses. Tempers flared, and the harried mint-master had 'lately had much vexation by the want of harmony between Lawson & Bouch [Busch], The last night or rather this Morn*g* 'tween 12 & 1 o clock they even got to Blows'.[29] A few days earlier, Boulton had managed to quell an incipient riot among 'all B & W Engine Smiths & other workmen' by a mixture of firmness (sacking the ringleader, Jo Turner) and conciliation (pledging himself not to alter the 'Old accustomd Hours of all Birm*gm* Manufacturers'[30]). His many trials at home tempted him to cast his eyes abroad. If he and his mint remained unappreciated in Britain, perhaps their luck would improve in France.

Such thoughts occupied his mind from the early months of 1791 to the spring of 1792. It is impossible to determine just how far he took these musings, or what he hoped to accomplish; perhaps he himself did not know. His mental processes are seen most clearly in a series of letters to his agent in Paris, a German chemist named Dr Swediaur, In them, Boulton discussed the preparation of a French coinage from bell metal. It would be Swediaur's responsibility to secure such a coinage for Soho, which might be done in England, *or in France*. If the latter, 'I impower you to offer to sell [the French Government] my Coining Mill with all its appurtenances; the powers, advantages, & properties of it you are already acquainted with'.[31] Swediaur met with Monsieur Cussy, President of the Comité de Monnoie, and 'I stated your offer to bring over the apparatus & coin all the money for a stipulated price'.[32] Boulton appears to have taken the idea of a Soho-made French coinage rather more seriously than that of the wholesale transfer of the Soho Mint to France: such an event must have appeared chimerical even to his lively mind. He abandoned that portion of the project once and for all in late April 1792, citing other commitments. But by then, he was already involved in a French coinage of sorts – tokens for the Monneron Brothers, whose demands for large, thick five-sol coppers were taxing his mint to the utmost. Swediaur was instrumental in securing Boulton's connection with this Parisian business house; earlier, he had searched for and secured the services of an artist to replace M. Dumarest, an engraver in his mid-twenties named Noël-Alexandre Ponthon. Ponthon was engaged on 16 June 1791, his £80-a-year post to commence at the beginning of July. His arrival at Soho was delayed, and Boulton retained the services of Rambert Dumarest for a few weeks longer than either he or that artist had desired. Ponthon finally made his appearance during August, and he eventually became one of Soho's more prolific and successful engravers. By the time of his arrival, there was more work to accomplish. The spring of the year marked the lowest point in Soho's fortunes; but as the year progressed, so did those fortunes improve.

Boulton's people were gradually adding to his mint's coining capabilities. To be sure, their progress was often a matter of two steps forward and one step backward (or sideways; or even two steps backward). Contemporary letters are illustrative. On 26 May 1791, James Lawson wrote that a fifth coining press was nearly finished, and that Peploe's new milling machine had been completed and was now ready for trials. But on 5 June, the same correspondent reported an accident at the rolling mill involving the master shaft. Six days later, he noted that the substitute shaft had broken and must be replaced in its turn. Meanwhile, Dumarest was ailing once again, and work on his obverse die for the Cornish halfpenny was accordingly delayed.

The designer recovered and the Cornish die was finished; for several months, we hear of no more internal crises. The Birmingham Riots came and went. They did not affect the progress of the mint, for which its proprietor was grateful:

Boulton at sixty-four, from a medalet or token of 1792; the reverse depicts Soho Manufactory. (Courtesy Birmingham Museums and Art Gallery)

> as all our Workmen obeyd orders during the late Riots I resolvd to give them one Treet & one Happy day before I dyed which I, with the help of the finest day we have had this Summer, accomplishd my Wishes & theirs in an eminent degree.[33]

The onset of coinage for Monneron Frères subjected Soho Mint to new stresses. Boulton desperately sought copper for the order (which commodity the knavish Thomas Williams made considerable efforts to withhold). Just as desperately, his people worked to bring more and better presses into line to meet the challenge of striking millions of large copper tokens. At times they made good progress: late in January 1792, Lawson reported that two presses were at work, striking precisely forty-five of the large Monneron tokens per minute. This slight reduction in speed had actually increased productivity and lessened wear and tear; so had the application of a double air pump to overcome the problem of recoil (the pieces being struck were heavy and thick; the violent recoil of the press arm posed a real problem). Moreover, the cutting out process was being improved, and there were ideas afoot which would likely double the speed of edge-marking.

So far so good. But by the end of that month, John Southern was reporting a series of minor but annoying accidents, brought on by the size and weight of the largest tokens. These problems worsened through the remainder of the winter, and Boulton duly reported them to the Monneron Brothers in mid-February:

> The great force which I find [must be used] to strike the 5 sous pieces has broke, bent, & deranged, most of the parts about the press's. ... But this is not the only misfortune for this Day one of the great Bars or Ballances of the Press broke & with the great weight, that is fixed upon the ends of it, fell down & has very much hurt one of my best Workmen & I fear hath broke his arm, this happend within this half hour[.] I have just sent for a Surgeon—[34]

Within a few days a second workman had suffered a similar injury. The Monneron tokens were so massive that they were tearing the mint apart, with dies breaking, presses being put out of commission, and workmen being endangered; 'I have not been able to keep more than one press going'. But Boulton adopted the long view, advising the Monnerons to adopt it as well:

> You must not conclude that my plan of Coining is any worse than I have always represented it & always thought it[.] I assure you upon my honor, it is not, but the Strengths & proportions of all the particular parts can only be ascertained by Experience & I am more confident than ever that all the imperfections will be overcome very soon[.][35]

It will be observed that he then still cherished hopes of selling his mint to the Monnerons, or to the French Government; but his advice was sound all the same.

By the beginning of March, Boulton was reporting that the difficulties had been overcome, that the mint was now striking better money than ever before. But James Lawson's letters were probably closer to the truth. One press broke, leaving two fit for coining and a third which would be repaired that evening (22 March 1792). A second press broke, again reducing the mint's effectives to two. A cash bonus was offered to anyone who could quickly get it back on line (26 March 1792). A *third* press broke (29 March 1792). And so it went: Matthew Boulton's first Soho Mint would not be fully operable until the later 1790s – at which time it would be pulled down.

New names entered the Soho story as old ones departed it. A young employee of William Matthews heard that Boulton needed a clerk for a few months and offered to fill the spot. This was William D. Brown, who volunteered in November 1791 and remained at Soho for the next thirty years. Matthews himself died at the beginning of April 1792. His passing occasioned genuine sorrow – and real anxiety. Mr and Mrs Matthews had been Boulton's bankers, and he had incurred debts to them which currently totalled £5,300. Much of their credit had been used to purchase copper for coinage; but while the coinage had been created, its creator had not yet been paid and would be subjected to acute financial embarrassment if the Widow Matthews were to demand her money just now. Since she was experiencing some fiscal difficulties of her own, she might well do so.

She did not, and the crisis passed. The widow and the entrepreneur remained on affectionate terms, and she would remain Boulton's financial adviser and personal confidante, her wise words cheering him in adversity and tempering him in triumph, all the way down to her own death in 1802.

Wax portrait of John
Phillp, by Peter Rouw.
From a private collection.
(Courtesy Birmingham
Museums and Art Gallery)

She would play a more direct role in our story as well. Finding that her
house and office in Green Lettuce Lane were now rather larger than needed,
Mrs Matthews began searching for more suitable quarters. She eventually
located a house at the corner of London and Fenchurch Streets, which she
purchased on 25 June 1795 for £850. She and her people moved in on

13 July, and the house would henceforth contain the London offices of Boulton, Watt & Company – as well as afford accommodations for the widow. It had two parlours, one of which 'would, I think, answer all my purpose of warehouse, and the other parlour I should occupy myself'.[36] The parlour-turned-warehouse would eventually serve as a repository for Matthew Boulton's first and second British copper coinages, and the image of the diminutive octogenarian carefully steering her way around hundreds of casks filled to overflowing with copper for the King is one of the more arresting images in the Boulton story.

Another figure arrived at Soho during these years, one still surrounded by controversy. This was John Phillp, who came to Soho as an apprentice early in 1793. He would one day rise to the position of assistant designer to Conrad Heinrich Küchler, and he would one day be involved with coinage for the East India Company, several medals, and the final pattern dollars for the Bank of England. The controversy surrounds his parentage. A persistent rumour has named Matthew Boulton as his father.

Dickinson had heard the story and included it in his 1936 biography. I have been unable to trace it to an earlier printed source, but there is at least a circumstantial plausibility to it. The fourteen-year-old Phillp was commended to Boulton's care by a Quaker named George C. Fox, whose Falmouth firm dealt in copper. Falmouth is in Cornwall, and Boulton had business dealings in the Duchy for many years, including the period of Phillp's conception and birth. But an examination of correspondence between George C. Fox and Matthew Boulton suggests that such a connection is doubtful: the wording Fox employed suggests a recommendation, not of a son to his father, *but of a worthy stranger to a prospective mentor*. Writing from Bath on 25 January 1793, Fox referred to Phillp as 'the poor Lad who thee wast so very kind as to permit me to place under thy Friendly protection'.[37] On 16 February, Boulton pledged to do what he could once Phillp arrived. Fox sent the boy on from Bath to Birmingham on 2 March, appending a brief introduction and begging Boulton's leave 'to repeat our best thanks for thy kindly patronising [of] this poor Lad'.[38] Unless Fox had been deliberately misled (or unless he and Boulton had agreed to an elaborate written deception for the benefit of future historians), I cannot see how any blood connection between Matthew Boulton and John Phillp can be assumed.

Whatever Phillp's origins, he arrived at Soho without incident and was soon put to work on a variety of tasks as an apprentice. He attained his majority in 1800 but remained at the mint, gradually taking over an increasing amount of work from Conrad Heinrich Küchler. He died around 1815.

The artistry of people such as John Phillp would someday win additional laurels for Soho Mint. The dedication of people such as James Lawson would plumb the depths of the new technology, carry it to its limits through patient trial and error, and make a visibly improving product year after year. And the vision of Matthew Boulton would bring artistry and technology together, creating a new, industrialized coin. But all that admitted, one must add that the purpose of any business is to make a profit; this was as true in the 1790s as it is today. By that standard, how was Mr Boulton's venture doing? By that standard, it was not doing well.

We have heard Boulton's earlier complaints: he had invested thousands, with nothing to show for the money. That was in the late 1780s, before Soho

Mint had become operative. But now that it was actually in motion, what were its fortunes? Materials are lacking for a detailed answer. But we do have a snapshot of sorts, taken at a particular time, during the late summer of 1792.

We owe it to Mr Brown, the clerk who came to Soho and remained. One of the reasons why Boulton had wanted him there was to straighten out the unorthodox and scanty records of John Roberts. In September 1792, Boulton asked Brown to create a concise statement of Soho Mint's profits and losses, using what materials he was able to cull from the records left by his predecessor, carrying the story from the beginning of the coinage down to the present. Brown did what he could and filed his report; dated 13 September, it cannot have made enjoyable reading for its recipient.

The loss on coinage prior to 1791 amounted to £6,475. Adding the cost of Thomas Williams' presses and sundry expenses on the mint buildings brought the total to £7,780. Against that figure, one must posit the 321 tons' worth of copper made into coinage and tokens since 1791, for which charges amounting to £5,285 had been levied. But that still left a net *loss* of £2,495. In other words, Matthew Boulton had struck nearly three-quarters of a million pounds of copper over the past eighteen months – and he was still £2,500 in debt! Brown observed that Mr Boulton might console himself by the reflection that he at least had a mint to set against all these losses; but the observation would have brought little comfort just then to the entrepreneur, or to his workers.

In truth, Soho Mint was *not* a going concern and would not become one until its master secured its first regal coining contract in 1797. Meanwhile, Boulton must scramble for such work as he could find (and he must scramble for the copper necessary to do the work). Inevitably, the new mint experienced brief periods of feverish activity (reflected in the breaking of dies and the breakdown of machinery), interspersed with lengthy periods of reduced activity, or no activity at all. The 'boom-or-bust' quality of the work brought heartache to Matthew Boulton and those who worked for him. During fat times, he was busily soliciting new people from John Rennie and his other industrial contacts; during lean ones, he was agonizing over what to do with the people he already had. And those people, of course, suffered still more.

The pattern and its results are clearly seen in a sequence of events in the last half of 1792. On 1 September, James Lawson received orders to halt production of the Monneron tokens. He replied that those working under him would find sufficient employment during the ensuing week in cleaning and oiling the presses; but the workers would then run out of things to do, and an atmosphere of anticipatory gloom was already permeating the premises. Eight days later, the mood shifted. Lawson had received news from France ordering a resumption of the coinage,

> & I hope every thing will go on again pleasantly[.] the Men are renovated as indeed a greater change in countenances I have never seen then there was on giving them the information of working again—[39]

The information was false, and in any case it arrived too late to be of immediate aid to those who had already been laid off. Boulton ordered the remaining copper which had already been cut into Monneron blanks struck, and Brown promised to get the work down 'as soon as possible by such persons as are retained'.[40] The lot of an early denizen of Soho Mint was not a happy

Soho Manufactory, 1797, from an undated medalet by Peter Kempson. (Author's collection)

one; nor was it a particularly predictable one. But unpredictability of employment was always the lot of Soho Mint and anyone attached to it, even in the years of its peak production.

Its proprietor did what he could. He borrowed more money from Mrs Matthews (drawing on her for nearly £2,300 in May 1793: he currently had some £3,500 owed *him* by the Sierra Leone Company and others, but the money had not yet come to hand). Hearing from Sir Joseph Banks that the Government was once again considering a coining contract, Boulton replied that he had been agitating for one for years, had finally offered to put the pieces in circulation himself, 'And if this plan is not acceptable I think [the Ministers] should purchase my apparatus, knowledge & Experience as a justice due to my Zeal'.[41] What Mr Boulton thought Government ought to do and what it *would* do were obviously two very different things. So while he continued to agitate and appeal for a coinage at home, he also kept an eye out for coinage abroad. Mid-February 1796 saw an appeal to Robert Wissett, his influential friend at East India House, in which the coiner pulled out all the stops: 'I remember you askd me if my Mint is employd to which I answer w*th* a Sigh, No except now & then a day for a few provincial ½ pence'.[42] Did Wissett think there was any likelihood of a new coinage for the Company? And if so, could he *please* steer it Soho's way?

Boulton's years in the wilderness were about to end: his continuing agitation, and the continuing deterioration in the nation's minor coinage (which had descended to a shoddy mixture of counterfeit regal issues and genuine and counterfeit private tokens), were about to produce results.

By the late winter of 1797, it had become clear that something would finally be done about the copper coinage. Accordingly, Boulton went to London to push the coining project along, to solicit the copper which he would need to pursue it, and to lay down ground rules with the Ministers about how the coinage would be placed in circulation. On 3 March, he received word from Lord Liverpool that a new regal copper coinage would indeed be his. The good news was communicated to Mr Brown, who immediately called everyone to a meeting and gave them their marching orders. The men set to work, Küchler on the first of the dies needed for the penny, James Duncan on plans for an improved press, others on improving and strengthening the six presses which then constituted the striking complement at Soho Mint.

The head of the enterprise remained in Town until the middle of the year, sending back such encouragement and counsel as he could. Through all his letters home there ran a single thread: the new pence would be larger and heavier than anything heretofore struck at the mint, and the twopence would be more massive still; Soho's machinery must be radically strengthened if it were to coin adequately, or even survive.

The twopenny coppers worried him most of all, even though they would form a very small percentage of the total production. He urged John Southern to strengthen the framing around the presses, to take steps to ensure that the violent motion was effectively checked by counter air-pumps. Southern put John Busch and others to work on the tasks of reinforcing the presses, creating new layers in, etc., and a good deal had been accomplished by the beginning of June. But not enough: realizing that he must begin coining within a fortnight, Boulton urged Southern, Busch, and the others to still greater efforts. And he had taken the logical next step: doubtful of the efficacy

Matthew Boulton's Empire, 1793: Soho Manufactory and Soho Mint were adjacent to Hockley Pool. From a hand-drawn plan in one of Boulton's notebooks. (Courtesy Birmingham City Archives, Birmingham Central Library)

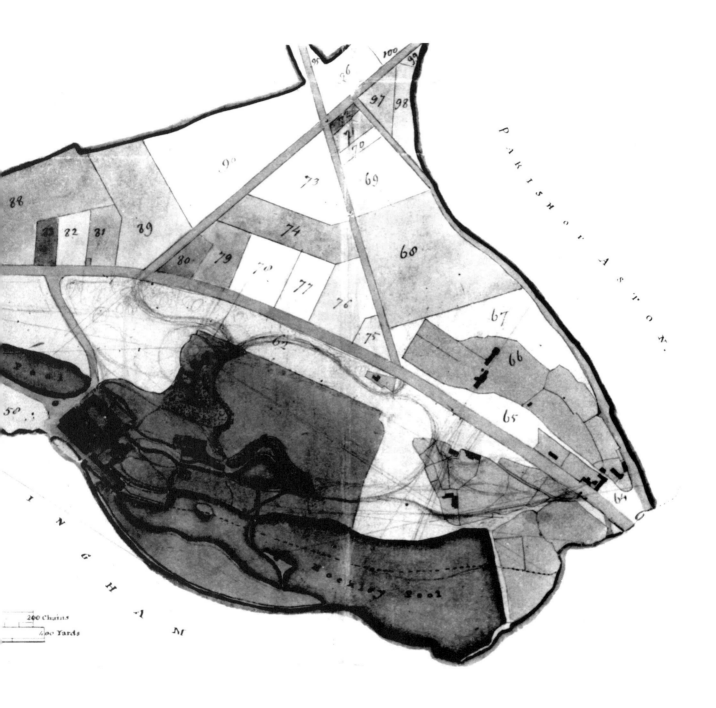

of his current mint regardless of patchwork reforms, he began to consider pulling it down and erecting an improved one in its place.

We cannot be certain when the idea first occurred to him. One of his notebooks from the spring of 1797 bore cryptic jottings on the subject, but it received its first confirmed expression in a note to John Southern of 19 May:

> I hope you have not lost sight of the new Mint for I am perswaded it will be far more compleat & harmonious than the present one, & the more I think about it the more I am pleased.[43]

This passage suggests that the idea was fairly new, and that it probably originated around the beginning of May 1797.

Coinage got under way on 19 June, and Boulton soon found that his fears were well-founded: all of the emergency tinkering and refitting did not alter the reality facing him and his mint. The coinage was virtually beyond its capacity. Presses broke, dies shattered, bottlenecks were created, and harried workmen were deafened by the noise. We may discount the effect of the latter, but we were not there at the time. The rumbling of the overhead wheel, making a dozen revolutions per minute, added to the cacophony as iron curves and rollers banged against each other, air pumps hissed and sputtered, and dies smashed images of Britannia and the King into pieces of metal weighing sixteen to the pound or even twice as much – all must have made a racket beyond our conception, even in these days of universal noise pollution. Matthew Boulton's mint would deafen anyone who long remained at work in it; and I have a feeling that one of the main reasons he wished to improve it was to muffle it.

But he would do nothing just yet. Noisy and breakage-prone his present mint might be; but it was a mint nonetheless, and its proprietor could scarcely advise the Government that, having finally granted its permission to coin money, it must now stand by while he constructed just the right apparatus for the purpose. Boulton would meet his commitments with what he had on hand and meanwhile dream of better days.

Before those dreams could become reality, a hard fact must be met and overcome. That is, a simple rebuilding of Soho Mint would not solve all or even most of his problems. The strongest presses conceivable would still make an infernal racket and shake themselves to death *unless a new way of linking them to the steam engine were devised.* Boulton and his mechanics mulled over the problem through the remainder of the year. Early in 1798, John Southern suggested a possible solution: abandon the overhead wheel-and-escapement linkage in favour of a simpler one featuring a vacuum pump, *directly communicating power from the engine to an individual press.* On 17 January, Boulton told him to fit up one press in the fashion he proposed; if the method worked, he would pay Southern £500 for the idea and make him superintendent of the mint machinery. It worked, Boulton paid – and it now paid to build a new Soho mint.

In a sense, it would have paid from the beginning. Boulton was perfectly aware that his method of linking coining presses to a steam engine was not the only possibility, or even the most eligible possibility. But it was his idea, and that counted for something. More significantly, he eventually sank so much money in a mint with the overhead wheel at its center that he dared not abandon it except for very strong cause. Through the mint's first eight years, such cause was absent: except for the Monneron tokens, the first Soho

Mint was never put to a real test of its strengths and weaknesses. And even in the Monneron affair, it had managed to win through – if only because the brothers' firm obligingly fell to pieces before the mint did.

Then came the first British copper coinage. Boulton worried that his mint might prove inadequate, knew that it might well remain so through the entirety of the coinage, wondered how he and it would look if it were not equal to the task. So the game had changed: the stakes had become so high that the coiner was now forced to think the unthinkable, to consider seriously the alteration of the very heart of his moneying process. Now he was ready to listen to new ideas. And now he would rebuild.

We are not certain when he began. While Boulton was reconstructing his own mint, he was also building one for St Petersburg; and those involved in both projects did not always take pains to separate them in the written record. But the best indication is that Southern's method was tested for the first time around the beginning of February 1798 (and exhaustively tested a second time, late in April), and on the strength of the initial results, Matthew Boulton ordered the first drawings prepared, the first of the new machinery cast. In both cases, activity began around 1 April 1798 and continued through the winter of 1800. But most of the drawings and castings for the machinery were done in 1799, and that, in fact, was to be the crucial year in the building of the second Soho Mint, which would be up and running that May.

Boulton relied heavily on John Southern to keep the project on schedule. We may therefore imagine his anxiety when one of the Lords of Privy Council suggested to him that Soho might be harboring a man of doubtful loyalty, the very person responsible for the completion of the project – John Southern. Boulton stoutly defended the patriotic intentions of *all* denizens of Soho, but immediately wrote to his superintendent, seeking assurances that he was in fact loyal. Southern reassured him and the work went on; but we are reminded of the tensions of those times, analogous to the climate of opinion in America a century and a half later,[44] when invasion or subversion appeared imminent and neighbour distrusted neighbour.

John Southern's idea had freed Matthew Boulton from the circular press arrangement of the first Soho Mint; as at St Petersburg, the coiner would adopt a linear press arrangement. He would also expand the number of his presses, creating a mint of the same size as the one he was building for the Tsar: from first to last, this new Soho Mint was always intended to have eight presses. There is a hint that the earliest scheme involved two rows of presses in the new mint (one of four presses and the other of three) and an eighth press in the old mint. This suggests that the new and old coining rooms were in close proximity to each other. As none of the buildings has survived, we are reduced to guesswork and close interpretation of the occasional hint left in the archival record.

Work on the building to house the new presses got under way in June 1798. It was at least two stories high, and the steam engine to power the presses would be located directly *above* them. This sounds odd at first, but it was an economical arrangement and worked well with the new method of powering the coining machinery. Work proceeded at a furious pace throughout the summer, Boulton putting any workman he could spare from the current coinage on this exciting new project. He had hopes of having the building completed and the presses operative by the end of the summer, so that he could invite those members of the Government now considering a new Royal

Mint to Soho, to see what steam and ingenuity could achieve. As in so many other instances, Boulton could not keep to his own schedule: the new mint would not be finished until the following spring.

What actually took place was somewhat complex. As presses were built, they were set up on a temporary basis in the old Soho Mint and brought into production there on the 'Cartwheel' coinage. They must have been powered by Southern's new method rather than the overhead wheel, for the latter would have occasioned much refitting and would not have produced any particular improvement over the old way of coining. And Boulton was adamant about the fact that there *had* been an improvement. Midway during the rebuilding process, he wrote his friend Sir Joseph Banks with the news:

> I have the pleasure to inform you that I have now finished & set to work my Leviathan, which turns out to be equal in perfection to all my hopes, wants & wishes — You will probably remember that my first Coining machine struck about 42 pence pr Minute with each press & made an unmusical [*sic*!] Noise. The present strikes 60 pence pr Minute pr Press, & is perfect[ly] silent. I am therefore now removing all my presses into the new Mint, & there being yet to make 4 more, it will be 7 or 8 weeks before the whole number will be at Work – after which I hope for the honour of Your & some of y*e* other L*ds* of Com*tee* [Lords of the Committee on Coin] to inspect it for I declare it to be a beautyfull, harmonious, Simple, & perfect Machine.[45]

Boulton's estimation of opening time was still optimistic, but the mint was indeed making good progress, going up far more quickly and with far fewer difficulties than had its predecessor. The fourth of eight presses had been set into motion by 19 September 1798; over the next few clement months, work centred on finishing the exterior of the new building and getting the steam engine into place. Once that had been completed, the difficult job of dismantling the new presses and re-erecting them at their final worksite got under way. This was a delicate process: Boulton's people were still coining copper for Great Britain, and due respect must therefore be paid to leaving enough presses in place to keep up some semblance of production in the old mint until work could shift once and for all to the new. By 21 February 1799, John Southern was able to report that two of the relocated presses had been set to work in their new home, and two more were on line by 12 March, all of which worked well.

That left four to finish, and Boulton offered a hefty reward to James Harley and James Duncan if they succeeded in bringing the final presses into motion by 1 May. They just managed it, as John Southern proudly reported on the morning of the first:

> Soho, *May Day*, 1799
>
> Dear Sir/
>
> I have the pleasure to write, what I hoped you could have seen *with your own eyes to day*, that all the 8 presses have been at work *together* for a considerable time this morning—
>
> 6 on pennies
> 1 on halfpence
> 1 on farthings[46]

Southern's comments deserve a word or two. Soho was still striking pence, for it was finishing Boulton's original contract with the Government. But it

56

had no business striking halfpence or farthings, for it had received no permission to do so and indeed would not for another six months. But Boulton assumed that a contract for the second coinage was imminent: having labored under a disadvantage on the first copper coinage (wherein the Government had desired its coppers quicker than he could initially produce them) he was determined not to be caught unprepared on the second. He had to halt production when the legal ramifications sank in, but the desire to steal a march was one reason for his insistence on getting the new Soho Mint to work as rapidly as possible. Another was the fact that he was expecting a visit from the Russian Ambassador, Count Vorontsov, during the first week of May.

As some of Boulton's men busied themselves with the presses, others were ordered to paint and paper the coining room's interior, papering being done to reduce the noise level. Boulton explained what he wanted:

> I … wish that you would order either Wyatt or Smallwood to hang the new Mint with Clean Cartridge paper & the Ceiling also, & let them put up the [ornamental] Iron roses— We can afterwards paint the Walls of a dark green & the Ceiling of a light Sky blew in Water Coulers but the Colums & door & window should be painted Stone Couler in oyl. In order to paper it they may stop y*e* Mint for a day & paint on Sundays for I fear it will [otherwise] not be compleat [in time for the Ambassador's visit][47]

Walls papered and painted, machinery perfected and at work, the coining portion of this second Soho Mint became a reality in May 1799. Although the record is silent, we are probably safe in assuming that the new rolling mill (for Boulton had decided to reform that area of production as well) had become operable about the same time. It was now time to consider the fate of the original mint.

Writing to Southern the previous March, Boulton had expressed his opinion that once all eight presses were in working order at the new mint, 'I dont think we shall want the old'.[48] While we lack precise information, it seems reasonably certain that the first Soho Mint was indeed pulled down in short order – perhaps during the summer of 1799, when Boulton and his people were awaiting orders to begin the second copper coinage and were therefore unexpectedly left with time on their hands. Bearing in mind Boulton's own figures on the mint's dimensions, its demolition would not have been an onerous task.

But what do we know about the new mint? Do we have better, clearer information about this second incarnation? We do; and most of it comes from a single source, an American Quaker named Joshua Gilpin.

Gilpin's ancestors had come to Pennsylvania from England in 1695. He himself was born in 1765 and died in 1840. With his brother Thomas, Joshua owned the Brandywine Paper Mill, one of the pioneers in the American chapter of the Industrial Revolution. Joshua's work and interests took him to Great Britain on several extended tours; during one of them, he collected data on behalf of the United States Mint. This activity inevitably led him to Soho.

Arriving there on 22 August 1799, Gilpin spent most of the next week touring Boulton's just-finished facility, inspecting its machinery (as well as that being made for St Petersburg) and receiving instruction from its creator. The moneyer first took him to see the new coining room, which Gilpin described as in form part of the Segment of a circle with its sides parrallel & ends square. this form is adopted I presume to regulate the machinery above—

This room contains the Presses only. 8 in number with the actual process of coining, but the presses are moved by machinery in the room above all from one steam engine.

Neither the movements above nor the cutting of the cobs, – the polishing of them, nor the milling of the edge, are at all shewn – this room simply exhibits the striking of the Dye.

The screw [of each press] is fixed to a large solid suction head from which a spindle extends into the room above when the motion is given to it …

A Boy attends each Press who stands in a square sunk in y*e* floor ab*t* 3 feet square & 3 deep as to bring him on a level with the Dye.

These boys are all about 12 years of age. nearly of the same size & are cloathed in an uniform of blue & red. one of them attends each press, merely to put the cobs [planchets] in the little hopper which feeds the dye, & to put the coins in a sheet iron box when coined— … The mint works have a distinct Engine of 16 horse power, which however will turn as many more works.

The speed of Boulton's presses could be regulated; as a general rule, the larger the coin the fewer which could be struck in a given amount of time. The rate for coins the size of farthings, shillings, or guineas varied between ninety-seven and one hundred pieces per minute; about eighty halfpence could be struck during that same minute and perhaps sixty coins the size of the 'Cartwheel' penny, whose production had just come to an end.

Gilpin later visited the other components of the new Soho Mint. He learned that Boulton used a single mill to roll all of the metal elaborated at Soho, including metal for coinage, and that this apparatus was now powered by steam. The mint's copper was rolled into fillets six inches wide by three feet long; once in strip form, it was taken to the cutting out presses, located adjacent to the rolling mill. Rolling and blanking were powered by the same steam engine. The mintmaster cleverly recycled his planchet-cutting operation:

The cutting out Mills are I believe also the same he uses for buttons – they consist in a number (I think eight) punches forcing the blanks thro – the punches are fixed perpendicular & on a Screw the whole of which are turned by a large horizontal wheel worked by the Engine; the punches are fed by women who put the sheet of copper in & run it backward & forward by hand so as to compleatly perforate it.—

Next came the milling process, which was also performed by boys. Gilpin pinpointed the locus of all of this activity:

Note all the above are done at the Soho building property [that is, Soho Manufactory], the blanks are then carried to what is properly the Mint distinct. I presume the reason of this is that all y*e* foregoing processes are done with the Button Machinery.

Having appreciatively viewed the new mint with its wonderful contributions to the moneyer's art, Gilpin and Boulton discussed what might be done for the United States. Boulton suggested a two-phase approach, wherein he would first provide the Americans with a new coinage ('This would be compleated in ab*t* 6 Mos & would furnish the UStates with a Copper coinage of ab*t* 200,000 dollars'). Later, he would provide a small mint and the steam engine to run it. He also volunteered to train two or three American citizens in the use of their new mint 'including the secret of copying the Dies ad infinitum and as fast as they can be broken, also refining *ye* Metals & every other part of the business'. Boulton proposed to furnish between two and four coining presses 'on a rough estimate under 5000. Stg [sterling] including rolling Mill & all the Iron work, with compleat plans &ca & also to include an Engine of 8 horse power'. Boulton's estimate was low, for Gilpin observed that the industrialist 'would also require a coinage from which he should derive some profit'.[49] The Americans would actually pay for much of their mint through these means rather than through a simple sale.

This series of conversations led to no more conclusive results than others earlier or later, and Gilpin eventually returned to Pennsylvania empty-handed. But we have been more fortunate: we now know the location of the new Soho Mint, the nature of its machinery, and something about those entrusted with its operations.

What Gilpin saw and what was actually at work under normal circumstances were at variance with each other. It would be far too harsh to suggest that Matthew Boulton created the numismatic equivalent of a potemkin village for the benefit of his transatlantic visitor: but the fact remains that he currently had considerably more mint than work, and he was about to lay off a goodly percentage of the smiling, uniformed operatives which the Quaker business-man had just seen.

Mr Brown had put his finger on the problem as early as the end of May, just as the second Soho Mint was opening for business. Boulton's first copper coinage having nearly concluded, Brown observed that the situation at the mint was now 'on the Eve of becoming very alarming indeed as certain heavy expences must fall on you [or] the poor people employed must be discharged either of which will be very unpleasant'.[50]

The clerk's correspondent was then in London, deeply involved in copper matters. He reluctantly gave his permission to discharge those who were truly superfluous, and for whom it would be absolutely impossible to find other tasks. And he intensified his efforts to secure a new coining contract, one which would allow him to put his employees, and his mint, back into full production. By the standards of the day (and indeed, by the standards of our day) Matthew Boulton was a compassionate employer. To be sure, he saw his workers as 'his people', both figuratively and literally, and he had difficulty dealing with them as equals. But he would also look out for them (his reaction to reports of John Southern's radicalism was typical: he worried about the ruin of a promising career as well as damage to Soho's reputation); and he would move heaven and earth to keep them employed and happy.

How large was this staff? How many people were affected by the vagaries of the first industrial coinage? At the beginning of June 1799 (immediately before the first Soho Mint workers were let go), Brown provided a useful tally. He counted thirty-two hands working on copper coinage in the rolling mill. At the mint itself, another ninety people found their livelihood. If we were to add those connected with the cutting out and milling processes, a total staff of 140 would not seem unreasonable. While the count diminished that summer, the final months of 1799 would see a reprieve of some workers, a re-employment of others: Matthew Boulton finally secured his second coinage contract, and the mint was working to capacity by the end of the year.

But its resurgence was limited. One of the results of Boulton's reforms was that his mint was now more productive than ever before. It would therefore take his moneyers less time to coin a given amount of metal than it had previously. The admittedly larger volume of the first coinage had kept the mint busy for no less than two years. The second coinage began in November 1799; alarmed by the speed of production, Mr Brown was advising Mr Boulton to slow down output as early as the following March: for the sake of the operatives, the work must be made to last as long as possible. But the mint nonetheless ran through its contract by the end of July, and a massive lay-off ensued. The mint boys were retained, but most of their older peers were let go; and the total staff at Soho Mint was reduced overnight by more than half.

But life went on. John Phillp turned twenty-two at Midsummer 1800; his apprenticeship ended and he would soon be employed in London and Soho designing coin and medal dies. There was a fire at Soho on 20 July of that same year; it broke out in the engine once attached to the first Soho Mint, an engine whose duties had been reduced to raising water for the garden. There was no damage to the new mint or to the adjacent tea room, but the blaze took an hour and a half to extinguish, even with the assistance of two engines from Soho Foundry. The garden filled with spectators, some of whom peered inquisitively through the windows of the nearby mint. This alarmed the Soho men; as soon as the fire was put out, they shooed everyone out of the area, moving them along with promises of free ale at an adjacent public house called Toneys. The mint's virtue was thus saved and the afternoon ended with general congratulations all round.

That eventful year concluded with a burglary attempt, the only one ever recorded at Soho Mint. It took place on the morning of 24 December, the thieves rightly supposing that there would be a considerable payroll in the Cashier's Office for distribution on Christmas Eve. The Boultons received advance warning that an attempt would take place, and they impressed twenty or thirty workmen into service as guards (for Soho Manufactory was so large and had so many entrances that so numerous a security force was necessary). The coiners-turned-constables were sworn to secrecy, and such was their loyalty that the aspiring burglars were totally taken by surprise.

There were five of them. Armed with false keys, they made their way into the Cashier's Office at 12:30 on the morning of the twenty-fourth.

> In about half an hour they had collected their booty & were returning with it when the Signal was made for seizing them. In a moment the posts which had been stationed to prevent their retreat sallied from their concealment & the scene of action was instantaneously illuminated by torches[.] the inflammation of combustible squibs had been prepared for that purpose. ... Gregory Murdock & myself were posted together & had the satisfaction of assisting to secure the two offenders who were first taken. Mr J Watt was placed in another part of the building, but soon joined in pursuit of the remaining visitants — None of the party received injury.[51]

One has difficulty imagining the sixty-four-year-old James Watt joining in a chase through the halls of Soho Manufactory; on the other hand, his partner had assisted in a raid on a nest of forgers the year before, at the age of seventy-one. Four of the five thieves were apprehended immediately, one of whom had been run through by a bayonet. The fifth was wounded but managed to get away after savaging a watchman. This miscreant was William

Fowld, who remained at large for four months; he was finally turned in near Manchester in May 1801 for the reward Soho had offered for his capture.

Life went on. On 9 January 1802 Matthew Boulton lost the person who had been his greatest confidant, and the Soho Mint lost one of its most generous champions: Charlotte Matthews died in London. James Watt felt the loss nearly as keenly as did Boulton, and he suggested an obituary notice for the newspapers, one which praised Mrs Matthews as 'a lady singularly eminent for her abilities in business and for her benevolence and liberality'.[52] The encomium was accurate, but it left rather more unsaid: there were times in the early and middle 1790s when Charlotte Matthews was the most important person connected with Soho Mint; there were times when her inspiriting counsel was the only buffer between Matthew Boulton and complete despair.

Life went on. If the coiners had time on their hands and empty pay-packets, their comrades and relatives working on other people's mints had as much work as they could reasonably handle, and more. Machinery for the Russian mint was being constructed; soon it would be joined by machinery for Denmark and later Tower Hill and even Brazil. And the coining business straggled along through 1801 and 1802, a few halfpenny tokens here, an order for Ceylon there. Then came a rapid increase in business. Soho was asked to coin for Madras: the order was large, and Mr Boulton must scramble to get the hands to fill it. There followed requests for Bombay and Sumatra. There came more interesting projects still: Boulton was asked to recoin Pieces of Eight into dollars for the Banks of England and Ireland, and he was soon striking new copper coinage for the latter island, and then for the former. Soho Mint's greatest days had got under way.

They lasted from the autumn of 1802 to the spring of 1811, less than nine years. But what years they were! Of all the coins and tokens produced at Soho during its two-thirds of a century, more than half were struck during this brief, golden time. And if we seek to see Soho Mint at its most populous, the year 1804 would be a good choice: during those twelve months, the facility was turning out coinage for India from new copper – and was also recoining dollars, a process which Zack Walker would later divide into no fewer than thirty steps! Several of them involved book-keeping (five) and packing (three); but the other twenty-two all centred on recoining, and they must have required an immense number of hands. During that one year, I would estimate that the mint numbered more than two hundred employees.

By the following February, the total had fallen but was still impressive – especially in light of the fact that the mint was currently between orders. MBP418 (Soho Mint: Coining, Rolling, Melting) contains a document from February 1805, called 'Process of Manufactory & List of Persons to be employ'd on the different operations'. Therein were listed the wages and names of all of the employees at work on all of the coining operations except for rolling. The list contains 110 names.

Matthew Boulton looked after them all; and to a limited degree, they were encouraged to look after themselves. The *Annual Register* for the year 1801 contained a fulsome description of Mr Boulton's manufactory and mint. After a general account of the history of the works, the account mentioned an 'Insurance Society, belonging to the Soho Manufactory'. One assumes that it embraced mint employees as well as those in other branches of the Boulton enterprise; among its by-laws were the following:

I.That every person employed in the Soho manufactory shall be a member of this society, who can earn from 2s. 6d. per week, or upwards.

II.Each member shall pay to the treasure-box, agreeable to the following table, which is divided into eight parts; viz. the member who is set down a 2s. 6d. per week shall pay $\frac{1}{2}$d per week; 5s. 1d.; and so on, in like proportion, to 20s. 4d.; and none to exceed that sum.

VI.If any member is sick, lame, and incapable of work, he shall receive, after three days notice to the committee, as follows, during his illness, viz. if he pays in the box, for 2s. 6d. he shall receive 2s. per week; and for 5s. 4s.; and so on in like proportion; &c.[53]

Just as the coining business was resuming with a vengeance, Boulton found himself disputing the claims of a detested former employee, Jean-Pierre Droz. The latter had not been idle since his return to Paris. He first secured work engraving plates for paper money under the Constitutional Monarchy and the First Republic; under the Directory, he became Keeper of Coins and Medals, a position confirmed and expanded by Napoleon some years later. Droz's continuing experimentation in coining technology is more important to our story, however: by 1802, he was making such serious claims to primacy of invention (claims thoughtfully supported by the Consulate, in the form of a printed pamphlet), that he was beginning to alarm his former employer, Matthew Boulton.

The latter made two responses. He authorized his nephew, who was then on the Continent, to circulate Soho's claims of primacy to anyone of importance who would listen to them; and he sent along a paper which Zack Walker might publish as he saw fit. Some years later, Walker observed that by the time he received this material, the French climate of opinion had turned so anti-British that he saw no point in publishing it.

Boulton also turned to another medium: as a counterblast to Droz's claims, he published his own on a handsome medal, struck in the autumn of 1803. Its obverse bore the bust of the entrepreneur; the style of the bust and the indented lettering have led many to assume that Küchler was the artist; but the dies were actually engraved in Paris by Rambert Dumarest, whom Boulton engaged for this last assignment. The reverse gave a brief history of Soho Mint and the number of coins of various sizes which could be produced there per minute. The medal is known in copper and in white metal; ironically, it may have been restruck by W. J. Taylor after the demise of the mint which had inspired it.

Boulton's growing worry over the security of his claims coincided with another decision taken at this time. Until 1797, the coiner had allowed relatively free access to the premises of Soho Mint, for a person of importance

Boulton at seventy-five, on a medal of 1803. (Author's collection)

SOHO MANUFACTORY.

THE PUBLIC are requested to observe,
that this MANUFACTORY cannot be SHEWN in Con-
sequence of any Application or Recommendation
whatever. Motives, both of a public and private
Nature, have induced the Proprietors to adopt this
Measure, and they hope their Friends will spare
them the painful Task of a Refusal.

SOHO, May 20, 1802.

who was suitably impressed was a potential customer. Entrance was restricted once Boulton's regal coinage began, but very important persons (such Lord Hawkesbury and Count Vorontzov) could still come by and see the machinery. But worry over potential and actual spies and annoyance over the resurrected claims of Monsieur Droz led Boulton to an ineluctable conclusion, which found expression in the printed advertisement reproduced above.

You will observe that this prohibition mentioned Soho Manufactory rather than Soho Mint. But that was deliberate, since most of the moneying processes were actually carried on at Soho Manufactory, and the notice would thus embrace coining as well as other activities. Boulton had discussed the idea with Mrs Matthews as early as the spring of 1800. She attempted to dissuade him, on the grounds that showing visitors around gave him much pleasure and ought therefore to be continued; but her passing, and his growing fears, counselled prohibition.

Matthew Boulton's health underwent a serious deterioration in 1805, one from which it never fully recovered. His interest in and grip on Soho Mint began declining as well. Like it or not (and there is evidence that he did *not* like it), he was increasingly forced to rely on his son to oversee the business of Soho Mint – and his other interests, too, which included the construction, dispatch, and erection of mints on the industrial principle at Copenhagen, St Petersburg, London, and eventually Rio de Janeiro. In time, the younger Boulton would also ship two steam-powered mints to India: it is deeply ironic that this man, who had so very little interest in the industrialization of money and lacked his father's vision of it or passion for it, should have done so much to ensure its success.

Matthew Boulton died on 17 August 1809. A simple but handsome commemorative medal was struck at Soho and given to each of his employees. By the time of his death, his mint's most productive years were over. The recoinage of dollars would indeed continue into 1811; but that would be the final work which Soho did for the British Isles – with the single exception of a small copper issue for the Isle of Man, produced and shipped in the summer of 1813.

For this sorry state of affairs, Soho must blame itself. Had Matthew Boulton not persisted until the British Government agreed to purchase one of his mints; had the productivity of the second Soho Mint and the quality of its product been less than they were; then his organization might well have continued coining for the British public power (or barring that, for the British private tradesman) well into the nineteenth century. After all, Soho's stepchild (the Heaton Mint) did just that well into the twentieth.

As it was, the second Soho Mint entered a period of decline from which it never recovered – at least, a decline never reversed in the place of its birth. And more than a decline, an eclipse: between June 1813 and June 1821, Soho Mint produced no coinage whatsoever. The mint made *planchets*, to be sure, and it made them by the millions, shipped to the United States, Portugal, and Brazil. But it let others stamp them, generally oblivious as to how that stamping was performed: with the exception of a half-hearted offer extended to the Americans in 1810, Matthew Robinson Boulton was content to leave the burden of monetary reform to others. And he was coming to a momentous conclusion: the best way to encourage others to effect a coining reform might be to sell them Soho Mint.

There were, I think, at least three forces at work here. While I regard psychohistory and its practitioners with some scepticism (and would cheerfully suggest that readers of this book do the same), I continue to believe that one reason for the younger Boulton's decision to sell the elder Boulton's mint was just that: it *was* his father's creation, brainchild of the parent who had constantly urged him to adopt greater business enterprise, better social skills, even better penmanship. By ridding himself of his father's mint, he would be proclaiming that his life was his own, that he was his own man – and that he had had the last word. Matthew Robinson Boulton never consigned a word of this to paper, so far as I know; and he may not have fully thought it out. But he would have been more than human, I think, had he not wished to move out of the shadow of his father. Ridding himself of the second Soho Mint was a step toward the light.

But there was more to the decision than that. Indolence formed part of Matthew Robinson Boulton's character, and he found it far more pleasant to play the country squire at Tew Park (or the man-about-town in London) than to remain in the Midlands, hustling for ever-more-elusive work for Soho Mint. To indolence were belatedly added the cares and joys of family life: nearing fifty, he took a wife early in 1817, who presented him with a daughter in the summer of 1818 and a son in the early autumn of 1820. The boy was named Matthew Piers Watt Boulton, and he would eventually oversee the demise of Soho Manufactory and Soho Mint. All that was far in the future: for the present, Matthew Robinson Boulton had all the more reason to withdraw from an active pursuit of the coining business.

And there was a final factor. Soho Mint was a drain on his finances. Whatever his other characteristics, the son appears to have been as kind-hearted as his father. Even in times when he had no work for them, he was extremely reluctant to discharge any of his mint's employees, as a notation from the end of 1813 attests. After recording a loss that year to the Coining Account of nearly thirteen hundred pounds, a clerk tersely added 'arising principally from Wages paid & little work done'.[54] By the following August, there were still twenty-three people on the mint payroll (including three mint boys), and there was virtually *no* work being done. Matters certainly could not continue down this path: Boulton must either make a determined effort to find new work for his mint, or he must sell it to someone who would. He chose the latter course.

He wrote to the Americans in the summer of 1810, offering to do their coinage or sell them his mint. Caught by surprise and hampered by the deteriorating level of Anglo-American relations, Mint Director Robert Patterson did not respond. Boulton's partner James Watt, Jr. approached the Dutch with an offer of an outright sale at the beginning of 1818. But Boulton wanted more than the King of the Netherlands was willing to pay and this attempt, too, came to nothing.

By the beginning of the 1820s, Boulton was holding conversations with the East India Company about the sale of *two* mints, one for Calcutta and the other for Bombay. It occurred to him that the now-silent Soho Mint might serve very well for the second spot, as well as freeing him from an unwanted and uneconomic possession.

The beginning of 1821 saw him supplying his partner Watt with 'the necessary information for your interview with M*r* Thompson'.[55] In order to convince the East India Company of the quality of his partner's mint, James Watt, Jr. solicited and received an order for copper coinage – Soho's first since 1813. This was prepared in the presence of the two Company engineers who would be going out to Calcutta and Bombay, William Nairn Forbes and John Hawkins. The coinage consisted of halfpennies for the island of St Helena, and what he saw convinced Captain Hawkins that *this* was the mint he wished to carry to Bombay. That was in mid-1821. It would require many more months before the East India Company would arrive at the same decision, more months still before it told Boulton of the decision that it had reached. But on 13 February 1823, Peter Auber of the Company finally gave sanction to the project. Matthew Robinson Boulton could at last rid himself of Soho Mint – and turn a profit into the bargain.

But he could not do so just yet. We may imagine that he wished the dismantling to begin as soon as weather permitted; but a new business opportunity intervened. A contact made with Argentina the previous year now resulted in a coinage of four million copper décimos. They left Soho Mint in mid-April, on the heels of another, fairly sizable copper coinage for Sumatra. Once these two issues had been dispatched, the work of dismantling the mint could begin.

By August 1823, most of it had been taken down, refitted, and made ready for its eventual resurrection at Bombay. But not quite all of it: enough machinery was left standing so that a small coinage could be prepared as a teaching aid for the managers of the future Bombay mint, should the East India Company desire such an education. It did; and a million or so copper coins in a single denomination (which was as much as the truncated mint could currently manage) were struck and sent away on 24 February 1824. John Hawkins received training; so, probably, did his foreman mechanist, George Cadenhead. And then the remaining apparatus was disassembled, greased, and crated – and what had once been the most modern coiner in the world awaited new adventures in a distant setting.

The mint departed for Bombay on board the *Florentia* on 14 September 1824. We might imagine its erstwhile proprietor perusing the *Times* for a record of the sailing, locating it, and breathing a sigh of relief: with the mint gone, he would truly be his own man, on the threshold of a life of uncomplicated leisure. We might imagine all this, but we would be wrong. For Matthew Robinson Boulton had already reached the conclusion that, like it or not, he must replace his father's mint with one of his own.

He came to this decision on the strength of lucrative new orders which appeared to be coming his way. Late in July 1826 (by which time the machinery for the third Soho Mint was completed but not yet erected), Boulton revealed why he had decided to rebuild what he had just torn down:

> I was induced to undertake the restoration of the Mint Establishment of this place by the expectations held out to me of a contract for an extended copper coinage for Buenos Ayres ... & also by concurrent similar overtures from Colombia with the additional inducement of that state becoming the purchaser of the Coining apparatus when the supply of Coin for their more immediate wants had been effected—

In other words, Matthew Robinson Boulton had been made an offer which even he could not refuse: build a new mint, make coinage on it for a profit – then sell the machinery for another profit and retire to a life of leisure, several thousand pounds to the good. These grandiose plans came crashing down during the financial crisis of the mid-1820s; but by the time they had done so, the younger Mr Boulton had a new mint.

It would be smaller than its two predecessors: it would in fact be very nearly a half-scale model of the second Soho Mint. It would feature four coining presses, six cutting out presses, and three milling machines. Coining would go on in the same separate, crescent-shaped building erected for the second mint, while all other processes would be relegated to Soho Manufactory, including rolling. Mirroring arrangements at the first Soho Mint, the rolling mill for this successor would be powered by water raised by steam.

While work began during 1824, the majority of the machinery was constructed during 1825 and early 1826. The total cost for the new mint came to £7,513. Building was halted in the spring of 1826, its owner having good reasons for curtailing the work:

> The present political state [of Argentina and Colombia] & more especially the disastrous failure of Messrs Goldsmithds [sic; Goldschmidt] have occasioned the suspension of both [coining and the sale of the mint] & with such a remote expectation of the revival of them as leaves me without an adequate inducement to incur the expence required for the erection & bringing into action of the remaining Machinery—[56]

The Soho Mint remained in an unfinished state for several years. To be sure, it effected another coinage for Buenos Aires in November 1824, and we can only assume that its presses were then moved by hand rather than steam. In July 1826, Boulton observed that while his mint could cut planchets, it could not strike them into money – at least, not by steam. This observation makes sense: planchet-cutting was a relatively simple operation, one fairly easy to resume in the Soho Manufactory. Since Boulton's sale of blanks to the United States was currently his sole reliable source of income from the mint, he would have made his best efforts to resume it. But actual coinage was another matter: the third Soho Mint did not coin by steam until the early 1830s.[57]

Boulton had once mentioned that he would be happy to mechanize his new mint, provided he had sufficient inducement. Prior to 1830, such temptation was lacking. Then two coinages beckoned in fairly quick succession, and the mint was finally completed. The first was small – so small, in fact, that it was apparently completed by hand on the new presses. This was an order for the Island of Guernsey, and the first denomination to be struck was so light (one hundred eighty-four doubles could be struck from a single pound of copper) and so limited (the Bailiff of Guernsey only wanted four tons of coins) that virtually any press would do a creditable job, with or without the intervention of a steam engine. The next denomination supplied was heavier (forty-five to a pound) but more limited still (only two tons). It was filled and sent in November 1830. By the time more coinage for Guernsey was ordered, Boulton's new mint was fully prepared for it.

The striking of the larger Guernsey coins would have predisposed Boulton in the direction of completing his mint. Two months later, an order appeared from another quarter: a gentleman named Colville wanted copper kepings for his associates at Singapore. These tokens were even smaller than the Guernsey doubles, and Soho could have limped along as it was. But this was the second time Boulton, Watt had been approached for kepings (the first had occurred in 1827 but nothing had come of it); aware of the island colony's booming trade, Matthew Robinson Boulton may have concluded that Colville's request was the tip of the iceberg. So while he discussed designs with that merchant, his people at Soho finished the mint. By 16 June 1831, an employee there reported that three of the presses were nearly ready for work, and that coining could commence within a few days; by 23 July 1831, Colville's order had been filled. It was indeed the tip of the iceberg. While this initial batch only amounted to seven hundred thousand tokens, Soho would strike over fifty million pieces for Singapore before it had done.

But this promise lay far in the future. For the first few years of its life, the third Soho Mint had very little business to fill, and its proprietor may have wondered why he had bothered to complete it. Except for issues for Guernsey in October 1831 and September 1834, the mint would lie idle until the middle of the decade. Then a modest upsurge occurred: Colville was supplied with more kepings and an issue of double-kepings, the islanders of Guernsey were supplied with modest amounts of four- and eight-double coppers, and the Chilean Government was supplied with far larger quantities of centavos and their halves. By 1837, the mint was a solid success; and the preparation of penny and halfpenny tokens for banks in Lower Canada would carry it into the middle of the next decade.

When the final Canadian orders were filled, Matthew Robinson Boulton would not be there to witness the event. He died early in the summer of 1842. An inevitable question arose: what would be done with Soho Mint?

For a time, it appeared that the mint would quickly be sold. Messrs Vivian & Sons expressed an interest in its purchase (this was logical: John Vivian had been Matthew Boulton's associate in the Cornish Metal Company, some fifty-five years before). An inventory of the machinery was prepared on 1 July. On the following day, John Vivian, Jr. and three other gentlemen came to Soho at one in the afternoon, remaining there until past six. They inspected the mint apparatus and the general state of affairs – and at that point, the transaction fell through.

We do not know why, and the fact that the Vivians took their time about delivering the inventory occasioned bad blood at Soho. Rebuffed by the Vivians, rebuffed again a few months later by a second firm, Williams Foster & Company, the three parties currently responsible for Soho Mint, Joseph Westley, Thomas Jones Wilkinson, and Charles James Chubb, reached a

Soho, 1835. (From the *Penny Magazine*)

momentous agreement: if no one wanted the Boulton facility, they would keep it open and run it themselves.

There followed one of the odder if least-known chapters in the saga. The three reduced the prices charged for coining. One of them, probably Joseph Westley, drafted a circular which was printed and sent to every foreign ambassador and consul then resident in Great Britain and personally handed to every manufacturer in Birmingham. The circular bore fruit almost immediately: on 7 January 1843, Westley reported that an agreement had just been completed for a coinage for New Brunswick. A few days later, an enquiry was received from a representative of the Swiss Confederation – although nothing came of this particular contact. The firm likewise agitated for a Mexican coinage, patterns dated 1843 bearing witness to the effort. Its efforts and the proven quality of its wares continued to bring business its way: it struck copper tokens for the Bank of Montreal during 1845, prepared blanks for Sardinia the following year, and manufactured tokens for Singapore as late as the autumn of 1847.

But an event had meanwhile taken place which cast the mint's future into jeopardy: Matthew Piers Watt Boulton had come of age. This last male descendant of Matthew Boulton would play no active role in the story of Soho Mint except for one decision which he took at the end of the decade: he elected to sell it.

And so he did: the mint was disposed of by Messrs Fuller and Horsey on 29 and 30 April 1850. We know the fate of parts of it at least: Ralph Heaton & Sons bought the presses and most of the other machinery, moved it all a few hundred yards closer into Birmingham, and set up the Heaton Mint. Its descendant still coins in Birmingham today – although any reminders of the way in which it began are muted at best. Although the Heatons got the lion's share of Soho, others bid successfully on smaller consignments. One of them was W. J. Taylor, whose winning offers enabled him to enter the coining business in a fashion particularly galling to generations of numismatists and scholars.

The auction concluded, the crowd departed, the machinery was crated and carried off – and a silence descended on this last pale reflection of Matthew Boulton's vision. His grandson's agents rented out portions of the old premises to all takers. William Vickers Toney leased a portion of the rolling mill on 1 January 1853; someone named Frederick Jenks leased the rest of it later that month, and the coining room went to a party named Southall on 15 February 1853, for an annual rent of £60.

And that was that, or very nearly so: the buildings themselves remained standing, and we may imagine that their new tenants continued to infuse them with noise and work. Then came the final act: 'in 1863 the buildings were razed to the ground, and no trace of them now remains'.[58] No trace indeed: the area where 'the Soho' once stood is now a mixed residential-industrial section of a Midlands city; and not one person in a hundred knows what happened here two centuries ago. But every time a coin jingles in the pocket of an immigrant walking up the Soho Road, a tiny act of homage takes place: for that coin is the direct descendant of the new money created at a new mint erected by Matthew Boulton, 'of Soho, near Birmingham'.

One of the last Soho patterns for Mexican coinage, a peso struck in copper, 1844. (Reproduced by kind permission of the Trustees of the British Museum)

SOURCES

The most important archival sources for this chapter will receive mention in the notes; but there are others which those interested in delving deeper into the story will wish to examine, other still which I may have mentioned in the notes but wish to emphasize again.

THE SOHO MINT, NEAR BIRMINGHAM.

To be Sold by Auction, by

MESSRS. FULLER AND HORSEY,

On MONDAY, APRIL 29, 1850, and following days, at 11 o'Clock,

AT THE WORKS, NEAR BIRMINGHAM.   IN LOTS.   BY DIRECTION OF THE EXECUTORS OF THE LATE M. R. BOULTON, ESQ.

THE VALUABLE MACHINERY AND PLANT

OF

THE SOHO MINT,

long celebrated and in high repute with the Government of Great Britain, as also with Foreign powers in Europe, Asia and America, the East India Company, and with mercantile and other firms of eminence in all parts of the world.   Also,

THE IMPORTANT COLLECTION OF DIES FOR COINS AND MEDALS,

(forming the well-known Soho collection), most beautifully executed, principally by the celebrated Kuchler, and by Droz and Philpp.

THE MACHINERY

may be pronounced as the most perfect of its kind in existence, having been constructed entirely under the personal superintendence of the late proprietor, whose genius and great mechanical skill are too well-known to render further allusion necessary; it includes

FOUR COINING PRESSES,

highly finished and worked by Pneumatic Apparatus.   Each Press is constructed in a massive iron frame, with 5½-inch screw, working in a heavy metal nut; the dies are placed in a steel collar, which rises as the blank is struck, thereby preserving a square edge to the Coin.   It is fed by a self-acting layer on, so formed as to reject an imperfect or improper Blank, and requiring merely the attention of a child in order to the efficient operation of the Machine.   The speed varies from 60 to 80 blows per minute, according to the size of the Coin.

SIX CUTTING OUT PRESSES,

(worked by the Steam Engine with pneumatic balance pumps;) they are highly finished and erected in a circular iron frame, with fly-wheel and gearing, and capable of cutting 300,000 Blanks per day.

THREE MILLING MACHINES;

2 Shaking Machines, with Drying Stoves; Washing and Pickling Cisterns; Annealing Furnaces and Muffles;

A POWERFUL MEDAL OR MULTIPLYING PRESS,

to work by hand, with 5½-inch screw, and metal nut, in massive iron frame; several smaller Punching Presses;

A 10 HORSE POWER CONDENSING STEAM ENGINE;

2 Steam Boilers: 2 Timber Beam Condensing Steam Engines, one of which will be considered highly interesting from the fact of its being the first erected by "James Watt;" 2 powerful Vacuum Pumps; 700 feet Iron Shafting; 100 pair Plummer Blocks and Brasses; self-acting Screw-Cutting Lathe; 1 self-acting Turning Lathe; 8 Engine and Foot-turning Lathes; Drilling Machines; an assortment of Taps and Dies, Stocks and Steel Tools; 50 dozen Files;

EIGHT PLATE AND BAR ROLLING MILLS,

the Rolls by "Wilkes;" Driving Pinions and Apparatus; the iron frame work for a Water Wheel; 100 Spur, Rigger and Pinion Wheels; Cutting Shears; Tilt or Stamping Hammer; Smiths' Forges, Bellows and Tools; Box, Beam and other Scales; 2 tons Weights; Crab Crane; Machine Crane and Jib; Grindstones and Frames;

AN ASSORTMENT OF EXPENSIVE PATTERNS,

including those of the Royal Mint and the East India Company's Mints at Bombay and Calcutta, also of the various Machines at the Soho Mint;

12 TONS OF THE FINEST DIE STEEL,

made expressly for the late Mr. Boulton, under his personal directions, and acknowledged to be the best Die Steel in the Kingdom; 2 tons Shear and Scrap Steel; 7 tons of best Die Iron; 6 cwt. forged Dies and Collars;

5 TONS OF COPPER AND LEAD,

in sheets and Scrap, Cisterns, Pipes, &c.; Swedish Copper for Alloy; 50 Brass Cocks;

THE EXTREMELY VALUABLE COLLECTION OF DIES

for the Coins and Medals, well-known as the Soho Collection, most beautifully executed, principally by the celebrated Kuchler, and by Droz and Philpp, also the Dies for many rare Coins, hitherto considered as almost unique, including a Dollar George III., 1798, a Britanniarum Penny, many specimens of proposed Coins, of various dates, and of the French Republic, 1790 to 1792, a pattern Half-penny George III. by Droz, and Provincial Tokens; also

A CABINET OF COINS AND MEDALS,

embracing 4 sets of the Soho Collection, and many others extremely rare.   At the same time will be sold

THE OFFICE FITTINGS AND FURNITURE,

including 2 Iron Strong-room Doors, an Iron Safe, Wainscot Presses, Desks, Copying Machines, Office Stove, and a large variety of miscellaneous property.

The Machinery may be seen in motion, and the other effects Viewed, on Thursday, Friday, and Saturday prior to the Sale.   Catalogues, without which no person can be admitted, may be obtained at One Shilling each, of Messrs. FULLER & HORSEY, Billiter Street, London.

End of the line: title page of the Soho auction catalogue, 1850. (Courtesy Birmingham City Archives, Birmingham Central Library)

Memorial medal to
Matthew Boulton, 1809.
(Courtesy Birmingham
Museums and Art Gallery)

Matthew Boulton's notebooks afford a priceless glimpse into the course of this magnate's thoughts about the conjunction of coinage and steam power. The most important materials will be found in MBP377, 378, and 379 – boxes containing notebooks 26–50, 51–79, and 80–96, respectively. Coinage first enters the picture in notebook 47, started on 1 June 1786. Early musings on the second Soho Mint are first found in notebook 77, begun on 1 May 1797. Boulton's notebooks frequently give us the earliest hints about his future actions or policies.

Materials on the construction of the second and third Soho Mints may often be found in the Boulton Mint Books, especially MBP30 and 38 for activities in 1798–9 and MBP68 for those during the mid-1820s. In the latter case, it will also be advisable to consult the boxes on the Bombay and Calcutta mints, especially MBP403, Bombay Mint, box 1.

For the story of the original Soho mint, our sources are less extensive; but one can usually follow the thread of its conception and construction through the Boulton-Droz correspondence (MBP27 and 28), as well as the former's outgoing letters of the period, copies of which will be found in MBP145, 148, 150, and 151 ([Private] Letter Books L, O, Q, and R, respectively); other relevant materials have already been mentioned.

For the story of Soho Mint as a whole, the specialist will wish to consult MBP416–419: Soho Mint; Soho Mint Accounts; Soho Mint: Coining, Rolling, Melting; and Recoinage of Spanish Dollars, 1804–11. Of the four, the first is probably the most useful. And material on the survival tactics of the middle 1840s will be found in MBP333 (Robinson, Westley, Chubb) as well as in the letter books of that period, especially MBP86 (Mint and Coinage Letter Book, 1840–1845).

The auction catalogue from the sale of Soho Mint has survived in several collections; I am indebted to Harrington Manville of Washington DC for his loan of a photocopy of that publication.

NOTES

1 MBP416, Soho Mint: James Lawson to Matthew Robinson Boulton, 2 January 1810; emphasis in original.
2 The concept in question was the minting of coins in low relief, their legends sunk into raised surrounding ribbons. Boulton was making pattern guineas along these lines by 1791, and it eventually led to the 'Cartwheel' coppers of 1797; but Watt suggested that Boulton was testing this idea (and that of striking coins in plain collars) as early as 1785. His sketch on Boulton was reproduced in H. W. Dickinson's *Matthew Boulton* (Cambridge, 1936), pp. 203–8.

3 MBP308, Garbett, Samuel and Garbett family, 1765–85: Samuel Garbett to Matthew Boulton, 5 December 1782.

4 MBP416, 'Minutes of a Conference held at Soho-House on the 7*th* of Jan*y* 1810.' John Southern claimed credit for the introduction of an air pump into Murdock's scheme.

5 One of the reasons for Boulton's attraction to Droz was that the latter was a superb engraver, one of the finest numismatic artists produced by the eighteenth century. Boulton grudgingly conceded this point even after Droz's many faults had driven him to distraction, and to the annoyance of legal recourse.

6 MBP145, Letter Book L: Matthew Boulton to Lord George Hamilton, 18 September 1786.

7 MBP28, Correspondence, Boulton to Droz: Matthew Boulton to Jean-Pierre Droz, 2 April 1787.

8 MBP28, Matthew Boulton to Jean-Pierre Droz, 15 April 1787.

9 Garbett continued to see himself and Boulton as a team, working together for coinage reform. But his interest was waning by mid-1787 (perhaps in recognition that very little was likely to be accomplished in the foreseeable future); and he played little further role in the story.

10 MBP148, [Private] Letter Book O: Matthew Boulton to Hodgells, Harrison, and Greenbaugh, undated but October 1787.

11 Boulton was referring to the small building which would house his presses, not to the complete mint. From other evidence, we know that the first Soho press room stood in Matthew Boulton's garden, behind the menagerie, facing Soho Manufactory. The builder announced its completion on at least two later occasions (in his letters to Droz of 17 December 1787 and 22 January 1788); by mid-April 1788, he had decided that his original structure was too small, had it pulled down, and started again. A second brick building, which Boulton intended to hold eight coining presses, had been finished by mid-June. It was incredibly tiny. An undated memorandum of 1789–90 assigns it a length of only eighteen feet and a width of thirteen. Attached was a vault measuring twelve by thirteen (MBP342, Soho Manufactory, 'Dimentions of Soho Shops & Buildings'; this document is in Matthew Boulton's hand).

12 One of the oddest elements of the Boulton-Droz story is that an otherwise hard-headed businessman became almost girlishly shy when it came to a formal contract. Droz's conduct might be explained by his perennial reluctance to come to a decision; Boulton should have known better.

13 MBP28, Matthew Boulton to Jean-Pierre Droz, 17 June 1788.

14 MBP145, Letter Book L: Matthew Boulton to Thomas Williams, 3 July 1788.

15 MBP306, Droz, John Peter: Matthew Boulton to the arbitrators in his dispute with Jean-Pierre Droz, 14 February 1791. Droz's offer was not taken up.

16 MBP145, Matthew Boulton to Thomas Williams, 8 October 1788; spelling in original. We may wonder at Boulton's candour in a letter to a past and future rival. But he must have Williams' active or passive co-operation in any future copper coinage and likely concluded that honesty now might prove rewarding in future.

17 MBP351, Watt, James, 1785–91 (box 4): Matthew Boulton to James Watt, 26 January 1789; spelling and punctuation in original.

18 MBP322, Lawson, James and Lawson, Archibald: James Lawson to Matthew Boulton, 27 June 1789.

19 MBP358, Walker, Z. sr., (box 1): Zacchaeus Walker, Sr. to Matthew Boulton, 4 September 1789.

20 MBP306, 'English agreem*t* between M Boulton & __ Droz drawn by M*r* Slaid Novem*r* 1789'. It is interesting that Boulton was now thinking about a refurbishment of the Royal Mint in connection with Droz. Soho would indeed rebuild the national coiner some two decades later – but Droz would play no part.

21 MBP150, [Private] Letter Book Q: Matthew Boulton to G. Foucaut, Jr., 9 November 1789; spelling and emphasis in original.

22 MBP351, James Watt to Matthew Boulton, 11 January 1790.

23 MBP150, Matthew Boulton to Jean Baptiste Barthélemy Dupeyrat, 18 March 1790.

24 Not by me, though.

25 Boulton's fears were justified, as Droz did just that a decade or so later.

26 Birmingham Reference Library, Boulton & Watt Papers, Portfolio 714, second part, 'Specification of Coining Mill [1790]'. The Patent was finally published in 1855 by Eyre and Spottiswoode, complete with drawings. The punctuation was slightly altered in the printed version, but the wording remained identical.

27 Dumarest was also something of a perfectionist, and his nerves were simply not equal to the slack periods punctuated by days of frenetic activity which were the lot of the early Soho Mint and anybody who worked for it. He was replaced by another Frenchman named Noël-Alexandre Ponthon in the summer of 1791. Ponthon worked at Soho until

September 1795, but he was soon overshadowed by the most durable of Mr Boulton's imported designers, Conrad Heinrich Küchler. Küchler began working for Soho on a piece-work basis in the spring of 1793, moved there in the summer of 1795, and continued in the firm's employ for the remainder of his career. He died in 1810.

28 MBP416, 'Inventory of Property belonging to Coinage-account taken 31*st* December 1790'. That Boulton's bludgeons might not be redundant was borne out by the famous Birmingham Riots of the following July, which represented in part a nativist reaction against all things French. Boulton's mint with its suspect machinery and French designer posed a logical target for the wrath of the mob; but the rioters concentrated their attention elsewhere.

29 MBP351, Matthew Boulton to James Watt, 26 March 1791.

30 MBP351, Matthew Boulton to James Watt, 23 March 1791.

31 MBP346, Swediaur, F: Matthew Boulton to Francis Swediaur, 7 February 1791.

32 MBP346, Francis Swediaur to 'Andrew Smith' [Matthew Boulton], 17 March 1791.

33 MBP325, Matthews, Mrs. C., (Box 1): Matthew Boulton to Charlotte Matthews, 18 August 1791; spelling in original.

34 MBP151, [Private] Letter Book R: Matthew Boulton to the Monneron Brothers, 15 February 1792; spelling in original.

35 MBP151, Matthew Boulton to the Monneron Brothers, 23 February 1792.

36 MBP325, Charlotte Matthews to Matthew Boulton, 19 June 1795.

37 MBP233, Letter Box F2: George C. Fox to Matthew Boulton, 25 January 1793.

38 MBP233, George C. Fox to Matthew Boulton, 2 March 1793.

39 MBP322, James Lawson to Matthew Boulton, 10 September 1792. Boulton was then in Truro, Cornwall on copper business.

40 MBP295, Brown, W. D: William D. Brown to Matthew Boulton, 20 September 1792.

41 MBP272, Banks, Sir Joseph and Miss Sarah: Matthew Boulton to Sir Joseph Banks, 9 June 1795.

42 MBP411, East India Company coinage: Matthew Boulton to Robert Wissett, 18 February 1796; spelling in original.

43 MBP385, 'A.W.': Matthew Boulton to John Southern, 15 May 1797.

44 A similar fear existed in the United States during this period. Alarmed by the possibilities of a war with the French, the administration of John Adams secured the passage of Alien and Sedition Acts that very year, 1798.

45 MBP272, Matthew Boulton to Sir Joseph Banks, 1 February 1799.

46 MBP343, Southern, John; Southern, Thomas: John Southern to Matthew Boulton, 1 May 1799; emphasis in original.

47 MBP385, Matthew Boulton to John Southern, 19 April 1799; spelling in original.

48 MBP385, Matthew Boulton to John Southern, 9 March 1799.

49 Manuscript Group Number 58, Joshua and Thomas Gilpin Collection, Pennsylvania State Archives (Harrisburg, PA), Joshua Gilpin Reel 2, Journal LXXXIII, 21–27 August 1799; spelling and punctuation in original. I am greatly indebted to my friend and colleague, Professor Eric Robinson, for alerting me to this priceless material.

50 MBP295, Brown, W. D: William D. Brown to Matthew Boulton, 30 May 1799.

51 MBP369, Wilson, Thomas, 1778–1812: Matthew Robinson Boulton to Thomas Wilson, 24 December 1800. The younger Boulton enclosed a handbill for Wilson to distribute at Cornish ports and other places, giving a description of the fifth burglar, who was still at large.

52 MBP352, James Watt to Matthew Boulton, 14 January 1802.

53 *The Annual Register, or a View of the History, Politics, and Literature for the Year 1801* (London, 1802), p. 406.

54 MBP60, Mint Day Book, 1808–1813, p. 372 (notation of 31 December 1813).

55 MBP403, Bombay Mint, (box 1): Matthew Robinson Boulton to James Watt, Jr., 9 January 1821.

56 MBP407, Calcutta Mint, (box 1): Matthew Robinson Boulton to Sir George Robinson, Bart., 31 July 1827. Boulton had been asked to coin twenty or twenty-five tons of copper for the East India Company; this letter contained the reasons for his refusal.

57 To be sure, it had the potential long before that; an entry of 31 December 1826 noted expenses on the 'Soho New Mint' of £668.7.0 for the metal materials of a ten-horse engine with a twelve-horse boiler – just the size we would expect for a mint with four coining presses (MBP68, Mint Book, Mint and Coinage Day Book, 1820–34, p. 146).

58 W. K. V. Gale, *Boulton, Watt and the Soho Undertakings* (Birmingham, 1952), p. 30.

CHAPTER 2

Russia

Among the foreign adventures of Boulton, Watt & Company, that experienced in Russia may well have been the most significant. There are a number of reasons for its importance.

First, it was a very large project – large at least compared with what had gone before if not with what came later. To be sure, with the Royal Mint and the East India Company mints, the Boultons would be working with projects involving sums several times greater than those seen here. But in the context of Soho's earlier adventures (and its current, still-shaky financial picture), the Russian project was very large, and very welcome.

The second key to the importance of the St Petersburg story is that it represents the first time Matthew Boulton moved from the talking stage to the doing stage. The inventor had discussed sending a mint to Prussia (and he had even thought of transferring his own operations to France); but this was the first modern mint which he actually built specifically for export, and then exported. The Russian project would mark an important stage in the story of Soho if only for this single reason.

But there were several other keys to its significance. It was the only one of Matthew Boulton's foreign adventures which changed the way he did business at home. The Russians informed him that their mint would have to be arranged in a particular fashion. Boulton panicked, then began tinkering with his invention. And he shortly emerged with a new idea, not only about how to dispose the Russian machinery in an acceptable manner, but how to arrange coin-making at Soho in a better manner too, and by extension any manufacturing process whatsoever. We shall examine this development in detail, because it may be the greatest single contribution made by Matthew Boulton to the history of technology.

For the fortunes of Boulton, Watt & Company, the greatest significance of the Russian affair was this: it forecast the future in a number of ways. The firm encountered difficulties here which it would meet elsewhere, again and again, for as long as it went on exporting mints. Indeed, it is difficult to think of any later problem or event which had not previously found its way into the St Petersburg story.

That affair was always subject to the force of larger events, both in Britain and elsewhere. The mint was conceived and constructed during the Napoleonic Wars, reaching its completion just as events were taking a turn against the interests of Britain and her people – including numismatic entrepreneurs. The conflict dogged the Russian project every step of the way, a preview of what would happen in dealings with Denmark, Brazil, even the United States. Of all of Soho's bad fortune (and on balance, the firm had more than its share), its lack of timing may have been the worst: for just as it was ready to export what it had learned, a diffusion which could only thrive in peace, the European wars were approaching their climax. Here as later, the Boulton operation would finally win through, but only by dint of sheer persistence.

The second harbinger lay in what happened when Boulton attempted to set up his mint. Having trained several Russians in the mysteries of industrialized moneying (and having been somewhat disappointed with the results), Boulton would send his own mechanics out to St Petersburg to erect the mint. But there would be incessant tension between the members of the team, and between Boulton's men and their Russian hosts. Authority and wages would form constant bones of contention, and their experiences would so scar Soho's men that none of them would ever participate in another foreign assignment. The Boultons would continue to send their people abroad – and the later emigrants would encounter the same tensions and disputes as the members of the pioneering group. In no case could the process be said to have been an unqualified success; again, Russia forecast the future.

But there was more. Matthew Boulton had assumed that the Russian monarchy viewed his machinery in the same way as he, desired it for the same purposes for which he had contrived it. But the monarchy had other ideas: *it* wanted a Boulton mint, not to provide secure money for its people, but as a symbol of its enlightenment and modernity! Matthew Boulton would have been greatly disappointed had he known this at the outset. By the end of the project, he and his firm would count themselves fortunate to receive payment for the mint, regardless of why the monarch wanted it. But Soho had been taught the first in a series of similar lessons: its industrial writ did not extend beyond the shores of Great Britain. Once one of its mints left the country (or was even paid for, preparatory to its exit), it passed from the control of the seller to the caprice of the purchaser. Boulton, Watt & Company eventually learned to live with this fact, but it was never entirely comfortable with it.

Two other malign qualities first appeared with the Russian project, and reappeared later. First, the building of the St Petersburg mint took far longer than anyone had anticipated or even feared. The project was initiated in 1796, and Boulton confidently expected to see its end within five years at most. Instead, between the time of the project's initiation and that of its conclusion, *twelve years* would elapse. Matthew Boulton and his firm were partly responsible. But the majority of the blame originated to the east: with rulers who countermanded each other's orders, with venal and incompetent officials, with mint buildings pledged but found wanting – and with the terrible Russian winters, which mocked all human timetables. What first happened here happened elsewhere later, with variations in the proportions of blame.

If Russia predicted the course of later events, it was nonetheless unique. Its cast of characters, ranging from deranged Tsars to squabbling Scotsmen, set it apart. So did the ever-present danger of industrial espionage, yet another legacy of the Napoleonic conflict. Matthew Boulton (whose nerves were none too steady after his long dealings with officials at home) saw French spies around every corner and under every bed in St Petersburg. He was over-reacting; but there *were* spies nonetheless. And industrial barons with whom he'd crossed swords in one country, now waiting in ambush in another. And rogues and mountebanks in general, including one whose mistress was a London pawnbroker. In short, an interesting tale for what it foreshadowed – and an interesting tale for itself.

It bears a final mark of distinction. In no other instance would the dealings of Boulton, Watt & Company with a foreign government, for a foreign mint, cause more harm to the general fortunes of the firm. For the fact that the Russian mint took far longer to construct than anticipated, the fact that Boulton's men could not be assigned to other projects until its completion, created problems in the construction of a mint at home, crises in the construction of a mint abroad. In the latter case, it would also mean the postponement of payment for services rendered for nearly ten years.

In the telling of the story, there are a few people you will wish to meet, or meet again. On the British side stand Matthew Boulton and his son, Matthew Robinson Boulton. Each will be invited to Russia to oversee the mint project. Neither will accept the invitation: by the time the offer is extended, the elder Boulton's health will be precarious, while the younger will have interests enough to keep him at home as well. But a member of the family will be sent out all the same, Matthew Boulton's nephew, Zacchaeus Walker, Jr. Two years older than Matthew Robinson, he shares some of the son's interests but is rather closer to the father, and becomes his troubleshooter in Russia. He sees the mint to completion, as well as acquiring a bride (to his own and everyone else's surprise: he has the reputation of a confirmed bachelor). Walker possesses no particular mechanical attainments, but he is good at smoothing over interpersonal difficulties, which is why he is sent. He is also an inspired if acerbic commentator on Russian life and manners.

In St Petersburg, he superintends four members of the 'Soho Corps'. The group's leader is James Duncan; he is constantly challenged by the three others, led by James Harley (James Walker and William Speedyman are the other members of the group). The constant squabbling between them (and the fact that progress on the mint is much too slow for Soho's taste) results in Zack Walker's eastward mission.

As to Soho's clients, the three rulers under whom the project goes (and does not go) forward need no introduction, as the saying goes. But character traits of Tsarina Catherine II and Tsars Paul I and Alexander I go far towards influencing the course of the Russian project, as you will see.

Beyond rulers (whose contact with Boulton, Watt is obviously limited), Soho deals with two sets of Russians over the years. One group is in London, consisting of the Russian Ambassador to the Court of St James's, Count Simon Vorontsov, and his secretary, the Reverend James Smirnov. Smirnov is the more important of the two from Soho's point of view, for he handles much of the correspondence with that firm's owner, Matthew Boulton. Both gentlemen are sympathetic observers of the Soho effort to reform their nation's coinage.

The second set of Russians with which Soho must deal is based in St Petersburg. Most important is Count Alexis Vasiliev, Minister of Finance and Treasurer of the Russian Empire. He wishes Boulton and the new mint well,

Count Vorontsov, from a
painting by Richard Evans,
c.1790. (Courtesy of
Randolph Zander)

but unfortunately dies just as it is completed, putting payment for it at risk. Alexander Deriabin comes under consideration as a prospective master of the new machinery, but he goes on to more important posts, ends at last as chief director of mines, salt works, and *all* Russian mints. Other Russians will move across the stage and will be introduced in their order. But these are the main players with whom Matthew Boulton, his nephew, and the Soho 'Mintaneers' will have to deal.

Or nearly all: a handful of Britons long resident in Russia deserve mention. Chief among them is Charles Gascoigne, son-in-law of Matthew Boulton's old associate Samuel Garbett. Gascoigne had enjoyed a shady reputation while still in Britain (he managed the Carron Iron Works); his reputation was scarcely enhanced when, one step ahead of his creditors, he allowed himself to be enticed to Russia by Admiral Grieg, who wanted him to set up a cannon works there. He tried to tempt several British workers to accompany him, but with limited success. He had better luck in obtaining massive quantities of cannon metal, fire brick, and fire clay – worrisome, because he would be able to set up a cannon works with British commodities whose products would undercut British guns, being produced by slave labour.

This was in 1786. Gascoigne prospered, and he eventually became *Baron* Gascoigne, to the consternation of Matthew Boulton and his other, more scrupulous acquaintances. And he would never forget that Boulton had been one of the leaders in the movement to prevent his departure, and to stifle the inception of the Russian cannon project.[1]

George Sheriff started out at Soho, where he was apprenticed to Boulton & Watt. He made his way to Russia some years later, and he was working for the Russian Government as an engineer when our story gets under way. His reconnection with Soho, while brief, will be worth scrutiny.

It is important to understand that the Russia story did not suddenly begin in the mid-1790s. Boulton's connections with St Petersburg may in fact be traced back at least as far as 1765, and trade with the Russians was promising enough to inspire his partner John Fothergill to set up shop there late in 1767. This was long before Boulton's connection with James Watt, and with the steam engine: Boulton & Fothergill sold the wealthy inhabitants of St. Petersburg and Moscow their usual assortment of useful and useless articles, ranging from clocks (twenty-six were shipped to St Petersburg in 1768), to ormolu vases and fancy shoe buckles.

When Boulton entered into partnership with James Watt, his range of trade expanded. He began manufacturing steam engines on Watt's principles, was selling them to Cornwall by the late 1770s. They were used there to remove water from mines; it was only natural that he would seek to sell them abroad for the same purposes. By now, he had a contact in Russia named Peter Capper, whom he asked to make inquiries in this regard. Capper dutifully did so and sent back an interesting reply:

> I have lately had some discourse with a great Iron Master he tells me that little Power for draining Mines is wanted as the ore is in such Abundance that they work none but what is cleared by a Level & if I understand him right that they work horizontally into the Mountains not sink Pitts & as one great Object of your Engine is a saveing of Labor – that as the Workmen are all slaves, this advantage is of no Moment – (NB. I dont comprehend the sense of this objection)[2]

Matthew Boulton may not have understood it either, but he would have done well to ponder it. For a country which saw no sense in labour-saving innovations to pump water from mines would probably not welcome such improvements elsewhere, including in the minting process.

Undaunted, Boulton continued to send a variety of typical Birmingham exports to Russia, even as he became more closely involved with steam power and its prospects. As we know, he had turned his attention to steam-powered minting by the late 1780s, and it became the subject claiming his interest and labour for the remainder of his life. By 1790, he had secured his patent and, having been rejected by officials at home, was now sending specimens of his new medals and coins to important persons abroad, in hopes that something might turn up.

And soon there were straws in the wind that, if Britons rejected his mint, Russians might well embrace it. For now, they were hints and nothing more: in 1791, an acquaintance named Park informed Boulton that Count Vorontzov would appreciate having two of Boulton's medals – wanting them perhaps as an aid in persuading his Empress of the suitability of Mr Boulton's machines to the reformation of Russia's wretched copper money. This would have been music to Boulton's ears: Russia's copper coin *was* abominable, and the reformation of money on the lower end of the scale was always his dream. But nothing came of it, at least not just now.

More straws: another Boulton acquaintance, a St Petersburg businessman named Wagnon, was approached sometime in the mid-nineties by members of the Russian Court. They wished his advice on the reformation of their coinage. Could he supply them with 'a Sample of some of the best English Coins'? He could, sending them 'the Collection in Tin & Bronze [Boulton] was so kind to present me with in 1794'.[3] And this straw led to greater things.

Boulton's wares found a favourable reception with Catherine II (who always viewed herself as a reformer, on the cutting edge of modern times). Their maker would soon be offered his first, and in many ways his most important, opportunity to extend his new way of coining beyond the place of its birth.

The Empress was interested in his coinage, not because of the ormolu vases he had once sent her, and not, at bottom, because of such enterprising intermediaries as Messrs Park and Wagnon. The truth was that the St Petersburg mint had become sadly outdated, was simply unable to produce the volume of gold, silver, and copper coinage required by a dynamically growing economy.

Set up by Peter the Great in the early 1720s, it had scarcely changed in the past seventy years. It was particularly deficient in motive force. While horses were used for the rolling process, the actual coining was done by hand on screw or *balancier* presses. The largest coin struck was the copper five-kopek or piatak, and it was in fact so large and thick that its production was generally farmed out to even more primitive mints, facilities where water-power could be employed. The products of these mints – located at Anninsk, Ekaterinburg, and Kolyvan – were so poor that they invited forgery, both unofficial and official (in the latter case by Sweden during a war with the Russian Empire in the 1780s). Catherine began to address the problem near the end of her reign. Two main possibilities existed. A new facility could be set up someplace else. Or the old one could be rehabilitated. Catherine opted for the latter. And here, at last, was the opening which Matthew Boulton would take – to his later regret.

The precise moment when the industrialist and the Russians began serious conversations is not known, but it is likely to have been during the latter half of 1795. Certainly, one of Boulton's notebooks contains several pages of jottings on the subject under date of 1 January 1796. By the end of the following May, the coiner was approached on the subject by one of his old St Petersburg acquaintances, Alexander Baxter. Baxter, a transplanted Scotsman who was now serving as the *Russian* Consul General in London, wrote to Boulton in the name of the Empress, making him an offer which was couched in such a way that it could scarcely be refused:

> As the Empress of Russia is very desireous to make some necessary Improvements in Her Imperial Mint at S*t* Petersburg – by procuring some masterly hands, to engrave Dies for Gold, Silver & Copper Coins, & to purchase the whole apparatus & machinery, that is necessary for Strikeing them. And as all the World knows that no person is better qualifyed to execute such a Commission Then M*r* Boulton – May I request the favor of you Sir! to inform me in return whether you chuse to make any proposal respecting the whole of this busines?[4]

Boulton was deeply interested but unwilling to commit himself on a precise estimate of the cost of such a mint. He had never before constructed one for export, and he had no real idea of the coinage requirements of his prospective customers. (As it happened, neither did they, but they failed to tell Boulton.) The summer of 1796 passed in a confused series of interchanges, wherein each side attempted to clarify the ideas and commitments of the other. By late July, Boulton was getting some of the data which he needed to set a price. The Russian requirement for coinage would, said Baxter, be enormous, and it would be concentrated in Boulton's favourite metal, copper.

Baxter estimated that the new mint must create £1,000,000 in coinage each year. While £100,000 in gold and £850,000 in silver coin would be wanted, that still left £50,000 in copper. And if that £50,000 were all struck into kopek pieces (the denomination most urgently required), this would mean a coinage of thirty million pieces in copper alone.

By late July, the Russians were thinking of more than a mint. Boulton must also send the hands to erect it, as well as the dies for its new coinage. The industrialist was peppered with questions as to reasonable wages, prices for dies ready for coining, etc. And always, there was a reminder that speed was of the essence: Boulton must commit himself *now*, while the Empress' interest was keen.

He was moving towards commitment by mid-August. In his papers in Birmingham, there is a press copy of the fifteenth of that month, which he titled 'An Estimate of the Expences of Erecting a compleat Mint (ou Hotel de monnoie)'. The original appears to have been signed and sent out, either to Baxter or to one of his Russian superiors. Boulton's use of French in the title suggests that he expected it to be translated into that language (then current in Russian correspondence) and sent on to the Tsarina's advisors at St Petersburg. The document names a cost (£6,520, half to be paid on shipment, the other half six months later) and describes a mint, to consist of eight coining presses, especially created to strike heavy Russian coins, an equal number of cutting out presses, three edge-marking machines, four contrivances for drying planchets, a turning lathe or two, various connecting mechanisms, one of Boulton & Watt's new steam engines to power the whole – and good solid British oak beams to fix all the machinery in place, Boulton having apparently heard that none was available in Russia. A rolling mill was not included but would be added later.

The day following, Boulton sent a letter of introduction to Count Vorontsov, along with a few medals and coins. Some could be sent on to St Petersburg; others were for the Count. Along with the numismatic items, Boulton (who was feeling somewhat guilty about the amount of the estimate, which he admitted was high) sent a list of all the *other* useful things one could accomplish with one of Soho's new steam engines. One could bore cannon with it. One could grind wheat. One could spin silk. One could do nearly anything, and one could do it whenever one wished – unlike water mills, whose power was interrupted by floods and frosts (no small consideration in a place like Russia), steam engines were always there, always ready to serve. The future beckoned, and its name was Steam!

Boulton's boilerplate[5] (or his medals and coins) apparently turned the trick: Vorontsov forwarded his proposal to St Petersburg on 18 August, where it was approved. Boulton heard the glad tidings from a letter to Vorontsov dated 10 October 1796 OS.

He also learned, finally, of the requirements of the mint he was now formally asked to construct. It would have to strike 240,000 gold coins, in two sizes, per year, and another fourteen million silver pieces, in four sizes. But the preponderance of the money would be in copper, as he had hoped, and the requirement there would be for a coinage greater than any Soho had ever approached, let alone surpassed. For the Russians wanted machinery capable of producing no fewer than *145,000,000* coppers, in five sizes, per year!

Copper medal commemorating the death of Catherine II, 1796; the treatment forecast Boulton's British copper coinage of the following year. (Courtesy Birmingham Museums and Art Gallery)

They also wanted Boulton personally to come over and superintend the construction of the mint – or if he were unable, to substitute two British engineers handpicked by him. The Britons would be joined by several Russians, who were already on their way to England to learn the new coining methodology at Mr Boulton's knee. And if Boulton had any concerns about securing the permission of the British Government for the export of his mint (a consideration which would indeed cause him anxiety later on), he need not worry: Vorontsov was authorized to act on his behalf.

Boulton's victory was complete. But it was also apparent rather than real. Vorontsov could not have received his authorization before the beginning of November. And the Empress who had approved the project died of apoplexy within a few days of its British receipt. She had favoured the project; would her unstable son, who now became Tsar Paul I?

For the time being, the project went on, the new ruler having more immediate concerns than British mints. The young Russians continued on their journey to Soho, arriving in London at the beginning of January 1797. Boulton awaited them impatiently, awaiting as well a wax model of the new Tsar, which Rev Smirnov had promised to obtain. He wished to put Paul on the new Russian coinage. He could have spared his efforts: the emperor would never appear on circulating Russian coins. And it soon seemed unlikely that Matthew Boulton would have any hand in making dies of any description – or indeed a mint – for this prince.

The Tsar countermanded his mother's approval. But he did so for a most curious reason. At the end of Catherine's reign, there were immense quantities of promissory paper notes in circulation, called *assignatsii*. Their value against the silver ruble had depreciated – and as far as the ruble went, it, too, was not what it had been when it was introduced as a coin during the reign of Peter the Great. Paul proposed to attack both problems at once. He would redeem and retire the inflated paper rubles, introducing improved silver rubles in their stead. He would do so at a single blow, without bothering to consider a fall-back position – which was how the new Tsar tended to address challenges in general.

He would need a mint, of course, and logic suggested that he would need a *large* mint, a productive mint, such as the one Mr Boulton was offering to build. But that facility would take several years to construct, and Paul wanted to get under way *now*. So he would quickly construct a new facility, locating it on the premises of the Assignat Bank. The Alexandrovsky Machine Works at Petrozavodsk would furnish the coining presses and a steam engine.[6] And to manage the new Bank Mint he would rely on a gifted if shady technocrat, an old friend of his and a former acquaintance of Matthew Boulton – Baron Charles Gascoigne.

It is impossible to say whether the Baron had anything to do with what shortly took place, although logic suggests that he did. It is also impossible to say when Matthew Boulton began realizing that matters were becoming complicated. At the beginning of 1797 his project still appeared to be moving smoothly along: Vorontsov initiated a request for permission to export the mint, at the same time asking for a *pro forma* confirmation of his mother's agreement from her son. And the Russians began to arrive at Soho Mint. There were five of them, the most important being Felix Schlatter, an experienced moneyer who would soon help Boulton draw up his preliminary plans.

The latter was busy thinking of the role he would personally play in time to come. He would not be able to go to St Petersburg to set the mint up, because his health was not robust and he had 'almost 1000 people in my employ [and] have contracted to erect a very great number of Steam Engines in England in the present year'.[7] He would, however, provide detailed plans for the installation and would also select and send the skilled personnel to carry it to completion.

But the Russians would first have to send him precise and detailed plans of the building where the new mint was to be erected. Schlatter could presumably help him here. Assuming that a new edifice was intended, it must be located on solid, dry ground, allowing for the construction of vaults or caves to hold the bullion prior to coinage. And it must be located near a canal or other navigation, so that heavy machinery could be easily got in now and hundreds of millions of copper coins could be easily got out in the years to come.

When Schlatter arrived, he confirmed that a new structure was indeed intended, and that the site first suggested had been rejected because it was too small to hold all the machinery and was in any case on boggy, unsound ground. This first site was the Fortress of St Peter and St Paul, and Boulton would eventually learn a good deal more about it than he desired. The Russian choice of mint location would eventually swing back to the Fortress, causing great difficulty for Boulton at Soho and his people on the spot.

But current difficulties arose closer to home. Vorontsov had promised to apply to the British authorities to secure permission to export the mint. He had accordingly written to Lord Grenville, Secretary of State at the Board of Trade. Grenville had passed his letter on to a functionary named George Hammond, directing it as well to the attention of the Attorney General, Sir John Scott. There ensued a complicated wrangle which lasted more than two years, Sir John eventually asking Boulton to prove that the export of a steam-powered mint contravened current British law in the first place! The matter would remain unresolved until the passage of a Parliamentary statute in July 1799; but even as he was attempting to extricate himself from problems at home, Boulton suddenly learned of serious difficulties abroad: on 6 February 1797, Rev Smirnov informed him that all orders for the new Russian mint had been suspended, by express order of the Emperor. Felix Schlatter was to abandon his studies and come home, along with his four companions. If Boulton had begun any of the machinery or any of the dies, he was to cease work immediately, then render a bill for the services he had provided.

What had happened? Paul's scheme for the Bank Mint must have now been in motion – even though the new facility would not be officially brought into existence until late spring. Its director would be Baron Gascoigne, and, while the alternative to Boulton's mint would eventually fail dismally, the early promise of success (Gascoigne was always eloquent, and the new Tsar was always credulous) must have cast Boulton's mint into temporary eclipse.

The industrialist was annoyed but hardly devastated. Vorontsov was sending him mixed messages – hold off on everything concrete, but continue with your plans, as this will only be a temporary halt to the proceedings. Moreover, he was receiving the first hints that the project for which he had turned mint-builder in the 1780s, a reformed copper coinage for Britain, was finally coming his way. And there was the first order of United States copper planchets, and an order of coinage for the East India Company. All in all, Boulton had enough to occupy him for now.

But he kept his hand in all the same. In late February, he sent a masterfully elegiac letter to Vorontsov, one calculated to inspire the Count with a keen sense of regret, with a realization of the magnitude of the lost opportunity – a letter which would, it was hoped, inspire its recipient to urge his Emperor to reconsider. Boulton said he would be sorry to witness the departure of Mr Schlatter and his four compatriots; but at least the former had been at Soho long enough to see 'all my presses working at the rate of 68 blows pr Minute which being multiplyd by 8 presses is equal to 544 pieces pr Minute & that number multiplyed by 60 Minutes is equal to 32,640 pieces pr hour'. He added that even larger coins, such as the Russian five-kopek coppers, would still come from his presses at the rate of forty-five per minute.

While Schlatter had been shown things from the outside, there had not been time to instruct him on the inner mysteries of the machinery, mechanisms whose principles were so radically new that neither Schlatter nor any other engineer in Europe could even guess at their nature. Boulton would be only too happy to show him all, however, if the Tsar would countermand his recent order.

Schlatter had also been introduced to one of the new Soho steam engines, which just happened to be 'of the very size & power proposed to be erected at S*t* Peters*bg*'. It was currently being employed to roll copper, iron, and steel into sheets – but it could be used for virtually any other purpose desired, from grinding musket barrels, to working forge hammers, to making copper sheathing for the Russian Navy. What a shame it would all come to nothing!

But perhaps the Tsar would reconsider. Boulton knew him as a rational prince[8]: surely he must see the wisdom of employing 'old Experience' in the building of a mint, of engaging a man 'who has not only invented but done the thing' rather than 'a Fancifull projector who only *Talks* about it'. (Boulton meant Gascoigne, although he did not name him; he knew his competition well.)

Whatever Paul's decision, Boulton proposed to continue drawing up plans for the mint, in the steadfast hope that there would one day be a mint to build. And he was doing something else as well, something which would not be fully realized for another year but whose beginnings may be traced to this period: he was toying with a new scheme of organization. Thus far, he had not got beyond a general statement of purpose: when he had the chance to build it, the Russians' new mint would be so arranged that

> every kind of work & every department should be kept seperate from each other and the people employd not permitted to enter into each others apartments. but the pieces [of money] pass through tubes [from one place to another][9]

From this modest beginning, a revolution would grow.

Five months after being informed that he had lost the right to build the Russian mint, Matthew Boulton was informed that he had regained it. It is not known whether his letter to Count Vorontsov (and to the Tsar, who stood in the shadows) had any material effect on the latter's decision to countermand his own order. Nor do we know whether Schlatter's enthusiastic reports of what he had seen found an audience at St Petersburg (although the engineer sufficiently impressed his superiors to win a return visit to Soho). The primary reason why Boulton regained the Tsar's favour appears to have been that Baron Gascoigne lost it. The Bank Mint was a fiasco from start to finish.

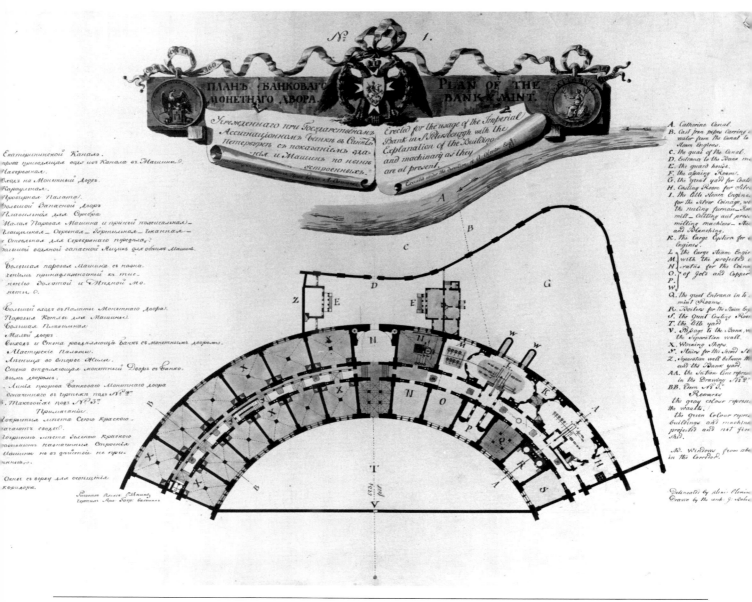

Plan of the ill-fated Bank Mint at St Petersburg. (Courtesy Collection of Richard Margolis)

Promulgated on 25 April 1797 OS by the Emperor, its tale is quickly told. A portion of the machinery stipulated was indeed set up in the Assignat Bank building, where it was joined by coining contrivances taken from the old Fortress Mint. But the coins it struck bear witness to the fact that the steam-powered equipment failed to live up to expectations – if it ever produced a single coin. The pieces struck at the Bank Mint are typical eighteenth-century Russian coins, their motive force the human arm not the power of steam.

The Tsar's loss of interest in the reform also meant that the coins made there would retain the traditional amounts of silver, rather than the higher amounts originally stipulated – while more assignats would be thrown into the money supply for good measure. So much for reform!

Baron Gascoigne would nonetheless head the new mint, at least for a time. It opened its doors for business late in 1799, its potential augmented at the end of that year when the Fortress mint was closed, the rest of its machinery transferred to Gascoigne's charge. It began serious coining in January 1800 and struck gold and silver until late 1805 – when its machinery was transferred back to the Fortress Mint! But by then, Gascoigne had long been separated from the project: a decree of 1 January 1801 OS placed the Minting Department and everything relating to it under the command of a new official, Alyabev, President of the College of Mines. The Baron was now out of office.

But we are getting ahead of the main story. Matthew Boulton had lost his mint in February 1797. He regained it in June, but there had been hints of things to come several weeks earlier.

Felix Schlatter had returned to St Petersburg, where he had extolled the virtues of Soho Mint to anyone who would listen. In mid-May, the engineer's uncle (Monsieur Schnese, who had once been attached to the Fortress Mint but was now with the Ministry of Finance) wrote an introduction and a recommendation for his nephew – who wished to perfect his understanding of coinage under the eye of the master at Soho. And if Schlatter were returning to study modern mints, that could only mean that he would soon have a modern mint of his own: the Russian project was still alive!

Schlatter duly sailed for England, arriving there late in June. And on the twenty-ninth of that month, Soho received official word:

> Sir!
>
> His Imperial Majesty the Emperor my Sovereign knowing the superiority of your inventions, and being further informed by Mr Shlatter [*sic*] of the great readiness, zeal and sincerity, which you had the goodness to shew in forwarding the design of His Imperial Majesty to erect a Mint in Russia upon the best Principles of construction, was pleased most graciously to approve of your Proposals for that Purpose, and as a mark of His approbation has sent a Letter and a gold Medal, which Mr Shlatter will have the honor to deliver into your hands.[10]

Boulton accepted the gold medal with thanks; but it was the letter which interested him more. His victory could have hardly been greater; providing his own government gave its approval, the industrialization of money could now spread abroad.

That approval was long in coming, would remain unresolved until the passage of one Act of Parliament (39 Geo. III Cap. 96 – allowing Boulton to export his mint and the skilled craftsmen required to set it up) had nullified the provisions of another (25 George III Cap. 67 – preventing the export of such commodities and people). Official blessing would only be secured in the summer of 1799, and it would not be the last hurdle to export that Soho would face. But the customer had at least reappeared and reordered, and Boulton set about satisfying him.

These were crowded times for Matthew Boulton. He was just beginning the massive 'Cartwheel' coinage (whose module and volume would nearly destroy his mint, encouraging more speculation on the reform of his machinery). He must draw up plans for St Petersburg to the degree possible with the scant knowledge he was being given. And he must make room for more Russian visitors, for Felix Schlatter's depression (the Russian worked too hard, ate and drank too little, and was desperately homesick; at one point he simply decamped, suddenly appearing on Smirnov's stoop in Richmond one day) was about to be turned to joy. No fewer than six of his countrymen were on their way to join him at Soho.

They appeared there early in 1798. Chief among them was Alexander Deriabin, who was to be taught the metallurgical side of minting. He would prove an apt student, and he would eventually achieve high rank. There were a father and son named Sobakin, sent to learn how to erect and maintain the machinery which Boulton would build. There was future tragedy here: the younger man would perish – from consumption, by the archival evidence. John Lizel was to receive training in sinking dies. In time he would do well, Boulton recommending him for important work at the new Russian mint. Tuganov and Grezin were to be trained in instrument-making, and Grezin would also learn how to make cutlery.

By the time these students arrived, their mint was beginning to take form. It is unclear when work began on the machinery, but a letter of 16 October 1797 from Boulton to Schlatter observes that mechanics had been engaged to work on two of the presses, 'which you have seen are already cast'[11]. Very probably, Boulton began work on the project as soon as he received word of the imperial assent to it.

Much had been prepared by the beginning of 1798; at that time, Matthew Boulton and James Smirnov drew up a contract of sorts, a stipulation of what was agreed upon. Dated 6 February 1798, titled 'Memorandum by the Rev*d* M*r* Smirnove of things required along with the Establishment of the Mint in Russia', the contract took a curious form, consisting of a series of questions from Smirnov, answers from Boulton. A copy of it still exists in Birmingham, signed by Boulton and witnessed by Andrew Collins, a Soho employee at St Petersburg.

There were twelve points, and they covered every conceivable aspect of the Russian project. The first four concerned the latest crop of Russian visitors, whom Boulton promised to instruct. The fifth clause asked whether a medalist should be sent to Soho to learn engraving, the sixth whether Boulton needed some Russian coins for inspiration. Boulton replied in the negative to both questions.

The seventh clause was the first suggestion of what would become a great personal disappointment. The Russian Government had decided to reduce the amount of coinage to be struck at the new mint. That being so, would it not be advisable to reduce the size of Boulton's mint package? Boulton replied in the negative – as we might expect: the man made money by selling machinery. But he gave a curious reason, and now matters become interesting.

He had originally intended to arrange the Russian presses in the same way as those at Soho – in a circle, powered by an overhead wheel connected to a steam engine with gears and shaftwork, the presses being engaged and disengaged by escapements on the wheel. But Felix Schlatter had just told him that the Russian Government would wish its coining done in separate apartments for gold, silver, and copper. This would be impossible under Boulton's original arrangement – unless the form of the coining room were to assume the shape of a pie, which was not likely. So Boulton sat down and thought, and soon announced that he had found a solution:

I have now invented the means of working any Number of Presses, placed almost in any direction in different Rooms & *at the same time* to strike very large Money with 1 Press, & very small money with another; ... I intend it to be more simple than that of my first [mint] plan. However before I attempt to erect any Part of it in Russia, it shall be erected & tried here, & then not sent 'till M*r* Deriabin & M*r* Sobakin tried it [and are] fully satisfied with its degree of Perfection.[12]

In light of his new plan, Boulton now proposed a coining room for each of the three metals, with two presses for gold, four for silver, and six for copper. This would add up to twelve rather than the eight machines the Russians wanted; but for now, let the earlier figure stand, with one press for gold, three for silver, and four for copper. The extra presses could be added whenever the Russians desired, with no trouble: Boulton's new power arrangement would see to that.

The eighth clause related to the provision of trained people to set up the mint and keep it running. Smirnov wanted an assurance of several people, for at least three years and preferably five. Boulton agreed to send out two men, one to set up the steam engine and another to erect the coining machinery. They would also instruct their native successors in their crafts, but it would hardly be necessary to detain them for three years, let alone five. A single year should suffice both for setting up the mint and training personnel. Boulton would come to rue his optimism on the eighth clause.

The ninth gave a detailed listing of the machinery to be sent out, and its cost. To strike modern money in Russia, a steam engine, eight presses, and twelve cutting out machines would be required; cost, £6,520. To roll out the metal, a fifty-five horse steam engine would be needed, along with an assortment of steel rolls; cost, £5,000. The cost of the mint would thus come to £11,520. Boulton admitted that this was a great deal of money, even for a Great Power. But the rolling mill could make sheathing for the Russian Navy in its hours of leisure, while the entire, integrated package was, to use Boulton's favourite word, 'philosophical' in construction. Considering all the time and trouble it would require, Boulton respectfully requested half payment at the time he shipped the mint (which he supposed would be in April or May of 1799), remission of the remainder six or seven months later. (Boulton would be grievously disappointed on both counts; let us hope that the 'philosophic' principle behind the Russian mint was a stoic one!)

The tenth clause would provoke disappointment and dispute as well. Boulton was asked about how much his men would expect to earn while working in Russia. He replied that wages in Britain were now very high – not less than two guineas per week for good hands – and that anyone he sent to St Petersburg would expect to receive at least that much, as well as travelling expenses. Boulton was not sanguine about finding anyone at Soho willing to undertake the project, for few artisans would consent to leave their families for extended periods. But he would look.

The eleventh clause concerned the building for the mint, whose construction Boulton asked be postponed until he had redrafted his plans. He may have regretted that clause too, in times to come. The final section attempted to establish a timetable: how long did Mr Boulton think it would be before everything was ready to send? Boulton answered that while any figure was an informed guess, he believed that the steam engines, the coining and cutting out machinery, and the connecting mechanism could all be ready to sail by April or May 1799; if that were the case, Boulton felt that the whole could be set up during 1799. Of all the optimistic pronouncements of Matthew Boulton, none would be more breathtakingly inaccurate than this.

But we are most interested in Smirnov's seventh clause, and in Boulton's response to it.

By the time it was written, Boulton had had an extended exposure to the circular press arrangement, had come to realize that it left much to be desired. This had been only one of several ideas discussed when the first Soho Mint was being built – but Boulton eventually invested so much money and effort in it that he was reluctant to abandon it. By the beginning of 1798, he was open to alternatives.

That January, John Southern came to him with a revived concept for powering presses, one involving a vacuum pump directly connected from the engine to a coining machine. On the seventeenth, Boulton agreed to a trial of Southern's idea – and his interest was indicated by his agreement to pay that engineer £500 outright and £100 annually for his occasional superintendence at Soho Mint! I suspect that preliminary suggestions that the revived method would work well explain Boulton's breezy response to the seventh clause: the new power connection would free him from the old restrictions.

But Boulton would take what was a modest if substantial improvement in minting into completely new realms. It is unclear whether he himself realized its implications at the time of his remarks to Smirnov on the sixth; a fortnight later, they were coming clear. What he was now seeing was shared with Smirnov on 20 February 1798, and it was an epiphany, a new way of thinking about the process of manufacturing itself.

It could be applied to coining – and Boulton so applied it here. But it could be applied to *anything*, whether coins or not, whether made by machinery or not. We take it for granted today; but Matthew Boulton may have been the first person in history to devise it; and he is almost certainly the first person to write it down.

His idea was that manufacturing should a *progressive* activity, in terms of the location of the various materials and movements which made it up. Listen to him:

> It is a decided & leading principle with me in the arrangement of so great a Manufactory of money
> 1*st* to apropriate an apartment for every distinct process or operation & not mix one thing with another
> 2*d* Never to permit the persons who work in one apartment to enter or pass through another
> 3*d* To *weigh* or *tale* the pieces in one room & pass them through a proper sized hole in the Wall forward into another
> 4*th* To arange the rooms in such an order that the Metal & the Money shall go forward progressively from one room to another untill it is compleatly packed & ready to deliver for circulation & never go backward & forward
> 5*th* That it shall proceed as above on the same horizontal ground floor & never be carried up & down, that being expensive[13]

Boulton added that cleanliness was important, and that he had incorporated these ideas into the latest set of plans – sent along with this covering letter for remittance to Russia.

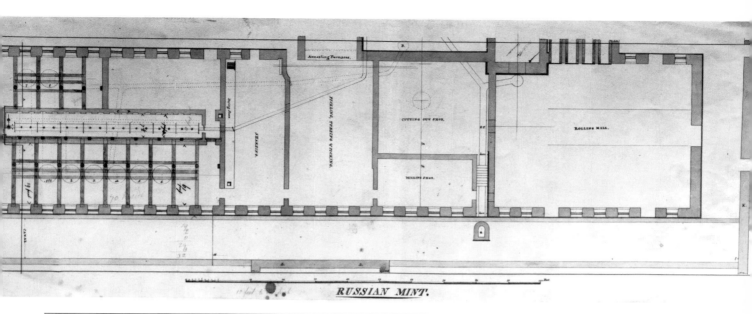

RUSSIAN MINT.

An early plan of the Russian Mint, clearly indicating Boulton's new, 'progressive' concept of manufacturing. (Courtesy Birmingham City Archives, Birmingham Central Library)

Where did he get the idea? As a manufacturer of small, intricate objects, whose elaboration naturally broke down into several logical steps, accomplished in a particular order, he must have been familiar with the basic concept for many years, even if only on a subconscious level. We take the progressive concept for granted today – how *otherwise* would you make all the products of our daily lives, ranging from washing machines to automobiles? But we take coins with shallow relief and perfect edges for granted too: and Matthew Boulton had a hand in both.

Along with general theory, Boulton included plans meant to put it into practice. They would have been general in the extreme, for the industrialist as yet had no idea of the actual appearance of the building which must be erected to house his machinery. But while cheerfully admitting that much would be subject to change, he at least put his new manufacturing arrangement on paper, spoke in general terms about the rooms (whose ceilings should be about twelve feet high and whose outer walls should be more than a foot thick, protection against the severe climate) and the preferred location for the mint (on the banks of a canal or other waterway). Theory addressed, Boulton returned to work on more immediate matters.

Mr Deriabin's education was looked to, and permission was secured for his residence in Great Britain for another nine months. Boulton continued working on the construction of the machinery (he had secured the imperial assent to receiving payment for it in the manner he desired, was still confident of shipping the mint in the spring of 1799) – and he was working with the Rennie firm as well, seeking a perfect marriage between their rolling machinery, a Boulton & Watt engine, and the striking portion of the mint. When we consider that he was still coining copper for Great Britain at this time, was sending planchets to America, was holding preliminary talks with a second country, Denmark, for a second mint – and was rebuilding Soho Mint, for good measure – we may conclude that Boulton was becoming seriously over-extended, and that unfortunate consequences might result. And they did: there was no possible way that he would be able to send out the St Petersburg mint on time.

This was only the first of a series of delays, but it was unquestionably the most important. For Boulton's lack of timely delivery would begin the process by which the entire Russian project would be delayed, year after year, until larger political events would intervene, casting this and other Soho schemes deep into doubt. And payment for them would also be endangered, Soho's foreign clients being able to argue that good intentions were simply not enough. So, to the long list of 'firsts' which we should ascribe to the Russian mint affair, we ought also to add Soho's lack of timeliness and its dire results.

In defence of his tardiness, Matthew Boulton might have observed that through honest ignorance he had been overly sanguine about the time it would take to build his machinery. But he would have been disingenuous in making such a plea: he was constructing a mint of nearly identical size for himself at Soho, and that mint, begun in April 1798, was striking coins scarcely more than a year later.

But he might also have mentioned a second problem by way of excuse, and here he would indeed have had a point: one of the difficulties about the Russian mint was that it took many months to pry permission to export it out of the sluggish British bureaucracy. It was finally secured by an Act of Parliament (39 Geo. III, Cap. 96, 'An Act to enable *Matthew Boulton,* Engineer, to export the Machinery necessary for erecting a Mint in the Domains of His Imperial Majesty, the Emperor of all the Russias'), passed on 12 July 1799. But the alert reader will have noted that the Act did not become law until some two to three months *after* Mr Boulton had promised that the machinery it mentioned would have exited Great Britain.

Let us quickly review the five clauses in the statute, for they would largely be echoed in later Acts, for later mints. First, the Secretary of State for Trade could authorize Matthew Boulton to erect a mint in Russia. Second, British customs officers could inspect the machinery and related parts but were not authorized to seize anything. Third, the Secretary of State could authorize Boulton to treat with workmen to leave Great Britain. Fourth, those workmen were authorized to do whatever was necessary for executing the project in Russia. And fifth, the Act now passed was proclaimed a Public Act and was to be so considered in all courts of law.

Boulton had continued to work on the Russian machinery even as the bill authorizing it was wending its way through Parliament. But his progress was slow, for he laboured under a major difficulty: he was unable to obtain precise, detailed ideas from his clients as to precisely what they wanted and precisely how and where they wanted to house it. His request for cooperation and its frustration formed a constant thread in Boulton's dealings with Smirnov and Vorontsov in London, and with those who stood behind them in St Petersburg. He suggested a specific architect for the project, an otherwise-unknown Londoner named Dixon. But Dixon (who, whatever his gifts as a builder, enjoyed the valuable one of speaking English as a first language, enabling him to carry out Mr Boulton's wishes to the letter) was rejected by St Petersburg, creating a potentially serious break in the chain of communications. Boulton did what he could, on one occasion sending an elaborate model of the entire arrangement of machinery he proposed. On another, he pleaded for the employment of Mr Deriabin as an intermediary between Soho and the mint architect (whoever that might be), for Deriabin understood the philosophy behind Boulton's machinery, would ensure its proper arrangement, regardless of the identity of the architect.[14] This emphasis on philosophy was no mere cant: Boulton saw mints in an essentially organic way (and how much more so, now that he had made the minting process itself organic!); while he naturally wanted to sell mints abroad, one suspects that his primary concern was that their recipients take them as seriously, and see them in the same light, as did he himself. When the Russians refused to do so, Boulton would receive his greatest disappointment.

Emboldened and spurred into greater action by his government's assent to the export of the mint, Matthew Boulton and his workers finished most of the machinery for the mint during the final months of 1799 and the first months of 1800. We know very little about the course of construction, for much of the labour was purely internal and no formal records would have been kept. But a Scotsman named George Sheriff did leave a brief account.

Sheriff had begun his career as an apprentice to Boulton & Watt, but was now resident in Russia, representing the interests there of the Clyde Iron Works. He had come to Soho to discuss the purchase of a steam engine for Russia, and he inspected the new Soho Mint and the St Petersburg machinery as well. Sheriff apparently visited the works during the last week of 1799. At that time, he saw the new Soho Mint at work on the second copper coinage for Great Britain, adding

> I likewise saw the 8 Coining presses & the 12 Cutting out presses quite finished which are intended to be sent to [St] Petersburg – However I wish it not to be mentiond, so as to come to M*r* Boultons knowledg least he should take it amiss but I could not forbear giving you this information as I thought it would afford some satisfaction to know that you will soon have the compleatest Mint in the World without plague vexation or risk of disappointment.[15]

Sheriff went his way, but he promised to send Soho accurate information on matters at St Petersburg, centring on the Russian choice of a mint site but extending to other things as well. His services to Boulton in the former instance will be detailed later; but he also rendered a service to us – by penning a description of an earlier attempt at mint modernization, one which owed nothing to Matthew Boulton *or* to Baron Gascoigne.

I include it here because I have never seen it anywhere else. According to Sheriff, it took place in 1795. A proposal had been put forth to purchase a steam engine belonging to a Mr Baird – almost certainly Charles Baird, another Scotsman who had set up shop in the Russian capital. It was thought that Baird's engine could be used to power a mint, movement being transferred from the engine to the presses by means of cranks and rods. The presses were simple *balancier* affairs, the very ones 'as at present used in the old mint in the fortress, only they work them by hand'.[16] Sheriff's terse sketch suggests that the project was not a success, indeed may have never gone beyond the talking stage. The rods and cranks might have worked; but Baird's engine may have lacked the power necessary to the work.

All of the information which Boulton was able to obtain from George Sheriff and others in England proved inadequate: in the end, he had simply to ship his machinery with all good intentions, and hope that it would be decently and intelligently housed once it reached Russia. The most important elements, the coining presses, the cutting out machines, and the steam engines to power them and the rolling mill, left Soho in April 1800. They would depart Hull for St Petersburg on 9 May on board the *Nottingham*, Thomas Minnitt, Master.

As Boulton was finishing and sending his wares, he was also turning to a related concern, the selection and dispatch of personnel adequate to erect the mint once it arrived in Russia.

Four Britons would be sent out for that purpose in 1802 – James Duncan, James Walker, James Harley, and William Speedyman. It was supposed that the first two were currently at work for George and John Rennie. Both were old hands, both would be most valuable employees in the St Petersburg project. In January 1800, Matthew Boulton requested their loan from the Rennies. That firm shortly replied that James Walker had moved on, was now working for another organization named Gardner Manner & Company. But the Rennies thought that Walker's release could be easily secured, and so it eventually was. Duncan and Walker would be the source of much dispute in St Petersburg and increasing headaches for Soho, as we shall see; and another member of the future 'Soho Corps' was now making his appearance too – James Harley. The son of a physician, Harley had evidently come down in the world and would prove deeply resentful and easily slighted in the harsh Russian environment in which he and his mates must labour. Harley would cause more trouble than all of Soho's other men combined. William Speedyman, youngest member of the Russian expedition, would join it somewhat later. Easily led, he looked up to James Harley and tended to fall in with the latter's plans and protests.

One question remained to be decided: Soho would be sending its mechanics; but would its master accompany and oversee them and the construction of his mint? Boulton declined with regrets: as the eighteenth century ended, he was already in his early seventies, burdened with coinage for Britain and mints for several countries – and his health, none too robust for the past decade, simply would not permit an extended absence of this sort. For a time, he and his son mulled over the dispatching of the latter in his father's stead, but Matthew Robinson Boulton now had Soho Foundry and a number of other concerns at home, and he, too, would decline the honour. But in time a Boulton relative would be sent, indeed would *have* to be sent, to superintend the project. This was Zacchaeus Walker, Jr. Walker would go to Russia in 1803, about a year after the other Soho employees had arrived. His tasks would be to oversee the project – and to prevent the four from doing mayhem to each other.

As mentioned earlier, the first of the shipments of mint machinery left Soho in the spring of 1800. At the time of its departure, its builder had still received no concrete instructions or plans as to its housing, and he was writing Vorontsov and Smirnov (for translation to their masters in Russia) that unless such plans were received in short order, nothing more could be accomplished at Soho; without those plans and detailed information, the entire mint project (which had already gone on longer than anticipated) would necessarily be postponed for another year.

It is unclear whether Boulton's arguments had any effect on St Petersburg and the fickle Tsar. At one point in the middle of 1800, it appeared that

Paul wanted the machinery installed in the building currently housing the *Bank Mint*. This prompted furious scurrying on Soho's part until it was learned that the mint was intended for the Fortress of St Peter and St Paul, and that this decision was final. Boulton learned so in late July 1800; and he also, at last, received the detailed plans for which he had been asking for the past two years. Now work could proceed in Russia. And just now another serious stumbling block made its appearance – not in Russia but in England.

When Matthew Boulton proposed to export a mint and the personnel necessary to erect it, he launched a series of events which would finally lead to public meetings and a petition of protest to Parliament, the famous Birmingham Memorial of 1800. Boulton himself saw the cause of the opposition as sheer envy and nothing more, and there was more than a grain of truth in that view: Soho *had* been successful, had got its way in the matter of the coinage and was now serenely sailing ahead with a lucrative mint for the world's largest country. Only Boulton and those around him could have known the price this success had demanded; but from the outside, Boulton looked all too fortunate for his own good.

But there was more to it than that. If Boulton's old business rivals were arrayed in opposition, so was the Birmingham millhand with no capital except his ability to do his job. The millhand was worried that such projects as Mr Boulton's mint could result in the transfer of technology – and ultimately jobs – to an area whose wages were so low (or non-existent: they had slavery in Russia, didn't they?) that an honest English workman could not hope to compete. Capital would drain eastward; so would jobs; and Birmingham would become a wasteland.

Boulton's rivals (including Thomas Williams and a former Boulton associate, John Hurd) tapped this popular discontent, but it would almost certainly have burst out in one form or another had they not been there to channel it into a written form. What eventually became the Birmingham Memorial began as a series of meetings held at various local taverns about the time Boulton was sending off the first batch of the St Petersburg machinery. Boulton was aware of the movement by late April, and despite his proud boast to Smirnov that 'I am better satisfyed to be an object of their Envy than of their Pity',[17] he was clearly worried. For trouble might erupt. Boulton remembered the terrible Birmingham Riots of July 1791: could history repeat itself nine years later? If it did, the current anxiety over the war with the French (and the seeing of French spies everywhere) might make matters very unpleasant indeed, for Matthew Boulton, for Soho Manufactory, for Birmingham, for the Russian mint.

And there *were* riots on the evening of 1 May, although they were nothing compared to the events of 1791. When all of the town's magistrates were absent from their posts (and we must remember that Birmingham had nothing resembling a permanent police force at this time, had not yet even achieved borough status), the disturbances had to be put down by the Birmingham Cavalry, the Birmingham Volunteers, and the Inniskilling Dragoons. Property damage was slight (in contrast to the events of '91, when much of the central city had been torched), and there do not appear to have been casualties. But the rioters promised to return, and the anxiety of the propertied remained high.

By the beginning of June, opposition to Boulton's mint was crystallizing. Papers had already been printed and distributed among those worried about their livelihoods; Boulton had got hold of one and sent it on to Smirnov as early as the end of April. On the evening of 3 June, a meeting was held at the Shakespeare Tavern (which still stands in New Street, near the railway station, in the centre of the city). Chaired by Jonathan Grundy and attended by twelve others (including Edward Thomason, a future coiner who appears to have volunteered for spy service in the cause of Matthew Boulton, and another fledgling coiner named Henry Kettle), the session produced three resolutions. First, it proclaimed that regardless of Boulton's right to export under the Act passed the previous summer, his sending of machines and workmen to Russia 'may be injurious to Birmingham, by enabling the Russians to execute most of our manufactures to the greatest advantage'.[18] Second, those assembled were requested to draw up a document to that effect, which was to be sent to the Secretaries of State most directly involved. And third, Matthew Boulton was to be told of the resolution. This was the genesis of the Birmingham Memorial.

It was published on 21 June 1800, signed by forty-seven merchants, including the coiners Henry Kettle and Peter Kempson. It was *not* signed by the man Boulton saw at its centre, Thomas Williams. But the Llanidan lawyer would have been far too clever to leave any traces of himself. The Memorial briefly discussed the passage of the 1799 Act allowing Boulton to export his mint and the personnel to erect it in Russia. It then discussed the dire effects which such exportation would surely have on the city, and on the country. A lucrative trade would pass from Britain to Russia. Of even greater importance, talent and genius, once resident in the latter country, might be persuaded to remain there, sharing the secrets learned at home, to the great detriment of British manufactures.

To be sure, the Act had been passed with the advice and consent of the Ministers of King George III, and they had undoubtedly acted in what they believed was Britain's best interest. But they had been misled by Matthew Boulton, and those who signed the Memorial now humbly petitioned them to reconsider their action, and to give those who had signed the Memorial 'a ready and patient hearing'[19] on the Act's repeal.

The Birmingham Memorial generated far more heat than light, far more annoyance than action. Becoming aware of the movement against him well before the formal drafting of the petition, Boulton spent the following summer engaging in what the twentieth century would call damage control, writing to Smirnov on the Russian side, Lord Grenville and the Earl of Liverpool (Lord Hawkesbury, a long-time correspondent) on the British, refuting the Memorialists' arguments point by point. Boulton also came to Town later in the summer, spending part of July and August there in case Lord Liverpool required his services at a summit conference. But while the cabinet discussed the Memorial, there is no indication that its authors ever received a hearing from the British Government. Boulton's closely-reasoned arguments may have turned the trick; more likely, William Pitt and his associates were acutely aware that, largely friendless against the French, Britain would secure no advantage in alienating the Russians by withholding the shipment of their mint – especially when they had already paid for half of it.[20] We hear no more of the Birmingham Memorial, and Boulton's second shipment of machinery exited Soho on 6 September. It consisted of flies and screw pins for the presses, the shaking machines, parts of the milling machinery, and virtually all other machine parts which had not gone out with the remittance in May. It sailed for Russia aboard the *Refuge*, John Bowser, Master, later that month.

And for the next months, the Russian affair proceeded smoothly – with a single exception. The exception was yet another Russian in search of instruction, a young mechanic named Kakoushkin. Smirnov had introduced him to Boulton while the latter was in London and had prevailed upon him to show Kakoushkin some of Soho's marvels once back in the Midlands. But the Russian had got on Boulton's nerves (the record is silent, but Kakoushkin would later prove all too inquisitive for comfort, and Boulton probably found him so on this occasion) and had been ejected from Soho Mint and sent back to London. He would prove troublesome in several future instances, both in Britain and back home.

Despite annoying guests, work went on well. Boulton finally received detailed plans from St Petersburg in late July 1800, enabling him to allocate space for the new mint. The largest element would be contained in a building 217 feet long by forty-five wide: here would be fitted the rolling mill (in a space measuring forty-five feet by forty-five); here too would sit the cutting out room, the annealing and pickling room (for preparing the planchets for coining, once they had been cut out), and a shaking room (for polishing them prior to striking). Each of these three rooms would measure forty-five feet by twenty. That left the press room and the melting room and engine house. Boulton was uncertain about the size of the former, but estimated that it would range between sixty-five and seventy-five feet in length (perhaps sixty-eight, if ten presses were to be eventually housed there), and measure forty-five in width. And the melting room and engine house would be forty-five feet on each side. Were Boulton's calculations correct, this would take up all available space. As it turned out, they were *not* correct, through no fault of his.

As the year 1800 closed, Matthew Boulton was approaching the Russian affair from three directions. He was creating those parts of the machinery left undone. He was fitting them and the items already sent out into a coherent framework, based on information received from St Petersburg. And he was addressing the matter of the British personnel to be sent out to erect the machinery in its new, Russian, setting. All of these activities would occupy him through 1801 and into 1802, and the paucity of archival records suggests that all was proceeding smoothly, at least at Soho.

This formed a contrast to events on the larger stage. Tsar Paul I had been a loyal adherent to the coalition against the French during the first two years of his reign. But he then inexplicably swerved off in a different direction, organizing a league of armed neutrality with Scandinavia which carried an implicit threat to British interests. His actions became more bizarre: he eventually assembled an army of Cossacks for the invasion of British India.

But it was his reign of terror at St Petersburg that proved his undoing. On the night of 11 March 1801 OS, a group of officers murdered him, certainly with the foreknowledge and possibly with the complicity of his son, who became Tsar Alexander I on the following day. The successor had certain mental problems of his own, an instability which was hardly tempered by the memory of what he had known and what part he had played in coming to the throne. But unstable or no, this man would henceforth be the most important element in Soho's Russian problem, for it would be he with whom the firm must deal as it erected its mint, struck its first coins – and finally sought to bring its people home.

Boulton's first reaction to the Russian turn of events was to halt work on the mint until reassured that the son would not repeat the *volte-face* of his father and suddenly reject the work. But the Tsar himself, through his Treasurer Vasiliev (and the latter back along the chain of command to Vorontsov and Smirnov), assured Soho that his intentions were honourable, and that its mint would find a good home in St Petersburg. Work was therefore resumed in the summer of 1801. But more precious months had been lost in indecision, and the shipment of additional machinery (and the passage of the Soho workmen to put it together) would necessarily be delayed until the following spring.

The choice of Soho personnel began receiving serious discussion late in 1801. But as Boulton was making his selection of Britons, he was encountering trouble with several of the Russians who had been sent to Soho for training. These were Lizel, who was still at the mint, and Kakoushkin, who had recently been shown the door. Lizel was the more promising of the two – indeed, Boulton thought him the most gifted member of the Russian delegation. But he tended to get above himself, had dreams of someday going on to better things, perhaps the Vienna Mint. Whatever his pretensions, he was a skilled mechanic and modeller.

And his model-making caused difficulties. Lizel had known Kakoushkin while the two men were still in Russia, and he seems to have given him one model of a coining press and another of a steam engine, created during Lizel's residence at Soho and therefore technically Matthew Boulton's property. Kakoushkin had either been given the models for safekeeping or for the advertisement of his friend's talents to the right people; after his return to London following the tiff with Matthew Boulton, Kakoushkin eventually pawned the models for fifty pounds to a woman with whom he was living in Bankside. There they lay unredeemed for several months until discovered by an acquaintance of Matthew Boulton named John de la Fonte. Signing himself 'John Dee', the latter wrote to Boulton with the news. Shortly thereafter, Kakoushkin's pawnbroker/inamorata offered to sell the models to James Smirnov for fifty pounds, a purchase Boulton advised the Reverend not to make. Their subsequent fate is unknown; but Lizel's credibility was diminished, while Kakoushkin (who had been living in London at the sufferance of the Russian Government, having already lost his credibility at Soho) was eventually recalled to St Petersburg.

Boulton initially had better luck with those Britons who would be going to Russia. An old Soho associate named James Lawson recommended his employee James Harley in the highest terms; Harley, who had long been interested in the Russian adventure, would indeed become a part of it. And by March 1802, his three associate 'Mintaneers' (the term is Matthew Boulton's) had been selected as well – James Duncan, James Walker and William Speedyman, in order of importance. By the end of that month, Boulton was writing an *aide-mémoire* called 'Memorandums of things I ought not to neglect'. Its contents ranged from 'a present of fleecy Hosary' for the four to the uttering of stern warnings to them to keep strangers away from the mint project as it was being erected. The latter was the first indication of a worry which would occupy much of Boulton's thinking over the next several years – the fear of spies, emissaries of Napoleon of France, stealing the secrets of Soho's success. A portion of his concern stemmed from his old troubles with Jean-Pierre Droz, whose cause and claims the First Consul had taken up as his own. Part of it stemmed from the fact that, in a war as total as the one with the French, skills and technologies had an importance greater than that which they enjoyed in times of peace. And part of it stemmed from the fact that, in this one instance at least, the normally-rational Mr Boulton gave free rein to his fears. But his concerns, first voiced only to himself, were later expressed in letter after letter to those to whom he had entrusted his mint – resulting in frazzled nerves all round.

Boulton's memorandum mentioned something else which would grate on nerves in times to come. Russians and Britons alike would be working on the mint, but all of them must obey 'one Superior & not [be] a Republik'. This was a perfectly legitimate observation: since the days of the Pyramids, any large, complex project – indeed, any project involving more than one person, must have a recognized, agreed-upon chain of command, with one person to whom, in the final analysis, obedience must be paid. The Russian mint project would suffer from too many superiors, none of whom was taken seriously by everyone, or sometimes by anyone.

A final observation was unsettling. Boulton had heard that one of the Soho men had a drinking problem. This was James Walker, chosen for his long experience as a mechanic. Walker would still go to Russia, but he must be cautioned against excess in the strictest terms.[21]

Matthew Boulton told the men of their new assignment by the end of March. He had not previously confided in them because he was not sure of their reaction. But they must have known something was afoot prior to his disclosure: the next shipment of machinery had left the works in mid-March, and its nature and mass (pumps and other oddments, with a weight of only ten tons or so) suggested that it would be among the last to go out, and that somebody must soon be sent to fashion it and its predecessors into the Russian mint.

So he told the four, and he told the Russians who would be accompanying them. All would travel to Hull, where they would meet the machinery, then depart with it for Russia. Boulton discussed his arrangements with Smirnov on 3 April, introducing him to the four Britons to be sent, and to the duties which each would perform, the offices which each would enjoy.

There was no question that James Duncan would be the most important member of the group. His responsibilities would be the greatest, for he would be entrusted with setting up the all the presses and erecting all the delicate parts of the mint. He would also oversee the others in their tasks. James Harley was next in importance: a skilled engine-builder, he would be entrusted with the two steam engines. James Walker was to erect the rolling mill and assist James Duncan as needed. And William Speedyman was to serve as a general hand, giving the other three any help in his power. All four were put under the protection of Alexis Olinien, the Emperor's architect, who would presumably be the general overseer of the mint project. Certainly Boulton hoped that Olinien would enjoy that role: he spoke English, and someone in authority in Russia with a command of that language would be essential. Olinien had created the drawings for the mint, and this, too, recommended him to Boulton.

Much remained to be done before the men could leave. Passports must be provided for the Britons, while permission to quit the country must be obtained for the Russians. And wages for Soho's people must also be discussed and agreements secured. Discussion on this latter point was under way by the beginning of April; while we lack details, the essential points have survived.

Of the four Britons, Duncan would receive the highest wages, three guineas per week, commencing on the day he left Soho, ending on the day he returned there. The Russian Government would pay his travelling expenses to and from St Petersburg. While there, he would work a twelve-hour day (meals included) and a six-day week. His pay would continue even if he were unable to work due to inclement weather or illness. If asked to do extra work, Duncan would perform it at the same wage rate.

James Walker would receive two guineas per week, working under the same conditions. William Speedyman would receive one and one-half guineas per week, while James Harley would earn two *pounds* per week for his services for the first year, two guineas per week thereafter. For a man of Harley's *amour propre*, this offer must have been galling indeed: with the exception of Speedyman (whose attainments were modest), Harley would be the lowest-paid of the four. Nevertheless, he signed on, as did the others. That aspect of the project had been dealt with by mid-April. By now, the various legal documents had been secured as well, and there were no further impediments to the departure of the Soho Corps. And so, with handshaking all around, it departed Handsworth on 18 April 1802, bound for adventure.

There were nine people in all – four Soho workmen (plus the wife and child of one of them, James Walker) and three Russians, Lizel, Grezin, and the latter's wife. The other Russians who have flitted across our stage had already departed – with the exception of young Sobakin, who died at Soho three days before his compatriots left for home. He is at Handsworth still.

The party left with Boulton's best wishes. But one of its members soon provoked concern. This was James Walker, who had been roaring drunk the morning he left – so inebriated that Boulton worried lest he be thrown from the top of the coach (where he was riding) before journey's end. Boulton sent along stern advice via James Duncan: Walker must become temperate or risk losing his position and his marriage as well.

But dissension among the members of the British contingent was soon causing Boulton much greater concern. He had been aware of potential difficulties from James Harley even before the journey began; but now he learned that matters were far more serious than he had feared.

James Duncan told him so, in a letter from Hull dated 4 May. By then, the group and the mint machinery should have cleared that city and been halfway to Russia. But a series of false starts had kept the crew and its cargo penned up in the town, and the frustrated voyagers had begun to get on each other's nerves. James Harley was the chief malefactor, doing his best to turn the others against James Duncan. Had the latter known how spiteful Mr Harley could be, he would never have agreed to travel with him. But they were nonetheless together; would Mr Boulton send a communication, setting forth in plain terms the nature of each man's work and the chain of command?

Boulton did so, in a letter sent to St Petersburg to await Duncan's arrival. After dispensing homely advice (the men should repair to coffee houses from time to time, where they would find good English newspapers and polite diversion), he answered Duncan's request:

> *Your Department* is that of erecting the great Presses, with their Framing[,] the Cutting-out Presses with their Framing & Machinery, also all the Air Pumps great & small, with their working Gear. *James Harley's Department* is that of erecting the two Steam Engines, with the two great Air Pumps. *James Walkers* is that of erecting the Rolling Mill, & I expect that each shall be accountable for their own Mistakes. And though each of these Apparatus s [*sic*] may correctly be erected separately, yet it is necessary these several Machines should be so harmoniously connected as to perform their several Uses perfectly, & therefore the four Engineers should be so harmoniously connected as to perform their Parts both separately & jointly correctly, so as to compleat *One perfect Mint*. Mr Harley to erect the two Engines & you to superintend all the Rest.[22]

– good advice, if anyone would follow it.

The squabbling 'Mintaneers' and their cargo finally cleared Hull on 6 May. After a rough sailing, they reached Kronstadt on the twenty-second, St Petersburg two days later. There they met George Sheriff, who would temporarily act as interpreter. They met Vasiliev, and they attempted to meet Olinien, who was absent and no longer connected with the mint in any case. His successor was an individual named Alyabev (the same person who had superseded Baron Gascoigne), into whose charge the Britons were placed in the matter of lodging. They had visited the Fortress, site of their future mint. Perhaps they would find permanent lodging there as well: the inn where they were staying was very expensive, the first indication that what had seemed like an adequate wage in Britain might fail to be so under the harsher conditions at St Petersburg. The author of this observation was James Duncan, and Boulton might have paid attention to what he wrote: of the four, Duncan was the highest-paid.

But Duncan's news (a new overseeing official, who presumably did not speak English; a high cost of living, potential source of discontent) paled in comparison with what George Sheriff had to say. Sheriff wrote on 6 June 1802 OS – that is, about a month after the arrival of the Soho Corps. He mentioned that they had indeed found spacious apartments in the Fortress. He added that a decent, permanent interpreter had been secured, a gentleman named James Furt. All well and good; but what of more substantive matters from the viewpoint of Matthew Boulton? Sheriff next spoke of them, and his recipient probably wished he had quit reading while he was ahead. For James Harley had entered Sheriff's room as he was finishing Boulton's letter, having just returned from visiting the mint building for the first time. And Harley opined that it was 'not at all suffisant [sufficient] being an old building and all cracked and rent = with the foundation bad'.[23]

And the closer one looked, the greater the problem became. Not only was the building structurally unsound (it had gone up nearly a century ago, and time had not dealt kindly with it). In addition, it was too small for the purpose for which it was intended: even if it were sound, it would still have been between nine and sixteen feet too short for all the machinery which Boulton had sent. In other words, the plans for which Matthew Boulton had so eagerly waited, about which he had praised Alexis Olinien so warmly – were worthless.

First panic, then resolution: Duncan and his mates came to a decision: if this building were inadequate, it must simply be pulled down and another raised in its place. That this would take time was unfortunate, but inevitable. Just how much time it would take was beyond their knowledge. Under the circumstances, this was a mercy.

Matthew Boulton's St Petersburg mint would not be finished until the summer of 1807. There were several reasons for the agonizing slowness of the proceedings. The first was that not all work could be pursued year-round. Outdoor activity, including the actual erecting of the mint building, could only go on from April to October. The harsh winters rendered outdoor labor during the other six months of the year difficult or impossible. And while work could indeed go on inside the mint (assembly of the machinery and steam engines, exhaustive testing of all components once assembled) nothing could be accomplished *indoors* until the mint was completed *outdoors* – in other words, the machinery could not even be uncrated until there was someplace secure and dry in which to work. The Russian climate was the single most important factor in the tortoise pace of Matthew Boulton's Russian mint; but there were others.

First, those Russian officials who, it had been assumed, would be ready and able to speed progress, to open doors and smooth the way – were either unable or unwilling to help. A pattern emerged, becoming evident at the very beginning of the Russian residency of the Soho engineers. Things which ought to be ready at the outset were not, and the one man who could set them to rights was all-too-often absent or unsympathetic. An extreme literality would be applied to everything: Boulton's men found spacious if gloomy lodgings in the Fortress, eventual site of their mint. But they were given rooms without beds or other furniture, for Boulton's contracts with St Petersburg on their behalf did not mention such amenities by name. So Duncan and his mates had to borrow the money to furnish their rooms from the Russian Government, with obligation of repayment in full. This may have been a minor point in comparison with larger events, but it was a very early suggestion of a long-term problem, one which would never be solved. Russian officials and British mechanics simply looked at the world through different eyes.

The dispute over furniture related to another long-term problem. The men discovered that the cost of living at St Petersburg was far higher than they had been led to believe when they had agreed to terms. Part of the greater expense was real: as any traveller has found, any journey is apt to include costs totally unforeseen at the outset, expenses which nonetheless have to be met. And it will always prove impossible to live precisely as one does at home on the same amount of money as one spends there. Part of the problem for Boulton's men was that, while they had signed contracts for wages in sterling in England, they were actually being paid in rubles, in Russia – and the exchange ratio between the two currencies constantly fluctuated, making budgeting very difficult. When James Walker (who had his family with him and therefore *had* to budget his money) struck a bargain with Russian officialdom to calculate his salary at thirty pence per ruble, then learned that the true ratio was closer to twenty-four-to-one, he applied for a revision of the rate but got little satisfaction from Count Vasiliev – or even the Emperor, to whom Vasiliev eventually applied.

To uncertainty or dissatisfaction over wages was added the extreme isolation under which the men lived and worked. The Fortress was distant from the markets where they must purchase their food, and the only way of getting there was by boat. Vasiliev had been applied to for the loan of a state vessel but had refused the request. And so every time the men ventured out of their gloomy apartments, it cost them money.

All this was true enough; but it was not the entire story. The leader in the discontent over wages was always James Harley, and Harley had an agenda which included dissatisfaction over wages but a more general dissatisfaction over status. He would not be happy until his wages were higher than anyone else's (and from his letters to Boulton, one suspects that he also wanted the post of foreman); and he was charismatic enough to carry James Walker and William Speedyman with him. At this distance, it is impossible to say whether the wages of the 'Mintaneers' were too low; but they do seem to have been low in comparison with the salaries paid to another set of resident Britons – the men working for Baron Gascoigne. Gascoigne's people frequented some of the same haunts as Boulton's employees, and, doubtless egged on by the Baron, were always happy to tell the Soho men about the lavish lifestyle which the Baron had secured for them – and which he would happily provide for James Harley, James Duncan, James Walker and William Speedyman too, if they but asked. (In passing, the arousal of discontent was almost the only weapon left to Gascoigne in his vendetta against Matthew Boulton – but it might have a major effect, if it were properly applied.)

Consider matters from the perspective of a Soho workman. Here he was, several hundred miles from home, in a country where the language, folkways, and religion not only were not his, but were completely divorced from anything within his limited circle of experience. He lived in gloomy surroundings, and he needed a pass to visit his own quarters. He seemed to pay too much for everything. It was dark and cold for half the year. He worked for bored officials who neither valued him nor, it now appeared, the objective he had been sent all that distance to accomplish. No wonder he was discontented; no wonder he wanted more money.

The question of wages was first brought up by James Duncan, on behalf of the lowest-paid individual of the four, William Speedyman. Speedyman was asking for a slight increase in his salary, and, considering the unexpectedly high cost of living at the Russian capital, Duncan thought he deserved it. Duncan's request to that effect was sent on 5 August 1802 OS. And this, the opening salvo in a years-long war over wages, would find Matthew Boulton in adamant opposition.

Let us now consider matters from his point of view. He saw much of the discontent as mere puffery, concocted by James Harley for his own purposes. He had received reliable advice that living costs were *cheaper* in Russia than in England, was convinced that his men would find them so if they merely applied themselves to the task. And he himself was in a very delicate position, one in which he must tread lightly. Here was his mint, several hundred miles from home. Less than half of it had been paid for. If he demanded higher wages on behalf of his men, there was no guarantee that the Tsar would not abandon the project, eject his men but keep his mint – and then refuse payment. If that took place, there was no guarantee that the British Government would come to Boulton's rescue: its need for benevolent neutrality from the fickle Emperor would carry far greater weight than the cause, however righteous, of a Midlands' entrepreneur. In sum, Boulton's men had better get used to living within their salaries.

By the standards of the early nineteenth century, Matthew Boulton was an admirable employer. But he was nonetheless typical as well: *he* would look after the interests of his charges, not they. And when the stream of letters began emanating from St Petersburg, telling Mr Boulton that in fact he had *not* acted in their interests, must in fact make amends, his feelings were hurt. By mid-March of 1803, he asked James Smirnov for advice on the matter: he had by then received complaints from all four of his men and was 'now too angry to write to them with discretion'.[24] But Boulton's anger was tempered with concern. *Did* the men have a point? *Were* their wages too low? Smirnov promised to send extracts of their letters to the proper officials in St Petersburg; if the wage complaints were justified, action could be taken there. And Boulton meanwhile wrote James Harley (whom he correctly identified as the instigator of the dispute), advising him and the others that, while their complaints would be examined, they were nonetheless now in the Tsar's employ rather than his. Let them therefore cheerfully resume their labours, in the expectation that a grateful monarch would reward their industry and cheer with tangible marks of his favour. But Mr Harley had the unparalleled gall to continue to disagree with Mr Boulton over the adequacy of his salary; and the pot continued to simmer to the end, even if it never quite boiled over.

What effect did all this have on the speed with which the Russian mint got built? Like any other human interaction which took place so long ago, we can only surmise on its precise influence; but common sense suggests that workers who feel they are well-paid and well-regarded are likely to work harder, give more of themselves, than workers who feel they are not. The wage dispute is thus likely to have had a malign influence on the fortunes of Boulton's Russian mint. And it certainly played a role in the relationship of the four Soho men to each other.

Interpersonal rivalries between James Duncan, James Harley, James Walker and William Speedyman plagued the project from beginning to end. With the wisdom of hindsight, one could say that it would have been better had all four been paid the same or similar salaries, for an important source of friction would have thereby been removed. But when one looks at James Harley and James Duncan, the parties responsible for most of the animosity, one concludes that nothing could have made these two like each other, or work well together.

Harley was bright, very bright; even Boulton viewed him as a person of great promise, had encouraged him in his studies – which only increased his sense of betrayal once his protégé arrived in Russia and began making complaints. Harley was also witty and charismatic, charming when he wished to be. He was, in fact, everything that James Duncan was not.

The latter was morose, a hypochondriac (when he surprised everyone by announcing his intention to marry, one of his associates remarked that his real and imagined illnesses made him 'a much fitter subject for a Nurse than a Wife'[25]), and tended to be sullen under pressure. He was also clearly appalled at the magnitude of his responsibility – especially as he seemed to be the only one to take it seriously. He asked for, and received, written confirmation of his senior status from Matthew Boulton himself, but had to stand by helplessly when James Harley and the others simply refused to accept his primacy. A pang of envy also twinged in the bosom of James Duncan. Here he was, fighting the good fight, living a life of purity – and there was Harley, who was

> particularly fond of Company[,] Card playing[,] Billiards playing & ca, For which vices is Petersburg a most Infamous place, and abounds with such numbers of Idle people who principaly give up there minds to such Diabolical practices[.][26]

Duncan added that Harley often stayed out for several nights at a time, consumed by his mania for gambling – at which he fared poorly. As the other two men, Walker and Speedyman, tended to side with Harley against Duncan, 'I am sorry to say that there is not that Sociableness and Society amongst us at home That there ought to be – which in general makes me very uncomfortable'.[27]

The discomfort and tension felt by all would play a part in the slow progress of the St Petersburg mint. It would also be a primary reason for the dispatching of a fifth Soho man to the troubled St Petersburg project. This was Zacchaeus Walker, Jr., who would go out to Russia in the summer of 1803. But for the first year, James Duncan would be on his own, extracting what co-operation he could from baulky Britons and Russians alike.

The decision having been made to pull down the old building and start afresh, Duncan set to work. An Italian architect named Porta was called in to inspect the site proposed for the new mint. He estimated a figure of slightly under fifty thousand rubles for the construction of a building 216 feet long by forty-seven wide – which would definitely hold all the machinery which Boulton had remitted, and all which was still to come. Urged on by his master, Duncan was soon busily drawing up plans for the organization of the mint once its building had been completed. But before building could begin, the old structure must be demolished to make way for the new. By the beginning of September 1802, Duncan had a small army of *muzhiks* doing just that.

For a time, things went well. The Tsar had come by late the previous month to view the machinery, had pronounced himself satisfied, and signed the plan and estimate for the new mint building. And more materials were reaching the site just as Alexander was inspecting what had already arrived. Late in August, the *Maister*, Robert Cowham, Master, left Hull for St Petersburg with a cargo of cement, iron pipe, and a beam for the rolling mill engine. These materials arrived in Russia in early September.

They would be joined by a final cargo in 1802, and a most important one. By now, Matthew Boulton was becoming aware that the Russian project would likely take far longer than anticipated to complete. He was also aware of the discontent of his men. Apparently concerned lest the Russian Government become dissatisfied with his efforts, he risked one last shipment of goods that autumn. It left Hull during the first half of October, and it consisted of the essentials of the rolling mill, including the delicate steel rollers, as well as four milling machines, two turning lathes, and various small parts for the cutting out machines. The vessel carrying these essential materials was the *Hope*, and she reached Kronstadt about the middle of November – just in time to get stuck in the ice in the harbour. It took two hundred men four days to get her freed and into her berth. Her cargo was anxiously examined by Duncan and his mates: the most delicate parts were carried on to St Petersburg, while the remainder wintered where they were.

The disposition of all this machinery was a particularly ticklish problem, because there was currently no mint building in which to secure it. The last of the old structure had been pulled down by the end of September 1802, the adjacent canal had been drained, and digging work for the foundation of the new mint was in progress. Soon, pilings would be sunk (the marshy nature of the ground meant that the entire area would eventually have to have pilings: St Petersburg was often called the Venice of the North, but like its southern namesake showed a disquieting desire to sink back into the primeval muck from which it had been raised). The men might get the pilings in by the end of the 1802 season (and if they were extremely lucky, they might get the actual foundation securely laid); but that would be the outer limits of their success. For the next half year at least, Matthew Boulton's mint would have to remain in the crates which had carried it to Russia. Some parts of it would stay at Kronstadt, and other parts would repose in the Fortress at St Petersburg. And *all* of it would be vulnerable – to French spies!

Or so Boulton feared, and he had some basis for his concern. To understand why a Russian mint might prove interesting to Frenchmen, we must briefly digress. At the same time that work was beginning at St Petersburg, another Boulton emissary was attempting to carry out Soho's bidding many miles to the west. This was Zacchaeus Walker, Jr., who was then in Paris, attempting to interest the government of the First Consul in a coining contract. He found the going difficult: Boulton's old adversary Jean-Pierre Droz was assiduously laying claim to Boulton's inventions for himself, was appealing to French patriotism over the dubious claims of an English promoter.[28] And while Boulton had an old employee named Rambert Dumarest engrave a handsome medal with his portrait and claims displayed thereon, neither his medal nor his nephew succeeded in obtaining the right to coin for the French.

Walker heard the bad news at the end of October 1802. But he also learned that Napoleon intended undertaking a vast recoinage of silver, melting down all previous money and restriking it into large five-franc pieces, bearing his portrait. In order to carry out the scheme, the Corsican would need new minting machinery – and Walker heard rumours that he would be obliged to get it from Matthew Boulton.

The rumours were false or the plan fell through; but Boulton realized that there was more than one way to obtain Soho machinery for France. Napoleon could purchase it. Or he could steal it: he could send industrial spies to St Petersburg, where they might pry and poke until they learned his secrets. His men must be warned lest they be 'entraped ... by subtile Crafty Spies'.[29] And the fact that they were discontented with their wages and living conditions was an additional concern. Surely they wouldn't go over to the Enemy for a few extra shillings, would they? As the year 1802 ended, Matthew Boulton was a worried man.

He need not have concerned himself about the loyalty of his men (who, on balance, were probably more patriotic than he: one somehow can't imagine a

James Duncan trading with the French, which was precisely what Duncan's employer had just tried to do). But his fears about malefactors in French pay seemed justified when Duncan wrote him towards the end of the winter with a piece of news: there had been a confrontation with foreign spies at the mint site!

This took places about mid-March 1803. Three gentlemen had come calling, having previously visited Alyabev, the head of the Bank Mint. They very much wanted to see the machinery for the new Boulton mint, said that Alyabev had given them express permission to do so. But they could not produce a written order from that functionary – which made Boulton's men very suspicious. The latter refused to show their visitors anything, on the reasonable grounds that nothing had even been unpacked as yet, let alone set up. They *had* agreed, however, to show the three the mint site – which in its current state was no breach of security: all the spies would have seen was the pilings and the foundations, and a bit of the framing for the building. With that, the three departed.

One of them had worn a Russian officer's uniform but spoke German. Another was dressed nearly in the English style but also spoke German. The third wore a *shuba*, a Russian fur-lined overcoat with cape – and he looked like a spy, and a French spy at that. He refused to speak to the others within earshot of the Soho men, but spoke rapidly to his fellows once out of range. While neither he nor the other two had been seen since, James Duncan and his mates would be on the alert in case they reappeared.

Earlier, another potential source of trouble had presented himself – Kakoushkin, who approached Duncan and Harley late in December in search of a job at the mint. They would send him packing, for they remembered his earlier mischief with Lizel's models. But his connection with the Russian Government had continued after his return to St Petersburg, and he would have to be watched.

The winter of 1802–3 was an unhappy one for the Soho mechanics and for their old employer. They continued working on the mint as weather permitted, got some of the framing done and arranged to have stones cut for the walls of the new edifice. But the weather took an abrupt turn for the worse at the beginning of November, and all outside work had to stop. And since they could hardly work on the inside of a mint which was not even built, they had too little to do and began to fight among themselves – and to resume their complaints about their wages. When two of them (Duncan and Harley) were approached by a Russian Vice-Admiral with an offer of employment, Boulton must have worried still more: the seduction of honest British craftsmen by clever Russians was exactly the sort of thing for which he had damned Gascoigne, and for which the Birmingham Memorialists had damned *him*. All parties at Soho and St Petersburg eagerly awaited the spring of the new year.

In Soho, Matthew Boulton readied what would be the penultimate shipment of mint materials. Consisting of twenty-two castings and fifteen cases of odds and ends, it left Soho on 11 April and sailed for Kronstadt on board the *Echo*, John Peck, Master, on the fourteenth. These portions of Mr Boulton's mint took their time reaching Russia: they do not appear to have been seen there until mid-June.

In St Petersburg, Soho's men on the spot were doing what they could to construct the machinery's future home. The foundations having been securely laid, the walls were now going up; it was hoped that the entire area would be under cover by the end of the summer of 1803. Duncan was getting the machinery cleaned, while his mates were finishing the framing for the press-room floor. But the work went on under difficult circumstances. Duncan and Harley barely spoke to each other, and there was ceaseless animosity between them and the others over who bossed whom, who was in charge of what. Wages were another source of unhappiness, but so was something else which had nothing to do directly or indirectly with Matthew Boulton.

His men there felt they had no one in the Russian bureaucracy to whom they could turn when progress was slow, or stalled. Duncan summed it up:

> On the part of the Russian Government there is no person hear [here] that we can apply to for the Least Advice concerning the building, or the convenience of the work in General[.]
> And in Short every thing as yet is left wholly To us; and I am apprehensive that if there should be any mistakes, blame would fall on me.[30]

Boulton agreed. He was also tiring of the dispute over wages, was apprehensive about spies, and was painfully aware that nothing short of a miracle could keep the Russian mint project even remotely on schedule. He must appoint someone close to him with plenary powers to act on Soho's behalf, someone energetic, someone diplomatic, someone who could push baulky Russians when needed, someone who could smooth the feathers of proud Britons when that was required. The man he needed had just finished a project in France, where even his skill and tact had been insufficient. But he was free just now, and Boulton would soon tell him of his new assignment. The man he needed was Zacchaeus Walker, Jr.

Walker wanders through several chapters of this book; here is as good a place as any to discuss him. He was born in 1768, died in 1822. While he was almost of an age with his cousin, Matthew Robinson Boulton, he seems to have been more at home with his uncle, Matthew – at least, according to the testimony of the correspondence. Both men had strong strains of curiosity, both were more cheerful than otherwise (although the Russian imbroglio would try their good humour), both were born letter-writers, in love with the English language and its descriptive potential – but Zacchaeus was the more literate of the two. He generally called himself Zacchaeus Walker, Jr. (for his father, who does not enter this story, was also named Zacchaeus). His associates at Soho generally called him Zack informally, Z. Walker, Jr. when they referred to him in writing.

No portrait survives of Zacchaeus Walker, Jr. But we know he had a tendency toward corpulence even when young and was somewhat careless about his appearance, his uncle advising him to pay greater attention to it if he wished to make his way in the world. He was deeply patriotic, fervently anti-French (so much so that, in an age which generally capitalized its nouns, Walker customarily spelled 'France' and 'French' with small f's). He was inclined to be stodgy, but an adventurer lurked within: otherwise, he would not have criss-crossed the world in the way he did.

When Walker first entered the Matthew Boulton Papers, he was twenty-one. It was 1789, and Matthew Boulton employed him as an emissary between Soho and the irascible Thomas Williams. Walker's role was minor, but he performed it well. Toward the end of 1792, he sailed for the United States, to represent a firm there called William and George Russell. He met John Mitchell of Charleston, and his shrewd observations regarding that knight-errant of American numismatic history gave a hint of the always perceptive, occasionally hilarious letter-writer to come. Walker resided in the United States for several years, finally securing dual citizenship in November 1797. This would allow him to trade in places where an ordinary Briton could not, given the edgy nature of Anglo-American relations at the time.

By then, he had returned to Europe, was representing his uncle's interests in France and Germany. He travelled under an alias, 'Henry Mortimer' - not particularly for the sake of security, but because the assumption of a *nom de guerre* amused him. He did his best to arrange for a French coinage made at Soho; when that project fell through late in 1802, Matthew Boulton deter-mined to send him out to Russia, where his services would be equally if not more important. Walker must go to St Petersburg, allay the ire of the four Soho workers already there, and somehow bind them and their Russian coun-terparts into a great, collaborative effort, the building and breathing of life into Boulton's Russian mint. Before he was done, Walker would need every atom of charm, patience, and innate good humour he possessed.

He was originally scheduled to go to Russia in the beginning of 1803, and he actually got as far as the Netherlands before being recalled because of his father's poor health. But the elder man rallied, and Walker was soon making preparations to resume his journey. As he did, Matthew Boulton was writing Count Vasiliev, explaining why he was sending Zack Walker and what he hoped to accomplish thereby. Walker had been granted

> full Powers to conduct on my behalf at S*t* Petersburg all such Affairs as may occur in the Course of the Erection of the Russian Mint ... & to take upon himself the entire Controul of the Workmen employed in that Business. I therefore request Your Excellency will be pleased to consider him as my Representative in the Completion of the Concern, & allow him in Consequence the Honor of transmitting any Communications you may deem it necessary to make either to the Workmen or myself on the Subject of the Mint.[31]

Walker's intended authority could not have been plainer, and Vasiliev even-tually granted an official recognition of it. Henceforth, Zack Walker would be the official middleman between His Imperial Majesty, Tsar Alexander I of Russia, and Matthew Boulton, Merchant, of Soho, near Birmingham.

But the middleman would still have to get to St Petersburg to assume his post, and he nearly failed in the attempt. Walker departed England on 3 June 1803, bound for Elsinor – today's Helsing, the normal half-way point for travellers going to Russia. Helsing belonged to Denmark, and Anglo-Danish relations were not good at the time. The resumption of war with the French also made travel risky, and Walker travelled to Helsing as part of a convoy.

The town is situated at the southern end of the Kattegat, that inland sea between Sweden and Denmark, and it must be approached from the north. But as Walker made for the port, his convoy caught a headwind which separated its vessels, blowing a tremendous gale and heavy seas for three days. Walker and his ship were tossed all over the Kattegat, the vessel's sails split, 'and we were scarcely able to bear as much Canvass as would permit her steer-ing.— Our Mate an old Man near 70 says he never passed the Kattegat in such tremendous weather in his Life'.[32] The second leg of Walker's journey was relatively uneventful, and he arrived at Kronstadt on 15/27 June, about the same time as Boulton's latest batch of machinery. Expecting to see an empty harbour induced by the resumption of the wars, Walker instead beheld a bustling scene with hundreds of merchantmen (largely British, except for fifty or so American vessels, there to acquire naval stores which they would then carry to France).

Travelling on to the capital, Walker soon had his first encounter with the Russian bureaucracy. He was not impressed: the officials he met comprised

> an endless List of shabby Secretaries & Servants who obstruct every Avenue & render it next to an impossibility to proceed beyond the first Anti-chamber for any one not wearing $\frac{1}{2}$ doz Stars, Crosses, & Ribbands, nor scarcely to gain admittance into the Court-Yard without a Carriage & four; as the only Criterion of human merit in this Capital of misery & magnificence seems to consist of the Number of Horses a person is entitled to drive, his nominal Rank in Society, & the quantity of money he can get at by whatever means, & squander foolishly away.

His Soho correspondent might excuse the preceding; his nephew was new on the scene and doubtless had much to learn. But Walker's next observations brought Matthew Boulton up short.

The latter had always assumed that the Russians wanted his mint for the same reason he had created it, to manufacture safe and abundant copper coinage for the labouring poor. They had drawn him to that conclusion – although he would not have needed all that much outside help to have arrived there himself. And now his nephew told him that, while the bickering officials of St Petersburg disagreed on most things, 'the only point on which they seemed clear & intelligible was, that the Copper-Coin will never be struck here, but in Siberia'. Nor would Boulton's mint be responsible for much gold or silver coinage: 'the Gold … will not amount to more than 400 lbs p*r* Annum english weight'. And while Walker was unsure of the silver, he had seen no more than fifteen tons' worth in the Fortress, in the form of ingots.

It will be recalled that the Russians had told Boulton that his new mint must strike 160,000,000 pieces per year. Now Walker told him the origin of that figure. Russian mints in Siberia were indeed coining that many pieces per annum; but they were using the labour of 'Slaves of the Crown', i.e., state-owned serfs, to do so. From the Russian point of view, this meant that the labour cost of creating the coinage was, effectively, non-existent, *and was thus more economical than Boulton's steam-powered mint*. In such a climate, that mint would be fortunate to receive any coining work at all.

But Walker added a note of cheer: if the fortunes of Matthew Boulton's mint were bleak, those of Baron Gascoigne's were even bleaker. Walker had visited it and sent his uncle a description of what he had seen; even allowing for some exaggeration, it is worth quoting:

> I met [the officers of the Bank Mint] in a place under the Building, which, on entering, would strike any person who had never been in a Coal-Pit, or a Copper-Mine with some degree of awe & trepidation. It is chiefly a Lamp-light occupation, & as far as a faint glimmering of Light & the collected filth & nastiness of Years would permit us to distinguish in this Cavern there is nothing

new in the process, which, however the Baron G[ascoigne] attributes to himself as an invention of his own. All the running down the Metal in the Furnaces, Rolling, cutting out, pickling & scouring ... & striking are completed under the same smoky Roof without partition of any kind.— the Rolls crack the Metal like Clay hardened in the Sun, & on account of it's [sic; Walker always included the apostrophe] inequality, they afterwards pass it thro' a Drawing-Machine similar to those used in England for drawing Wire, the Cutters-out & Coining Presses are some of them like the Button-Stamp ... & others resemble the Old [balancier] Press badly constructed; but I feel quite of their opinion that they are extremely well adapted for the Country & ought not to be changed, for rely upon it that any thing requiring either accuracy or attention to it's use here will soon be destroyed.[33]

Walker reported progress on Boulton's mint building: when he first saw it, its walls were within a few feet of their final level, and it promised to be ready for storage of the machinery by the following winter. But he reported no progress on the discontent over wages. There were several points of friction and low morale which his master could not possibly have anticipated: the Russian officials entrusted with the project had been ousted from higher positions and were taking out their frustrations on the members of the Soho Corps. Moreover, the official attitude seemed to be that the Russian Government had become the men's owner when it became their paymaster.

But the most important point threatening morale was disillusionment: the men found that no one particularly cared whether they made their best efforts, and that no one would be able to judge of their labours once they had finished. This point must have been as disquieting to Matthew Boulton at Soho as it was to his men at St Petersburg.

Zack Walker's dealings with Russian officialdom never mellowed. He was forced to attend endless meetings, during which much time was wasted and very little was accomplished. The ostensible purpose of the gatherings was to see whether Boulton's machinery would be accepted as it was or altered to fit the whims of the current bureaucratic favourites. After a number of these gatherings, during which Walker was informed that the arrangement of the machinery must be altered, and altered again, the Soho emissary finally lost his temper; observing that Boulton had been contracted to build a mint and send it to Russia, and had done so, Walker opined that it must now 'either be erected according to our Plans & Directions, *or not at all*'.[34]

At this, the elderly Mint President (whom Walker never names in his letters, perhaps fearing censorship) eased his meddling, as did his subordinates. Work on the mint building went on through the summer and early autumn of 1803, its architect receiving promises of the extra hands necessary to get the walls finished and the site completely covered over before the end of September. And a final, small shipment of castings left Hull for Russia on board the *Mercury*, Thomas Martin, Master, on 12 September 1803. Once she arrived, the men building the mint should have everything they could possibly require.

But the mint site itself posed problems. While enjoying better communications than the original site because it was closer to the canal, the new location was starved of light, surrounded by old buildings and high walls within the Fortress area. Walker thought the locale looked more like Bridewell (a notorious seventeenth-century jail in London) than a site fit for moneying. The

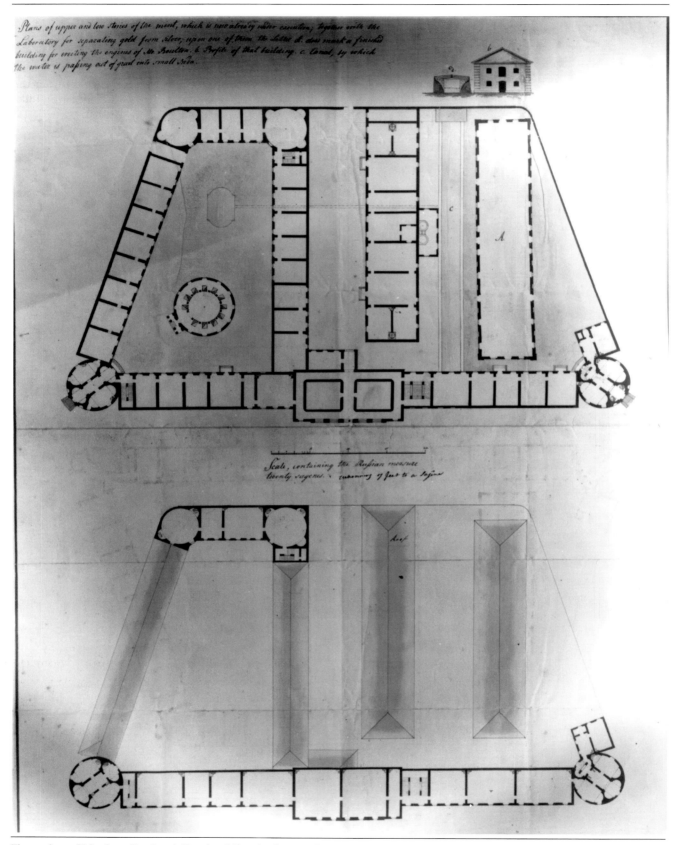

Floor plan of Matthew Boulton's Russian Mint; in the top drawing, the cutting out presses would occupy the circular area at lower-left, and the coining machinery would fit into the eight small rooms at the right. (Courtesy Birmingham City Archives, Birmingham Central Library)

problem was intensified by the Russians' insistence on putting heavy grates in the windows – which may have been unexceptionable from the viewpoint of security but made it still harder to see. The room for cutting planchets would present particular problems, for more light was needed there than anywhere else. It was initially suggested that the roof be glassed over, but someone soon realized that it would be covered with snow for half the year, rendering it useless. Then James Duncan had suggested a cupola with vertical windows, and this idea was adopted. But light would always be a problem – although it would be many months before Boulton's people would have to deal directly with its consequences.

For even after the walls had been raised and the roof put on (and this was essentially completed before the onset of winter in 1803), so much mortar had been used in the mint's construction that, combined with the cold, damp climate of the region, it would take many months for it all to dry, ready to be painted and populated. Since the members of the Soho Corps could no longer work outside (and could not yet work inside), they inevitably fell to quarrelling with each other once again. And once again, the problem of their wages came up, and they approached Zack Walker about it: had he heard anything from his uncle?

Walker had not: he had written Boulton for advice and a decision on salaries as soon as he had a moment to spare from superintending the building project. That was in November 1803. He was still waiting for an answer several months later. The men's patience was exemplary, and they merely asked him from time to time whether he had heard anything from home concerning their complaints. Always he had to reply in the negative.

Boulton's silence may be partly explained by his aversion to causing dissatisfaction to his client (who still owed him several thousand pounds). It may also be explained by Soho's involvement in other fields – actual activity in a massive recoinage of Spanish dollars for the Bank of England, potential activity in negotiations for a mint for Denmark. And Boulton's declining health played a role as well: henceforth, his letters to Walker, Duncan and the others decline in frequency and length. But the squabble over wages might have given Boulton something to consider: if he would not stand up for his men in St Petersburg, did he realistically think they would stand up for him in Copenhagen?

The spring of 1804 saw renewed activity at the Russian mint. The finishing touches were given to the building. Its walls were plastered over twice, inside and out; the outer walls were then painted stone gray and the iron roof pea green. Within, the flooring was completed except in the coining room (left undone there until the heavy presses, which would otherwise mar its surface, had been got into position). The steam engines and rolling mill machinery had been moved into their general places but were not yet set up. And no fewer than sixteen stoves had been installed in various corners of the structure, to combat the damp natural to the building, to attempt to safeguard the health of those who must work in it.

But much remained to be done. Taking everything into account (including the ongoing feud among Boulton's men and their difficulties with meddling Russian officials),

> I should say that the Machines will not be completed, set to work, & sufficient trials made of their powers, so that our people can return to England, before the latest of next Fall-Ships[35]

111

– that is, until the late autumn of *1805*. Already far behind schedule, the Russian mint seemed to lose ground as it progressed.

The winter of 1804–5 marked the nadir of the 'Russia Mint-Expedition'. Its members were discontented, sick (James Duncan's ailments were real as well as imagined, while James Walker, the eldest member of the band, was very nearly chronically ill, so that it was doubtful whether he would much outlive his Russian assignment), and sick of each other's company. And to cap off everything, Kakoushkin the meddler returned to the scene.

He had last appeared at the mint near the end of 1802 with a request for a job – any job. The employment of Russians at the mint (after they had been sent to Soho to receive their training) had been a major concern of Matthew Boulton, had become of equal or greater importance to Zack Walker, who feared that untrained hands would ruin the delicate machinery of the new mint. He had accordingly made frequent requests to Count Vasiliev that promising people be selected and sent to England; in the autumn of 1804, Vasiliev (who otherwise appeared to be losing interest in the entire mint project) decided to send three or four good Russian workmen to the Boulton mint at St Petersburg rather than Soho, so that they could receive training on the very machines they would later manage, from the very Soho men who were then erecting them. The nobleman told Walker of his decision, adding that one such artisan had already been picked and detailed to come to the new facility and make sketches and notes about it – but that James Duncan had churlishly refused him entrance. Thus was Kakoushkin reintroduced into the proceedings.

He had pursued a checkered career since his ejection from Soho. He had returned to Russia, eventually finding work at Baron Gascoigne's engine factory at Kronstadt – and had been exiled from it when it was discovered he was stealing parts of the machinery. Then,

> after these valuable certificates of Service rendered his Country, my friend M*r* [Mint] President picked him up, put an Uniform over his ragged Shirt, stuck a Sword by his Side, gave him a Rank which places him a few degrees above the dread of being flogged for future peculations, & thus equipped sent him into the Mint to look over our people's shoulders whilst at work, & collect all the information he could.—[36]

Kakoushkin visited the site on several occasions in the early autumn of 1804, each time without identification or authorization. On one occasion, he sat down in the middle of the floor and began to make drawings while the work continued around him. The irascible Duncan thereupon threw him out, and Kakoushkin lodged his complaint with the Mint President. The latter approached Vasiliev, who was by now exasperated with all parties on all sides. The Count wearily signed a document giving Kakoushkin an appointment as superintendent of the mint machinery – which gave him the power to pry anywhere he pleased.

Zack Walker was outraged. He advised his men to be perfectly polite to the intruder but make their answers to his questions as vague as possible. And if Kakoushkin made any more attempts to sketch the machinery, he was to be stopped at all costs, Walker taking full responsibility for the action.

The tension died down nearly as quickly as it had blown up. Once the Mint President realized that, document or no, his writ did not extend to the inner

A Soho teaching aid for
aspiring Russian coiners,
1804. (National
Numismatic Collection,
Smithsonian Institution)

secrets of Soho's Russian mint, and that Walker and his people were willing to defend those secrets by force if necessary, he ceased his meddling. And he withdrew his man of straw as well: Kakoushkin did indeed visit the mint a few more times, but he was even more polite than the Britons, asked no questions, made no drawings. And we soon cease to hear about him. We only have Walker's explanation for the change of Russian policy; but his impression was probably correct.

At St Petersburg, the Boulton mechanics continued their assembly of the machinery. At Soho, their master turned to other considerations. One was relatively minor, and soon accomplished. This was the provision of dies to the new mint. Boulton never seems to have seriously considered making *all* of the dies for St Petersburg: leaving aside the extraordinary logistical problems created by the European war, even a modest Russian coinage would turn Soho's attentions in a direction of limited interest at a time when they were most urgently required elsewhere. Instead, Boulton proposed to send the Russians dies in various stages and pieces struck from them as a teaching aid, for the instruction of those persons who would someday become responsible for the mint. With that in mind, an elaborate package was sent to Russia in the fall of 1804. It consisted of sets of dies in dollar and halfpenny sizes. Their obverses depicted Tsar Alexander, with a legend in Latin; their reverses bore a simple Greek cross. One of the 'coins' struck from the dollar-size dies is illustrated. The package would have reached St Petersburg before the end of the year.

This consideration was minor: by trial and error, the future master of the mint and whomever he hired would eventually learn how to make dies even without Soho models. But the other consideration was major indeed: if he and his subordinates did not learn correct procedures for the use of their new machines, the refurbished St Petersburg mint might be ruined, never striking coins from Boulton's dies or any others. As 1804 closed, the assembly and training of skilled Russian personnel at Soho assumed a paramount importance for its master, Matthew Boulton.

There was a reason for this which the inventor must keep to himself. He was now committed to sending a second mint abroad, to Copenhagen. And he was on the verge of committing to construct yet a third facility according to his principles, on Little Tower Hill, in London. All of this led him to an inevitable conclusion: he must get one or more of his 'Mintaneers' out of Russia and on to other projects – especially the Danish, the more pressing of them. And in order to get any of his people *out*, he must get Russian replacements *in*.

This conclusion may have been unavoidable, but it was also beset by difficulties. The Russian mint was not yet finished, and any or all of Soho's men could scarcely leave until it was up and coining. And Soho's men hated each other. Whom could he prevail upon to go to Copenhagen? Would anyone be willing to accompany anyone else? Would they work together in Copenhagen any better than they had at St Petersburg?

These considerations occupied Boulton through all of 1805 and much of 1806. Meanwhile, he signed a formal agreement with the British Government and finished and shipped the Danish mint to Copenhagen. The sending of personnel to Denmark (with an eye to a brief sojourn there before the final assignment in London) became increasingly important with time. Boulton would attack the problem from two directions. He would confer with Russians, in London and St Petersburg, for the native workers he needed. And he would attempt to persuade his own men to accept the Danish assignment, once they were free to take it.

He achieved success in neither case. In March 1806, he wrote directly to Count Vasiliev, pleading with him to send competent people to Soho for training in the machinery of the new mint. He wanted mechanics, not artists:

> for although an artist might make the finest organ in the World yet he would not be able to play upon it unless he understood music & was in the habit of playing. In order therefore that the Machine, when completed, should be able to coin money (which it cannot do of itself) it must receive the aid of some intelligent beings properly instructed for the purpose[.]

Were either Deriabin or Lizel to be posted to the new mint, the personnel problem would be solved. But Deriabin was too old to learn a new trade (and was also destined for greater things), while Lizel, though competent, lacked the fire and drive which would be needed. He might also have an eye out for greener pastures. Nor were James Duncan and his mates fit subjects: they were millwrights, not moneyers, and they could not be expected to do the work of coiners. New personnel must be chosen; but before sending them to England, Vasiliev would do well to send them to James Duncan (most qualified among the Soho residents); they must pass this Scot's muster, secure his approval, 'for you had better let the Mint remain inactive, than put it under the care of an improper Workman'.[37] Duncan might not know moneying, but he knew mechanics. In the event, the Russians sent no additional people to Soho for training; they sent them instead to St Petersburg, where James Duncan and the others did their best to train them – or at least look after the machinery as best they could.

While progress on the mint limped along (Zack Walker was finally able to report that it was likely to be finished by mid-1806; he was off by a full year), Matthew Boulton addressed his second objective. He would try to get one or more of the British mechanics to agree to go on a second mint adventure, proceeding to Copenhagen as soon as the Russian affair had been concluded. He had modest success at best: only James Duncan would agree to go out, none of the others wishing to have further dealings with him at Copenhagen or anywhere else. And Duncan himself would eventually be unwilling and then unable to leave when desired. None of the Soho men would ever go on another of Soho's foreign expeditions; and only one of them, William Speedyman, would ever work on another mint for Soho.

By mid-1806, basic work on the Russian machinery was finally nearing completion, and the first trials of the machinery were beginning. Both steam engines were fired up and performed admirably; James Harley and the others might have been difficult characters, but they were also superb artisans. The cutting out machinery was also tried and found operable. And the rolling mill performed to specifications. That left the coining machinery; here, many months were lost as the insecure James Duncan (who was responsible for the final arrangements of the delicate mechanisms) spent endless hours tinkering, testing, and re-testing. Harley and the others slowed down their pace to match his, so that the final few months of work on the mint must have been the most exasperating of all. But progress was real, work was coming to an end. That being the case, might Mr Boulton receive the remainder of the sum due him for his Russian mint?

Zack Walker thought he might, and he so advised his uncle. The latter wrote Count Vasiliev on 19 March 1806, with a polite, almost diffident request for remuneration. He observed that he could have asked for the payment of the second part of his fee as early as the end of 1800. Not wishing to appear greedy, he had not done so; nor was he now asking for the money justly due him as interest since the time when the second payment had come due. All he wanted was the remainder of the original sum charged for the mint, or £6,020. He did not press the issue, however, nor did his man in St Petersburg – at least not yet. Both were painfully aware that, until the mint was finished, or so close to completion that even the densest bureaucrat could see the future for himself, Soho's case was weak.

By the summer of 1806, the firm's case was much stronger, as construction was now moving rapidly towards a conclusion. Walker had been told that Count Vasiliev was coming to the mint to see the engines and rolling mill at work in a few days' time; when he visited, said Walker, he would present his uncle's claims, and he thought there was a good chance of their being honoured. He wrote to Boulton in this vein on 20 June 1806 OS; for the next several months, Soho anxiously waited for word of success. Boulton's men remained immured at St Petersburg – and were therefore unable to advance the old man's other schemes. His health in decline (brought on in part by worry over the interminable Russian project), Boulton's grasp on the affair weakened, even as his concern over it strengthened. Walker had said he expected matters to be cleared up in six weeks? What was going on?

His nephew was doing all he could, but in truth the project could not be accelerated. Duncan fiddled with the machinery, testing and retesting, painfully cognizant that James Harley and the other two workmen were waiting for him to fail. In such an atmosphere, this senior mechanic very nearly became catatonic, afraid that *any* action would be a mistake. Work slowed to a crawl: while Walker was silent, he was undoubtedly waiting for Duncan to make his final adjustments before aggressively pursuing the matter of payment.

But despite all obstacles, the mint was finished at last. Around the middle of June 1807, a very nervous James Duncan fired up the boilers and produced the first trial coins; the earliest pieces for circulation emerged from the presses on 20 June 1807 OS.

Russian pattern ruble with head of Alexander I, 1807. (National Numismatic Collection, Smithsonian Institution)

They were rubles, and according to Zack Walker, the artist responsible for them was a man named 'Liebricht'. This was Carl *Leberecht*, a well-known designer active in Russia at the time. Leberecht was born at Meiningen, Germany in 1749, was appointed engraver to the Russian mint at the age of twenty-six, and henceforth enjoyed a long and distinguished career there – as a medallist. Full of years and honours, he died in 1827. No coins have previously been ascribed to him; nonetheless, he produced pieces of at least three types – two groups of pattern rubles and a third group of actual coins for circulation, maiden efforts of the new Boulton mint.

The first pattern group employed a rather anaemic-looking portrait of the new Emperor, Alexander I, along with the date 1801, the year of Alexander's accession; Soho contributed nothing to its creation. A second group featured a better portrait of the ruler – but his head seemed in danger of disappearing into his stock;[38] a typical example from this latter group is pictured. It bears the date 1807, and it bears the appearance of a typical Soho product. But the artist's name is featured at the truncation, and it seems certain that it was made in Russia, perhaps one of the trials which Duncan produced before he got down to the business of regular coining.

The actual money for circulation bore less ambitious designs. A double-headed eagle, with the denomination and date, adorned the obverse. The value was repeated on the reverse, placed within a wreath with the imperial crown above. This arrangement was pedestrian but deliberate, chosen with Boulton's industrialized coining in mind: with money created in a single, rapid blow of the press, any designs featuring obverse-reverse relief in the same general spots would result in imperfectly struck coins. The 1807 rubles might not inspire (although James Duncan was likely deeply moved when he first beheld them) – but their designs worked well. Yet these were hardly perfect coins.

Leberecht refused to take the time to finish his dies with the care demanded and received at Soho. And their forging was even worse: Lizel had been hired to oversee this branch of the process,

> but, as he finds more profit in working at home for his own account, it is left chiefly to Subalterns who employ common slaves, who slight the work, & leave it unsound both from ignorance, & the want of any motive of personal interest to do it well; nor, do I perceive that it is much mended in Lizel's own hands (tho' he affects to understand the detail of the business better than it is done at Soho) he having sunk two pair, from the sides of which the water started at the first blow, & the Dies cracked; nor does it appear to me that they are likely soon to remedy this evil … omitting what I recollect was always considered amongst workmen the best material in sound forging, viz, the liberal use of Elbow-grease—[39]

Russian ruble, 1807, with prominent die crack. (National Numismatic Collection, Smithsonian Institution)

Russian ruble, 1807, showing weakness in the central portion of the designs. (National Numismatic Collection, Smithsonian Institution)

Russian ruble, 1807, with prominent adjustment marks on reverse. (National Numismatic Collection, Smithsonian Institution)

The dies also suffered from a minor but vexing problem of design: while Leberecht's overall concept was sound, he had engraved one portion of his obverse too deep, the depiction of St George on the eagle's breast. Deep as it was, it could not be brought up in one blow, and the opposite area on the reverse suffered from a similar weakness at the same position. And the appearance of the new coins was scarcely helped by the Russian method of weight adjustment for heavy planchets: they scraped them with a coarse file until they came into tolerance. Some of the file marks were so deep that they remained visible even after striking.

Lest we assume that the foregoing complaints were another example of Zack Walker's spleen in the face of all things Russian, I have illustrated three coins from the Smithsonian's Numismatic Collection which bear him out. While the mint would ultimately do fine work, this was not the case in its earliest days.

At first, no more than two of the coining presses were set to work, but Duncan was able to strike between sixty-seven and seventy rubles per minute on each. His success in imparting life to the first two presses emboldened him: he soon told Walker that he could have the other six ready for work in two to three weeks' time. In fact, they would not be operable until mid-August, but progress that summer stood in happy contrast to the snail's pace of the previous months and years.

Zack Walker believed that now would be the time to demand payment for the mint; now, no one could conceivably harbour any doubts, raise any objections. To clinch the matter, Walker proposed to have Duncan coin ten or fifteen tons of the silver bullion now stored in the Fortress; that should quell any lingering doubts, should act as a powerful argument with Count Vasiliev, paymaster to the project. So Duncan got to work with a will, and even with his first two presses succeeded in striking nearly half a million rubles, even as he was getting his remaining half-dozen machines ready for coining.

All of the presses were finished by 9 August OS. Walker called on Count Vasiliev that evening. He begged the Treasurer to receive the mint as complete, to order passports for the returning Soho workmen, and to name a day when payment for the mint might be received. After a frank discussion, Vasiliev ordered that Walker should receive bills of exchange for the remaining principal of £6,020, plus interest calculated from the time in late 1800 when Matthew Boulton might have asked for the rest of his money. He would also be given a rebate for the expense of keeping his nephew in Russia during the four years of the latter's residence there. This sum was estimated at between £2,000 and £2,500.

And if Walker's expenses were now met, the long-festering question of the workmen's wages would also be addressed. Just as Boulton had promised, they would be rewarded: each would be allowed an extra guinea per week (Duncan, as foreman, would get an additional adjustment; he had earned it) 'from the time of their arrival in this Country to that of their departure'. No one would grow rich from his Russian experience, but each would do rather well by the modest standards of those days.

The Count promised to see the Emperor on 14 August, obtaining orders thereby to carry everything into effect. And when Walker came calling on the following day, he could get Boulton's bills of exchange, and the entire Russian mint affair would now come to an amicable conclusion. Let Walker tell what happened next:

> I began to revive again, enlivened by a ray of hope that this business would at last terminate to the satisfaction of all parties … when, on the 15*th* the golden dream vanished by intelligence that this Minister died very suddenly on the preceding night.— On reviewing the principal occurrences of my life, insignificant as it has been, I can scarcely avoid yielding up my reason & common-sense to the false & pernicious doctrine of an evil Genius or, unfortunate fatality, hovering over all the actions which some men are either directly or indirectly concerned with, & that I belong to the ominous Class of whom it may be truly said "Lo! whatsoever those men do it shall *not* prosper".—
>
> The Count's Papers are all sealed up, & no new Minister yet appointed, every thing material to the Mint-Department may therefore be considered as at a stand until a nomination takes place … Jas Duncan is in the hands of the Physician with a low putrid fever, so that nothing is doing in the Coinage … [40]

As far as the Russian affair was concerned, the future proved not as black as Walker feared: the bureaucracy moved far more rapidly than accustomed, appointing a temporary successor to Vasiliev within a few weeks. This was Fedor Golubtsov, and he took up the Russian mint arrangements precisely where his predecessor had left them. A settlement was being hammered out by the middle of October, and Matthew Boulton finally received his remaining principal plus interest in December 1807. He also received a showy ring, personal token of Tsar Alexander's favour.

The delay in proceedings between Vasiliev's death and Golubtsov's succession thus created no real difficulty in the matter of payment. But it raised problems elsewhere. Duncan and his family could hardly leave St Petersburg for Copenhagen until they had been provided with passports, and the Count's death held up their provision for several crucial weeks. By the time an exit was legally possible, two more events had taken place, one personal and the other international. The personal was that Duncan's wife was in the later stages of pregnancy and could not travel safely; and Duncan had no intention of going to Denmark without her. The international was that Britain and Denmark stood on the brink of war, stepped over that brink early in November. All of this meant that, once the Duncans could safely travel from the perspective of health, they would not be able to do so from the perspective of the international scene. And *that* in turn meant that Boulton could not keep the letter of his agreement with Denmark – and so would not soon receive the remainder due from the Danes. The elder Boulton would have been in his grave for seven years before that score was settled.

James Duncan never returned to Great Britain. He grew acclimatized to the Russian environment (he appears to have been the only one of the Soho people who took the trouble to learn Russian – he had to, for the job of paymaster to British *and* Russian mint workers had been added to all his other duties), staying on as foreman at the mint he had done so much to create. In 1814, he wrote to Matthew Robinson Boulton for supplies, proudly advising that 'his' mint was now coining more than ten million silver rubles per year, another million rubles or so in minor coinage – five, ten, and twenty kopek silver pieces. He added that new steam engines were now entering his adopted country in quantity – which must have created mixed feelings at Soho, after the many difficulties experienced in trying to introduce some of the first ones, at the St Petersburg mint. James Duncan died in Russia in the mid-1820s.

His sparring partner James Harley stayed on in Russia too, lured to Siberia by promises of great wealth there for the enterprising. The elderly James Walker went home to Scotland with his family, there to spend his final years. He and his associate William Speedyman left Russia for Great Britain in November 1807, arriving safely towards the end of the month. That left Zack Walker. The final chapter in his story was the most surprising of all.

Just as he was observing the first coining efforts of Mr Duncan, Napoleon and Alexander I were sitting on a raft in neutral territory, dividing the world between them. The vacillating Tsar had swung against Great Britain – for the time being. He would swing decisively in the opposite direction in a few years' time; but for now, all intercourse between England and Russia was cut off, the British Minister resident at St Petersburg was handed his travelling papers – and other Britons would do well to leave as well, while they still could.

The James Walker family and William Speedyman left in time, having no further business at St Petersburg. But Zacchaeus Walker took his time; he was still attempting to secure his uncle's money, and he also had personal reasons for delaying his departure.

We might feel safe in assuming that the thirty-nine-year-old Walker was a confirmed bachelor. And we would be confounded: he abruptly surprises us (as he must have surprised his friends and relatives at Soho) by taking a wife. There is a hint that his marriage, which took place in midsummer 1808, was not entirely voluntary, and that he was as dumbfounded as anyone else. Surviving evidence suggests that he rued the action even as he was taking it. But married he now was, which would mean more time spent in securing a second set of exit papers. These proved difficult to obtain; Walker's efforts to secure them and the monies due Matthew Boulton for unforeseen expenses on the mint project would carry him through most of 1808.

He finally achieved both missions by the end of October 1808. Not wishing to tempt fortune, he and his wife left St Petersburg within a few days. As Walker observed to his cousin just prior to their departure, 'To-morrow I hope to have passed two happy Days in this City, the first being that on which I arrived in it, & the last that on which I shall quit it'.[41] This was unkind, but pardonable.

But Zack Walker's adventures were not quite over. He and his bride had a rough passage by land to Riga, where their vessel was stuck in the ice for several days. After a horrendous voyage across the Baltic, they fetched up at Goteborg, in Sweden – where their further passage was again postponed by ice. After a dangerous crossing by packet, during which they were chased by privateers, the Walkers finally reached Harwich, and safety. That was in mid-March 1809: the journey home had taken four and one-half months. Zack Walker may have been overly dramatic in describing himself as a star-crossed man; but as one reads the account of his harrowing voyage, one begins to understand his point of view.

Once returned to Soho, Walker remained there, his travelling days at an end. He performed faithful service for his cousin, just as he had for his uncle. Zacchaeus Walker, Jr. died in April 1822, aged fifty-four.

What conclusions might we draw about the mint which had brought him and his mates to Russia? It was the most ambitious and the most frustrating of

Soho's foreign adventures – ambitious because of its size, especially in light of its early date, frustrating for reasons now obvious to the reader. What did the Russian experience finally 'mean' to those caught up in it, involved in its course? What lessons might Soho and later generations draw from the story of the 'Russia Mint-Expedition'?

Perhaps the basic moral which might be drawn is that technology does best when it is 'neutral', when it is true to its simplest definition: a way of linking a particular group of objects and their parts, in a particular way, for a particular goal. It is obviously permissible to hope for the better, to foresee the improvement of a project to the benefit of the daily life of the average person. But that hope must always be tempered with reality – the recognition of the force of tradition and habit, of personal turf, of events and collective personalities larger than the individual. An example: Matthew Boulton believed in the paramount importance of the amelioration of copper coinage. He believed that his Russian customer felt as he did, wanted his mint for the same purpose. He continued to hope in this way, long after it was apparent that his client wanted his product for other purposes, none of which had anything to do with Matthew Boulton's objectives. Zack Walker was unkind, but he was far more realistic than his uncle, when he made an observation which will be familiar to any student of the history of technology:

> the Russians in general may with propriety be still considered as great Babies, who, when they hear of a novel & pretty thing cry after it, & must have [it] 'coute qui coute' [whatever the cost] whilst the fit lasts, but it is seldom of long duration, & as soon as the attention is diverted by some fresh object, the former is totally forgotten—[42]

In time, the Russian Government would indeed begin coining copper coinage at Matthew Boulton's mint, on Matthew Boulton's model. Copper patterns were prepared in 1810, and the first coinage for circulation entered the commerce of the capital later that year. But it must be emphasized that this coinage was undertaken, not out of deference to the aspirations of a recently-deceased entrepreneur from the English Midlands, but because a Russian Tsar decided that it would be so.

At that point, Matthew Boulton's ideas received their final consideration, acceptance, and justification. But now they had solid roots in their new soil, would do well there since they now belonged to it. At bottom, Soho's Russian experience leads us to a simple conclusion: we may hasten technology if we choose, but we must not pin all our hopes on the results. And we must await those results with patience.

SOURCES

The majority of the Russia story will be found in MBP414 and MBP415, Russian Mint, box 1 and 2; but a good part of it lies elsewhere.

Matthew Boulton's early connections with Russia are delineated in a number of letter books not normally visited by students of numismatics, or indeed by those interested in industrial history. They include MBP134, 135, and 136 – Letter Books B, C and D, respectively, covering the period between 1764 and 1773.

Crucial material will also be found in the Letter Boxes – notably MBP219 (Letter Box B1), MBP225 (C1), MBP227 (C3), MBP228 (D1), MBP229 (D2), MBP236 (H1), MBP248 (P1), MBP253 (S1), MBP254 (S2), MBP260 (W1) and MBP262 (W3). Four of Matthew Boulton's private notebooks come into our story as well. They are no. 72, compiled in 1796, no. 76, 'Coinage, 1797–1805', no. 79, compiled during 1797–8 (all to be found in MBP378, Matthew Boulton's notebooks, nos. 51–79), and no. 86 ('1800'), in MBP379 (Matthew Boulton's notebooks, nos. 80–96). Several other boxes contain significant materials. The most important of them is MBP360, Zacchaeus Walker, Jr.'s box. But details of the rolling portion of the Russian mint will be found in MBP332, Rennie, John.

MBP343, Southern, John; Southern, Thomas, affords data on the construction of the mint machinery by one of the participants. Charles Gascoigne's father-in-law left a voluminous account of his shady dealings; this will be found in MBP309, Garbett, Samuel, 1786–97. Additionally, the papers on the Danish mint (to be found in MBP410) contain some materials on the Russian project not found elsewhere – testimony to the fact that the same men were, in theory, to be responsible for the erection of both facilities.

Most of the details of times and types of shipments of mint materials appear in MBP414 and 415; but those interested may also wish to consult MBP43, 44, and 46 – Mint Books covering the years between 1798 and 1805, during which the component parts of the mint made their way to St Petersburg.

Several non-archival studies were also used in the preparation of this chapter. They included Grand Duke Georgii Mikhailovich's *Monnaies de L'Empire de Russie, 1725–1894* (trans. Nadine Tacké, reprinted 1973) and Randolph Zander's 'The St Petersburg Mint', *Journal of the Russian Numismatic Society* 45 (Winter 1992). I took my information on Carl Leberecht from the third volume of Leonard Forrer's monumental *Biographical Dictionary of Medallists* (8 vols., London, 1904–30).

NOTES

1 All the same, one of his old associates at Carron observed that it was probably as well that Gascoigne had left:

    Speaking of Gascoigne, [Walter Hog] shook his Head, & said he was a Clever Fellow, it was well for the Creditors he was gone out of the Kingdom, had he remained they would never have got one Shilling[.]

(MBP309, Garbett, Samuel, 1786–97: copy of a letter from Samuel Barker to Samuel Garbett, 3 October 1793.)
    Gascoigne died in Russia in the middle of 1806; he left a daughter (Anna, Countess of Haddington, *née* Gascoigne) and a collection of creditors to mourn his passing. I am greatly indebted to Professor Eric Robinson for welcome help in understanding this complex early industrialist.

2 MBP225, Letter Box C1: Peter Capper, Jr. to Matthew Boulton, 24 November 1777 OS; spelling and punctuation in original. Russia used the Julian calendar (OS) until the October Revolution. In the eighteenth century, this dating system was eleven days behind the Western, Gregorian calendar. The discrepancy widened to twelve days in the nineteenth century and thirteen days in the twentieth.

3 MBP260, Letter Box W1: H. S. Wagnon to Matthew Boulton, 11 November 1796.

4 MBP219, Letter Box B1: Alexander Baxter to Matthew Boulton, 27 May 1796; spelling and punctuation in original.

5 No pun intended.

6 How the Tsar proposed to connect the engine to the presses is not known. His engineers were not privy to Boulton's first method of harnessing steam power to coining, and Boulton himself had yet to devise his second. But that is why Tsars have engineers rather than engineering degrees.

7 MBP415, Russian Mint, (box 2): Matthew Boulton to Simon Vorontsov, 21 January 1797.

8 Suggesting that his acquaintance with the Emperor was slight indeed!

9 MBP414, Russian Mint, (box 1): Matthew Boulton to Simon Vorontsov, 20 February 1797. Emphasis and spelling in original.

10 MBP414, Simon Vorontsov to Matthew Boulton, 18/29 [sic] June 1797.

11 MBP415, Matthew Boulton to Felix Schlatter, 16 October 1797.

12 MBP415, 'Memorandum by the Revd Mr Smirnove of things required along with the Establishment of the Mint in Russia', 6 February 1798. Soho customarily appended the e to Smirnov's name. Emphasis in original.

    Boulton was being less than forthcoming here. The second Soho mint was indeed constructed partly as a testing of the new arrangement for Russia. But it also *had* to be rebuilt, for the massive Cartwheel coinage had uncovered many flaws in the original design.

13 MBP414, Matthew Boulton to James Smirnov, 20 February 1798. Spelling and emphasis in original.

14 Deriabin in fact would play no intermediary role, his direct importance to the St Petersburg project essentially disappearing after 1800.

15 MBP253, Letter Box S1: 'A Sketch for Mr Sheriff to write to St Petersburgh Jan 1800'. The sketch is in Sheriff's hand, and the spelling and punctuation are his. Although Boulton must have inspired the missive, meant to be read by the right people upon Sheriff's return to Russia, there is no reason to suppose that Sheriff did not agree with its contents.

16 MBP253, George Sheriff to Matthew Boulton, 16 January 1800. Sheriff's description of presses at work in the Fortress Mint is confusing until we remember that, when he had last been in Russia, those presses had not yet been moved to their new if temporary location at the Assignat Bank.

17 MBP254, Letter Box S2: Matthew Boulton to James Smirnov, 24 April 1800.

18 MBP415, 'Resolutions of the Birm m Memorialists Shakespear Tavern June 3d 1800'.

19 MBP415, contemporary copy, 'The Merchants of Birmingham Memorial to His Majesty's Principal Secretaries of State, Birmingham, 21 June 1800'.

20 Under the provisions of his agreement, Boulton drew on the agents of the Russian Empire, Messrs. Harman & Company, for slightly less than half the amount due him. The precise date of his claim (amounting to £5,500) has been lost, but it must have been made around 20 May 1800.

21 MBP376, 'Notebook 10, Coinage, 1797–1805', pp. 3–5 (notation of 28 March 1802).

22 MBP415, Matthew Boulton to James Duncan, 13 May 1802. Emphasis and spelling in original.

23 MBP415, George Sheriff to Matthew Boulton, 6 June 1802 OS.

24 MBP415, Matthew Boulton to James Smirnov, 21 March 1803.

25 MBP415, Zacchaeus Walker, Jr. to Matthew Boulton, 20 June 1804 OS. Duncan got married all the same in September 1804, by proxy. His bride was a Miss Twycroft, of Coventry. She came to Russia, and her middle-aged husband soon surprised his fellows once again, fathering at least one child and probably two by his young wife.

26 MBP415, James Duncan to Matthew Boulton, 15 December 1802 OS.

27 MBP415, James Duncan to Matthew Boulton, 5 May 1803 OS.

28 Droz was Swiss, of course, but gracefully surrendered his national identity for the greater good of France – and for the greater injury of Matthew Boulton.

29 MBP415, Matthew Boulton to James Harley, 8 November 1802; the spelling lapses suggest great agitation.

30 MBP415, James Duncan to Matthew Boulton, 5 May 1803 OS.

31 MBP415, Matthew Boulton to Alexis Vasiliev, 1 May 1803. The introduction had originally been dated 10 September 1802, a clear indication that Boulton was convinced that Walker's hand would be needed very early on. But he could not set out until the success or failure of Soho's dealing with the French.

32 MBP415, Zacchaeus Walker, Jr. to Zacchaeus Walker, Sr., 12 June 1803.

33 MBP360, Walker, Z. jr. box: Zacchaeus Walker, Jr. to Matthew Boulton, 23 June 1803 OS.

34 MBP415, Zacchaeus Walker, Jr. to Matthew Boulton, 22 July 1803 OS; emphasis in original.

35 MBP415, Zacchaeus Walker, Jr. to Matthew Boulton, 4 October 1804 OS.

36 MBP415, Zacchaeus Walker, Jr. to Matthew Boulton, 5 November 1804 OS.

37 MBP415, Matthew Boulton to Alexis Vasiliev, 19 March 1806.

38 The Tsar apparently posed grave problems for those who would put him on coins, and he never appeared on ordinary Russian money during his reign.

39 MBP415, Zacchaeus Walker, Jr. to Matthew Boulton, 21 June 1807 OS.

40 MBP415, Zacchaeus Walker, Jr. to Matthew Robinson Boulton, 18 August 1807 OS; emphasis in original. Walker's agonized cry might aptly serve as the motto of the 'Russia Mint-Expedition'!

41 MBP415, Zacchaeus Walker, Jr. to Matthew Robinson Boulton, 19 October 1808 OS.

42 MBP415, Zacchaeus Walker, Jr. to Matthew Boulton, 15 February 1804 OS. When writing my dissertation on industrialization in Latin America, I frequently encountered this same, unrealistic, attachment to new technology simply because it *was* new, and supposedly conferred a mantle of modernity on its possessors. My favourite story along this line arose in Paraguay during the mid-1950s. A project to set up a washing machine factory in Asunción was received enthusiastically until someone recalled that the capital lacked a dependable source of running water.

CHAPTER 3

The Limits of Success: Denmark, 1796–1816

Soho's dealings with Denmark offer interesting points of comparison with, and departure from, its adventures in other parts of the world. The flat, welcoming landscape of this small Scandinavian kingdom offered no challenges of geography or climate, as did India, Mexico, or Brazil. Denmark was welcoming in another way: unlike Russia, unlike Brazil, the Danes (including their ruling class) had every intention of employing Mr Boulton's new mint for the purposes for which he had created it – that is, for safer money for the average citizen, rather than as a totem of modernity.

Nor would there be problems with the mint site – another point at variance with events elsewhere. The Danes chose, and Soho accepted, a building for the new mint which proved to be sufficiently large and adequately situated for the purpose.

So far, so good; and we might expect that Boulton, Watt's Danish experience would offer a welcome respite from its more arduous labours, a blessedly simple, quick and profitable injection of the new moneying process into a problem-free arena. And we would be completely mistaken.

For in proportion to its size, no other project would cause the Boultons greater annoyance than this one. A combination of malign events at home and abroad would stretch the affair (which should have occupied a year or two at most, based on its size and complexity) into a process taking nearly two decades to complete. And the Boultons found to their surprise that a mint could be quite as troublesome after it was done as while it was building.

They themselves bore part of the blame. Throughout the negotiations leading up to the signing of the formal contract between the Kingdom of Denmark and Boulton, Watt & Company, the latter always had more important matters on its mind. It wanted the connection, and the cachet and profits it might be expected to bring. But it was always engaged in larger and more prestigious and lucrative matters at the same time – the Cartwheel coinage, the Russian mint, eventually the Royal Mint – and was inclined to put the Danes off until able to give them its undivided attention. This annoyed Copenhagen, which accordingly played the same game. And so many months were wasted, at a time when punctuality and enterprise would, as it happened, have been crucial.

Most of the responsibility lay in the world of high politics, in areas beyond Soho's control, and even beyond Denmark's bidding. In no other instance were the fortunes of the firm more shaped by the unfolding of the Napoleonic Wars. The Anglo-French conflict (and the attempts of the two powers to draw others into the vortex on their respective sides) influenced every step of the Danish story. Soho would suffer from it in the most direct way imaginable: it would not be paid for its services until nearly a decade after they had been rendered. In the sense that it could have easily got its mint constructed and payment received in the years before the war, Boulton, Watt's timing was off. But as Matthew Boulton sadly observed on another occasion, the times themselves were out of joint during those early years of the nineteenth century; and Soho must take its chances in this real, hostile world.

There are rather more gaps in the Danish record than in that of its Russian counterpart, but enough has survived (most of it in MBP410, the Danish Mint box in the Birmingham Archives) to make possible a detailed telling of the tale. While contacts between Copenhagen and Matthew Boulton had existed for decades (in part because the Danes served as factors for Norwegian copper), any idea of a numismatic connection does not come to light until the latter part of 1796.

This new direction involved correspondence and conversations between Matthew Boulton and Baron Gustavus Buchwald, a high official of the Danish Government. We are uncertain as to how the contact was initiated; but we know that Buchwald had been entrusted by his superiors at Copenhagen with a number of missions in England, and it seems safe to guess that exploratory talks with Matthew Boulton about the reformation of Danish coinage were among them. The Baron was provided with coinage samples, which served to convince him that Matthew Boulton was definitely the man for the job. Prior to his return home in October 1796, Buchwald wrote the Danish Minister of Finance, Count Ernst G. Schimmelmann[1] to that intent, receiving an almost instantaneous reply requesting him to ask Boulton for his terms.

Boulton replied about two weeks later, explaining that he could offer no more than generalities until the Danes gave him more precise information about the extent of new coinage their nation might require. He would also need to know whether a rolling mill would be wanted; if so, it could provide copper sheathing for the Danish Royal Navy when not busy rolling metal for the coinage. Those observations made, he attempted to provide rough data as to the price of a new mint. If the Danes wanted one the same size as Soho, it would cost them what Soho had cost him – and we know from other sources that Boulton had sunk around £10,000 into that project by the mid-1790s. If they wanted something smaller (and there is a hint throughout that this would be *his* preference), they could have it at his cost plus a thousand guineas. This price would include the training of a Dane or two in the new coining. With his letter, Boulton sent complete sets of production coins and medals to the Baron and his employer, the Count, including one piece which was not yet in production but shortly would be: the Cartwheel penny. And here was the first hint of a complicating factor in the story of Soho's dealings with Denmark. When the British copper coinage finally became a reality, Boulton would, and indeed would have to, abandon smaller pursuits in its favour. And when we add the project of the St Petersburg mint, for which talks were also beginning in 1796 (and in comparison to which the Copenhagen mint was of a lesser importance), we begin to see the emergence of a pattern.

Unmindful of Soho's other projects and prospects, Baron Buchwald went about showing its wares to the right people in the Danish Government and discussing the mint project with his superiors, especially Count Schimmelmann. The latter wrote Boulton several enthusiastic letters late in 1796 and early in 1797, forwarded to Soho by the London agents of the Danish Government, Wolffs & Dorville. Preoccupied with mint and patent matters, Boulton did not bother to reply to the Count's communications until April 1797 – which annoyed Wolffs & Dorville and served as a basis for that firm's later attitude toward Soho.

When Boulton finally got around to resuming contact, he put the best face he could on his current press of business, especially the British copper coinage. While it would certainly delay his work for Denmark, it would just as surely make it that much more satisfactory when it was finally pursued, because his machinery would be undergoing its most demanding testing to date with the execution of the gigantic Cartwheel order. The Danes would be the first beneficiaries, for they would be receiving machinery of the same type, whose defects had now been identified and resolved; a wildly optimistic Boulton told them that they could expect to have their new mint during the following year, 1798.

Schimmelmann and Buchwald (to whom Boulton wrote similar explanations at about the same time) were not particularly pleased with Soho's excuses, even as they admitted their validity. While the paucity of correspondence makes interpretation difficult, it seems clear that Boulton and his correspondents at Copenhagen were approaching the mint question from two very different directions, had two very different sets of ideas as to what had been promised. Boulton seems to have assumed that everything was still in the conditional tense (*whenever* time permitted, he would build a mint for Denmark). The Danes appear to have viewed the matter in the indicative tense (Boulton *would* build them a mint, period). Buchwald and Schimmelmann may have been misled by Boulton's perennial optimism, wherein possibilities were presented in a rosier light than reality might admit. Boulton had adopted this stance as a necessary weapon in dealing with British officialdom (and in keeping up his own spirits during the lean years which were just now ending). He had only himself to blame if it created misunderstanding, disappointment, and eventually anger on the part of Danish officialdom.

In the summer of 1797, the Danes attempted to revive the project. Conceding that Boulton had his share of troubles, Count Schimmelmann gently reminded the industrialist that the Danes had theirs as well, and that Soho's temporary shelving of the plans for their new mint might turn them in other directions. Assuming that Mr Boulton was *not* interested in refurbishing the Copenhagen mint (a conclusion arrived at by careful perusal of his earlier letters) would he nonetheless mind if Denmark sent an intelligent traveller of a scientific bent (who would be in England anyway, perfecting his knowledge of mathematics and astronomy) over to Soho, to speak of mint matters? It would be Boulton's choice whether or not to receive him; and it would also be Boulton's choice whether or not to keep the Danish project alive.

The coiner had more than enough on his plate at this point, for the Cartwheel coinage was just getting under way, and he was virtually living at his mint, checking and rechecking the machinery which must strike the massive penny and twopenny coins. But this latest Danish appeal caught his attention: the businessman counselled the wisdom of keeping Copenhagen on the burner if not on the boil, and the self-taught man of science was always happy to see and speak with a kindred spirit, regardless of other commitments. And so he invited the Danish savant over for a visit, meanwhile reiterating that nothing concrete could conceivably come of it for the time being. The Danes accepted this response, and they sent their man to Soho.

This was Professor Olaus Warberg, who now began his long connection with Soho, and with the Boulton family. Warberg's first visit probably took place in the late summer of 1797. He and Matthew Boulton took an immediate liking to each other, for the Dane proved a quick student, eagerly exploring the intricacies of Soho's coining machinery – at a time when the problems inherent in its current design, exacerbated by the strains of the British copper coinage, were becoming obvious to Soho's proprietor.

It will be recalled that Boulton had arranged his presses in a circle, powered by an overhead wheel with escapements. At the time, this had seemed the only practical method allowing a steam engine to be added to the coining equation. But it was not an optimal arrangement, tending to create bottlenecks in the moneying process. With the undertaking of the Cartwheel coinage, Boulton's attention had been forcibly drawn to the problem as never before, and Warberg spent much time with him as he grappled with and finally overcame it in the first months of 1798. The Dane was impressed with his British friend's persistence and ingenuity, concluding that Boulton simply *must* be enlisted in any reformation of the Copenhagen mint. And Boulton agreed, perhaps rendered more sanguine by the fact that he now seemed to be on the road to solving his problems with his own mint, the Russian mint (as related elsewhere, Russian dislike of the circular press arrangement provided the actual impetus for Boulton's solution to it), and the Cartwheel coinage.

All of this resulted in a curious document of collusion between Matthew Boulton and Olaus Warberg, composed in March 1798. A rough draft exists in Birmingham: presumably, a clean copy would have been forwarded to Copenhagen. Consisting of two parts, the first, dated 4 March, consists of seventeen questions from Professor Warberg, centring on Boulton's possible contributions to the Danish moneying process. Boulton's answers to these questions is dated some three weeks later (26 March), but the way in which the questions are intertwined with the answers, the way in which Warberg phrases them so as to put Boulton's responses in the best possible light (and the way in which wording by Warberg is crossed out and re-phrased, in Boulton's hand), suggests to me that the two men composed it in each other's presence and with each other's counsel. The flavour of the exchange is suggested by Warberg's tenth question and Boulton's answer:

> *10* Are all those Machines, belonging to the [proposed Danish] Mint, to be worked by Steam Engines, without applying Men, is the Machinery constructed in such a manner, that they all may be worked at one, or as many as wanted, and can any single one, at any moment, when it is required, be stopp'd in an easy and convenient manner, without stopping or disturbing the motion of the others.
>
> 10 One Steam Engine will be applyd to the Cutting out the Blanks, the Milling of the Edges, the Shakeing the Blanks dry, the Coining, the turning of the Dies[.] Any one of the Cutting out presses or any one of the Coining presses is Stoped in an Instant & set going agin in an Instant without the least interuption to any other press[.]

The above suggests the tenor of the whole. The ability of stopping one part of his mechanism while keeping the others in motion was one of Matthew Boulton's greatest sources of pride, and it tended to creep into any account he wrote for outside consumption. The document runs the entire gamut of moneying, from rolling to finished coin. In its course, the inventor observes that his mint could be adapted to run by water-power, or even consist of ordinary, pre-industrial machinery, convertible to steam at a later period. He also pledges to adapt his machinery to fit in the premises of the current Copenhagen mint (a strong indication that he has solved the press-arrangement problem which had limited him previously), as well as agreeing to provide continuing technical advice. And he hints broadly at a new and improved method of coining ('that is not yet carried into Execution [but] which is of a Capital nature')[2] – presumably the lineal arrangement of his moneying presses and indeed his entire moneying process. All of this suggests that Boulton was now eager to pursue the mint project, was keen on getting it on any terms.

But by now the Danish Government was losing interest. As Boulton had once been reminded by Count Schimmelmann, Denmark was an actual *country*, and therefore had other pressing business in addition to Mr Boulton's mint. The Danes appear to have decided to get on with their business in light of Boulton's manifest inability to get on with his. And Boulton certainly hurt his own cause by a letter to the Count (of which an undated draft remains, firmly attributable to the spring of 1798), wherein he admitted that the press of copper coining and the beginnings of an involvement in yet another project (the reformation of the Royal Mint) would force him to put off the Danish project still longer: he would not be able to complete construction of the machinery until the spring of 1799, while it would not be up and running until the following autumn.[3] With this additional bit of information, the Danish Government decided to let the mint matter lapse for the next several months. And for reasons of his own, so did Matthew Boulton.

When he resumed it in the middle of 1799, he took a surprising new tack. Previously, he had always spoken of providing a Danish mint; now, he offered to provide *coinage* instead.

Why had Boulton retreated from his earlier objective? In part, his offer to coin for Denmark stemmed from the fact that he was about to cease coining for Britain, at least for the time being. And while he was agitating for a second Soho copper coinage, nothing had yet been signed. So a window of opportunity now existed: assuming that a few months' grace might exist between the first and second British coinages (or a few months of costly inac-

Two of Boulton's patterns for a proposed copper coinage for Denmark – undated, but struck in 1799. (Reproduced by kind permission of the Trustees of the British Museum)

tivity, viewing it in a less optimistic light) Boulton estimated that he could strike five to six hundred tons' worth of penny- or halfpenny-sized copper pieces for the Danes. He would be happy to do so – so happy and so eager, in fact, that he was essentially willing to trade good Danish copper for made-at-Soho Danish coins. This money would be struck from dies approved by the Copenhagen Government, Boulton charging between fourpence and fivepence per pound, depending on the size of the coin, as well as a carriage charge of £3 or £5 per ton, depending on whether the coinage was shipped from Hull, Bristol, Liverpool, or London.

Boulton sent along patterns of the sorts of coinage he had in mind. While we cannot be absolutely certain as to their identity, the British Museum contains several undated copper pieces, unquestionably of Soho origin, with the peculiar, 'thread-milled' edge which Boulton was about to apply to British copper coinage. He extolled the virtues of this new type of edge in his offer to the Danes (among other things, it would be impossible for forgers to cast such coins in sand, because they would not come cleanly out of the moulds). He also preached the virtues of coins struck with inward-curving fields (their edges were so much thicker than their centres that anybody attempting to replicate them unofficially would simply break his dies). When we reflect that the British Museum patterns have such special fields and variable thicknesses, it seems fairly certain that they were the sorts of patterns which Boulton was sending to Denmark to strengthen his proposal.

In his mind, a Danish coinage would achieve several goals. It would keep a connection alive until such time as a mint could be conveniently constructed. It would provide his employees with work. It would create a cordial atmosphere with a major copper-exporting power, which would be of obvious use once Boulton was asked to resume his coinage for Great Britain. But the Danes never bothered to accede to his offer (and apparently never even deigned to reply to it). And when Boulton merely proposed to purchase Danish copper (with no mention of coining it for Denmark) he had an equal lack of success, even though he attempted to enlist Professor Warberg's services on his behalf. These efforts went on through late 1799 and early 1800, by which time Boulton had begun his second round of British copper coinage, having scraped together supplies of the red metal from other sources. And by now, Professor Warberg had gone home, and Boulton was confronted with what appeared to be a missed opportunity, for which he bore a majority of the blame.

But his luck turned for the better early in the summer of 1800. Warberg had apparently kept up the good fight even after he had left England, and he was finally, triumphantly, able to report success on 6 June:

Sir

I am desired to inform you that the Danish Ambassador in London, Count Wedel Jarlsberg, is, by order of His Excellency Count Schimmelmann and the Board of Finances, requested to apply to the British Government for an Act of Parliament to enable you to export a mint for Denmark. I believe that our Ambassador must according to diplomatic rules apply to Lord Grenville, who brings the business before Parliament. Count Schimmelmann is informed of your good promises to do all in your power, & to forward the affair as much as possible; I shall therefore request you to give yourself the trouble to speake to the Minister & other Members of Parliament, as His Excellency very much wishes, that an Act like that granted to His Imperial Majesty of Russia, may be granted to His Danish Majesty still during this Session of Parliament. As to further particulars, His Excellency or the Board of Finances will probably open a correspondence with you, or order me to do so.[4]

For once putting aside other concerns, Boulton leapt at the renewed Danish opportunity. He wrote Count Schimmelmann on at least one occasion during that summer (a letter, now lost, of 25 August). Based on the evidence of Schimmelmann's reply, this letter contained at least an informal offer to sell Denmark a mint, as well as a proposal to coin the country's copper until its new facility came into operation. But larger events now intervened. Matthew Boulton would have a new culprit to blame for slow progress on the Copenhagen project: he could damn his own government.

The problem had fairly deep roots. War between France and Great Britain had erupted after the beheading of Louis XVI in 1793. Like the United States, Denmark had been attempting to steer a neutral path between the French and British colossi, as they busily tried to destroy each other – and anyone in the way. At first, Andreas Peter Bernstorff, who was entrusted with Danish foreign policy until his death in 1797, refused to align his country with the monarchist coalition against republican France. But Great Britain began complicating his policy soon after declaring war on the French in 1793 by conducting a series of annoying raids on Danish merchantmen. Bernstorff then allied his country with the other neutral Scandinavian state, Sweden. This caused the British to reflect, and to temper their attacks; so did a series of French victories on land. But France was soon taking Britain's place in the harassment of Danish waterborne commerce, forcing Copenhagen to adopt the convoy system. Henceforth, she would refuse to allow her merchantmen to be stopped and searched on the high seas by Britons *or* Frenchmen.

The matter of sea power remained in tenuous balance until the mid-1790s but began to swing in Britain's favour as that decade ended. Danish convoys now increasingly became involved in clashes with the Royal Navy. Early in 1800, an actual engagement took place between a Danish frigate, escorting a convoy through the English Channel, and a British squadron; it ended in the capture of the frigate. And in August 1800 (just as Mr Boulton's hopes and agitations for a Danish mint were ascending), a British mission called at Copenhagen, backed by a fleet of nineteen vessels in the harbour. The mission forced the Danes to abandon the convoy system – which meant in effect that Great Britain could henceforth meddle in Danish commerce whenever the inclination took her. Copenhagen replied four months later by signing a pact of armed neutrality with a wider group of nations, including Prussia and Russia. And London replied to that by seizing all Danish ships in British ports (January 1801). But the worst was still to come.

Late in the winter of 1801, a fleet of fifty-three warships under the command of Hyde Parker arrived off Copenhagen. A few days later, Parker's second-in-command was ordered to attack the Danish fleet. Horatio Nelson did so with an élan which brought him glory (and smoothed the way for his appointment with destiny at Trafalgar) – and introduced a new if temporary addition to the English language (to 'Copenhagen' – to attack suddenly and without warning).

Outnumbered three to one, the Danes fought well, and they badly mauled Nelson's squadron. But his threat to burn all captured vessels brought a peace party into power (one of whose members was Count Schimmelmann), and an armistice was arranged. Subsequent parleys led to Danish withdrawal from the league of armed neutrality, purchasing a few more years of peace between Briton and Dane, a peace more technical than actual and tense for all concerned.

This was the thicket into which Matthew Boulton's hopes for a Danish mint had wandered. It would take them nearly three years to find their way out again.

The coiner was beset by problems from both sides. He had made a proposal to send a mint, or coinage, to Copenhagen on 25 August 1800. Several months later, he received his reply from Count Schimmelmann: for reasons both practical and patriotic, the Danes could not accept his offer of coin – while the British Government had decided for them that they could not accept Boulton's mint either: with the deterioration of Anglo-Danish relations, Pitt's administration had determined to withhold permission for the exportation of the machinery. And the turn of the year brought even worse tidings, as we have seen. Victim of forces in which it had no direct or even indirect interest, Soho's Danish ambition had to be shelved.

And there it remained for over two years: between February 1801 and July 1803, not so much as a single scrap of Danish correspondence appears in the Matthew Boulton Papers. But if war had frozen the course of events, peace could thaw them.

The peace was the Peace of Amiens, that vernal breathing spell in the midst of the carnage of the Napoleonic Wars. By the beginning of 1802, Great Britain appeared to be in the ascendancy: it was winning the war on the sea, had captured former Dutch and Spanish colonies ranging from Trinidad to Ceylon, and had evicted the French from Malta and Egypt. But Britain's people were weary of war, even a war that was going well. Pitt's administration was aware of growing peace sentiment at home, and it decided that this would be a favorable time to treat with the French. The result was the Peace of Amiens: it was concluded in late March of 1802, and it lasted just fourteen months.

It proved a disappointment for the British Government. If it had assumed that Napoleon would now obligingly reopen the Continent to the nation's commerce, it was soon disabused of this hope. But many individual Britons benefitted all the same. Thousands of travellers resumed their sight-seeing junkets to the Continent – among them, James Watt (although it is difficult to imagine the morose Scot kicking up his heels on holiday). And Watt's friend and former partner was about to reap an advantage of his own. He would resume his talks with the Danes, and he would finally sell them a mint.

Dealings between Soho and Copenhagen were resumed in July 1803. To be sure, this was some months *after* the breakdown of the Peace of Amiens: but the armistice had also served to ease Anglo-Danish tensions, at least for the time being. While the two countries would indeed go to war late in 1807, there was a reservoir of good feeling at the moment, one sufficiently full to allow for the necessary official negotiations and paperwork which must go on if Boulton's Copenhagen mint were to become a reality.

Olaus Warberg restarted the proceedings. He had returned to Britain (presumably during the truce period), had seen Boulton, had talked over the resurrection of the mint project with him. He had undoubtedly done this on orders of the Copenhagen authorities, who by now had irrevocably decided to go forward. Warberg communicated what he had learned to the chargé d'affaires, Gyldenpalm. The latter would have to see Boulton's old acquaintance Lord Hawkesbury, because his Lordship would be essential in obtaining Parliamentary sanction for the exportation of the mint.

As explained elsewhere, there was currently a law on the books (25 Geo. 3, Cap. 67) forbidding exportation of coining presses and other machinery – and the skilled personnel to erect and operate them. Matthew Boulton had been able secure an exemption for his Russian mint in 1800, and his son would do the same for a Brazilian mint in 1810. But the fact remained that every time Soho wished to export what it had learned about the art of moneying, a special Act of Parliament had to be passed for the purpose; and the Danish case was no exception.

On 17 January 1804, the Danish Treasury Board formally authorized Olaus Warberg to come to a definitive agreement with Matthew Boulton for a new mint. The Board wanted a smallish facility, evidence that Boulton's advice to think modestly and realistically had been taken to heart by the Count and his colleagues. Four coining presses would be required, with cutting out machinery and other parts of the apparatus in proportion. A rolling mill would also be wanted, and someone must be trained at Soho in the operation and necessary repair of the whole. Five Danish Lords of the Treasury signed Warberg's set of instructions. Permission had thus been obtained from one of the two countries whose blessings Boulton must have. But the sanction of the other would be more difficult to obtain.

Warberg remained in London through most of 1804, doing what he could to prod the British Government into granting its sanction to the project in the form of a Parliamentary Act. Boulton remained at Soho – partly for reasons of health, partly because his involvement with dollar recoinage for the Banks of England and Ireland (and conversations about a copper coinage for Ireland) left him little spare time for other considerations. The Professor was aided by the Danish Ambassador to the Court of St James's. But the combined efforts of the two Danes were insufficient to move matters forward at more than a snail's pace. Another of George III's mental breakdowns brought the leisurely proceedings to a full stop in the spring of 1804. But the educator and the diplomat remained sanguine (as did Matthew Boulton, who in any case lacked the leisure to worry about it); and they kept up pressure on Lord Hawkesbury, who loudly protested that he was doing all he could.

By the beginning of June, Copenhagen was losing patience, demanding that Warberg return home with all convenient speed. It may have done so to put pressure on him or the Britons with whom he was dealing; but it left him in a quandary. While he would naturally rather not disobey his government, he feared that his departure at this point would only serve to complicate matters. And in any case, Parliament now appeared inclined to close its current session with the export bill still unpassed. Could Boulton write Lord Hawkesbury, or anyone else, to break the log-jam?

Boulton could do little, for he was having Danish problems of his own. Just when he had finally got the silver recoinage settled to everybody's satisfaction:

> new plagues arose; for upon the [proposed] Act, relating to the Danish Mint,
> appearing in the papers the very same set of Ignorant, Envious, shabby fellows
> [who had penned the infamous Birmingham Memorial of 1800], assembled, &
> endeavourd to raise a Clamor against me with an intent to prevent the passing
> of the Act of Parliament[.] but by a little exertion on my part I turned the
> Tables against them— ... I have wrote a letter to my friend Lord Harrowby [a
> newly-appointed member of the Pitt administration, who was also doing his best
> to forward the Danish mint proposal] least the malcontents should take any
> further steps but I have now not the least Expectation of further trouble.

Boulton next gave Warberg – and us – a glimpse into the sort of thing
which might be expected were the Danish mint project to collapse altogether.
For Birmingham forgers were not confining their attentions to the coinage of
their own country, rather:

> within this fortnight as a Man was driving a Cart along the Birm*gm* Streets it was
> observd that there were 2 Casks in it & from one of them a considerable
> quantity of Counterfeit prussian Coin issued which attracted the attentions of
> the passengers. The Cart Horse & Coin was immediately arrested but the Driver
> made his escape. The 2 Casks contain about Seven Hundred weight & one was
> in the possession of a Constable. I have wrote to Lord Harrowby upon the
> subject & it is probable he may speak to the prussian Ambassador upon
> it ... [5]

Happily, the adulteration of the Danish monetary supply by the clever forgers of Birmingham would never be a problem. At the time Boulton was writing, the export bill was receiving its third and final reading, becoming law a
week later. The Act (44 Geo. III, Cap. 70 – 'An Act to enable his Majesty to
authorize the Exportation of the Machinery necessary for erecting a Mint in
the Dominions of the King of *Denmark*') – empowered the Secretary of State
to authorize anyone employed by the King of Denmark to export machinery
to Copenhagen to set up a mint, such apparatus being inviolate to search and
seizure by British Customs. Workmen for the project were also authorized:
the Secretary could pick anyone he chose to engage with such personnel for
that purpose. All of this pointed directly to Matthew Boulton, and it meant
that he had now cleared the second of the two hurdles which had stood in his
way. Now he could get to work.

And Boulton could begin work with the assistance of Olaus Warberg. The
Danish savant's health being none too robust, his superiors had decided to
leave him in England, and he came to Soho within a month or so of the passage of the Danish Mint Act. He was soon in consultation with Boulton, who
was hard at work on the coining machinery by early September 1804.

When examining Soho's efforts to export its industrialization of money, we
must always think on two levels. The first and most obvious one is the shipment of machinery and the other representatives of the material culture of
the new technology. Our interest here centres on coining presses and rolling
mills, but this first category could also include bronzing powder for the
United States and dies for Mexico.

But there was a second, human level to Soho's work, representing a second
export product. In its turn, it was made up of two components. The first was
the training at Soho of nationals of the countries where mints would be sent.
The second was the sending of Soho's sons (and sometimes their wives and

children) to the host countries, to erect the mints in the first instance, and to give advice and initiate new hands and new lands into the new ways in the second. Having secured all necessary permission to export members of the first, material dimension, Matthew Boulton now turned his attentions to its human counterpart.

He first considered the training of a Danish national. In October 1804, Boulton was in London. He had come there on business (possibly related to the proposed new Irish copper coinage), but had remained much longer than expected due to poor health. His enforced stay in the capital had given him the opportunity to meet a Danish national who had been sent over to learn the secrets of the future Copenhagen mint. This was probably Fridrich Holst, whom Boulton pronounced 'a sensible Man & a good Workman, but he can't speak English, which he finds puts him to some inconvenience in a Country where they won't speak Danish to accommodate him'.[6] When the coiner could finally go home, he would bring the monoglot Dane with him.

Holst was to prove a somewhat troublesome character, who extorted the equivalent of £20 from one of Warberg's acquaintances in Copenhagen for the upkeep of his wife, who had been left behind in Denmark. This outraged the Professor, for the lady in question had been very well provided for prior to Holst's departure. But Holst would partially reform, and he would eventually perform good service at the Copenhagen mint. This would be as well, because Boulton's plans to send his own people there would fall through.

His experiences with Russian workmen (which had not proved especially successful) had convinced him that primary reliance must be placed upon Soho natives, especially those with experience in erecting mints abroad. There was only one pool from which Boulton could pick: the tiny contingent of 'Mintaneers' now resident in St Petersburg. They alone had the necessary combination of background and skills. A plan inevitably took shape: after their successful launching of the Russian mint, the Soho mechanics would not go directly home. Instead, in the words of the formal agreement between Boulton and Warberg, they would 'come down to stop and dwell at Copenhagen', where, provided with the necessary parts, they would construct 'a compleate and useful Mint'. And if any of them were unable to serve, due to death, 'dispersal', or too-tardy arrival in Denmark, Boulton would procure and train other mechanics in their stead.[7] This simple agreement would soon become very complicated indeed: due to circumstances beyond his control, Boulton would not be able to send the workmen stipulated in the pact, and his inability literally to fulfill his end of the bargain (combined with still other outside circumstances) would mean that Soho would not be paid in full for its mint until ten years after its delivery.

But all this lay in the future. A few days after his formal agreement with the Danes, Boulton wrote to James Duncan, foreman mechanic of the Soho workmen now resident in Russia. He asked for an exact accounting of the current state of affairs and the completion date for the mint (data he would need for providing an accurate timetable to the Danes). He then formally requested that Duncan stop in Copenhagen on his way home and set up the new Danish mint. Realizing that the mechanic and his wife might by now have had their fill of foreign adventures, Boulton noted that a visit to Copenhagen would not actually lengthen their voyage, because Denmark was about equidistant between Russia and Great Britain. In any case, this would be a very short job in comparison with the Russian project. Duncan might have countered that, as compared with Russia, any other job would *have* to be minor in duration; but he seemed amenable enough to the request – with two conditions. First, he wanted Boulton clearly to spell out the matter of the wages he was to receive, for a lack of precision here had produced much discomfort at St Petersburg. Second, he demanded complete authority at Copenhagen, with no outside control. And he could do the work himself, with the assistance of such Danish mechanics as he deemed necessary: his mates from Soho would not be needed. In time, he would agree to take one of them, young William Speedyman, along; but he had had so much trouble with the others, especially James Harley, that he never wanted to see them again, much less work with them. Zack Walker (who had been sent to St Petersburg to oversee the foundering mint project, and who had had troubles of his own with the fractious Harley and his friends) tended to agree with Duncan, feeling that if anybody were to accompany him to Copenhagen it would have to be Speedyman. Boulton favoured James Walker instead (presumably for his experience rather than his personality). But the important thing was to finish the St Petersburg project quickly; precise details of personnel could come later.

While waiting for his Soho mechanics to complete their labours, Boulton was training their Danish counterparts. Holst had blossomed, becoming something of a specialist in the laying-on mechanisms attached to Boulton's presses. The fact that Boulton gave him the responsibility for constructing these intricate bits of machinery suggests that he had become a very good workman indeed. Professor Warberg was also receiving instruction in all aspects of the mint machinery and its management, for it had been decided that he would become its superintendent once it was operable. Holst and Warberg would have much larger roles than Mr Boulton had intended: along with a British mechanic named John Gillespie (with whom those at St Petersburg were apparently unacquainted – his previous experience had centred on steam engines rather than coining presses), the two Danes would actually set up the Copenhagen mint.

By the beginning of 1806, the shape of things was gradually emerging. James Duncan and James Walker were still at loggerheads, Zack Walker speculating that it probably had something to do with a spat between their wives. More importantly, the St Petersburg mint was still unfinished: Duncan had the last of his work to perform (tasks involving such precision that he seemed to be putting them off), while his mates assiduously slowed down their pace to match his.

Something would have to be done, and soon: by February 1806, the machinery for the Danish mint had been completed, and the Danes were understandably anxious for its shipment. And so was Matthew Boulton: his work had now been done, and he wanted to get his machinery to Copenhagen, get it set into motion – and get the money due him for his services.

There is a topsy-turvy quality to the Copenhagen story, one distinguishing it from most of the other foreign adventures of Boulton, Watt & Company. Instead of signing a contract and then starting a mint, Boulton started the Copenhagen mint and finished much of it before his contract was signed. The coiner's perennial optimism had never been more obvious, but his luck had held, and he had got his agreement in May 1805.

He would be paid £6,587 for his mint, the first half once the machinery was shipped and the second once it had been set to work. (Parenthetically, this would net him a profit of around £2,000 – fairly generous, considering the size of the order.)

He would provide two sorts of machinery. The first consisted of the actual mint – four coining presses, six cutting out presses, two milling machines, a die multiplying press, a turning lathe, and a shaking machine. This apparatus would be powered by a fourteen-horse engine, connected to the machinery by the now-standard arrangement of vacuum pumps, initially devised for Russia, but now current at Soho as well. The second category consisted of a rolling mill with spare rolls and communicating mechanism; this machinery would be powered by the same fourteen-horse engine, available for rolling when it was not seeing employment for moneying. Boulton would also provide duplicate parts and carriage to Hull as part of his services.

The agreement contained two riders. The first said that the mint must be erected within nine months of the date it left Hull for Denmark. The second, as we have seen, pledged Boulton to provide replacements for any workers who had been earmarked to come to Denmark to erect the mint but were unable to do so. And this rider would cause enormous difficulties, as Boulton found that he was unable to fulfill it to Danish satisfaction.

He could not do so because he could not retrieve his men from St Petersburg in time. While it was initially hoped that they would be finished in Russia by the early months of 1806 (which would mean that the Danish mint could sail in the spring, as soon as the ice broke up), Boulton found that none of his people could get to Copenhagen in time to meet it when it arrived. He stalled the Danes for the next few months but eventually capitulated and shipped their mint to Hull, whence it sailed in mid-August, reaching Copenhagen by the end of the month. But James Duncan was not there to meet it, nor were any of his mates. Nor were Professor Warberg or Fridrich Holst (although it had once been supposed that they would sail for Denmark ahead of their mint). Instead, it was met by the engine fitter John Gillespie.

He had no experience whatsoever with coining machinery, his expertise lying solely in the area of steam engines. But he was all Boulton had on the spot, and his role was critical during the first few weeks. When he heard of the arrival of the machinery, he immediately went to the dock to look it over; what he found was not encouraging. The vessel which had brought the goods to Copenhagen was leaky, and salt water had got into some of the machinery – Gillespie was unsure about which portion of it, because he had not actually been allowed to open the crates for visual inspection. When official blessing was finally granted, Gillespie looked things over and concluded that the damage had been sustained to the worst place possible: the four coining presses.

As it happened, Gillespie was an alarmist, who may have known a great deal about steam engines but nothing whatever about the machinery they drove. Professor Warberg made separate inquiries among his friends on the Danish Treasury Board and found that matters were scarcely as critical as Boulton's engineer (or his colleague James Adamson, who had been sent to Denmark by the Rennies to erect the rolling mill) imagined. The presses were *not* damaged, and Warberg gave orders that everything was to be laid aside, dried, and oiled, to await the arrival of Fridrich Holst, who would set things right. And Gillespie was to mind his own business, tend to the steam engine, and leave the mint alone.

Holst had left Soho for Hull long ago but had been detained in Hull until the arrival of the convoy, which was late. He finally cleared England on the fourteenth of September, sailing to Copenhagen on the *Oxenholme*. He arrived there on the twenty-first.

Immediately hastening to the mint site, he found that Gillespie was carrying matters forward in a satisfactory way, but was now apparently seeking to have his duties expanded to include work on the mint. Between the nosy Gillespie and the self-promoting Holst (who had reverted to type and was now attempting to wheedle a testimonial from Matthew Boulton to advance his fortunes with the Danish bureaucracy), Soho had nearly as many woes with its small Danish contingent as it had with its much larger Russian one. But the latter was more on Boulton's mind as the year 1806 drew to a close.

For the members of this group were *still* at St Petersburg, and Boulton had no real idea of when they would finally finish the Russian mint, be allowed to leave, and then 'come down to stop and dwell at Copenhagen', do the work which Holst and Gillespie could not or ought not perform, and allow Mr Boulton to receive the money still owed him.

Wolffs & Dorville had remitted the first half of the payment (£3,293.10.0) on schedule late in August 1806, after the machinery had left Hull for Copenhagen. But the second half appeared unattainable for the foreseeable future – at least, if the Danes and their British fiscal representatives were to take a literal view of their contract. Matthew Boulton decided to press them for payment now, putting as decent a face on matters as he could. He wrote the Danish Board of Finances at the very end of 1806, reminding it that he had supplied its mint, had carefully instructed Professor Warberg in its operation and maintenance, had in fact done everything possible to fulfill his portion of the contract. True, he had not yet supplied the specially-trained people mentioned therein, but that was hardly his fault. They were still unavoidably detained in Russia but would certainly be sent on the minute their mint was operative, their Russian duties concluded. Indeed, he made ironclad pledges to that intent; now, could he please have the rest of his money?

The Board of Finances agreed that he had certainly kept many of his promises. But he had not kept all of them – and he would certainly not get the remainder of his money until and unless some important alterations were made to the 1805 agreement. Discussions now took place between the same two parties responsible for the original pact, Matthew Boulton and Olaus Warberg. They began in March 1807; by the time they ended a month later, Matthew Boulton had bound himself to two related and potentially disastrous actions. First, he pledged that those who were still at St Petersburg would be the men sent to set up the new mint at Copenhagen, provided they could leave Russia in a timely fashion. Second, if they could *not* do so, in return for payment of the other half of his money, Matthew Boulton would find other people to do the work. Soho pleaded for and obtained minor Danish concessions: these included a written dispensation for not having trained possible replacements as soon as it became obvious that the Russian project would be delayed, and a time extension to train them if and when necessary. But these small victories scarcely changed the intent of the amended contract: Matthew Boulton would send adequate people to set up the Danish mint, or he would not get paid. And new events were about to conspire against him, to ensure that he would never personally see just recompense for his labours.

For the Danish project was now entering alien and dangerous waters. The first hazard was the ongoing delay in extracting Boulton's expert mechanics from the Petersburg imbroglio. The second was a deterioration in Anglo-Danish relations, which British stupidity succeeded in elevating into a shooting war by the autumn of 1807. Soho was responsible for neither of these circumstances; but the firm and its founder would feel their effects all the same.

In the summer of 1807, the St Petersburg mint was at last set into motion, striking its first coins: surely, the last barrier to the free exit of Soho's people had been removed! While one of them would elect to remain in Russia (the ambitious James Harley, who had been seduced by dreams of wealth in Siberia), another, James Duncan, had agreed to go to Copenhagen, to erect Mr Boulton's new mint in that capital. Once the Danish mint became a functioning reality, Duncan could come home, Boulton could receive the rest of his money, and his firm's foreign adventures could become the subject of amused recollection rather than ongoing anxiety. So the theory went. But misfortune excessive even by Soho standards once again intervened on the Russian project, with an even greater if indirect effect on the Danish one.

The linchpin of Soho's Russian adventure was that nation's Minister of Finance, Count Vasiliev. He it was who had been dealing with Boulton's engineers from the start; he it was who had guided the project from the Russian side since the very beginning; he it was who would be rendering final payment upon the affair's conclusion; and he it was who suddenly and most inconsiderately died, late in August 1807. The whole rhythm of the Petersburg affair was interrupted. Until a successor to this indispensable man had been named, Soho could not be paid and Duncan could not come to Copenhagen.

As it happened, the sluggish Russian bureaucracy moved more quickly than might have been anticipated. An interim Minister of Finance had been appointed by mid-October – Count Fedor Golubtsov, who treated the settlement of the Russian mint business as a matter of the first priority. He visited the new facility, pronounced it admirable, and arranged for Boulton's payment in the closing days of 1807. But this did nothing to aid the Copenhagen project.

Two factors, one personal and the other international, now conspired to keep James Duncan in Russia. The mechanic had a sickly wife who was in no condition to travel at this time. He would not leave her in Russia while he went to Denmark, which meant that any help he might render at the new Copenhagen mint would have to be postponed until at least the following spring.[8]

But the international factor would have shaped matters as well. World events did not stand still while mechanics dawdled, counts died, and Soho dithered. At the time that the new Russian mint was preparing to strike its first shiny silver rubles, two emperors meeting on a raft in the middle of the Niemen River were preparing for a shift in direction for their respective countries. They signed the Treaty of Tilsit, which linked Russia with France in an alliance against Great Britain. And just as Golubtsov was promising that directions for payment would soon be leaving Russia for Britain, an English gentleman named Sir Robert Wilson was heading in the same direction. Sir Robert had been the British Minister to St Petersburg: he was leaving there because Russia and Great Britain had just broken off diplomatic relations.

Would there be war? No: indeed, Britain and Russia would eventually become allies against Napoleon. Would this rupture delay payment for Boulton's Russian mint? Again, no; payment (and a number of generous presents, including a diamond ring for Mr Boulton) would be rendered at the end of the year. But would Anglo-Russian tensions make matters more difficult for the *Danish* project? Yes.

James Duncan could not leave Russia on time for his Copenhagen assignment for personal reasons; but international tensions would soon render it impossible for him to travel there at all, even had he been otherwise able to make the journey. This meant that Duncan's employer risked non-compliance with the rider it had signed in March 1807. And if the Danes chose to read that rider in a literal fashion, Soho might not receive the second half of its money.

There was a way around this impasse: let Boulton train and send replacement personnel to erect the Copenhagen mint and all would be well. But when Soho prepared to do so, it encountered a new and most unwelcome fact of international life: Great Britain's relations with Denmark were even worse than those with Russia.

The background to this deterioration may be ultimately found in the strains on British nerve caused by fifteen years of warfare. By 1807, George III's ministers were seeing spies everywhere, uncovering opposition where none existed – in sum, becoming the victims of something akin to official paranoia. Denmark fitted neatly into this climate of alarm: despite its size, the nation had an important navy, which, were it allied with that of the French, might inspire an effort to avenge Trafalgar. That Danish fleet must not be allowed to fall into the wrong hands: to see that it did not, Foreign Secretary Canning pressured Denmark to give up her fleet for the remainder of the war and conclude an alliance with her heavy-handed suitor. Denmark vacillated. Albion dithered. France waited.

In the same month as Tilsit, Canning sent a fleet of forty-six warships into Danish waters under the command of Admiral Gambier. It was accompanied by an army of thirty-one thousand under the command of Wellesley. The arrival of these forces caught the Danes by surprise. King Christian VII was currently in Kiel, keeping his eye on his southern borders, and was not about to be bullied into precipitous action to the north. So the king and his ministers delayed talks with Francis James Jackson, Britain's representative at Copenhagen.

Jackson seems to have been of an impatient mien and in any case had specific instructions from Canning. If Denmark would not parley, the diplomat would increase his pressure. He reiterated his government's insistence upon an alliance, threatening forcible seizure of the Danish fleet if his demand went unmet. Since he simultaneously admitted that Great Britain could not protect Denmark against a determined French attack, his argument lost a portion of its punch. King Christian refused these conditions and hastened north to defend his capital. Great Britain chose to regard this as an act of war and replied with one of its own, on 16 August 1807.

Wellesley's men landed north of Copenhagen, which place they proceeded to invest. The future Duke of Wellington hesitated for several days, perhaps in hopes that the Danes would capitulate without the necessity of bloodshed. But they did not, and he finally opened fire on 2 September.

The bombardment continued for five days, by which time more than a thousand buildings (including the university, former home of Olaus Warberg) were destroyed. The king yielded under fire what he had previously refused: the entire Danish fleet, some fifteen line-of-battle ships, an equal number of frigates, and many smaller vessels, was surrendered to the enemy. Another four warships still on the ways were torched. And Copenhagen would be occupied by a victors' garrison for the next six weeks.

All of this prompted the Danes to action, but not to the kind which Britain had desired. In October 1807, they concluded a formal alliance with France, declaring war on England at the beginning of the following month. The two nations would be enemies for more than six years. Bad news travels fast: by the eleventh of November, Olaus Warberg was on his way from Soho to Denmark.

The Professor was a curious mixture of perfectionist and realist. He had been one of the most vociferous advocates of sending part or all of Soho's Russian contingent to Denmark – and of putting everything in Copenhagen in abeyance until it could arrive. But as Anglo-Russian and Anglo-Danish relations deteriorated, Warberg also became aware that the Copenhagen mint might have to be constructed by agents less perfect, less experienced than those he desired. And so he asked for and received more detailed instructions about the machinery he would eventually be superintending, and he secured the agreement of another Soho mechanic to come out and help him. This was Thomas White. White would never serve in the Danish project, his departure for Copenhagen being put off indefinitely by the outbreak of war; he would eventually have adventures aplenty in Brazil. And Warberg would have to rely on his own efforts, joined to those of Fridrich Holst and John Gillespie. These three latecomers and specialists in other fields would build the Copenhagen mint and set it running. And Matthew Boulton's industrialization of money would take root in another country, even though planted by the wrong hands.

Warberg's sudden decampment alarmed Soho and created confusion. The Dane had left many matters unsettled, including details of the final payment for the mint. Warberg was not especially concerned about this aspect of things, for he had had a long conversation with Boulton's nephew George Mynd and assumed that remuneration would soon be rendered, war or no war. But he did not reckon with Wolffs & Dorville.

That firm was not in the best of fiscal health, and it may have decided that, with Great Britain and Denmark now at war, it and not the Danes could be held liable for what was due to Boulton, Watt & Company. It embarked upon a brilliant career of procrastination, combined with judicious amounts of vituperation; these tactics held the Boultons at bay until bankruptcy put it permanently beyond the reach of its pursuers.

Boulton, Watt did not make a determined effort to get paid until September 1808. Why this longish delay with a substantial sum at stake? The answer seems to be that one of Soho's hands did not know what the other was doing. The elder Boulton was aware that Wolffs & Dorville had agreed to render the second half of the payment in a timely fashion as early as October 1805; but he had lost the letter containing this pledge, and the younger Boulton was unaware of its existence. And one wonders whether the son knew about the riders added in March 1807: all in all, Soho had a reasonably strong claim for payment, provided it acted fairly quickly. This it did not do. By the time the 1805 letter was resurrected, Wolffs & Dorville was fiscally unsound, and war with Denmark had been a fact of life for nearly a year. The trail was very cold; but no choice existed but to take it up all the same.

Soho's representatives in London did so, and they were promptly rebuffed. In the eyes of Messrs Wolffs & Dorville, Boulton, Watt had simply not performed its part of the bargain. While it had indeed trained a mechanic to go out to Copenhagen as a replacement for the one marooned in St Petersburg, it had not actually got him to the Danish capital. And while Soho might blame the outbreak of war for its involuntary non-compliance, an agreement was still an agreement: no mechanic, no payment. To this argument, the ingenious if impecunious Wolffs & Dorville added a second. The original agreement had pledged Boulton, Watt to ship the mint before April 1806, while the actual remittance had not taken place until several months later; might not this too invalidate any obligation to pay? Wolffs & Dorville certainly thought so, and it defied Boulton, Watt to prove otherwise.

Meanwhile, life went on: whether the personnel were ideal or not, there was a mint to be set up and Olaus Warberg proceeded to erect it. We know very little about the actual process, for the rupture in relations on the major, diplomatic scale was mirrored by a hiatus on the minor, purely private one. But we know that Fridrich Holst was there, probably working on the presses under the superintendence of Professor Warberg. Holst remained true to form and attempted to extract a character reference out of the younger Boulton (which he said had been promised him by the elder). According to Holst, he could not obtain a fixed salary from the Danish Government without such a testimonial; but Boulton never replied and Holst seems to have remained at his post all the same. He was joined by John Gillespie, who would be working on the engines – and was likely barred from all else by the Professor. And Warberg himself oversaw the whole.

Unlike St Petersburg, we do not know when this mint struck its first coins. But it was most certainly sometime in 1809, based on the testimony of the coins themselves. Matthew Boulton would have been satisfied. These first specimens of the new money were the very sorts of coins for which he had always laboured – copper money of modest value, for the secure commercial dealings of the poor.

The Danes began with two-skilling pieces, shortly adding similar coins ranging from one skilling to twelve (until 1813, sixty-four copper skilling equalled one silver krone; after 1813, ninety-six skilling made up a new dollar-size coin, the speciedaler). A double skilling of 1810 suggests that Warberg and his charges were having troubles with their new mint: while the obverse is successful enough, the right-hand portion of the reverse displays a wide, circular gouge, suggesting problems with the ejection mechanism. Die cracks and failings on that side indicate that the Danes were also finding difficulties in securing steel of the quality demanded by the new technology. But compared with earlier issues, this Danish coin was very advanced, offering hope that, after an initial period of learning and adjustment, Denmark's coinage would be among the most modern in Europe.

Growing pains: the reverse of this Danish 2 skilling copper coin, one of the first struck at Matthew Boulton's Copenhagen Mint, suggests that the tyro coiners had not yet perfected their craft. (Author's collection)

Silver struck on the new machinery was not introduced until the reform of 1813, while gold had to wait until the mid-1820s. While the leisurely pace of improved precious-metal coinage may be ascribed in part to the dislocations of war and its aftermath, it also hints that the Danes were first turning their attentions toward the weakest area of their money supply, copper. In this respect, the Danish story stands in notable distinction to the Russian, which it otherwise resembles in a number of ways.

If the Copenhagen mint were up and running by 1809, surely *now* payment for it must be due. And so it would be in an ideal world; but in the real one, Soho would have to wait for another seven years.

For five of those years, it probably felt it had little choice. It had been rebuffed by one of the two logical sources of money, Wolffs & Dorville. It could hardly take its case to the other – at least not while Britain and Denmark remained at war. And Soho had a great deal else on its mind during these years: the death of its founder, the squabble over who had invented which portion of his presses, one mint for the Tower, another for the Portuguese in America. But the primary cause of Soho's long inactivity was probably the war: for as soon as peace was concluded early in 1814, the Birmingham firm swung into action.

It moved on several fronts. It attempted to inspire Professor Warberg to act on its behalf. This was not the most realistic of tactics: having been forced to construct Soho's mint for it, Warberg was not likely to be particularly sympathetic. And in fact he took little if any part in what was to follow.

Boulton, Watt also made attempts to secure its due from those originally responsible for payment – Wolffs & Dorville, or what was left of that firm. But it had no greater success now than previously: after nearly a year's worth of efforts to extract blood from a stone, Soho pinned the remainder of its hopes on the basic decency of the Danish Government – which had, after all, got a new mint, even if not under the most favourable conditions.

It made its first approach to the new Danish Minister in London, Edward Bourke, in the summer of 1814, stating its claims at £3454.17.0.[9] But it was soon demanding much more, including the unpaid principal plus interest for seven years, two months, and seven days (from 27 May 1807, the day it reckoned final payment had come due). Soho's claim had much validity, the strongest suit being those new Danish coppers with its signature on them. But it would be very lucky to get its basic payment, and it would never recover more than a fraction of the interest it felt its due.

Finding Warberg disinclined to provide assistance, the firm relied on two other acquaintances, one recent and the other of long standing. The new player was Augustus John Foster, Britain's new envoy to Copenhagen. Foster occupied his post early in the autumn of 1814, and he would eventually prove to be most helpful. But Matthew Robinson Boulton decided to bring a second player into action as well.

This was Erich Erichsen, who had visited the Boultons at Soho many years before; an infrequent correspondence had been maintained since then, even through the war. Erichsen had certain connections at Copenhagen, and his unofficial labours might nicely complement the official ones of Mr Foster.

Erichsen performed a signal service: being Danish himself, having dealt with Copenhagen officials during a successful business career, Erichsen was a pragmatist who knew what one could and could not expect to achieve.

Boulton's demand for interest during the duration of the war was simply unrealistic, and Erichsen gently told him so. But interest on the unpaid balance since the end of the conflict might reasonably be expected, and Erichsen pledged his best efforts on behalf of his old friend. Treating on Boulton's behalf with Møsting and Rosencrantz (the Danish Ministers of Finance and Foreign Affairs, respectively), the businessman worked in tandem with Augustus Foster to secure a reasonable percentage of the Boulton claims. Taking Erichsen's advice, Boulton submitted two bills of exchange to Møsting in February 1816, one for £1900.14.0, the other for £1922.6.0, the first payable in three months and the second in six. These sums included a charge for interest since war's end, and the Danes honoured this additional claim: perhaps they had simply grown tired of the tedious correspondence, one scarcely worth maintaining over a matter of a few hundred pounds. Sometime in the summer of 1816, the lengthy Danish business was settled at last. The actual date is unknown – an irony, in light of all the paperwork which has survived concerning the earlier stages of the Danish dispute.

Matthew Robinson Boulton commemorated the event in his own way: not too long afterwards, Minister Foster received an elaborate ornamented box ('deliver'd free of all expences'), while Erichsen was presented with other products of Soho's artistry ('so much admired by every body that sees them').[10] The giving of gifts – or bribes, if you prefer – was one of many ways in which an eighteenth-century firm made its way in the world. And Soho always remained a resident of the eighteenth century, regardless of the date on the calendar.

Within a short time of its establishment, Boulton's Copenhagen mint was doing what its creators intended, providing safe and plentiful money for the people of Denmark. But a final question must be posed: at bottom, why did the Danes want such a mint? Their country was largely rural, its population was small, and it was scarcely concerned with the larger issues of the Industrial Revolution until much later in the nineteenth century. Lacking a mass wage-earning class, the number of coins needed by the nation was relatively small; so was the number of counterfeits threatening the public. So why this new mint on the leading edge?

It is possible that the Danish monarchy wanted such an importation precisely because it *was* on the forward edge of modern technology, would serve to advertise the progressivism of the country's ruling house. But unlike the Russian tsars, the Danish kings seem to have been practical souls, and we are somehow unable to ascribe to them the same, slightly pathetic hankering after 'modernity' that we see in Catherine, Paul, and Alexander. I can advance no obvious, unanswerable argument on behalf of the new mint, and I must therefore fall back upon the possibility that the Danish monarchy simply wanted one of Matthew Boulton's products because it believed that the new apparatus was desirable on general principle. And surely there are less substantial reasons for entering the modern era than that.

SOURCES

Reflecting the Danish mint story's close connection with contemporaneous events in Russia, much of the raw material for the present chapter will be found in MBP411 and 412 (Russian Mint, box 1, Russian Mint, box 2), as well as MBP360 (Walker, Z., jr.). Most of the remainder comes from MBP410, Danish Mint.

Letters of some of the major players in the Denmark story not found in MBP410 are distributed as follows. A portion of Baron Buchwald's correspondence will be found in MBP224, Letter Box B6, while letters from the irascible Wolffs & Dorville appear in MBP262, Letter Box W3, as well as in the Danish Mint box; similarly, a few of Olaus Warberg's letters will be found in MBP260, Letter Box W1. One of John Gillespie's letters is in MBP234, Letter Box G1; the remainder are in the Danish Mint box. And Fridrich Holst is represented by one letter in MBP237, Letter Box H2; for other correspondence, consult the Danish Mint box.

Records of Soho's payments from the Danes can be found in MBP50, Mint Book, Mint and Coinage Day Book, 1805–1808, and MBP61, Mint Book, Mint and Coinage Ledger, 1808–1819. And an excellent overview of the larger historical picture, against which Soho and the Danes played out their smaller dramas, will be found in Stewart Oakley's *A Short History of Denmark* (1972).

NOTES

1 This long-suffering dignitary had greater liberties taken with the spelling of his name by the Boultons than anyone else outside Russia. It appears in the Boulton correspondence as Schimmellmann, Schimmellman, Schimelmann, etc., etc., enjoying the wide number of possible permutations which a series of double consonants suggested to the fertile British mind of the day. The Count (who should have known) favoured Schimmelmann.

2 MBP410, Danish Mint: joint rough draft of Olaus Warberg and Matthew Boulton, 4–26 March 1798. Spelling and punctuation in original.

3 MBP410, 'Proposed Letter to Mr Warbrough, suppose 1799'. This draft certainly dates from the first half of 1798, and the recipient of the final copy would have been Count Schimmelmann, Warberg being with Boulton at Soho at the time. To sweeten the bad news, Boulton adds that he has actually carried out his experiment with a new industrial layout, '& that it fully answers all my Hopes and proves to be a most capital Improvement in the art of Coining' - which would someday be of benefit to patient Danes.

4 MBP260, Letter Box W1: Olaus Warberg to Matthew Boulton, 6 June 1800.

5 MBP410, Matthew Boulton to Olaus Warberg, 3 July 1804 [spelling in original]. Boulton adds that, while 'I have had many applications made to me by merchants & men of property ... I never struck an unlawfull piece of Money in my Life'. This was not self-promotion: his papers contain evidence of at least one such request. It is as well that Matthew Boulton was never attracted to forgery: he would have been very good at it!

6 MBP410, Matthew Boulton to Olaus Warberg, 13 October 1804.

7 MBP410, 'Memorandum of Agreement with O:Warberg Esqr May 21st 1805 — for the Construction of the Danish Mint Machinery'.

8 As it happened, Duncan never did come to Copenhagen, becoming instead the chief mechanic of Matthew Boulton's Russian mint. He was still there in the mid-1820s.

9 This amount represented the second half of the mint payment, with an additional charge for dies and spare parts provided later.

10 MBP410, Erich Erichsen to Matthew Robinson Boulton, 28 September 1816.

CHAPTER 4

The Royal Mint

The rebuilding of the Royal Mint on Little Tower Hill, its recasting in Soho's image, should have formed the crowning achievement of Matthew Boulton's career. The provision of plentiful money in all metals for all classes, money which was cheap to coin but prohibitively expensive to counterfeit, had been at the centre of his thoughts for many years: how could he and his son not regard its adoption by a once-sceptical British Government as their greatest triumph?

But an odour of acrimony hangs over the project, one born of mutual mistrust, of promises made (or assumed made) and later broken or forgotten. Matthew Boulton did not have full confidence in the British Government, having suffered many prior disappointments. That polity did not fully trust *him*, realizing that his ambitions and its welfare did not inevitably correspond.

Throughout the period of the Royal Mint's reconstruction, such mutual incomprehension was always at or near the surface. And when the facility was nearing completion, an additional misunderstanding emerged, one which would mar Soho's relations with its offspring down to the end of the parent concern: Matthew Boulton and his son had enjoyed (or assumed they enjoyed) a gentleman's agreement with the Royal Mint. Once it had been refurbished with Soho machinery and steam power, it would strike gold and silver coinage, *but not copper, whose provision would be reserved to Soho.* The officials in London saw matters differently: for the time being, no copper coinage was needed at home (the sheer bulk of the most recent Boulton coinage proving a glut in commercial channels); but whenever such coinage was required, either for Britain itself or for any of its possessions, *the Royal Mint would strike it, if convenient.*

It recognized no prior arrangement with the Boultons – at least, none which would limit its future course of action. In all of my review of the Matthew Boulton Papers, I have never found any official pledge on the part of anyone connected with the Royal Mint project that the new facility would specifically *not* strike copper. Hints and innuendoes there were to be sure, and gold and silver coinages were mentioned by name, and not copper. But two decades of prior experience should have taught the Boultons that, if a promise were not made in writing in plain English, it probably did not exist. Reckoning on good faith and reasonableness were not enough; and Soho's relations with its London offspring were never happy ones.

Through most of this study, I have relied on the Matthew Boulton Papers for the telling of the tale: no other sources exist for the story of the construction of the mint at St Petersburg, or Copenhagen, or Calcutta, or Culiacán. But in the matter of the Royal Mint, additional sources exist, demonstrating other points of view. Sir John Craig's *The Mint: A History of the London Mint from A.D. 287 to 1948* was published by Cambridge University Press in 1953, and it contains some information about the Boulton contribution to the institution's fortunes. It has been largely superseded by *A New History of the Royal Mint* (edited by Christopher E. Challis, with additional contributions by Graham Dyer, Peter P. Gaspar, Nicholas J. Mayhew, and Ian Stewart, published by Cambridge University Press in 1992). I recommend this new study most highly, and its account of the rebuilding should most certainly be read along with my book. The reader can emerge with an excellent general account of mint doings from the Challis study alone: what I want to do here is relate the Boultons' side of the story.

From their perspective, that story began in the early 1780s; but it would be years before they would play an active role in it. In the beginning, the primary players were one of Matthew Boulton's Birmingham associates, Samuel Garbett, and his son, Francis. The Garbetts had friends in high places: Francis, for instance, may have served as private secretary to the Marquis of Lansdowne, Lord Shelburne. Both Garbetts had weight in the councils of the mighty, that weight increasing during the brief Shelburne ministry of 1782–83. When dissatisfaction over the current Royal Mint inspired a demand for a thoroughgoing investigation in the early 1780s, Shelburne put Samuel Garbett in charge of it. This Midlands businessman received unlimited powers to go over the facility's coining reports, investigate its practices, and render a report.

He received his orders at the beginning of September 1782. Garbett poked, prodded, asked indelicate questions, and reached a number of probably foregone conclusions. Aided by his son, he drew up a report of his findings at the end of November; wending its way through bureaucratic channels, the Garbett memorandum finally reached the hands of William Pitt and Lord Shelburne early in March 1783. These gentlemen declared themselves well-pleased with the results, awarding the Garbetts £500 for their trouble.

But would they act on the report? Throughout its pages, it stressed the same themes: mint officials were overpaid, and their products were of variable quality and insufficient quantity. Samuel and Francis Garbett recommended fundamental change in the way the mint was organized, in the chain of command by which its coinage was produced. Reforms of this degree would be difficult to implement; and after Lord Shelburne resigned his post over the American peace treaty in late February 1783, much of the impetus was gone. William Pitt was asked to succeed him; he declined at first but finally agreed at the end of the year. The new, very young prime minister soon had more important matters on his mind than mint reform; and so the project was allowed to sleep, the public coiner carrying on its proceedings as usual. But by now, another factor was entering the equation: Matthew Boulton was beginning to take an interest in mint reform.

Boulton had known about Garbett's appointment from the beginning, and he agreed that the mint and its products certainly begged for improvement. But he did not become personally interested for the first few months of the

Garbett investigation: just now, his attention was concentrated on Cornwall, where recalcitrant miners were refusing to pay him for the use of his engines.[1] But the miners soon gave way, and Boulton now had the time to begin serious thought on what was to become his enduring passion. He began to think about mints, and minting, and how he would go about improving them. And by December 1782, the future was forecast: while the Garbetts advocated reform through reorganization of mint personnel, Boulton had 'the Idea of introducing other Modes of Manufacturing'[2] to secure the desired result. But for the next few years, it would remain a theory, a desideratum, and nothing more. Matthew Boulton too had more pressing matters to consider than the reform of a mint.

But the idea of reform never quite disappeared, either for the Birmingham industrialist or for certain members of the British Government. Boulton's interest in coinage and coining grew after the middle of the 1780s: his role in the Cornish Metal Company attracted him to copper coinage, while his experiences with the East India Company's order for Sumatra gave him crucial, 'hands-on' experience with the pre-industrial processes then in use – and reinforced his desire to improve them and his conviction that he could do so. And when a contract copper coinage appeared imminent – and when he and Thomas Williams competed to secure it, lining up governmental support in their respective favours – Boulton took a crucial step, from which everything else developed. He began putting his ideas on paper, and then, by the first days of 1788, translating them into action. He began building a mint.

Thomas Williams built a mint too, and he had finished before Matthew Boulton had even begun. But it is a measure of the difference between the two men that Williams never thought in terms of steam, while Matthew Boulton never thought in any other.

Through trial and error, and despite the assistance of Jean-Pierre Droz, the first Soho Mint went up. Boulton's optimism led him to make excessive claims for it and the new methodology. In the middle of 1788, he sent specimens of Droz' pattern halfpence to William Pitt, boasted that all British copper coinage could be made as beautiful at his new mint (which still largely existed in his mind at the time; Droz had made the patterns in Paris). In the late summer of the following year, he promised to send similar coins to his friend Sir Joseph Banks, and made more claims for the virtues of his mint (which was indeed nearing completion by that time). And in both cases, Boulton looked beyond Soho, and to the Tower. His 1788 letter to Pitt is instructive: Boulton saw the possibility of a regal copper coinage struck at Soho as much more than a convenience to the public, and a laurel for him: he hoped that the minting experience gained

> will probably enable me (before my declining Years have abraded my Powers) to offer some improvements to his Majesty's Mint, that may perhaps be deemed of importance in the Coining of Gold and Silver—[3]

For his part, Samuel Garbett also tried to keep the reform idea alive. In 1792, he published a pamphlet called 'General Heads of Memorandums Relative to Coins and Coinage'. In it, he repeated the findings which he and his son had presented to the British Government a decade previously, and he made the same recommendations – that sinecures be abolished, that more and better coins should be provided, at reasonable rates of manufacture. But

Garbett's slender work would bear no better fruit than Boulton's letters to the mighty – at least, not just yet.

But reform would come. Having managed to keep his mint semi-active in spite of official indifference (by striking coins for the East India Company and several colonies and tokens for businesses in the British Isles and France, all dealt with elsewhere), Boulton was gaining invaluable experience, was literally reinventing his technology as he went along. And in 1797, the elusive contract for British copper coinage finally came his way. Its execution nearly wrecked his mint, as he himself admitted; but once again he learned from the experience.

It must be emphasized that the British Government had undergone no basic change of heart between during the past ten years. Rather, the minor coinage situation had become so intolerable by the mid-nineties that wide segments of the public were joining their voices to those of Matthew Boulton and his few early supporters. And when the next logical step in the story took place, and Soho was entrusted with the reconstruction of the Royal Mint, similar, pragmatic, considerations would shape the issue.

These considerations involved silver coinage. The primary problem was that there currently *was* no silver coinage in regular production – nor could there be, for a general rise in the price of silver versus gold, whose beginnings roughly coincided with the accession of George III, meant that silver struck for circulation was hoarded as soon as it left the mint. A small issue of shillings in 1763 had been augmented by a larger coinage of shillings and sixpences in 1787, but none of these coins were in current circulation. By 1797, the situation was so desperate that the Bank of England began purchasing Spanish and Spanish-American Pieces of Eight, or dollars, having the Royal Mint countermark them with the head of King George, and then reissuing them as pieces worth four shillings and ninepence. But the emergency issue was extensively counterfeited (ironically, many if not most of the fakes originated in Birmingham), while false countermarks were applied to good coins and bad, and occasionally, good countermarks were stamped on bad coins. The public (which had once thronged to get the converted coinage) soon tired of it, for it could not be trusted. And the Bank of England soon admitted defeat: in September 1797, it called in countermarked dollars, paying four shillings and ninepence for each dollar in lots of twenty. The coins were demonetized after the end of October, and this first attempt to address the silver shortage was declared a failure.

But there would be others: in its pursuit of a plentiful silver coinage which could remain in circulation, British officialdom would turn to Matthew Boulton on two occasions, for two products. The Bank of England would ask him for recoined dollars. And the British Treasury would ask him for a new mint, so that it could coin dollars of its own – or anything else it chose.

The three months after the end of the first, failed dollar experiment occasioned serious thought in official circles: obviously, something must be done about the nation's silver famine, and the simple countermarking of other peoples' coins did not appear the answer. Lord Liverpool would be a key figure in the search for a better solution.

Born Charles Jenkinson, created Baron Hawkesbury in 1786 and Earl of Liverpool a decade later, he was now semi-retired, his sole remaining contributions to government centring on currency reform. It was this interest

The Bank of England, depicted on a medalet by Peter Kempson from the mid-1790s. (Author's collection)

which produced his best-known work, *A Treatise on the Coins of the Realm; in a Letter to the King* (1805). But it was also this interest which led him to invite Matthew Boulton into the struggle for a better silver coinage.

At the end of January 1798, Liverpool wrote his old Soho correspondent, requesting the latter's opinion on four points. How much did Boulton suppose it would cost to strike the four major silver denominations (crowns, halfcrowns, shillings, and sixpences) on his machinery? Supposing Boulton started with crowns and halfcrowns: how many did he think he could coin in a month? Could Boulton '& some one of your ablest *Mechanists*' come to London, make an inspection of the current mint (accompanied by a subcommittee of the Privy Council) 'to inspect their present Instruments & Mechanical Powers, in order to form a Judgement, what Alterations & Improvements should be made therein'? And that being done, 'What Time [do] you think it would require to erect your Machinery (so as to be in a Condition proper for beginning to coin) at the Mint, in the Tower'?[4]

Two observations should be made. First, Liverpool was only speaking about coinage in *silver* – because that was the metal in shortest supply. But the lack of mention of other metals may have helped persuade the Boultons that the copper coinage would be theirs in perpetuity – which was of course exactly what they desired. Second, a new mint would be wanted on the site of the old, the Tower of London. But a number of difficulties would eventually be raised, and a change of venue would result.

Boulton's written response to Liverpool's overture has been lost; but the next two months saw him taking what time he could from the copper coinage for calculations on how best to coin silver money, how best to refurbish the Royal Mint. Early in April, he received an official invitation from Sir Stephen Cottrell of the Privy Council Office to come to London 'and bring with you one of the able'st Mechanists of Birmingham'; Boulton and his aide would go with the Lords of the Committee on Coin 'in an Inspection They intend to make of the Mint, on Tuesday the 20*th* of this Instant April';[5] expenses would be paid.

Boulton already had an 'able Mechanist' in mind: John Rennie. Rennie was not from Birmingham, but Boulton wanted him anyway, because he was more gifted than anyone in the immediate neighbourhood. So Rennie it would be, and thus was an important player introduced to the industrialization of money.

John Rennie, his two sons George and John, Jr., and the Rennie firm, would figure in Soho's mint exports for the next thirty-five years, and they, their products, and their artisans will be found described in many portions of this book. It will be as well, therefore, to say a few words about John Rennie, Sr.

Like so many other engineers of the period, Rennie was a Scot. He was born in 1761, died in 1821. His acquaintance with Matthew Boulton dated back to 1783, when a mutual friend introduced the two men in Edinburgh. Boulton saw a skilled engineer in the making; Rennie saw an opportunity for wider horizons and work for a prestigious firm. When he returned to Birmingham at the end of 1783, Boulton mentioned the new man to his partner; accordingly, Rennie was invited to join the Soho combine and eventually accepted, in June 1784.

Boulton had a precise assignment in mind for Mr Rennie. He and Watt were just then constructing the Albion Mill in London, and the young engineer was soon put to work designing the flour-grinding mechanism – thereby gaining his first experience in the general sort of machinery with which he and his successors would remain associated. When the mill was completed, Rennie stayed on in the capital, setting himself up in Holland Street, Blackfriars. His relations with his former masters remained cordial (and so did those of his sons with the sons of Boulton and Watt): when asked to attend at the mint with a skilled mechanic, Boulton knew precisely whom he wanted.

Postponed for a week, the meeting at the mint finally got under way on 27 April. Boulton recorded the proceedings in one of his notebooks (Notebook 81, covering the years between 1798 and 1803). Besides he and Rennie, Lord Liverpool, Sir Joseph Banks, and several other sympathetic members of the Privy Council attended. They investigated all aspects of the facility, paying particular attention to the melting and refining aspects of precious-metal coinage. They adjourned for the week-end, convened again on the thirtieth, and had one final meeting on Friday, 4 May.

Out of all this would eventually come a report by John Rennie, under date of 10 July 1798. More immediately, Matthew Boulton made a report of his own, written while still in London and dated 8 May. He listed four crucial objectives: absolutely precise assaying; a greatly enhanced coining capability; improved workmanship; and cheaper workmanship. He did not go into detail about how to achieve such reforms, and he was particularly reticent about what the mint needed to do to improve its coining: any discussion of the latter

> would extend this Report to a tedious length; and would tend only to plunge me into Disputes with Persons, whose habits & customs have establish'd Prejudices in favor of their old trades in their old ways; but whose Occupations have not allowed them to gain that Mechanical and Philosophical Experience, which more general and more extensive manufactories afford to thinking men.[6]

But he added that were *he* running the mint, he would manage it far differently, would abandon some current practices and improve upon others.

Intrigued, the Lords met on the following day and asked Boulton for elaboration. The industrialist replied in predictable fashion: the mint ought to adopt his new presses, powered by a steam engine. Coinage could thus be augmented and improved, while the number of staff could be reduced. By his figures, the steam produced from a single bushel of coal would yield a power equal to that of fifty-five men for one hour. Eight small boys could coin as many guineas, on new steam presses, as could those fifty-five men, working eleven old-style presses.

Advice on the ideal coin (shallow relief, struck in a plain collar) followed; in all, Boulton's report ran for more than twelve closely-written pages. He had answered every conceivable question and now confidently awaited developments.

They were slow in coming. Boulton maintained an amicable correspondence with Lord Liverpool and Sir Stephen Cottrell through the early summer, and John Rennie rendered his own report (which enthusiastically recommended Soho's methodology and machinery for the Royal Mint) that July. And then the project was allowed to lapse by both sides. We may hazard the guess that Boulton had so much on his mind (the Russian mint, the

Danish mint, the winding down of his first British copper coinage and the pursuit of his second) that he was content to let the matter rest; but what had happened in London? Had the British Government lost interest, and if so, why?

The full answer may never be known, but several obvious possibilities exist. Lord Liverpool's health (he was a year older than Boulton) began to decline, and he would withdraw from public life by mid-1800: one of the most vociferous and effective voices for change would thus be muted. A greater obstacle was the fear and loathing which Matthew Boulton's coining activities had inspired at the Tower. From the mint's point of view, here was a man who had already cast it into disrepute with copper coinage, whose friends such as Garbett had been making rude comments and inviting unwelcome scrutiny for the past decade and a half. Further, Boulton's cheeky observations on his own merits versus those of the traditionalists, typified by the extended quotation above, were hardly calculated to win him support at the mint. Beleaguered officials there did what threatened bureaucrats have always done: they dug in their heels and vowed that whatever successes the intruder might one day enjoy would receive no assistance from them.

The interloper quickly became aware of the cooling of interest, and he blamed such officials as James Morrison, deputy master of the mint, for delaying progress. Boulton maintained a lively correspondence with anyone who would listen, damning the institution for having 'never made the least improvement for a Centry [century] past, they have never Coind 1/4 of the quantity I do in equal time (even in their common Gothick manner)'.[7] Samuel Garbett did what he could in the cause of reform, crowning his efforts with a detailed report to Lord Lansdowne on 5 February 1800. Once again, he charged that the current mint did too little, did it too poorly, and did it for too much money. But even Garbett's persistence could not bring results; and the question of a rebuilt Royal Mint disappears from the Boulton archives for the next four years.

Beneath the surface, events were nonetheless moving in the direction of reform. Presented with several years' worth of grace, the current mint did nothing (and perhaps could do nothing) with it. The silver shortage worsened – so much so that the Bank of England placed another order for countermarked dollars (which this time featured an octagonal rather than an oval countermark). Launched in early 1804, this attempt proved no more successful than the experiment of 1797; as before, forgers quickly copied the validating mark. As related elsewhere, the Bank soon turned to Matthew Boulton for assistance, and Boulton came up with an improved countermarking technique – in the guise of two complete dies, with which he was able to obliterate virtually all of the original designs. While there was some talk of a minor silver coinage of the same type, it never went beyond discussion; but Matthew Boulton's Soho Mint struck slightly more than a million five-shilling Bank of England tokens and slightly less than eight hundred thousand six-shilling token pieces for the Bank of Ireland during the middle six months of 1804, all of which had started out as Spanish or Spanish-American Pieces of Eight. The excellence of the Boulton products (contrasted with the easily-forged improvisations from the Royal Mint) seems to have rekindled interest in that facility's renovation along Soho lines. From the spring of 1804, while there would be much vacillation over details and participants, there would never again be serious doubt that Great Britain would get a new mint, and Matthew Boulton a new mint contract.

While the Committee of Coin reported in favour of a refurbished mint on 5 March 1804, we cannot say precisely when matters began moving forward at Soho. A Boulton notebook for 1804 contains jottings about the possible power requirements for a new Royal Mint (and another hint that he assumed its activities would be restricted to precious-metal coinage). But these notes are undated, and the thread of events remains tenuous until July. Then, on the twenty-eighth, word was received that attendance in London was required. But the command was sent to George Rennie, not Matthew Boulton.

It was repeated a few days later by George Chalmers, another functionary at the Board of Trade; a two-day meeting ensued on 2 and 3 August. Rennie was entrusted with the preparation of drawings of the current mint buildings, with new machinery substituted in place of the old. He was to carry out this task with the help of his mentor at Soho, and all of the machinery 'I understood was to be entirely on your plan'.[8] Rennie added that the Lords of Privy Council wanted the new mint to be at work by the following summer.

While naturally pleased with the prospect of another order for a mint, Matthew Boulton was annoyed with the manner in which it was presented. He, not Rennie, should have been contacted first! His London agent John Woodward looked into the matter, concluded that, while the Lords should certainly have approached his master first, there was probably no malice intended. But Boulton's reaction to what was probably an innocent mistake is significant. A climate of mistrust and misunderstanding, born of past disappointments, would surround the Royal Mint project from start to finish.

On 9 August, Cottrell summoned Rennie to the Tower of London; as in 1798, the engineer was to undertake a minute inspection of the current mint, recommend improvements of the latest type 'with a view to executing in the most perfect manner the Coinage of Gold and Silver Moneys'.[9] Note that Cottrell made absolutely no mention of *copper* money: if this letter were not a guarantee of a future Boulton monopoly of the lower end of British coinage, what was?

While Rennie busied himself in London, Boulton fretted at Soho. He trusted Rennie (who in any case could not devise new mint machinery without his help); but the lure of glory had turned the heads of many another man, and no one, not even John Rennie, was beyond temptation. Boulton especially disliked the cavalier manner in which the government had simply ordered Rennie 'to take possession of my Secrets & Inventions without proposing or promising any thing to me'.[10]

The old man's unease was scarcely helped by the state of his health, which currently confined him to his bed. But so worried did he become that he proposed to travel to London on a specially-equipped canal boat, in which he could lie horizontally for the entire length of the journey – and being Boulton, he actually conducted a series of experiments on Hockley Pool! But by the end of the summer, his apprehensions were diminishing: Rennie was proving faithful, and the British Government was proving sincere in its quest for a mint.

During September and October, Boulton was actively discussing plans and prospects for his new creation, in constant correspondence with John Rennie on all aspects of the project. And the new mint began to take form. It would be about the size of Soho Mint, with eight coining presses. It would feature Boulton's concept of progressive manufacturing. But it would not be built at the Tower.

During the autumn of 1804, it became increasingly apparent to Boulton and Rennie that the old, jury-rigged minting space, which had served well enough for a pre-industrial coinage, simply would not suffice for the new, progressive technology. Rennie's initial solution was an exchange of space with the Ordnance Office, wherein the mint would give up some scattered holdings but gain buildings in contiguity with each other. Military authorities were initially favourable to the plan, but not even a swap of buildings could change a central fact: the ancient warren represented by the Tower of London was not the best place for a factory.

Matthew Boulton saw this clearly, and he drew the logical conclusion: build a new mint, on a new site. In coming to this view, he had the experience at St Petersburg in mind, wherein an extant building had finally proved inadequate for his requirements – and much time had been and was still being lost while a new one was erected in its place. Boulton made a forceful plea for a new mint edifice in a letter to Rennie on 5 November, and the swift adoption of the idea (just three days after he had made it) suggests that Rennie and the members of the Committee for Coin had come to the same conclusion, were simply waiting for someone to put it in writing.

Certainly, Boulton's arguments made good sense. If new buildings were constructed, they could be made to fit the machinery – rather than the machinery having to be compromised to fit *them*. Moreover, the old mint, in its old space, could still coin while the new mint was being erected. That point was telling, for the erection of a new mint on the old spot would have meant a cessation of coining for many months. The current mint might be inadequate, but it was obviously better than no mint at all. When one added the possibilities of cleanliness and light at a new mint, compared with 'a certain prison like gloom within the Walls' of the old,[11] the Birmingham coiner believed that there was every advantage to his plan. And the British Government agreed.

The site it selected was on Little Tower Hill, a spot currently occupied by the royal tobacco warehouses. Preliminary surveying got under way before the end of the year. On 8 January 1805, John Rennie submitted his report to the Lords of the Committee on Coin; it was essentially identical to the document of 1798, and it recommended a new, larger, modern mint built on Matthew Boulton's principles of progressive manufacturing. His report was approved, and William Fawkener at the Board of Trade was soon asking Matthew Boulton what portions of the machinery he wished to construct. There ensued several months of tripartite correspondence between Matthew Boulton, John Rennie, and various functionaries at the Treasury. Boulton's suspicions were once again aroused (this was inevitable: unable to travel to London, he felt himself, and indeed was, at the mercy of the good conduct of his former employee and the faceless officials of the British Government); but he was mollified when it became obvious that Rennie was deferring to him upon every occasion. As matters finally stood, Soho would construct the engines and the coining and cutting out machinery, while John Rennie would manufacture the rolling mill.

More precisely, Soho would construct the following: two steam engines, one of sixteen horse (for the cutting out presses and milling and shaking machines), the other of ten (for the coining presses);[12] all of the necessary connecting apparatus between engines and implements; eight large coining presses of the Soho type; twelve cutting out presses (four more than Soho's complement); six double milling machines; four double shaking machines; a die multiplying press; the ironwork for four furnaces for annealing blanks and four more for annealing dies; four turning lathes; and a steam apparatus for warming the coining rooms (so as to avoid the necessity – and the hazard – of fires and stoves).

In exchange, Matthew Boulton would receive the sum of £16,990.

This agreement was long in coming: Boulton's poor health delayed a final arrangement for many months, for he was not yet ready to relinquish control of the Royal Mint project to his son but was too frail to conduct it himself. While a preliminary accord was reached in April 1806, the final contract was not signed until late July, by which time the building process was actually under way.

The proceedings encountered one last obstacle in the early summer of 1805. We know very little about it – and we would know even less, were it not for a report from John Rennie to William Fawkener, dated 26 June. The Committee on Coin may have been moving in the direction of a totally new mint, but Rennie's elation the previous autumn had been premature: it had not arrived there yet. It wanted to be persuaded, and it therefore requested data on the competing costs of the two possibilities – a completely new mint, and a refurbished mint in the Tower. James Johnson, the architect entrusted with the project, was asked to produce both sets of figures, which John Rennie then incorporated in his report, along with advice and arguments from Matthew Boulton. The resulting document put the cost of a new mint in a new building at £126,490 and new machinery in the Tower at £86,510.

Rennie had a difference of nearly £40,000 to explain, and he attempted to do so with ingenuity and verve: he made the disparity more palatable by observing that the old mint could become a barracks for soldiers, easily worth £15,000 alone. He never came close to balancing his figures, but he argued so forcefully for the new site that he swung opinion in its favour all the same. His efforts were aided by a change of mind in the Ordnance Department, which decided that it needed all of its current space in the Tower, and then some.

On 31 July 1805, the Board of Trade held a plenary meeting to which Rennie was summoned. He was told that a new mint had been agreed to, to be constructed on the site of the old tobacco warehouses, and that he and James Johnson could proceed with it. The news became official on 18 August, and workmen immediately set about removing the warehouses' contents, preparatory to pulling the buildings down. The project had finally begun!

Demolition work must have begun early in September; by the end of the following month, the old buildings were down and the foundations for the new were being dug. Work on them and negotiations for the mint package they would contain proceeded without incident through the final months of the old year. Then events at the beginning of the new cast everything in doubt: the essential man, prime minister William Pitt, died on 23 January, and the wheels of government abruptly ceased to turn.

They remained motionless for nearly two months, during which time very little was accomplished at the Treasury, on Little Tower Hill, or at Soho. But Pitt's replacement took office, the government returned to life – and mint work resumed in March. Drawings for the new buildings shuttled back and forth between London and Soho, while work at the site was resumed and Matthew Boulton completed his calculations for the machinery he would supply. His final proposal went out on 3 April, and a contract was signed on 30 July. But the final arrangement contained an additional passage requested by Matthew Robinson Boulton, who had now become the primary Soho party dealing with the affair.

The clause which the younger Boulton sought and obtained conceded an extension of the time allowed for the erection of the mint machinery once it had arrived at the Little Tower Hill site. The elder Boulton had initially supposed that a mere six months would suffice for that aspect of the work, because he expected the services of the workmen he had sent to construct the St Petersburg mint. But matters had developed contrary to expectation: not only were his people still immured in Russia, but James Duncan, the only member of the squabbling group likely to accept another mint-building assignment, was pledged to proceed to Copenhagen to erect a second Boulton mint there, for Denmark; and only after the conclusion of that additional task could he be expected home to work on the Royal Mint. Matthew Robinson Boulton assumed that new workmen would have to be procured and trained for the London project, and he therefore requested an extension of the construction time from six months to a year. This was granted.

As it happened, the only person supposed to return to Britain and accept additional employment stayed where he was: James Duncan finally made his peace with Russia, and he would spend the rest of his life there. But two other members of the 'Soho Corps', James Walker and William Speedyman, would one day surprise everyone by accepting employment at the new mint. Returning to England at the end of 1807, they went to Soho, settled their affairs, and were soon at work on Little Tower Hill.

The mint affair proceeded on a satisfactory course through the last months of 1806. On Little Tower Hill, the walls for the new buildings were going up, and some of the roofing had been completed by the end of the year. At Soho, Matthew Boulton mislaid his signed copy of the contract (which occasioned sleepless nights for his solicitor, Ambrose Weston: his master's unease had communicated itself to the lawyer, who fretted that without a contract, the British Government could back out of the bargain at any time). But the old man located the document, Weston was relieved, and work on the machinery went on. Much of it had been completed by the end of 1806, and the remainder would be done by the summer of 1807.

By then, British officialdom was concluding that it would be advisable to train someone in the operation of the machinery which Mr Boulton was supplying. Current master of the mint Earl Bathurst commissioned three people to come to Soho for preliminary talks – his deputy, James William Morrison, Robert Bingley, the King's Assayer, and Henry William Atkinson, a member of the Company of Moneyers. Boulton would not have looked forward to the visit, for he had already encountered difficulties with Morrison – and the positions of the other two would have reminded him of everything he was pledged to reform. Nonetheless, the visit was agreed to and apparently took place on 3 July. But as Boulton observed to Sir Stephen Cottrell, an extended observation of a collection of machine parts in packing crates was scarcely likely to benefit anyone; he who came to Soho for instruction must look at Soho Mint itself.

The man finally selected to superintend the erection of the London mint machinery could not have been more appropriate. For he already knew a great deal about Soho Mint: he had had a hand in building it.

James Lawson was a Cornishman, who made his appearance at Soho at the beginning of 1789. He was then looking for a temporary position, and, since Matthew Boulton was looking for new hands just then, the two men agreed that Lawson would work at Soho until he found another, more congenial spot. But he never found a better and remained at Boulton's works.

By the first years of the nineteenth century, Lawson had become Boulton's troubleshooter – a replacement for the absent Zack Walker – manager of difficult people and situations. He would need all of his expertise in his latest and, as it happened, his last assignment.

He appeared in London at the end of 1807, his way paved by introductory letters from Matthew Robinson Boulton to a number of mint officials, most notably the new architect, Robert Smirke, who had acceded to the post on the death of James Johnson at the end of June. This new man has received much praise as a designer; Soho's view of him was far less charitable.

Immediately upon taking command, Smirke had demanded alterations in the die multiplying and cutting out rooms (and the latter area would be a continuing source of aggravation, the last part of the mint to be completed). Smirke would later refuse to turn over drawings and plans when asked, on the grounds that he had done them in his spare time and deserved extra payment for them. When we consider that Lawson's position was still being financed by Soho (which received regular subventions from the government for that purpose); and when we learn that the buildings were by no means ready to receive Boulton's machinery at the time of its delivery, we begin to see parallels with the St Petersburg story, and we begin to entertain sympathy for Mr Lawson. Never in the best of health, he appeared to be coming unhinged by late February 1808: for by then, he had come to understand the challenges he faced.

He faced challenges from London *and* from Soho. One of Lawson's many talents was expertise in die multiplication. Just as he was settling into his post at the new mint, emissaries of the old came to enlist his aid: they were preparing dies for a new coinage for the Bank of Ireland,[13] and their designer Lewis Pingo needed guidance in the production of dies for the issue. Lawson agreed to assist in this worthy cause – only to find himself the recipient of an angry letter from Matthew Robinson Boulton. That old mistrust had resurfaced: Lawson was being used, was taking too much on faith, and was absolutely prohibited from doing anything other than hastening the erection of the machinery, the completion of the new mint project. Lawson saw things somewhat differently: regardless of character clashes at the top level, he and Pingo were colleagues. This evidence of an unaccustomed independence (along with the sudden announcement that he was thinking of marrying; Lawson had always been considered a confirmed bachelor) convinced the people at home that their representative was having a mental breakdown. He was invited to Soho for a rest cure at the end of February.

He would need all his wits to face the coming spring. The new mint was woefully over budget by the first days of 1808 – by as much as £80,000, according to John Rennie. The buildings proceeded at a snail's pace, partly due to Rennie's insistence on having Dundee stone for the foundations of the cutting out and press rooms – only to find a shortage of masons capable of working with it. Contrary winds kept shipments of Portland stone from entering the Thames: this stone, too, was essential for the project. And overall, there was a shortage of skilled building personnel; Smirke made great efforts to secure the hands he needed, but he had only limited success.

Minor and major annoyances continued to distinguish the Royal Mint's rebuilding. Some problems were due to sheer stupidity: when Soho dispatched the last of its engines, the sixteen-horse mechanism for the cutting out department, from the Midlands to the Metropolis, it encountered a cloth-headed official of the Wolverhampton Boat Company who was uncertain of the location of the Tower of London – and therefore sent the engine to Brentford. It took Lawson two weeks to locate the truant machine, four days more to get it delivered to the Tower and safely uncrated. Once he had done that, the relieved superintendent decamped for a long-deferred Scottish holiday; he would be absent from the scene for the next two months.

But work went on at a gradually accelerating pace; the space for Rennie's rolling mill engine was completed and work on its installation was under way by the time of Lawson's departure. Soho had been asked whether it wished to manufacture the heavy steel rollers for this mill. It declined, and John Rennie turned to another early industrial pioneer, the Eagle Foundry, for help. James Walker and William Speedyman appeared at the site early in the year and were soon put to work: they had been earmarked for the cutting out mechanism, but the delay in the appearance of its engine forced their employment at other tasks.

The cutting out room posed a particular problem. The structure was circular, in recognition of the arrangement Soho required for its blanking presses. They were set in a circle, worked by an overhead wheel and escapements, and represented the final vestiges of Boulton's original arrangement for coining. A dome with a skylight formed an essential part of the cutting out room's plan, because good light was more important here than at any other stage of the minting process. But the scaffolding necessary to construct the dome and the thick supporting columns upon which Smirke insisted took up all the interior space: until the final touches had been applied to the structure, nothing could be done about the machinery it was intended to contain. So Lawson complained; and Walker and Speedyman must be otherwise employed.

By the summer of 1808, the foundations for the multiplying and coining presses were in place, and a skilled Soho millwright named John Harris had been dispatched to London to set up this delicate machinery. He began his labours late in July, and he was still at them the following October. By then, the construction of the coining room had been completed; the addition of locked doors would mean that Harris could soon carry on the rest of his tasks in the privacy which was always a first consideration at Boulton mints.

As Harris was tinkering with his presses, Soho was receiving payment for them and the other portions of its package. Late in August 1808, John Woodward called at the Treasury and found that a warrant for Soho's £16,990 had long ago been made out, was simply awaiting registration by the

157

appropriate official. This gentleman's assent was secured (Woodward reminding him that the money was long overdue) and the sum was placed to the Soho account on 5 September. One major hurdle had been surpassed.

But troubles remained. Harris was making good progress with the coining machinery, as was John Rennie at the rolling mill. But work in the cutting out room remained at a stand while the basic construction of that area remained incomplete. Manpower shortages existed in some areas, while shortages of useful labour existed in others. The latter exacted its toll: William Speedyman was taking to the bottle and was carrying others with him, 'for it is very difficult to keep men working when they see the work not wanted'.[14] For his part, Matthew Robinson Boulton could only advise his amanuensis Lawson to keep after Smirke – or Mr Pope, the Clerk of Works most immediately concerned with the machinery: he was to remind Pope of the 'serious loss and inconvenience which I suffer from the deferred completion of the erection of the machinery'.[15] Lawson's thoughts on reception of this advice went unrecorded.

But the final months of 1808 marked the nadir of the project. By the beginning of the new year, Smirke and Pope had evidently been told by their superiors to find the necessary personnel and get the project finished. Workmen suddenly appeared from nowhere, and plastering of walls, hanging of doors, and installation of locks went on with a will. By mid-March, the cutting out room was finished, so that Walker and Speedyman could finally begin their appointed labour on the machinery it would contain; morale immediately improved.[16] Harris' work in the coining room was meanwhile coming to a successful conclusion; he made his final adjustments on the final press at the beginning of the summer. The rolling mill proceeded apace.

By the middle of 1809, the entire mint was so far along that the Lords of the Committee of Coin made two closely-related requests. They asked Matthew Robinson Boulton to instruct the Royal Mint's people in the operation of the new machinery. And they asked James Lawson to stay on as the machinery's caretaker.

But they shortly abandoned the first request in favour of the second, reasoning that if Lawson's services were secured, *he* could train the future moneyers. Lord Bathurst made a verbal offer of £600 per year until a house had been found for Lawson and his family (for the engineer had indeed found a wife), £500 per year thereafter, the house free. The engineer accepted provisionally – and he was immediately told that his duties would henceforth include training on as well as maintenance of the new mint. And Matthew Robinson Boulton was then informed that his services would not be required.

All of Soho's mistrust of the British Government resurfaced, bolstered by the fact that a potentially lucrative coinage for Bengal had just been countermanded. The bureaucrats were up to their old tricks, and an angry, apprehensive Matthew Robinson Boulton warned Lawson against accepting the post as it had been offered to him.

Lawson was miserable: he wanted the job, but he also wanted Soho's good will. If he took the post, he would have to have his old firm's assistance – in securing personnel, in filling future orders, especially in getting quick and correct advice when something went wrong. If he did not take the post, he could return to Soho – but he would be giving up a good deal of money, heightened prestige, and those roots which he had set down in the

Unexpected competition: this half-cent for Penang was the first production of the new Royal Mint, now poised to take over Soho's role as coiner. (National Numismatic Collection, Smithsonian Institution)

Metropolis. After a week of indecision, Lawson opted for the future, meanwhile doing his best to maintain his amicable connections with the past, and with Soho.

He would dispense with the services of James Walker and William Speedyman. Walker would remain in London for the time being; Speedyman would visit Scotland. But John Harris was asked to remain at the Royal Mint and accepted; so did another Soho man named Joseph Vale, who would continue to serve as Harris' assistant. Work on minor portions of the mint occupied the two – and their new, government-paid supervisor, James Lawson – through the final months of 1809 and the first months of 1810. But it was far enough along by late January that Lawson was ordered to a meeting at the Board of Trade, where he was told to get dies forged and punches engraved for a maiden coining attempt.

On the following day, 30 January, Lawson broke the news to his old superior at Soho; and now, two decades of mistrust on the part of two generations of the Boulton family came into sharp focus at last. For the first thing the Board of Trade wanted struck was *copper* coinage.

To be precise, it wanted the new mint to create twenty-five tons of copper half-cents, weighing forty-two to the pound, for the East India Company's Prince of Wales Island – Penang, in Malaysia. The metal for this coinage would have to be obtained in the form of rolled fillets, because the Royal Mint's new rolling mill remained inoperative until a connecting tunnel could be finished between its reservoir and the Tower of London's ditch. No matter that the upstart coiners had only half a mint with which to do the work; no matter that the work was minuscule, compared with the previous copper exploits of Soho. A precedent was being established, and an advertisement was being given, that any gentleman's agreement which may have existed once existed no longer. And insult was soon added to injury when George Harrison had the effrontery to ask Matthew Robinson Boulton to honour that portion of the contract which pledged him to train personnel.

Boulton must have anticipated what was coming. In April 1809, he heard rumours that the East India Company was thinking of having its copper coinage done at the new Royal Mint. This evinced an angry reaction: he complained that Soho had been told that the new mint would only be wanted for silver and gold and had designed and priced it accordingly. He added that he had been promised the copper coinage by John Rennie, relaying the pledge of Rennie's contacts in official circles. Finally, an informal agreement between Rennie and the Boultons had led the latter to assume that, if the British Government ever did decide to strike copper, it would purchase another mint from Soho for the purpose. Boulton's blandishments were ignored; a year later, he was able to return the favour.

He took nearly a month to reply to Harrison's request for help and then categorically refused such assistance, recapitulating the unjust and shabby treatment which he and his late father had received at the hands of the British bureaucracy. He capped his litany with a request for additional remuneration to cover the cost of the suffering; he got no further with this line of argument than had Harrison with his original request.

As winter turned to spring, and as the new mint made good on its promise to coin copper, with or without Soho's assistance (and the relative crudity of those first coins proclaims that it did so alone), Matthew Robinson Boulton and the directors of the new facility angrily turned their backs on each other, refusing to communicate or compromise. But they would soon resume communication: the connections between the private firm and the public institution were too intimate and too general to allow for a permanent estrangement. Simply put, the Royal Mint needed Soho's help and could not do without it. And on a curious level, Soho needed its daughter's help as well: the survival of the elder institution during the lean years to come was aided in no small fashion by the requirements and demands of the younger.

In some cases, contact continued whether or not it was desired. John Harris and Joseph Vale had indeed been retained at the new mint – but their wages were still being paid by Matthew Robinson Boulton, who was regularly reimbursed for his pains by the Royal Mint. The two men only became 'official' employees of the mint – and therefore paid directly by it – in May 1811.

More generally, dealings persisted because of Soho's expertise in machinery, its unparalleled experience with the intricacies of industrial moneying. Orders for machine tools were regularly made and filled throughout the period of coolest relations: on 15 June 1811, Lawson and Henry William Atkinson, a senior moneyer, requested a complete set of stocks and dies for making all of the different screws belonging to the machinery which Boulton had supplied. Not hearing from Soho for more than a week, they reiterated their request on the twenty-fourth. This crossed a reply from Matthew Robinson Boulton, whose tone suggested that he was still angry, still felt betrayed: he would supply the parts in question, but only with due regard to prior engagements. Since he was then in process of sending a mint on the first leg of its journey to Brazil, he had a point. But the order from the Royal Mint could have easily been filled by someone else at Soho, had Boulton allowed it. Yet he did fill the order all the same, in his own good time; even during the worst period of the association, the two parties remained on speaking terms.

Often enough, they spoke at cross-purposes. One of the Royal Mint's presses broke in mid-1812 and was sent to Soho for repair or replacement. Boulton received the apparatus, awaited instructions to proceed. These were not forthcoming. He then put his people to work on another project, whose completion he had deferred upon hearing of the Royal Mint's problem. Meanwhile, the press or its replacement became badly-needed for the latest production of Bank of England silver three-shilling and one-and-sixpence tokens. James Lawson came under increased pressure to get a new or repaired press in service; writing to Soho, he found that nothing had been done due to lack of instructions. The press was finally repaired and sent back to London at the end of August. But this sort of exchange would be typical of dealings between the Royal Mint and Matthew Robinson Boulton for many years.

Yet those dealings continued, could not be abandoned. How important Soho remained was abundantly indicated in the aftermath of a major fire at the Royal Mint on the morning of 31 October 1815. Starting in the shaking shop near the chimney of the stove used for drying planchets, the blaze quickly spread to the roofs of the buildings and to several apartments adjacent to the shaking room. The greatest damage occurred in the cutting out room, but the rolling and coining rooms also suffered extensive injuries.

On 3 November, a desperate James Lawson enlisted Soho's help, and the first of several orders for new castings went out on the ninth. In this instance, Boulton put the common good above personal pique, and the replacement parts were quickly prepared and sent. And grateful officials at London wasted no time in remitting payment for Mr Boulton's trouble.

The mint was quickly repaired and was back in business in time to undertake the ambitious reform of 1816. Its continuing dependence on Soho may be illustrated by two developments during the recoinage. About a month prior to its start, Lawson wrote Soho, pleading for the loan of any workers with expertise in coining or cutting out (8 June 1816). Matthew Robinson Boulton was unable to accede to Lawson's request, because prolonged inactivity had forced him to lay off most of his skilled personnel; only a few boys and women remained in his coining and cutting out departments, while the few adult males remaining on duty 'have been employed by me from motives of charity and at a considerable loss for more than two years'.[17] Lawson was more successful in obtaining parts than personnel: an order for collars and layers on for the new coinage was swiftly filled and remitted, as was a later order for two additional coining presses.

If Soho could not provide further trained personnel for its offspring on Little Tower Hill, it could nonetheless train those people at Soho. As part of the recoinage effort, the services of a talented immigrant from Rome were enlisted. Benedetto Pistrucci's expertise was in an Italian specialty, gem-engraving. He had come to London in the spring of 1815, where he made the acquaintance of Matthew Boulton's old friend, Sir Joseph Banks. The following year, Sir Joseph presented him to *his* friend, William Wellesley Pole, who was the new master of the mint. Pistrucci's career with the nation's coiner was about to be launched – except for one slight problem: he worked in stone; the mint worked in steel.

This brought Soho into the equation. Around Christmas 1816, Pole wrote to Matthew Robinson Boulton: could his new artist come to Soho to learn how to make a master punch, in relief? The record is silent, but the design intended for the punch was probably that of a jasper cameo of St. George and the Dragon: Pistrucci had suggested the design as suitable for the reverse of the upcoming gold coinage, and Pole had commissioned him to carve it in stone.

On Christmas Day, Matthew Robinson Boulton declined seeing Pistrucci at Soho, explaining that the press of business made any instruction there impossible. (One may doubt the validity of the excuse: Boulton had absolutely nothing on his plate at Soho Mint at the time, with the exception of a small order of cent planchets for the United States Mint.) But he rethought his refusal and soon relented. James Lawson and Benedetto Pistrucci visited Soho at the end of the year, with favourable results but a difficult return to London:

> We have had rather a tedious journey, owing to the bad roads, &c. The first day Mr Pistrucci's large trunk was badly fixed and got loose, which detained us more than an hour, and after this the axletree of the hind wheels of our chaise broke near *Bradley's* the horsedealer's, and let us down with a good *hard* thump, though the chaise did not upset, and as the *Post* man thought he could bring on the chaise slowly by mending the axle, I thought it best to walk on to Shipston, which I did, through mud to mid-leg, leaving Mr Pistrucci to guard the *Luggage* till I sent *back* a chaise, so that we only got to Enstone that night, and I was so

much fatigued and wet that I caught a violent cold, and on getting *home* on Friday evening near *seven* o'clock, I was quite *knocked up*, so much so that I could not sleep, and from both my head and throat being much affected, accompanied with slight fever, confined me to bed all day on Saturday, and to the *House* still. ... M*r* Pistrucci is quite delighted with the punch you *did*, and will begin upon it immediately.[18]

James Lawson died in the Royal Mint's employ on 9 April 1818. Soho's advice was solicited on the choice of his successor. For a time, the leading candidate was William Murdock, Jr. He declined the position in favor of the delights of country life; and the man who replaced Lawson was another individual known to Soho, John Rennie's elder son, George.

Matthew Robinson Boulton and James Watt, Jr. gave the young engineer their whole-hearted support, Watt telling his contacts at the Royal Mint that his partner at Soho would be happy to give George any instruction he might need before taking up his duties. This seems to have been crucial to George Rennie's appointment, and Boulton kept his promise later that spring, with a brief but thorough introduction to the art of modern coining.

George Rennie took up his post at the end of May, held it until early 1826 – during most of which time he was also in partnership with his younger brother, John, Jr., the two sons carrying on the multi-faceted business left to them by their father. Rennie's years at the Royal Mint were not particularly happy ones: most of his time was devoted to making dies – which is not particularly surprising, considering the facility's rather heavy responsibilities during those years. Like his predecessor, he relied a great deal on Soho, and on Matthew Robinson Boulton, for advice on coining and on personnel. (The crowns struck during the final years of George III's reign proved especially difficult, as did their designer, Benedetto Pistrucci.[19]) And like his predecessor, Rennie served as Boulton's informant on affairs at the Royal Mint.

It was in this latter capacity that he bore word of a final disappointment. The Ionian Islands had become a British possession at the end of the Napoleonic Wars. In 1818, it was proposed to send them a copper coinage. On 4 January 1819, George Rennie advised Boulton 'that *you were thought of* but the Government preferred the execution of it themselves'.[20]

The blow was bitter; Rennie added that upwards of £30,000 worth of coinage, corresponding to copper pence, halfpence, and farthings, were to be struck, which would have given Soho Mint much employment. Boulton responded in a predictable fashion. Rennie was sympathetic ('this I must say that you have not been treated well[.] you have furnished them with Arms to fight against you & they will not rust for want of use'[21]). But he could do nothing, for the decision was not his to make; and when the final indignity took place and the Royal Mint resumed the coinage of copper for the British Isles in 1821, Soho did not even bother to complain.

In any case, its connections with its offspring were drawing to a close. With George Rennie's departure in 1826, the last direct link between Soho and Little Tower Hill was severed. Business dealings between the two facilities virtually disappeared after the middle 1820s – but we shall find Soho supplying small machine parts, and another coining press, as late as 1844.

The swift attenuation of contact was based on far more than the death or departure of particular people, although these occurrences underscored the larger play of events. At bottom, the decline and death of the link was based on an essential difference between Soho Mint and its descendant on Little Tower Hill. The former was a personal creation of two men, father and son, a phenomenon whose rise and fall would be measured in generations, in decades. The latter was an *institution*, created by no one in particular, whose existence extended far into the past, would stretch far into the future. When advice and help were solicited, notice was being given that those entrusted with the mint were uncomfortable with its current incarnation. When advice and aid were no longer requested, notice was being given that the mint had achieved stasis, was doing what it currently wished to do. Matthew Robinson Boulton might have reflected that the severance of the connection meant that Soho's London mission had been brilliantly realized – but he would have needed a philosophical detachment beyond him, and beyond most men, to draw that conclusion.

SOURCES

Most of the material for this chapter came from four locations in the Matthew Boulton Papers. Samuel and Francis Garbett's early investigations into practices at the old mint were found in the first of the three boxes devoted to that family (MBP308, Garbett, Samuel and Garbett family, 1765–85) – although their 1782 report must be sought in MBP303, the box which otherwise contains the papers of the Cornish Metal Company. MBP413, Royal Mint, was another major source of material.

Two other sources were essential. MBP332, John Rennie, contains correspondence from *all* of the members of the family, and most of what we know about the continuing connection between Soho and Little Tower Hill in the late 1810s and early 1820s will be found there. And for the day-to-day frustrations attendant on the actual construction of the new Royal Mint, consult MBP322, Lawson, James and Lawson, Archibald.

But additional archival sources had to be consulted to round out this chapter. Matthew Boulton's letter books were valuable, especially MBP148, [Private] Letter Book O, 1783–1788. Several of the incoming letter boxes were also critical, particularly MBP227, 232, and 243 (boxes C3, F, and L2, containing the correspondence of Sir Stephen Cottrell, William Fawkener, and Lord Liverpool, respectively). Matthew Boulton's notebooks contributed material at critical junctures, particularly Notebook 81 (1798–1803) and Notebook 93 (1804); both are located in MBP379. And the post-1799 correspondence of Ambrose Weston (MBP363) was useful, especially that from the year 1804, a crucial period for the Royal Mint project.

As one might expect, MBP406, British Coinage, contains some materials relating to the British *mint*. And I have already recommended the modern studies of Craig and Challis; I do so again.

NOTES

1 You may recall that in the early days, Boulton & Watt did not sell its engines outright but rather charged rent for them, computed as one-third of the difference between the amount of coal actually consumed and the amount which would have been consumed with a Newcomen engine.

2   MBP308, Garbett, Samuel and Garbett family, 1765–85: Samuel Garbett to Matthew Boulton, 5 December 1782. This is the earliest direct reference I have found connecting Matthew Boulton with a reform in the manufacturing processes of moneying.

3   MBP148, [Private] Letter Book O: Matthew Boulton to William Pitt, undated but mid-1788. Note Boulton's early division of labour: he will strike the nation's copper coinage, while the Royal Mint will confine itself to gold and silver. Neither Boulton ever abandoned the conviction that that was the preferable arrangement.

4   MBP243, Letter Box L2: Lord Liverpool to Matthew Boulton, 30 January 1798.

5   MBP227, Letter Box C3: Sir Stephen Cottrell to Matthew Boulton, 5 April 1798.

6   MBP413, Royal Mint: Matthew Boulton 'To the Lords of the Committee of Privy Council appointed to take into Consideration the State of the Coins of this Kingdom', 8 May 1798. One imagines he rather enjoyed writing this report.

7   MBP406, British Coinage: Matthew Boulton to Sir Joseph Cotton, 25 November 1799; spelling in original.

8   MBP332, Rennie, John: John Rennie to Matthew Boulton, 3 August 1804.

9   MBP413, Sir Stephen Cottrell to John Rennie, 9 August 1804.

10 MBP363, Weston, Ambrose, post-1799 (box 2): Matthew Boulton to Ambrose Weston, 7 September 1804.

11 MBP332, Matthew Boulton to John Rennie, 5 November 1805.

12 An engine for the rolling mill was *not* included in this list. Rennie's notes assumed that one would in fact be required, and he estimated that something of the order of thirty horse would be adequate for a coinage in silver and gold. A rolling mill engine was indeed erected at the new mint, along with the rest of the machinery. But the provenance of the engine is unclear or at least went unrecorded in the Matthew Boulton Papers. It is possible (but not likely) that John Rennie constructed it himself. It is more likely that he purchased it from Boulton & Watt, but that fact somehow went unrecorded. In any case, the engine was adequate for gold and silver (for which it had been designed), inadequate for copper (for which it had not) – as surviving correspondence informs us.

13 This effort culminated in the thirty-pence (i.e., halfcrown) token issue of 1808, one of the last silver coinages undertaken at the old mint.

14 MBP322, Lawson, James and Lawson, Archibald: James Lawson to Matthew Robinson Boulton, 20 October 1808. Again, the parallels with the recently-finished St Petersburg mint are interesting.

15 MBP322, Matthew Robinson Boulton to James Lawson, 19 October 1808.

16 Speedyman returned to sobriety once his proper work began – although, as Lawson observed, he was 'certainly not well named' (MBP413, James Lawson to Matthew Robinson Boulton, 17 March 1809).

17 MBP413, Matthew Robinson Boulton to James Lawson, 10 June 1816.

17 MBP322, James Lawson to Matthew Robinson Boulton, 6 January 1817; emphasis in original. No one ever said a career in numismatics was easy.

19 Pistrucci blamed Boulton's presses, which he said were too weak fully to strike up the reverse design. Rennie blamed the designer, who had made the reverse relief too deep.

The crowns were finally created in the following manner: the reverse die was applied first, acting with a blank die in place of the obverse. The half-struck coin was annealed, softened, then placed atop the bottom, reverse, die for a second strike. But this time, the obverse die would be used in place of a blank die. One would thus obtain a coin with clear impressions of both sides. This explains the great sharpness of strike common to this issue. But the methodology slowed down coining to a crawl: instead of sixty or more pieces per minute, no more than fifty pieces *per hour* could be struck in this fashion. 'You will well conceive how the moneyers like it' (MBP332, George Rennie to Matthew Robinson Boulton, 28 August 1818).

20 MBP332, George Rennie to Matthew Robinson Boulton, 4 January 1819; emphasis in original.

21 MBP332, George Rennie to Matthew Robinson Boulton, 12 January 1819.

CHAPTER 5

Brazil –
A New World Fiasco

By the middle 1790s, Matthew Boulton was ready to disseminate what he had learned about creating the unforgeable coin, ready and eager to ship the mints to make it, happy to send the technocrats necessary to set those mints up. Now all the world could create its own safe money on Soho's model. But by the time he was ready to act, he found that the times were already playing host to another, larger, group of circumstances. In time, historians would call these events the Napoleonic Wars; in time, they would play a major role in the creation, channelling, and success or failure of his exportation enterprises.

The Wars' effects upon Boulton, Watt & Company's varied concerns were largely negative. When Boulton constructed a new mint for the Danes, the international situation held up payment for it for years. When he created a similar facility for the Russians, the same unsettled circumstance threatened the same results, and it long postponed the return of the man sent out to superintend the process, Boulton's nephew Zacchaeus Walker, Jr. A related and dependent conflict, which Americans call the War of 1812, put a temporary halt to a lucrative trade in copper planchets between Boulton, Watt and the United States of America, a commerce which might had led to greater things had it not been interrupted.

But the wars could yield positive results as well. Some of the agitation for an improved Royal Mint may be imputed to a wartime economy and its increased need for coinage – even though the new facility's major efforts only began in 1816, the year after Waterloo, even though agitation for a better mint went back to the early 1780s. And there is a second case where the connection between the Napoleonic Wars and a business opportunity for a numismatic reformer is far more plausible, stands up to scrutiny far better. This is the case of Brazil.

As the Napoleonic Wars began, Brazil was the most backward area in all of Iberian America. This vast colony's masters had never had the manpower necessary fully to develop an American territory which was some three hundred times the size of Portugal itself; moreover, as long as the European situation remained in rough equilibrium, neither metropolis nor colony was likely to be forced to modernize from exterior pressure. And so Brazil slumbered in the tropical sun: incredibly wealthy in some respects (gold and diamonds were exported, as were sugar and brazilwood, a dyestuff after which the colony had been named), it was miserably poor in others. No newspapers existed. No books were printed here – nor were there libraries, had there been books to fill them. No universities enriched local minds. Other than extractive pursuits, no industries provided employment for that minority of the population which was free. And as long as the international scene remained in stasis, very little if anything would happen.

Change was imposed from outside, in the wake of Napoleon I. Late in 1807, the Corsican's generals invaded Portugal, whose location and traditional alliance with Great Britain were creating an unwelcome hole in the continental blockade. Prince Regent Dom João (who was ruling for his mother, mad Queen Maria), the servants, and most of the court scuttled for the safety of Brazil, just as General Junot's frustrated troops arrived on the hills overlooking Lisbon. The British Navy provided ferry service to the New World: this was as much as England could currently do for its oldest international partner.

After a miserable voyage of two months, the monarchs and their court reached Rio de Janeiro (January 1808). While most of the court sniffed in disdain, their leader was spurred to reform by what he beheld. It was abundantly evident that Portugal had served her American daughter poorly, and Dom João determined to make up for lost time. He would try to achieve the work of two centuries within a few years.

Change was dramatic. Universities were launched, as were printeries for newspapers and books. Sewers and roads were built; so were a national bank and the colony's first medical academy. Brazil was thrown open to the winds of intellectual and economic liberation. Given the realities of the day, most of these winds would be blowing from Great Britain; and some of them might carry Matthew Boulton and his people on a new and profitable course.

Soho's connections with the Portuguese actually predated the Napoleonic conquest of their Iberian homeland. In 1798, the firm had supplied five and one-half tons of copper blanks to a London firm called Lucena and Crawford. While the record is silent as to the final destination of these planchets, the fact that they were made in weights and sizes corresponding to those of the Portuguese five, ten, and twenty *reis* coins presents us with an obvious possibility – as does the fact that someone with the same unusual Portuguese surname would soon be involved in matters unquestionably connected with Brazil. But it would take a French occupation at home, and a reforming prince abroad, before the next step could happen.

On 5 July 1808, Boulton, Watt received a letter from Manoel Antonio de Paiva, suggesting that the Prince Regent's zeal for reform might extend to coinage as well as universities. It is worth citing in full:

Mess*rs* Boulton & Watt

London 5 July 1808.

Birmingham.

Private.

Gent*n*,

    I beg leave to enquire upon what terms you would undertake to deliver a Mint at Rio de Janeiro in the Brazils, and to provide English Coiners to set it on foot and to remain a sufficient time to instruct other Workmen to take their place. It is of course intended that the mint shall be complete in every respect for the coinage of gold, silver and copper, and I understand that the only additional expence that will thus be incurred will be that of a dye for each metal. It is also in contemplation that a means be provided for giving a second impression to existing coins, as was done by your house in respect to the Spanish Dollars. In replying to these points in the detail which your knowledge of the subject cannot fail of suggesting, I should wish to know whether by taking 2 or 3 mints, to be erected in different places, any facility would be allowed in the terms. I remain with great regard,

Gent*n*
Yr M*t* Ob*t* H*ble* S*vt*
M. A. de Paiva[1]

The letter speaks of two possible phases in the Soho connection with Brazil. The first, the supplying of a mint (rather than several mints, an idea which was soon abandoned), would actually come to fruition. But the second would not, and it raises several interesting questions.

When De Paiva mentioned a 'second impression … as was done by your house in respect to the Spanish Dollars', he was of course referring to Boulton's Bank of England dollars and their Irish cousins. But was he asking the industrialist to overstrike Spanish-American pesos *at Soho*, for shipment to Brazil? This seems unlikely, given the disturbed state of transatlantic commerce at the time: anyone shipping rich cargoes of silver coinage to and fro under the noses of the French Navy would be asking for trouble. But Boulton, Watt did prepare pattern coins on the Brazilian model, one of which is illustrated. If not intended as the harbingers of a Brazilian coinage made at Soho, might these essays have been struck to inform the Prince Regent of the quality he might now expect to see on new coins struck *in the colony* from Boulton dies in a Boulton mint? The latter is somewhat more likely than the former – at least based on the evidence available to us. But a new Brazilian overstruck silver coinage on the Soho model would never take place; and regardless of their purpose, Soho's splendid Brazilian patterns, probably created by the talented designer John Phillp, would lead nowhere.

But a steam-powered Soho mint would indeed be prepared and sent out. Shortly after receiving De Paiva's letter, Boulton, Watt invited him to Birmingham for discussions about the recoinage and the mint. The merchant was greatly impressed by what he saw, and he brought two additional gentlemen into the equation on the Portuguese side: his nation's ambassador to Great Britain, the Chevalier Domingos Antonio de Souza Couttinho, and a young Portuguese engineer named Gaspar Marques. Marques currently

Patterns for the proposed Brazilian recoinage, 1809, in silver and copper. (Reproduced by kind permission of the Trustees of the British Museum)

resided in England, but he would be sent out to Brazil to oversee the mint project.

Souza Couttinho and Marques came to Soho early in September 1809: the long hiatus between De Paiva's visit and that of his two colleagues is largely explained by slow communications: a year was required for the former's mint recommendation to travel from London to Brazil, wend its way through the transplanted Portuguese bureaucracy there, and then return to London with the Prince Regent's approval. But progress now appeared satisfactory: on 2 October, Matthew Robinson Boulton sent the Portuguese an estimate of costs for a mint capable of recoining up to two hundred thousand Spanish dollars per week – our strongest indication that the recoinage was indeed intended to be carried out in South America rather than at Soho.

The proposed mint would be slightly larger than the one recently supplied to Copenhagen, but much smaller than the one now working at St Petersburg. It would consist of six coining presses, four cutting out presses, three milling machines, two shaking machines, and a die multiplying press, all to be powered by one of the latest generation of Boulton, Watt's ten-horse engines. Spare parts and a second boiler would be included, in frank recognition that the primitive Brazilian technological environment would preclude finding these articles locally. Detailed plans would be remitted, and one of Soho's craftsmen would be sent as well, following Soho's established pattern.

Matthew Robinson Boulton also proposed remitting a modern rolling mill with a twenty-four-horse engine to power it. Presumably, the Rennies would have supplied the rolling machinery, just as they had recently done at the much larger site on Little Tower Hill. But despite Boulton's spirited arguments on its behalf, this portion of the proposal would finally be rejected by the Portuguese. Soho would lose the opportunity to sell another steam engine, a fairly large one by the standards of the day. But the people of Brazil would lose much more, for the new mint would not be the holistic, 'philosophical' creation its inventor and his son had intended it to be.

Negotiations proceeded through the remainder of 1809 and into the following year. Matthew Robinson Boulton prosecuted them in a somewhat distracted fashion: he was still clearing up the paperwork stemming from his father's death in August 1809, dealing as well with an attempt by John Southern to claim more credit in print for the invention of the Boulton mint than was his due. The Portuguese were hardly more assiduous: nothing could be finally decided in London without being first submitted to Rio de Janeiro, subjected to the inevitable delays and risks of a double transatlantic passage. But as time went on, one thing became clear: if any recoinage of Spanish-American pesos was to be done, Soho's dies would probably not play a role in it.

One of the firm's recurrent problems was an inability to deliver goods on time. We shall see this phenomenon in its dealings with North America; we see it to the south as well. Ambassador Souza Couttinho, and the two Portuguese merchants who would ultimately be entrusted with paying for whatever was done, John Charles Lucena and Manoel Antonio de Paiva, were initially quite serious about a Soho die production for Brazil. By the late summer of 1809, dies for most Brazilian gold and silver coins were in contemplation, production of which could have yielded great profits to Boulton, Watt & Company, the recoinage envisaged by the Portuguese being a very large one.

But the firm could not muster the speed necessary to get impressions from proposed dies to the Prince Regent while he was still keen on the idea; it literally missed the boat, the Brazil packet intended to convey its wares being forced to leave without them. By the end of the year, the chance of improving Brazilian coins through the intercession of British dies had receded, well on its way to becoming another of the 'might-have-beens' we associate with Soho. But the possibility of improving those coins through the intercession of a British mint was still alive. It would finally become a reality, but with a subsequent history very different from what anyone had anticipated or intended.

Despite Matthew Robinson Boulton's earnest entreaties, he never got his way on a steam-powered rolling mill, for the Chevalier and his agents were simply not empowered to agree to it. And by the beginning of 1810, Boulton was beginning to worry about losing the half-loaf he possessed: the Portuguese were unaccountably stalling on signing a contract with him for their mint.

For once, his own government was to blame. In 1785, a law had been passed by Parliament to prohibit the exportation of machinery and skilled workmen, it being feared that such exportation might give foreign industries an unfair advantage over British ones. Matthew Boulton had often railed against the inanity of the law, which affected Soho every time it sought to export a mint. But it remained on the books, not to be repealed until the 1820s. Now his son was introduced to its effects.

The younger Boulton appears to have been unaware of the existence of the law, or of the fact that it could put a damper on his dealings with Brazil. In fact it was already doing so: while anxiously awaiting word that the Portuguese had accepted and initialled his proposal for their mint, he was unaware that his correspondents were waiting in their turn for final British approval to export that mint. This must come from Richard Colley, Marquis Wellesley, Foreign Secretary under Spencer Perceval. Until the Marquis agreed, nothing would move. The Portuguese might be Britain's oldest allies, but when it came to the export of technology, they had to take their place in the queue along with everyone else, biding their time until their export of Mr Boulton's mint was deemed *not* to constitute a threat to the security of Great Britain. Messrs. Lucena and De Paiva, or the Chevalier de Souza Couttinho, might have done well to inform Matthew Robinson Boulton of the reason behind their lassitude regarding his contract. And we are somewhat surprised that the younger Boulton had managed to remain blissfully unaware of the 1785 ordinance, which had bedevilled his father on several former occasions; but such was the case. Official blessing for the shipment of the Brazil mint was finally granted on 9 June 1810, codified as 50 Geo. 3, Cap. 63, 'An Act to enable His Majesty to authorize the Exportation of the Machinery necessary for erecting a Mint in the *Brazils*', and a formal 'Articles of Agreement for preparing Coining Machinery for the Brazils' followed seven days later. It was signed by Matthew Robinson Boulton and John Charles Lucena and Manoel Antonio de Paiva, on behalf of the Chevalier de Souza Couttinho.

While waiting for the bureaucratic tangle to be unknotted, Boulton had done what he safely could to keep the project alive. Assuming that a mint would eventually be approved for export, it would need skilled representatives to erect and look after it. The final months of 1809 and the first months of 1810 had therefore been employed in personnel-related activities of two varieties. First, Gaspar Marques must be initiated into the mysteries of industrialized moneying as practised at Soho, for he would eventually be responsible for its latest incarnation, once it arrived in Rio de Janeiro. Much instruction was given, and Marques returned for a refresher course early in 1811. Second, qualified workmen from Soho itself must be selected for the initial phase of the project, the actual assembly of the mint in Brazil. After their selection they must receive additional training prior to leaving Birmingham; but before all that, their acceptance of their posts must be secured. In practice, this meant that once again Soho would be placed in the middle, mediating between skilled artisans from the first days of the industrial era, workers very conscious of their importance and rarity, and a somewhat miserly foreign government, which intended to hire them on the cheap.

Several prospective workmen came to Boulton's notice. The first was William Speedyman, one of Soho's millwrights. Speedyman was by now a seasoned numismatic campaigner, veteran of not one 'mint-expedition' but two (to St Petersburg and Little Tower Hill), and, despite Zack Walker's ungenerous opinion of his abilities, probably the best man to send out, due to his experience abroad.

The second candidate was Thomas White, another millwright. White had had no experience in foreign service, although he had been selected to go to Copenhagen a few years previously, his appointment rendered nugatory through no fault of his own. He was highly qualified in the erection of steam engines and appears to have been more highly regarded than Speedyman, at least in terms of expertise. The third man was Richard Clough, a jack-of-all-trades, who would be entrusted with the fitting together of the coining presses and other machinery in Brazil; he would serve as subordinate to whomever else was sent. At one point, it was in contemplation to send out all three workmen; in fact, only one of them, Thomas White, would ever make the journey. And he would bitterly regret having done so.

Speedyman had been receiving wages of three guineas per week in St Petersburg, his salary having been paid from the time he left England until he returned. He had also got his passage to and from Russia. These arrangements essentially formed the basis for Soho's discussions with the Portuguese, as it did battle with them on behalf of its people. Bearing in mind the considerable inflation in prices which had taken place during the past few years, the salaries Boulton, Watt proposed were not unduly generous. But Messrs. Lucena and De Paiva disputed them every step of the way. The sticking point appears to have been the matter of portal-to-portal wages, which the Portuguese dismissed as excessive, and upon which Boulton insisted – along with a cash award at the end of service as had been granted by the Tsar upon the completion of the St Petersburg project. No agreement having been secured after several months of effort, Boulton finally threatened to wash his hands of the entire affair, to abrogate unilaterally that portion of his agreement with the Portuguese in respect to the selection of Soho workmen and leave his foreign client to his own devices. This would be unfortunate, for 'without the aid of such men there will be the greatest difficulty in bringing the Machinery into Action with proper effect'.[2] The log-jam would not be broken for another six months, the Portuguese at last coming to Boulton's conclusion that a well-paid, happy workman would be far more valuable in a project of this complexity than an ill-paid, unhappy one. But by then, the workman in question (for it had finally been determined that only *one* Briton would be sent out) had been waiting in limbo for more than a year while his current and prospective masters discussed his fate; and he now decided to increase his demands.

After much discussion, it had been decided that Thomas White (the eventual winner in the Brazilian sweepstakes) would receive a wage of three and one-half guineas per week, plus his passage out and back. And while the record is not entirely clear, it appears that Boulton had won his point for the commencement of White's wages upon his departure from England rather than his arrival in Brazil. But the mechanic now presented Soho with a bill for an additional payment of £117.9.6, representing the difference between his ordinary Soho wages (three guineas per week) and what he had been promised by the firm if he agreed to go to Brazil to set up the mint. He had so agreed in June 1810 but had been kept in suspense for over a year; now he had come up with this figure as compensation for his time and general aggravation.

He had raised his demands for foreign service as well. White now wanted passage for his wife as well as himself, suitable lodgings in Brazil for them both, a medical plan, and the establishment of an account upon which he could draw for provisions for the journey. Amazingly, he appears to have got his way in most of his new demands, for the Brazilian mint was now ready to leave England, and his accompanying of it was regarded as essential. White's position was established in late August 1811, and he then hurried to London on the heels of the machinery.

Work on the latter had begun well before any agreement had been signed, and we can trace parts of it back to the early autumn of 1809. A convention of 16 June 1810 formalized matters, and it essentially followed the pattern of Matthew Robinson Boulton's initial proposal of October 1809. A ten-horse steam engine (to be sent with two spare boilers and duplicates of those parts most liable to wear out) would form the heart of the new Brazilian mint. Connecting machinery to supply power from the engine to the blanking and coining apparatus would also be remitted: this would have centred on a series of vacuum pumps, devised by Soho in 1798 and employed in all of its subsequent mints at home and abroad. The connecting mechanism allowed the machinery to be operated in a line, encouraging the progressive arrangement of the manufacturing process.

The moneying apparatus would consist of four coining and six cutting out presses, a pair of milling machines (to upset or mark the edges of the coins), and two shaking machines (to polish the planchets before they were struck). Annealing furnaces would be supplied, as would two turning lathes, all items essential for the making of dies. Punches and models would be included for the same purpose. Duplicate parts of all of the more delicate machinery rounded off the list. Everything would be finished and made ready for shipment to Brazil within twelve months, as would all necessary general and detailed drawings of the mint buildings and their machinery arrangements. And Boulton pledged his best efforts to procure likely Soho workmen to accompany the mint to Brazil.

In return for his wares and good offices, he would receive the sum of £8,550, payable upon shipment by bills of exchange. He might expect to receive half of his money in bills at two months' sight, and half at four.

It proved easier executing the terms of the agreement than enforcing them. As we have seen, the Soho workman chosen to accompany the mint to Brazil had successfully struck for higher wages, temporarily casting the remainder of the agreement into doubt when he did so. But more serious difficulties arose on the Portuguese side.

The Brazilian mint machinery and its engine, all sixty-six tons of it, had been completed by early May 1811, well ahead of schedule; Boulton naturally expected that it could soon be sent to London (thereby relinquishing the precious space it was currently taking up at Soho Foundry). His interest in moving the machinery went beyond the question of a tidy warehouse, for his agreement with the Portuguese said that he could not be paid until their mint had departed Soho and had been safely deposited at the London Docks, bound for Rio. But a letter of inquiry of 15 May 1811 met at first with procrastination and then with a response which cast the entire project into doubt. For Souza Couttinho now informed him that Soho's tardy delivery of plans for the mint would greatly delay the proceedings. Prior to anything else, Gaspar Marques – unaccompanied – must carry the drawings of the machinery and the mint buildings to Brazil. There they must be studied and approved *before* the mint could sail! Until such approval was obtained, the new mint must stay where it was, at Soho.

This request was reasonable at first glance – after all, one could hardly erect a mint in an open space, and one could hardly construct a suitable building for it without detailed plans. But the timing of the request was devastating: if it were all that important, why hadn't somebody said something earlier? And what did Souza Couttinho expect Boulton to do with one or more disgruntled Soho workmen, who had already been left dangling for nearly a year, wondering when or whether they would ever be going to work in the tropics?

All of this found expression in an angry letter which Boulton addressed to the Portuguese Ambassador on 3 June. Any delay in preparation of plans for the mint was the fault of the Portuguese, who had not provided Soho with any concrete ideas about its proposed site until very late in the game. As for the British workmen, it was essential that they go out with Marques as soon as possible, for they would be greatly needed even during preliminary phases of the construction. Moreover, their patience was wearing very thin, they were likely to abandon the enterprise if additional delay took place, and Boulton was unlikely to find others as qualified. Nor was he likely to expend much effort looking for them. Boulton demanded payment for his mint now, since he felt he had done everything required by his part of the agreement. And if the Portuguese still wished to delay the shipment of their machinery, he would be happy to comply with their request, meanwhile charging them rent for its storage. Such was Boulton's reply on the higher level; on the lower, he sent a note to Messrs. Lucena and De Paiva that same day, informing them of Souza Couttinho's request and his response – with another demand for payment for the mint. It was obvious that he was prepared to be most persistent, had no intention of giving way or backing off. And behind his polite words loomed the possibility of a suit to obtain what was owed him, such as was already being considered in conjunction with the Danish mint.

This was a possibility worthy of reflection. While the Portuguese Government could hardly be found liable for non-payment, it was distinctly possible that two Portuguese businessmen with long-established ties in London could be so found in British courts. And so Lucena and De Paiva gave way, as did Souza Couttinho, who was hiding behind them. The mint would be shipped rather than retained at Soho. And its builder would get paid sooner rather than later.

The Portuguese yielded early in July 1811. Lucena and De Paiva now instructed Boulton to begin sending the apparatus to London, and he in turn divided it into two large groups. The first, labelled 'ZK', consisted of the steam engine and its related parts, whose combined weight amounted to over twenty-two tons. This consignment was packed into eighty-six crates and sent off to London by canal boat slightly ahead of the coining machinery. This second consignment, weighing nearly forty-four tons, was marked 'BM' (for Brazil Mint), and it was crammed into 138 boxes and crates and sent on its way. The entire lot reached London by the end of the month – although there was a minor panic when it was feared that two boxes of machinery had been lost somewhere between Soho and the London Docks. The two were eventually accounted for by an embarrassed captain of the vessel for Brazil (who had miscounted the packages as they came aboard), but the misunderstanding held up any prospect for Boulton's payment until a suspicious Senhor Lucena personally checked each item in the master's receipt against its counterpart on the original invoice. He and his partner then demanded a written guarantee that all machinery and plans had been supplied and that all conceivable instruction had been given to Gaspar Marques – culminating in the solemn pledge to make good on anything left undone, unshipped, or untaught. This Boulton refused: it now appeared that Lucena and De Paiva might be replaced by other intermediaries, and if this were to happen before payment for the mint had been secured, it might be long indeed in coming. So Boulton continued to press for payment now, and the obdurate merchants finally gave way, accepting his drafts upon them. This took place at the end of September 1811.

Events finally seemed to be moving ahead in a satisfactory fashion. Soho had its space back, Boulton his money, Thomas White his favourable deal with the Portuguese. He and their mint were soon en route to Brazil. And Gaspar Marques had already set out for the same destination, accompanied by the plans: here, at least, the Chevalier and his representatives had got their way. Marques left England about the middle of August, well before the final disputes over Thomas White and payment for the mint had been worked out. But it was deemed necessary for him to leave early, for he must make the crucial arrangements necessary for beginning construction on a building for the machinery, regardless of when it was paid for or who set it up. After an uneventful voyage of fifty-seven days, Marques appeared at Rio de Janeiro (16 October 1811). He only reported his arrival to Boulton early the following February, citing the press of business. And the business was going very badly indeed.

Matthew Robinson Boulton had learned a lesson from his father's experience with the St Petersburg mint: never rely completely on a foreign guarantee that a building suitable for your machinery already exists. You may find that it is not strong enough for your purposes. You will then have to pull it down, and you and your people may waste months or even years in replacing it. It will be far better to start from scratch, to include a new edifice, built along your lines, in your plans. The experience of his father before him, the younger Boulton had drawn up such plans for a new building for the Rio mint.

And so Gaspar Marques arrived at the capital, blueprints in hand – and immediately ran foul of the authorities, who had already chosen an extant structure to house the new mint. The leader of this oppositionist group was the Count of Aguiar, one of the transplanted noblemen who had come over with the Prince Regent some four years previously. He was to be a thorn in Marques' – and Boulton's – side from that point onward.

There was nothing inherently wrong in using a building already in place instead of one that was not. Both Boultons would have agreed that, providing the edifice were strong, correctly laid out, and appropriately situated, their machinery might indeed find employment there. (The Danes had presented them with just such a site back in 1805, and they had installed their machinery in it with satisfactory results.) So new wine could be put in old bottles.

But not *this* bottle. The building Aguiar and his confederates had selected was ill-suited to the purpose, for half of it must be demolished before the machinery could be made to fit within its walls. Nor was this all: water stood some four inches deep on the structure's stone floor, 'as it is in all part of this City'. The problems of size or layout were one matter, but that standing water was another: were personnel to be provided with waders upon their employment at the new mint?

Marques said that the proposed site simply would not do, whereupon a second was offered. This one was no better: an abandoned church, it had too little available water rather than too much.

By now, official interest in the new Boulton mint was on the wane. A debate sprang up on whether it would be better to erect a new building (which was what Soho had assumed had already been agreed upon) or simply drop the whole project. The local champion of coining reform was the elderly Count de Linhares, who did what he could but whose death in January 1812 damaged the cause of innovation. But the Court finally agreed to erect a new structure, and by the beginning of February an architect had been selected for the purpose. However, he had demanded an enormous sum for his services, far more than the state was willing to pay.[3] An impasse had been reached. Yet Marques was guardedly optimistic: perhaps when Thomas White and the mint arrived, the local officials would be emboldened to pursue the project.

The engineer must have written his letter over a protracted period, for between this account and the time the letter containing it was posted, an incident occurred which changed everything, and which Marques mentioned by way of a laconic aside:

> P.S., the ship his [is] lost near Pará, having save all the Crew & sume part of the Cargo.[4]

It has proven impossible to pinpoint the exact site of the wreck: the person most intimately concerned with the event, Thomas White, said it had taken place at 'Cape Dillon',[5] but no such name appears on any current map of Brazil. Based on shipping routes and on the eventual course of events, I would guess that the event took place off Cabo Maguarinho, at the mouth of the Pará River.

Marques proved a desultory correspondent. Having put Matthew Robinson Boulton on tenterhooks, he proceeded to leave him there for the better part of a year. Not until December 1812 did he bother to tell the latter that matters were not as bad as originally supposed. The mint equipment was actually safe and sound, having been transported from the wreck site to Paraíba, near Pernambuco, the present-day João Pessoa. While Marques did not explain how the equipment got carried all the way from the mouth of the Pará to João Pessoa, a distance of a thousand miles, we can only conclude that Thomas White somehow brought it there himself.

This engineer was in an unenviable position. He was currently stranded at Pernambuco, stuck there until the Portuguese Government could decide what to do about him and about his mint. And he was meanwhile receiving no salary and was by now in desperate circumstances.

There was an excellent reason for official delay, although neither Marques, nor Boulton, nor probably even White, was yet aware of it. When news of the wreck reached Rio de Janeiro at the beginning of February 1812, the Portuguese Government, like Marques, had been informed that at least some of the machinery had been lost. It chose to enter an insurance claim with the London underwriters as if *all* of it had been lost, and it had accordingly received payment of seventy per cent of the assessed value of the cargo. It would have to repay these monies were the apparatus to be found in good order. And so White was ordered to remain in hiding, along with his charge, while nervous bureaucrats debated their plan of action, and his fate.

Not that Marques' position was all that enviable: having been entrusted with the superintending of the building of a mint, he would lose his post if no mint could be built. His most important champion, Linhares, had died a few days before the wreck had been reported – driven mad, said Marques, by the constant intrigues at the Court. Linhares' successor Galvim would be far less sympathetic to the plan and to Marques' role in it. In addition, there had been an earlier attempt by the Interior Ministry to reform Brazilian coinage. This scheme, which had involved the erection of a new building to house superfluous Lisbon coining machinery of the traditional type (to be moved by cattle in this latest translation), had not come up to expectations, 'so at present we have no Money. but we have two Mints'.[6]

Attempting to make headway against bureaucratic intransigence, Marques had spent months shuttling between the various offices of the transatlantic Portuguese Government, telling anybody who would listen about the advantages of the Boulton product – just as Matthew Boulton had had to do with another administration in another country so many years before. In time, the Portuguese engineer had managed to patch together an agreement with Linhares, agreeing to install the mint in any building selected for the purpose, providing only that it had proximity to running water. But Linhares had died, and Galvim had been less sympathetic to the idea, even as amended by the desperate Marques. And the latter had had his ground completely cut from under him on 7 February 1812, when an affable Galvim had told him about the wreck: no mint to set up, no job setting it up. Marques had been advised to look for other employment, and we soon find him writing to his friend Boulton, offering to represent Soho in Brazil, not as a constructor of mints but as a salesman of steam engines.

Late in January 1813, the final element in the Brazilian farce made its appearance. Thomas White showed up in Rio de Janeiro, along with most of the machinery which had been entrusted to him.

Apparently disgusted with bureaucratic delay, he had decided to take matters into his own hands. If the Portuguese Government were incapable of taking over Boulton's mint at Pernambuco, White would facilitate matters by securing the necessary means to carry it all the way from there to Rio de Janeiro. And so he did, sailing and dragging the apparatus nearly two thousand miles this time, triumphantly appearing at the gates of the capital like a water-logged phoenix, his machinery in tow.

He was the last person the venal authorities expected or desired to see. They had no intention of repaying the insurance money; yet here stood White, with his accursed mint, visual testimony that all had *not* been lost. What to do?

The answer was obvious – at least to the bureaucrats. Marques had been pestering them with concerns about the well-being of his friend, was now asking that White be allowed to return freely to England, taking along the wages he had been promised. And Marques wanted out too: he was tired of intrigue, and he had been sick during most of his stay in the tropics. That being the case, why not let White and Marques have their wish, get them away from Brazil, and then sequester their machinery, keeping it safe from the prying eyes of claims agents?

And this was done. Thomas White was paid off and sent home, arriving back at Soho in mid-July 1813. He shortly drew up a list of materials salvaged after the wreck of the previous year, and the extent of the Portuguese fraud now became known, at least to Matthew Robinson Boulton. For White had managed to save nearly everything: the Portuguese could have had their mint, had they wanted it.[7]

Gaspar Marques thought so too, at least at first. He had stayed on after White's departure, in part to check on the condition of the mint apparatus, which had been lodged in the Rio de Janeiro custom-house. He was finally granted entrance to the building in September 1814 (that is, more than a year after White's departure and nearly two years after the machinery had arrived at Rio). He was appalled at what time and neglect had wrought.

Everything was corroded. Some of the parts were broken, others had been stolen. What had certainly been a functioning mint when it had left England, and a potentially functioning mint when it had arrived at Rio, was now an inert mass of rusting iron and brass. Marques requested and secured official permission to take the machinery into his own safe keeping, for he wished to clean it and perhaps even render it operable, were that in his power. But he appears to have given up on the idea, and we do not know his final fate or that of the mint.

But we can at least hazard an educated guess about the latter: in 1833, Brazil's coinage began taking an abrupt turn for the better. Starting with gold, soon extending to silver and then to copper, coins were now struck in a collar in the precise way we associate with Boulton, and with steam. A revolution was taking place: it seems reasonable to surmise that at least some of the earlier, initially rejected Soho machinery figured as a participant in the event.

There is a curious footnote to the fiasco of Soho's Brazilian mint. In September 1814, just as the firm was receiving the last of Gaspar Marques' depressing letters from Rio, a Boulton agent received a visit from a Spanish nobleman. The Marquis de Apertado informed John Mosley that Spain was interested in sending one of Boulton's mints to New Spain, presumably to Mexico City. Mosley passed on the information to Zack Walker, who wrote his cousin with the news near the end of the month. Boulton never seems to have responded, and the Marquis broke off contact. We hear no more of a mint for the Viceroyalty of New Spain.

But the episode is significant from two perspectives. First, while leading to nothing directly, it was another of Soho's early contacts with Mexico, connections which would eventually involve it with no fewer than five mints over twenty-five years. And second, the Portuguese Government's London representatives introduced De Apertado to John Mosley. While these representatives are unnamed, it seems reasonable to suppose that they included one or more of three men we have already met – John Charles Lucena, Manoel Antonio de Paiva, and the Chevalier de Souza Couttinho. Were these gentlemen feeling a trifle guilty over the shabby treatment afforded to the Boulton mint and Thomas White, and were they attempting to make amends by steering another customer in Soho's direction, one more willing and capable of taking advantage of its products and people than the Portuguese in Brazil?

It is of interest to reflect that Soho's dealings with the two largest nations in the Western Hemisphere followed very similar paths. In each case, the Boultons began with visionary, expansive ideas of fundamental change in the nature of the moneying process, ideas which had to be dramatically cut back in the face of contemporary reality. In the United States, ambitious plans to create an American coinage or an American mint eventually yielded place to a humbler but still-profitable occupation, the supplying of copper planchets for cents and half-cents to the Philadelphia Mint. And exactly the same sequence of events took place in Brazil – where, as in the United States, the copper blanks would be turned into coins by the traditional processes which Soho was attempting to supplant. But unlike the United States experience, which continued to involve direct contact with high officials at the Philadelphia Mint, Soho's dealings with the Portuguese colony and new nation of Brazil were indirect, carried on through British intermediaries.

Through most of the Brazilian planchet trade, these would be members of a London firm called May & Lukin. The first indication we have that anything was under consideration is a brief document labelled 'Estimated Prices & Copper-Blanks. For Messrs: Maye & Lukin', dating from June 1816. This is merely a set of columns, but it suggests that Soho was thinking about the exportation of planchets to Brazil about a year before it actually began.[8]

Thought about such a commerce would have been logical at this point: Boulton, Watt was currently seeing its United States position under attack by a rival Birmingham firm called Belles & Harrold, and an opening door in South America might go far to compensate for a closing one in the north.

Between March 1817 and late 1820, May & Lukin purchased nearly £30,000 worth of copper blanks from Boulton, Watt & Company. The first shipment set the tone for them all. A Soho entry for 3 March 1817 notes that fifty-five casks of copper blanks had been sent from the mint on 25 February, making their way to Liverpool on one of Worthington & Company's canal-boats. They were then transhipped by Soho's Liverpool agents, Thomas and William Earle & Company, to the *Ann*, whose master was John Ware. This vessel left the Mersey on 3 March 1817, bound for Rio de Janeiro. For its services, Boulton, Watt charged £1,241.16.6.

The planchets the *Ann* carried were of two weights, thirty-two to the pound and eighty-one and one-half to the pound. This would give them theoretical weights of 14.19 and 5.57 grams. From the second shipment onward, they were joined by pieces of a third, smaller size, cut out at 107 to the pound, for a theoretical weight of 4.24 grams. These dry figures belie the drama of the sheer numbers of planchets sent out: between March 1817 and September 1820, Soho produced and shipped over thirty-nine million copper planchets to Brazil! The majority, nearly twenty-two million, were of the medium size. Large-size planchets came next, over nine million. The smallest size accounted for nearly eight million more. We can put this figure in perspective by noting that it represents nearly four-fifths of the figure for the entire forty-year planchet exportation to the United States, accomplished in just three and one-half years. Boulton, Watt had compensated for its partial loss of the American trade with a vengeance.

The firm's prompt delivery of goods on favourable terms seems to have emboldened May & Lukin, and the government it represented, to a much more ambitious project. Not only would Soho be asked to make copper planchets; it might also be asked to make silver ones, *and strike both into coins for export to Brazil.*

That May & Lukin would make such a proposal is the best evidence we have of the sorry state of Brazilian coinage at that time. It is unfortunate that the 1811 Boulton mint had been allowed to deteriorate, because it would have put an end to the crude, inferior coinage which was currently flooding the country.

This coinage emanated from mints in two cities, Rio and Bahia, from facilities which had scarcely changed since the introduction of milled coinage to the colony in the late seventeenth century. Bad presses made bad coins. In the case of copper, official issues were so crude that they were forged all over Brazil – and abroad as well, in Britain and the United States. But the copper coins had little value, and no one was hurt all that much by the frequent appearance of counterfeit coppers, whether emanating from Brazil, Birmingham, or Belleville, New Jersey.

But silver coin was more important. It will be recalled that the restriking of Spanish-American Pieces of Eight into their Brazilian equivalents had been one of the earliest projects discussed by Matthew Robinson Boulton and the Portuguese Government. The mint Boulton sent had not been called into such service, but the recoinage had proceeded nonetheless, with distinctly mediocre results: the old Brazilian presses were simply not up to the task of restriking something as large as a Spanish dollar.

In pre-industrial moneying, the easiest part of a coin to strike was its centre, the most difficult its periphery, because striking power diminished as it moved from the centre outward. A restraining collar would have helped channel the metal into the dies' outer areas, but collars were rarely employed for coinage struck on the old, manual presses. There was thus a tendency for the central area of such coins to be more sharply struck than the area along its circumferences.

In the case of money struck on ordinary planchets, this would pose no particular problem, and the legends of the pieces would probably be legible enough. But in the case of coins struck on other coins, pieces *which already had legends around their peripheries*, it was perfectly possible to strike a coin which was literally indecipherable. This is what faced the Portuguese authorities in Brazil by 1820, and this is probably the reason for May & Lukin's exciting new proposal to Boulton, Watt & Company in the middle of that year.

Talks about a Soho coinage for Brazil occupied most of the second half of 1820. As they progressed, it became clear that Soho would not be restriking Spanish dollars; rather, it was expected that silver would be shipped to Birmingham in ingot form. The ingots would already contain the correct proportion of copper for the finished coinage (slightly less than ten per cent, relative to silver). Thus received, it should be possible to strike money from it, wrap the pieces in paper rouleaus, pack the rouleaus in wooden casks, and send the whole to Rio de Janeiro for between one shilling and one shilling and twopence per troy pound – that is, for about a penny per coin. If Boulton had to pay for shipment of the silver to Soho, a further cost of £5 per ton would be incurred. So much for precious-metal coinage. If it were desired to strike Brazilian copper at Soho, this too could be done, for a fee ranging from £15 to £18 per ton over and above the ordinary charges for planchets, depending upon the size of the coin.

Soho prepared models of what it had in mind, sending them to John May in mid-December 1820, accompanied by a letter from Zack Walker describing what May was receiving. The models were submitted in three designs. The first, a pattern for a copper ten-reis copper coin, was probably engraved by a young artist named as Wells,[9] who is otherwise unmentioned in the Matthew Boulton Papers. Walker's verbal description of this piece matches a trial now in the British Museum, illustrated with its permission. Its designs were intended to give May and his clients a general idea as to what Brazilian coinage might look like, were it to be entrusted to the Soho Mint.

The second pattern was a silver coin:

> The Design of the Obverse is emblematic of the advantages of Union in States as exemplified by the trite fable of the bundle of sticks, whilst the Reverse is a copy from a Die which was once prepared for the English Bank-Dollar instead of the one since adopted, & which may be considered a fair sample of the appearance which would be given to any Silver coin struck at Soho.[10]

The only coin which fits this description is a piece more generally listed under Great Britain, a concoction featuring a Hercules figure left over from the Monneron five-sols coinage of 1792 and the British arms from a Küchler pattern dollar of 1798; it, too, was intended to give an idea of the quality of the Soho coinage rather than serve as a precise design proposal.

The second of the two silver patterns was a close copy of the Portuguese dollar – presumably one of the proofs left over from the coinage deliberations of 1808–9, since no such piece with an 1820 date has come to light. All three patterns left Soho on 14 December 1820 – and nothing more was ever heard about a Brazilian coinage at Soho. The problem lay not with the patterns' designs, nor with their finish, nor indeed with Boulton, Watt itself. Rather, it lay with the British intermediary between Boulton and Brazil, May & Lukin.

By late 1820, that firm was encountering financial difficulties. It had ordered another batch of planchets from Soho earlier that autumn; when informed that they were ready for shipment, it had requested Soho to keep them for the time being. Boulton thought little about the request at first: May

Two patterns concocted for the delectation of the Portuguese, 1820. (Courtesy Birmingham Museums and Art Gallery)

& Lukin was among his most reliable customers. But it eventually became apparent that the company did not wish the planchets shipped because it could not pay for them: there ensued a correspondence of increasing acrimony between Matthew Robinson Boulton and John May which lasted through 1821 and into 1822. With an initial diffidence which deepened to a nasty persistence, Boulton, Watt attempted every trick it knew to persuade John May to pay up; he finally agreed to do so in March 1822, after learning that Soho had simply sent the planchets on to Brazil without waiting for his approval. Boulton received his fee, plus interest for the time the hundred casks of unwanted cargo had been sitting in his warehouse. A year later, John May ordered another seventeen and one-half tons of planchets, and Matthew Robinson Boulton readily agreed to supply them. Business was business.

But this final order was held up for two months by the prospects of a war between Great Britain and the Holy Alliance, that congeries of reactionary powers which was bent on recovering insurgent Spanish America on behalf of the appalling Ferdinand VII. British pressure on the members of the clique, particularly on the French, succeeded in putting an end to the project, but the price of many commodities ascended during the war scare, including that of copper. Boulton was approached about the planchets in mid-February 1823, but he was uncertain about procuring copper on reasonable terms until early April. By then, the war panic had dissipated and the work could proceed. John May's final order, some 1,254,400 planchets made at thirty-two to the pound, left Soho on the fifteenth of May and were eventually shipped to Rio on the *Ann*, the same vessel which had figured in the beginning of the trade back in 1817.

There would be one last order and shipment of copper planchets, but May & Lukin would not be involved in it. A merchant named Samuel Winter placed an order for ten thousand pounds of copper planchets sometime near the end of 1823. Winter does not appear as a correspondent in the Matthew Boulton Papers, nor can we even be sure that the planchets he ordered were intended for Brazil. But blanks corresponding to two of the same odd series of weights – thirty-two and eighty-one and one-half pieces per pound – were stipulated and prepared, and since no other client of the day wanted blanks of comparable weights, we are, I think, on firm ground in assuming that their destination was Brazil. They left Soho on 28 January 1824, some 160,000 pieces of the larger size and 407,500 of the smaller, presumably meant to be turned into coins of the new, independent Empire of Brazil.

But which coins? Put another way, *what were all these planchets for?* This question is not as frivolous as it seems. Colony and empire, Brazil struck copper coinage in denominations of ten, twenty, thirty-seven and one-half, forty, seventy-five, and eighty reis. Unfortunately, in terms of actual observed weights, none of these issues precisely corresponds to what Soho was sending to Brazil.

At thirty-two pieces per pound, each of the firm's largest planchets ought to weigh 14.19 grams – at least, if we are speaking in terms of the English pound[11]. Each of its medium planchets, at eighty-one and one-half pieces per pound, should weigh 5.57 grams. And each of the small planchets, at 107 to the pound, should weigh 4.24 grams. These weights roughly correspond to actual coins of forty, twenty, and ten reis, but a real emphasis must be put on that qualifying adjective: coins of those three denominations in the collection of the Smithsonian Institution, Washington, and the American Numismatic Society, New York, vary greatly in weight.

For example, Smithsonian forty-reis pieces do tend to cluster around 14.2 grams, but they range from a low of 8.16 to a high of 23.13! Twenty-reis pieces at the Smithsonian average 5.3 grams but vary from a low of 3.93 to a high of 5.97. And ten-reis coins do cluster at 4.15 grams, but individual specimens range from 3.94 to 4.22 grams. Similar weight spreads exist for specimens at the American Numismatic Society.

How can we explain these anomalies? And if Boulton, Watt's planchets were not being used in Brazil to elaborate official coinage, why were they being sent there? The answer, I think, is that the planchets *were* being turned into forty-, twenty-, and ten-reis coins. But they were probably only being struck into money at a single mint; and even there, they very likely had two types of competitors.

I believe that Matthew Robinson Boulton's planchets were indeed being turned into coins, at Rio de Janeiro. But Brazil had another mint which struck the three denominations at this time – Bahia, which persistently produced lightweight coinage. For example, while Boulton's planchets for ten-reis coins weighed around 4.2 grams, the American Numismatic Society has an extensive run of Bahian coppers which averages between 2.5 and 2.9 grams – and which is therefore unlikely to have been struck on Soho blanks.[12] We should probably take the record of shipments to Rio de Janeiro literally: that was where Mr Boulton's planchets would be made into coins. If we do so, we find a much closer correlation between planchet weights and actual coins.

But the fit is still not perfect, and this may be explained by two types of competitor. One may have been legitimate: the Brazilians could have been getting their planchets from several sources at once, with a corresponding confusion and variation in quality and weight. But the second was definitely *il*legitimate: the simple designs on Brazilian coppers offered tempting targets for counterfeiters, as did the thinness of the real coins. Virtually *anybody* could make a plausible Brazilian ten-, twenty-, or forty-reis piece, and there can be no doubt that many forgers did so, both at home and abroad. In the process, the criminal would have probably struck his products at a lighter weight than their targets: and here may be another explanation for the wild gyrations between theoretical and observed weights on Brazilian copper coinage.

I believe there can be no doubt that Boulton, Watt & Company was a major contributor on the lower end of late Portuguese colonial and early independent Brazilian coinage; just as with the humble United States copper cent and half-cent, Soho played a real if overlooked part in the creation of Western Hemispheric numismatics. But just as with the firm's experience in North America, its successful role in South America was something of a disappointment, at least in comparison to its aspirations. And the gap between aim and grasp was even more frustrating in the south than it was in the north.

For one can scarcely imagine a worse course of events than that which actually took place. A firm receives official sanction to create a mint for the largest colony in South America. This mint must be on the leading edge of technology – welcome news to the firm in question, which has always fought for this very goal. It creates the machinery, using the finest technology in the world. Pledged to help find and train people to erect and operate the new mint, it does so. But its client resists paying for its product and refuses to follow its recommendations as to personnel. At length, the firm does prevail: payment is rendered, a technocrat is agreed upon. Mint and man sail for the New World.

… And then everything unravels. The product over which it has taken such pains, injected so much of itself, is lost at sea. When it is recovered, it is received with a singular lack of enthusiasm by those who were initially so keen to have it. It is allowed to sit idle and decay. The firm's expert (who had single-handedly rescued its wares from oblivion) receives no thanks but is ingloriously cashiered and sent packing. And its customer, in which the firm had reposed such high hopes, announces that it, and the colony it rules, have decided to turn their backs on the firm, and by extension on the modern era.

Such was the course of events: it is difficult to view Soho's Brazilian experience as anything other than a total failure, probably the worst it ever suffered.

We might be tempted to impute Boulton, Watt's troubles to the clash of advanced European ideas with a backward American environment. Such an attribution is true, but it is not the complete story. For Soho had two adversaries rather than one. To be sure, the first was the primitive American environment, where no one had ever seen steam technology and was likely to view it with suspicion. We see this hostile atmosphere at work in another American nation (Mexico) – but in a European one as well (Russia). The latter instance should inform us that there is nothing distinctly 'American' about a rejection of new technology, that resistance to the novel is not conditioned by place alone, but by time as well – in the form of an area's general state of technological development when a new methodology becomes available.

Soho's Russian experience also affords us a clue as to the nature of the second Brazilian adversary. This enemy, and not the American environment, would determine that the mint for Brazil, once lost and later found, would nonetheless be allowed to rust in inactivity. This enemy was not native to the New World, but was one of the crowning governmental achievements of the Old. This enemy was the time-serving bureaucrat, and his weapon was a species of inertia. The heroic Thomas White might be able to snatch a mint from the grip of the sea; he might be able single-handedly to transport it for thousands of miles; but he could not overcome the government functionary, who knew the rules.

Twenty years later, a modern mint would at last be established in Brazil. As I mentioned, there is at least a possibility that some of Soho's machinery came into service then, vindication of Thomas White and the firm he served. And we may draw a final lesson from the climate wherein this modern mint struck its coins.

That atmosphere had evolved in the two decades since Boulton, Watt had made its abortive attempt to reform the process of moneying in South America. Then, steam engines were a rarity, so much so that they excited hostility. Now, they were relatively common, their reception much more enthusiastic than before. And the idea of the modern, whose roots were exotic and surface-deep in 1813, was cautiously probing downward into the soil of Brazilian official and popular consciousness by 1833. When a steam-powered mint began striking its first coins in the latter year, no one viewed it as a threat, but as a desirable inevitability. No one attempted to sequester *this* mint, or to dispute the virtue of its products. In short, Brazil joined the ranks of industrial coiners at the precise moment she was ready to do so. There was a lesson here for Boulton, Watt & Company, and there is still a lesson here for us: every good intention in the world cannot guarantee the favourable reception of an idea whose time has not yet come.

SOURCES

Most of the raw material for the Brazil story will be found in MBP405, Brazil, Haiti, Argentine, USA and San Salvador mints. Soho's Portuguese planchet production for Lucena & Crawford is noted in MBP34, Mint Book, Day Book Mint, 1795–1798, while the firm's later planchet work for May & Lukin and Samuel Winter are recorded in detail in MBP61, Mint Book, Mint and Coinage Ledger, 1808–1819, MBP64, Mint Book, Day Book or Rough Coinage Journal, 1814–1819, and MBP68, Mint Book, Mint and Coinage Day Book, 1820–1834. But the memorandum of June 1816, the first suggestion that a trade in planchets might be in the offing, appears elsewhere (in MBP416, Soho Mint). Actual letters regarding these later dealings will be found in MBP65, Mint Book, Mint and Coinage Letter Book, 1820–1823, and MBP360, Walker, Z., jr. Walker was frequently employed in Boulton, Watt's dealings with John Charles Lucena, Manoel Antonio de Paiva, and the Chevalier de Souza Couttinho; his correspondence detailing these activities forms part of the contents of MBP360. For details on the weight, cost, and time of shipment of the various packages making up the Rio de Janeiro mint, consult BRL, MBP60, Mint Book, Mint Day Book, 1808–1813.

Treatment of larger contemporary events, the backdrop against which the mint story was played out, may be found in any decent history of early Brazil. I particularly recommend Caio Prado, Jr., *Formação do Brasil Contemporáneo* (7th edition, translated and published as *The Colonial Background of Modern Brazil*, 1967), and C. H. Haring, *Empire in Brazil: A New World Experiment with Monarchy* (1958). And readers should be aware of F. F. Gilboy's article 'Misadventures of a Mint – Boulton, Watt & Co. and the "Mint for the Brazils"', which appeared in the *British Numismatic Journal* in 1990 (vol. 60, pp. 113–20). Gilboy utilized many of the same materials in the Boulton papers as have I, and he presents a viewpoint differing slightly from my own.

NOTES

1 MBP248, Letter Box P1: Manoel Antonio de Paiva to 'Mess*rs* Boulton & Watt', 5 July 1808.
2 MBP405, Brazil, Haiti, Argentine, USA and San Salvador Mints: Matthew Robinson Boulton to John Charles Lucena and Manoel Antonio de Paiva, 23 February 1811.
3 The architect was demanding two hundred thousand *cruzados*, which at current exchange rates worked out to something over £25,000, a sum three times the cost of the actual machinery!
4 MBP405, Gaspar Marques to Matthew Robinson Boulton, 5 February 1812. Marques' grasp of the English language is fully comparable with mine of the Portuguese.
5 MBP405, 'At Cape Dillon Parts of Michenery Belonging to the Mint'. This list is in White's hand, and it is dated 17 July 1813. Unfortunately, no precise date is given for the actual wreck, here or elsewhere in the Boulton Papers. But it likely took place sometime during January 1812.

6   MBP405, Marques to Boulton, 15 February 1813. Aguiar had been entrusted with this earlier project, which might explain his opposition to the Boulton mint.

7   Thomas White resumed his duties at Soho, but his experiences in Brazil may have unhinged him. In September 1815, he threw himself in the Severn near Tewkesbury and drowned (MBP360, Walker, Z., jr: Zacchaeus Walker, Jr. to Matthew Robinson Boulton, 18 September 1815).

8   The correct spelling of the senior partner's name was May, not Maye. The document will be found in MBP416, Soho Mint box.

9   This is the name given in Walker's letter to Matthew Robinson Boulton of 27 July 1820. Is it possible that Walker was referring to Thomas *Wells* Ingram? According to Forrer (*Biographical Dictionary of Medallists*, Vol. 3, p. 26), Ingram began his career at Soho around 1820. If he were new to the mint, Walker might well have mistaken his name. And we may be seeing a very early work by a medallist who would later become well-known.

10 MBP405, Zacchaeus Walker, Jr. to John May, 14 December 1820.

11 Alain J. Costilhes of Sao Paulo reminds me (letter, 12 April 1993) that the Portuguese and Brazilian pound varied slightly from the English one – 459 versus 454 grams. And according to Kurt Prober, *Catálogo das Moedas Brasileiras* (2nd edition, 1966, p. 16), the official weights of the forty, twenty, and ten reis pieces were 14.34, 7.17, and 3.58 grams respectively, based on that slightly heavier pound. If we divide our pound of copper into coins weighing 14.34 grams each, we could indeed get thirty-two forty-reis pieces; but we could also obtain sixty-four twenties or 128 tens, numbers dramatically different from the stipulated planchet weights (of 81–2/3 and 107 pieces per pound). If we possessed the initial 1816 correspondence between May & Lukin and Boulton, Watt & Company, we might be able to ascertain which pound was being used as a standard for planchet weight, the British or the Portuguese. But in the absence of such correspondence, I must opt for the former. In any case, the identity of the pound does nothing to explain the wide spread of weights seen in Brazilian copper coinage.

12 Of the fifteen Smithsonian forty-reis pieces whose average gave me my figure of 14.2 grams, two come from Bahia, weighing 10.98 and 11.99 grams respectively. The remaining thirteen coins are all from Rio, and their average weight amounts to 14.62 grams – significantly heavier than they should be regardless of whose pound was being used. I would be the last to make a sweeping generalization on the basis of two lightweight coins, however, especially in light of the fact that the two *lightest* coins of the entire group (at 8.16 and 8.90 grams) both bear the 'R' mint mark of Rio de Janeiro. While they indeed appear to be counterfeits, I cannot be certain of this imputation.

CHAPTER 6

India

There is an old saying that trade follows the flag. Applying this adage to Soho's activities in British India, one might expect that the firm's business there would proceed more smoothly than it did in sovereign states, places where Britannia's writ might or might not run. To some degree, the course of events at Calcutta and Bombay bears out this expectation.

Given the size of the two projects, the building of Indian mints was the easiest of Boulton, Watt & Company's large undertakings – at least, from the point of view of the principals of that firm, Matthew Robinson Boulton and James Watt. Jr. There was no real need to convince customers of the virtues and viability of the new minting technology – unlike the cases of St Petersburg and the Royal Mint. There was a fairly brief period between the preparation of a mint and its actual coming into production – at least, in comparison with the cases of St Petersburg and Copenhagen.

Moreover, the new Calcutta and Bombay mints first turned their attentions to the very coinage which Soho deemed most important – copper. This stood in contrast to events in Russia – and on Tower Hill, where the new Royal Mint would strike no British copper for nearly a dozen years after its opening. All in all, the owners of Soho could look upon their Indian projects, compare them with those undertaken elsewhere, and congratulate themselves – except for an additional distinction between their experience here and elsewhere. Success in India may have been easier to obtain, but it only came at the cost of human life.

While Boulton, Watt & Company may have been extraordinarily lucky in other instances, the fact remains that the firm lost precisely one individual (a smith named Joseph Griffiths, sent out to Culiacán in the early 1830s) in all of its non-Indian projects combined. In India, it and its subcontractors lost *seven*. And to this sorry roster could be added the name of the guiding spirit behind the Bombay mint, Major Hawkins. While most of the other men succumbed to disease, Hawkins simply worked himself to death, so intent was he on breathing life into Mr Boulton's mint.

Beyond human cost, there would be a second parallel between Mexico and India, one worth noting now for discussion later. That is, the men of Guanajuato found that some of Soho's products were not applicable to the conditions extant in an isolated Mexican mint. And so they began to modify them and the larger coining technology which they represented. The men of

Calcutta and Bombay would make the same discovery, react in the same fashion. And they too would leave their mark on the course of the industrialization of money.

All of the mints which the Boultons built came about as part of a progression, a reflection of the fact that the world was smaller then than it is now. Matthew Boulton sold items ranging from candlesticks to fancy buttons to members of the upper classes in Great Britain and elsewhere. As he did so, he was making contacts of potential use in other fields, because the man who bought his silver plate might very well occupy a high position on the Board of Trade, be a sitting Member of Parliament, be the owner of a business or a factory. In time, the member of the Board of Trade might advance Boulton's interests with the Government – and the busy merchant might need copper tokens prepared for the use of his customers. The interconnections of the high-born and the prosperous and their relationship with Matthew Boulton run like a broad thread through his story and the story of his firm. The thread is far less visible in the story of his son; but by then, it had accomplished its purpose.

So when we look at a mint built by Matthew Boulton or Matthew Robinson Boulton, we do well to investigate previous dealings between the principals. And what we tend to discover is the prior provision, to a satisfied customer, of something bearing no earthly relation to coinage. The happy purchaser might be in the position of helping Soho obtain a contract for coining machinery; more likely, there would be an intermediate phase, wherein excellence, friendship, and influence would yield a contract for coinage. This was how matters moved in Great Britain, how they moved in India. And in both cases, it would only be a slight exaggeration to suggest that the quality of coinage led directly to the sale of mints.

Soho's dealings with the Subcontinent and those lands attached to it were always channelled though 'The United Company of Merchants of England Trading to the East Indies' – better known as the East India Company, that hallowed public-and-private, high-minded and cheerfully corrupt organization set up in the reign of the first Elizabeth to trade with the East. By the time the Boultons dealt with it, it was growing sclerotic, increasingly becoming the despair of believers in rationality and progress; but the businessmen and lords who steered its course in London knew of opportunities in India, alerted Soho to them. Matthew Boulton had sold fancy goods to John Motteux and Robert Wissett; as related elsewhere, these two denizens of East India House would help Boulton get his first coinage contracts, and a good deal more besides.

The Boultons minted money for the East India Company on numerous occasions between 1786 and 1824; the story is told elsewhere. In time, one of Soho's offspring (and a translated Soho Mint itself) would be turned to for more coinage; but in the meantime, the East India Company's people in India and those in London were impressed with the quality of the Boulton product, especially as compared with what was being manufactured in India itself.

That coinage was crude, inconsistent, and easily forged. These qualities largely stemmed from the way in which it was produced; for the hammering method still held sway. Moreover, this hand-done coinage cost a good deal to produce, even in a land where human labour was poorly paid. As one of his arguments in favor of the adoption of a modern mint at Calcutta, Lieutenant William Nairn Forbes of the Bengal Engineers observed that

> the *loss* sustained from the imperfections of the [pre-industrial] Calcutta Mint amounted *in one year* to a sum which would *have built a new one* – That improved Apparatus would produce a *saving* to the Amount of *£45,000 Per Annum* ... [1]

This was one of the most trenchant arguments which could have been made. Matthew Boulton and the Garbetts had stressed the point in the 1780s and 1790s; Forbes and his counterpart at Bombay, Captain Hawkins, reiterated it some three decades later. If your cost per coin went down, but you kept the cost to the public unchanged, your profits from seigniorage would inevitably go up. Officials at East India House were thus attracted by the same sort of logic as their counterparts at the Anglo-Mexican Mint Association. The argument would hold good for India even if it would not for Mexico.

There was one final element in the East India Company's decision to adopt mechanized coining. The Subcontinent was gradually becoming more unified, trade between its component parts expanding. But there was no currency in universal use: instead, a bewildering series of gold, silver and copper coins, inherited from the earlier contributors to India's monetary history, made buying and selling between one place and another a challenge at best, a virtual impossibility at worst. In time, there must be a single, reliable, rational coinage; and the East India Company must provide it. The only way in which all the millions of new coins required could be quickly and reliably struck was by the application of the most modern processes to the task, married to the power of steam.

Because of earlier contacts and contracts, there was never any serious doubt that Boulton, Watt & Company would have a major role when it came time to industrialize the coinage of India. But the firm only achieved that position at the end of a lengthy process, carried on by fits and starts. We have an indication that the East India Company first turned its thoughts to simple screw presses – the very sorts of machines which Matthew Boulton was seeking to replace with his new, steam-powered ones. A request for manual screw presses went out in the late winter or early spring of 1796, Boulton's old acquaintance and Company functionary Robert Wissett acting as messenger. Nineteen machines were finished around June of that year, and they left Soho for London at the end of November. The East India Company was charged £746.15.6 for the package, including transportation and insurance.

Unfortunately, it is impossible to ascertain the purpose of these presses. I would like to assume that they were intended for the Calcutta mint (and it is a matter of record that they were designated for the Bengal Presidency). But were they constructed for moneying? At no place in the scant record are these machines referred to as *coining* presses; but on one occasion they are called *packing* presses, and on another, the screws which drove them are referred to as *packing* screws. I am unaware of any other East India Company project at the time requiring the services of screw presses of any type, and my examination of Calcutta coinage manufactured in the closing years of the eighteenth century suggests a modest technological improvement, consistent with the application of this type of machinery. I therefore believe that the presses sent out were indeed intended to improve the quality of coinage in British India. But were that their purpose, they evidently failed to satisfy the

Company's nabobs in India and England. For there would eventually be talk of another Boulton contribution, this one powered by steam and unquestionably intended for the making of coin.

Discussions along this line began early in 1808: the Company was interested in striking gold and silver coinage for circulation throughout its territories, requesting an estimate from Boulton, Watt of

> the cost of a Mint apparatus rolling mill Steam Engine &c capable of coining a Million Rupees weekly … a rough estimate I mean in round numbers is all that is required in the present stage of the business but to it sho*d* be added the probable expence of the persons necessary to be sent out with it from this country and in the latter consideration must be included that of two such mints being required and the persons who erect one at Calcutta first might then proceed to Madras to put up the other[.][2]

The man making the first contact was apparently Joseph Thompson, a senior official with the East India Company. Thompson was also interested in a Soho coinage for Bengal. Matthew Robinson Boulton was intrigued with both prospects – but he was also cautious: Thompson's superior in coinage matters was Soho's old friend Robert Wissett, and it would be unwise to alienate the latter in pursuit of a deal with the former. Wissett was made privy to both prospects and promptly expressed his concerns over the mint exportation idea. Might it not be wiser to keep Soho's special minting processes safely at home? While we cannot be certain, Wissett's doubts may have played a major part in what soon happened.

For the ambitious mint idea was progressively curtailed until it was abandoned altogether. By the beginning of February 1808, the idea of two mints had been rejected in favour of one, at Madras. And the size of that proposed establishment began shrinking. While the Company first wanted something the same size as the new Royal Mint, consisting of eight coining presses, it had lowered its requirements to five by the spring of 1809. This smaller establishment had also undergone a change of venue: reversing its earlier stand, the East India Company decided that its new mint should go into service in Bengal rather than Madras. And only if mechanization proved successful in the first place would an apparatus of the same size be sent out to the second.

Thus amended, plans and estimates went back and forth during the first part of 1809. The Boultons decided to subcontract the rolling mill (for such, powered by steam, would also be wanted in India) to the firm of John & George Rennie – specialists who were represented in most of Soho's foreign projects through the years. The Rennies would want about £12,000 for their part of the work, while Boulton, Watt & Company could supply the mint and all necessary steam engines for another £18,000. As spring approached, it appeared very likely that Soho would receive orders to export a mint to Bengal. It would indeed send one there – and also one to Bombay; but not for another fifteen years.

For everything began unravelling later that season. We can only speculate about the reasons, for the Matthew Boulton Papers are silent. But we know that orders for a large copper coinage for Bengal were suddenly withdrawn, after a good deal of effort had been expended by Soho to produce dies and find copper for the purpose. The East India Company was likely annoyed at

Soho's recent mistake in coining twenty-two tons more of a particular denomination for Madras than had been desired; in any case, the Chairmanship of the Court of Directors was about to change, and it may have seemed pointless for the outgoing Chairman to agree to a Bengal coinage which his successor might immediately countermand. Both sides were angry, and the Boultons became a good deal angrier when they learned that both copper coinage for the British Isles *and for the East India Company* would henceforth be struck by the Soho Mint's descendant on Tower Hill. That this represented fulfilment of sorts of the elder Boulton's dream made it no easier to accept. Other areas of the family papers contain much recrimination on his son's part; and the Indian mint project may have guttered out in Birmingham and not in London. But whoever bore the greater blame, an opportunity was lost: and we shall hear nothing more of it for the next ten years.

But time was on the project's side. During the decade of silence, much had taken place. Matthew Robinson Boulton had arrived at the conclusion that what he would most like to do with his father's mint was sell it. He made a determined attempt to do so at the beginning of 1818, using the good offices of his partner, James Watt, Jr. Watt travelled to Holland on this and other business in January, turning up at the Hague on the twenty-first of the month. While he encountered initial enthusiasm for the purchase of the Soho Mint, the enthusiasm soon waned. Watt spent several more weeks in the Dutch capital, finally returning home in mid-March; perhaps his abrupt departure would galvanize the Netherlanders into action. But it did not, and the younger Boulton found himself the continued possessor of the elder's mint. But the attempt (and an earlier, even less successful appeal to the United States of America) had cast his mind in a particular mould: given a reasonable opportunity, he would indeed sell that mint.

Meanwhile, in India, events were conspiring to give him a customer. For the years since 1809 had not seen an improvement in the Subcontinent's coinage; if anything, it was even less adequate now than it had been then. Worse, growing quantities of silver were coming into the ramshackle mints at Calcutta, Madras, and Bombay – so much bullion, in fact, that it could not all be made into money even with the rather undemanding techniques then in use. A crisis was reached in 1819: during the first seven months of that year, the Calcutta mint was unable to turn much more than half of the twenty-two million rupees' worth of silver metal submitted to it by private parties into coinage. Its inability left its customers inconvenienced and the Treasury out of pocket – for it was obliged to make interest payments on the uncoined balance. Matters could not continue thus, and the local officials of 'John Company' had a series of meetings, discussed a series of possible solutions. They eventually concluded that the most efficacious remedy would be the dispatching of someone to England to obtain a steam-powered mint similar to that now at work on Little Tower Hill. That someone would be Lieutenant William Nairn Forbes, lately attached to the Bengal Engineers as Surveyor of Embankments.

The Bombay authorities were reaching similar conclusions about the same time. They determined to send their own man to England, entrusted with a similar mission. Their emissary would be a somewhat older soldier with a similar engineering background, Captain John Hawkins.[3] Hawkins left a vivid vignette of the state of the mint whose coining he had sworn to improve:

> Urgent as the demands were for complete & powerful machinery in the Calcutta Mint, the Records before your Hon*ble* Court will fully bear me out in declaring the demands of the Bombay Mint to be infinitely greater.— In proof of this assertion I need only mention the fact of the Hammer, Chisell, & Punch, being to this day the only Coining tools in use — With such Barbarous implements, which are in every mans hand, it is impossible to produce a coin which may not be easily imitated – The Public are consequently exposed to every species of fraud, & to the vexation delay & expence, of submitting every Rupee, in the commonest money transaction, to the examination of a Shroff or money changer.—[4]

Hawkins was to take his mission to improve Bombay's coinage very seriously indeed – giving his life for it in the end.

Lieutenant Forbes seems to have left Bengal about the beginning of 1820 and was definitely in Great Britain by the early days of May. Hawkins probably arrived later in that year, or perhaps even at the beginning of 1821. When Soho was reintroduced to the discussion over Indian mints, its earliest dealings would be with Forbes, and from that point onward the Bombay mint project would occupy a position somewhat subordinate to that of Calcutta.

A few words are needed about the two emissaries from India. Both were engineers, Forbes working with dredging and harbour improvements, Hawkins with a variety of projects during his twenty-odd years with the Corps of Engineers. Both had made some sacrifices when they agreed to rescue their respective mints. Forbes found that his salary abruptly diminished, even though his duties and responsibilities grew, and kept growing. Hawkins encountered the same problem, although he was not nearly as verbose about it as was Forbes.

Forbes was Scottish, from the vicinity of Aberdeen. He was probably in his early thirties when entrusted with the Calcutta mint project. His counterpart Hawkins was about ten years older than he and was probably of English birth. Hawkins had a wife and family; Forbes apparently was unmarried. And while both men complained about the harsh Indian climate (and watched their mint-builders die from its effects), Hawkins succumbed to it while Forbes flourished in it: he remained at Calcutta, serving as Master of the new mint he had constructed from 1836 to 1855.

These were the men to whom the fortunes of modern coining in India would be entrusted. From a description of the men, let us turn to the mints they built.

CALCUTTA

The Calcutta project was the more important of the two – indeed, it would be of a size and complexity fully comparable with the Royal Mint in London and the St Petersburg mint in Russia. The East India Company was adamant concerning the output of which the new facility must be capable – it must be able to strike no fewer than two hundred thousand rupees in a working day of eight hours. This was precisely twice the minting prowess to be demanded of Bombay. Another indication of the greater importance of the Calcutta project was the fact that Forbes was already in England seeing to it at a time when Captain Hawkins had yet to leave the East.

Forbes reached England early in May 1820. Already acquainted with the elder John Rennie, he naturally thought of Rennie's firm in conjunction with the new machinery. And the Rennies naturally thought of Soho, with whom they had collaborated on several earlier projects. This Rennie/Boulton connection would be responsible for the machinery for both Indian mints; it was joined, however, by a third, unwelcome interloper.

Henry Maudslay of Maudslay, Sons, and Field had the ear of Joseph Thompson, one of the primary movers in the Calcutta project. So while Forbes had assumed that all the work for Calcutta would be carried out by the Rennies and by Boulton, Watt, he suddenly learned that Maudslay's firm might well be entrusted with the entire machinery order, had actually begun to manufacture portions of it. His protests (and quiet manipulations by James Watt, Jr. and George Rennie) helped prize most of the machinery from Henry Maudslay's grip. So did the latter's construction of a rotary coining press which the prolific American inventor Jacob Perkins had devised for the Indian coinage. The contraption failed so signally that Maudslay's credibility (and his lock on the construction of machinery for India) was weakened. He would nonetheless be entrusted with a portion of it,[5] and he would occasion considerable annoyance to those constructing the rest.

As the year 1820 drew to a close, a new division of labour was gradually taking shape, to be fully realized by late March 1821. Boulton, Watt & Company would provide the coining and cutting out presses for the new Calcutta mint. John and George Rennie would supply the rolling mill. Henry Maudslay would be relegated to the construction of various odds and ends, including the drawbench, lathes, and melting furnaces for the new facility. And the steam engines to power the whole would come from Soho. The East India Company called for estimates from the various suppliers, and the latter began serious thought about what would be required, and how much it would all cost.

Soho's role would grow over the next few months: it would soon be made responsible for the entire mint order, the Rennies and Maudslay acting as its subcontractors. One suspects that the controversy surrounding Henry Maudslay and the dilatory way in which the Rennie concern responded to its requests for an estimate led the East India Company to this decision. And from the Company's point of view, it made good sense to delegate responsibility if at all possible. Boulton, Watt was the recognized coining expert: let it shepherd things along. In time, Soho would gather the component machinery together; ship it to the Regent's Canal, where it would be loaded on vessels bound for Calcutta; and receive payment for the entire project, dispersing monies to the subcontractors.

It would also act as intermediary between the East India Company and those mechanics wishing to go out and set up the machinery. It would look for likely hands. It would do its best to keep the Company and those hands satisfied with their arrangements with each other. And in time it would look for new hands to replace those who died in 'John Company's' service.

Estimates began arriving at East India House in late January 1821. On the twenty-seventh, Boulton, Watt & Company sent its proposal to Joseph Thompson in London. It offered to construct steam engines with an aggregate power of 138 horses (including a rolling mill engine larger than that now at work at the Royal Mint, which had sometimes been found wanting); the requisite coining and cutting out presses (twelve of the former and eighteen of the latter); nine milling and six shaking machines; a die multiplying press; and all the requisite drawings, spare parts, etc. for a modern mint, for a grand total of £30,260. If copper boilers were substituted for iron ones (which might be a good idea, given Calcutta's climate), the cost would ascend by another £3,060, to £33,320. Maudslay's estimate was tendered about the same time: his total amounted to £10,820 for the melting and refining machinery. John and George Rennie took their time providing a figure: aware that the rolling mill was perhaps the most important single part of the proposed new mint (due to the volume of silver to be rolled into strips for rupees), the Rennie firm remained annoyingly vague as to terms.[6] But general approval of its part in the project was secured at a meeting of the Committee of Correspondence on 9 March 1821; while the role of Soho received unconditional approbation two days later:

> It was … determined … that the whole order should be given to us, with powers to issue that for the Rolling Mill &c to Mr Rennie, and that for the Smelting House to Maudslay.[7]

Lieutenant Forbes happened to be at East India House that day and quickly communicated the news to James Watt, Jr. The lieutenant was meanwhile drawing up plans for the buildings required for the new mint, as well as making preparations to come to Birmingham to receive instructions in modern coining processes as seen at Soho Mint.

Built at the close of the 1790s, that facility had been the apple of the elder Boulton's eye; the younger Boulton viewed it somewhat less favourably, had in fact been making efforts to sell it since 1810. By the beginning of 1821, he had decided to offer the mint to the East India Company (for a reduced sum) as one of the two facilities it was interested in purchasing. At this early point, its definitive destination had not been established; it was currently still *in situ*, fully functional, and ready for Forbes' inspection whenever he chose to drop by.

Realizing that it would be more useful to see a mint in actual operation than one sitting idle, James Watt, Jr. asked his contacts at the Company about the possibility of a coinage for the East Indies. He learned that an issue was indeed in contemplation – one of copper, for the island of St Helena. By the sixteenth of March, it had been decided that Soho Mint would coin for this distant flyspeck – copper halfpennies to the value of £1,000 – and that Lieutenant Forbes would be involved in the project. At the end of the month, sanction for the coinage came from Leadenhall Street, while the plans for the mint building which the lieutenant had laboriously drawn up also received official blessing. Made of brick and stone, embracing an area of 501,216 cubic feet, the new mint building would cost £27,207. We know the dimensions of the various rooms: the rolling mill would sit in a huge apartment measuring 118 feet by 54, the cutting out room would be a square, measuring 46 feet on each side, while the coining room would be nearly as long as the rolling room (102 feet) but rather narrower (30 feet). The dimensions of the cutting room suggest that machinery there would be arranged in a circle (a pattern Soho retained for blanking, having abandoned it for coining). And the oblong press room tells us that the coining presses would be arranged in a line, just as they had been at the second Soho Mint and its relatives at St Petersburg, Copenhagen, London, and Rio de Janeiro. Forbes' plan received the Company's approval on 2 April 1821.

This was a crowded time for the lieutenant and for his Soho correspondent. He and Boulton had been in constant communication while the Calcutta plans were being drawn up, and he was about to make his way to Soho to receive his education in the steam-powered minting process. But the times were even busier for Matthew Robinson Boulton: from London, Watt had confirmed that the East India Company wanted Soho to form the focal point of the mint-building, with all other suppliers subordinate to it. This entailed great responsibility as well as honour, and Boulton's duties grew more onerous still when he turned from matters of machinery to those of personnel.

No formal agreement between the East India Company and Boulton, Watt appears to have survived; perhaps none was ever drawn up. But when Soho constructed machinery for India, there was an implicit agreement to select people to erect it and operate it as well. Certainly Matthew Robinson Boulton had agreed to instruct those chosen to go out: a letter to Joseph Thompson survives from late January making just that pledge. And was Lieutenant Forbes not journeying to the Midlands for the same purpose? Every prior Boulton mint had involved the firm in the choice and instruction of personnel, the service as intermediary between strong-willed mechanics (who naturally wanted as much for their services as they could get) and a series of tight-fisted bureaucrats (who naturally wanted to hire them as cheaply as possible). And the Calcutta mint would be no exception to the rule.

The first prospective hands began knocking on Boulton's door at the end of March. One was sent packing without ado. This was John Westwood, nephew of one of the elder Boulton's old adversaries in the token field. This young man observed that he had recently heard that Boulton, Watt was building a mint for Calcutta; he would be more than happy to go out and run it, or to engrave dies for it. Westwood's current employment as restriker and vendor of his uncle's tokens appears to have been insufficient recommendation, and we hear no more of him.

A second candidate was taken more seriously. This was James Haden, who met Forbes in London late in March, then journeyed to Soho to speak with its proprietor. Haden seems to have been under consideration for a senior position, but he would eventually decline going to Calcutta.

By the beginning of April, Lieutenant Forbes was being brought into the equation, as was James Watt, Jr. The Company was now asking the former 'as to the establishment of European workmen which it would be desireable to send out and the Wages which should be given them'. And George Rennie was now asking the latter for help in the same direction, only stipulating that 'the Man he sent out to erect his Machinery should be put upon the same footing in regard to Wages &c'[8] as those sent by Soho. Watt pleaded ignorance, thereby dropping the matter in his partner's lap. And Matthew Robinson Boulton would henceforth be the single most important person involved in personnel selection – and replacement.

All hands were soon at work on various branches of the Calcutta project. At Soho, construction of the first of the machine parts got under way early in April, while the extant mint was being cleaned and made ready to coin. In London, Forbes was soliciting likely hands for the project, meanwhile preparing for his own journey to the Midlands, the commencement of the St Helena coinage. And a third player would now make his entrance, coming to Soho too. This was Captain Hawkins. He too would be viewing the coining process as carried on at Boulton's current mint because he would eventually erect and operate that machinery at Bombay. We do not know whose idea it was – perhaps that of Peter Auber, the new Assistant Secretary of the East India Company. But it was a brilliant concept, whoever its author: for one man could be instructed on *a* mint, another on *his* mint – while the East India Company could get its coinage into the bargain!

Selection of the workmen to accompany and erect the various components of the Calcutta mint went on very slowly: the East India Company questioned every shilling's worth of wages suggested, to the despair of its own man, Lieutenant Forbes, and Forbes' minting instructor, Matthew Robinson Boulton. And the men selected sometimes held up the proceedings. Several of those initially keen on the idea later thought better of it, and declined. Others accepted but made last-minute demands for better terms. Combined with the lassitude endemic to the bureaucratic process, all of this meant that the selection process would take slightly more than two years to complete.

Soho would send six men to Calcutta. In descending order of importance, they were the following.

Thomas Hughes, of Boulton, Watt & Company. Hughes was an Irish millwright and mechanist, would be employed as foreman and mechanist at Calcutta. He would superintend and assist in the erection of the coining machines. He would receive a salary of £400 *per annum* during the five years of his contract. If he became ill and had to return home, he would receive a retirement annuity of £90 per annum. He would also enjoy an advance of £100 for the purchase of necessities prior to the voyage. Hughes was married, and he solicited and succeeded in obtaining a guarantee that a percentage (apparently unrecorded, but likely £150 or so) of his salary would be retained at home for the support of his family.

Edward Gozzard, currently employed by Matthew Robinson Boulton, would serve as a general workman and, later, as a die multiplier. He would earn £250 annually for the first two years of his contract, £300 per year during the final three, pending satisfactory conduct. Gozzard's pension would be £70 per year, and he was to receive an advance for the same amount to purchase his outfit for the assignment.

Joseph Mears, also currently employed by Matthew Robinson Boulton, would serve as a general workman, turner, and fitter, with special responsibilities in the cutting out department. His salary would amount to £300 per year from the outset; his allowances for retirement and outfitting were the same as Gozzard's.

John Lewis, who was now working at Soho Foundry, would serve at Calcutta as a general workman and engine erector. For his services, he would receive the same terms as Mears. He was married, and his wife would accompany him to India. Lewis appears to have declined the opportunity at the last moment, then being replaced by Gregory Wilkinson. Wilkinson's wife would accompany him to Calcutta.

Josiah Stratford also worked at Soho Foundry. He would go to Calcutta as a workman and engine erector, serving under Hughes. His salary (£250 for the first two, £300 for the last three years) marked his subordinate status; but the other terms of his engagement were identical with those of John Lewis.

These men were all residents of Soho. But a Londoner named William Lewellyn had also applied for and secured a berth. He would serve as a general workman for the present and a die setter in the future. His salary would stand at £300 for each of the five years of his contract, and he would receive retirement benefits of £70 per year and an advance for an outfit of that same amount. Lewellyn too was married, and his wife would also come with him.

Besides their salaries, all of these men would receive free accommodation for themselves and their families (if applicable), either at Fort William or elsewhere. They would enjoy free medical care from the time they left England until the time of their return, and they could also, permission secured, perform other jobs for pay in their free time.

Thomas Hughes, Joseph Mears, Gregory Wilkinson, and William Lewellyn would die in Soho's service at Calcutta. Josiah Stratford would succumb to drink and be shipped home for his own good. Mercifully, none of this was known to the hopeful young men who signed their indentures, waited to go aboard their vessel with the mint they would set up.

Boulton, Watt and the Rennies had made solid progress on the construction of that facility by the middle of 1821. The first of the rolling mill apparatus had been sent off by mid-July 1821, and George Rennie estimated that the remainder of the order would be finished by the following spring. Henry Maudslay was preparing his plans for the melting house by late May 1821 – although it would be many months before blueprints were transformed into apparatus. As for Soho, Forbes' and Hawkins' visit had indeed taken place, coinage created, instruction given. This had occurred during the middle of May, and the coinage – some 44 casks of halfpence, with a net weight of slightly over six and one-half tons – was finished near the end of the month, leaving Soho for the East India Company's docks at the beginning of the next.

St Helena halfpenny, 1821. (National Numismatic Collection, Smithsonian Institution)

As Boulton was demonstrating the prowess of his old mint, his workers were progressing with the new. By September 1821, they were about half-way through the preparation of their part of the package, exclusive of the steam engines.[9] The latter seem to have been completed toward the end of November. The projected total weight of engines and minting machinery then stood at nearly three hundred tons, a figure which would rise by another ten tons or so when everything was finished. The sheer mass of the package would mean that not one ship but *three* would have to be employed to send the new mint to its destination. And there would be much agonizing over whether any of the Indiamen currently in service had a hold large enough to contain the gigantic boilers for the steam engines. It was suggested that the boilers be cut in two to accommodate them – risky indeed for their future service in India. In time, adequate vessels would be found; but the difficulties of shipping something of the size and weight of an entire steam-powered mint down the Atlantic, around the Cape of Good Hope, and across several thousand miles of open ocean to Calcutta afforded many sleepless nights to all concerned. But while the agonizing went on, so did the mint. Even with delays, Soho was able to advise Joseph Thompson (13 March 1823) that all of the machinery was finished, ready for inspection by Captain Boulderson, the Company's Master Attendant. Boulderson approved the whole. Boulton, Watt & Company had requested and received the first half of its payment the previous summer, dispersing the relevant portions of the money to its subcontractors: Boulderson's acceptance of the package in March 1823 assured remittance of the remainder, which was made the following June. A commonly encountered problem (getting paid in a timely fashion for its work) would not distinguish the Calcutta experiences of Boulton, Watt & Company.

Ships were now engaged to take the men and their mint to India. Forbes argued that it would be better for him to venture out first and survey the ground where the mint would be built (near Fort William and under its guns). The East India Company took the opposing position (partly because it deemed it extremely important to get Thomas Hughes and his machinery to India as quickly as possible). After considerable discussion, the Company won the argument. The mint machinery and the six men Soho had selected sailed on the *Potton* at the end of May. The rolling mill went out on the *Florentia*, while Maudslay's melting furnaces voyaged to India on the *Abberton*. We are ignorant of the details, but the three vessels and their cargoes had arrived at Calcutta a short time prior to Forbes' landfall there (21 October 1823).

We also know less than we would wish about those made responsible for assembling the Rennie and Maudslay packages. The man in charge of the rolling mill was Thomas Pigg (who was soon to be thrust into a much larger role than anyone expected); Pigg's salary was £350 per year. Pigg was married, and he brought his wife and child out with him. His son would die at Calcutta. One of those serving under Pigg was a millwright named Richard Burley; his salary is unknown. Two other names eventually appear in the record, those of John Rose and William Dunn. One of these men would have worked on the rolling mill, the other on the melting house; but anything beyond that simple statement is still conjecture, likely to remain so.

That left Forbes. The lieutenant made a flying visit to Scotland to see friends during the first part of June, but he was back in London by the ninth, had left for the Downs a few days later, where he was to meet the *Minerva*, the vessel which would carry him to Calcutta. She left British waters on the sixteenth, her passenger having just prized some £2,500 in back pay from the Company and therefore feeling modestly optimistic about the Calcutta project and his role in it.

We are accustomed to the quick gratification of instantaneous communication. We become impatient when someone is absent half a world away, their telephone engaged, their fax machine turned off: they cannot provide us with instant answers to our insistent questions, instant answers we have come to view as ours by right. If there is one outstanding difference between the people of the 1820s and those of the 1990s, it may well be the nature of patience. For we deliberately cultivate it as a virtue. Our ancestors would have naturally acquired it as a necessity.

When Forbes and his men sailed away, they literally left the known world. They would eventually emerge in another known world and provide tidings of their arrival. But it would take several months for them to reach their destination, several months more for the news to get back. During that intervening period, which could be expected to last anywhere from six months to a year, they might as well have been on the moon. One might wonder how they were faring. But there was no point in spending much time in such reflection, for there was absolutely nothing one could do.

More than most experiences, the Calcutta adventures of Boulton, Watt & Company took on a surreal quality once the firm's men and machinery left home. Events, which had previously been chronicled on an almost daily basis, now became disjointed, jerky: now, it is as if we watch them unfold under a stroboscopic light. But for those viewing them at the time, they must have appeared ordinary enough. How else might the story progress?

So Matthew Robinson Boulton would not be unduly surprised when he heard nothing from Lieutenant Forbes through 1823, and nothing through the year following. Forbes indeed wrote him a long letter in October 1824 – so long, in fact, that he started it on the seventh and only finished it on the nineteenth. Boulton would not receive it until March 1825 – that is, a year and three-quarters from the time he had last seen the lieutenant. Forbes maintained a somewhat more faithful (and, one hopes, briefer) correspondence with his masters at East India House, and from them Boulton would learn some of what was going on at Calcutta.

But the long letter he finally received from Forbes supplied him with the details. Observing that 'I landed on this blessed Region of eternal heat, fog and fever' on 21 October 1823, Forbes added that he immediately set to work on selecting a place for the new mint. He was offered a site on ground owned by the Company near a new quay along the Hooghly, in handy proximity to many of the governmental offices with which he would have to deal. The fact that there were empty brick warehouses nearby (in which the machinery could be stored until the new building was ready to receive it) was decisive: Forbes embraced the offer.

The next step was to off-load the mint apparatus. The machinery was landed with reasonable dispatch, checked for damage during the long months of shipment (there was remarkably little, all things considered), and safely stowed in its temporary home.

The site selected for the mint formed a shallow basin of the Hooghly. While the new embankment cut it off from the river, it was nonetheless covered with water when Forbes first saw it, for there was a drainage tunnel under the adjacent quay which connected with the river. The basin's soil was discovered to be composed of sand and clay, interspersed with small springs from the Hooghly. Before anything could be built there, Forbes would have to remove all that water.

This he did, in quick order. The tunnel under the quay was bricked up, and one of the mint engines was put to work drawing water out of the basin. The jury-rigged pumping system performed admirably, raising over three tons of water per minute when necessary. Forbes estimated that, 'had it not been for this contrivance', it would have been necessary to have 'from 700 to 1000 men daily at work for the last 16 months', and for nearly half of that time 'we should have had ... several feet depth of water over our commencements'. The ingenious engineer put another of the engines to work grinding bricks into dust which, when mixed with lime, formed an excellent cement – thereby saving the labor of another hundred workmen.

Now the foundation walls were laid, Forbes making them five feet thick at the least, and a solid mass of masonry in those places of heaviest future weight, including the engine house. The lieutenant had nearly a thousand natives currently employed in the work. Once the foundation walls had risen to an average height of twenty feet, work on the actual mint apartments could get under way. At present, Forbes was about half-way through with his foundations, 'but when we have arrived at that level – half the labor of building will have been accomplished'. Forbes' cautious optimism must have caused much satisfaction at home; what he had to say next would not.

For the solid if modest progress just reported had demanded a terrible price. Three of the ten people sent out were already dead.

Two of them were Soho men, Thomas Hughes and Joseph Mears. The third was one of those attached to the rolling mill, Richard Burley. Hughes and Mears had died of fever within two days of each other, in April 1824. Burley's constitution was delicate, and he succumbed to the ravages of the climate in mid-September of that same year. Even allowing for a generous dose of self-pity, Forbes and his mint were in trouble:

> The loss of Hughes is in some respects irreparable.— The distress it occasioned me you can well imagine.— Nothing could exceed his enthusiasm and anxiety to forward business — qualities which with others he possessed attached me much to him.— His death and that of Mears within two days of each other, the sickness of the rest of the workmen — and my own bad health made the additional load of trouble and responsibility which fell upon me sufficiently distracting — and it was sometime, from the alarm of the men, and their expressed anxiety to be permitted to return to England, before I saw any chance of being able to carry on the work.—

Even for Europeans new to India, this had been an unusually high casualty rate. Forbes was doing what he could to preserve the lives of those remaining under his care:

> I allow them each 5 R*s* [rupees] a month for a man to carry a chatta (or umbrella) over their heads when they are at work outside the warehouses and I have procured for them comfortable houses on account of which each is permitted to draw 80 Rupees per month.—

Forbes slowly managed to get the project moving again, and the construction of the building was resumed. But the outbreak of war along the Burmese border was another complicating factor, the Company's fiscal expenditures for its prosecution creating a scarcity of resources for other projects, including mint-building. Happily, the war was brief, and construction work resumed.

Nonetheless, the loss of the three mechanics would soon have to be made good, for as soon as the building was finished the East India Company would naturally want the mint machinery assembled and readied for coining. Forbes responded by attempting to plug the holes with surviving workmen. He approached Wilkinson about erecting the engines – who declined, citing a complete lack of experience in that line and a fear of undertaking it now. Nor did Stratford have the requisite experience – and he was rapidly sliding into alcoholism, and thought to be near death. In a desperate attempt to address the most important casualty, Forbes finally hit upon a practical expedient. He would replace Thomas Hughes with the foreman of the rolling mill, Thomas Pigg. Pigg had never worked at Soho, but he had the experience with steam engines which both Wilkinson and Stratford lacked and was sincerely anxious to succeed in this new challenge. And since Lewellyn only knew coining machinery and Gozzard die hardening, Pigg it would have to be.

Meanwhile, Forbes was seeking more British workmen. He was less than sanguine, for the news of what had happened to Messrs Hughes and Mears was likely to dissuade their mates at Soho from undertaking their replacement – at least on the same terms. And the process would be tortuous in any case. Forbes could not simply write directly to Matthew Robinson Boulton. Rather, he must make a public application through the local government to the Court of Directors back in London, which would in turn (if it approved the idea) speak to Mr Boulton on the staffing problem. That was the theory. But Forbes went around the bureaucracy, appealed directly, and desperately, for help:

> If you can get two men, good — bad or indifferent, to come out to expedite matters a little in the erection of the machinery for Mercys sake do it. ... If [the Rennies] could send us out a millwright in the room of Burley it would be a God send.[10]

But it would be many months before Forbes' plea could be answered (and indeed many months before Soho would even hear it): in the interim, the lieutenant muddled along as best he could.

Matthew Robinson Boulton had become aware of the personnel crisis somewhat prior to hearing directly from Forbes. The engineer had written to his superiors in London a month after the first two deaths, and he specifically stated the nature of his needs. He would require two men. One of them must have experience in setting up large land steam engines, should also possess a working knowledge of coining and cutting out machinery. The other must be an expert turner in iron and steel, capable of preparing beds, punches, collars, and dies for the coining and cutting out presses. Forbes suggested Boulton, Watt & Co. for the engine-man; the turner might be found either at the Royal Mint or at Soho Mint. Joseph Thompson wrote to Matthew Robinson Boulton in February 1825, enclosing a copy of Forbes' letter. Boulton had already heard the news, which was apparently floating around London during the last weeks of the old year, and he was now searching for new hands.

He was having little success, for news of the deaths had naturally reached Hughes' and Mears' shop-mates as quickly as anyone else. George Rennie had located a suitable turner by late February – only to find that he declined going out, fearing for his health. The Rennies tried again, and they eventually found a replacement, not for Hughes or for Mears, but for the deceased millwright Richard Burley. This was Thomas Obrien, who expressed a keen interest in sailing for India, and who would accept the same terms as the first group of mechanics.

Obrien emerged in late May – after more than three months of diligent search. Boulton, Watt had meanwhile been looking for Forbes' other two replacements, with a signal lack of success. Soho was itself now short of hands, because Mr Boulton had found that he needed a new mint almost as soon as he had sent his father's old one to Bombay.

But another substitute was eventually located, a married man named Henry Daniels, late of the Eagle Foundry. Daniels drove a hard bargain: he wanted his wife and children well taken care of in his absence, electing to settle half of his salary on his spouse, to be directly remitted to her by Matthew Robinson Boulton. While reducing his family's allotment from £150 to £100, the East India Company agreed to most of the smith's other demands, a suggestion of how desperate things had become. Agreements between the Company and the two mechanics (Daniels had insisted on being addressed as an 'engineer' rather than a millwright) were drafted and signed at the end of July, Daniels receiving £300 annually for five years and Obrien £250 for the first two years and £300 for the final three. The men left Great Britain on the *Hibberts*, which sailed for Calcutta in late August.

The two new smiths missed a letter written by Forbes on 21 November to his superiors at East India House. It contained more bad news:

> Of Ten Mill-wrights and Engine men who arrived in Calcutta along with the Machinery, four are now dead.— A fifth of the name of Stratford has, I am sorry to say, so materially injured his health by the habit of hard drinking as to have become an encumbrance to the Establishment[.][11]

The new casualty was William Lewellyn, one of the better workers, who must have died during the summer of 1825. In July 1826, Joseph Thompson so informed Boulton, Watt & Company, requesting replacements both for Lewellyn and for Richard Burley. But Thompson wanted other commodities as well: upon Forbes' urging, he was asking for dies, collars, steel bars for the edge-marking process, beds and punches for the cutting out presses, and a host of other specialized machine parts, all of which could only mean one thing: despite all odds, and with the diminishing personnel at his disposal, Lieutenant Forbes was finishing the Calcutta mint!

Soho could provide all the dies and most of the other commodities Forbes needed. It was going to have extreme difficulty supplying one item, however – manpower. It promised a sincere effort in that direction but also candidly told East India House that, with the sorry record of deaths thus far, it was not especially optimistic. Any skilled hands at Soho would have known most or all of those who had perished and would thus be reluctant to hire on at Calcutta. And anyone who did not know the deceased men would probably lack the skills Calcutta required. Soho suggested that, if enthusiastic-but-unskilled people could be found, the Royal Mint might perfect their training. Soho could not, having no current plans to coin (and no inclination either: at Midsummer 1826, it rejected an overture from Joseph Thompson for a small coinage for Prince of Wales Island, along the line of the earlier St Helena halfpence).[12] For the time being, Forbes would simply have to get along with the people he had.

Early in September 1826, the lieutenant reported more bad news. Gregory Wilkinson had died. The two replacements for earlier casualties (Thomas Obrien and Henry Daniels) were both ill – so ill indeed that they were not likely to recover. And Josiah Stratford had become a statistic of another kind: he had ruined his health by drinking, had in fact become totally useless to the mint project. He, Obrien, and Daniels would be sent home on the next available vessel. Accompanying them would be Wilkinson's widow – who personally delivered Forbes' report of the tragedy to Matthew Robinson Boulton.

The effects of this sickness and death on the building of the Calcutta mint were less catastrophic than might be imagined. While Forbes sincerely lamented the dead men, while he was desperate for their replacements, there was never any question that his mint would in fact be finished, would one day start to coin. The outer building was done: what Forbes now needed was the skilled personnel to set the engines it contained in motion and, still more, to superintend the coining process.

Despite his constant criticism of the local authorities, they had been most generous with their time and cooperation: in erecting the Calcutta mint buildings, Forbes never encountered the obstacles that Captain Hawkins found at Bombay. And so the mint situation by late 1826 was indeed serious, but not critical.

And against all logic, Boulton, Watt was able to recruit two more workmen – George Hudson and Charles Cashmore. They were Soho men, and, lacking the skills needed at Calcutta, must be educated at the Royal Mint. Forbes would not know of them for many months, and they had in fact been engaged in November 1826, well before Boulton could have received Forbes' cry for additional assistance. The Royal Mint was at first less than welcoming, but the two newcomers were eventually able to obtain the training they needed. They left for Calcutta in the spring of 1827.

Hudson and Cashmore would eventually be joined by another neophyte, an individual named Taylor, and by an old hand, Henry Daniels. Daniels had nearly died at Calcutta of a liver complaint, but the long sea voyage home had done him much good and he and Taylor went out to India together, probably in the fall of 1827. Daniels acquitted himself well on this second engagement, serving to the satisfaction of all concerned, coming home with honours at the end of his tour of duty. He was back in Birmingham in December 1830, and he subsequently entered the service of Soho.

We hear very little of the Calcutta mint between the summer of 1827 and the summer of 1830. The dies ordered in August 1826 took many months to prepare, but some two thousand of them, all intended for rupees, finally left Soho on 7 February 1827, along with three hundred collars, screws of various sizes for the milling machines, sheet steel, etc.

These dies were shipped out blank, but attention was now turning to the designs which would appear on them, and thus on the coins they would eventually strike. In May 1827, Soho sent Calcutta and Bombay master punches featuring a wreath as their design, but we have no word of the identity of the designer. Since the coinage of rupees was to be a primary consideration at both mints, we may probably conclude that the punches were intended for eventual use on that denomination – and indeed, the reverses of the 1835-dated rupees of William IV featured a wreath as their central type. But the first rupees of Calcutta and Bombay would not employ this design, or any other representational art. Instead, as the illustrations suggest, they would be true hybrids – new coins struck on old models.

There is evidence that the Calcutta mint was finished in the summer of 1829: Mr Philip Mernick of London has kindly drawn my attention to an article published as part of an appendix to the *Journal of the Asiatic Society* in 1834, called 'New Calcutta Mint'.[13] I include an illustration which accompanied the text. If you look closely, you will see that the path taken by the moneying process is 'progressive', in line with the elder Boulton's concept. But you will also see that the illustration states that the mint was begun on 31 March 1824 and finished on 1 August 1829. I think we may accept the starting date as reasonable; but the date of completion does not fit with our other testimony.

Certainly there is no evidence that *moneying* began at the new mint that early. In fact, we can put the commencement of coining no earlier than the summer of 1830 – and Forbes could not have managed even that without the reappearance of Henry Daniels. But we are indeed on safe ground in attributing it to that later period, for we have Forbes' own testimony to the event.

Ground plan of the
Calcutta Mint, as
published in 1834.

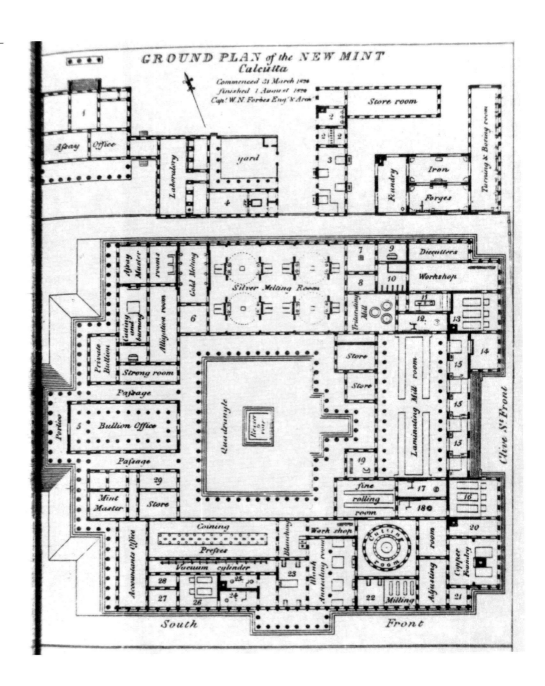

This was contained in a letter to Soho of 23 August 1830. Forbes' account
was slightly breathless, but his enthusiasm was understandable:

> Every part of the Mint Machinery has proved itself capable *of doing more* than I as
> its Godfather *promised* for it; In *confirmation* of such assertion we have recently
> struck at the New Mint upwards of *(10,000,000)* millions of pieces of copper
> money.— The coining presses part of this time having thrown out upwards of
> 32,000 pieces per hour, the contract for the machinery (as I have stated) having
> stipulated in the same period of time an hour but for the issue of 25,000
> pieces.— the great expense of the undertaking has in these economical times of
> course *much* been objected to— I must however say that even on this score I (on
> its account) have had no reason to complain.[14]

Soho's founder would have been proud: a Boulton mint was striking what had always been his own top priority, copper money for the labouring poor. But there is a difficulty: *no copper coinage firmly attributable to 1830 is known from the new Calcutta mint.* There were indeed copper pies and half-annas, and they were struck in vast quantities, for they are readily obtained today. Undated, they have always been attributed to 1831 (the pie) and to the years 1831 to 1835 (the half-anna) – for the legislation authorizing them was passed on 9 August 1831, and the coins were made current on 18 October of the same year. But that does not necessarily mean that they were *struck* in 1831: if Forbes were prudent enough to order dies in advance of needing them,[15] he was certainly wise enough to strike a plenteous coinage in advance of launching it into circulation. Since he seems to have been working amicably enough with his superiors at Calcutta, would it have been impossible for him to secure permission to begin coining in one year, for circulation in another?

With all this in mind, I am reasonably certain that what Forbes was striking at an accelerated rate was the diminutive one-pie piece, the very sort of coin with which he could exceed everyone's expectations. And while the half-anna coins may indeed date from 1831 and later, we should probably attribute the pies to 1830, making them the earliest representatives of the new, industrialized Indian coinage.

The first coinage from the new Calcutta Mint: pie, undated but struck 1830. (National Numismatic Collection, Smithsonian Institution)

This new mint had its share of growing pains. Forbes sent a large order for dies, collars, and other 'stores' to the Company in the spring of 1830, and it in turn communicated his request – for six hundred collars and no less than 14,500 die forgings (for the rupee and its quarter and half) – to Soho on 10 September 1830. But it was one thing to order stores, quite another to get them where they were needed. While Boulton, Watt worked on the order through the remainder of 1830, all of 1831, and into the beginning of 1832, Forbes had received none of it at the time of his next letter to Soho, written on 5 May 1831.

By now, his relations with his superiors were decidedly mixed:

> Gov*t* [had] agreed to my being continued in charge of the Mint Machinery, and having called me Superintendent of all the Machinery belonging to Gov*t* have reduced my allowances 500 Rupees per month. Thinking this rather a hard dispensation (inasmuch as my duties have at the same time been rendered much more extensive & laborious), I have strongly protested against *the Reduction*.[16]

But Forbes' charge, at least, was doing well. It was still striking copper fairly exclusively, for the demand for minor coinage continued to be great – as were the mint's profits with copper and therefore its zeal in supplying such money to the public. At times, nearly a quarter of a million pieces had been struck in only six hours: Forbes did not say, but these were probably still pies, small coins which could be minted more rapidly than any other denomination, and which, in a country as poor as India, would have been in very great demand. There was also a hint that silver coinage might now be under way: Forbes complained that 'we still go on striking the old Indian letter'd barbarous looking coins'[17] – which, while profitable to make, were so crude in appearance that he was ashamed to send Boulton any specimens. The only pieces which merit such comment were undated silver rupees and their subdivisions, minted between 1830 and 1833, for the copper coins bore part of

The industrialization of India's money: traditional rupee, struck at old Calcutta Mint (top); transitional rupee, struck at new Calcutta Mint but retaining old designs (centre); Western-style rupee, struck at new Calcutta Mint – signed 'F' for Forbes (bottom). (National Numismatic Collection, Smithsonian Institution)

their legends in English. Forbes may have complained of their crudity, but they represented a quantum improvement over what had gone before.

By 1831 then, the new Calcutta mint was approaching full production. Forbes' die requirements were ascending accordingly. On 23 April, Soho sent another large portion of his order – nearly two thousand dies and five hundred collars – out to India. But even these were not enough to feed the presses. The East India Company begged Boulton, Watt to hurry with the remaining dies ordered in September 1830, and some four thousand more left Soho on 9 February 1832. But in its eagerness to keep its mint busy, the Company was now flouting British law.

It wanted to smuggle dies into India, and it was asking for Soho's connivance. In theory, anyone wishing to ship such tools abroad had to secure an Order in Council to do so legally. The East India Company did not wish to expend the effort – and particularly the time – in doing so, and it therefore asked that its dies be disguised as something else. As John Mosley, Boulton's business representative in London, advised the people at home,

> The Dies must not be called *So* in the Invoice which you send to the E I Co for Entry at [the] Custom-House— but '*Steel Lumps*' to save the trouble of applying for an order of Council to ship them which must be done if entered as *Dies*—[18]

Such subterfuge was seen on several occasions in another faraway place to which dies were shipped – Guanajuato.

The Calcutta mint expanded its activities and production during the 1830s and beyond. It struck gold in and after 1835, and its silver and copper acquired Western designs to accompany their Western fabric at the same time. For the first few years, Forbes worked under a Master of the Mint named Robert Saunders, who had been granted the post on 7 April 1826, well before there was any coinage to superintend. But Lieutenant, now Captain, Forbes became Master in January 1836, enjoying that post for the next nineteen years, only relinquishing it a few months before his death.

The links between Soho and Forbes, and his mint, continued through the end of 1839. The vast majority of later archival evidence consists of brief exchanges between the East India Company and Boulton, Watt, concerning the supply of dies and other coining tools, and they confirm that the traffic in dies continued heavy throughout the decade. For additional detail, we must rely on other sources, Major Pridmore's two volumes on India, part of his monumental *Coins of the British Commonwealth* outstanding among them. But the Matthew Boulton Papers still have something to offer, and they offer it during the final eighteen months of the Calcutta connection.

When the Calcutta mint began striking rupees with the portrait of William IV (in 1835), it had asked a local artist named Kasinath Dass to create the effigy. This he had done, employing a William IV halfcrown as his model. Probably combined with the wreath punch sent out by Soho years before, the new portrait served well enough; and when William died in 1837, it was decided that the old king's head would continue to grace the rupee and its subdivisions for the time being.

By the latter part of the year, the Company's representatives were approaching the gifted William Wyon, soliciting his services for the new Queen's portrait. But Wyon had work enough – he was redesigning the obverses for British coinage at the time – and his lack of enthusiasm and celerity seems to have led Dr Wilson of the East India Company to approach Soho for the work. On 17 August 1838, Wilson wrote a letter, now lost, to Boulton, Watt & Company, asking it to make the original die.

Soho soon got to work on the project. The Matthew Boulton Papers record a charge of £25.10.0 to the East India Company on 24 November of that year – £24 for engraving an original die with Victoria's head and the legend VICTORIA QUEEN, and £1.10.0 for taking a punch from it. The new matrix was laid before the Court of Directors in mid-December, and it was approved on the twentieth of that month.

The master and its punch could have gone to Calcutta on any of several occasions during 1839, for Soho was shipping stores to the mint throughout that year. But it would not be used for Indian silver coinage until it had been radically altered at Calcutta, the head retained but the lettering redone. And the new head, perhaps the product of Thomas Wells Ingram, would never appear on any Soho dies sent out ready for coining. In this respect, the story of the Calcutta mint would differ from that of its contemporary at Guanajuato, to which ready-engraved dies were often sent.

But Calcutta shared a similarity with Guanajuato. Writing in July 1838, John Potts observed that the Mexican coiners were now creating their own dies and improving on those Soho had sent them. And writing three months after Potts, from the other side of the world, Captain Forbes made a very similar claim: the Soho product might be of high quality, 'but for top [reverse] dies, those we make ourselves of cast steel bars we find best'.[19] In both instances, ingenious men were adapting European models to non-European realities, changing the nature of technology as they did so.

As in Mexico, so in India: Captain Forbes was serving notice that what had once been an alien dream had become a productive institution, had taken root in its new soil, was healthy, was growing. Now let us turn to its counterpart at Bombay.

BOMBAY

The story of Bombay shared many points in common with that of Calcutta. The same three firms would be involved in the preparation of a mint – with the addition, however, of a fourth company late in the game. Senior responsibility for constructing machinery and selecting personnel would again rest on the shoulders of Matthew Robinson Boulton. As at Calcutta, several of the men chosen to go out would be found wanting, while others would die at their tasks. A similar amount of time would be required for building the two mints. In sum, the two projects appear very much alike, at least at first glance.

But there was a difference between them all the same, and it was a major one. For Calcutta, a new mint would be supplied; for Bombay, an old one would be refurbished and remitted. This choice of machinery benefitted all parties. The East India Company saved money, but nonetheless got a superb coining facility. And Matthew Robinson Boulton rid himself of an unwanted memory.

The recycling of the Soho Mint, taken apart in one country and put back together in another, suggests something of the relative importance with which Bombay was viewed by the Company – at least as compared with

Calcutta. The former project was always seen as subordinate to the latter. We can see this attitude from the beginning (Forbes came to Great Britain prior to Hawkins, began dealing with his suppliers months before the latter's arrival) to the end (when Calcutta would supply engraved dies for Bombay). In practice, the Bombay mint would be about half the size of the Calcutta mint – but its costs would be nearly identical.

The earliest connection between Boulton, Watt & Company and a mint at Bombay went back to the autumn of 1808, and it was modest indeed. The East India Company was contracting for a steam engine, and it desired Soho's advice on a suitable person to go out to Bombay, erect the engine there, and then stay on as superintending mechanic at the Company's mint at Fort St George. The mint in question was *not* steam-powered, and there was apparently no intention of making it so in the foreseeable future. And in any case, surviving documents suggest that Matthew Robinson Boulton declined to help. But a precedent had been set, a link established, between Soho and Bombay.

Nothing would be done to expand that linkage for the next dozen years. But by the end of 1820, plans were afoot at East India House – and at Soho. Joseph Thompson's letter to Boulton, Watt (of 27 December 1820) requested estimates for two mints, one at Calcutta and the other at Bombay, and it set the desired output of the latter at precisely half of that of the former – one hundred thousand rupees in a working day of eight hours. Matthew Robinson Boulton's response for Calcutta received attention above; what did he have in mind for Bombay?

He proposed the sale of Soho Mint, and he seems to have had it in mind from the beginning. Less than two weeks after Thompson's letter of inquiry, Boulton penned an answer to James Watt, Jr., which the latter could carry back to East India House. Boulton estimated that a new facility would cost £18,515. But the East India Company could have the present Soho Mint for a mere £12,000. Boulton was to adjust his figures over the next two years, while the East India Company would oscillate between choosing a new mint or a rebuilt one – or indeed any mint – during that same time. But it would finally and definitively opt for modernization at the beginning of 1823; and when it did, it would choose the current Soho Mint.

It would do so partly from motives of price. But it would also do so because of the advice of the Bombay emissary, Captain John Hawkins. Hawkins visited Soho along with Lieutenant Forbes in mid-May 1821, witnessed the striking of the St Helena coinage, and was convinced of the worthiness of this 'most Philosophical & perfect apparatus'. In June 1821, the engineer came out firmly in favor of a mechanized mint – *this* mechanized mint – listing his reasons and comparing Soho Mint to what now existed at Bombay.

There, the most primitive conditions imaginable produced a coinage which was easily counterfeited. A modern mint would eliminate this evil; it would also serve to standardize the currency (due to its greater output), and it would make money cheaper to produce, thereby augmenting the profits of the producer – the East India Company. In summation,

> The incalculable advantages which would result from the abolition of all the petty [native] mints on the Bombay Establishment, by the creation of an efficient mint with perfect machinery, & by the introduction of a well executed & uniform currency ... are consequences which I am persuaded must be obvious to your Honourable Court.—[20]

The Honourable Court would arrive at the same conclusion at last, and Hawkins' recommendations would then be acted upon in a manner favourable to Boulton, Watt & Company. But the Company took a great deal of time to get there: less than two weeks prior to Hawkins' report (with its unconditional approval of Soho Mint), it was wondering whether *hand* presses might not achieve the same results. This suggests an important feature of the Industrial Revolution – at least as it applied to moneying. There was no single, unanimous conversion to a new methodology. Rather, new ways won out over old as much by luck and persistence as by intrinsic superiority.

In the present case, the ultimate issue of the sale of Boulton's mint could and did hang by a thread while discussions over subcontractors and erectors of the facility went on. The participants couched everything in the conditional tense: assuming that a mint *were* to be built, how many suppliers would be needed for the parts, how many men to bolt those parts to one another? I suspect that more of history is like that than we suppose, only acquiring an appearance of linearity well after the event.

Part of the disjointedness stemmed from the fact that the Calcutta mint took priority over Bombay, both in the eyes of the East India Company and in those of Matthew Robinson Boulton. For Calcutta, Soho must actually construct a large body of machinery; for Bombay, it need merely refurbish what it had constructed long ago. And so Hawkins languished in London, first prodding the Company, and then Boulton, Watt, with little result in either case. Not until the summer of 1822 (by which time most of the machinery for Calcutta had already been finished) would the Bombay mint move forward.

On 25 June 1822, the East India Company requested an estimate 'of the expense of renovating your mint … and including also the Rolling mills, melting apparatus and every charge connected with the mint'.[21] It also asked Soho to act as primary contractor, so that the nabobs need only deal with one firm rather than several. Boulton, Watt had previously agreed to do so in the case of Calcutta; now it was served notice that it *must* do so in the case of Bombay.

Matthew Robinson Boulton was agreeable, and a preliminary estimate for the steam engines and coining machinery was drawn up on 5 July. For eight coining machines (rather than the six which had been mentioned in an earlier estimate: this would bring his father's mint up to its original complement of presses), nine cutting out machines, and three steam engines (a rolling mill engine of forty horse, a second engine for coining and cutting out of twenty-four, and a third of ten, for the triturating process), Soho would charge £17,638. The coining and cutting out machinery would be the rebuilt Soho apparatus of 1798; the engines would be new. Messrs Rennie and Maudslay, Sons, and Field were also invited to submit estimates – the latter, one suspects, because of Henry Maudslay's friendship with the mighty at East India House. Matthew Robinson Boulton delivered their figures and his own to the Company's Chairman and Deputy Chairman on the following day: the Bombay mint, complete with its rolling mill and melting house, could be had for £37,824 – which price would include duplicate parts and instruction.

It would be pleasant to report that, once estimates were given, they were eagerly accepted by the East India Company so that work could begin. It would also be erroneous: work on the Bombay mint would not receive official sanction from its customer for another seven months. On 13 February 1823,

Peter Auber, Assistant Secretary of the East India Company, finally gave official blessing to the sale and construction of machinery for the Bombay mint. By then, the amount of the estimate had ascended by slightly more than two thousand pounds, reaching a final figure of £40,016. Most of the extra charge came from the preparation of cast iron plating for the floors of the melting houses – which would soon inject a troublesome new subcontractor into the Bombay project.

Part of the reason for the months of delay was that the Company vacillated over whether it wished to purchase a second-hand mint, even for a secondary coiner. Soho might solemnly guarantee the worthiness of its product, but doubts nonetheless lingered. Additional uncertainty stemmed from personnel conflicts at East India House: the current Chairman, Reid, was becoming favourable to the recycling of Soho mint, while his Deputy, a gentleman named Wigram, was distinctly unfavourable – as was the powerful Joseph Thompson, who still hoped to steer the order for coining machinery to his friend Henry Maudslay. These difficulties were slowly resolved during the last months of 1822, and on 29 October the senior officials of the Company told Hawkins that 'they had made up their minds to take the [Soho] mint on the terms proposed by you ... some time since'[22] – adding that the entire package must be ready for shipment by January 1824. This left little time, and the machinery would not in fact be sent to India until the latter part of that year.

Provisional approval obtained, Captain Hawkins now busied himself in drawing up plans for the new mint. This activity engendered further dispute, the Company informing him that the buildings he envisaged were far larger than required, Hawkins defending his plans in their present state. Boulton, Watt & Company busied itself in extracting estimates from its subcontractors – including Henry Maudslay, who would be as annoying here as he had been with Calcutta. Estimates were nonetheless being obtained and forwarded during December 1822, and the East India Company approved the whole and gave final, official permission to proceed in mid-February 1823. Work on new machinery got under way at Soho at the end of that month. The Rennies waited a month or two to begin their portion of the apparatus, while Henry Maudslay was still quibbling over terms at the end of spring.

As with other mint exportations, Boulton, Watt and its subcontractors were not only sending out machinery but *men* – the skilled personnel to erect and tend Bombay's mint, symbol of technological modernization for a backward area. As we might expect, even preliminary discussions over manpower began very late – the record is silent until after the East India Company's formal blessing of the Bombay project in February 1823. By 20 March of that year, George Rennie had located a suitable foreman for his firm's portion of the project, and he so informed Boulton that day. But we hear little more of personnel until the autumn.

Meanwhile, work on the actual mint went on at a satisfactory rate at Soho, much more slowly elsewhere. By late August, a note to Captain Hawkins observed that the milling machines had been taken down and refitted, as had all but one each of the coining and cutting out presses. That portion of the equipment had been left standing, for Soho hoped to use it to strike a small issue of coinage for the East India Company, both for the instruction of that person chosen as mint foreman, and to give a visual guarantee that the old mint was good as new. Discussion over such coinage for the island of Sumatra had been spoken of in general terms as early as August 1822, but the rise in the price of copper (partly the result of a scare concerning a possible war with France) had put the project in limbo for several months. In time, the East India Company's establishment at Sumatra would be blessed with *two* issues of Soho copper, the last coinages Matthew Boulton's unmoved mint ever prepared for that or any of the Company's other possessions.

The first and far larger issue left Soho for the London docks early in April 1823 – some £7,000 worth of coins in three sizes. These bore the date of 1804 (the date of the last Sumatran issue), but the copper crisis was reflected in the fact that the coins were lighter than their earlier counterparts. This issue was completed before the mint was disassembled for remittance to Bombay.

The second coinage was much smaller, and it left Soho on 24 February 1824. It consisted of ten tons of copper pieces, all struck at fifty-three to the pound, a weight corresponding to the lightweight four-keping coin.[23] The East India Company was charged £1,522.10.0 for this coinage, which was struck on the sole coining press yet uncrated. Unfortunately, it is impossible to distinguish between these coins and the four-keping pieces minted the previous year.

Nor do we know the identities of all those who witnessed this final coinage. Certainly John Hawkins would have been there; so would George Cadenhead, who, as the foreman mechanist chosen to erect the machinery, was one of those most immediately concerned. And others likely attended; for by now, the roster of those who would go to Bombay was nearly complete.

At the time of the striking of the Sumatran coins, six men had been chosen for Soho's part of the Bombay mint.

We have just met George Cadenhead, who was now employed at Soho Foundry. About twenty-eight years old, Cadenhead was married and secured the same arrangement for the support of his family as had his counterpart for Calcutta, Thomas Hughes. His salary was identical to that of Hughes – £400 *per annum* during the five years of his contract, with an advance of £100. At the last minute, Cadenhead's wife decided that she would like to go to India with him; and so she did.

George Cadenhead would die at Bombay.

James Howard was engaged as a die-setter, pressman, and general workman. He was only twenty-two, and his salary arrangements reflected the fact: he would receive £250 per year for the first two years, £300 for the last three – by which time his experience would presumably merit the raise.

John Clough was the same age as Howard, and he would enjoy the same salary. These two men would also receive advances of £70 apiece to purchase supplies for the trip. Clough would serve as a turner and tool fitter for the cutting out department; he would also fill in as required as a general workman.

Henry Bellamy and Henry Ingle were younger still: Bellamy had yet to turn twenty-one, and Ingle had just done so. Their salary arrangements would be the same as Howard's and Clough's, Bellamy to serve in the die department, Ingle to work on the steam engines. The latter was currently employed at Soho Foundry. All of these men were from the Birmingham area, Howard from Handsworth. A second engine fitter and general workman was searched for and found somewhat later, an individual named Enderwick. He worked at

Soho Foundry, and he volunteered to go out on the same terms as the other junior workmen.

That Bombay was of secondary importance to Calcutta may be deduced from the above list of men and their salaries. For with the exception of Cadenhead, all were very young, and all would receive less money for their labours than the people at Calcutta. This disparity would also be seen among those going out on behalf of Messrs Rennie. The foreman of the rolling mill was John Scott, from Christchurch, in Surrey. Currently working for John and George Rennie, the thirty-year-old Scott agreed to go out to Bombay for a five-year term in return for £300 during the first two years, £350 during the final three. His counterpart Thomas Pigg received £350 per year from the beginning. After some grumbling, the Royal Mint agreed to teach Mr Scott the finer points of the rolling process – for it had subsequently been decided that Scott would erect the rolling machinery, then operate it once minting began. He would be accompanied by two other, subordinate millwrights, Joshua Humphreys, aged thirty, and George Bilton, now twenty-four. The latter two (who were also Surrey men) would receive the same wages as Boulton, Watt's junior employees for Bombay. Except for their salaries, the employment conditions of the various men sent to Bombay would be identical with those of their colleagues at Calcutta. Maudslay, Sons, and Field sent no men out with its portion of the mint; its part of the package would be constructed by members of the other two groups.

John Scott would die at Bombay.

Other prospective workmen emerged as the Bombay machinery neared completion. Having heard that a post for engraver might be in the offing, one of the numerous Wyons wrote to Boulton in February 1824, offering his services. This was James Wyon II – whose skills were deemed insufficient for the position – at least, if original punches were required.[24] And a former employee at Soho named Joseph Turner offered himself but was rejected by the East India Company as mentally incompetent, afflicted with a religious mania.

By March 1824, the machinery the men would be paid to erect was nearly complete. On the twentieth, Boulton, Watt informed Joseph Thompson that everything would be ready for forwarding on the first of the following month – and on that same day wrote its various subcontractors, in a desperate effort to ensure that they would enable it to keep its word.

One of the main threats to Soho's promise was Samuel Walker & Company, which did business at the Gospel Oak Iron Works. Walker & Company was called in at the last moment, when it had been decided that iron plates would be required for the flooring of the melting rooms. The firm was a specialist in this type of commodity and had therefore been given the order, in January 1824. But it proved dilatory in filling it; and Boulton, Watt was still waiting for the materials well beyond its deadline.

Fortunately, the *Potton* (which had served admirably to transport the Calcutta mint the previous year and was now wanted for Bombay) proved as tardy as the worst of Boulton, Watt's subcontractors. She was expected home in late May but had still not docked by the summer of 1824 – by which time other arrangements had had to be made, were the machinery and its personnel to be got on their way to India. Whatever annoyance it may have engendered at East India House, the non-arrival of the *Potton* afforded a welcome breathing space to Matthew Robinson Boulton and John Hawkins.

Boulton employed his time to chivvy his subcontractors along, and the Rennies and Maudslay had completed their parts of the package by the middle of April, Samuel Walker & Company by the end of that month. Boulton was also acting as intermediary between the East India Company and the proposed workmen, keeping both sides as contented as possible. George Bilton wanted an allowance for his wife, who would remain at home; Boulton's assistance was sought to secure it. Then the family changed its mind: Mrs Bilton would be going out to India too; Boulton secured *that*.

On his part, Hawkins drew up an elaborate list of specialized needs for the eyes of Joseph Dart, a senior Company official in charge of supply. Hawkins' requirements ranged from Swedish copper for alloy to an experienced melter – or at least a bricklayer – for the Bombay melting department, a personnel requirement which Lieutenant Forbes had overlooked the previous year at Calcutta. Hawkins also suggested that, even if matrices for dies were retained in Britain, it would still be advisable for the Company to hire two engravers, one for Bombay and the other for Calcutta, and send them blank dies and punches taken from the matrices on a regular basis. In this way, a constant supply of moneying dies could be maintained. The East India Company rejected Hawkins' advice in this instance, but it may have adopted it in another: the captain's counsel may help explain the anomaly of frozen dates on coinage of the East India Company. Hawkins observed that

> If the original Matrix be annually altered in the date ... it will be necessary to have a new Matrix, as often as such alteration takes place; and in that case it will be requisite to have an eminent Die Engraver in India capable of doing it— But if the date be not yearly changed ... the original Matrix may then perhaps be prepared & kept in England[.] ... In this case a common Die Engraver at each Mint will be sufficient—[25]

Whether in India or in Great Britain, the East India Company believed in cutting corners whenever possible; and rupee dies dated 1835 would be used until 1840, while those dated 1840 would be used down to the end of the Company itself – and even beyond.

By the time of his good advice to Joseph Dart, Captain Hawkins was within a few days of leaving for India. He sailed on the *Upton Castle* on the morning of the eighteenth of April, one of

> 29 passengers on board, four married ladies, five single, and 20 gentlemen, all pleasant people, good ship, captain, crew, and sumptuous living; but after all it is a *ship*, on board of which we have the prospect of being confined at least three and one-half months.[26]

The captain left without his mint, for the *Potton* obstinately refused to come to port. Matthew Robinson Boulton, his subcontractors, and the mint employees were in the uncomfortable position of having made a major effort, taken a major decision – with no apparent result.

But much could still be done during the ensuing months of enforced waiting. The agreements with the last of the workmen must be signed and forwarded to East India House, advances for the nine artisans secured. Payment for the mint must be obtained and disbursed to the various partners in the enterprise. The mint machinery and engines must be sent to London, to await their journey to Bombay. The mechanics must also be got to Town – and kept out of trouble until they could sail. And finally, either the *Potton* or some other vessel or vessels must be engaged for the long journey to Bombay. This last would fall to the Company's responsibility; everything else was Matthew Robinson Boulton's problem.

The latter did remarkably well – especially considering the fact that, having just dismantled one Soho Mint, he had come to the reluctant conclusion that it would be necessary to erect another. While mulling over his future in coining, he found time to secure work indentures from the Company, see that everybody signed them, and handle the inevitable last-minute details. Cadenhead's wife opted to go to India with her husband. Boulton smoothed the way. By the early part of May virtually everything to be agreed to was on paper, initialled by all parties.

Now Boulton addressed the matter of payment. Unlike the cases of Russia or Denmark for mints (or that of the United States for copper planchets), there was never any difficulty in this regard. Soho presented its bill on the seventh of May – urged on by the fact that the Walker firm was demanding £1,000 from *it*, having become exasperated with a warehouse filled to bursting with made-to-order cast-iron plates (which could not be moved until the East India Company secured a place for them). Boulton, Watt & Company made out a warrant for £40,016 (£39,915.9.0 for the actual payment, another £100.11.0 for various fees) on 24 May. Samuel Walker & Company, John and George Rennie, and Maudslay, Sons, and Field were likely paid the following month – although the only archival notation is a remittance of £1,000 to Samuel Walker, under date of 7 June.

After months of fruitless waiting for the *Potton*, the East India Company gave up on her and engaged two other vessels, the *Florentia* (which had carried the rolling mill to Calcutta the previous season) and the *England*. These were large ships, although not as capacious as the *Potton*; as matters were finally arranged, Boulton's machinery and engines, all of the goods from Samuel Walker and about half of those from Maudslay, and all of the men and their families would sail first, on the *Florentia*. The boilers and the remaining machinery would leave a few weeks later, on the *England*. If all went well, the mechanics and their apparatus would be met by Captain Hawkins at the site of the new mint.

All of this had been determined by the first days of August, and the mint began moving out on the fourth day of that month. There was much confusion attending the shipment. Samuel Walker's wares were delayed so long that part of them had to be sent on the *England* rather than the *Florentia*. A box of machine castings went missing, to be replaced at the last moment by a harried Mr Boulton. The last of the materials would not reach the docks until 22 September.

The men proved nearly as difficult as the machinery. Shortly after their contracts had been signed, they had been given advances for the purchase of supplies. They had spent the money during the long summer weeks of waiting for the call to London – for they had meanwhile been unable to work. When the summons finally came, Boulton's six charges arrived in London with scarcely a shilling between them.

That was on 10 September. The *Florentia* would sail on the fourteenth, and the men simply had to have more money to purchase the necessities for their voyage. Boulton's London agent John Mosley took a chance: he advanced

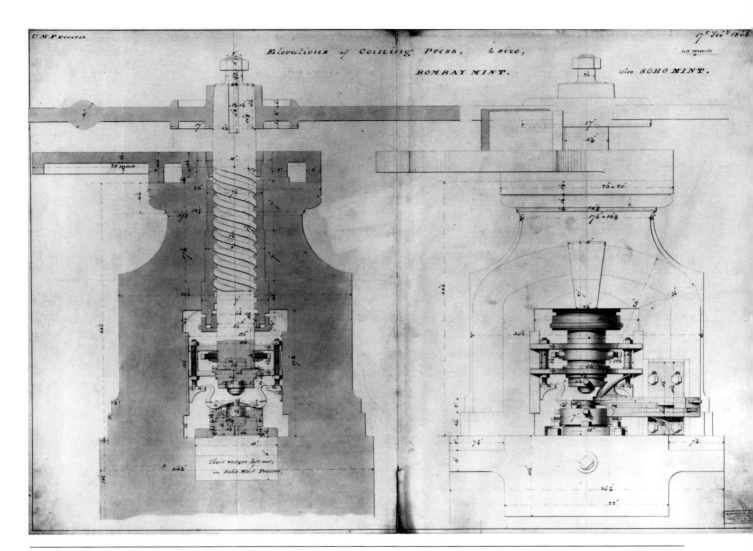

Boulton, Watt coining presses of the 1820s. (Courtesy Birmingham City Archives, Birmingham Central Library)

each man thirty pounds, in hopes that the East India Company would reimburse him. This it agreed to do.

The *Florentia* sailed on schedule on 14 September. The *England* left Great Britain on 1 October. All told, the cargo which sailed on the two Indiamen weighed nearly seven hundred tons – far more than the shipments for Calcutta. Much of the disparity was due to the addition of the heavy iron columns and floor plates ordered from Samuel Walker & Company, which weighed 125 tons; but the Rennie rolling mill added 200 tons to the total, the three steam engines (of ten, twenty-four, and forty horse) another 142. Maudslay's melting apparatus added another twenty tons, leaving a weight of about two hundred tons for the boilers and Matthew Boulton's former mint. No wonder they needed two large ships!

By the time the first of the machinery was leaving Britain, the person entrusted with it was arriving in India. John Hawkins had had a number of difficulties early on – a month's sailing had only got him as far as Madeira, and he had also discovered that plans drawn up in 1798 did not always correspond to the mint he would begin to erect in 1825. But when we remember that the machinery was now nearly thirty years old, and that Matthew Boulton and his people had been tinkering with it ever since its creation, it would be highly surprising if all of the plans and the machinery *were* in agreement with each other.[27]

The captain's difficulties rapidly intensified once he reached Bombay. He had had a standing agreement with the local government that it would begin work on the mint buildings the moment he returned, so that the machinery could be safely housed indoors as quickly as possible. But when he reached Bombay, Hawkins learned that 'the Government have not yet determined the site – and the materials ordered by the Court [in London] to be in readiness are not procured'. Nor would it be a simple matter to obtain what he needed on the spot: the current system of supply was both corrupt and inefficient. Hawkins' views are worth quoting in some detail, because the supply system would bedevil the Bombay project from beginning to end.

> It is now the practice here ... for all supplies of materials to be made by the Commissary General who is an Infantry officer & knows little or nothing of the matter; when an indent is made on the Commissary, he gives the supply to the lowest tender by contract; the consequence is, the natives bid one against another, & take the contract at a lower rate than they can fairly furnish good articles; their only hope to get out of the difficulty thus engendered is, by furnishing bad supplies,— or to bribe the agent who reviews the supply, hence delay, intrigue, vexation, & evil consequence to the public service.— If I am to receive my materials in this manner, God only knows how I shall get on—[28]

By mid-December 1824, slight progress had been made. After considerable agitation on Hawkins' part, the local officials had conceded him the right to make his own arrangements respecting supplies – with several very large exceptions. Chief among the latter were timber and stone, and their omission might stand as an excellent example of bureaucratic idiocy in the Bombay Presidency: Hawkins could have obtained all the stone he needed for his mint locally – but was prevented from doing so by Company regulations. Instead, he had to wait for his requests slowly to push their way through channels, while work remained at a stand.

His morale could have scarcely been lower. No site had yet been selected for the mint, although all agreed that it must be near Fort George. Water for the steam engines would be a recurrent problem, and the Company's resident engineers suggested that Hawkins build a fourteen-hundred-foot wooden conduit to bring water from a small ditch connected to the main moat surrounding the fortress. The fact that water travelling over a quarter of a mile in Bombay's climate would be scalding by the time it reached the mint site convinced Hawkins that the plan was unwise. So did the fact that the largest city sewers discharged their filth into the same ditch: even assuming that he or anyone else at the mint could abide the smell, anyone using that water would soon see the steam engines clog and fail to perform. Alone and isolated, the captain waited for the new year, and for the arrival of his men.

On 12 February 1825, the *Florentia* docked in Bombay harbour. The Soho Mint was unpacked, and it appeared to be in generally good condition – although parts of it had rusted from their lengthy detention in crates prior to leaving England. Unfortunately, a good deal more of the machinery might soon be rusty or worse: although Hawkins had been seeing officials since his own arrival five months before, none had yet deigned to tell him where to store the mint once it had arrived. And the men and their families had no place to reside either, the Company having overlooked that consideration as well. For the moment, Hawkins lodged everybody in a local tavern and considered his next moves.

In a sense, the machinery was even more vulnerable than mint personnel, and Hawkins soon managed to find a safe and inexpensive warehouse for it. But he had worse luck with his human charges: had they arrived even a few weeks earlier, it would have been easy to find them lodging close to the work site; but this was no longer the case.

Hawkins now had time to take a long look at his employees. Most of the men seemed adequate to their future tasks, and two of them, Henry Ingle and Henry Bellamy, had received very good reports from the captain and passengers of the *Florentia*. These two young mechanics had become very close during their months at sea, and Hawkins would try to find them lodging together at Bombay. He had no way of knowing that one of them would one day pose a major difficulty for the mint; but it was already clear that he would experience trouble from another source. This was George Cadenhead, who 'I am sorry to say has taken to *drink*'.[29] Cadenhead's addiction would eventually kill him; for now, it meant a possible gap in the chain of command.

On 1 February 1825, the foundation stone of the new mint was laid, and work on the walls began. Hawkins used such stone as he could wheedle out of the bureaucrats, and the foundation walls of the new structure, raised by the labour of two thousand men, had soon attained an average height of eight feet. Hawkins believed that he could have done even better, had he been left to his own devices. He was not so favoured, of course. Red tape, incompetence, and graft were omnipresent: its builder estimated that the new mint would cost the East India Company at least fifteen thousand pounds more than estimated, simply because favourites were making off with lucrative contracts for supply. But this cost overrun would be several times greater by the time the mint was finished.

By late March, the remainder of the machinery had arrived at Bombay. By now, Captain Hawkins had minutely examined the entire cargo of the *Florentia* and had found it in remarkably good order. He was not nearly as sanguine about the rolling mill and other cargo of the *England*, because that vessel had run into violent weather off Mauritius, losing her topmasts and taking on much water; but for now, the Bombay engineer had more immediate worries, originating with his men rather than the machinery they would construct.

Cadenhead's drinking was growing worse, and he was now incapacitated. The other Soho men ranged in quality from excellent (Ingle and Bellamy), to tolerable (Enderwick and Howard), to poor (Clough, 'the laziest fellow I ever saw').[30] Those connected with the rolling mill looked promising enough; but the morale and hence the potential of all of the Europeans was at risk because of the policies of the East India Company. We see a curious parallel between officials at St Petersburg and their counterparts at Bombay more than twenty years later. The same mindless literality characterized both groups of officials. By late March 1825, Hawkins' people were constantly encountering it, and they were becoming sullen from their treatment.

As in Russia, housing was a major problem at Bombay. The Britons were still living at the tavern, because the Company had not found them suitable quarters anywhere else. The Mint Committee proposed to house all nine of the Soho people – six men, two women, and one child – in a single small house. Moreover, this dwelling was not even furnished, because the men's contracts merely mentioned 'quarters', not 'furnished quarters'. Worse still, they had no medical aid – which they badly needed, two of them already requiring the attentions of a doctor.

The workmen decided that two could play the same game. If the Company held to the letter of its agreement concerning lodging, they would hold it to the letter of its agreement concerning pay: they demanded to be paid in pounds sterling, because that was how their contracts had stated their remuneration. They also demanded that a doctor live at their quarters – because one could read the Company's obligation that way if one chose. All of this animosity could have been solved at the beginning by a few tables and chairs; but the contract of mutual respect between proud men and their inflexible employer had been broken, and would not be mended.

Despite all this, work went on. Hawkins' builders had got most of the foundation walls completed by late March, and he estimated that they would be done with that part of the building within two months. His estimate proved accurate: by June, the foundations were finished, and much of the infrastructure for the future mint had been completed as well. From his letters, one gains an impression that Hawkins drove the mint project along through sheer force of will – encountering and defeating obstacles ranging from the Bombay Mint Committee to the annual visitation of the monsoon. But the captain's success came at a heavy price: he had already collapsed once, during the spring of 1825, and he would someday work himself into the grave. But from his point of view, what choice did he have?

By the late spring his health had somewhat recovered, and Hawkins now turned to the Rennie and Maudslay machinery. What he found confirmed his earlier apprehensions: Maudslay's cargo had been damaged to a degree – although it would be fairly easy to repair. But the rolling mill was another matter. Here, he found the machinery 'in a shocking state, the bright work was not properly protected [by those who had crated it back at the Rennie works] & the Rolls are one mass of rust'.[31] The rolls could be scoured and repaired, but the labour would divert precious manpower from other, more pressing concerns.

As Hawkins was forcing his mint along in India, his friend Boulton was seeking to smooth its path in London. Shortly prior to his departing England, Hawkins had requested a large order of supplies for the nascent mint, including dies. Some of this material (but no dies) had been sent off in January 1825; in July, 750 rupee-size dies and an assortment of collars, beds, and punches finally left Soho, more than a year after they had been ordered. Whenever Hawkins got his machinery up and running (and he was confident he would be able to do so prior to Forbes at Calcutta, even with his problems, even having got started a full year after the lieutenant), he would have something with which to strike coins.

Boulton sought to extend help for the present as well as the future: quietly working behind the scenes, he prevailed upon the London officers of the East India Company to reorganize the Bombay Mint Committee, granting

Hawkins the same relative freedom of action as that enjoyed by Forbes. Henceforth, many of the problems of supply should disappear – and the surviving correspondence does suggest that the captain henceforth had a somewhat easier time of it.

For example, he was now granted permission to solve the problem of water for the new mint in his own way – and he promptly abandoned the imposed idea of a wooden conduit, was soon writing to Boulton & Watt for over four thousand running feet of cast-iron pipe. The pipe would convey water from a relatively unpolluted location of the fort ditch to a reservoir within the walls of the mint. Shut-off valves would prevent water being used in the mint, and hence heated nearly to the boiling point, from flowing back into the ditch and raising the water temperature there. The valves could be opened and the water returned to the ditch for cooling once the day's work had ended. In order to reduce the temperature of the water as it flowed from the ditch to the mint, Hawkins proposed a tunnel through which the pipe would travel, and he was granted permission to construct it. He requested his friends at Soho to supply the valves and pumping hardware as well as the pipe. While Hawkins had to forward his request for supplies to his superiors on the Bombay Mint Committee (in late October 1825), the fact that the Mint Committee approved it without comment and sent it on to the next rung of the bureaucratic ladder suggests that he was indeed being given a freer hand, even if he still had to respect channels.

By the end of 1825, Hawkins' report on progress was decidedly mixed. Even with his new authority, delays on supplies were still taking place – most notably the delivery of bricks, for which he had been waiting for the past five months. But the purely material part of the project was proceeding at an adequate pace. Hawkins was constructing his buildings and the machinery which they would contain at the same time, and the close of the year saw the foundations done, the walls from one to two stories high, and most of the heaviest machinery in place.

But there was another side to the Bombay coin: just as Hawkins was solving material difficulties, he was encountering real and growing problems with his personnel. And while his material progress made him modestly sanguine that he could still beat Forbes in the race to strike the first new Indian coin, his labour difficulties put that and much more at risk.

The greatest problem was still George Cadenhead, who had become a confirmed alcoholic, and whom Hawkins could no longer trust with even the simplest work on the mint. The other men might be decent workers in their limited spheres, but none of them had the general sort of knowledge which was currently necessary – and which should have been supplied by the foreman, Cadenhead. And so 'every thing falls upon my shoulders'. But Hawkins' persistent optimism still obtained: 'I have as yet met with no difficulty that has not been overcome, nor do I expect any; always excepting the *Committee* & the *Commissary*'.[32] The captain was being half-humorous; and he had no idea that his situation would soon grow worse.

His relationship with the Bombay Mint Committee shortly deteriorated. The recent vote of autonomy had angered several of its members, and Bombay now attempted to take away what London had granted. The Mint Committee decreed that, while Hawkins could indeed draw up his own orders for supplies, he must henceforth submit 'all contracts I might wish to make & the prices of all materials I intend to purchase'[33] to it, prior to placing them with his suppliers. The engineer protested angrily – the Mint Committee seemed to be accusing him of venality. It backed down – but matters now reverted to the place they had occupied prior to Hawkins' grant of greater autonomy. The result was more delays and an ascending cost overrun. And progress on the mint now slowed: the buildings were nearly completed, but work on the actual minting machinery nearly came to a halt.

That was in early February 1826; by mid-June, matters had scarcely improved. Now Hawkins was not only wrangling with the Mint Committee; he was also battling Nature. The rainy season was upon him, and he had anticipated indoor work until the monsoon ended. But the Commissary had meanwhile intervened, and the materials which he needed to keep his men employed inside (including timber, which had been ordered in *1824*) were not forthcoming. As in Russia, so at Bombay: under conditions of enforced idleness, personnel difficulties would deteriorate. But Zack Walker and James Duncan had never had to contend with another aspect of the natural world which Hawkins endured at Calcutta: white ants were busily eating the wooden cogs of his rolling mill wheels! The engineer must have often wondered why he had gone into engineering in the first place, and why, particularly, in the tropics.

The months of involuntary idleness soon put the Bombay project at risk. In June, staffing matters were still more or less under control, although Hawkins was plainly worried about what the future might bring if work could not be resumed. By August, he was finding out.

To no one's surprise, Cadenhead remained useless. But the well-regarded Henry Bellamy was also creating difficulties, acting in concert with John Scott and James Howard. None of these men had given trouble before; but their involuntary idleness was destroying their civility and their usefulness to the mint. Hawkins did what he could, employing the men in those few areas where they could be kept busy, and useful. He got them occupied with the melting furnaces, even though he was no expert on the subject and had once cherished the hope that the Company would send him a specialist for the purpose. But any labour was preferable to none, at least at this time.

Hawkins' personnel problems multiplied, reaching a crisis stage near the end of the year. In one of his efforts to keep his men employed (and out of a real belief in the young man's worth: Hawkins had once gone so far as to write a letter of praise to his parents in England), the captain had made Henry Bellamy his personal assistant and receiving clerk. Bellamy repaid his regard by loafing on the job and eventually stealing from it; after several articles had been embezzled, Hawkins had been forced to demote him.

Bellamy then had a falling-out with his room-mate, Henry Ingle, and moved in with the foreman of the rolling department, John Scott. Scott, 'who was one of those fellows who subscribe in London to *strike* for wages', now joined Bellamy in retarding the work wherever possible. Hawkins allowed them to set their own hours; when they took advantage of him, he obtained an order from the Mint Committee fixing their workday at six hours – nine to noon and one to four. They and their mates petitioned the Committee to reduce their shifts from six hours to five, and when Hawkins refused to countenance the reduction, everybody combined against him and left an hour early anyway.

Work on the machinery now threatened to cease altogether. In a desperate effort to re-establish control, Hawkins sacked the two men he rightly considered the ringleaders, Scott and Bellamy, and docked the remaining employees £50 per year (except for Ingle and Enderwick, who had never joined the uprising in the first place). Bellamy left, and John Scott came to a bad end before he was able to leave: while drunk, he fell off his horse and died from the fall.

These two events broke the back of the opposition, and Hawkins was able to shepherd his people back to work – except for George Cadenhead. The latter had to be kept *away* from the machinery, lest he break something. In case his superiors in London wondered how he could manage with approximately half of his personnel, his next sentences were meant to inspire confidence:

> I shall not require a man in Scotts place or in Bellamy's; and now I find the advantage of making myself master of the *practical* in England.— I think however I may fairly claim remuneration for teaching a roller [to replace Scott], and a Die Multiplyer [to replace Bellamy] &*ca*[;] there are steady men to be had from the Regiments, and they are under better command, and will work for one third of the pay.—[34]

Hawkins would indeed adopt this policy in future: any personnel replacements would come from the military rather than from England. But he was once again volunteering for yet more responsibilities, putting his own health on the line, so that a mint could be finished on time, so that a contract he had made with himself could be kept. In the end, he would prove unequal to his task, only fulfilling his contract at the price of his life.

But at least he had succeeded in getting mint construction resumed. Much of his machinery was operable by the end of 1826; early in 1827, Hawkins began the trials of the engines which would power the presses, and he had those presses in place, the die department and coining room ready for moneying, by the end of February.

He also had one less man – George Cadenhead, whose alcoholism had carried him off on 1 February. Hawkins' epitaph was brief, and brutal:

> no man ever brought a finer constitution to India, & no one ever took greater pains to destroy it— he has done no work for the last year, & happy would it have been if he never had done any—

The other workmen were now performing well, and they seemed to regret their earlier insurgence. Accordingly, Hawkins countermanded his own order, restoring their salaries to their original levels. So much progress was being now being made that 'if the Mint was supplied with water we might soon be ready to commence a copper coinage, & even now I do not despair of *rolling* copper during the next monsoon'.[35] Hawkins had not yet received his cast-iron pipe, of course, so moneying would have to wait.

As work proceeded, Hawkins began thinking about the types of coins which would be struck at his mint, and of the relationship between them. These musings would soon make him a pioneer in the story of Indian numismatics. For he may have been the first person to make a serious argument for a single, decimal coinage for the Subcontinent, anticipating what was actually circulated there by nearly a century and a quarter.

Many of his ideas were contained in a report to the President of the New Bombay Mint Committee, J. D. Devitre. Devitre's people were now discussing the denominations, weights, and finenesses of future coinage from the new mint, and Devitre asked Hawkins for his ideas.

The latter responded with a detailed plan for new denominations and a new relationship between them. Instead of the current systems of the Presidencies of Bengal (3 pies = 1 pice; 4 pice = 1 anna; 16 annas = 1 rupee) and Bombay (16 reas = 1 anna; 16 annas = 1 rupee), let everything be multiplied and divided by tens. Thus, one would have copper coins worth ten, twenty, fifty, and one hundred reas – the latter piece the anna of the current systems. In silver, there would be pieces worth five, ten, and twenty annas, corresponding to one-half, one, and two rupees. There would also be gold pieces, worth five, ten, and fifteen rupees. (The fifteen-rupee piece was, admittedly, a departure from the decimal idea, but Hawkins had had to retain it because it was the mohur now current at Bombay).

Of course, a new decimal arrangement would not bring a numismatic millennium to India; there must also be a reform in design, to render counterfeiting as difficult as possible. Hawkins reflected on this requirement and concluded that major change was necessary here as well, one which would alter the basic appearance of the money:

> Of all devices, the native characters [in current use] are perhaps the easiest to be copied by the native Indians; and I apprehend the human head, is the most difficult; animals, and trees, follow next; because they require animation and gracefulness in the delineation, which the native artists have never yet attained—[36]

These designs should be current on *all* of the coins, regardless of metal; and let the new, decimal issues with their new designs pass current across all of British India. It would take independence to bring decimalization to India; but Hawkins' ideas on designs may have borne fruit in the uniform coinages of 1835 and later.

Meanwhile, the captain still laboured at his mint – which must be finished prior to the striking of *any* coinage, reformed or unregenerate. By early September, virtually all of the facility was habitable, and Hawkins was now considering a simple yet attractive ornamentation for its front. He was also addressing the problem of manpower once the mint was completed, making an offer to the Mint Committee to train soldiers to augment his dwindling band (especially for the rolling mill: Scott was dead and Bilton had also succumbed to drink and could no longer work). The record is silent; but a deal must have been struck, for Hawkins would soon have his new personnel. He estimated that everything would be finished and ready for coining by the end of 1827, but he was wildly optimistic; while a few trials would be struck in the early months of 1829 (one is illustrated through the kindness of Joe Cribb and the British Museum), actual coinage for production would be held off until 1830.

Hawkins himself bore very little responsibility for the delay – although he probably would have seen things differently. In November, he suffered another breakdown and went to Candalla to recuperate. But he was soon back at his post at the mint, desperate to drive the project through its final days of construction. His absence may have retarded progress by a few weeks, but he was still able to report proudly to London that, as of 6 January 1828, the mint machinery was ready to coin.

But it would not see employment for many months. The curved pipe and valves were still on their way, and until they arrived, Hawkins' charge would literally be at the mercy of the elements as far as moneying was concerned. The water supply was still in limbo by the middle of the year,[37] but by then Hawkins had more pressing concerns, his mint more serious obstacles.

Many months of potential production would be lost because the East India Company's Court of Directors seemed unclear about what to do with its new mint. Much of the problem arose from the severe illnesses of two of the men in senior positions, Sir George Robinson and James Pattison, illnesses which eventually led to their retirement. Not knowing any of this (and powerless in any case) Hawkins and his people impatiently waited for the arrival of the Company's ships of the 1828 season, which they supposed would convey the order to begin work. But the ships arrived, and they carried no word: the new mint remained inactive month after month, a prey to the moisture and salt in Bombay's atmosphere.

But even if the orders to coin had come, Hawkins' mint would have had difficulty in responding: years before, the captain had stressed the advisability of sending along masters or punches for creating working dies and a skilled melter for preparation of the metal; as yet, he had received neither melter nor coining implements.

In the belief that these shortages would eventually be overcome, the mint someday asked to coin money, Hawkins employed the early months of 1828 in patching together a work force for the purpose. Ingle, one of the two men who had *not* joined the strike, was made foreman of the coining operation, where he showed great promise. He and a recruit from the artillery named Norton were also learning how to turn and harden dies – a prime necessity once the order to coin was received. With an eye to the future, Hawkins had chosen another military man as his assistant and possible successor, Lieutenant Charles Grant. But Grant's current duties in Gujarat (where he served as the only engineer in the entire province) would keep him absent from his new post for some time, and Hawkins continued his desperate search for helpers. He eventually commandeered one European soldier for die turning, another for the rolling mill, a third, general, man to work under Enderwick (the other loyal mechanic, who had meanwhile been promoted to head engineer) – and he now had a fourth British soldier at the mint, being trained in the annealing process. These men, plus two young half-caste men, were how Hawkins proposed to meet the demands of his new mint – whenever the order came to set it to work. He was aware of his expedients' shortcomings, aware of his unenviable position in comparison with that of Forbes at Calcutta. For there was at least a sizeable reservoir of industrial talent in Bengal, a collection of people who knew something about machines. Here, such persons were in critically short supply.

In England, the East India Company was slowly shaking off its lethargy of the previous months. In September 1828, Joseph Thompson sent a large order for stores to Soho. Matthew Robinson Boulton soon put his part of the order in train – largely dies and collars for rupees, but such oddments as copper tubing for annealing and an elaborate series of scales for weighing as well. And he alerted his former subcontractors that their services would again be required. A portion of the order left Soho on 11 November 1828; the inclusion of four magnifying glasses and ten dozen bags of die-hardening compound suggests that the Bombay people were serious in their intention of creating their own dies. The whole of the order, including those portions supplied by the subcontractors, had been delivered at the East India Company's wharf by the end of the year.

As the supplies for the new mint were leaving Great Britain, its director was cautiously beginning a coinage with what he already had on hand. Sometime at the beginning of 1829 – Hawkins omitted the precise date – he put his presses in motion:

> I have sent you a few *pice* coined a few weeks since in the old mint, & some pieces of copper struck from blank Dies in our presses last month; I had hoped to have sent you others, with the Lion and palm on one side & a *star* & inscription on the other, of the same size, done by a lad of my instructing here, but they are not ready — You must not expect them to be perfect, it is only a first attempt.—[38]

And there would still be many months between the first attempt and a regular coinage.

Part of Hawkins' difficulty was that he was making do with a skeleton force, any diminution of which would loom large. Having made Ingle his foreman, he now had to stand by helplessly as that young man's health deteriorated to the danger point. Ingle would have to be sent home for his own safety – when he left, Hawkins would be short of a valuable ally. Then the millwright Humphreys thought matters over and decided not to renew his contract, and the captain was again caught off guard: Humphreys was frequently troublesome, and he tended to put on airs; but he was also a trained European mechanic and would therefore be missed. Hawkins asked Soho for assistance in selecting the successors to these two workmen; but even had he had the men to make a coinage, he still lacked many of the stores for the purpose.

It will be recalled that he had written a long letter of advice to Joseph Dart at East India House in April 1824, a few days prior to leaving for Bombay. Hawkins had given much good counsel – but he had also requested an extensive and expensive list of articles which he must have before he could begin coining. His request had been ignored in 1824; it returned to haunt the mint five years later, as did Hawkins' pleas for personnel, made at the same time. In April 1824, he had suggested that it was time to begin thinking about a die engraver and a melter and refiner, who ought to be in place prior to the opening of the mint. These requests, too, had been ignored. So it was now that

> The new Mint machinery has all been put up ready to commence working Sixteen months ago, extraordinary exertions both mental and bodily were made to accomplish the great work to the ruin of health &c all of which now goes for nothing; and the Company have been put to great and unnecessary expences in keeping the machinery clean and in the payment of salaries & so forth, all to no purpose—[39]

And while Hawkins was doing his best to train replacements for those who had died or been dismissed, even their instruction became difficult in the absence of the right supplies.

Trial piece from the Bombay Mint, dated 1828 but apparently struck early the following year. (Reproduced by kind permission of the Trustees of the British Museum)

The captain persevered: if it were humanly possible, the Company *would* have a new coinage from Bombay. On 8 March 1829, he sent Boulton a few strikes with the designs he had mentioned earlier; their quality was less than perfect, but they were a beginning.

But more men must be secured before Bombay's minting could go beyond this initial stage. The success of the mint demanded that a replacement be speedily found for Henry Ingle. By April, Lieutenant Grant was also too ill to remain at his post. He, too, would be going home – and just, Hawkins bitterly remarked, as he was becoming useful. And the captain himself was coming to an unwelcome conclusion: regardless of the success or failure of the new enterprise, he would have to abandon it for his own good.

The remaining months of Hawkins' residence at Bombay saw him feverishly exerting his diminishing strength to get his mint in motion prior to giving it up. In April 1829, a large shipment of materials left Soho for Bombay – including many of the stores for which Hawkins had been agitating for the past five years. But they would not reach him for many months – and indeed he had no means of knowing that they had even left the Midlands.

Perhaps as a reward for his perseverance, he was promoted to Major in July 1829. But as he observed at the time, his rise in rank signified very little beyond an increase in worry and responsibility. In addition to his normal duties, Hawkins was expected to train all incoming employees; but whenever he approached the Mint Committee about an increase in salary commensurate with the increase in his work load, he was put off. Meanwhile, the object of everyone's concern, the new mint was

doing nothing, excepting working all the machinery now & then to show Visitors of whom we have a great number— [Meanwhile] the want of Copper Coin is so great, that I have been ordered to send a large part of the Copper lately rec*vd* from England to the *old mint* to be coined in the old way— But I am getting a greater Philosopher than I was, & these things do not annoy me as much as they once did— I console myself that my part has been done to the best of my ability—[40]

This growing detachment would serve him well in the months to come. For while the Court of Directors finally gave the order to commence coining, in the autumn of 1829, it still refused to send out a melter or a die engraver, advising Hawkins to make the best of what he had. It also refused to take a stand on new designs for the coinage, and so Hawkins was ordered to retain those in current use. This helps explain the curious, transitional rupees struck at Bombay and Calcutta in the early 1830s, struck in a new way but bearing old designs.

But the Bombay mint would strike copper before it began minting silver, and Hawkins would oversee it, his final connection with the mint that he had built. A brief reference to copper coinage is contained in the last letter he wrote to Soho, under date of 15 November 1830. He was very ill by then, not least because all of his efforts seemed to have yielded very modest results. Several of his people were sick. No fewer than four of the soldiers sent to be trained by him in various mint matters had died – while one of his half-caste engravers had quit upon learning that the Court of Directors was unlikely to send out anyone to help him. Through all of this (and Hawkins' calendar of woes included machinery which he was unable to get to work as well as he

One of the first coins from the new Bombay Mint, quarter-anna, 1830. (National Numismatic Collection, Smithsonian Institution)

had seen it perform at Soho, parts of which were already wearing out), the copper coinage was commenced and continued. Hawkins admitted that the machinery was currently working at half capacity if that. Nonetheless, a milestone had been reached; and the fact that his old mint was striking in the metal he had deemed most important would have cheered its builder, Matthew Boulton.

Hawkins was silent as to the identity of the coins being struck, but from other testimony it appears that they were quarter-annas.[41] The new Bombay mint would extend its activities to other circulating copper coinage in 1832 and to silver that same year. But by then, the man who had built it would be gone.

At the beginning of July 1831, Matthew Robinson Boulton received a brief communication:

London July 1*st* 1831

Sir

Major Hawkins made me promise that on my Arrival in England, I would Acquaint you That the Bombay Mint was Completed. and the First Issue of Copper Coinage was in Circulation.

My Husband, Departed this Life on the 19*th* February. And was Buried at Sea[.]

I am Sir Your Ob*t* Servant Susan Hawkins[42]

Some months later, one of Hawkins' colleagues added to Susan Hawkins' spare account. His friend had died of overwork: although warned by the doctors, he had overexerted himself on behalf of the mint, and there could be no doubt that it had cost him his life. In January 1831, his health having broken completely, Hawkins was ordered to the Cape of Good Hope to recuperate. Nearly too weak to walk, Hawkins left India accompanied by his wife, leaving his children behind. They had only arrived at Bombay a few weeks previously, and the shock of separation from them weakened the engineer's health still more. Hawkins and his wife sailed on the *Triumph* on 3 February; he died and was buried at sea sixteen days later.

His demise spared him a final disappointment: after years of indecision (and years of badgering by the late major), the East India Company finally came to the conclusion that Bombay did not need an engraver, and that dies for the facility would be engraved and forged at Calcutta. All of Hawkins' written reports, and all of his verbal arguments, had gone for nothing.

This decision was handed down on 12 August 1831, but it had little immediate effect. One part of the East India Company was either unaware of or unconcerned with what the other part was doing. The nabobs in London may indeed have decided that all dies must be made at Calcutta. But their representatives at Bombay had other ideas, and they requested and received dies from Soho until the end of 1836, engraving them at the new mint and striking coinage from them until the design reforms of 1835 took effect.

When importation ceased, it had several causes. The authorities at Calcutta were becoming insistent on their right to provide Bombay with finished dies, and their persistence eventually wore down the latter's independence. But Boulton, Watt bore a share of the responsibility too: many of the rupee dies it was sending to Bombay were defective.

These were included in the shipments of 1833 and 1834. The second batch, sent on the *Mermaid,* was particularly poor, and a report from F. McGillevray, the new Bombay Mint Engineer, to his superiors on the Mint Committee observed that the *Mermaid*'s consignment was so bad that it was threatening to bring work at the mint to a halt. For the moment (McGillevray was writing in January 1835), coining could still go on if the presses were adjusted so as to strike the coins with a minimum of force: for the designs of the rupees were so simple that a weak impression would do.

But conditional adequacy deteriorated into complete inadequacy once the new rupee designs were adopted. Bombay had received matrices for the new designs by the end of 1835 and attempted to make a coinage from them, using the Boulton dies. Now their inferiority became insurmountable:

> out of the Dies received from England [i.e., Soho] not one could we find, prepare them as we might, which would withstand for half an hour together the force of the blow necessary to give the impression to the new Rupee. I speak here of those used as bottom [portrait] dies many of which flew to pieces whilst being set, many others before they struck 20 Blows; ... I took off from the strength of the blow, until the money was quite unfinished in its appearance, but still with little benefit, for the whole day in the coining room was, in spite of this, taken up in changing and setting Dies, instead of striking money, until it became evidently apparent that the case was hopeless.

Despite vigorous denial, Boulton, Watt would receive no more orders for dies for Bombay, although it would continue to supply that mint with other stores until mid-1845. But Bombay's problems with Soho dies were to yield a most interesting result.

McGillevray faced a major challenge: he was expected to prepare a large coinage, and he lacked decent imported dies for the purpose. *Could he make his own?*

He decided to try. Having located some tolerably good steel, the engineer set to work. He wanted a cylindrical steel core, surrounded by an iron ring to prevent shattering. This posed a difficulty, for if the ring were welded to the core, the heat involved was likely to destroy the goodness of the steel. So he adopted another course: he had the ring and the core forged separately, then contracted the former onto the latter without the application of heat. The first die thus made was engraved, put in the press – and served for the next three days, striking fifty-six thousand impressions of King William IV, and wearing out several top dies in the process! McGillivray had solved his problem, and

> since this time all the bottom dies used in the Department have been prepared at our own forge, and we find that according to the quality of the steel of which they are formed they may be depended on for striking a smaller or greater number of pieces of money[.][43]

What this skilled craftsman was accomplishing at a large, modern mint was being duplicated elsewhere – by others on the opposite side of India, in another modern mint, and by others still on the opposite side of the world, in a not-so-modern mint in Mexico. All were engaged in the common work of making the Industrial Revolution conform to their particular requirements, fitting universal theory to local reality and practice. But whether in Bombay, Calcutta, or Guanajuato, they were constructing their improvements upon the common ground provided to them by a faraway firm in the British Midlands.

SOURCES

The great majority of the material for this chapter comes from MBP403–4 (Bombay Mint) and MBP407–8 (Calcutta Mint). But for antecedents, several other archival sources were consulted.

MBP411 (East India Company coinage) has material on the shadowy press exportation of the late 1790s, as does MBP262, Letter Box W3 – which contains a portion of Robert Wissett's correspondence with Matthew Boulton. MBP322 (Lawson, James and Lawson, Archibald) is also useful. The actual records of shipment are detailed in MBP34, Mint Book, Day Book Mint, 1795–1798.

Much of the early discussion about steam-powered mints will be found in MBP374 (Woodward, John, 1808–10, box 5).

James Watt, Jr. played a very important role in the resumption of talks about Indian mints at the beginning of the 1820s. His relevant correspondence will be found in two boxes, MBP 354 and 355 (boxes covering the years 1811–21 and 1822–27, respectively). The details of the shipment of the two mints (and a variety of stores later on) will be found in the Mint Books for the respective periods. Finally, among archival sources, MBP332 (the John Rennie box) was helpful – although much of the Rennie correspondence is included in the Calcutta and Bombay mint boxes.

In addition to original papers, there are two volumes which any student of the two Indian mints must consult. These comprise the fourth part of Major Fred Pridmore's monumental *Coins of the British Commonwealth of Nations* (London, 1975, 1980). His first volume takes the story of British coinage in India from its beginnings in the seventeenth century down to 1835; the second volume brings it forward to the end of the Raj.

NOTES

1 MBP407, Calcutta Mint, box 1: '(Copy) L*t* Forbes's memorial addressed to the Chairman [of the East India Company] respecting the engagem*t* of Workmen to be sent out with the Calcutta Mint Machinery Aug*t 1821*'. Emphasis in original.

2 MBP374, Woodward, John, 1808–10, box 5: John Woodward to Matthew Robinson Boulton, 13 January 1808.

3 Until recently, the captain's given name was unknown to me: he signed all his correspondence with the simple initial 'J'. But a colleague, Dr Brian Weinstein, was recently in Bombay, and he kindly discovered Hawkins' first name for me. I thank him for this bit of information – minor if you have it, major if you do not.

4 MBP403, Bombay Mint, box 1: John Hawkins to Thomas Reid, 25 June 1821. Reid was then Chairman of the Court of Directors of the East India Company.

5 James Watt, Jr. observed that the East India Company had put Maudslay to so much trouble in building Perkins' rotary press that 'they cannot dispense with employing him to execute the Cranes & other Castings of the Melting Departm*t* & Refinery, the Shaking & Triturating Machinery' (MBP354, Watt, James, jr., 1811–21 [box 2]: James Watt, Jr. to Matthew Robinson Boulton, 7 January 1821).

6 I have been unable to locate a precise figure for the rolling mill in the Matthew Boulton Papers. But a letter from James Watt, Jr. to Matthew Robinson Boulton on 3 February 1821 (MBP354) noted that 'M*r* Rennie's Est*e* [estimate] as far as I recollect was about £29000' –

and since Watt remembered Boulton's figures for the engines and coining presses accurately enough, we may accept him on that for the rolling mill.

7 MBP354, James Watt, Jr. to Matthew Robinson Boulton, 11 March 1821.
8 MBP354, James Watt, Jr. to Matthew Robinson Boulton, 6 April 1821.
9 There would be *five* steam engines – two of forty horse each for the rolling mill, one of twenty-four for the cutting out machinery, one of twenty for the coining operation, and a final one of fourteen horse for the 'triturating' process – wherein silver was pulverized prior to melting and refining. The aggregate power was 138 horse, very large for those days. Forbes, the East India Company, and Matthew Robinson Boulton were taking no chances: this mint *must* be able to do everything desired, consistently and from the beginning; for there would be no simple way of materially altering it in Calcutta. That explains the two rolling mill engines: rolling was perhaps the most critical of all the activities at this particular mint. The advice of the experts was taken, and copper boilers were included in the package, raising its total price by around £3,000.
10 MBP407, William Nairn Forbes to Matthew Robinson Boulton, 19 October 1824.
11 MBP407, William Nairn Forbes to unnamed East India Company correspondent, 21 November 1825. The correspondent was probably Joseph Thompson.
12 'I beg to state … that my Mint Machinery has been restored for the present only so far as is requisite for the preparation of Planchets' (MBP407, Matthew Robinson Boulton to Joseph Thompson, 26 July 1826). The only reason that the blanking machinery had been set up was to prepare copper planchets for American cents and half-cents, a trade which predated the sale of the second Soho Mint.
13 'New Calcutta Mint', in [James Prinsep,] *Useful Tables, Forming an Appendix to the Journal of the Asiatic Society. Part the First. Coins, Weights, and Measures of British India* (Calcutta, 1834), p. 38 and facing, unnumbered page.
14 MBP407, William Nairn Forbes to Matthew Robinson Boulton, 23 August 1830; emphasis in original.
15 He sent a huge order to London in the early spring of 1830, an order placed with Soho on 10 September of the same year. It consisted of 14,500 dies, mostly for rupees and their halves, and 600 collars. While Forbes should have had several thousand rupee dies on hand from the original shipments of 1823 and 1827, Soho had once estimated that the number of rupees proposed to be struck would use up eight thousand dies per year; Forbes was obviously anticipating a large coinage and preparing accordingly.
16 MBP407, William Nairn Forbes to Matthew Robinson Boulton, 5 May 1831; emphasis in original. Despite threatening to sail for China, and thence for home, Forbes stayed at his post, vigorously complaining of his mistreatment. His troubles with the miserly East India Company seemed to have inured him against the climate, however, and he remained in India for many years, finally dying there on 1 May 1855.
17 MBP407, William Nairn Forbes to Matthew Robinson Boulton, 5 May 1831.
18 MBP408, Calcutta Mint, box 2: John Mosley to John Robinson, 24 January 1832; emphasis in original.
19 MBP407, William Nairn Forbes to James Watt, Jr., 15 October 1838.
20 MBP403, Bombay Mint, box 1: John Hawkins to Thomas Reid, 25 June 1821. Reid was the new Chairman of the Court of Directors. Hawkins' use of the word 'philosophical' is interesting: Matthew Boulton had often employed the same adjective in describing his new machinery.
21 MBP403, John Hawkins to Matthew Robinson Boulton, 25 June 1822.
22 MBP403, John Hawkins to Matthew Robinson Boulton, 30 October 1822.
23 The single denomination was struck because Matthew Robinson Boulton was convinced that, with the rise in the price of copper, he literally could not afford to manufacture the Sumatran coinage in more than one size. The fact that he must soon disassemble the remaining mint machinery, were he to send it to Bombay on time, also led to his decision (see MBP403, Matthew Robinson Boulton to Joseph Thompson, 29 October 1823).
24 There was brief discussion of employing James Wyon at Bombay as a 'secondary' engraver, i.e., to retouch and finish dies created in England, from matrices retained there for the purpose. But so far as we know, this discussion never materialized in an appointment; and Bombay's engraved dies would in time be supplied by Calcutta, not Great Britain.
25 MBP403, John Hawkins to Joseph Dart, 15 April 1824.
26 MBP403, John Hawkins to Matthew Robinson Boulton, 25 April 1824; emphasis in original.
27 On a personal note, the captain requested 'the favor of your sending me from your Manufactory of Soho two pairs of [silver] plated Curry dishes with silver edges, which I find are omitted in *my list of stores*—' (MBP403, John Hawkins to Matthew Robinson Boulton, 16 May 1824; emphasis in original). Tasteful dining accoutrements are important, even for empire-builders.
28 MBP403, John Hawkins to Matthew Robinson Boulton, 25 September 1824.

29 MBP403, John Hawkins to Matthew Robinson Boulton, 20 February 1825; emphasis in original.
30 MBP403, John Hawkins to Matthew Robinson Boulton, 26 March 1825.
31 MBP403, John Hawkins to Matthew Robinson Boulton, 22 June 1825.
32 MBP403, John Hawkins to Matthew Robinson Boulton, 28 November 1825; emphasis in original.
33 MBP403, John Hawkins to Matthew Robinson Boulton, 4 February 1826.
34 MBP403, John Hawkins to an unnamed correspondent at the East India Company, 19 November 1826; emphasis and spelling in original.
35 MBP403, John Hawkins to Matthew Robinson Boulton, 18–27 February 1827; emphasis in original.
36 MBP404, Bombay Mint, box 2: John Hawkins to J. D. Devitre, 28 August 1827 (copy); Hawkins appended this copy to a letter to Matthew Robinson Boulton of 6 September 1827.
37 Hawkins must have secured it and constructed his pipeline by the autumn of 1828, although that fact was unrecorded in the Matthew Boulton Papers.
38 MBP404, John Hawkins to Matthew Robinson Boulton, 9 February 1829; emphasis in original. Hawkins' description of the piece with the lion and palm tree/star design tallies with Pridmore 335, reproduced elsewhere, and suggests that this pattern must have been struck early in 1829.
39 MBP404, John Hawkins to Joseph Thompson, 20 March 1829.
40 MBP404, John Hawkins to Matthew Robinson Boulton, 30 July 1829; emphasis in original.
41 The evidence was contained in a letter from Hawkins' friend George Fulljames, which also gave details of Hawkins' death at sea. As an afterthought, Fulljames remitted some copper coined at the new Bombay mint – all of them quarter-annas. He added that the coiners had struck nearly 150,000 coins of that denomination, but no silver as yet – and no other copper, except for a few pie specimens (MBP404, George Fulljames to Matthew Robinson Boulton, 11 September 1831).
42 MBP403, Susan Hawkins to Matthew Robinson Boulton, 1 July 1831. She appears to have asked Boulton's help in securing a remuneration promised to her husband upon his completion of the Bombay mint. No evidence survives that Boulton acceded to her request.
43 MBP404, 'Extract of a Report from the Mint Engineer at Bombay dated 25*th* March 1836'.

CHAPTER 7

Mexico: Five Mints and their Stories

In the lengthy career of Boulton, Watt & Company, the firm's adventures in Mexico have a special interest for the historian of technology and for the numismatist. The attraction springs from several sources.

First, Soho's activities here illustrate one of the primary and recurring themes of this book, and they illustrate it more fully than anywhere else. They proclaim that wherever Matthew Boulton's technology was sent, its acceptance was never absolute, but only relative. The firm and those whom it chose to do its bidding, carry out its mission, found that compromises must be made, corners must be cut – found in fact that a forward progression might include pauses or even retreats along the way. To be sure, Soho experienced some of the same ambiguities and disappointments elsewhere, and the firm could always argue that half a loaf (*some* coining improvement) was far better than none (*no* coining improvement), in Mexico as elsewhere. But this new Latin American nation witnessed the full development of many things seen only incompletely in other places: if we wish to see how a modern Western technology was really exported during the first half of the last century, if we wish to see how it really fared in an essentially non-Western setting, we could do far worse than examining the Mexican fortunes of Boulton, Watt & Company.

These adventures have other points of distinction as well. First, they were Soho's only foreign contacts which owed nothing directly to its founder, Matthew Boulton. In fact, they only began in an organized fashion in 1825, nearly two decades after the founder's death. They were largely played out in the 1820s and 1830s – but they continued into the 1840s, and a good deal of the final business conducted by Boulton, Watt was connected with Mexico. The major player in Great Britain was Matthew Robinson Boulton, and, while this gentleman manifested certain unappealing characteristics in a number of other circumstances, he conducted his Mexican business with a flexibility, enterprise and grace which would have done his father credit during his own times of trial.

There is another observation to be made. When Soho's mint projects foundered elsewhere, the Boultons could at least place part of the blame on the 'natives' – people belonging to the host countries, ranging from a capricious tsar to a transplanted Lisbon functionary. These individuals stood in the way of Progress, at least as the Boultons defined it. But in the case of Mexico, the firm must blame its co-nationals when anything went wrong – fellow Britons who should have known better.

Two other circumstances lent Mexico a special place in the Boulton story. First, Soho's dealings there involved not one mint but *five* – Guanajuato, Mexico City, Culiacán, Chihuahua, and Zacatecas – and its fortunes differed in all five circumstances, fluctuations and variations based on time, place, and personnel.

And here is the final point of difference between Boulton, Watt's adventures in Mexico and those it found elsewhere. In other places, even including India, the firm dealt with a single set of people in England and (largely) on the ground in Calcutta and Bombay. In Mexico, it would deal with four sets at home, plus a fifth individual on the ground in Mexico. So this story is an unusually complicated one for us; we can only imagine what it must have been like for those at Soho, much of whose livelihood would ultimately depend on keeping all those strands separated, productive, and happy.

Boulton, Watt & Company must deal with so many groups because it was dealing with five mints. And it was dealing with five mints because of the recent turn of Mexican history.

Under Spain, and particularly after the coming of the House of Bourbon in 1700, Mexico had a highly centralized government, with control emanating from a single source (the Viceroy) and a single place (Mexico City). The Napoleonic invasion of the mother country in 1808, and the abdication of one Bourbon prince (Charles IV) and the deposition of another (Ferdinand VII) in quick succession, led to an unravelling of affairs in Spain's American dominions. The very nature of legitimacy and the preferred form of government were called into question for the first time; by the autumn of 1810, an armed struggle for Mexican independence had begun.

This conflict was far more confusing and complex than anything experienced in English North America in the 1770s. Indeed, Mexico's war for independence was probably the most complicated of any of the Spanish-American freedom struggles, and it left scars which are still incompletely healed. The event had the characteristics of a civil war in the broadest possible meaning of the term, wherein the colony's diverse races and classes were all pitted against each other – and only incidentally and intermittently against Spain.

Localism was the order of the day, as old scores between villages and regions were settled and new ones born, desperate struggles fought in the absence of any mitigating restraint from Spain. (For that country had its own problems: liberation from a foreign tyrant, Napoleon, and subsequent resistance to a domestic one, Ferdinand VII; during most of the period of the Mexican fight for independence, Spain's role there would be slight.) The Mexican war lasted between 1810 and 1821, eleven years. When it was over, much of the country lay in ruins. And it would take almost a century for the population level to return to what it had been before it all began.

With the departure of the last Viceroy, comically-named Juan O'Donojú, the new country settled into an unquiet truce. Never having enjoyed the experience of self-government, the next few decades would see Mexico's people investigating many avenues of political expression. There was a brief flirtation with Empire (the first of *two*, the second being imposed from abroad some four decades later). The lucky prince was Agustín de Iturbide, whose Army of the Three Guarantees (Religion, Independence, and Union) had finally lined up the support of the Mexican upper classes in the late summer of 1821, without which the Spanish Viceroy would have doubtless retained his seat. But Agustín the politician proved more skilful at conciliation than Agustín the emperor: overthrown in the winter of 1823, when he made an attempt to regain power the following year, he found that his successors were sincere when they promised to shoot him if he dared return.

After much debate, the successors in question decided that the country must be a republic, and a thoroughly federal one. Their decision found legal expression in Mexico's first organic law, the Constitution of 1824. The new national compact was a curious mixture of realpolitik and idealism, both tending toward the same result. Realism observed that Mexico was not a single *patria grande* but many *patrias chicas* – smaller, beloved entities with local loyalties and lores, whose nature had been proclaimed, indeed strengthened, during the struggles for independence. As most of Latin America severed ties with Spain between 1815 and 1825, a natural desire to avoid the centralization which had been the rule in the days of the colony combined with the liberalism then fashionable in Europe to create a luxuriant federalism. Surely, that (national) government must be best which governed least. For Mexico, the result was an organic law which borrowed heavily from the spirit at least of the Articles of Confederation, the pre-Constitutional federal compact of the United States. In the Mexico of 1824, as in the United States of 1777, the states were independent entities and the central government essentially their creature, set up to oversee those matters deemed beyond or beneath their notice. One of the avenues taken by the new Mexican liberalism would have a particular importance for Soho, and for ourselves: since the right to strike and circulate money has always been a salient trait of sovereignty, the Mexican states were now accorded that right, unmistakably spelled out in Article XI of the *Ley de Clasificación de Rentas*, passed on 16 November 1824.

Here, current political theory, fashion, and aspiration were strengthened by previous experience. Mexico's eleven years of tumult had disrupted virtually all aspects of the wider economy, shattering it, atomizing it into many local units. This was as true in the mining regions of the centre and north as anywhere else; indeed, in frank recognition of the practical impossibility of safely channelling all precious metals from these provinces to a single mint at Mexico City (and then getting the coins struck there safely distributed throughout New Spain), colonial authorities had allowed or encouraged the establishment of several auxiliary facilities in or near the mining country, at Guadalajara, Chihuahua, Zacatecas, Durango, and Guanajuato. These branches primarily struck silver, although Guadalajara also coined a tiny amount of gold, while Durango minted a fair amount of copper. Their products' designs attempted, with varying success, to approximate Spanish colonial norms. Zacatecas was undoubtedly the best coiner from an aesthetic point of view, while Chihuahua was unquestionably the worst. But aesthetics were secondary at most: the emergency mints all rendered yeoman service to the Crown during a time of troubles and were still functioning entities at the time of the transfer of power in 1821.

And from that point, poor and risky communications, localism, and the federalist view of the world combined to keep the coiners in operation, and even to add others from time to time. Between 1821 and 1905, the Mexican Republic would see no fewer than fourteen official mints, ranged from Hermosillo and Chihuahua in the far north to Oaxaca in the far south. Several of these facilities were extremely short-lived, but eight or nine of them were likely to be in service during any given year of the nineteenth century. They provided much silver coinage (particularly the peso or Piece of Eight, that most popular of players in the Far Eastern trade of the period). But they also struck some gold – and some copper, first for the states, later for the nation. As these mints sought to modernize (from motives of prestige, profit, or better service to their customers), they would have to look abroad to secure the machinery and engineers they required, for the commodities and skills they required were not to be found at home.

So one final element must be in place before concerns such as Boulton, Watt & Company could make their entrance: the new Mexican nation must invite the participation of European capital, and Europeans, especially Britons, must be willing to provide the influx of money and skills to rebuild shattered local and national institutions. These pieces of the puzzle were being fitted by the beginning of the 1820s, and a speculative boom based on new investment in new American nations had reached its climax by the middle of that decade. And just as it was being reached, and just as it began to seem impossible for an Englishman *not* to make money there, Soho was brought into the picture. In the summer of 1825, it would be asked to reconstruct two Mexican mints, one in Guanajuato and the other in Mexico City. Let us examine the fortunes of each in turn, then proceed to the lesser lights, and to Soho's adventures at Culiacán, Chihuahua, and Zacatecas.

GUANAJUATO

Guanajuato was by far the more important contact – indeed, it enjoys the distinction of being the most varied and longest of any of Boulton, Watt's Latin American connections. It would involve virtually every aspect of Soho's contribution to numismatics, from the purveyance of pattern coinage (hopeful harbingers of regular issues to come) to the sending of machinery, dies, and the gifted personnel necessary to put and keep everything in motion – in short, the equipment and manpower necessary to transform this backward, up-country mint into a leader in Spanish-American coinage of the period. The Birmingham firm and its American client would be partners for a quarter of a century, and the only cause for an end to the relationship was the end of Soho itself.

As I noted in an earlier study on this facility,[1] Boulton, Watt & Company did not deal directly with the Guanajuato mint, much less with the state or federal authorities in that place. Instead, it did business with a succession of British intermediaries who had ties with the state in which the mint was located.

This tended to be the case with all of Soho's dealings in the Mexican Republic, and it formed one aspect of the *empresario* (contractor) system, whereby foreigners were allowed to run Mexican mints, a system which prevailed until the end of the nineteenth century. The outside contractors were an affront to national sentiment, and it was widely believed that they were sucking the country dry; but they were also the only way by which bankrupt state governments could modernize their mints, improve coinage, and increase their revenues from seigniorage.

Guanajuato had a connection with two closely-related British firms, the Anglo Mexican Mining Association and the Anglo Mexican Mint Association. The two companies shared personnel in their London offices and on the ground in Mexico. The Mining Association had become a major player in the resurrection of Guanajuato's silver mining by the mid-1820s; its search for a secure market for its wares drew it into the business of minting, focusing its attention on the local coining facility.

When it looked there, it saw a challenge and an opportunity. The mint was ramshackle, having never been upgraded from its hardscrabble days as an emergency facility. Its machinery was abominable, its products crude, tempting targets for the forger; and its production was inadequate to the rumoured wealth of the mines it served. An irascible gentleman named John William Williamson proposed to change all that.

Williamson was the Mint Association's representative in Guanajuato. At the end of May 1825, he signed an agreement with the state to refurbish its mint. Local authorities would have concluded that they were getting the best of the bargain: Williamson and the Mint Association agreed to rebuild the facility, pay the salaries of the Mexican employees whose presence the law required, strike copper money for the state at cost, and allow the state to inspect the mint whenever it wished. Moreover, the Britons agreed to allow the abrogation of their contract if a better firm made its appearance, and best of all, the end of the ten-year contract would see the mint's reversion to the state – with all the improvements wrought by the Mint Association – for free!

The Britons were no fools, and they had their reasons for agreeing to such an ostensibly one-sided deal. Provided the Guanajuato mines were as rich as everyone said, and provided the Guanajuato mint could be made as productive as everyone hoped, anyone connected with the mint scheme would (so to speak) make a great deal of money.

It was all there in the contract. Williamson had agreed to a low price for each mark (about seventy ounces) of silver coined. If the mint's output remained at present levels, no one would get rich. But the mint's output, of course, was not intended to remain where it was: the Mint Association proposed to turn the facility into the numismatic powerhouse of Latin America, striking silver pesos by the millions. And when that happened, everything would change. If one assumed that there would be a one-time cost of £10,000 to upgrade the machinery, the refurbished, more productive mint could make that investment back during the first year, *and £26,000 besides.* After that, it would all be pure profit for the next nine years. Williamson in Mexico and Robert Mushet (the director entrusted with the project in London, who was also cozily serving as melter at the Royal Mint) had discovered an enduring secret of manufacturing: if you make and distribute enough of anything, it doesn't particularly matter what you charge for any one unit; volume will take care of you.

But volume would have to be enormous in the case of Guanajuato. Robert Mushet estimated that, for the mint to reach his minimum target of

£1,000,000 worth of coinage in one year (and thereby achieve the £36,000 annual profit), it would have to strike about seven million coins in a working year of three hundred days, or 23,530 pieces daily. The only way to reach or surpass that level was by applying the latest machinery to the coining process. And Mushet's mind instantly leapt to his old friends from the mint-building days at the Tower, Messrs. Boulton, Watt & Company.

A working relationship was established between Matthew Robinson Boulton, of Soho, Robert Mushet, of London, and John William Williamson, of Guanajuato. Acting on what he assumed were Williamson's instructions, Mushet would tell Boulton what to build, what to prepare. For all concerned, and for the fortunes of the Guanajuato mint, full and accurate communication was essential. As the story developed, this critical element would be in short supply.

But matters moved smoothly enough at the beginning. The Mint Association began making general inquiries of George Rennie, among others, during the first week of August 1825. Robert Mushet was made director for the Guanajuato project a few days later and was soon asked to oversee the provision of new machinery for the mint. He was approaching his old friends at Soho by the eighteenth, requesting an estimate for a package roughly the size of the one now building for Soho – with four coining presses, eight cutting out presses, a die multiplying press, and the various other oddments associated with a Boulton mint. There was an important distinction, however: while Mushet wanted something which could be adapted to steam or horsepower in the future, the mint must be workable by hand for the present. The Association was thus in the ambiguous position of wanting to modernize and expand a coinage while eschewing the primary item necessary to do so. But it had its reasons: as Mushet observed, 'the scarcity of fuel [at Guanajuato] puts the Steam Engine out of the question'.[2]

Had he recalled these words, he, the Mint Association, and Matthew Robinson Boulton would all have been spared a great deal of trouble. Instead, he would talk himself into a different, and malign, conclusion.

Boulton helped him get there. As on several other occasions, Soho would be assisted by the Rennie firm in the preparation of a machinery package. Boulton seems to have advised George and John Rennie to incorporate a steam engine in their plans for a rolling mill, something which the Rennies would have likely done in any case. Meanwhile, Boulton prepared an estimate for his part of the work – £4,478 for four coining presses, six rather than eight cutting out machines, three milling machines rather than the two Mushet had originally suggested (Boulton may have heard that virtually all Mexican coinage was edge-marked, which meant that a third machine might well be required), a die multiplying press, lathes, and the remainder of the supplies and tools necessary to refurbish the coining branch of the Guanajuato mint. He said nothing about steam power, however, perhaps assuming that the Rennies' estimate and Mushet's prior experience would lead him to draw the correct conclusion.

Mushet was already moving in that direction. Boulton's estimate went out on 24 August; by the beginning of September, Mushet was convinced that steam power was indeed essential, and he had managed to convince the fellow-members of his Board of Directors by the sixth. A vote was taken that day: steam it would be. Boulton had meanwhile prepared a new estimate, incorporating steam power into the equation. The final total for Boulton's presses, plus two steam engines to power them and the Rennies' rolling mill, would come to £8,281.

This was an enormous amount of money to invest without a shilling's worth of profit to show for it. While the Mint Association approved of what Mushet had done and what Boulton proposed to do, both men would have to move quickly. The sooner the new mint was built, the sooner it was striking those silvery symbols of the wealth of the New World – the sooner it and its backers would begin to turn a profit. George Rennie had promised that his people could prepare their portion of the machinery within six months; what about Boulton, Watt & Company?

That firm was not inclined to make promises it knew it could not keep. It was engaged elsewhere with three extant mints (at Calcutta, Bombay, and, of course, Soho), and it was entertaining conversations about a fourth, for Mexico City. But it moved with due alacrity, beginning construction of its portion of the package in October or November. It worked in accordance with the instructions it received from Robert Mushet, who was in turn advised by John William Williamson. The latter counselled that, if steam engines were to be used (and Williamson does not appear to have asked *why* they were to be used – at least, not at this point), they must be fuelled by wood, there being no coal or charcoal in the vicinity of Guanajuato. As it happened, another element was in short supply as well, but Williamson left that for later.

For now, other matters made their presence known. Prime among them was the question of mint personnel. It was all very well to provide new machinery to a needy mint. But coining is a human activity, even in the age of the machine: without skilled, caring people on the site, Guanajuato's new coinage might be scarcely more successful or plentiful than its old.

Much would be asked of the master of the new mint, for upon his shoulders would fall the greatest responsibility for the success or failure of the modernization effort. Mushet mulled over the choice of master, finally recommending a young but very skilled civil engineer for the post named George Cumming Scott. Scott must have been well-qualified indeed, for Mushet recommended him to his Board of Directors at a salary of no less than £750 per annum – an enormous sum by the less-than-generous standards of the Mint Association, and three times the money to be paid to a simple mechanic. The Board complained, but it finally gave way. Scott would be sent to Soho for final training; meanwhile, that firm was asked to select someone to go out and actually erect the apparatus.

We have seen such requests for help in personnel elsewhere, especially in India. But Mushet's next query was distinctly unusual: on 4 March 1826, he asked Boulton whether, provided the Mint Association could obtain master punches for the purpose, Soho could provide dies for a Mexican coinage at Guanajuato. When he did so, he was crossing the line from enterprising business practice to illegality – and he was asking Boulton to come along.

The provision of Soho dies was against current Mexican law, which said that all such tools must be created from masters made at the primary mint in Mexico City. While a more rational arrangement would have been to have die blanks sent to Mexico City, hubbed there, and sent back to the individual mints, the Mexican authorities preferred to send the *masters* out, have local impressions taken, and have the originals returned to the capital. This was not a particularly safe or speedy way of doing business, and it wasn't even especially efficacious in the primary cause for which it was employed, die standardization; but it was the law.

The Mint Association rightly saw this practice as a potentially serious bottle-neck to its own concerns. Mushet was well aware that mass production of coinage with steam power would necessitate an enormous number of dies, while the demands of the powerful presses would mean that those dies must be made from best-quality steel. The Mexican system would fail in both respects; might the British system be employed? That its employment was ille-gal, would in fact involve smuggling if it were carried forward, does not appear to have concerned Robert Mushet or his prospective supplier. And dies would soon provide an interesting if clandestine chapter in the story of the Guanajuato mint. But not just yet: by the summer of 1826, the Anglo Mexican Mint Association (and shortly its business partner at Soho) had more pressing concerns.

For if the truth were told, Robert Mushet and his confederates were far bet-ter at spinning tales than they were with dealing with facts. The Mint Association had been set up to make money for its stockholders, paid in the form of dividends. It had secured an opportunity to make these monies over a ten-year period when its man Williamson had struck his agreement with the state of Guanajuato. It had expected to begin making money almost at once.

Then reality intruded. Ten years was not that long a time to get rich, and more than a year had already been expended in building the machinery. And there was still the matter of getting the apparatus to where it could begin to perform its miracle: it now appeared that transporting the mint to Guanajuato might actually cost more than the machinery. And even if it got there, a site for it must still be selected and buildings constructed. And finally, even if all this were solved in a timely fashion, three crucial elements must still be in place were success to be assured. There must be fuel. There must be water. And there obviously must be silver.

And by the summer of 1826, it was becoming clear that two of these three elements were in short supply.

First, the water. While Williamson had said nothing about it, another employee named James Baird had been sending back reports to London warning that running water was non-existent during several months of the year. Baird was at frequent loggerheads with Williamson about most aspects of the mint project, and Mushet took what he said with a grain of salt. But Baird had a point in this instance: water *would* be a problem, and Williamson had known about it but remained silent. The water problem put the Guanajuato affair in an entirely new light.

So did a second revelation: despite Williamson's rosy estimates, there apparently wasn't all that much silver in the region either. Any profits which would accrue would therefore come much more slowly than anticipated, to the annoyance of current and the discouragement of future investors. Precious months, even years, of the contract would inevitably slip away. From over-optimism, Mushet now swung to the opposite pole. It would take between fifty-seven and sixty thousand pounds to set the mint in motion, not the ten thousand he had previously supposed; and it would take no less than two years to do so. The aspiring minters would have no more than seven years to recoup their investment and to profit from it.

Mushet and his London associates conferred madly, then settled on a two-pronged approach to solve their problems. In Mexico, John William Williamson must somehow get their contract extended. In Soho, Matthew Robinson Boulton must somehow be persuaded to take back their mint.

Williamson was successful: despite initial opposition, the state eventually extended the Mint Association's contract, which would henceforth run until 1842. But Mushet and his cronies had much less success at home.

They let Matthew Robinson Boulton in on their difficulties by degrees. He had nearly finished their mint by mid-July 1826, had also secured the agreement of two Soho mechanics to go to Mexico as mint employees. On 19 July 1826, Boulton was advised that the machinery would not be wanted just yet, and that the two mechanics should be retained on half pay for the time being. Soho would receive additional instructions in due course.

For the next year, Boulton waited for further orders. In London, mutual recrimination was the order of the day, as Mushet, Williamson, and Baird all blamed each other, as members of the Board of Directors took sides in the controversy. By late December 1826, Robert Mushet was quietly asking James Watt, Jr. whether the two steam engines might be taken back, and if so, for how much. By February 1827, a decision had been made to abandon steam power; and by mid-July of that year, Matthew Robinson Boulton was being asked to provide a second, pre-industrial mint, and to find a buyer for the first, industrial one!

This new mint was an altogether more modest affair, but it did enjoy the distinction of actually seeing service in Guanajuato. It consisted of two coining presses rather than four, three planchet-cutters rather than two, a single milling machine, and a single die multiplying press. All of this machinery was to be operable by hand, and it was precisely the sort of apparatus which the old Royal Mint had used before the elder Boulton had taken it in hand.

But business was business, and the younger Boulton showed himself inclined to take his profits where he found them. If the Mint Association wanted to turn its back on the industrialization of money, that was its affair, not his.

And this modest approach certainly accelerated matters. Cannibalizing as he went along, Matthew Robinson Boulton estimated that the Mint Association could have its machinery in a month or six weeks, which was good news. The machinery would weigh only ten and one-half or eleven tons, a small fraction of its previous weight, which was better news. And the whole package would only cost the cash-poor Mint Association an additional ten or twenty pounds, which was the best news of all.

The log-jam was finally broken, and the Guanajuato mint would become a reality – albeit one to nobody's particular taste. Boulton was given his marching orders on 20 July 1827, and the reduced machinery finally left England on its long westward journey early in October. But a number of loose ends remained. A sum for the unwanted steam engines must be agreed to and secured. The nature of mint personnel must be readdressed. And the remainder of the redundant machinery must be sold.

The first two problems were solved fairly quickly. A sum of £2,187 for the two steam engines had been previously broached, and it was formally agreed to on 11 February 1828. And the second problem was temporarily solved around the same time. Since the services of a skilled engineer were no longer needed, those of the expensive Mr Scott were dispensed with, and two of Soho's regulars were sent out in his stead.

These were Edward Riley and Robert McLeish. Riley was a blacksmith, a man who enjoyed a reputation as a teetotaller among his mates – a rare bird indeed in this time and place. He would receive a salary of £150, rising to £175 and £200 over the life of his three-year contract. He had a wife and child, but they would stay behind, the Mint Association refusing to pay their passages. Loneliness and the pressures of a tropical environment turned poor Riley in new directions: he began drinking heavily and ran away in the spring of 1829, never to be seen again.

Robert McLeish was a good general mechanic, capable of erecting a steam engine in the unlikelihood he was sent one to erect. His current tasks would include turning dies and working with the coining and cutting out machines. His salary is apt to have been somewhat more generous than Riley's, but no precise figures have survived. Riley and McLeish would join John William Williamson and James Baird, who already loathed each other. McLeish and Baird seem to have taken an instant dislike to each other as soon as McLeish and Riley (along with much of the machinery) appeared on the scene early in 1828. For the next few years, personnel rivalries would be nearly as great a problem at Guanajuato as they had once been at St Petersburg.

All of this could be worked out in time – after all, the men's contracts were for a set period of years and a regular turnover might be expected. The problem of the remaining, unwanted machinery was far less tractable, and it took no less than fifteen years to achieve even a partial solution.

This was not due to lack of effort on the part of Matthew Robinson Boulton – who had generously if unwisely agreed to store the redundant machinery at Soho. Nor was it the fault of the Mint Association – whose interest in recouping its loss was and would remain keen. But while schemes were floated by both sides year after year, ranging from sale to an unnamed party in 1827, to sale to the Austrians in 1828, to sale to the Americans in 1829, to sale to the Dutch a decade later, nothing had been done by the close of the 1830s. Early in the following decade, however, it appears that a transfer of the apparatus was consummated. If my reading of the scant documentary evidence is correct, an individual named John Potts was the recipient, on two occasions during 1841. Potts had worked for the Anglo Mexican Mint Association in Guanajuato in the 1830s. At the end of that decade, he hired on at the Chihuahua mint, but retained some of his ties with his old employers. Through their good offices, he obtained coining dies from Boulton, Watt in 1840, and he was also then requesting an estimate from the firm for a die multiplying press and a pair of cutting out presses – a project which did not go beyond the preliminary stage. But early the following year, I believe he asked the secretary of the Mint Association, George B. Lonsdale, to help him obtain the unwanted Guanajuato machinery.

Lonsdale approached Boulton, Watt that February, asking that the two coining presses remaining at Soho be cleaned, packed, and shipped to the Mint Association's offices at 9 New Broad Street, London. The fact that he was requesting all parts of the machinery below the 'trumpet' (the horn-shaped connection between the press and a steam engine) tells us that the presses had originally been steam-powered but could be converted to work by hand, and were in fact the two unwanted Guanajuato machines from 1826. The ten boxes with press machinery left Soho on the eighteenth of the month, and Lonsdale was billed £7.10.0 for cleaning and retouching the apparatus.

But this would not be the final word. The letter generating this shipment has unfortunately been lost, but it apparently asked for information about new machinery as well, particularly about three cutting out presses and the pneumatic linkage necessary to connect coining presses to – a steam engine! Lonsdale later settled for the linking apparatus constructed back in the mid-twenties, and this machinery too left Soho, at the beginning of June 1841.

What happened next is uncertain. While there *is* an improvement in the quality of Chihuahua silver and gold coinage between the late 1830s and the early 1840s, Boulton's presses alone could have accounted for it, even without steam power. And there is no hard evidence for the employment of steam at that mint until the end of the 1850s. But Potts may have been looking to the future, or a contract for a steam engine from an unknown supplier may have been discussed, then rejected.

In any case, the remainder of the original Guanajuato machinery was now out the door, and all parties in London and at Soho breathed easier.

As efforts were getting under way to sell the unwanted parts of the mint, those portions of it which would actually see service in Mexico were slowly making their way to the New World. The Rennies' rolling mill got there first, then a portion of the Boulton machinery, early in 1828. But packages containing parts of the Guanajuato mint were strung all the way back down the tortuous road to the port of Veracruz, and the final portion of it, the all-important milling apparatus, was not even *shipped* until the spring of 1832. All of this meant that what was left of the industrialization of Mexico's money would have to be applied piecemeal, weakening its effect.

Before the mint machinery could be put to work, a building must be found to house it. The original place selected was an abandoned tobacco factory, soon rejected because it was too small. A second, larger site was chosen, the Hacienda de San Pedro – but it, too, was spurned, although we do not know the reason. Perhaps it was deemed too distant from the centre at Guanajuato; certainly the site finally picked was near the city centre, on Calle Sopena. The new mint formally opened here on 14 November 1827. And its first coins were as disappointing as anything which had gone before.

The Mint Association sincerely desired to upgrade the quality of its product, hopefully turning a profit at the same time. This twin objective explained its flirtation with steam, a project which had failed. But there was another way of improving the appearance if not the quantity of its wares, and that was by having the dies which struck them produced in Great Britain by the same firm which had supplied the machinery, Boulton, Watt & Company.

Robert Mushet had always been interested in the possibility, and he had gone to the trouble of selecting a prospective engraver for the project as early as the autumn of 1825. This was probably William Wyon (1795–1851; Wyon was already connected with the Royal Mint, as was Mushet), and the initials W.W. appear on pattern pesos and onzas (eight-escudo gold coins) from this time. But the letters might as easily stand for (John) *William Williamson*, as has indeed been suggested by Alberto Francisco Pradeau, among others. In any case, Wyon wanted far more for his work than Mushet was willing to

Soho pattern peso for Guanajuato, with final digit of the date left blank. (Courtesy Richard Ponterio)

countenance, and the Mint Association would henceforth call on Soho's engravers to place the designs on Soho's dies.

But it made their work difficult, demanding two qualities for its dies, two attributes which effectively cancelled each other. Soho's dies must be identical with the Mexican product, so that they could safely be employed once they had reached Guanajuato. But they must also be *better* than the Mexican product – more attractive, more artistic, more refined – so that they would serve as a deterrent to forgers.

Boulton and his artists did their best to achieve the impossible, beginning with dies for the most popular of Guanajuato's coins, the peso or Piece of Eight. A pair of master dies was made at Guanajuato in the latter part of 1829, sent on to Soho (to be slavishly copied while improved upon there), and an agreement to provide some six hundred 'dollar' or peso dies was drawn up at the end of the year. Soho was ordered to proceed with the project on 5 January 1830.

It will pay to take a close look at the Mexican peso and its designs. The coin was extremely popular in the Far Eastern trade, and any obvious design modifications would have led to rejection by merchants there – as would indeed happen in the 1870s, when an unfamiliar design adopted by the Juárez government in 1869 failed miserably a few years later. The designs so popular with Chinese businessmen featured an eagle clutching a serpent for the obverse, surrounded by a wreath below and the legend REPUBLICA MEXICANA, Mexican Republic, above. The reverse design incorporated a Phrygian or liberty cap, surrounded by rays, with the denomination, the abbreviated name of the mint, the date, two initials representing the assayer or assayers, and a guarantee of silver fineness. The elements of the obverse die remained unchanged between 1825 and 1897, legend included. The reverse legend was altered in accordance with mint, date, and minting personnel.

Soho's maiden attempt at die supply was not particularly successful. Its shipment left Great Britain several months behind schedule, only beginning its journey in mid-May. It arrived in Guanajuato some ten months later, and, when excited mint officials opened the crates, they found the dies badly rusted from the salt in the Russian tallow in which Soho had packed them. (On instructions from those on the site, subsequent shipments were packed in white wax, which left the surfaces of the dies unscarred and could later be recycled into candles for lighting.) Along with the first dies, two other commodities were shipped which would never see employment (single-piece collars and layers-on, in case the mint ever modernized in the Boulton fashion) and a third which would see a good deal of use. This last was a matrix plate for making letter and number punches, and it would have to be available virtually from the beginning of coining.

To see why, think back to Mexican coin designs and legends. The obverse did not change, so dies could be sent out from Soho in a hardened or finished state, with all elements in place. But elements on the reverse *did* change – the date every twelve months, assayers' initials ordinarily less frequently, but unpredictably. Reverse dies must therefore be shipped with gaps where these elements would appear, and they must be sent out soft. They would be finished in Mexico with punches taken from the matrix. Hardened, they would then be married to the obverses for coining.

The matrix plate too must yield a product identical with the Mexican, yet superior to the Mexican.

In time, the trade in dies became a regular feature of Soho activity. Dies were generally sent out with obverses ready for coining, reverses left uncompleted, but in times of emergency risks were taken. In the summer of 1830 and again at the beginning of 1832, dies were ordered with all elements added at Soho, probably because the Guanajuato coiners were in such acute difficulties that their need transcended the off-chance that the assayer combination displayed on the dies would no longer be current by the time they arrived. And other variants came about from time to time: at the beginning of the 1840s, there was a shipment of peso dies from Guanajuato *back* to Soho – reverses which had been dated 183- in England and which must be redated 184- there to serve in the new decade. Soho did the necessary, charging £17.5.0 for the work, sending its recycled wares back across the sea in November 1840. And the dies got used, as coins struck from them testify.

There was one element of this commerce which went beyond the confines of normal business activity: it was illegal. Its pursuit therefore depended upon subterfuge and smuggling on the part of that venerable pillar of the business community, Boulton, Watt & Company.

The firm and its customer thought of a number of stratagems over the years, the most successful one being developed by those on the ground in Mexico, whose acquaintance with local conditions gave them an interesting idea. Mints were always short of iron cylinders or pillars for machinery – in fact, mints in Mexico tended to be short of iron in all forms. If you were to provide iron *tubes*, whose diameters matched those of the bottoms of peso dies, fill the tubes with dies (along with suet, to keep the dies from rattling, and lead pellets, to give the packages the weights of solid pieces of metal); if you were to then seal both ends of your tubes with flanges which were heat-sprung into place; and if you were to then paint the whole gray, you would have something which would look like pillars or rollers for mint purposes, 'which I think will completely avoid suspicion [of Mexican customs agents at the port of Veracruz, who were told to be on the lookout for British-made coining dies]'.[3] This advice was taken for succeeding die shipments here and elsewhere, and it seems to have been successful.

A typical Guanajuato peso struck from Mexican dies, 1830. (National Numismatic Collection, Smithsonian Institution)

Because of the popularity of the Mexican dollar within and outside the country, fewer liberties were allowed and greater smuggling precautions were taken with dies for this denomination than with those for any other. A careful examination of Guanajuato pesos struck from Soho dies reveals no major points of departure: obverse, reverse, and edge all fall within the admittedly fairly broad range of admissible variation for nineteenth-century Mexican coinage. There is a minor point of difference, however, and it has generated a certain amount of confusion.

Other Mexican pesos featured a single dot after the date; between 1830 and 1843, Guanajuato's pesos featured *three*, arranged in a triangle. Pradeau and others have speculated that the three dots bore an arcane relationship to Freemasonry, a hint for those in the know that the Guanajuato coiners had an allegiance to this proscribed creed. But the three points are more likely to have been an arcane reference of a different kind: since we also find them on pesos from Chihuahua, whose dies were also made at Soho, I tend to see them as a privy mark of Boulton, Watt & Company. Whatever their significance, they only appear on silver, and then only on pesos.

A typical Guanajuato peso struck from (smuggled) Soho dies, 1832. (National Numismatic Collection, Smithsonian Institution)

Soho's onza pattern for Guanajuato, 1831; these designs would be adopted for normal coinage at the end of the decade. (Courtesy Birmingham Museums and Art Gallery)

Other denominations saw less frequent use, and greater liberties could be allowed with the designs for their dies. By the summer of 1834, minor silver coinage was being reworked on orders of the Mint Association, the artist responsible being John Sherriff. Dies with distinctive, realistic eagles and triangular[4] liberty caps and delicate rays, intended for half-reales, reales, and two- and four-real pieces, were finally created to the Mint Association's satisfaction by February 1835, and they left Birmingham for Mexico at the end of that month. The new designs would see use at Guanajuato through the early 1840s.

Soho was sending out dies for gold coins by 1831, but design reform took longer to achieve for gold than for silver. The first dies shipped were for the largest gold piece, the eight escudo or onza, which also happened to be the most popular gold coin in commerce. Popularity might inspire close scrutiny, and Soho was accordingly instructed carefully to copy the Mexican originals, without variation. By 1838, however, it was being encouraged to reform the design of the onza and its half. John Sherriff again appears to have undertaken the work, and the artist's distinctive, realistic eagles (along with a slight improvement in the reverse design) testify to his work. (Those eagles would also be featured on onzas from Chihuahua, struck between the early 1840s and the mid-1860s, about which more later.)

Thus amended, dies for gold and silver coins went out to Guanajuato year after year, playing their quiet role in the development of Mexican numismatics. But British dies were nonetheless illegal for Mexican coinage, and they could be seized by local authorities at any time. Moreover, they could not be relied upon to appear in a regular and timely fashion – like its planchets for American cents and half-cents, Soho's dies for Mexican coinage were subject to the hazards of the sea, and the firm which made them enjoyed an imperfect record for punctuality in any case. The risks and associated difficulties were turning the Guanajuato coiners towards two major decisions by the end of the 1830s.

The first, and the more important of the two, was to make coin dies in Mexico in addition to importing them from abroad. The Guanajuato mint's inadequacy as die-sinker had attracted it to Soho back in 1829–1830. But the local coiners had learned much in the ensuing years, and they now discovered that they could industrialize their own coining processes *and improve upon the Boulton model in the process.*

They found they could mass-produce dies for their peso coinage. This denomination was always a problem, because the mint struck more Pieces of Eight than any other member of the series – heavy coins which soon wore out the dies used in their creation. The mint was importing more peso dies than those for all other denominations combined by the middle of the 1830s. Now trial and error would find a local solution.

The coiners found that they could harden Soho reverse dies (which had been shipped out soft), then put them in a coining press and replicate their designs and legends onto soft steel die blanks. The final digit of the date and the assayers' initials could then be added, the new dies hardened, and new coining tools produced. The coiners could replicate obverses as well – with even less trouble, because obverses never changed, needed nothing added. The results might not have had the needle sharpness of British dies, but they would certainly serve well enough.[5] And the Guanajuato moneyers took their die-making one realistic step beyond the practice of their English supplier. The latter was still sending out dies with precise, right-angle relationships between top faces and sides. This configuration was absolutely necessary in moneying with restraining collars and layers-on (with which tools Guanajuato was also regularly supplied through most of the 1830s, in the vain hope that such mechanization would still someday occur). But such dies made no sense in the primitive conditions under which the Guanajuato mint actually struck its coins: such tools crumbled along their peripheries, marking their products and shortening working life. So John Potts and his colleagues reformed the shape of their dies, even as they were discovering new ways of replicating their designs. They would abandon the sharp, right-angle edges in favour of broad, rounded corners, and their dies would work far better and last far longer.

In the process of industrialization of any commodity, including money, due attention must be paid to what *can* be done as well as to what *ought to* be done. While the Guanajuato coiners may have wished for steam power, hankered after the most modern, productive mint imaginable, they were forced to adapt to circumstances: there is no water here, you are thousands of miles from the centre of the Industrial Revolution, whose writ, taken literally, now has no force. You must therefore make compromises, coin as you can, produce the finest commodity possible under the circumstances. This the Bairds, the Williamsons, the McLeishes, and the Potts' did; and while the Boultons and the Lonsdales must have been disappointed with the results, *we* may view the undertaking with a greater charity, and as part of a larger story.

The second decision taken was to bring the appearance of Guanajuato's coinage into line with that seen elsewhere. The fact that they were now taking their own die impressions would have tended toward a greater visual similarity with the products of other Mexican mints, many of which were weakly struck. But in the early 1840s, the coiners made determined effort towards local compliance with the national norm.

They may have been inspired by the fact that the Guanajuato mint's contract was due to expire in 1842, and that the Mint Association wished to gain its extension.[6] They must have also been influenced by the constant fear of discovery of imported dies: the authorities will have a good deal more trouble proving your guilt if your foreign dies look like everyone else's domestic ones. For whatever reasons, the years between 1842 and 1844 marked an abandonment of English-style Mexican coinage at Guanajuato.

Sherriff's eagle yielded to an uglier but more plausible bird. The triangular cap was abandoned, as were the three dots. And the die axis of the coins (the relation of the faces to each other, which numismatists refer to by the numbers on a clock face) changed from twelve to six – an orientation adopted in several other Mexican mints from the 1820s onwards, but one in which Guanajuato had defiantly refused to participate. From the early 1840s, therefore, that facility's coins are essentially indistinguishable from those products of other Mexican mints: and while Boulton, Watt would still send dies to the coiners there until 1848, they could no longer be distinguished from the native product. Here as elsewhere, a larger environment was having a determinant effect on the fortunes of Soho. Earlier, it had attempted to reform coining, then coin design. And it had finally found its way blocked in both instances.

It had meanwhile made another attempt at amelioration in an area dear to its original mission, minor coinage. Here, there might be less worry about conformity of design, thanks to the workings of that Mexican federalism we examined earlier. Under the Constitution of 1824, states had the right to create state coinage as well as federal. This power was restricted to issues at the very bottom of the monetary scale, coins worth between one-sixteenth and one-quarter of a real. State issues were augmented on this level by federal coppers as well, about which more later. But the important point to be noted here is that the states could place any designs they pleased on their base-metal issues.

In Guanajuato as elsewhere, the ambitions of the local coiners exceeded their coining prowess. The state's issue featured designs which, properly handled, would have yielded an impressive coinage, with a seated female figure emblematic of Guanajuato on the obverse, a liberty cap in a glory of rays plus the date on the reverse. But the state was incapable of giving its base-metal coinage the finish these designs deserved. In addition, the metallic content of its coins varied from something approaching pure copper to something much closer to brass, and, all in all, its quarter- and eighth-real offered convenient and easy targets for local forgers.

George B. Lonsdale of the Anglo Mexican Mint Association thought that the designs deserved better treatment, and late in 1831 he asked Soho for help. Could the firm replicate them on a new state coinage, struck in collar by steam in Britain and exported to Mexico? Matthew Robinson Boulton was interested: at this time, his people had nothing in particular in hand except for the United States Mint's latest order for planchets and John Colville's latest order of kepings for Singapore, neither project overwhelming in difficulty. So he instructed his designers to create a perfect version of the imperfect Guanajuato model.

By the turn of the year, Lonsdale and his associates were having second thoughts, worrying that their new state coin would invite detection if it were *too* perfect. And as comparison between one of the originals and Boulton's collar-struck masterpiece (minted in January 1832 but dated 1828, deliberately inviting comparison with the original) suggests, their fears were justified. Lonsdale determined to absolve himself of any decision-making: provided Soho quickly dispatched the lovely patterns to Guanajuato, and provided the people there thought them worth the risk, Boulton, Watt might indeed find itself venturing into coinage for a Mexican state. But that concern spent far more time over shipping arrangements than it had over the actual preparation of the patterns. The Mexican packet set sail without them, and all we have left is a dozen or so of these lovely, hybrid cuartillas, or quarter-reals, mute witnesses to an opportunity lost.

They are related to another, slightly later essay into Mexican copper coinage, this time for the federal government. You will recall that the nation as well as the state had the right to strike copper coinage for small change. The primary mint at Mexico City accordingly struck base-metal pieces worth a quarter, an eighth, and a sixteenth of the silver real. They were authorized on 28 March 1829; within a few years, they were becoming a major problem on the lower end of the nation's monetary scale.

As originally authorized, the quarter-reals (the only pieces struck at first) were so large and heavy that they broke machinery and cost nearly as much

Original Guanajuato quarter-real (courtesy American Numismatic Society, New York) and Matthew Robinson Boulton's suggested improvement (author's collection)

Pattern Mexican quarter-real, 1836. (Author's collection)

to strike as they were worth. Even with a reduction in size that summer, the federal quarters (and their smaller brothers, whose production began in 1830) proved a major disappointment for the national mint, and a major annoyance for the common people. The new coins were poorly struck and were almost immediately counterfeited on a major scale. So great did the problem with false federal – and state – coppers become that the national government finally suspended all base-metal coinage, including its own, on 17 January 1837. And it is at this point that an odd, 1836-dated pattern copper quarter-real piece fits in.

Struck in collar, this is unquestionably a Soho product. Its reverse is very similar to the Guanajuato trial, except for the date. Its obverse displays the familiar 'Soho-style' eagle surrounded by the national legend REPUBLICA MEXICANA. The pattern came about in the following way.

By the mid-1830s, opposition to the crude federal copper coinage was already reaching serious proportions. Someone at Guanajuato must have written home to Lonsdale mentioning the problem; by a letter of 16 December 1835, Lonsdale advised Matthew Robinson Boulton that another opportunity to create a copper coinage for Mexico had just opened up.

The pattern cuartillas dated 1836 were the result, work on them beginning a few days before Christmas 1835. The designer, probably John Sherriff once again, altered the 1828-dated Guanajuato reverse die to reflect the new year, combined it with one of his eagles – and Lonsdale was sent three dozen new specimens on 12 January 1836. These pieces fared no better than the Guanajuato essays of 1832. And while there would be more correspondence concerning a Mexican copper coinage done at Soho in 1839 and again in 1841–1842 (the latter featuring a long series of letters between Matthew Robinson Boulton and his executors on the one hand and George B. Lonsdale on the other), neither these talks nor related ones in 1843 (which would see Soho producing pattern silver pesos by way of inducement) ever resulted in actual orders for a Boulton coinage at Guanajuato, Mexico City, or anywhere else.

For Guanajuato as elsewhere in Mexico, Soho's accomplishments were more modest. But they possess a satisfying depth and richness all the same. Elsewhere in this story, we have usually spoken of activity on a single level: coins are sent out, or a mint is shipped out. If the latter, any personnel sent by the firm will be home in a few years' time, repatriated as soon as they have set their charge in motion. And that charge will move in accordance with stipulations set down in the offices and on the shop floors of Boulton, Watt & Company.

That was not the way things happened at Guanajuato. In that case, machinery was built according to the rules, changed when the rules were found not to apply. When Soho's people went out with the redesigned mint, some of them shortly returned – but rather more of them stayed on, apparently finishing their careers in the new land.

That land changed them, and it changed they way they carried on their business. Frequently left to their own devices for many months at a time, the men found themselves in a technological tension of which Matthew Boulton could never have dreamed; and they found that what worked well in the pleasant British Midlands might not work at all in Mexico, and that the elder Mr Boulton had not in fact had all the answers. As they relied evermore upon themselves, striving to retain as great a portion of his technological model as possible, they were achieving something more important than the making of coin in a faraway mint. They were changing the face of the Industrial Revolution itself.

MEXICO CITY

Compared with the Guanajuato experience, Soho's other adventures seem incomplete. But each has its significance: if Guanajuato demonstrates what can happen to advanced technology when it encounters a traditional setting, events relating to Mexico City show that pitfalls can exist at home as well, that it is as easy to blunt a technological cutting edge at home as abroad.

When Boulton, Watt & Company first considered the matter of Mexican mints, they thought of Mexico City. As the administrative centre of New Spain, a mint had been established there as early as 1536, at a time when no other mints existed in the future Mexico – or indeed anywhere else in the Western Hemisphere. And there were two brief possibilities, late in the colonial period, that Soho might re-equip the venerable facility with machinery on the new model.

The first of these windows of opportunity came in the summer of 1789, when Matthew Boulton himself was still formulating his plans, arranging his machinery. Through a friend, he had been introduced to a resident of Cádiz named Don Pascual Mensa y March. This Spanish gentleman was traveling through Great Britain on a technological mission, and he and Boulton met and spoke about the possibility of exporting Soho steam engines to Spain – and to New Spain. Boulton immediately seized upon the matter closest to him at the time – the harnessing of steam power to the making of coinage – and was soon sending Mensa the usual collection of Droz's halfpenny patterns and his own claims relative to the merits of the new moneying apparatus he was just finishing at Soho. He would be amenable to striking Spain's coins at Soho – or would 'furnish & erect in his [Spanish] Majesties Mint or Hotel de Monney at Madrid or in any other part of Spain, a Steam Engine with all its necessary parts made for the purpose of Coining of Money'. He added that such 'Machines would be of great importance in New Spain & are applicable to the Coining of all the Metals'.[7] While impressed, Don Pascual left Great Britain at the end of the year with no mint arrangement concluded, and Matthew Boulton would eventually look elsewhere to sell coinage – and mints.

A similar contact took place in 1814, as related in the chapter on the Brazilian mint. There, the correspondent was a high-ranking Spanish nobleman, the Marquis de Apertado: in late September, Matthew Robinson Boulton learned that the Marquis was interested in holding conversations with him concerning the dispatching of a steam-powered mint to New Spain – presumably for Mexico City, as none of the other Royalist facilities was currently large enough to support such an improvement. The noble proposed to come up to Soho to see the Boulton mint (and Zack Walker thought it might be a good idea to take him around to Little Tower Hill and show him the Royal Mint as well). But Matthew Robinson Boulton does not appear to have responded favourably (the fact that the Marquis had been placed in contact via Portuguese agents may have reminded him of what had happened the last time Soho had shipped a mint to Latin America); and the opportunity was allowed to slip away.

By the time the next chance came along, a world had changed. Mexico was no longer part of the Spanish Empire. And where Spanish grandees had once strutted, British businessmen now scurried, their entry into all of Latin America having been facilitated by the disappearance of the exclusory arrangements of Lisbon and Madrid. There was money to be made – including, it appeared, money to be made in selling mints. And so Britons and others came to Latin America, and several of them eventually arrived at Soho's doors with a proposal.

The new arrivals were called Barclay, Herring, Richardson & Company. They approached Boulton, Watt through the good offices of Robert Mushet. On 16 November 1825, Mushet asked Matthew Robinson Boulton for an estimate of costs for a mint virtually identical with the one now building for the Mint Association, the only major exception being a ten-horse engine rather than the fourteen-horse one for Guanajuato. 'This Mint is for the City of Mexico, and on account of the Mexican Government. The Agents here are Messrs Barclay, Herring Richardson & Co who have requested me to get the order executed for them'.[8]

Boulton would have been impressed: the Barclay group was one of the jewels in the financial crown of the City of London during the 1820s: an order from this source would be prestigious as well as profitable. But appearances were deceiving: Barclay, Herring, Richardson & Company was not as strong as generally supposed, would soon go bankrupt. And anybody working for it would encounter difficulties.

Soho knew nothing of this, and it duly delivered an estimate of terms. As the estimate evolved, it would finally embrace a mint package identical with that for Guanajuato (to the eternal confusion of anyone working in the Mexican Mints Box of the Matthew Boulton Papers!), with an identical price tag, £8,281. Barclay, Herring agreed to the package in mid-January 1826, and work on the Mexico City mint began. Much of it had been finished by autumn of that year, and all of it was scheduled for completion by Christmas.

Meanwhile, its supposed recipient was about to renege on the deal. The several members of the Barclay concern squabbled over finances (this was the period of a massive economic slump in the City of London, whose effects spread across the nation): they parted company by mutual consent on 14 September 1826 – without, of course, telling Soho of the event.

When Barclay, Herring, Richardson & Company dissolved, a number of the defunct house's concerns went to other London firms. Baring Brothers & Company gained responsibility for the Mexico City mint. This was unfortunate: Baring Brothers had floated a massive loan in London on behalf of the fledgling Mexican Republic; the loan had not gone well, and a cash-strapped Mexican Government at length decided that it could not afford the new mint – and certainly wanted no part of it, if the Barings had had anything to do with it. And so history repeated itself: just as he was finishing a shiny new mint for Mexico, Matthew Robinson Boulton was finding that his purchaser had left the shop.

The final months of 1826 and the first months of 1827 are a complicated story of Soho's efforts to get someone – *anyone* – to pay for the unwanted coining apparatus. Boulton agreed to take back the two steam engines (for they could be easily sold elsewhere), allowing what was left of Barclay, Herring, Richardson & Company £2,187 against its bill. The remainder owed was £6,094, and a complicated scheme was eventually worked out to secure Soho its money, plus interest. In hopes of quickly securing the former, Boulton abandoned the latter: he was paid his £6,094 on 25 May 1827.

But the mint stayed right where it was: that was one of the conditions to which Boulton had had to agree. He also pledged to keep it well-crated and ready for a buyer, should a buyer happen to appear. And he promised that he would diligently search for one. It would take him and his partner James Watt, Jr. nearly a decade to succeed.

Nothing happened for several years, and the crates sat there in Soho Warehouse, getting in everyone's way and on everyone's nerves. A gentleman named Frederick Grellet examined the machinery early in 1834, acting on behalf of an unnamed, foreign power. Nothing came of that; but a sale *was* on the horizon. It would involve another foreign power, and it would be conducted by another British intermediary.

The power was Portugal, and the intermediary called itself Willcox & Anderson. Based in London, it came to James Watt, Jr.'s attention in the early spring of 1835. Watt was soon writing his partner that here, at last, might be a real opportunity to divest Soho of the unwanted Mexican mint. Willcox & Anderson had a dual mission. First, they were acting on behalf of the Spanish Government, and in that capacity they solicited information on the costs of a *new* mint, constructed along the lines of the Barclay, Herring machinery of 1826. (This may be one of the sources of a persistent tale that such a mint *was* built and shipped by Soho, but left to rust on a dock somewhere on the Spanish coast; as far as I have been able to determine, the event never happened, and Soho never went beyond the preparation of an estimate, if that.) The Londoners were also acting as agents for the Portuguese Government, which was interested in the purchase of the Mexico City machinery.

The record of subsequent events is somewhat sketchy, but its main outlines are clear enough. Willcox & Anderson must have inspected the machinery early in April 1835 and, finding it in good order, purchased it for Lisbon. The elements of the apparatus were taken out of their cases, cleaned, regreased, repacked, and shipped to the Willcox & Anderson offices at 46 Lime Street, London during the latter part of April and the first part of May. The mint package probably left Great Britain in May 1835 – followed in September by some odds and ends which had not been part of the original package but which Willcox & Anderson deemed useful all the same.

Meanwhile, at least one Briton had been dispatched to Soho to learn about the machinery he would shortly erect and superintend. He was James Pennywick, and we next find him in Lisbon in 1837, where he had encountered some minor difficulties with the apparatus and some major ones with his new employers, the Portuguese. The Lisbon Mint continued the connection with Soho, purchasing collars, annealing pots, layers-on, and especially dies, all the way down to 1849. Since all of these purchases were intended to serve at a mechanized mint, we can say that Soho's second Mexican experience had at least a partially happy ending, even if an unexpected one. Here at least technological pretensions had saved face. For its third encounter, they would not even enter into consideration. This encounter took place far from the centres of population, at an isolated, northwestern town called Culiacán.

CULIACÁN

Soho's adventures here began abruptly in the summer of 1832, and they ended just as suddenly less than two years later. The brief contact had a positive result: a functional mint was constructed and shipped out, along with the personnel to set it up. But Boulton, Watt & Company had learned from its two previous experiences with Mexican mints: at no time did it suggest that the Culiacán mint be equipped to run by steam, and at no time did it suggest that anything larger than a basic facility be built. In this, its sober realism was abetted by the wisdom of the British intermediaries with whom it dealt: Finlay, Hodgson & Company of London.

That firm already had a representative in Sinaloa state (a new jurisdiction, which had only come into existence in 1830). On 11 April 1832, this unnamed employee wrote to his people in London, informing them that, in line with its new sovereignty, the new state wanted to set up a mint of its own.

Beyond local pride (and the Constitution of 1824, which enshrined local pride), there were cogent reasons for a mint in this isolated corner of Mexico. The very fact that the state capital at Culiacán was so distant from the centres of commerce and power meant that it was extremely difficult to get coinage to it from other mints. And the area surrounding Culiacán had the raw materials necessary for a coinage: isolated it may have been, but it was also blessed with productive veins of copper, lead, iron, silver – and gold.

Miners were already there, seeking to exploit the subsurface wealth. But as matters currently stood, they were forced to transport their precious finds all the way to Durango or Guadalajara to get them made into coin – this so that the Mexican Republic could collect its share of the booty in the form of taxes. A mint at Culiacán would obviate that, add to the local economy, and strengthen local pride. The federal government saw matters in a favourable light, and it authorized the state to set up its mint, probably late in 1831 or early in 1832. The Finlay, Hodgson employee resident in the coastal hamlet of Rosario duly made his appeal to the parent firm in London, and based on his stipulations, Finlay, Hodgson would soon set to work.

That firm had been given an accurate idea of what to expect, and of what would be required. Since there was no possibility of steam power at Culiacán, the rolling mill necessary for coining must be constructed to work by six mules. And duplicate rollers must be included in that package, because they would never be found locally.

Soho would have no part in that machinery, but its own contributions would have to be made on an equally modest level. A fly press, 'to be moved by Six Men to coin $10,000 and upwards daily' must be sent, along with two cutting out presses, a heavy one for peso blanks, a somewhat lighter one for smaller coins (the first to be worked by an adult, the second by a child). A turning lathe and duplicate tools rounded out the order: the unnamed representative left their details to Finlay, Hodgson & Company, but he was more specific as to the personnel to be sent out along with the mint.

Sketch of a mule-powered rolling mill for Culiacán, 1832. (Courtesy Birmingham City Archives, Birmingham Central Library)

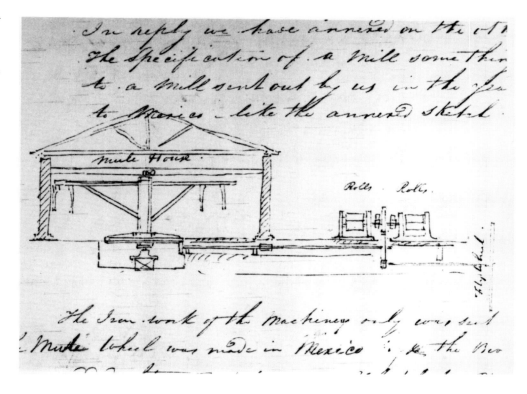

The most important figure would be 'an English Engineer', whose duty it would be to set everything up 'and devote himself exclusively to the work' for a term of at least five years – a tacit recognition of the difficulty the local authorities were likely to encounter in finding a replacement. For his pains and his time, he ought to receive two thousand dollars per year – about £450 sterling. This was a large sum of money, especially compared with what Boulton engineers were receiving at other mints, but it was suggested in frank recognition of the challenges the new employee would certainly encounter once at Culiacán.

The engineer must be assisted by two other Britons, a blacksmith/engraver and a carpenter. Their salaries might range from six to eight hundred dollars per year (£140 to £180, not overly generous even by the standards of the time). The state would pay return passage for all three workers, but they, and their machinery, must leave for Mexico with all convenient dispatch.[9] So the representative wrote, and so Finlay, Hodgson informed Matthew Robinson Boulton, bringing him into the project nearly as soon as the representative's letter had been received.

Boulton entered the equation in July 1832. He suggested that George and John Rennie be given the order for the rolling mill – and a sketch of it, reproduced above, has survived in MBP418, Soho Mint: Rolling, Coining, Melting; the drawing dates from late July 1832. Such a rolling mill would cost around nine hundred pounds, while the machinery produced at Soho (to which he appended a milling machine and a die multiplying press, items absent from the Rosario correspondent's list) could be provided for around £1,375.

Boulton generally concurred in the latter's ideas as to salary, but he cautioned that such roving Britons be kept on a very short chain, be chosen extremely carefully, attention being always paid to the difficulty not to say the impracticability of finding amongst the class of our Mechanists parties upon whose discretion reliance can be placed, when left in controul in a distant Country[10]

– and as he wrote these words, a parade of troublous if gifted engineers and smiths, the Harleys, McLeishes, and Bairds, spiritual descendants of Jean-Pierre Droz, must have filed past in Boulton's memory.

Finlay Hodgson agreed to pay Boulton the amount of his estimate at the end of August, also instructing him to set the Rennies to work on the mule-powered rolling mill. But now and later, Finlay, Hodgson demanded one thing above all else from its subcontractors – *speed*. Above all else, the mint materials simply *must* be sent off by the end of October. Was there an element of financial shakiness or chicanery here, or did Finlay, Hodgson simply hope that it would be able to get its mint in place before the local authorities found a better offer, or simply abandoned the idea? Having had experience in both areas, Boulton did what he could, and so did the Rennies. And for once in its career, Soho actually sent something ahead of schedule – eight days early, to be exact.

While seeing to one requirement, Matthew Robinson Boulton was also seeing to another, the selection of qualified mint personnel. His choice for the senior post fell upon William Callow, while Joseph Griffiths was chosen for the junior position. Griffiths is otherwise absent from the Soho record, but Callow has left faint traces there. He was a general fitter, who had begun his career as a press boy back in 1822 (helping produce the last Bencoolen coinage for the East India Company) and had since risen in rank. He would need some training to go with his new duties, which was no particular problem. But he had a sickly wife and a young child, and that was a problem, from the viewpoint of Finlay, Hodgson & Company.

The problem lay in the difficulty of getting to Sinaloa from Great Britain in the early 1830s. There were only two feasible paths, each with its own set of challenges. You could cross the Atlantic, sail around Cape Horn, then proceed north along the entire west coast of the Americas to San Blas or another port near Culiacán. This was the safer of the two routes, but it took many months, and the passage around the southernmost tip of South America was always risky. The other route was quicker, but far more dangerous. There, you would cross the Atlantic to the Isthmus of Panama, risk contracting fever while traversing that fetid strip of land between the seas, and then, health permitting, proceed north along the American west coast as before. Callow's wife and child suggested the first alternative; the necessity of getting the machinery to Culiacán as speedily as possible suggested the second.

Callow solved Finlay, Hodgson's problem by deciding against taking the appointment. He yielded his place to an engineer named Job Peat. Peat seems to have been one of Soho's contacts in Manchester, who was fortunately free of 'the encumbrance of a wife, or at all events ... from the necessity of taking her out with him'.[11] Peat got the post, which would extend over five years. His salary

varied from £220 to £300 p r Ann m with some few other advantages such as passage out & home & medical attendance when not caused by any imprudence on his part[.]

> The Smith [Griffiths] was allowed from £150 to £200 for the like term with the same advantages as the Foreman[.][12]

But the idea of an imported carpenter was abandoned, Soho arguing that his position could be adequately filled in Mexico.

Peat and Griffiths were trained at Soho during the final months of 1832 and the first months of 1833. They left Birmingham for Culiacán in mid-February, travelling by the more dangerous Isthmian route, which would, it was hoped, get them to the mint site in time to meet the machinery, which had left Soho by the long way late the previous October. With them they carried a selection of tools of various sorts, bringing the final cost of the Sinaloan mint to £1,731.6.0. Unlike his experiences with this mint's two predecessors, Matthew Robinson Boulton appears to have encountered no difficulty in getting payment for it.

At rates current in the 1830s, Soho's portion of the Culiacán mint amounted to nearly eight thousand Mexican pesos. This was a considerable sum of money – but the leading Mexican numismatist puts the cost of the mint at five times that amount:

> Sinaloa persistió en su deseo de tener casa de moneda propia, y en … el año de 1834 [sic] se invertieron cuarenta mil pesos para traer de Europa maquinaria de amonedación. [Sinaloa persisted in its desire for a mint of its own, and in 1834 forty thousand pesos were spent importing coining machinery from Europe.][13]

Even if we added the Rennies' rolling mill and generously assign it a value of a thousand pounds (almost certainly too high), we cannot arrive at a figure larger than around £2,700 – about twelve thousand pesos, less than a third of Pradeau's figure. I have no explanation for a discrepancy of this magnitude, but its importance diminishes in the face of an even greater one: if the Culiacán machinery sailed in 1832, and the men who were to erect and manage it sailed in 1833, *why did it take them or others some thirteen years to get it into production?*

Culiacán only began producing gold and silver coinage in 1846, copper a year later. While various reasons have been advanced for the thirteen-year hiatus between reach and grasp (delays in getting the mint packages to the mint site, an unco-operative attitude on the part of those who held the mint contract in the 1830s and those who inherited it in the 1840s), even collectively they cannot explain it. But a third factor would have played a part: one of the Englishmen sent out from Soho died within a few months of arriving in Mexico.

This was the all-purpose smith Joseph Griffiths, and the record of his passing is in fact the last news we have from Culiacán within the Matthew Boulton Papers. The time of the tragedy, and the cause of it, went unrecorded. We can only surmise that Griffiths died in the winter of 1833–1834, perhaps from the cholera which was still raging across Mexico at that time. But even his death should not have held back the project for a period of years: he was, after all, subordinate to Job Peat, who had survived to work on the mint.

And so the meagre parts we have cannot add up to a plausible whole. But there may have been local opposition to the project, while the endemic unrest put many another scheme on hold during the 1830s. We only know that a mint was sent out in the early 1830s, and that a mint began operations in the mid-1840s. But we are at least on safe ground in assuming that it was a Boulton mint: neither Pradeau nor any other expert has ever postulated the existence of a second mint, from a second source.

Did the Culiacán mint employ Soho punches and dies when it finally began coining? It may have done so, but we cannot know. When the mint had been shipped back in 1832, blank dies at least had been sent along in the peso and half-peso sizes, as well as specimens of engraved dies and punches. But the first Sinaloan coinage shows none of those peculiarities of design one associates with dies made at or inspired by Soho. Of course, word could have got to Culiacán of the increased demand for conformity to federal models by the time its mint got into operation. We lack data to reach firm conclusions; all we can say at present is that no additional dies were sent to this federal facility after the early 1830s. And in that respect, Culiacán stands in contrast with the final two mints with which Boulton, Watt did business, Chihuahua and Zacatecas.

CHIHUAHUA

Both facilities had been established during the unsettled days of the war for independence, when dangerous roads encouraged implosive economies and monetary localism. But while Zacatecas continued coining through the entire period of the Mexican Republic (and indeed, down to the definitive monetary reforms of 1905, from which *no* branch mints emerged), Chihuahua temporarily ceased activity in 1822, once the warfare which had called it into being had temporarily abated. But it reopened in 1831, and until its closure in 1895, it would function as a typical Republican-era mint, striking a fairly crude state copper coinage, augmented by silver and gold on the federal level.

It was typical in another matter: by the late 1830s, its operation had been farmed out to foreign impresarios, in this case a British firm named Kelly & Company, whose principals were John Jennison and John Potts. We met Mr Potts at Guanajuato; he would now serve as the liaison between Soho and the mint of Chihuahua.

We do not know when Potts left Guanajuato for greener pastures, but the new connection certainly must have been in place by the end of 1839, for the beginning of the following year found him at Soho, where he requested an estimate 'of the expence of original & moneying dies of the doubloon [onza], dollar, real, & half reals, similar with a slight variation to those made for the Anglo Mex*n* Mint Asso*n*'.[14] After initial confusion over the identity and sincerity of Potts (which the Mint Association quickly cleared up), Soho set to work. Potts wanted his dies as quickly as possible, because he was anxious to proceed to Chihuahua immediately. But what he wanted and what he received were slightly different.

Matthew Robinson Boulton proposed to assign the engraving work to Thomas Wells Ingram, who was one of Soho's finest artists, if not the finest. But Ingram was currently at work on a medal celebrating the recent marriage of Queen Victoria, and this work must naturally take precedence. At length, Soho hit on a reasonable alternative. It secured permission from the Anglo Mexican Mint Association for the use of its master dies for *Guanajuato* to provide working dies for *Chihuahua*.

This was easily done: the G*o* mint mark could be removed and a C*a* (for Chihuahua) substituted, while the date could be rendered 184- instead of 183- and the space for the assayers' initials simply left blank, as it already was on the masters. But even with these short cuts, Potts would not be receiving his dies as quickly as he wished. They only left Soho on 7 March 1840 bound for Liverpool, where the impatient coiner managed to intercept them on his way out of the country. The twenty-four pairs of dollar dies and six pairs each of real, half-real, and 'doubloon' dies were packed in iron tubes to sneak past Mexican customs; packing arrangements for the letter and figure punches requested and remitted are not known.

As mentioned earlier, Potts was interested in securing machinery as well as dies from Soho, and his mint at Chihuahua may have been the final resting place of apparatus originally destined for Guanajuato. This point is still not definite; what *is* known is that the Boulton dies were used for coinage at Chihuahua, and that the minter came back for more.

This was at the end of May 1848, long after Matthew Robinson Boulton's death and only months before his heir disposed of the firm. But on 30 May, Potts wrote for more dollar dies (nine pairs, '*deeply* impressed',[15] and six reverse dies for onzas, obverses not being needed. Potts also requested twelve pairs of blank dies; and then he lodged a complaint.

The gold dies he had received back in 1840 had been plagued with concentric cracks along their peripheries – a complaint borne out by Chihuahuan onzas in the National Numismatic Collection in Washington, which indeed display breaks of this nature. The coiner sent along a drawing of what he wanted, a die with the profile of a tombstone, whose shoulders were rounded. From this, it is evident that Soho's first shipment had consisted of dies meant to work within collars, dies which therefore crumbled at their edges when collars were not used. Potts had remembered his earlier tinkerings at Guanajuato, was attempting to replicate them at his new post; the industrialization of money would take another minuscule directional shift at another Mexican mint. And Potts' request for '*deeply* impressed' dies and die blanks suggests that he was intent on repeating another experiment from his days at Guanajuato: the use of working dies as masters for other working dies. This would help to explain the lack of definition on many later pesos from Chihuahua, a characteristic seen earlier at Guanajuato.

John Potts' second and final order was filled and departed Soho on 13 November 1848 (the long gap in filling so small an order suggests the distracted nature of Soho during these final months); and another link between the Midlands firm and the Mexican Republic was severed. A connection with a final Mexican mint was also ending at this time – and now we have come full circle, again encountering the Anglo Mexican Mint Association.

ZACATECAS

Lonsdale and the members of his group had become contractors for this busy north-central coiner through their new overlord, Manning & Marshall. Having greased the palm of dictator Antonio López de Santa Anna, Manning & Marshall had been granted a fourteen-year contract to manage the

Zacatecas facility in the autumn of 1842. And Boulton, Watt & Company would be a modest participant during four of those fourteen years.

Its activities were primarily confined to providing coining dies for Mexican dollars and their halves, but it began the connection by creating three screws for the mint's coining presses (which were manually-operated: this was a large coiner but not a technologically advanced one) in mid-1844. Soho sent a similar part for the multiplying press in 1845, a piece which also gave satisfaction. It was soon venturing into more familiar territory, the provision of coining dies.

There would never be a dispute over design, because all of the dies were sent out blank: Zacatecas may have been backward, but it was perfectly capable of sinking its own dies. (It was also close enough to Mexico City to encourage conformity in design.) Die blanks of good steel were another matter, and Soho supplied such orders from the summer of 1845 until the spring of 1848. It primarily sent dies for eight-real coins or pesos, but it shipped several hundred dies for four-real pieces as well, Zacatecas being one of the few Mexican mints striking this denomination in any quantity. The final shipment of dies was just leaving Soho as that venerable firm was preparing to close its doors.

*   *   *

In all, some sixty years passed between Soho's first and final contacts with Mexico. The middle portion of those years is of particular interest, not merely because of the events which happened but also, as I hope to have suggested, because of what did *not* happen. For a thread of misunderstanding, unreality, runs through our story: people wishing to modernize a country's coinage really had no idea of what is required, and they must be rescued from their costly mistakes by those on the scene. Expectations must be lowered if the process was to go on at all.

But it did go on, at a modest level. It seems clear that Mexico's coinage was better for Soho's intervention than it otherwise would have been, even if the improvements actually effected stood in stark contrast to what might have been done under better fortune. But the gap between intention and reality, and the tension between them, make the story of the 'mints for Mexico' one of the most interesting tales to be reconstructed from the papers of Matthew Boulton – not least because the way in which it ran, its combinations of boom and bust, hope and disappointment, high ideals and low comedy, would have appealed to him as they do to us.

SOURCES

Most of the raw materials for this chapter came from two sources, MBP412, Mexican Mints, and volume Mint 13/200 in the Public Record Office, London, the account of the early years of the Anglo Mexican Mint Association. The latter source is crucial to the story of early events at Guanajuato.

Additional references in the Matthew Boulton Papers, other than as indicated in endnotes, are as follows.

The charges for Soho's services to various Mexican mints will be found in MBP58, Mint Book, Soho Mint, Memoranda Calculations, Estimate and

Charges of Coinage and Coinage Machinery, 1807–1844; MBP68, Mint Book, Mint and Coinage Day Book, 1820–1834; and MBP81, Mint Book, Mint and Coinage Day Book, 1834–1849 – charges which are sometimes but not always replicated in MBP412 as well. While most Mexican correspondence will be found in the latter box, two other sources are important – MBP355, Watt, James, jr., 1822–27 (box 3), and MBP356, Watt, James, jr., 1828–48 (box 4): these two boxes add much detail to the story of the new mint for Culiacán and the sale of the old one for Mexico City. Some correspondence related to Mexico will also be found in a series of Mint and Coinage Letter Books running from 1824 to 1827, 1824 to 1833, 1827 to 1830, 1831 to 1835, 1835 to 1839, and 1840 to 1845 (MBP70, 71, 76, 80, 84, and 86, respectively).

Among outside sources on coinage of the period, the outstanding text is still Alberto Francisco Pradeau's monumental *Historia Numismática de México* (4 vols., 1957–61), of particular use because of its generous citation of nineteenth-century Mexican documents.

NOTES

1   '"A Mint for Mexico": Boulton, Watt and the Guanajuato Mint', *British Numismatic Journal* 56 (1986), pp. 124–147.
2   Public Record Office, London, Mint 13/200 (the record book of the Anglo Mexican Mint Association, May 1825 to October 1827): Robert Mushet to Matthew Robinson Boulton, 19 August 1825. I am greatly indebted to Mr Graham Dyer, Librarian and Curator of the Royal Mint, Llantrisant, for bringing this essential archival source to my notice.
3   MBP412, 'Extract [of] Mr Potts's report 20*th* July 1838.' Potts' report was initially made to members of the Mint Association; a distillation from it was sent to Soho with a covering letter on 26 October 1838.
4   Was this another privy mark for Soho? This seems unlikely, but the triangular shape is very obvious, even on worn specimens, and it and the naturalistic eagle disappear in the early 1840s, at the same time as the 'Masonic' dots are removed from the peso reverse.
5   The new activity explains the appearance of a new commodity among Soho's exports to Guanajuato after 1840, cast steel plugs. The plugs could be quickly turned into coin dies once they reached Mexico – and they were far safer to send than actual dies.
6   The Anglo Mexican Mint Association's contract was in fact renewed in 1842 for another fourteen years, but only in the face of strenuous local opposition, an opposition which continued for some years and which must have reinforced the coiners' new fidelity to official design models.
7   MBP150, [Private] Letter Book Q: Matthew Boulton to Pascual Mensa y March, 14 August 1789.
8   MBP412, Robert Mushet to Matthew Robinson Boulton, 18 November 1825.
9   MBP412, unnamed correspondent to Finlay, Hodgson & Company, 11 April 1832.
10 MBP412, Matthew Robinson Boulton to Finlay, Hodgson & Company, 30 July 1832.
11 MBP412, Finlay, Hodgson & Company to Matthew Robinson Boulton, 27 September 1832.
12 MBP333, Robinson, Westley, Chubb: contemporary copy, Joseph Westley to James Brown, 24 June 1833. Westley added that the two men had been paid £40 each for the three months they spent at Soho 'receiving instruction in the Soho Mint to enable them to undertake the erection & subsequent working of the Mint Apparatus destined for Culiacan.' But how they were instructed in the niceties of mint machinery which had already been sent out is something of a mystery.
13 Alberto Francisco Pradeau, *Historia Numismática de México* (Mexico City, 1957–61), II, p 315.
14 MBP86, Mint and Coinage Letter Book, 1840–1845: Joseph Westley to R. F. Davis, 28 January 1840.
15 MBP412, John Potts to Boulton, Watt & Company, 30 May 1848; emphasis in original.

CHAPTER 8

Ones that got away: The other side of the Coin

For every coinage Soho struck and every mint it built and sent away, there was another project discussed, perhaps even agreed to – but left undone. As soon as I began my research on the major portions of this book in 1983, I began encountering traces of music in a minor key, of schemes which never came to fruition. I shall speak of them here, on the general principle that they formed part of Soho's history and hence *should* be available to the interested reader, and the idea that they may tell us something about the background climate in which Soho's successful projects grew to maturity. Some of these missed opportunities and might-have-beens may surprise you; they surprised me.

They paralleled Soho's better-known, more successful enterprises. The first of them emerged in February 1788, just as Matthew Boulton was creating the preliminary drawings for the parts of his new mint. On the twenty-second of that month, a businessman named Otto Jakob Finck from Altona (a city near Hamburg which was currently under Danish rule) wrote to Soho on behalf of a colleague. Would Boulton be interested in preparing a hundred thousand copper coins, each weighing about seven pennyweights, three grains?

The identity of the coinage was never named, but its weight would correspond to the copper sechsling or sixth-schilling. Seven pennyweights, three grains works out to 171 grains, or 11.08 grams; the seven Smithsonian specimens of 1787 (the only year of issue) average 11.02 grams for fairly worn coins.

Boulton remitted his prices for copper blanks and coins on 7 March – which were shortly dismissed as excessive by his correspondent. But the two men remained in contact until 1790. On one occasion, Finck suggested that Boulton might also be interested in striking silver coins (the double-sechsling; and he sent along four of the tiny pieces on 25 April 1788, by way of instruction). In another instance, he came up with a complicated scheme whereby Boulton would receive copper blanks from Sweden, strike them at Soho, then ship them to Altona. But the two entrepreneurs were never able to reach an agreement for coining – a shame, for the right arrangement would have greatly profited Boulton during the early, lean days of his mint.

As the Schleswig affair faded, a much larger opportunity seemed to be emerging: during the final months of 1790, an Austrian nobleman named Baron Vay de Vaja put out cautious feelers on securing a Boulton mint for Vienna. Soho's reply was favourable, not to say anxious: its British proposal was in limbo, and the terms of the settlement with Droz threatened its resources still further. Nothing came of the project at the time – although it was to resurface a decade later, with conversations in two directions.

In February 1800, James Watt introduced a Mr Oliver to his partner Matthew Boulton. Oliver was carrying a letter from Le Comte de Saureau, Austria's Minister of Finance,

> who wants to engage us to erect a Mint at Vienna, with one of our Engines & wishing one of us to come over to establish it, for which every facility will be given—[1]

What happened next is unclear: but neither Watt nor Boulton was able to make the journey to Vienna, and the distracted state of Central Europe during the Napoleonic wars would have made the project difficult if not impossible in any case.

A second tack was taken during the summer of 1800, when Soho was evidently approached to make a copper coinage for the Austrian Government. Correspondence is lacking, but the coins under consideration were copper kreuzer, about the size of Boulton's farthings of 1799. This project was much to his liking, for his second copper coinage for Britain had just been completed, and Soho Mint would stand idle if other business were not obtained. Two of his notebooks (81 and 86, both covering the year 1800) contain his jottings on the subject through the summer and autumn of that year. But larger events again intruded, while his construction of the Russian mint and preparation of additional copper coinage for the East India Company would soon keep Soho fully occupied.

At the beginning of the 1790s, it appeared possible that Boulton, Watt might receive orders for *two* Central European mints: a fairly extensive correspondence between March 1789 and April 1791 might have led to a mint for Berlin.

This Prussian possibility grew out of Matthew Boulton's earlier connections with the influential people of his time. He and Baron Reden of Clausthal evidently knew each other from previous business dealings; on 30 March 1789, the Baron introduced his nephew, Count Reden, with a general request that he be accorded Boulton's advice on steam engines for the royal mines and forges of Silesia; these were the younger man's official responsibilities. The counsel was supplied, and talk soon turned to Boulton's prime interest, the improved coining of money.

Count Reden visited Birmingham in January 1790; having visited Soho, he bluntly asked Boulton his price for a new mint, built on his principles, sent to Prussia. Boulton's reply has not survived, but he seems to have remitted the by-now standard package of coins and claims in mid-February. Taken ill shortly thereafter, he was unable to receive the young Count prior to the latter's departure for Prussia. The younger Reden promised to act as Soho's emissary in the pursuit of the Prussian mint – and he did. Nearly a year after the nobleman's departure, Boulton received a letter from Berlin:

> I am ordered by His Majesty the King of Prussia, to let you know that His Majesty highly approved of your Methode of Coining and that the Pattern for the Half-pence exceeded all Expectations. Accordingly His Majesty being determined to have an Engine for Coining established here at Berlin after your Inventions. I therefore am to ask you, What Remuneration you would chuse to accept for the Discovery of your Secret, by which it is supposed that the Coining will be more forwarded, executed more handsomely & performed with less Expense than ordinary.
>
> Besides I am to ask you, whether you yourself would chuse to come over to undertake the Ordering of it and see it set agoing. I beg the favour of your speedy Answer[.][2]

The preceding was written by Count Reden's secretary, whose command of English was better than his own. But the Count added a few words in his own hand. The King and his ministers were deeply intrigued by the scheme, but much would depend on Boulton's previous engagements with his own government, which must surely take precedence over a commitment abroad. And Reden was by no means certain that *all* of Boulton's improvements could be adopted at present (left unsaid was the fact that Frederick the Great's wars had left the monarchy strapped for cash); but some, at least, could be acquired, were Boulton willing to sell.

Boulton must have been amused when he read the Count's postscript: in February 1791, he had no commitments whatsoever from, or to, the British Government – indeed, matters were such that he would soon be thinking of moving Soho itself. But he tried to put the best face on things in his answer to the Count. While Soho was positively thronged with orders for steam engines from parties all over Europe and even beyond, he promised to fill any orders within five months of their receipt. 'And in regard to the Coining Mill if I cannot send a person to my own Satisfaction I will come my Self, for I have much to say & to shew your Coiners besides what relates to the mill.—'[3]

Boulton's letter of 24 February was shortly followed by another, wherein he gave his advice on the nature of the revivified Berlin Mint. It should consist of eight coining presses, worked by a ten-horse engine, joined by eight cutting out machines. Based on his own experiences at Soho (where he was currently coining between sixty and seventy coppers per minute per press for the East India Company) Boulton reckoned that the Prussians could rely on an output of approximately half a million pieces daily from their new mint. Concluding with advice as to training of staff and the size of the coining room, Boulton confidently waited for the Prussian order.

Within a month, the project for Germany began to recede. Reden wrote from Berlin on 3 April, acquainting his correspondent with the real requirements of the King of Prussia. They were far more modest than Mr Boulton had supposed. No copper coinage was in contemplation – and thereby much of the rationale behind a Boulton mint abruptly disappeared. In this reduced climate, Reden estimated that Prussia would be content with 'one Laminoir, one Coupoir and one Coining press perfectly complete, all of which will serve as Examples for the making of others at Berlin'.

All of this was a disappointment, but the Count had worse news still. The present Berlin mint was situated on the bank of the Spree and could be worked by water power. With that in mind, and considering that coal was as expensive in Berlin as it was in London, 'we should wish to avoid the use of the fire Engine'.[4] In sum, if Boulton were seeking to export his new technology, he must look elsewhere.

The industrialist replied to the disappointing news a fortnight later. He made a spirited justification for a steam-powered mint, regardless of present conditions and requirements – although he conceded that four presses, powered by a six-horse engine, might suffice for the time being. But if the Prussians persisted in their desire for a pre-industrial mint, they could have one for around £4,200. Regardless of their decision, he suggested that they send a qualified workman to Soho to view *his* mint, probably in the belief that such a witness would return to Berlin and sell the concept of a bigger and better mint to Prussian officialdom in a way that mere claims made by letter could never achieve.

But the Prussians sent no emissary, and this mint project also died. Years later, there was brief discussion of a coinage of Prussian thalers to take place at Soho. This was in 1807, and the scheme was said to have the blessing of British and Prussian Governments alike. But it, too, came to nothing. And when Prussia finally chose to modernize its money at the end of the Napoleonic Wars, it would call upon other men, with other technologies, for the purpose.

The six years between 1791 and 1797 constituted the time of greatest trial for Matthew Boulton: he had a new mint, which had cost him an immense amount of money to construct. But his preferred and most logical customer had left the shop before a sale had been concluded: now Boulton enjoyed great prestige but little more. He must try to keep his establishment busy until the preferred client came to his senses: he must coin whenever and wherever he could. The activity would be good for Soho Mint, because potential trouble spots could be located and eliminated prior to the major event, the British copper coinage. At the same time, Boulton and his people would gain crucial experience in the new technology, definitely useful at home, potentially so abroad. And the profits from making other people's money would help to defray expenses until better times arrived.

Matthew Boulton's hard times coincided with the phenomenon of the eighteenth-century token. When it became clear that the British Government would not soon create a major copper coinage (or appoint Mr Boulton to create it), merchants across the British Isles took matters into their own hands, ordering the minor private coinage which the public authorities could not or would not provide. The first of their copper tokens appeared in 1787. By 1789, there were half-a-dozen issuers, by 1791 a score or so, and by 1794–5 (by which time the objects had been discovered by coin collectors, not least because of the localism they enshrined), literally hundreds of different issuers had engaged a score or so of coiners to strike copper tokens on their behalf.

In one sense, these pieces were anathema to Matthew Boulton, for there was no official control over their quality or quantity. But in another, they provided opportunity – and the realistic entrepreneur bowed to the old advice of collaboration with what you cannot defeat. He joined the token issuers, at first as a subcontractor, later in his own right.

Boulton's trade tokens tended to fall into two categories. First were the tokens which he produced in quantity – or fully-realized projects, if you prefer. The second group embraced tokens which got past the planning stage – but which were rejected for one reason or another, to survive only as patterns. These included the halfpence for the Copper Company of Upper Canada (the subject of a series of excellent articles by David Vice[5]), the Ibberson halfpenny (upon which I published a brief article in 1986[6]), and the Myddelton and Swainson tokens. The former was the precursor of a coinage for an intended British settlement in Kentucky by Philip Parry Price Myddelton – whose dreams were abruptly shattered by an unfeeling bureaucracy, who saw his settlement as a potential drain of talent from the British Isles.[7] The latter was probably aborted when it was discovered that the designer had misspelled the intended proprietor's name – but I have found nothing about this piece in the Matthew Boulton Papers. While unsuccessful, all of these attempts did reach the metallic stage. But there were other possibilities which never got that far.

The first was discussed in the autumn of 1791. A Stockport merchant named Burry wrote Matthew Boulton about his terms for striking copper tokens. Burry's letter did not survive, and all we possess is Boulton's reply, a press copy to 'Burry', dated 4 October. In it, the coiner quoted general terms for the preparation of a coinage, at a price ($14\frac{1}{2}$ pence per pound) which suggests that Mr Burry was probably interested in halfpence. Boulton offered to send examples of what he had already created for others; but if specimens were sent they were wasted effort, for we hear no more of this correspondent.

The next two possibilities occurred at the beginning of 1795, during the height of the token craze. The first involved a London firm called Lockwood Morris & Company. On 14 January, a gentleman named George Bowser placed an order for a ton of halfpence with Matthew Boulton, tokens which were to weigh a third of an ounce each and bear very simple designs – the letters L M & Co on one side, T & Co on the other, along with a legend making them payable at 26 Bush Lane, London.

What happened to this issue? While small, it was no more so than a number of others created at Soho, from which specimens have survived. But no known eighteenth-century token exists with these designs, and we can only suppose that one party or the other decided against the project. I would guess that the prospective issuers did so, for their order coincided with rumours sweeping London that all such private issues would soon be declared illegal. And the second project from January 1795 may have been halted for the same reason. This involved another London concern called Hutton, Jackson & Magrath, silk manufacturers located in Angle Court, Friday Street. The firm wrote to Soho in mid-January, and Zacchaeus Walker, Sr. forwarded its letter on to his master in London with a covering letter on the twenty-sixth. But nothing more is known about this project, which apparently never even reached the stage of the Lockwood, Morris correspondence.

Tokens prepared for William Wilkins got much further. In fact, tiny orders were actually prepared and sent to him in January 1802 and March 1803 – some years after Boulton's Cartwheel and later copper issues should have rendered such private monies both unnecessary and irrelevant. But Wilkins' pieces were different: they were passes for the theatre rather than more general substitutes for coin.

I have included them at this point because I know nothing about them save the fact that they *were* struck by Matthew Boulton. I know nothing of William Wilkins: the only other reference to a man of that name in the Matthew Boulton Papers comes from a letter written from Norwich in July 1791: was our token-issuer of 1802 and 1803 the impresario of a local theatre in Norfolk?

Whoever he was, Wilkins had only modest ambitions for his tokens. They were not created from ordinary dies. The issues of 1802 were simply listed as '4,158 pieces of Copper Mark'd Pit, box &c [with] 8 different punch marks'. Wilkins was charged for the cutting of letters and the creation of punches for the work, as well as 'Octagon Tools': like a number of other theatre passes of the day, his tickets would be deliberately distinguished from copper coinage by their shape. This first order left Soho early in January 1802, at a cost to Wilkins of £8.6.8 – which he had prepaid.[8]

In those days, it was common practice to order and award silver passes to valued clients and friends. Thus, William Wilkins returned to Soho for a second, even smaller issue of silver tickets early in 1803. On 2 March of that year, he paid seven pounds for fourteen of the pieces, which had been created from actual dies and engraved with recipients' names. These tickets were large, weighing nearly an ounce apiece – and since Wilkins only paid ten shillings each for them, labour included, we may conclude that he received very good value for money! But it would be gratifying to know what they looked like.

While we are ignorant of the appearance of the Wilkins passes, we know far more about the results of another project under discussion at the time. This was a coinage for the German state of Württemberg, and patterns for it have survived at the British Museum, the City of Birmingham Museum, and in several private collections.

The key person here was Nathaniel Marchant, who deserves a brief introduction. Born in 1739, Marchant was a gem engraver and medallist, employed at the Royal Mint from 1797 to 1815. His work did *not* centre on the engraving of dies: rather, Marchant was the probationer, or designer, who modelled the heads that the Pingos and Wyons would finally place on the dies, and on the coins. In this capacity, he created the model for the head of George III for the Bank of England tokens of 1812–16. He died in the latter year.

Marchant had been one of Matthew Boulton's correspondents since 1790, and Soho regularly supplied him with its latest products in the medallic line. The origin and nature of his connections with Württemberg are not known, but he seems to have travelled in the highest circles of this major German state. It was probably Marchant who arranged for the Soho visit of Prince Friedrich at the end of April 1797; and it was definitely Marchant who acted as midwife to the coining schemes of 1803.

They must have originated during the previous year, for by January, matters were sufficiently along for Marchant to send two pairs of dies to Soho. The first would be used for the production of a medal; but

> The other pair of Dies are to be explained to you by Mr Küchler[.] you will please to tell him I will send the Drawing of the Duke's Arms with the Directions[.] Mr Küchler proposes to make a Poncheon from the Head, one hundred Crown peices are to be struck from it when the Die is properly compleated[.][9]

Matthew Boulton's thaler
for Württemberg, dated
1798, struck 1803.
(Reproduced by kind
permission of the Trustees
of the British Museum)

This letter gives us the identity of the designer; it also forecasts the fate of
the coinage.

Küchler set to work as soon as he received the dies. His first efforts were
sent to the Duke, and to Nathaniel Marchant. Neither was particularly
pleased, Duke Friedrich being especially critical of the low relief, typical for a
Soho coin but atypical for a pre-industrial German one.

There followed months of dispute between Marchant and those who stood
behind him at Stuttgart, and Boulton and Küchler at Soho, over the relief of
the coin, its depiction of the Duke's hair (definitely 'not the way I think Hair
should be treated'[10]), the minutiae of the Württemberg arms, etc., etc. The
Duke continued to complain about the low relief; Boulton continued to
defend it as the only way a modern *coin*, as opposed to a medal, could be
manufactured. But after much debate, a workable design was agreed to, dies
were prepared, and a hundred silver planchets for the trials were cut out. At
that point (5 May) the die for the head cracked, slowing the project while
Boulton gingerly tested the tool to see whether it would serve for the trials, or
whether a new die must be made.

As it happened, the die had to be replaced. By now, Marchant was becoming annoyed with the whole project ('I have had nothing but trouble about it
… and it makes me sick of steel Engraving'[11]). And he now informed Boulton
that, even if his dies were perfectly done, they were not likely to become the
basis of a sizable coinage for Württemberg. It appeared that Duke Friedrich
wished to retain the dies and the coins which they struck merely as mementos
and would continue to circulate coinage of the traditional variety. And when
Boulton finally managed to strike coins with the new pair of dies, after receiving them Marchant told him that they were altogether too heavy! In brief,
nothing Soho did seemed to meet these customers' demanding requirements. The project petered out in Midsummer 1803.

An entry of 27 August tells the remainder of the story. Boulton charged
Marchant £50.2.2 for preparation of five dies, for striking one hundred
'German Crowns' (thalers) from ninety-three ounces of silver, and for the
boxes and carriage of the package to London. But an aside at the foot of the
entry tells what Boulton really thought of the entire affair. Opposite 'my own
troubles, the Use of my Machinery[,] the loss sustained by neglect of other
Work[,] copper Cases to prevent tarnishing[,] finding the Silver &c', Boulton
placed the single word 'nothing'[12]. All of that aggravation had been to no
purpose.

Most of Boulton's activities regarding tokens took place in the early and
middle 1790s, and they centred on actual and possible issues in copper.

But there was another token opportunity which arose much later, in 1804: had it come to completion, Soho would have created silver tokens for Ireland.

Boulton's contact here was an old acquaintance named James Woodmason. Woodmason had been born in South Carolina, had emigrated to London, where he set himself up as an agent for James Watt's new letter-copying press. He and Boulton had been corresponding since 1785; nine years later, Woodmason removed his business to Dublin, and it was from that city that he now made a request for silver tokens.

He did so through the agency of his son Alfred, who visited Soho on 10 April 1804. Boulton learned that the lack of small silver coinage in Ireland had reached a critical state, that the island would soon be flooded with worthless counterfeits, to the ruin of honest merchants everywhere. A person of reputation must step forward to address the problem; and Matthew Boulton was that person.

What the Woodmasons wanted was an initial production of four thousand guineas' worth of tokens, two in silver and two in copper. There were to be silver pieces for shillings and sixpences, to contain eightpence and fourpence in silver; a copper halfpenny, whose intrinsic value must nearly match its stated one; and a copper penny. The elder Woodmason believed that so great was the shortage of decent money in Ireland that 'the demands will exceed any thing I can imagine, and it would be necessary to make such plans, as would insure a quick & constant supply'.[13]

But he would soon be disabused. At the time he shared his idea with Soho, its master was already in process of addressing the shortage which Woodmason lamented – through official means. And while he and Boulton continued to discuss the matter through the media of Alfred and the written word, James Woodmason gradually abandoned the idea of circulating his own money, in favour of helping his friend Boulton circulate that which he would soon be striking for the King. He sent Boulton an offer of assistance on 24 April 1804, but his tender was not accepted, a firm called Puget & Bainbridge being selected for the distribution. The Woodmasons thus lost on both counts, and what would have been Soho's last private tokens were never produced.

A proposed coinage for an island in the Caribbean was no more successful. Soho had struck coinage for a number of British possessions in the area, and on 28 March 1804, Matthew Boulton's old friend Sir Joseph Banks suggested that Antigua might soon join the list. Local authorities had decided to have £5,000 in minor silver and copper coinage struck in Britain on their behalf. Banks had learned of the project through his connections with the Board of Trade, and he naturally thought of Soho.

We hear nothing more of the idea for nearly two years, but on 27 February 1806, the island's agent Anthony Brown wrote to 'John Bolton' with a request for the manufacture of £5,000 in silver coins and another £500 in copper. Brown was precise about the denominations and designs desired. The silver must be struck into pieces worth four shillings (to the value of £750), two shillings (£750), shillings (£1,000), sixpences (£1,250) and threepences (£1,250) – for a total of £5,000. Copper coins were wanted in two denominations, pennies and halfpennies, and £250 should be struck of each. As to designs:

Every Piece is to bear the Impression of His Majesty's Head encircled by his Name and Titles on the one Side. And on the reverse the Impression of a Windmill encircled by the Letters of the word Antigua.[14]

Boulton refused Brown's order, with regrets and an explanation. His health was abominable; more than that, his massive copper coinages for Great Britain and Ireland were taking up all the capacity of Soho Mint and would continue to do so for the remainder of the year. The preparation of a totally new coinage, in no fewer than seven denominations in two metals, was simply beyond him and his designers: and so he must decline the opportunity, with thanks.

One of the reasons he continued to be overburdened was his inability and unwillingness to place more responsibility on the shoulders of his son, Matthew Robinson Boulton. The younger man would have been perfectly capable of overseeing this Caribbean project. In any case, his father's continuing poor health and onerous work load would soon find the younger Boulton involved elsewhere in the Antilles, in Haiti.

For the century prior to the French Revolution, Haiti, or Saint Domingue, was France's richest colony, and one of the richest agricultural lands anywhere. Haiti grew sugar, and she grew so much of it that she accounted for fully half of France's colonial trade. But in the way that sugar was grown there rested a tale.

For Haiti was a hell on earth – at least, if you were one of the half million slaves toiling there in the sun. Once you arrived on the island – in chains, delivered from the fetid hold of a slaver – you might expect to live five years, ten at the most, before you succumbed to the island's many sicknesses or to simple overwork. Above the slaves was a tiny white aristocracy – and between these two rested a slightly larger mulatto group, looked down upon by the others.

The French Revolution brought immediate repercussions to this island in the sun. Slavery was outlawed – whereupon the planter class agitated for independence from the homeland. But it watched its control over events slip and fall to the mulattoes, and finally to the blacks.

There followed more than a decade of riot and war. First Consul Bonaparte made a concerted effort to recapture the island, sending in his brother-in-law General Leclerc with twenty-three thousand men. But the French died in droves – mainly from disease, occasionally from the bullets of the insurgents; faced with this early nineteenth-century equivalent of the dilemma a later generation would face in Southeast Asia, Napoleon cut his losses. Haiti was free.

For the first two years, she lived under the dictatorship of victorious general Jean Jacques Dessalines; while essential to the rebuilding of the island's shattered infrastructure, Dessalines' harsh rule led to his assassination in 1806. The island then passed under the control of not one regime but two. In the south, Alexandre Pétion ruled ineffectively but gently between 1808 and 1818. In the north, from the city of Cap-Haïtien, the last of the revolutionary generals held sway. He was an ex-slave named Henri Christophe. He would one day crown himself King Henri I. And he would soon provide an interesting opportunity for a Midlands firm named Boulton, Watt & Company.

At the time Christophe took command, coinage was in short supply, and what little was in circulation was poorly made and of variable quality and weight. He was thinking about the problem even as he consolidated his power, and his ruminations soon led to concrete developments. In his capacity of 'Président et Généralissime des forces de terre et de mer de l'État d'Haïti' Christophe proclaimed the creation of a new coinage in September 1807. It would be uniform, made of silver, and struck in three denominations, the escalin or real, its double, and its half. These coins' designs were carefully stipulated:

> Ces pièces porteront sur la face la figure de la liberté, la valeur de la pièce et le millésime, avec l'inscription *Monnoie d'Haïti*, et sur le revers le chiffre du président, surmonte d'une couronne de laurier, et pour inscription: *Libertas, Religio, Mores*. [These pieces will bear the figure of Liberty on the obverse, along with their value and fineness, with the inscription *Money of Haiti*, and on the reverse the cypher of the President surmounted by a laurel wreath, and as an inscription the Latin for *Liberty, Religion, Morals*.]

They were to be placed in circulation at once. Those who had old escalins must bring them to 'la fabrique de la monnoie, pour en faire l'échange pour la monnoie nouvelle'.[15] Full-weight old coins would be exchanged for new ones of equal value. Lightweight pieces would be exchanged for their value in silver.

What Christophe decreed, Christophe would have. But he and his island faced a problem: the escalins of 1802 and 1807 had been wretchedly struck, but there was no possibility that Haiti's new money would be any better than its old if it were made on the same presses, designed by the same artists. Two possibilities existed: either get new machinery, and improve your own coinage, or contract for it and have someone else improve it for you. The Haitians would explore both possibilities, and Boulton, Watt & Company would be their sounding board.

In late January 1808, the firm was approached by Christophe's London representative, Jean-Gabriel Peltier. Christophe ordered Peltier to hire an English engraver for the island's mint. But the agent concluded that it would be far simpler to have the engraving done in Great Britain. He accordingly approached Soho with a request to manufacture dies for three denominations – thirty, fifteen, and seven and one-half sols, corresponding to the double escalin, escalin, and half-escalin. Peltier stipulated the designs he wanted. Instead of Christophe's initials in the form of a cypher, Peltier preferred the name of the country and the value of the coin surrounded by a laurel wreath. He also requested a seated figure of Liberty for the obverse. Christophe's decree was silent on the figure's pose, but if he were seeking a simple improvement of the original designs, he would have envisioned a standing figure of the goddess.

There was nothing conditional about Peltier's request: Soho was asked to enlist the services of one of its artists to create the three denominations as quickly as possible. Once the dies were finished, a few sets of specimens must be struck in silver and in various silver and copper alloys. The emissary promised payment whenever requested.

Soho set to work. On his part, Peltier repaired to the Board of Trade, initiating the lengthy process by which an export licence must be secured. He wrote Matthew Boulton at the end of April, reporting that his quest for permission had finally succeeded. But he added another bit of news which cast the Haitian affair in a new light:

> Since I had the honour of applying to you, I have received a further demand from general Christophe for a fly, or what is called in french a *balancier* for coining. I send you the Specimen and explanation of it, such as I have received it from St Domingo. I beg you would prepare it with the 6 dies. The soonest will be the better, as I will have in the course of 4 weeks a very safe opportunity of sending the whole.[16]

Word of the Board of Trade's permission to export the dies and machinery was sent to Matthew Boulton on 30 April. By now, his declining health had forced the surrender of the project to his son's care; the latter carried out his duties in a subtle, tactful manner.

Tact was required in dealing with Peltier and his impoverished island. The agent (and doubtless his employer) assumed that any coinage made from Soho dies would produce coins which looked like Soho coins. And Matthew Robinson Boulton had gently to disabuse them of this idea. Haitian coins would look like Soho products *only if they were struck on Soho presses*. And presses of that type were far beyond the island's financial capabilities.

In point of fact, even a new, manually-operated coining press might be too costly for them. The younger Boulton hurried along the production of the dies, meanwhile mulling over the question of the press. Within a week, he had a satisfactory answer to all aspects of the problem, and he henceforth led Peltier to the same conclusion. The dies should be designed to work with a pre-industrial press, one which the agent could very likely find at an establishment which was about to abandon them – the Royal Mint. Armed with traditional dies *and* a traditional coining press, Haiti should be able to create perfectly acceptable coinage. Boulton volunteered to look for such a second-hand apparatus, or construct a new one at Soho if Peltier insisted. Meanwhile, his dies and puncheons would cost Haiti £110.

Peltier accepted the estimate, embracing as well Boulton's offer to find a suitable press. Progress on the dies now became fairly rapid, and the entire package of dies, punches, and specimen coins left Soho at the beginning of August. By that time also, Matthew Robinson Boulton had located a suitable press, which he was in process of reconditioning. It would cost Haiti £73.10.0, and Boulton proposed to ship it to London within a few days.

The press probably left Soho around the twentieth of August – at least, a draft for £73.10.0 at three months' sight was made on Peltier on 24 August and paid on 4 October. But there is no indication that this emissary carried his machine back to Haiti – and the wretchedness of the country's coinage until the middle of the nineteenth century suggests that, even if it arrived there, it never was put to use. Nor does there appear to be a record of payment for the Haitian dies and specimens which Soho was asked to prepare.

But we are on firmer ground here: we know that specimens were struck, for a few have survived in each denomination. They adhere to the designs set down in the amended decree – and they look completely different from other Soho products, as the illustrations suggest. I never suspected that they came from the Boulton mint until I found incontrovertible written evidence that they had. And they may well be the only survivors of yet another failed Soho scheme.

Patterns for a Haitian silver coinage, struck at Soho, 1808. (Courtesy Craig Whitford Auctions)

The Haitian project came to its conclusion just as another Latin American opportunity was opening up – a mint for Brazil. In time, Boulton, Watt & Company would send mints to Mexico as well as Brazil, besides creating copper blanks for the latter country and actual coinage for two other South American nations, Argentina and Chile. These activities were part of a larger shift of orientation on the part of the firm, from a predominantly European base to emphasis in what would one day be called the 'Third World'. As one might expect, Soho's concrete accomplishments in a non-European setting were paralleled by a number of other projects which never went beyond the talking stage.

One of them was mentioned in the Mexican chapter, a mint for the Spanish colony of New Spain. There was also a brief discussion about a new mint for the second of Spain's four vice-royalties, El Perú. This involved a reconstruction of the busy mint at Lima, and an enterprising native of Guayaquil named Vicente Rocafuerte. Around the end of 1813, James Drummond[17] introduced Rocafuerte to James Lawson, Soho's old employee who had accepted permanent employment at the Royal Mint. The South American

> expects to get permission from the Spanish Gov*t* to erect a Mint (at Lima)— He goes in a few days to Spain— and wishes to know previously— what would be the expence of a Mint— to have 4 Coining & 6 Cutting out Presses— with 2 Double Milling Machines— With a Steam Engine capable of working the whole. For Coining Dollers [Lawson meant the popular eight-real piece]. M*r* Rocafuerte has been at S*t* Petersburgh & seen the Mint there.[18]

Lawson added that Rocafuerte had told him that coal had recently been discovered near Lima, so that there would be no problem in powering steam engines. Since the South American would be leaving England in a few days speed was of the essence, and a preliminary estimate would do. Boulton's estimate of £8,600 for a steam-powered mint with four coining presses went out on 30 December, reaching Rocafuerte a few days prior to his departure for Madrid.

That is the last we hear of the Lima mint.

Either side might have broken the contact. Boulton, Watt & Company was still learning from the unpleasant Brazilian episode, and it may have decided to await developments in a less-than-quiet corner of the world. And the Spanish Government, embroiled in the ending phases of its war with the French, had reasons of its own for not pursuing coinage reform on the other side of the globe. In any case, Chinese merchants liked King Ferdinand's Lima dollars just the way they were – and here lay another possible brake on technological reform. Lima would someday purchase a steam-powered mint. But it would acquire it from the Americans, some five years after Boulton, Watt's demise.

While most of Soho's dealings during this and succeeding decades would be with India and with Latin America, it did not sever its connections with Europe. In the summer of 1822, it briefly seemed that Boulton, Watt & Company might be asked to equip a mint at Florence, for the Grand Duke of Tuscany.

As so often occurred, Matthew Robinson Boulton only learned of this possibility through indirect means. A Florentine named 'Fabbronie'[19] had approached William Wellesley Pole, Master of the Royal Mint. The latter had spoken with George Rennie – and Rennie wrote Boulton.

The Florentines were interested in machinery made specifically for their largest silver coin, the dollar-size francescone, and they wanted information on three points. First, how large a steam engine would be needed for the work? Second, how much would it cost to coin a million francesconi on a steam-powered press? And third, could an engine be adapted to burn wood in place of coal, which Tuscany lacked? Matthew Robinson Boulton was asked to send his answer to Rennie, who would then direct it to Signor Fabbronie, presumably through the offices of Wellesley Pole.

Rennie had written on 30 July. He dispatched Boulton's answer on to the Tuscan around the fifth of August, accompanied by a request for more data, so that he and Boulton could decide precisely what must be supplied. By the ninth, the project looked far less hopeful than it had previously, and in fact it seems to have gone no further. Both Boulton, Watt and the Rennies were hard at work on the Calcutta and Bombay mints, and neither would have been able to give the much smaller Florentine facility the attention it deserved. And it is always possible that the Italian received instructions to break off discussions.

From the early 1820s forward, most of the remaining mint possibilities would centre on the newly emergent nations of Latin America. There appears to have been brief conversations about a mint for Buenos Aires. These took place late in 1823, and they followed naturally enough from the copper coinage which Soho had been providing to Argentina. Talks centred on a rolling mill powered by a twenty-four-horse engine; the package would cost between £4,700 and £5,000. But discussions broke off at the beginning of the new year: Soho would continue to send coins to Argentina – but someone else would get the contract for a mint.

The failure in Argentina was compensated for by qualified successes in Mexico. And as Boulton, Watt was manufacturing its machinery for Guanajuato and Mexico City, another opportunity seemed to be emerging to the south.

This would have led to the refurbishment of the mint at Bogotá, Colombia. A mint had existed there since the beginning of the 1620s, but its production had never been large during colonial days, and it was now viewed as inadequate to the requirements of an independent nation. The record of a possible connection between Boulton and Bogotá consists of a single letter from James Watt, Jr. to Matthew Robinson Boulton in March 1826 – but it gives us many essential details of the conversations, and a broad hint at why they were abandoned.

Watt was approached by a Colombian gentleman named Hurtado, who wanted a mint constructed and shipped to his capital. From a letter written after the fact and cited elsewhere, it appears that he wanted a steam-powered facility, and that Matthew Robinson Boulton agreed to sell him the new Soho Mint. A coinage was also wanted, to be struck in England to demonstrate the superiority of the Boulton machinery. Hurtado had the funds necessary to pay for the package – securely lodged with reputable bankers named Goldschmidt. Unfortunately, Messrs Goldschmidt went bankrupt later in the year, and Hurtado's money disappeared in the general crash. Watt estimated that he might be able to recover fifty per cent of it, if he were very lucky, 'at some distant period'. The emissary remained cheerful, assuring that his government would send more money 'as soon as it can provide the means'. Watt deemed this unrealistic; worse, the South American had no concept of how a mint would have to be moved on the long and arduous trek between the Caribbean coast and the nine-thousand-foot level of Cundinamarca, where Bogotá sat.

> He does not think they can carry more than 2 or 3 Cwt [hundredweights] along the road to Bogota, which I told him would never do, that he must find means of taking at least a ton.[20]

The Bogotá episode was apparently not pursued by either side. Hurtado likely found his government less forthcoming than he had anticipated, while Boulton, Watt & Company must have eventually been very grateful *not* to have got the order, after all of the difficulties it would encounter in getting machinery to Guanajuato – along a route far less demanding than the road to Bogotá.

Correspondence for hypothetical Latin American mints continued through the late 1820s and early 1830s. The summer of 1827 saw Soho holding talks with Messrs Gibbs & Sons, who had been entrusted with the refurbishment of the old Lima mint. Matthew Robinson Boulton prepared an estimate for manually-operated machinery on 20 August, arriving at a total figure of £1,604 for two coining presses, three cutting out machines, a double milling machine, and a lathe for turning dies. Gibbs & Sons soon raised their sights to a larger mint (which would be powered by water, not steam), and they requested advice on costs of such a package and solicited Soho's advice on the personnel needed to accompany it to Lima. But when Boulton sent along a cordial letter with an estimate of around six thousand pounds for the mint, either the Peruvians or their London representatives decided that the cost was excessive and that Peru could do without the blessings of British technology in this instance.

Soho would be approached by emissaries from two other Latin American nations, for two different products, in two different decades. In the early 1830s, El Salvador would solicit information about a mint. And a dozen years later, Venezuela would inquire about a coinage.

The connection with the tiny Central American state of El Salvador lasted from August 1830 to May 1831. The British representatives of this new nation were Messrs Ellice Kinner & Company of London, which addressed a general inquiry to Boulton, Watt on 20 August. El Salvador wanted 'a mint for coining dollars and small pieces, also doubloons if necessary'.[21] How much would one cost? Boulton expressed mild interest in the project; but to come up with a reasonable estimate he must first know the size of the coinage contemplated, whether steam power would be wanted, whether a rolling mill would be included, and (with an eye to the suffering coiners of Guanajuato) how difficult it would be to get the mint from the coast to the capital, San Salvador. Ellice Kinner & Company wrote off to its representative in Central America, and it, and Matthew Robinson Boulton, let the matter sleep until an answer might be received. Its man replied on 2 January 1831, and his report was forwarded to Soho as soon as it arrived, some four months after it had been written. When Boulton scanned its contents, he rapidly lost interest in the project.

For it would mean a tiny mint indeed, which must only be capable of striking two thousand pieces *per day* and be worked by water. When he reflected that even in its present reduced state Soho could easily strike that many coins in a quarter of an hour; when he reflected that the package could not weigh over five hundred pounds if it were to be conveyed by Indian carriers over wretched mountain roads – or else must be sent by way of Cape Horn; he concluded that the Central Americans had no idea what they wanted – or at least what he could give them. And he wrote to Messrs Ellice Kinner & Company to that effect. Another Latin American project had come to nothing. In the cases of Mexico and Haiti, Matthew Robinson Boulton could be accommodating, altering or diminishing a new technology in the face of local conditions, local demands. But he had his limits.

The final contact with Latin America came eleven years later, in the summer of 1842. This concerned a copper coinage for the Republic of Venezuela. Again, Boulton, Watt dealt with Latin Americans indirectly through a British firm – in this case, Reid, Irving & Cox. The latter approached Soho on 16 July with an inquiry about a copper coinage in three denominations, centavos, half-centavos, and quarter-centavos. (The name of the intended recipient was nowhere given in the correspondence, but Venezuela was the only Latin American country to use coinage in all three denominations.) Writing for Soho, Joseph Westley solicited more information, which came in gradually over the next two weeks. By 5 August, Boulton, Watt was able to present a formal coinage proposal.

Assuming that the centavos, halves, and quarters were to be struck at 48, 96, and 192 to the pound respectively, Soho could make them for £127.13.0, £132.6.0, and £136.19.0 per ton. Around twenty pounds would be charged for the original dies, the exact sum dependent upon the complexity of their designs. But no reply was received from Reid, Irving & Cox, or from Venezuela – and this final Latin American connection came to an end, as had so many of its earlier counterparts.

This is not to say that Venezuela did not order and circulate copper coins, struck in Great Britain, of those three denominations: she did, in 1843 and again in 1852. Soho obviously would have had nothing to do with the second coinage;[22] but what about the first? Here, we must go back to the weights of the three denominations. *If* Westley were accurate in his assumptions, the centavo should weigh 9.46 grams, its half 4.73, and its quarter 2.36. And these weights do not correspond with those of extant specimens, either for circulating coins or for patterns. In every case, the coins are far heavier than they should be had Westley's understanding been correct, and had Soho been given the order: centavos weigh around 12.5 grams, with the halves and quarters in proportion. The 1843-dated coppers were in fact to be struck at the Royal Mint.

But if the Royal Mint got the order, why did it receive it, and not Soho? I surmise that it was successful because it was ready to coin and Soho was not. Matthew Robinson Boulton had recently died and the Soho operation was still in an uproar, as surviving members debated whether to solicit new business or simply sell the old mint. Soho clung to life for a few more years – but it is interesting to note that most of its later efforts, largely directed at Singapore, Mexico, and Canada, were continuations of contacts fully developed years or even decades before. The firm would cut little new ground in its last years.

There was one final opportunity which might have directed a revivified Soho into surprising new paths, had it worked out. For toward the end of 1838, interest was expressed in a Boulton connection with *Egypt*.

That nation was then part of the Turkish Empire, and therefore theoretically ruled from Constantinople. But the power of the Sultan had long since waned, and Egypt was currently under the harsh but effective control of Pasha Mehemet Ali. In an effort to modernize Egypt and consolidate his regime, Mehemet Ali cautiously invited in British technicians and British industrial products – and sent intelligent young Egyptians to Britain to see and learn about the Industrial Revolution in the land of its birth. One of these young men was an officer named Selim Aga: in the autumn of 1833, he was completing his studies at Woolwich, stealing time away from his courses to explore industrial byways with a young businessman named Sanderson.

On 17 September, Selim Aga and Sanderson dropped by Soho to see to some engines which had been ordered and were currently being built. Matthew Robinson Boulton was in London, but his partner happened to be at the works and showed the visitors the engines – and the Boulton mint, for good measure. Selim Aga was highly impressed, and Watt believed that he would deliver a favourable report on what he had seen – a report which might lead to further business.

If this officer's words were indeed favourable, they would not be acted upon for some years. But they may have had an impact all the same: in November 1838, James Watt, Jr. wrote his partner that another Egyptian functionary had been at Soho. This was

> Edham Bey, who is at the head of Mehemet Ali's arsenal, and appears deputed by him to enquire into such Inventions as might be successfully introduced into Egypt … He explained himself quite satisfied with our Engines; … [He] thought it likely the Pacha might incline to have a Mint, and M*r* Westley in consequence shewed yours and referred him to you for Estimates, which he will not apply for until he has written to the Pacha.[23]

The Egyptian's interest and Westley's enterprise might have led to either of two concrete results. Soho might have been able to construct a new mint for Egypt, which would have been a fitting climax to its decades of dedication to the improvement of coining. But Westley and Edham Bey might have also been discussing the sale of an extant mint, Soho Mint – a transaction which received far more discussion immediately after Matthew Robinson Boulton's death. The lack of archival evidence means we are unable to discount either possibility.

The Egyptians chose to pursue neither. Tensions between Great Britain and Egypt worsened at the end of the old decade and the beginning of the new, and Watt's letter stands as a lonely testimony to yet another numismatic might-have-been.

The interrupted stories of mints for Egypt, Prussia, Colombia, and Peru, of coinage for Schleswig and Württemberg, of tokens for James Woodmason, all suggest paths which Soho might have taken. That other mints were not built, other coins and tokens not struck in addition to the ones we know, must remind us of the interconnection between Boulton, Watt & Company and a larger world, an imperfect world. Considering the international and internal difficulties against which they struggled, the Boultons did remarkably well for themselves, their firm, and the history of coinage. But we may still regret that much remained undone, that Berlin and Cairo never struck their coinage on the model provided by an enterprising Midlands' merchant named Matthew Boulton. The loss was his, theirs – and ours.

SOURCES

Many areas of the Matthew Boulton Papers were explored for the preparation of this chapter. The interested researcher will find many of them grouped around those documents from which I have quoted directly. Thus, those interested in pursuing coinage for Altona should look in MBP232, Letter Box F1, and in Matthew Boulton's letter books for that period – MBP148 and 150. In the same fashion, letters from the Redens will be found in MBP251, Letter Box R1, and Boulton's replies to them in MBP150, [Private] Letter Book O.

This rule must be applied with care. The documents on the Haitian project will be found in MBP409 (Correspondence re coinage); they will *not* be found where one would expect them – in MBP248, Letter Box P1. (The record of payment for M. Peltier's press will be found in MBP59, Mint and Coinage Journal, 1808–1811.) And while information on the Antiguan coinage will be found in MBP223, Letter Box B5, the beginnings of the idea must be sought in MBP272, the box of correspondence from Sir Joseph Banks.

James Watt, Jr.'s correspondence is always useful, no more so than for this discussion of coins and mints that never were. MBP355 and 356 are especially important, covering the period between 1822 and 1848. And several of the letter books at Soho may also be of use, especially MBP70, 71, 76, 80, 84, and 86, which contain outgoing correspondence between 1824 and 1845.

NOTES

1 MBP352, Watt, James, 1792–1821 (box 5): James Watt to Matthew Boulton, 3 February 1800. The letter from Vienna bore a date of 3 October 1799.
2 MBP251, Letter Box R1: Count Reden to Matthew Boulton, 4 February 1791.
3 MBP150, [Private] Letter Book Q: Matthew Boulton to Count Reden, 24 February 1791.
4 MBP251, Count Reden to Matthew Boulton, 2 April 1791.
5 'The Copper Company of Upper Canada Halfpenny Token', *Numismatic Circular* 85, 3 (March 1977), pp. 99–101; 85, 4 (April 1977), pp. 144–7; 85, 5 (May 1977), pp. 201–3; and 85, 6 (June 1977), pp. 254–6. Vice utilized the Matthew Boulton Papers for his article – and indeed for his other excellent work on the Boulton enterprise.
6 'Notes on the Ibberson Token', *Numismatic Circular* 94, 2 (March 1986), pp. 39–40.
7 At Birmingham, the archival story will be found in MBP245, Letter Box M2. A printed account will be found in *Walter Breen's Complete Encyclopedia of U.S. and Colonial Coins* (New York, 1988), pp. 106–7.
8 MBP46, Mint Day Book, 1801–1805, p. 61 (entry of 9 January 1802).
9 MBP244, Letter Box M1: Nathaniel Marchant to Matthew Boulton, 27 January 1803; spelling in original.
10 MBP244, Nathaniel Marchant to Matthew Boulton, 25 February 1803.
11 MBP244, Nathaniel Marchant to Matthew Boulton, 26 May 1803. We may imagine what Boulton thought of the project by this time!
12 MBP46, p. 156 (entry of 27 August 1803).
13 MBP262, Letter Box W3: James Woodmason to Matthew Boulton, 9 April 1804.

14 MBP223, Letter Box B5: Anthony Brown to Matthew Boulton, 27 February 1806. Boulton's last name (and frequently his first) was often mangled by his correspondents. But he would have probably observed that such practice was admissible, so long as they spelled *their* names correctly on their remittances to him!

15 MBP409, Correspondence re coinage: *Gazette Officielle de l'État d'Hayti*, 19 (10 September 1807), p 76.

16 MBP409, Jean-Gabriel Peltier to Matthew Boulton, 30 April 1808.

17 This was not the only chimerical project in which Drummond played a role. Early in 1815, he wrote Soho on behalf of a friend who wanted a mint for *China*, preferably in time for the next sailing of the first ships in March. He was discouraged – a shame, for the possibility of a Peking connection for Boulton, Watt & Company piques the imagination.

18 MBP322, Lawson, James and Lawson, Archibald: James Lawson to Matthew Robinson Boulton, 23 December 1813.

19 This man is otherwise unmentioned in the Matthew Boulton Papers; but he may have been related to an earlier master of the Florence mint named Giovanni *Fabroni*. The latter had written Matthew Boulton at the beginning of the 1780s – but in regard to gardening, not moneying.

20 MBP355, Watt, James, jr., 1822–27 (box 3): James Watt, Jr. to Matthew Robinson Boulton, 14 March 1826.

21 MBP76, Mint and Coinage Letter Book, 1827–1830: Matthew Robinson Boulton to Ellice Kinner & Company, 23 August 1830. Boulton quoted that portion of their letter to him of 20 August in his reply to that firm on the twenty-third.

   A cursory glance at Salvadoran coinage of the period will suggest why a new mint was wanted. No 'dollars' or pesos were then being produced, probably because the country's old machinery was simply incapable of striking them.

22 Curiously, Soho's presses, if not Soho, did produce some of the Venezuelan coppers of 1852: when Boulton, Watt retired from business in 1850, its four coining machines were purchased by Ralph Heaton & Sons. Along with the Paris Mint, the Heatons produced the 1852 contract coinage. The mint's name will be found spelled out in full on the obverse of each coin that it struck.

23 MBP356, Watt, James, jr., 1828–48, (box 4): James Watt, Jr. to Matthew Robinson Boulton, 12 November 1838.

CHAPTER 9

A case apart:
The United States of
America

Elsewhere in this book, we have been examining the story of Boulton, Watt & Company in simple terms of success or failure. Our approach has been a generally linear one: a contact is made, a request goes out for a mint, for coins, for tokens, or for copper planchets. The request is honoured – or refused or retracted by either side. And the story can usually be told in a logical progression from beginning to end.

Soho's dealings with the United States were otherwise. Throughout the long years of the contact between the Birmingham firm and the new republic, there was a peculiar note of tentativeness, of diffidence, of something approaching suspicion; this note was sounded on both sides of the Atlantic. Again and again, opportunities would loom up, catching one or both sides unprepared. When either Soho or the Americans were ready to act, chance, mutual distrust, or a curious lethargy would set in, and the contact would be broken off, the opportunity lost. The five decades of business dealings between the Boultons and the United States can only be written with an eye towards what might have been, as well as what actually happened. While mints might have been built, coinage might have been supplied, and America's money might have been stamped with a new industrial aspect, what finally came to fruition was almost anticlimactic: the United States Mint needed planchets for copper coinage, and Soho supplied them.

Significant events on the larger stage shaped events on the smaller. The American War of Independence meant many things on many levels, for Briton and American alike. But one result, unexpected at the time and generally overlooked since, was that thereafter neither side could convincingly claim to know the other as well as it had previously assumed. A nervousness set in, an insecurity in dealing with former members of a single family. And citizens of Great Britain and those of the United States would regard each other warily, suspiciously, inconsistently: for they could no longer see each other clearly.

From the larger stage to the smaller: Englishmen were ambivalent about their American cousins, and vice versa. And the very English Matthew Boulton shared in the ambivalence, as did a succession of American statesmen, Mint Directors, and simple travellers. Let Boulton speak for them all: at the beginning of 1775, well *before* the actual outbreak of the American War for Independence, he was one of the leaders in a Birmingham petition to Parliament, demanding that that body uphold the law against the American malcontents, come what may.[1] But a few years later, he was able to write to an American correspondent that he wished the new country and its new government well.[2] He was surely sincere in the first instance, almost certainly so in the second. For the Americans might well be ingrates, but they held a fascination and an attraction as well, so like and yet so unlike their transatlantic relations.

It is appropriate that the first coinage contact between Matthew Boulton and the United States had the substantiality of smoke, dissipating into thin air, leaving virtually no trace. This involved Charles Borel of South Carolina, and it took place during the year 1786. At that time, the states were essentially sovereign powers: because the striking and distribution of coinage has always been considered an attribute of sovereignty, a number of them either had coinage made for them (Connecticut and New Jersey), struck their own (Massachusetts), or considered the idea but did nothing (New York). In addition, another entity which called itself a *republic* rather than a state had a contract coinage of its own: this was Vermont, whose land dispute with neighbouring New York would keep it out of the federal compact until 1791.

The Matthew Boulton papers prove that another jurisdiction was thinking about the contract coinage idea. Some American numismatists will have heard of John H. Mitchell, an ambitious young merchant from Charleston, South Carolina. But they are unlikely to have heard of Mitchell's neighbour, Charles Borel. Borel was French-speaking, and he had apparently settled in the French-founded Carolinian city some years previously. He prospered, and when he made a coinage proposal to the South Carolina legislature in the late winter of 1786, his influence sufficed to obtain legislation empowering him to solicit coinage for the state.

This ordinance was enacted on 22 March, and it stipulated coinage in copper and *silver*, £10,000 in copper pieces, divided equally between pence and halfpence, and £20,000 in silver shillings and sixpences, three of the former coins to one of the latter. Borel was given fifteen months to import such coinage into the state. The weights of the coins were to correspond to their British counterparts, but the fineness of the silver was to be on the French standard – an interesting monetary holdover from the days of Gallic control. The state's Governor was to select the designs.

Once Borel had secured his contract coinage, he was to submit it for assay; if it were found to be to the state's standards, he was to receive payment for it in the state's paper, value for value. It is difficult to see what advantage would accrue to Mr Borel for his pains; but so the ordinance read.

Charles Borel now set to work to secure a moneyer. It is unclear when he thought of Matthew Boulton, and his known connection with the then-fledgling coiner will be found in precisely two letters in the Matthew Boulton Papers. The first, written on 19 August 1786, requested Boulton's terms for striking five tons of copper coins for use in South Carolina – *with no mention of a silver coinage.* Boulton's reply naming terms is lost, but Borel agreed to them on 14 September. He asked for most or all of his coppers within three weeks' time, likely intending to take them back to America with him. But Boulton either could not or would not comply (his coinage for Sumatra was just getting under way) and we hear no more of the project in the Matthew Boulton Papers.

Had it proceeded, we may assume that Borel's coins would have been simple affairs, struck on manual screw presses, during time left over from the larger order for the East India Company. But the project never left the preliminary stage, and the mantle of *soi-disant* purveyor of Carolinian coinage passed to another, John H. Mitchell.

We know a good deal more about Mitchell than Borel – in part because an eventual descendant published most of the correspondence between Mitchell and Matthew Boulton in 1931; while scarce, enough American numismatists have seen copies of the Mitchell-Boulton letters to have realized that plans for an American coinage struck at Soho were under active discussion by the late 1780s. But there was rather more to it than that.

From the very beginning, Mitchell thought in grandiose terms. At a time when he had not yet informed the Governor or the General Assembly of his plans (let alone secured their agreement to them) he invited Boulton to participate in the plentiful supply of a state coinage (a drawing of the proposed design has survived; it is essentially a rendition of the state arms). When it became apparent that the government under the new federal Constitution would take a dim view of state coinages (this was the very sort of rampant federalism which the new organic law was intended to stop), Mitchell blithely suggested a new *national* coinage, all to be struck at Soho! The Americans would need no less than £200,000 worth of coin, an amount divided equally between gold, silver, and copper – and this would merely be the first of many orders. Mitchell clearly saw himself as the middleman, supplying Congress with Mr Boulton's coinage, paying Mr Boulton with rice, indigo, or any other local commodity of interest. Speed was of the essence: all of the coinage must be made by the autumn of 1791, two years from the time of the proposal. And Boulton would do well to state his terms quickly and precisely, for Congress would be meeting at the beginning of January 1790 and a concrete proposal must certainly be in place by then.

While harbouring doubts, Boulton dutifully produced an estimate of charges in late November 1789; with luck, it would reach Mitchell in time to inform the Congress. Copper coinage could be made for £46.13.4 per ton, provided the Americans found their own metal. If Boulton had to find it, the price per ton would rise by about £84. Mitchell could pay for his coinage by shipping indigo, rice, tobacco (or any other American products of value) to London, the articles to be sold there on the coinage account. This highly unusual arrangement suggests that Matthew Boulton was desperate to do business with America, at a time when it seemed increasingly unlikely that he would do much with England in the foreseeable future.

Unfortunately, his proposal only reached its audience in mid-March 1790. All the same, Mitchell submitted it to Congress, and his native optimism cheered him with the thought that a Boulton proposal received several months late was still better than a proposal anyone else delivered on time. But influential people in the new government would see things differently.

Chief among them was Thomas Jefferson, Secretary of State and the leader of an emerging political opposition group to the Federalist party. Jefferson was somewhat anti-British and decidedly pro-French. But his observations concerning John H. Mitchell's proposals, and the Birmingham magnate who stood behind them, transcended parties and pettiness.

Jefferson's report of 14 April 1790 acknowledged that Boulton could coin in the manner which he and Mitchell claimed. But technical excellence must yield place to national interest and safety: the Mitchell-Boulton proposal was admirable, *provided it could be carried out in America*. If it had to be effected in Great Britain, it could not be seriously entertained.

It could not be entertained because it would be far too risky. In times of war, ships laden with coin for America would make tempting targets for enemy vessels. Even in times of peace, such cargoes would always run the risk of mutiny and piracy by the crews to whom they were entrusted. And since coinage was a visible aspect of sovereignty, how could the new nation, whose nationality was still in process of formation, transfer coinage, which stood very close to the centre of the identity of *all* states, recent and established, to the safe keeping of another nation? In sum, Matthew Boulton could not be allowed to strike America's money at Soho.

Back home in Charleston, Mitchell learned the bad news in mid-May 1790, about a month after Jefferson had handed down his opinion. The merchant wrote Boulton almost immediately, stressing that the Secretary had invited Soho to extend its operation to the United States. But Boulton was unprepared for such a drastic step (and was perhaps becoming aware that Mitchell was not the go-between for the job, a dreamer more interested in turning a profit than in reforming a coinage); and the two men henceforth restricted their dealings to the more prosaic articles of the Anglo-American trade. Some years later, when Boulton's nephew Zacchaeus Walker, Jr. visited Charleston, South Carolina, he made a point of visiting his uncle's old acquaintance. He found Mitchell charming as always, but 'with the unlucky talent of trying to preserve the splendour of a Gent*n* [Gentleman] without adequate means'[3] – not the sort of person to carry off an American coinage for Soho.

The Borel and Mitchell contacts envisioning South Carolina coinage were an accurate reflection of interest in coinage on the state level. But the United States national government was also interested in a coinage, and its concern would yield another potential opportunity for Soho.

When the federal government looked around, it saw a sort of monetary chaos. There was no standard firmly in force for the lower end of the nation's monetary scale, and American citizens were treated to an unappetizing concoction of state coppers of varying weights, worn-out British and Irish genuine and counterfeit halfpennies, other copper coins or tokens of the same general size as the old British halfpence – and American counterfeits and evasive pieces of several descriptions. The country's citizens used all of these monies as they came their way, for they were starved for small change; but Congress believed they deserved better.

So that body determined to circulate a decent copper coinage, one which would henceforth serve as a standard against which other peoples' monies could be judged. It passed the enabling legislation on 21 April 1787. The next step was to choose a coiner: Congress may have had the power to legislate a coinage into being, but it lacked the necessary establishment to strike it.

Early on, there were two major contenders for the honour. The initial edge was enjoyed by General Matthias Ogden, of Rahway, New Jersey, who produced interesting patterns called 'Immunis Columbia' coppers. But he lost his position to a Connecticut resident named James Jarvis, who produced a ten-thousand-dollar bribe for the head of the Board of Treasury, Colonel William Duer. Jarvis got the contract. And he also got nearly thirty-two tons of copper from the complaisant colonel, with which to begin the coinage. For his trouble, Duer was to receive a portion of the profits.

For there *would* be profits. If one figures that Jarvis owed the United States government $11\frac{1}{4}$ pence per pound for the copper, and that he was federally-authorized to strike forty-four and four-ninths coins from each pound of copper (coins which would then circulate as halfpence or cents), a quick calculation suggests that Jarvis and Duer would be making a profit of roughly one hundred per cent, less the cost of coinage!

Of course, it was one matter to secure a lucrative contract, quite another to grow rich from it. Jarvis's plan for fulfilling his agreement was to buy controlling interest in a private mint in New Haven, which was currently striking coppers for the state of Connecticut. He had gained control by the beginning of June, whereupon he called a halt to the production of state coins, directing his designer Abel Buell to begin making dies for national ones. These would feature a sundial and the Latin motto 'Fugio' (I fly) and 'Mind Your Business' for the obverse, thirteen linked rings for the reverse. (The designs had originally been conceived by Benjamin Franklin for national paper and coinage back in 1776, and Congress had stipulated their resurrection for this new attempt at a federal coinage.)

James Jarvis' 'Fugio' cent, 1787. (National Numismatic Collection, Smithsonian Institution)

As Buell set to work, Jarvis was faced with a major problem. His contract with Congress called for 345 tons of copper coins. He had thirty-two tons of copper on hand (an amount soon to decrease, as Jarvis' father-in-law and mintmaster, an enterprising gentleman named Samuel Broome, found that he could turn a greater coining profit resuming lightweight Connecticut coppers than by undertaking fullweight federal ones; Broome merrily mulcted the national government to the tune of some three million state coppers). Jarvis had to get more metal, and quickly. And it would obviously help if someone could roll it out and blank it for him in advance. These considerations led him to Matthew Boulton's door in the late winter of 1788.

Boulton was Jarvis' first choice for the job, although he apparently let it be known that he was in contact with Boulton's competitor Thomas Williams as well. By late February 1788, the American was ready to make his first proposal.

Boulton's jaw must have dropped when he saw it. At a time when he was desperately attempting to extort a few halfpenny specimens from the baulky Droz, for the delectation of a still more baulky Committee on Coin, here was someone who wished to place an order for no fewer than three hundred tons of coppers! This was a gigantic order by Boulton's current standards, and it must have looked like salvation at the time, a tempting prospect indeed.

For Jarvis had decided that he wanted *coinage*, and not coinage blanks – a hundred tons on 1 September 1788, the second hundred tons a year later, the final hundred a year after that. This would presumably allow Boulton to test and perfect his new machinery in a leisurely fashion, rather than risk everything with a single, larger, order. Better still, Jarvis hinted that there might be funds available 'for an impressing apparatus': with luck, Boulton might be able to sell a mint as well as coinage to this amiable American. But there was a catch. Boulton must deliver his first hundred tons on the first day of September, 1788. He could not expect payment until the first day of September, 1789. 'This advance [Boulton's first hundred tons, at Boulton's risk] will be a leading principle in any contract that I may make'.[4]

The delay in payment gave Boulton pause, but not for long. In an undated memorandum from early March 1788, he proposed reducing the total amount of coinage by half, deliverable at around five tons per week, shipment to commence about a month after his agreement with Jarvis was signed. Instead of the other 150 tons of coins, Boulton would supply 200 tons of blanks – and 'a Coining Machine & six Pair of Steel Dies properly hardened, Tempered, & finished and exactly conformable to the Dies which strike the 150 ton aforesaid'.[5] The coins could be supplied at £122.16.8 per ton, copper included, while the blanks alone would cost £105.10.0 per ton, cut out, milled, and ready for pressing. Casks and carriage to Hull or Bristol would add another two pounds or so to the cost. But Boulton expected payment for his workmanship at the time of delivery, not a year down the road; this insistence on quick payment suggests he was having second thoughts about the American possibility.

And he was being urged to be careful by those around him. While Jarvis searched for ways to make the proposal more attractive (several letters to Boulton have survived, wherein Jarvis puts forth various, and increasingly elaborate, security arrangements, finally having to fall back lamely on the claim that 'no security can be more valid than what I offer, as the whole United-States of Am*a* gurantee me——')[6] Boulton's London banker sourly advised that he had learned that 'Mr J. ... has no Security to offer that it would be proper for you to accept & therefore it wou'd be better to let the Business drop.——'.[7] And Boulton came to agree.

Jarvis left Britain for America on 21 May 1788, still hopeful that an agreement with Boulton could be concluded. He arrived in America to find the federal coinage in a state of collapse. Samuel Broome had by now appropriated virtually all of Colonel Duer's copper for Connecticut coinage but had wisely kept a portion back to retain appearances. On 21 May, just as Jarvis was beginning his homeward journey, his New Haven mint shipped a trifle under nine thousand pounds (or 398,577 pieces) of copper coins to the national government, then located in New York City. Broome and his cronies then turned back to the more profitable Connecticut coinage, using most of the remaining copper for that purpose.

Modern collectors call these coins 'Fugio' or 'Franklin' cents, from the motto and the man who inspired their designs. Those who actually used them in trade called them 'Congress coppers'. But they were not popular with anyone. Their unfamiliar designs made them unpopular with the public (for whom a 'normal' copper coin featured a man's head on one side, a seated female on the other), and Congress found that, owing to the peculations of the Jarvis combine, the 'standard' coppers were scarcely heavier than those lightweight pieces which had inspired their creation. Jarvis arrived home in time to find that an exasperated Congress was about to void his contract. It did so on 16 September 1788, and it eventually fined him $10,842.24 for his failure to live up to his contract. Typically, it was unable to collect a cent of the money owed: the Fugio fiasco was a powerful argument in favor of a new, stronger national government, one which could get its policies carried out, one strong enough and enterprising enough to establish its own mint and do its own coining.

Meanwhile, with no further legal reason for existence, the current coinage contractors disbanded and went their separate ways. Samuel Broome sold the New Haven mint's machinery to Captain Thomas Machin, whose establishment near Newburgh, New York was able to expand its production of light-weight coppers (including a few Fugios, whose club-like rays proclaim their identity); Broome sailed to Europe on the proceeds. Aware of his role in the massive embezzlement of federal property, and remembering the consequences of his previous brush with the law (a brand mark on his forehead and the loss of part of an ear – the common penalty for counterfeiting), Abel Buell left for Europe as well. James Jarvis and his brother Benjamin left the United States too. They made for Paris, where they reunited with Samuel Broome. And Broome and Benjamin Jarvis, at least, made a final proposal to Matthew Boulton.

This did not involve coining, but something even more chimerical in the context of the times. They proposed to establish a gigantic, steam-powered flour mill in Paris, something along the lines of Boulton's Albion Mill in London. And they wanted Boulton's help in setting it up.

Their timing could scarcely have been worse. Benjamin Jarvis' initial approach came in a letter to Boulton of 27 August 1789, the American observing that profit might be made and civil calm restored by turning steam power to the service of the Parisian poor. But events were already beyond the control and even the conception of a group of failed, somewhat shady businessmen on one side of the English Channel and an enterprising industrialist on the other. The industrialist saw most clearly: while Jarvis continued to regale him with plans and data through much of the autumn of 1789, Boulton finally put a close to the project in early November, advising the Americans that continuing French unrest, as well as the magnitude of the project, had persuaded him and his partner Watt to 'determine against engaging in the concern as Partners & Proprietors; but as Engineers we offer our best services'.[8] Since Jarvis and his friends wanted Boulton's money as well as his mind, the great French flour mill scheme collapsed.

The creation of a new American government under the Constitution of 1787 presaged the collapse of Matthew Boulton's more ambitious dreams for the Western Republic as well. The new compact specifically forbade the states from coining money, and it implicitly pledged the federal government to do so instead, a pledge made explicit with the Mint Act of 1792. Coinage denominations and designs were stipulated, and a national mint was ordered to be built in the national capital, then Philadelphia. In time, Matthew Boulton would find that his opportunities in America had been dramatically curtailed. The new mint would take advantage of his services in carefully circumscribed ways, allowing him to do only those things which it was impossible or impracticable for it to do – with enough hints at larger vistas to keep him – and later his son – hoping for more for the next forty-five years.

In 1790, chances looked bleak. Thomas Jefferson had just served notice that a Soho coinage for the new government was out of the question. But within two years, matters were taking a more promising turn. If the

Americans persisted in striking their own coinage, they could obviously use some assistance in doing so. And by 1792, it began to appear as though they would turn to Soho for help.

As would be so common elsewhere, Matthew Boulton conducted his business with a public power through a private intermediary. In this case, the emissary was an Englishman named Ralph Mather, who was about to sail for Philadelphia, there to join his father-in-law in a business venture. In mid-1792, he was travelling between Birmingham and Manchester, apparently taking notes on all manner of British manufacturing activity (and the profits which it might reap from an American trade), including coining. He visited Boulton in late June or early July and was shown the best of Soho Manufactory, including Soho Mint. The two men entered into an informal agreement; provided Boulton gave him samples to display in America, Mather would do his best to drum up business in Soho's various products, including coining machinery.[9]

Mather sailed for the United States about the first of August. He carried with him a two-part proposal concerning an American coinage connection, a proposal which he eventually delivered to Thomas Jefferson. The latter was more favourable to this scheme than he had been to that delivered by John Mitchell. For Mitchell seemed to be suggesting a permanent connection between Soho Mint and America. This new prospectus assumed a temporary one: Boulton would produce coinage for the United States only until the fledgling federal mint was ready to take over the work. Meanwhile, he would sell the United States copper coinage for $5\frac{1}{4}$ pence per pound over the cost of the copper.

The second part of the proposal dovetailed nicely with the first. To ensure that the national mint would soon be up and running, and running well, Boulton offered to sell it machinery on the model of that now at work at Soho Mint. A rolling mill and a coining apparatus (the latter capable of striking from two to three hundred thousand pieces per day, many times more productive than anything the Americans could make on their own) could both be prepared and sent out, at a cost of about £10,000.

Jefferson was indeed impressed, and tempted, by the offer of coinage if not by that of a mint. Mather advised Boulton that stressing the temporary nature of coinage exports was a stroke of genius, going far to allay the fears of the Secretary of State. But a contract was still not a foregone conclusion. While everyone from President Washington down was pleased with Boulton's samples (they should have been: Mather had given them some of Droz's halfpenny patterns), the American minister must first come to Soho, examine Boulton's mint, treat with Mr Boulton, and then report home. His report would come before a Congressional committee, which would make the final decision.

So Mather reported early in February 1793; by the time Boulton got his letter, matters were beginning to unravel.

Rufus King, the American emissary who later got Soho the right to prepare the first struck United States Indian peace medals, may indeed have visited Soho at the end of 1792 or the beginning of 1793. But he left no record of his passing, and Matthew Boulton would soon find that events in America were working against him. Much to everyone's astonishment, the Americans were actually able to get a mint of their own in operation, a makeshift facility which opened its doors to regular coining at the start of 1793. The

Philadelphia mint only struck copper during its first year of operation, and it only made two sorts of coins, cents and half-cents. It cautiously added other metals and denominations as time went on. It was never very good at what it did. *But it was unquestionably American,* and its products, while crude and scarce, were immensely satisfying to public and private opinion. And when foreign events conspired with American ingenuity (Britain declared war on France early in 1793: now American sensibilities were tugged in yet another direction), the prospect of the sale to America of Mr Boulton's coinage, much less that of the sale of Mr Boulton's mint, vanished like a puff of smoke.

But there was still the matter of Mr Boulton's planchets. Over the next few decades, the sale of copper blanks for cents and half-cents would define the relationship between the world's first industrial coiner and the world's largest republic.[10] And both sides would attempt to expand the contact into something greater, leading to the purveyance of modern coinage or a modern mint to the Philadelphia moneyers.

These hopes would never be realized: but those in Britain might have indeed taken note of what had been accomplished, for it was no small thing. Between the 1790s and the late 1830s, the most likely coins to be seen in circulation by the average resident of the United States were the cent and half-cent. So typically 'American' are these coins considered that a sizable percentage of American collectors and researchers have specialized in them, to the exclusion of other denominations. And yet, of all cents struck between 1797 and 1837, more than two-thirds were made of Soho-supplied planchets. And *all* half-cents struck during the first third of the nineteenth century started out in Matthew Boulton's workshop.

Students of coining technology have tended to see the process of striking as the most difficult step in the making of coin. But there is another, anterior step which was far more challenging in the early days of mechanical moneying, and that was the rolling of metal into a consistent strip suitable for blanking into planchets. The metamorphosis of a thick block of metal into a thin fillet for coining required two articles, both of which were in short supply at the beginning of the industrial age. It demanded several sets of heavy steel rollers of high, unvarying quality. And it demanded a massive motive force, allowing those rollers to squeeze and shape the otherwise-useless ingot into a useful strip of metal. The scarcity of good steel and sufficient power meant that a bottleneck was always possible during the rolling stage.

The next step, the actual cutting of planchets from the fillet or strip, would pose no particular problems for the pre-industrial technology then in common use – except if a very large number of planchets were wanted. And then a second obstacle would arise, based partly on the motive force required to cut planchets from strip, stemming also from the fact that it was not possible for one man to cut more than a few dozen such planchets per minute by hand.

Both bottlenecks existed at the early Philadelphia mint. Heirs to the British coiners' disdain for copper, officials of the new United States Mint would have greatly preferred to restrict their efforts to the 'noble' metals, gold and silver. And common sense strengthened their preference: it obviously took one hundred times as much rolling, blanking, and coining to make a dollar's worth of copper cents as a dollar's worth of silver dollars. But economic and political realities dictated that, like it or not, copper must be struck, and struck in sizable quantity.

The economic reality was that, at a time and in a place where wages and prices were low, copper coins (which occupied the lowest rungs on the monetary ladder) were extremely important to most buyers and sellers. Matthew Boulton had recognized this truth in Birmingham; a succession of Mint Directors was forced to recognize it as well in Philadelphia. And while other nations' coins might be used in the higher echelons of the nation's new monetary system, there was much less available at the bottom of the scale. Congress was confronted with the unwelcome fact that, were it not to act decisively, the only low-value coins which most of its citizens were likely to see would be counterfeits of one sort or another (unpalatable on general principle), state coppers (which had been repudiated by the new Constitution) – or genuine British halfpence and farthings. And if the latter, what would that say about the nature of the new national sovereignty, about the plausibility of the new national government? From a political point of view as well, a reasonably plenteous copper coinage must be provided.

The United States Mint wrestled ineffectively with the copper problem for the first few years of its existence (and with an additional difficulty, which would have likely turned its eyes to Europe even had it had modern machinery: a lack of available native copper). It began making cents and half-cents in 1793, but by the beginning of 1796 had still struck only a million and a half cents and a quarter of a million half-cents – Soho's production during a fortnight. After three full years of operation, the harried Elias Boudinot, Director of the Mint, was looking for help in the striking of copper. He would turn to Britain, and to Matthew Boulton.

Despite the record of earlier contacts between Soho and the Americans, it was not inevitable that he would do so. Early in 1796, Boudinot made *two* proposals to Britons for the supply of planchets to the United States Mint. He had his nephew, Samuel Bayard, approach Boulton, Watt & Company, while he himself wrote to a second firm, the Governors and Company of Copper Miners in England. One of the proprietors of this second firm had a father-in-law named Thomas Clifford, who was currently a major force in Philadelphia politics. This political consideration suggested that the Company of Copper Miners be approached; so did the fact that it had important ties with the former Welsh copper power-house, the Parys Mines Company. It is unclear whether Matthew Boulton ever knew that the old rival to his Cornish Metal Company was in contention for the American planchet contract; he would not have been amused had he known.

But he need not have worried. While the Company of Copper Miners were first off the mark, their planchets reaching Philadelphia in October 1796, nearly *fourteen months* ahead of the competition, their rival managed to undercut their price per pound when he finally acted. Of still greater importance, his products proved to be suitable for coining at once, whereas those sent by the Company of Copper Miners were so rough as to be virtually useless, even after they had been cleaned and scoured. Rather than winning the favour of the United States Mint for his planchets, Matthew Boulton saw his rivals lose its favour for theirs.[11]

Boulton's maiden shipment was received in America at the beginning of December 1797. Early the following year, the first of what Boudinot anticipated as a regular series of remissions left Soho, arriving in the Schuylkill off Philadelphia in May 1798. The Mint Director looked over the new planchets, was delighted with them, and happily anticipated the establishment of a regular, easy production of good American copper coinage based on good British copper planchets.

What he anticipated and what he got were two different things. While Boudinot assumed that Boulton was as interested as he in a regular planchet trade, the Birmingham industrialist showed a curious and then an alarming disinclination to act in an appropriate manner – or even answer Boudinot's increasingly importunate letters. Boulton, of course, had problems of his own: he was just then rebuilding the Soho Mint, was also winding down one British coinage and desperately looking for another. He was also talking with officials of several countries about building mints for Russia, Denmark, and Britain. He was in fact a man of many parts, and while he might frequently be at the centre of the United States Mint Director's concerns, the latter and his planchets could scarcely expect reciprocal attention.

This led to some strange occurrences in 1798 and 1799. As the months went by without the arrival of new copper planchets from Mr Boulton, Mr Boudinot was forced to curtail production. The total cent coinage for 1799 was 42,540 pieces. Striking seventy pieces per minute, Boulton's eight Soho coining presses could have produced the same coinage in just an hour and a quarter. But then, he had the copper as well as the technology.

The coinage totals for 1799 represent the nadir of American cent production from the birth of the denomination to the present day. Boudinot curtailed coinage, stretching Boulton's planchets as far as they could be extended. But did he look elsewhere for his blanks? In the collection of the American Numismatic Society, New York, there is a curious 1798 cent, which began its career as one of Thomas Williams' 1788 Parys Mines halfpenny tokens. We know its origins because the United States Mint's coining presses were not strong enough to efface the earlier impression – and we can see parts of a lettered edge, guaranteeing payment in Anglesey, London, or Liverpool. Considering the fact that an Anglesey halfpenny was about the same size as an American cent, are we to conclude that Elias Boudinot had become so desperate for copper planchets that he was commandeering other people's money to secure them? We probably should not: this piece is the only one ever seen with a clear, recognizable undertype. And yet the timing of its appearance is so perfect that one is tempted to draw the logical conclusion. And it is difficult to explain the origins of this particular coin: other people's money rarely gets into a mint unless it has both purpose and assistance.

Matthew Boulton belatedly sprang into action. On 18 April 1799, nearly ten tons of cent planchets left Soho on the long journey to Philadelphia. Soho sent another seventeen tons about two months later, suggesting that its master was now determined to make up for lost time. For the United States Mint, the days of desperation would soon be over.

In all, fifty-seven separate shipments of cent planchets went out between 1797 and 1837. Beginning in 1800, they were joined by cargoes of blanks for half-cents. The latter were never sent with the regularity of their larger brothers; indeed, none at all were sent between the summer of 1807 and the spring of 1825, whereas most years saw two shipments of cent blanks and a few (1801, 1802, 1826, 1832, and 1833) saw as many as four. The sporadic nature of remittances of the smaller planchets suggests the relative unpopularity of the half-cent compared with the cent. The former was largely used to make change against the Spanish-American real, which happened to be worth twelve and one-half cents in American money; the latter was used everywhere.

Earlier planchet shipments ranged from ten to twenty-five tons; later ones tended to be smaller but sent more frequently, the risks of the sea being thus lessened for any given shipment. This practice was wise: there *were* risks, both man-made and natural. As a result, the consistency of the planchet trade between Soho and the United States Mint after 1799 was more apparent than real.

The purveyance of British copper to the American mint always functioned within the larger context of British-American relations. When they entered a period of serious decline during the first decade of the nineteenth century, a deterioration which led to open warfare in 1812, Soho's American connection was threatened, then cut. Shipments became sporadic after 1803: there was one in September 1804, but the next did not occur until August 1807, to be followed by a shipment in July 1809, and a final one in February 1812. Then the war intervened, and the commerce would not be resumed until the autumn of 1815. By that time, despite having doled out its planchets with increasing rigour (represented by a progressive decline in cent production from 1812 through 1813 and 1814), the United States Mint finally exhausted its supply of copper blanks and simply shut down production of the cent. The year 1815 is in fact the *only* date unrepresented in the entire story of the cent between its inception and the present day. With the end of the war, the connection was indeed resumed; but those on either side of the Atlantic would never again be able to take it for granted. For it had been abundantly proved that the consistency of the relationship was not immune to the human factor.

Nor was it immune to the influences of nature. Weather was always a threat, and the fact that fifty-five of the fifty-seven cent planchet shipments got through unscathed or nearly so says much about the sailing skills of the captains and skippers of the *Adriana*, the *Amelia*, the *Alleghany*, and all the other wooden ships of the day – especially when the Boultons sent their wares around the calendar, endeavouring from pride and enterprise to anticipate and fulfill the demands of a succession of Mint Directors over forty years. But two of the fifty-seven shipments were not so favoured.

In the first case, Boulton, Watt and the American mint got off fairly lightly. On 8 October 1832, the *Algonquin*, a frequent carrier in the planchet trade, cleared Liverpool with a cargo of twenty-nine casks of cent planchets (representing almost precisely five tons of copper, this was a common cargo size during the 1830s) and a few hundred pounds of fine Swedish copper for alloy in precious-metal coinage. The vessel was wrecked off the British coast, but all the planchets were recovered and brought back to Soho, where they were refinished, annealed, repacked, and reshipped. They then successfully made their way to America, where they were turned into copper cents at Philadelphia. A few uncirculated 1832 and 1833 cents in the cabinet of the American Numismatic Society show light corrosive damage consistent with brief salt-water immersion prior to striking; I hazard the guess that these pieces are metallic witnesses to a minor disaster at sea.

The second disaster was far more serious. This involved the *Delaware*, and it took place twelve months after the *Algonquin* affair. And while the latter vessel was refloated and her cargo recovered, the *Delaware* would never sail again, and the loss of her cargo would have important repercussions for the United States Mint, and for Boulton, Watt & Company.

The *Delaware* left Liverpool on 26 October 1833 with the usual twenty-nine casks of cent planchets. She had been involved in the copper trade the previous summer; but the speed with which she had sailed back from Philadelphia to Liverpool, and the haste with which she now returned to America with this second planchet cargo, may have told against her. She went down off Wilmington, Delaware in weather so foul that attempts to salvage her were fruitless. Of her cargo of planchets, nine casks and parts of two others were totally lost. The remaining copper was eventually salvaged and acquired by the mint – at a price reduction reflecting the fact that it was useless for coining in its present form and could only be remelted and used as alloy. The dispute over responsibility for the accident and for payment for the planchets went on for nearly two years, and it joined other, ongoing disappointments, frictions, and complaints between the British concern and its American customer, difficulties which would eventually lead to the end of the relationship.

Each partner felt it had grounds for dissatisfaction. Boulton, Watt had a great deal of difficulty extracting payment for its planchets from the United States Government, whose scant resources had generally been allocated for more important purchases many months prior to the arrival of the copper blanks. Soho usually suffered in silence, but on at least one occasion the firm refused to send more planchets until payment had been received for earlier remittances.

The Americans could reply that Boulton, Watt sometimes took less than strict care of the quality and shipping of its product. On one occasion, planchets ordered had an annoying, projecting burr along their edges; on another, the kegs containing the planchets had been carelessly placed in 'a very wet part of the Ship, by which means about one fifth part of them are almost spoiled'.[12] And on many occasions, planchets arrived inconveniently late. A number of other customers suffered from Soho's cheerful inability to deliver its goods in a consistently timely fashion; but the Americans did something about it. They found other suppliers.

In the record of Soho deliveries of planchets to the United States Mint, there are two long gaps. The first, extending from early 1812 to late 1815, has an obvious cause, the unravelling of Anglo-American relations, culminating in the War of 1812. But the second gap, which lasted from April 1821 to May 1826, has no such obvious explanation: the two countries were at peace, and economic relations were normal, even excellent, during most of the period. But there was an explanation, even if it eludes us at first glance.

The United States Mint had found a second British supplier for its planchets. This was Belles & Harrold, based in Birmingham but with a branch in Philadelphia. In January 1816, the principal on the American side, William Harrold (who may have started his career at Soho – at least there was an individual by that name employed there in the 1790s), approached Mint Director Robert Patterson with an offer to supply cent and half-cent blanks at very favourable rates. Since Patterson had just been refused planchets from Boulton, Watt until payment had been rendered for those shipped back in 1815 and *1812*, the Mint Director was naturally receptive to Mr Harrold's offer of assistance. An agreement for an initial five tons of planchets was signed on 1 February, the day after Patterson had been approached by

William Harrold. And for the next seventeen years, the Philadelphia Mint would be receiving copper planchets from this second British concern.

Patterson and his successor Samuel Moore seem to have had fewer difficulties with the new supplier than the old, and after a disappointing Soho shipment received in mid-1821 (the *Kensington* had been carrying a cargo of salt as well as a cargo of copper, and the presence of sea water had yielded predictable results), the United States Mint informally cut its connection with Boulton, Watt – at least in the matter of copper planchets. The link was not resumed until the spring of 1826, and, while Belles & Harrold was gradually phased out of the trade in the early 1830s, the position of Soho would never again be as secure there as it had been prior to the War of 1812.

Of course, that firm's connections with the United States were never solely dependent on the sale of a single commodity. The Americans had originally come to Matthew Boulton for expertise in *coining*, not coin blanks, and they continued to do so in bad times as well as good. Thus, even during the lean years of the middle 1820s, we see a Mint Director asking for advice from Soho on 'the process by which the covering or finish called bronzing, or browning, is prepared and applied to Medals'.[13] The Philadelphia Mint wished to try its hand at special presentation pieces, including proof cents, and the Boulton establishment had a world reputation for expertise in preparing proof coins and medals with glossy brown surfaces. Samuel Moore's predecessor Elias Boudinot had asked for help in more substantive areas, requesting Matthew Boulton's assistance in procuring good steel for dies and, especially, advice on how to employ that steel to best advantage once it reached Philadelphia. The United States Mint's lack of success in die hardening gave it particular difficulty during the institution's early years and for many years thereafter. Out of these modest requests for commodities and advice on their employment would emerge more important requests for assistance, more substantive offers of help. The years of the planchet trade were studded with the potentials at least for a far greater, far more intimate connection between the Boultons and the United States Mint. But the diffidence, miscommunication, and distrust mentioned earlier – plus most generous helpings of ill fortune and bad timing – ensured that offers once made were misinterpreted, ignored, and lost.[14]

Yet such overtures distinguished Soho's American experience from the beginning until very nearly its end. In the early 1790s, the United States Government had set up a mint of its own, an establishment which owed nothing to the earlier discoveries and improvements made by Matthew Boulton and the members of his circle. The new federal mint was small, composed of cast-off and jury-rigged machinery, and was staffed by rank amateurs, who learned (or made up) their professions as they went along. Understandably, it achieved less than spectacular results: thus far, we have been focusing on its problems with copper, but it encountered similar difficulties with *all* metals. It was in fact producing little in the way of coinage: this was perhaps just as well, for what it was making would have proved a tempting target for the forger had it been struck in sufficient quantity to become better-known.

Even the most patriotic of mint employees and Members of Congress were aware that the United States Mint needed help. And there was, at bottom, only one place where that assistance could be obtained. If the new coiner were to achieve the goal of Alexander Hamilton and the other hard-money men who dominated the new national government, the provision of abundant and safe specie for business transactions large and small (thus weaning the misguided American public away from the allure of paper money) – then Boulton, Watt & Company would have to be let into the United States Mint's affairs.

Mint Director Boudinot was given official blessing, and he made an approach to Matthew Boulton in April 1799:

> I have had it in Contemplation to request you to let me have an Estimate of the Expence of a Mint compleat in all its parts, but on a small Scale, to be executed by you, & sent out here with full Directions for putting it up, including the Engine &c. &c. If you could favour me with such an Estimate, accompanying it with such Explanations as would enable me to induce Congress to agree to it, I should be much obliged, as it might render the Business more expeditious & easy in future.[15]

Matthew Boulton would have been well-advised to grasp this opportunity with both hands, and yet he did not. He sent a tepid reply to the harried Mint Director (whose presses were regularly breaking down, who could not get the copper planchets he needed, and who was again about to vacate his establishment prior to Philadelphia's annual visitation of yellow fever). Boulton merely said that he would take Boudinot's request under advisement. When the latter had still heard nothing substantive by mid-autumn (that is, nearly half a year after he had made his request), he repeated it, this time in even more unmistakable language:

> I am preparing to lay before Congress, an entire new Plan of a Mint, as I am dissatisfied with our present Establishment— To enable me to do this with Precission, will you be so good as to let me know what you will charge for a compleat Apparatus of a Mint on your own best approved plan, with a Steam-Engine equal to the Force of 8 Horses constantly at work— the whole shipped on board a Vessel bound for this Port, so that Congress may have a View of the entire Expence by adding the Freight & Insurance—[16]

Amazingly, Boulton allowed this second approach to go unanswered, and negotiations ceased at that point.

I am unable to explain why this most enterprising of early industrialists should have let such an opportunity escape him. True, the proposed American mint would have been on a modest scale, certainly smaller than the Russian venture, possibly even smaller than the Danish one. And true, Boudinot's second plea would have arrived on Boulton's doorstep just as the latter had finally got regal permission to undertake a new copper coinage (and now had major concerns about how and where he was going to get the metal he needed to carry out his hard-won coining privilege). And yet … had he shown more of his accustomed enterprise, shown himself willing to go just a bit further, the history of his firm, and of American coinage, would have been very different.

Rebuffed by the elder Boulton, the United States Mint does not appear to have made any further, official calls for help during his lifetime.[17] The next move came from Britain, and from Matthew Boulton's son and business successor, Matthew Robinson Boulton.

I have elsewhere observed that the relations between father and son were frequently strained, the younger man apparently resenting his position in the shadow of the older. After Matthew Boulton's death in 1809, Matthew Robinson Boulton redoubled his efforts to emerge from the shadow. One of the most telling ways in which he tried to do so involved the Soho Mint. I suspect that he wished to sell this facility for a very obvious, if unacknowledged, reason: that mint had been at the centre of Matthew Boulton's concern over the last twenty years of his life. If it were gone from the premises, the memory of the father would go with it, and the son would emerge in his own right.

And so several attempts were made to sell the facility. Two of them are related elsewhere, the unsuccessful approach to Holland in 1818 and the successful one to the East India Company in 1824. But there was a third, and it was made to America.

It predated later attempts by several years, and it was in fact made almost exactly a year after Matthew Boulton's death. His son's thinking at this point was still somewhat imprecise: while recognizing the profit-making potentials of Soho Mint, he nonetheless resented it. And so, while offering to strike the Americans' planchets into coins in England, adorning them with the regular designs 'or any other device' they might choose, he also stood ready to sell them 'my coining apparatus'.[18] The United States Mint was caught by surprise, and no reply appears to have been made. And the outbreak of war would have soon rendered the scheme impracticable in any case.

In 1815, Soho's American connection was resumed, but it was restricted to planchets, and even that trade soon saw a curtailment. But it was revived in the mid-1820s, and it would soon provide more possibilities for greater things.

By the middle of the decade, Boulton, Watt & Company had supplied mints to a host of overseas destinations – to Russia, Denmark, Brazil, Haiti, and India. It had also prepared mints for Mexico – but had not shipped them, owing to circumstances beyond its control. Mint machinery prepared for Barclay, Herring, Richardson & Company had not gone out to Mexico City due to the bankruptcy of that firm. And coining apparatus prepared for the Anglo Mexican Mint Association had not gone out to Guanajuato when principals in that firm came to the belated recognition that it was unwise to ship a steam-powered mint to an area where water was in short supply. In 1827, both sets of machinery were sitting forlornly in a warehouse at Soho, their owners (through the good offices of their builder, Matthew Robinson Boulton) looking for new buyers.

And by 1827, a purchaser for at least one of the mints seemed within reach. The United States Mint, which may have been barely adequate to the nation's coining requirements in the 1790s, was definitely inadequate by the 1820s. Talk of change was in the air, talk of a sumptuous new building and powerful new machinery to effect the country's coining business. While Congressional permission to expand the United States Mint would not be granted until 2 March 1829, it had been confidently expected for many months. In the summer of 1827, Matthew Robinson Boulton was let in on the project, told that he might have a role to play.

On 31 August, Mint Director Samuel Moore wrote to Soho, requesting information on the number of presses and amount of horsepower likely to be required for a mechanized American coinage. It seems apparent that Moore was thinking about an establishment of a size comparable to the new Soho Mint, with four presses, and that he was primarily interested in improving the striking of the most common American precious-metal coin, the half-dollar. If such an apparatus were to be constructed at Soho for the United States, how much was it likely to cost? Boulton took his time in replying, and his letter of 10 November 1827 has not survived. But we can partly reconstruct its contents, especially its heart: the United States could have its new mint for around £7,000, delivered at Philadelphia.

The Americans debated the matter through the remainder of 1827 and the year following. But their attention was now turned in a new direction, as they learned of the existence of the redundant mint for Guanajuato. This machinery offered two advantages. It was already in being, essentially ready for shipment on short notice. And it would cost about half the price Boulton had quoted for a new mint, £3,824 instead of £7,000.

Moore would have learned of the purchase possibility at the end of 1828. The person informing him of the unwanted mint's existence was probably the American representative of the Anglo Mexican Mint Association, Major W. G. Buckner. Buckner was based in New York City, and Moore seems at first to have thought that the machinery was there as well – which obviously would have represented a huge savings in transportation costs to Philadelphia. He learned of the true site of the machinery by early 1829, but the additional costs of transportation by no means discouraged him: soon he was asking Major Buckner to get detailed plans of the apparatus from Boulton, Watt & Company.

The Major did his best, without success. Soho was perfectly willing to act as midwife to the sale of someone else's mint (while doubtless regretting that Philadelphia had learned of its existence, knowledge which had cost the firm several thousand pounds); but it was disinclined to let the Americans look at the plans and likely copy them without benefit of payment. The plans would remain at Soho, and Major Buckner would come away empty-handed.

And this latest round of negotiations for Soho machinery would soon collapse. The company chosen to ship the Guanajuato machinery refused any sort of personal guarantee, arguing that the name of Boulton, Watt & Company should be bond enough. And when the United States learned that it would have to make payment *prior* to shipment from England (something Soho had never asked it to make for copper planchets), it quickly lost interest in the unwanted machinery of the Mexican mint. The apparatus would languish in Soho's warehouse for another decade, parts of it, apparently, finally going to another Mexican mint with British connections, Chihuahua.

By the beginning of the 1830s, the United States was erecting the outer shell of a new mint at Philadelphia. The nature of its inner heart was still unclear. As it happened, the machinery to strike its coins would be finally made in America; but as the decade opened, there was one last chance that it could be made in England, by Boulton, Watt & Company.

On 19 August 1830, Samuel Moore made a final attempt to open negotiations for British coining machinery. But this time the Mint Director had no intention of skimping on expenses: observing that the new United States Mint would have a floor plan large enough to accommodate the best and most powerful machinery, Moore asked Matthew Robinson Boulton to come up with an estimate for a new, modern facility which would serve the

Republic well for decades to come. His sincerity was evidenced by the length of his letter (eight closely-written pages, including a floor plan), its inclusion of the mint's requirements in great detail, the fact that Moore was fully prepared to change the current proposed layout if Boulton deemed it necessary. But an early reply was essential.

Boulton's reply was hardly swift; by mid-October, he was still mulling over the finer points of Moore's request. But he had come up with a cost for the mint apparatus by the fifteenth (£6,997), and he communicated it to Moore two days later. The latter received it on 9 January 1831, and after five weeks of discussion, rejected it. No specific reason was given, but a logical guess is that the Mint Director had encountered patriotic opposition in Congress (or from the White House: Andrew Jackson had built his reputation on an anti-British stance) to his plan to equip an American mint with British machinery. Holding out the prospect of limited possibilities in the future, Moore nonetheless dashed any hopes for business in the present.

The new mint opened its doors, *sans* Soho machinery, in January 1833. So long as the production of cents and half-cents continued, so long as Soho planchets were used to produce them, Matthew Robinson Boulton could console himself that another opportunity on the larger scale might still emerge. He was strengthened in his consolation by the fact that the Philadelphia coiners might very well be in a new edifice but were still using the inadequate machinery they had employed in the old: it had been carried to its new site, set up, and once again forced into service until agreement could be reached on what kind of machinery, and from whom, would succeed it. Remembering the proverb about old wine in new bottles, Soho looked forward to better times. What it found was otherwise: far from extending its contacts into additional profitable lines, the firm would soon see the last of them taken from it.

In the early and middle 1830s, several events occurred in quick succession. They buttressed each other, and, taken as a whole, they would soon spell an end to Boulton, Watt's forty-year career as planchet supplier to the United States of America. We have noted one such event, the wreck of the *Delaware* late in 1833. That set minds to thinking on the American side: perhaps the United States had been extraordinarily fortunate thus far in not losing more vessels and more planchets to the whims of the sea. Perhaps it would do well to find another, domestic supplier.

Here was the second event: a plausible source of planchets was now emerging at home. This was Crocker, Brothers & Company, of Taunton, Massachusetts. The firm had shipped its wares to Philadelphia on an experimental basis late in 1833; at the beginning of the following year, the remittances became regular. Crocker, Brothers offered two distinct advantages over Boulton, Watt: first, this was an American firm, on American soil. Any wares it sent would reach Philadelphia in far less time, and such products would be virtually immune to the hazards of weather or war. And second, the Taunton firm agreed to take payment for its planchets *in the form of copper cents struck from them*; obviously, Soho would not do so. To be sure, the Crocker, Brothers products were slightly inferior to those of Boulton, Watt, their weights varying greatly. But all things considered, they would do.

The fact that the United States Mint was now able to find its planchets at home suggests two larger developments. First, more native copper had been found than had been available before the turn of the nineteenth century, when Cornwall was king. And second, the fact that the copper could now be transported hundreds of miles from mine to factory, could be rolled and blanked there, and then swiftly sent to Philadelphia to be processed into coinage suggested that the United States was now becoming an industrial nation, was approaching the point where it would no longer need other people's technology, could in fact create its own. And Soho would be under a misapprehension if it thought otherwise …

The ability to industralize was soon extended to something more important than planchets. In the summer of 1836, Robert Maskell Patterson (who had succeeded his brother-in-law Samuel Moore as Mint Director in May 1835; Moore was a son-in-law of the earlier Director, Robert Patterson) wrote a generally prosaic letter to Matthew Robinson Boulton, which contained a sting in the form of a postscript:

> It may not be uninteresting to you to mention that we are coining your copper, very successfully, with a Lever press, moved by a Steam Engine. The press is a modification of one made in Paris by Tonnelier. It is striking, with great ease, and without noise or jar, 80 pieces per minute, and we think of increasing its speed to 100. The motion is communicated from a drum shaft, by a strap and pulley. We are preparing similar presses for all our coining.[19]

The person responsible for the press was the gifted inventor Benjamin Franklin Peale, who had left for Europe in mid-1833 on a fact-finding tour for the United States Mint. He visited the Royal Mint, where he had seen the Boulton presses at work. He may have visited Soho. He definitely visited Karlsruhe and Paris, where he saw a press of a new type in operation. Featuring a toggle action invented by Uhlhorn around 1815 and subsequently improved by Thonnelier, this apparatus represented a great improvement over the mechanism invented and popularized by the Boultons. It was smaller, was marginally faster, broke down less frequently, and was much gentler on dies, because it progressively squeezed its designs onto planchets rather than relying on a single, traumatic blow to impart them. Peale had taken some notes on the new press, but he had consigned much more to memory. When he returned to the United States in 1835, he was able to recreate the machine he had seen in Europe in America, with improvements. He was hired by the United States Mint as Melter-Refiner in March 1836, graduating to the post of Chief Coiner in 1839.

The ingenious Mr Peale put paid to the hopes of Mr Boulton. Henceforth, the United States Mint would never need Soho's help in coining machinery. And it was about to discover that it could dispense with Soho's services for planchets as well.

Most of the pieces were in place which would lead to that discovery. The Philadelphia coiners now had a domestic source for their copper planchets; at the same time, they were finding Soho's planchets accompanied by unaccustomed risk and accustomed frictions. They no longer needed that firm's advice on anything relating to coining or coining machinery. And then, larger events intervened, and the final elements made their appearance.

In the spring of 1837, an economic panic and depression spread across the United States, a fiscal implosion resulting in part from the unbridled speculation and shoddy banking practices of the later years of the Jackson administration, in part from business failures elsewhere – including Great Britain. The transatlantic planchet trade, which had been difficult in good times, now became impossible in bad. The Philadelphia Mint soon found itself unable to pay for Soho's planchets in the usual way, by sterling bills of exchange, for economic uncertainty had driven this form of money from commerce. And hard times created economic nationalism as well: in times of crisis, charity began at home, and one's own businessmen took a natural precedence over those of other countries, however fine their wares might be.

And so a decision was reached in Philadelphia and announced to Soho. Citing the miserable state of 'pecuniary relations' between Britain and America, Mint director Patterson advised Soho that, until they improved, 'I cannot feel myself justified in giving you any additional order for planchets'.[20] The long connection had been severed at last.

Not yet aware of the new, domestic supplier, Matthew Robinson Boulton was taken by surprise, but gamely drew up his final account as his American correspondent had requested. And when Patterson paid the remainder of the bill, Boulton learned the remainder of the truth – about Crocker, Brothers & Company and about the advantageous arrangement which the mint enjoyed with that firm. Boulton's reply, the final document in the long correspondence, has an elegiac quality, summing up the entire story of Soho's American connection:

> It is with much regret I observe … that the Commands of that Establishment with which I have been honored for a long series of years, are directed into another Channel; the interruption of a commission of nearly 40 years duration & one always esteemed as a valued mark of Confidence & Distinction cannot be otherwise than deeply felt, altho' it is no inconsiderable mitigation to know that the event has not proceeded from any cause within my control. Beside [?] this impression I need merely add [?] that should circumstances hereafter allow of the renewal of it, you may rely on every disposition existing on my part to avail myself of the opportunity— For your obliging exposition of the sentiments accompanying the communication of your intentions I beg you to accept my best acknowledgements, as also the assurance that a lively sense & recollection of the attentions uniformly experienced with the Directors of the [United States Mint] Establishment, along with great respect & esteem will not cease to be entertained by
>
> <div align="right">Sir
Yours very faithfully
M Rob<i>n</i> Boulton[21]</div>

In the Matthew Boulton Papers, in a box containing materials on Brazil, Haiti, Argentina, the United States, and El Salvador, there is a ledger with rough computations of planchet shipments to the United States over the years. The entries stop with the year 1837 – but spaces have been provided for the record of transactions through 1842. It is evident that Soho chose to believe that the commerce might yet be resumed, that its severance was not yet absolute. But an era had ended nonetheless, and those spaces remained unfilled.

Soon Soho itself would pass from the scene, the contribution of the Midlands firm to American numismatic and technological history was forgotten by those few who had ever known about it, and the hybrid natures of the copper cent and half-cent were forgotten as well. Had Matthew Boulton, or

Matthew Robinson Boulton, been chosen to make America's money; had father or son succeeded in building a new United States Mint (and the fact that they did not strikes me as rather more surprising than the alternative); their places in the history of American numismatics, American technology, and American economics would have been assured. The commonplace nature of those wares which they *did* succeed in exporting told against them. Their American legacy may have been important, and it was certainly voluminous; but like Matthew Boulton's new concept of coinage itself, those who first saw it tended to accept it quickly if gratefully, while those who see it now have forgotten what it meant. And those of us who know the meaning then and now must regret that more was not done, that the contact was not as deep as the underlying community of shared British and American identity suggests that it might and should have been. But there are times when more can be accomplished between very different peoples than among members of a single family.

SOURCES

The material for this chapter largely comes from two places. Most of the correspondence between Soho and the United States Mint, as well as sizes, costs, and shipping information concerning planchets will be found in the Matthew Boulton Papers in the Birmingham Reference Library. But materials in the National Archives, Washington, D.C. are also of the highest importance. They will be found under Bureau of the Mint, RG104, and they frequently provide a priceless American explanation for events otherwise difficult to interpret.

In Birmingham, Elias Boudinot, Benjamin Rush, Samuel Moore, and the Pattersons all left traces in the incoming letter boxes (MBP222, 252, 245, and 248). So did earlier correspondents Charles Borel (MBP222), James and Benjamin Jarvis (MBP240), Ralph Mather, and John H. Mitchell (both MBP244). If not located in the appropriate letter boxes, Matthew Boulton's replies to these earlier correspondents will sometimes be found in MBP148 and 150 (private letter books covering the years 1783–8 and 1789–92, respectively), while Matthew Robinson Boulton's letters to a succession of Mint Directors will ordinarily be found in the appropriate letter boxes in Birmingham or in RG104 in Washington.

MBP405 (Brazil, Haiti, Argentine, USA and San Salvador mints) has some useful material for the closing days of the planchet trade. But for detailed notations on the actual sizes and times of shipments, the reader is advised to consult the succession of Mint Books – MBP34, 38, 43, 46, 50, 60, 64, 68, and 81 – which cover Soho's production of American planchets from beginning to end.

For background on and later adventures of Benjamin Franklin Peale, the reader may wish to consult my article in *America's Gold Coinage* (1989), '"An onerous and delicate task": Franklin Peale's Mission South, 1837'. For the trials of the early United States Mint, the best non-archival source is still Don Taxay's *The U.S. Mint and Coinage*.

I am indebted to two American numismatists, Raymond Williamson and Eric P. Newman, for their help in fleshing out the story of Charles Borel. Incidentally, the ordinance which Borel secured will be found on pp. 743–4 of the fourth volume of *Statutes at Large of South Carolina* (Columbia, 1838).

NOTES

1 The petition was delivered on 26 January 1775, and it was reprinted in *Swinney's Birmingham and Stafford Chronicle*, vol. 9, no. 3 (2 February 1775), p. 3.

2 MBP150, [Private] Letter Book Q: Matthew Boulton to John H. Mitchell, 25 November 1789.

3 MBP360, Box Walker, Z., jr.: Zacchaeus Walker, Jr. to Zacchaeus Walker, Sr., 19 February 1793.

4 MBP240, Letter Box J: James Jarvis to Matthew Boulton, 24 February 1788.

5 MBP240, 'M. Boulton's estimate of costs for Jarvis proposal' (undated but late February – early March 1788).

6 MBP240, James Jarvis to Matthew Boulton, 8 March 1788.

7 MBP325, Matthews, Mrs. C., Box 1: William Matthews to Matthew Boulton, 9 April 1788.

8 MBP150, [Private] Letter Book Q: Matthew Boulton to Samuel Broome, 3 November 1789.

9 I am obliged to Raymond Williamson of Lynchburg, Virginia for bringing Ralph Mather to my attention.

10 Those interested in an extended discussion of the Soho-Philadelphia planchet trade may wish to consult my 'Early United States Copper Coinage: The English Connection', *British Numismatic Journal* 57 (1987), pp. 54–76. Of the 73,830,369 cents coined between 1797 (the year of Boulton, Watt's first planchet shipment) and 1837 (the year of the firm's final shipment), Soho's planchets (assuming that all were used for copper coinage – a reasonable assumption, considering the United States Mint's inability to supply its own blanks) would have accounted for 49,219,935 coins. And for half-cent production during the same period, some 7,054,862 pieces, Soho was responsible for *all* of the planchets used for that denomination.

11 William J. Coltman, one of the directors of the Company of Copper Miners, persisted in his attempts to turn the tide until late 1798, using his father-in-law Thomas Clifford as intermediary with Elias Boudinot. But Boudinot had made his choice and remained wedded to it – even though Soho's slow delivery came close to driving him to distraction in 1798 and 1799.

12 MBP222, Letter Box B4: Elias Boudinot to Matthew Boulton, 3 July 1799. Considering the note of desperation found in the Mint Director's immediately preceding correspondence, this observation strikes me as somewhat churlish. But Boudinot had had to go to the trouble of laboriously cleaning the damaged planchets prior to using them, and this aggravation, along with Boulton's dilatoriness in sending him planchets in the first place, explains his ingratitude.

13 MBP245, Letter Box M2: Samuel Moore to Matthew Robinson Boulton, 16 February 1825.

14 As an example of bad timing, consider the fate of a possible coining opportunity which presented itself at the end of 1797. One of the Foxes, Boulton's Quaker correspondents in the copper trade, had presented one of Soho's new proof pennies to 'my Friend the Secretary of State at Philadelphia', who promised to show it to the President and other high officials. The enterprising correspondent offered to sell the Americans copper for a new, high-quality coinage, '& I believed thee would be pleased to Manufacture it into Money'. All were eagerly awaiting Boulton's agreement to do so – which would not be forthcoming, probably because of the strain the current British copper coinage was putting on Soho Mint (MBP233, Letter Box F2: Robert W. Fox to Matthew Boulton, 11 December 1797).

15 MBP222, Elias Boudinot to Matthew Boulton, 22 April 1799.

16 MBP222, Elias Boudinot to Matthew Boulton, 6 November 1799.

17 The visit of Joshua Gilpin to Soho Mint and his discussions there with Matthew Boulton in August 1799 appear to have been unofficial and in any case led to no concrete results. Gilpin's valuable description of the second Soho Mint will be found in the appropriate chapter.

18 MBP252, Letter Box R2: Matthew Robinson Boulton to Benjamin Rush, Treasurer of the Mint, 24 August 1810.

19 MBP248, Letter Box P1: Robert Maskell Patterson to Matthew Robinson Boulton, 25 August 1836.

20 MBP405, Brazil, Haiti, Argentine, USA and San Salvador mints: Robert Maskell Patterson to Matthew Robinson Boulton, 30 September 1837.

21 MBP165, Copies of Letters Soho, 1836–1840: Matthew Robinson Boulton to Robert Maskell Patterson, 29 January 1838.

CHAPTER 10

Enduring Impressions: What Soho Struck

Las estadísticas son poesías.

— *A wise Mexican saying*.

Matthew Boulton received his first order for coin in June 1786. His grandson honoured the final one in January 1850. During the intervening years, the Soho coiners created nearly two-thirds of a billion coins and tokens.

We can make the figure more precise: Boulton, Watt & Company was responsible for *at least* 646,396,767 coins and tokens. Some of these formed parts of gigantic orders: the third British copper issue of 1806–1807 totalled nearly 166 million pence, halfpence, and farthings. Other orders were tiny: Boulton, Watt struck less than eleven thousand tokens each for Hornchurch and Kings County. But the extent of any given order was largely irrelevant to Soho's primary aims, which centred on making a good and durable product, making safe money for all.

This chapter will summarize Soho's coining activities over nearly two-thirds of a century. The figures you will see were obtained in several different ways, based on the differing traces left in the Matthew Boulton Papers. A few of the totals which follow are exact: included in the documents and simply carried over to this chapter. Thus, a figure of eight million copper décimos for Buenos Aires was carefully recorded at the time: the Argentines wanted that many coins, and that was the precise number they received. Whenever I have encountered such a figure, I have alerted the reader to that fact.

Unfortunately, such exactitude was the exception rather than the rule. In ending with the figures you are about to review, I have been forced to rely on other sources and methodologies. But my totals are very firmly grounded in the records Soho kept. And on the few occasions where I have been forced to guess, I always announce that fact; in those few instances, the figures I present *will not form* part of the general total for Soho's tokens and coins.

As you will see, much or most of the uncertainty centres on the very beginning of the record. This is perhaps understandable: Matthew Boulton and his employees were learning their crafts as they went along, and they had far more on their minds than precise record-keeping for a coinage in copper, a commodity which was bought and sold by the long ton. But particular blame can also be assigned: until 1791, the primary book-keeper assigned to keep the coinage accounts was John Roberts; upon his dismissal, Roberts either took the account book with him (Matthew Boulton's suspicion) – or there was never an account book, and the clerk's rough notes were destroyed by someone else (Roberts' defence). Whatever the reason and wherever the blame, those earliest figures never resurfaced, to the temporary annoyance of Matthew Boulton and the continuing despair of this researcher.

The records improved after mid-1791, and they essentially consisted of two different types of data. The first included a notation of the number of pieces which were theoretically struck from a given pound of metal – usually copper, one pound avoirdupois or 454 grams – and the actual amount of copper struck, by tons, hundredweights, quarters, pounds, and sometimes ounces. So our process becomes one of simple multiplication and addition: if we have ten tons, nine hundredweights, three quarters, twenty-one pounds, and eight ounces of copper, struck into pieces at forty-eight to the pound, we emerge with $23,513\frac{1}{2}$ pounds of copper ($2240 \times 10 + 112 \times 9 + 28 \times 3 + 21\frac{1}{2}$), or 1,128,648 coins.

The earliest Soho shipments were remitted in boxes and kegs. Eventually, a cask capable of containing three hundredweights (336 pounds) of coins became the rule. When Matthew Boulton began wrapping his products in *rouleaus* to protect them from contact with each other during the long voyage from his mint to their destination, he gave us another method of computing mintages. The coins were generally wrapped up in packets of one pound each, 336 packets to the cask. When the number of pieces per rouleau was included in the shipping information (as was usually the case, especially as time went on), a slightly more precise method of mint estimation was created – and one slightly easier for the modern researcher, who must merely multiply and need not keep long tons, hundredweights, and quarters in mind. There have been occasions in the following figures where both types of numbers were given; there, I have adopted the second method over the first.

A final word, and we shall be on our way. Most researchers and collectors are aware of proof or specimen strikes of many Soho issues – of most if not all of them, in fact. They may also know that the firm retained many of its dies and made later strikings of coins and tokens for particular friends, to encourage new orders, etc. These later productions have no place in my figures – for it seems to me that the primary purpose of a Boulton coin or token was *to circulate at the time of its issue, or to commemorate the arrival of a new coinage*. With this in mind, I have included specimen and proof strikings in my totals *only when they appeared in the records at the same spot as the pieces made for circulation*. Of course, there may (and most likely will) not be any way of distinguishing between specimen coins made at the time and those made later; but that is another story.

Matthew Boulton's career affords a splendid illustration of how one activity might lead into another in the career of an eighteenth-century man of business. Thus, while it would surely be an oversimplification to say that his connection with James Watt and the improved steam engine led him to an interest in Cornish copper mining, and that in turn to an interest in Cornish copper mining companies, and *that*, in turn, to an interest in a market for their wares, and the copper coinage, one could nonetheless make an argument for each and every link in the chain. In the case of copper coinage, Matthew Boulton was a reformer, and in the application of steam to the coining process, he was a visionary; but he was also a businessman, and the remembrance of earlier journeys helped determine his arrival at this particular destination.

But his first copper coinage was *not* for the deserving British poor. Rather, it was for a possession belonging to the East India Company called Bencoolen (today's Benkulen) on the southwest coast of the island of Sumatra. Bencoolen was the Company's most important settlement in the East Indies until eclipsed by Penang, founded in 1786. The local authorities wanted a dependable currency in copper for trade with the natives; one of them mentioned this desire to London at the beginning of 1785. The request reached East India House about a year later, and officials of the Company duly mulled the matter over, drafting a report in June 1786. A copper coinage would indeed be provided; the nabobs had been in contact with personnel at the Tower Mint, but they subsequently inclined to a gentleman named Matthew Boulton. And another of Boulton's earlier activities (for example, the supply of silver plate to John Motteux, who successively served as Director, Deputy Chairman, and Chairman of the East India Company) was now to lead our Midlands entrepreneur in an interesting new direction.

We know very little about the workings of this first coinage enterprise. No formal contract appears to have been signed, but the Company must have applied to Boulton in the early part of June 1786. It wanted Sumatran coin of three sizes, 150, 100, and 50 grains (that is, of 9.72, 6.48, and 3.24 grams: coins worth three, two, and one keping).

Matthew Boulton would strike the coins, but not at Soho.

He currently had no mint, although he did have a water-powered rolling mill, enabling him to roll metal from ingots into sheets. He could also commandeer the presses necessary to do the blanking on Soho's premises. But the actual coining would be another matter.

That would be carried on in London, at a mint for whose machinery the Company would pay but which Boulton would equip. I must stress that this new facility would *not* be powered by steam, the aspiring coiner having devoted no concrete thought to that alternative at the time he was first asked to coin. As it happened, he and his people would make modest additions to the current state of pre-industrial coining technology (especially in the case of an improved layer-on); but the coinage would nonetheless remain firmly grounded in the traditional technology.

The earliest trials probably took place in October. They were followed by two regular coinages. The first, whose coins bore the date 1786, were made from slightly more than eighteen tons of copper (to be precise, 40,393 pounds of that metal) contracted for by the East India Company at the beginning of August 1786, delivered piecemeal on several occasions between then and the end of the year. Boulton was not able to coin nearly as swiftly as he had anticipated, and the entire operation, which had to be carried out in two places rather than one, was always difficult to control and subject to stoppages in London, at Soho, and on the canals and roads in between. The industrialist did not get his first coining order completed before late May

You have to start somewhere: Sumatra, 2 kepings, 1786. (National Numismatic Collection, Smithsonian Institution)

1787, several months behind schedule. He was philosophical ('In all new manufactures & new establishments there will be both losses in time & money at first setting out'[1]); the Company was annoyed. But it gave Boulton a second order (12 May 1787) for a second batch of Sumatran coins – thirty tons' worth, all to be dated 1787.

By now, his people at Soho and in London were somewhat more at ease with their craft; and it proved easier to get the copper to him this time than during the previous attempt. By the beginning of December, his men at Soho had rolled and blanked nearly eighteen tons' worth of 'dubs' (blanks for the Bencoolen coin), while William Harrison, the man to whom Boulton had entrusted the actual striking process at the makeshift London mint, confidently expected to see the conclusion of the project by mid-January 1788. The actual time of completion went unrecorded[2], but Boulton was soon soliciting Motteux for another issue. There was a modest profit to be made, while another assignment carried to a satisfactory conclusion would be the best form of advertising for still other gainful opportunities. But while Motteux was courteous enough, Matthew Boulton would receive no third order for Sumatra – at least, not immediately. His tardy delivery of the 1786 coinage had told against him. On Boulton's side, a recomputation of the profits from the first two coinages had convinced him that they were modest indeed, and, were he to pledge himself to the same rates for a new issue, he would actually lose money in the process of making it. And so he, too, allowed the matter to rest for the time being. When he again considered the matter of coinage, it would be through new eyes. He would *not* operate in two places, but in one – Soho. And he would not coin by hand, but by steam – for steam was cheaper.

But there is still the matter of the earlier coinage to consider. How many pieces did Matthew Boulton blank and strike?

We are faced with a virtual absence of detailed, contemporary records – a virtual absence, but not a total one. We can cite two pieces of information. The first will be found in a letter from John Motteux to Matthew Boulton, written sometime during June 1786: therein, Motteux guessed that the Company would want most of its 1786 coins struck in the largest size, 150 grains. This would have pleased Boulton, because it would mean fewer coins to be struck from the same amount of copper, and less work for a new moneyer who had yet to find his way.

If there is a hint that the largest pieces made up the majority of the 1786 coinage, there is definite testimony that the smallest ones enjoyed that distinction in 1787. Writing to his sometime ally and usual competitor Thomas Williams a few months after the conclusion of the second coinage, Boulton complained that 'I lost considerably by the operation of Coining the last 30 Ton in London, As you may readily Conceive, when you reflect, that the greatest quantity were pieces of 50 grains'.[3]

What can we derive from these data?

If the larger pieces made up the majority of 1786 coins, and Boulton struck eighteen tons, two quarters, and seventeen pounds of coinage (that is, 40,393 pounds), let us suppose that he made ten tons of the largest size, four of the medium, and four tons, two hundredweight and seventeen pounds of the smallest. At the rates stipulated in the 1786 agreement, that would yield 1,052,800 three-kepings, 627,200 two-kepings, and 1,264,620 kepings. If we apply the same methodology to the second issue, and allot, say, five tons for the largest size, five for the medium, and twenty for the small, we arrive at production figures of 526,400, 784,000, and 6,272,000 pieces, respectively. I lean toward this interpretation of the data; but all it does is suggest the way that the coinages are likely to have fallen, not how many of each year and of each type within each year were created in this, Matthew Boulton's first venture into coinage.

That venture was not a total success, and the crudity of the pieces must have annoyed the coiner as much as the tardiness of delivery irked his employer. But the entrepreneur would persevere; if the delivery of his product continued to leave much to be desired (a tardiness not completely solved until the advent of railroads, late in his son's tenure at Soho), the product itself would improve. And so, happily, would the recording of its production. But the latter must wait until the early 1790s: the end of the 1780s saw Boulton coining once again, and our records, and his products, were still very imperfectly realized.

Unlike his maiden attempt, Boulton's next adventures in moneying were a direct result of events at home. By 1787, the British Isles were being flooded by a host of counterfeit copper halfpence and farthings; but the public coiner refused to produce an official alternative. Soon, one of the rising industrialists of the day (who had a large payroll to meet in North Wales, an area especially lacking in dependable 'small money') took matters into his own hands. This was Thomas Williams: his Parys Mines Company began issuing copper penny *tokens* from a temporary mint at Holywell, Flintshire at the beginning of 1787. The 'Druid pennies' were an immediate success. Williams moved his operations to Great Charles Street, Birmingham in late spring; henceforth, that city was to be the centre of token production.

Enter Matthew Boulton. As you know, he was attempting to gain a contract to manufacture regal copper coinage in 1787–8, even as he was building a new mint at Soho to take care of the gigantic contract which he assumed must soon be his. Thomas Williams was also vying for the coining privilege. He and Boulton sometimes worked together to secure a joint appointment; at other times, they double-crossed each other as circumstances and connections at Court permitted. Their actions probably cancelled each other out; but both men's ambitions proved hostage to larger issues – the madness of the King, more major concerns at home and abroad, the opposition of the coiners at the Tower. By the end of the summer of 1788, it had become apparent that the regal coinage order would not soon be filled – not by the Tower, not outside the Tower.

Various people reacted in different ways. Thomas Williams expanded his output, adding halfpenny tokens to the pence he was already producing: his 1788 tokens were struck by the millions. The popularity of his issues (and the growing awareness that no regal competition to them would soon be forthcoming) emboldened other merchants and industrialists to circulate copper tokens of their own, pieces which would benefit cash-starved local economies and serve as cheap forms of advertisement for firms and their wares.

New issues began appearing in 1789. Their ranks would slowly swell over the next three years, then increase dramatically, as people of leisure began to notice the odd-looking coppers in their change, and began collecting them.

A craze ensued, which reached its zenith in the middle of the 1790s. Books were written about the new collectibles, which so admirably combined a growing interest in antiquarian and local topics with an expanding financial means for collecting. Nothing like the token mania had ever been seen before – and so long as the Government refused to do anything about it (either making the tokens illegal or providing copper money to replace them) it might well go on forever.

Matthew Boulton's reactions to all of this were complex, changing through time and circumstance. He had developed a set of responses to the lack of official copper coinage; and the issue of tokens was not numbered among them. On the other hand, he was constructing what he rightly viewed as the most modern mint in the world, and there seemed little current likelihood that his primary customer would be calling anytime soon. If he looked elsewhere for orders, three advantages would ensue. His machinery and his people would both receive essential experience in the making of small coinages, so that they would be masters of the situation once a large one beckoned. He would help defray the enormous expenses incurred from the building of Soho Mint. And the products of that facility would enable him to test new ideas on design, and if successful, could be brought to the attention of the mighty – the best possible advertisements for a new mint and for a new regal copper coinage.

While Matthew Boulton decided to join in the provision of copper tokens from practical considerations, he would later discover that he rather liked the medium. This is the only way of explaining the artistic excellence of so many of his tokens: had Boulton possessed no deeper feeling for them, the form they took would have been very different. And Soho would in fact be involved with it for several years *after* its proprietor had become the King's official coiner.

Boulton's first forays into the field took place in 1789, and they were essentially the actions of a subcontractor. John Westwood had agreed to coin halfpenny tokens for two closely-related firms, Roe & Company, of Macclesfield, Cheshire, and the Associated Irish Mine Company, of Cronebane, Co. Wicklow. As with the first Sumatran issues, virtually no hard data has survived as to these two token coinages. But a letter of 30 May 1789 noted that 'Westw*d* [Westwood] hath sent me 10 Ton blanks, milld on y*e* Edges & ready for annealing Cleaning &c— Westw*d* informs me he hath 4 Ton more ready'[4]. And on 29 October 1804, W. D. Brown drew up a list of tonnages for Soho's copper orders up to that time and noted that twenty tons, fourteen hundredweight, one quarter, and twenty-five pounds of copper had been turned into Roe and Cronebane tokens.

Unfortunately, Mr Brown did not record how many tokens had been struck from each pound of metal; nor did Mr Boulton. But an informed guess, based on the actual weights of tokens of both types at the Smithsonian Institution, suggests that they were probably struck at thirty-six to the pound; and if that were the case, then some 1,671,161 pieces could have been struck from that amount of metal. But how many of each type were struck? And when?

The second question is easier to answer than the first. The tokens were created in the summer of 1789, at a time when Boulton's engineers had got the first steam-powered machinery erected and were beginning to experiment with it. There is a faint indication that the Roe pieces took priority over the

One of the first pieces struck by steam: Matthew Boulton's halfpenny for Roe & Company, 1789. (Author's collection)

Cronebane halfpenny, 1789. (Author's collection)

Cronebanes, and a stronger one that some or all of the coinage was ready for shipment from Soho by 10 September. To be sure, the moneying could not have been that difficult, for the copper had already been blanked and edge-marked. Nor need it be struck in a collar, because Soho had yet to devise an effective collar and ejection mechanism. So Matthew Boulton's presses were activated, and these odd, hybrid pieces, reflecting at once the technology of the past and of the future, were the result.

As to the first question, based on the amount of copper which was made into Roe and Cronebane tokens, *any* modern estimate flies in the face of traditional accounts. Writing at the turn of the nineteenth century, Charles Pye, a Birmingham publisher who knew many of the token issuers of the previous decade, put the total for 1789 Roe tokens at two tons – slightly more than 103,000 pieces. He did not give estimates for the Cronebane pieces, or for any other tokens in the Irish series. My own estimate for Roe & Company is several times higher than that of Charles Pye: based on the apparent relative scarcity of Roe and Cronebane halfpennies, a figure of 600,000 to 700,000 for the former and about 1,000,000 for the latter seems plausible.

The Macclesfield and Wicklow tokens of 1789 would not be repeated; but while they were being elaborated at the new mint, Boulton was also turning to the first of several orders for a most surprising customer. This was Thomas Williams. He had decided to abandon the coining field to Matthew Boulton (he would still be heard from in the years to come, doing his best to strangle Boulton's new enterprise by cutting off its source of nutriment, copper). The productivity of Parys Mine was now in decline, and Williams was losing a personal interest in the token field; but Anglesey pence and especially halfpence remained very popular with the public. So the summer of 1789 saw a complicated business arrangement, wherein Matthew Boulton would purchase Williams' coining presses (which he certainly did not need) as a means to an arrangement to strike more tokens (which he certainly could use). The Anglesey pact was satisfactory to neither party; but it went on long enough to generate more and better records. With the Welsh tokens for Thomas Williams, we begin at last to emerge into the light; we begin to see our way.

The great majority of Boulton's labours for Thomas Williams centred on halfpenny tokens. They broke down into two major issues, the first dated 1789 and the second 1791. The 1789s were hybrids of the Macclesfield and Cronebane type, blanked in one era and struck in another. They were probably done at about the same time as the other two token issues, with Boulton contracting to create 'about 30 Ton of Coin'.[5] This figure is unsatisfactory: with the aid of Brown's notes from 1804, we can come rather closer to the truth.

This clerk recorded a *total* mintage of all Anglesey issues of twenty-nine tons, thirteen hundredweights, and twenty-four pounds. Subtracting the other coinages from this total (and for the issues dated 1791 we have precise figures for the copper employed), we arrive at a figure of 28,350 pounds of copper for the 1789 tokens. This copper was delivered to Soho in the form of copper blanks, already edge-marked. Extant specimens weigh about thirty-five to the pound; we may therefore estimate that Matthew Boulton struck some 992,250 tokens from Thomas Williams' copper blanks in 1789. Boulton may

One of Boulton's first halfpennies for Thomas Williams, 1789. (Author's collection)

Anglesey proof halfpenny, 1791. (Author's collection)

Matthew Boulton's penny for Anglesey, dated 1791, struck 1792. (Author's collection)

have assumed that he had contracted to strike 'about 30 Ton of Coin'; but had he actually done so in 1789, the total minted would have amounted to more than two million pieces. Sloppy book-keeping, or Boulton's perennial optimism, may have been responsible for the discrepancy.

The coiner's second issue for Thomas Williams consisted of more halfpence – to be exact, some sixteen tons, one hundredweight, and ten pounds of tokens, with a stipulated weight of thirty-two to the pound. Delivery appears to have taken place around 1 September 1791 – that is, about two years after the first issue. But between the first coinage and the second, a world had changed.

The new order was struck in a collar, for Boulton had finally managed to perfect the collar/ejecting mechanism on his press. The absolutely vertical edge, the precise, shallow relief inform us that here is a modern piece of money. This is no hybrid: there is nothing pre-industrial about this 'commercial coin'. It looks forward to new opportunities and to a new century.

In all, Boulton struck approximately 1,150,784 Anglesey halfpence bearing the 1791 date. They were joined in the summer of 1792 by a small issue of pence, struck at sixteen to the pound. An obverse die left over from Williams' own 1788 coinage was married to a new reverse die at Soho, and some nineteen hundredweights of tokens (or 34,320 pieces) were struck there and shipped to Williams in July. They were struck on copper planchets which had been edge-marked in 1787–8 but not struck when Williams had had his own means for doing so. The fact that Matthew Boulton had created a new coin for Thomas Williams by the application of one of Williams' own dies to pieces of Williams' own copper spoke volumes about the ascent of the former and the descent of the latter. So did a later entry in a Soho ledger: on 11 November 1797, Thomas Williams was charged for a cask of new 'Cartwheel' pence, sent to Holywell to pay workers there. A circle had closed.

With Thomas Williams and Matthew Boulton, John Wilkinson completed the triumvirate of industrial pioneers with an interest in coinage. Wilkinson had been providing crucial precision parts for Boulton & Watt engines since the 1770s. In 1787, this 'Iron Master' (for whom self-effacement held no charms) decided to circulate his own tokens. He had Williams strike the first of them, in Holywell, and when the latter moved his mint to Birmingham later in 1787, he continued to make copper tokens for John Wilkinson. The latter circulated his wares first as pence and later as halfpence: they were very popular at the latter valuation.

Williams struck Wilkinson's halfpence along with his own. But he had left the moneying trade by the summer of 1789, which meant that Wilkinson must look elsewhere for more tokens. He looked to John Gregory Hancock, Sr., who had designed his original tokens (and Williams' Druids as well). Hancock struck the later Wilkinson tokens featuring a reverse with a seated Vulcan. But Wilkinson also looked to a second coiner, Matthew Boulton. For his pieces, the latter would retain Hancock's original reverse design, a man at a forge.

His first efforts for Wilkinson took place in June 1790, and there were not many of them. Having turned slightly more than a quarter of a ton of copper into halfpence at thirty-two to the pound (which would yield a run of slightly over nineteen thousand coins), Boulton received an irate letter from Wilkinson, demanding that the weight of future issues be reduced to thirty-six

One of the later Soho halfpennies for the 'Iron Master' John Wilkinson, 1793. (Author's collection)

to the pound. Boulton acquiesced, and Wilkinson ordered five more tons of 1790-dated tokens on 8 December. This order was filled and sent by the end of January 1791. My estimates of 1790-dated Wilkinson tokens struck by Matthew Boulton run to 19,296 heavy tokens and 404,217 light ones, for a total figure of 423,513. Wilkinson placed another order in 1792, desiring tokens lighter still. Again, Boulton complied, his new tokens weighing forty to the pound. Some 94,183 of them left the mint on 11 August 1792. Members of this issue bore the current year; at the end of 1793, a similar number (92,553) of 1793s were sent off, followed by 86,448 1795-dated pieces remitted to Wilkinson in mid-March of that year. All these later coins were struck at forty to the pound. In all, Matthew Boulton struck some 696,697 halfpenny tokens for John Wilkinson; but just as the first of them were getting under way, he was receiving an order which would dwarf anything he had accomplished thus far.

This was a request for the East India Company's settlement at Bombay. While the coiner's performance in his maiden attempt had angered some, there were still enough good feelings (and beneficial connections) to accord him another chance. A major Company man named Robert Wissett acted as emissary: on 11 December 1790, he advised Boulton that there was a Bombay coinage for the asking.

At first glance, it would scarcely be worth pursuing: Wissett said that only a few tons of coin were wanted. But it soon expanded dramatically, and Wissett was now talking about one hundred tons of coppers for the deserving inhabitants of the Bombay Presidency. There was, however, a catch: the East India Company had agreed with Thomas Williams for delivery of his copper in mid-1790[6]: the 'Copper King' now proved remarkably slow in remitting it, once he had learned who would be turning it into coin.

Under pressure, Williams eventually turned over his metal, but he did so with tardiness and ill grace. In the meantime, discussions over designs had gone back and forth between East India House and Soho, and they were finally approved by all on 18 February 1791. A week later, Boulton received the go-ahead from Robert Wissett; three weeks after that, the first of many shipments of coin left Soho for the London Docks, the first leg of their journey across the sea to India.

The first pieces were remitted on 19 March, and they consisted of eighty casks of $1\frac{1}{2}$ pice pieces, struck at forty-seven to the pound. This remittance worked out to nearly a million and a half coins, but it was merely the tip of the iceberg. A second denomination soon made its appearance: the first pice coins, struck at seventy to the pound, were sent off on 13 April, and a second batch was sent six days later. Together with the larger coppers, they made their way to India on the Company's spring vessels.

Boulton was told to halt production a few days later, then ordered to resume it for the autumn shipment to Bombay. He finished the coining of the pice at the beginning of July, then began that of the fifty-grain, half-pice early that autumn. These pieces were struck at 140 to the pound, and they would form the bulk of the 1791 order. They were joined in November by the largest coin in the series, the double-pice or half-anna. Struck at thirty-five to the pound, these last were about the same size as the halfpenny tokens which the coiner had recently created; simultaneous striking of the largest and smallest sizes continued until the first day of December. Ten days later,

Bombay proof 2 pice and ½ pice, 1791. (National Numismatic Collection, Smithsonian Institution)

Southampton proof halfpenny, 1791. (Author's collection)

Boulton proudly advised John Motteux that 'I have [now] deliverd all the 100 Ton orderd by the E I Co'.

He had a valid reason for pride. In nine months' time, he had struck over seventeen million copper coins for Bombay. This would have represented a hefty output for any public mint of the day; but Boulton's private one at Soho had achieved it and several other projects as well. One of them was 'a suit of Historical Medals for Mess*rs* Mon*ns*'[7] – the ill-fated Monneron tokens.

In all, Boulton created 17,241,001 coins for Bombay – 7,903,280 half-pice, 5,472,740 pice, 2,690,351 one and one-half pice, and 1,174,630 double-pice. His success in filling this order sealed his fortunes with the East India Company.

The autumn of 1791 saw Boulton coining for John Company and Monneron Frères; it also saw him coining for several parties closer to home: Taylor, Moody & Company of Southampton, John Vivian of the Cornish Metal Company, and Gilbert Shearer & Company of Glasgow. All three firms wanted halfpenny tokens; in filling their orders, Matthew Boulton set the tone for much of his firm's later production of tokens – and coins.

All of these pieces would be struck in a collar, by steam. All would contain a generous amount of copper, made as heavy as practicable given the cost of the metal. And all would display an artistry rarely if ever achieved on tokens made outside Soho Mint.

Boulton had been in contact with Walter Taylor of Taylor, Moody & Company since 1789. Taylor was a brewer, a man in logical need of small change for his workers and patrons. He very nearly gave his order to another token-maker, John Westwood; but the latter's delay in filling it turned the brewer toward Matthew Boulton. The latter put Taylor off for some months: since he was very likely to obtain a contract for regal issues, he advised that private tokens from Soho or elsewhere would soon be redundant. But the British Government failed to cooperate, Taylor persisted, and Boulton finally assented.

The dies were designed by Rambert Dumarest, a French designer whom Boulton had persuaded to take the place of the difficult Jean-Pierre Droz. Dumarest worked on the project through the spring of 1791, a time when Boulton's people were scrambling to get all of Boulton's steam presses on line and involved in the Bombay coinage. The first trials were remitted to Boulton on 2 June, and Taylor received the first portion of his order in mid-July.

He was not happy with it. He had assumed that his tokens would have the glossy appearance of Boulton's specimen strikes; the pieces he actually received were tarnished, nicked, and scratched. He complained to Boulton, and the latter, desperate to retain the order, promised to do something – *anything* – to make amends. He offered to clean Taylor's tokens and send them back to him postpaid. He also struck a box of pieces from polished dies and sent them to Southampton: let Taylor give these out to his friends and business associates!

The brewer was mollified, and the order was saved. Boulton indeed took back the tokens, cleaned them, and shipped them off to Southampton in October. This remittance included fourteen boxes, or 168,000 halfpence. There was a second, smaller order of another 26,255 pieces, sent off on 25 August 1792. When we add these two shipments, as well as 150 silver

Cornish halfpenny, 1791.
(Author's collection)

Glasgow halfpenny, 1791.
(Author's collection)

specimens and eighty-four copper ones (struck during the summer of 1791, to counter Taylor's disenchantment with the turn of events thus far), we arrive at a grand total, in all metals, of 194,489 Southampton pieces. These are handsome, fairly heavy pieces; but Boulton would soon improve on them.

His next venture into the world of the token took him closer to home: John Vivian of the Cornish Metal Company (which Boulton had helped found, in which he retained a keen interest) wanted a Cornish halfpenny token to serve as a direct competitor to Thomas Williams' Anglesey pieces.

Vivian so advised Matthew Boulton on 23 August 1789. Boulton could do little immediately, and the project would lie fallow for a year. But having successfully persuaded Rambert Dumarest to come to Soho and take Droz's place there, Boulton put his new employee in charge of creating dies for Vivian's token. Dumarest lacked self-confidence and was also something of a perfectionist – as, indeed, was John Vivian: the designs would not be finished to everyone's satisfaction until mid-June 1791

Meanwhile, copper for the project was arriving from Cornwall, and the actual coinage soon got under way. Boulton sent specimens in August, and the actual order went out toward the end of October. There were eight boxes of tokens, or 76,070 pieces, each weighing half an ounce – and each piece proudly displaying that fact. The Cornish pieces gave an excellent demonstration of Boulton's ideas about intrinsicality: money should contain an amount of metal as close to its stated value as possible. And another Soho concept, artistry, was reflected in the delicate rendering of the Druid's head, one of Dumarest's better efforts.

But the time taken in the securing of artistic excellence may have told against the success of the project: Vivian had originally thought in terms of circulating a hundred tons of Cornish halfpence. But by the time he finally received his tokens at Truro, he was having second thoughts. He first wrote Boulton for another twenty tons (3 January 1792), then countermanded his own order (2 February 1792). Of the hundred tons, just a trifle over a ton, all of which were sent out in October 1791, ever saw circulation.

Dumarest's progress on the Cornish token was held back by his work on another piece, concocted for the Glasgow firm of Gilbert Shearer & Company. Talk about such a token dated back to the spring of 1791. There had first been discussions about a joint issue for the cities of Glasgow, Paisley, and Greenock; after those conversations fell through, Gilbert Shearer approached Matthew Boulton for a token specifically for Glasgow.

The result was spectacular, and popular. Dumarest's allegory of the River Clyde was one of the most artistic representations seen on any eighteenth-century token. The pieces upon which it reposed were actively counterfeited – the clearest indication of the popularity of an eighteenth-century token! The quality of Dumarest's work argued in favour of the token, and so did its solid weight, struck at thirty-six pieces to the pound, and its precise edge, made possible by the Boulton manufacturing process. Two orders were filled and sent, the first on 14 October 1791 (82,148 pieces) and the second on 4 February 1792 (401,693 tokens). Adding the seventy-two specimen strikes in gilt copper (remitted with the second order) we reach a grand total of 483,903 Glasgow halfpennies for Gilbert Shearer & Company. The autumn of 1791 saw one more token issue from the Soho Mint, but one destined for

Matthew Boulton's French connection: a five-sol token for Monneron Frères, 1792. (Author's collection)

Sierra Leone proof cent, dated 1791, struck 1793. (National Numismatic Collection, Smithsonian Institution)

circulation in France rather than Britain. This was a series of large coppers in two denominations created for Monneron Frères, a major mercantile house in Paris.

Those interested in the detailed story of this firm, its financial doings, and Matthew Boulton's connection with it can do no better than consult Richard Margolis' excellent article, 'Matthew Boulton's French Ventures of 1791 and 1792; Tokens for the Monneron Frères of Paris and Isle de France', which appeared in *BNJ* 58 (1988). Here, I merely add that the first contact between Boulton and the French firm came at the beginning of 1791, with John Motteux acting as intermediary.

The opportunity to strike tokens for France would have certainly appealed to the Birmingham coiner: earlier, he had talked about an actual coinage for that country – and he would one day become so disenchanted with his mint's prospects in Britain as to actually consider moving it across the Channel!

His French connection would finally prove more modest but still impressive. The first Monneron tokens left Soho on 3 November 1791; these were two-sol pieces, struck at twenty-seven to the pound. They were soon joined by five-sol coppers. Both denominations continued to be struck into the summer of 1792, although each suffered a diminution in weight, a reflection of the troubles through which the firm which had ordered them was passing. In all, some 3,675,289 two-sols and 3,886,194 fives were struck for circulation (plus an indeterminable number of silver and gilt two-sols, created late in November 1791); the total number of Monneron tokens coined for commerce would amount to 7,561,483 pieces. About 1,371,000 of the twos were melted down, as were 22,000 of the fives. And at least one of the former got recycled into an official coin: the American Numismatic Society has a double-sol of the First Republic visibly struck over a double-sol Monneron! Comparison of the overtype with the undertype shows how great a contrast existed between the works of Soho and those of the mints it was making obsolete.

A final coinage dated 1791 would come from Soho, consisting of copper and silver pieces for a new British enclave on the west coast of Africa. This was the Sierra Leone Company, and its coinage has been covered in detail in David Vice's 1983 publication, *The Coinage of British West Africa and St. Helena 1684–1958*. The date 1791 which appeared on so many of the Company's coins referred to the organization's date of founding, not to the year the money was minted: the first of it was only ordered in August 1792, and none of it was minted prior to December.

Involving a coinage of less than a million pieces, the Sierra Leone story nonetheless was fairly complex. Dollars and pennies were struck at the end of 1792 – 805 of the former (including five proofs) and 214,764 of the latter. The first dollars bore a '1' as their mark of value; in May 1793, a second, much larger group of dollars was struck, the denomination being changed to '100', for one hundred pieces of a new copper coin, called a cent. Some 6,560 of the redenominated dollars were minted at that time, accompanied by 498,932 cents. It is interesting to note that this Sierra Leone dollar was the first such decimal coin, directly related to the other members of its monetary system through the number *ten*. Smaller silver coins were struck to round out the arrangement – 4,622 fifty-cent pieces, 5,200 twenty-cent coins, and 4,200 tens. All of these pieces were minted at Soho in May 1793.

Bermuda proof penny, 1793. (National Numismatic Collection, Smithsonian Institution)

Even allowing for the destruction of many of the cents in a fire shortly after their arrival, the monetary needs of the colony were modest and had largely been met by Boulton's initial coinage of 1792–3. But another order of 50,129 cents was sent in August 1796; unlike their predecessors, these coins bore the correct date. And some 9,027 1796 tens trickled forth from Soho between that date and 1803, to be joined by a final issue of 6,100 pieces dated 1805. The total Soho coinage for Sierra Leone amounted to 800,334 pieces struck for commerce or for presentation at the time – plus a modest number of specimen coins struck after the fact for gift and for sale, which have not been included in my total.

Shortly before Boulton began the Sierra Leone coinage, a gentleman named John Brickwood approached him about coinage for an older British possession, Bermuda. Brickwood's proposal was dated 8 November 1792; it would involve coinage in a single metal and a single denomination. This colonial agent wanted copper pennies, and he wanted them fairly quickly. The nature of the order, as well as Boulton's genius for making the best of a bad situation, would lead to an interesting response.

Back in 1788, when there had seemed to be excellent prospects for a copper coinage for Great Britain, Matthew Boulton had engaged Jean-Pierre Droz to create halfpenny dies with the head of George III on the obverse, a seated Britannia on the reverse. By late 1792, the prospects for a British coinage had receded, and Boulton and Droz were no longer on speaking terms. But the entrepreneur still had those dies. He decided to recycle one of them, using it for the obverse of Brickwood's Bermuda pennies. And Brickwood could receive his order that much quicker.

The Bermuda pieces were attractive and heavy coins, weighing slightly less than half an ounce each. They left Soho on 7 May 1793 in seven casks. There were 81,942 normal, or 'business' strikes, to be followed two days later by fifty bronzed proofs and another fifty proofs in copper. Each of them bore the inscription DROZ.F. on the truncation; that artist's reaction went unrecorded.

Matthew Boulton would profit from the experiment: some thirteen years later, he was to repeat the lesson with another coinage for another island, recycling the work of another artist.

The year 1793 saw Soho's re-entry into the provincial token trade. For Henry Brownbill, a watchmaker and silversmith of Leeds, Boulton created two batches of halfpenny tokens, the first remitted on 12 March 1793, the second sent some five weeks later. In all, Boulton struck some 172,233 regular tokens, plus one hundred fifty proofs in copper, bronzed copper, and silver. The relatively large amount of collector coinage is explained by the fact that Boulton's contact for the Leeds tokens was not Brownbill himself but a business associate named Samuel Birchall who would soon write one of the earliest books on eighteenth-century trade tokens.

Leeds proof halfpenny, 1793. (Author's collection)

The Leeds token was one of Soho's outstanding efforts. The portrait of Bishop Blaize was sensitive, while the use of perspective (the double row of buildings represented the Mixed Cloth Hall of Leeds) was skilful indeed. The creator of these designs was Noël-Alexandre Ponthon, Boulton's other French designer during the 1790s.

A second token issue got under way in 1793; unlike the first, it would persist over more than three years. On 13 December 1793, Boulton shipped the first pieces to an Inverness firm called Mackintosh, Inglis & Wilson. These

Inverness halfpenny, 1795. (National Numismatic Collection, Smithsonian Institution)

The Ibberson halfpenny, withdrawn because its prospective issuer feared arrest. (Author's collection)

halfpence appear to have been struck at forty-two to the pound; if so, Boulton would have sent some 122,577 of them to Inverness on that first occasion.

They bore the current date, 1793. His Scottish correspondents renewed their order in 1794, and their second shipment, now dated 1794, exited Soho on 19 November. Again, these appear to have been struck at forty-two to the pound, so that 96,668 halfpennies must have comprised the second order. A third shipment (definitely struck at forty-six to the pound, a figure given in the Soho records) was sent away on 31 October 1795, comprising 79,316 halfpence of that date. And a final order, probably struck at the same weight, completed the Mackintosh, Inglis & Wilson story on 25 February 1796. This last consignment was made up of 85,524 pieces (which is surprising: one sees a good many more 1795s than 1796s); in all, Boulton's Inverness coinage totalled 384,085 pieces.

These commercial coins represented the advent of a new, and as it happened, permanent artistic addition to the Soho staff: Conrad Heinrich Küchler, who would remain at the firm until his death in 1810. Küchler would soon gain immortality as the man who created the 'Cartwheel' penny and its double; but he started out with tokens and medals.

By the summer of 1793, Boulton would need as much engraving talent as he could muster. There was serious talk of a second coinage for Bombay, Boulton scrambling to find copper for the order, Küchler meanwhile learning his way around his new employer's industrialized coining establishment. The talk soon materialized into action: on 1 January 1794, the first of the Bombay coins left Soho for the London docks, and for India.

They were pice, struck at seventy to the pound, and they were identical with the 1791s except for the date. By the beginning of February, Boulton was shipping their doubles, and another week saw his mint undertaking the coinage of their halves. In all, the first four months of 1794 saw Soho strike and ship 1,569,330 two-pice, 2,371,779 pice, and 4,711,998 half-pice, a total of 8,653,107 coins. An issue of 1½ pice was discussed, but it never went beyond the pattern stage.

The years 1794 and 1795 represented the zenith of the British token craze. The first books on the subject were appearing. Some dishonest coiners (and collectors) were finding that aspiring hobbyists would pay good money for anything new, especially if they could obtain it and their fellow-collectors could not. Matthew Boulton did not participate in some of the sharper practices of the day; but the years between 1794 and 1796 saw him much-occupied in the production of a commodity whose existence he had once deplored.

Some of his pieces never went beyond the pattern stage. They included the Myddelton token, Swainson's token, a piece for Christopher Ibberson (withdrawn when the latter began fearing prosecution for his pains) – and lovely pieces for the Copper Company of Upper Canada, upon which David Vice contributed a detailed study in *Spink's Numismatic Circular* in 1977. A few specimens of each type are known; the Ibberson pieces are the most numerous, the Myddelton pieces (minted for a British settlement in Kentucky which never saw the light of day) are the most beautiful.

Other Boulton pieces were struck for commerce and in quantity, and several of them are outstanding for one reason or another. That made for a Lancaster gadfly named Daniel Eccleston is one of the more interesting. You can read about Mr Eccleston in Robert C. Bell's useful *Commercial Coins,*

Myddelton halfpenny token, 1796. (Courtesy Bowers and Merena Galleries)

Daniel Eccleston's halfpenny, whose designs anticipated Boulton's regal coinage. (Author's collection)

1787–1804 (1963); Eccleston was an eccentric of the first water, once publishing a notice of his own death, then circulating a letter purportedly written from the Other Side! He was a deist and wrote a tract on religious toleration. He was also something of a deadbeat, cheerfully promising payment for his tokens year after year, upon one occasion sending the younger Boulton 'half a Doz Cocoa Nuts' (Eccleston had trading connections with the West Indies) which 'seem full of Milk, and expect they are very good ones'[8] – but no money for the tokens which he had ordered and actually received many years previously. Eccleston never did pay up. But we may excuse him when we see his token; and it surely afforded Matthew Boulton fifty-odd pounds' worth of coining instruction.

He shipped Eccleston slightly over a ton of copper tokens (109,247 pieces) on 25 August 1794. Eccleston had provided his own copper, and so he was charged £51.17.6 for coining and casks, and another five guineas for the dies. And it is those dies which most interest us.

They were made by Noël-Alexandre Ponthon, and they directly reflected Boulton's current concept of the ideal coin. The Eccleston halfpennies were struck in a collar. They featured very low relief, which nonetheless treated its subjects in a tasteful, successful manner. But the most salient aspect of this token was its raised border, into which the legends were sunk. Boulton was experimenting with a gold coin of this type, which he thought would be beyond the abilities of the Birmingham forger. But such a design element recommended itself to copper as well, especially combined with low relief elsewhere: such a coin would virtually never wear out. His trial with the Eccleston token encouraged him, and he would eventually introduce the new design concept to a larger British audience. But he would first introduce it to Madras.

It would form an element of that Presidency's coinage from the beginning. Ponthon was working up various design concepts by the spring of 1794, and on 16 July Boulton sent coppers in three designs to his contacts at East India House, asking them to make the final determination. A week later, the choice had been made: Madras' coinage would feature the Company's arms on the obverse, its bale mark on the reverse, along with the date. The obverse legend would be partly incused, partly in relief, while that for the reverse would be entirely incused. Boulton had received his orders to proceed with the coinage by the end of the month.

Madras 1/48 rupee, 1794. (National Numismatic Collection, Smithsonian Institution)

His initial problem lay in getting copper for the project; this occupied most of the remainder of the summer but had been solved by the beginning of September. The coiner then went to work: by December, he was able to report that he had shipped no fewer than 457 casks of coins to St Botolph's Wharf, where they would soon be loaded on board the Company's vessels for their passage to India. He had in fact sent so many coins that the person in charge of docking arrangements there pleaded with him not to send any more, there being no place to store them.

The 1794 Madras coins were struck in two denominations, a forty-eighth part of a silver rupee, struck thirty-four to the pound, and a ninety-sixth part, struck at sixty-eight. The odd denominations represented an attempt to create a monetary medium which would fit into a number of local coinage systems. The larger pieces were the first to leave Soho, the initial shipment departing on 8 November 1794 and the final one three weeks later. Delivery of the smaller coins got under way on 2 December 1794 and continued until 4 March 1795. In all, some 4,616,129 large and 9,102,868 small coins made up the 1794 coinage for Madras, a total of 13,718,997 pieces, struck over a period of about four months. This order would be repeated in 1797: except for date, the later pieces would be identical with the earlier. The first of them struck were the ninety-sixth rupees – which were actually being shipped by 15 December 1796, regardless of the date. By the time of the final remittance (9 February 1797), Soho had made some 10,540,223 of them. They would be joined by the first of the forty-eighth rupees about a week later: shipment of the larger coin continued until early May – by which time the coiner had more pressing matters on his mind. The 5,994,666 larger coins added to the 10,540,223 smaller, give us a total for 1797 Madras coinage of 16,534,889.

The advent of the first British copper coinage, long desired and long deferred, has tended to cast Boulton's other activities during the mid-nineties into shadow. But there *were* other coinages going on, in addition to Madras, prior to the 'Cartwheels'. Boulton continued to make private tokens – in fact, the years 1795 and 1796 would see no fewer than four such issues – none of them plentiful but all of them interesting, and one of outstanding artistic merit. And there would also be a coinage for another African colony, the Gold Coast.

First, the tokens. The earliest was a halfpenny for George Cotton, of Romford, Essex. Robert C. Bell (*Tradesmen's Tickets and Private Tokens, 1785–1819*, 1966) suggests that Cotton's piece may have been intended as a medalet rather than a halfpenny token; but Cotton's letter of 20 June 1795 specifically stated that he wanted his tokens 'to see how they would take as a substitute for Halfpence'[9]. Boulton obliged him with exactly 10,563 tokens, struck at forty-eight to the pound, sent away on the second of October. The pieces were undated, and they featured plain edges, so that no issuer's name could be deduced from the tokens themselves. But Boulton was abandoning edge-lettering by that point anyway, convinced that his collar-struck products needed no such additional adornment for their protection.

William Croom's token was also undated, struck with a plain edge. Croom was a draper in the city of Dundee; on 16 December 1795, he was sent the first of two shipments of tokens, struck at forty-six to the pound. The second remittance took place about two months later, and at that point twelve bronzed proofs and two in silver were sent as well. If we add together both of Croom's shipments of tokens for commerce, plus the fourteen 'special' pieces, we achieve a total of 53,499 tokens.

The Croom story has a sequel. The draper would have received the last of his tokens by early March 1796. He evidently succeeded in putting them in

George Cotton's (Hornchurch) proof halfpenny undated, struck 1795. (National Numismatic Collection, Smithsonian Institution)

Croom proof halfpenny token, undated, struck 1795–6. (Author's collection)

circulation and wrote Boulton for more in late July. The coiner replied that since the price of copper had risen, so had the price of his wares. Croom indignantly took his business elsewhere – to another Midlands' coiner named Peter Kempson. Kempson's products can be easily distinguished: they were not struck in collar, and the work was less fine than that seen on the originals.

Bishop's Stortford proof halfpenny, dated 1795, struck 1796. (Author's collection)

And the finest work seen on any of Boulton's tokens – and very nearly the finest work seen on *any* token in the eighteenth-century series – was emerging about the time that the Dundee merchant had run out of tokens for small change. This artistic high point may be found on halfpenny tokens minted for Sir George Jackson, of Bishop's Stortford, in the county of Hertfordshire.

The Baronet had long been interested in the improvement of navigation on the River Stort, and his token was intended to serve a dual function: to commemorate the improvements which had been made, and to provide small change for the people who lived along the banks of the Stort. He approached Matthew Boulton through a mutual acquaintance named John Knill at the beginning of May 1795, and Boulton agreed to the project at once – only to lose track of it for more than half a year. But he was gently reminded of his pledge, and apologizing profusely, he detailed Küchler to design the dies late in the winter of 1796.

The Bishop's Stortford tokens were struck in May and June 1796, and the Baronet must have considered them well worth waiting for. Küchler's landscape, rendered in astonishing detail and perfect perspective, was a *tour-de-force*, an artistic accomplishment with no competition among Boulton's other tokens and coins, and with few rivals anywhere else. The halfpennies were evidently struck at forty-four to the pound, and the 562 pounds of copper which we know were used would have yielded 24,728 tokens. In addition, Sir George wanted, and received, forty-four copper specimens and thirty-six gilt ones, as well as six pieces struck in silver: the total for the Bishop's Stortford halfpenny therefore stands at 24,814.

One final token saw the light in 1796, with the misleading date of 1794. This was a piece struck for George Chapman George of Penryn, Cornwall. George and Boulton had known each other since at least 1787, when Boulton had spent a good deal of time in the Duchy on matters related to copper. With the outbreak of hostilities with France, the patriotic George had helped raise 150 volunteers to go to war. On 31 May 1794, he wrote to his old friend Boulton concerning the purchase of some breast plates for bayonet belts, according to drawings he was sending with his letter. It is not known whether Boulton filled the order (which was so small as nearly to be beneath his notice). But more than two years later, a token for the Penryn Volunteers made its appearance.

Penryn proof halfpenny, dated 1794, struck 1796. (Author's collection)

It was very ornate, and in its design we may be seeing a faint echo of George's original drawings. The piece makes reference to Baron de Dunstanville, commander of the Volunteers; but there is no question that the Penryn token was George's brainchild, and that he was charged for its creation. Some 19,092 ordinary tokens were struck, shipped to Cornwall on 29 August 1796. They would be joined by forty bronze proofs, sixty silver strikes, and a single piece in gold – which George had manufactured either for himself or, more likely, for the Baron.

One other coinage occupied Boulton's attention during this time, money for the Gold Coast. The African Committee of Merchants made an initial approach on 21 October 1796: Soho was requested to strike four denominations of sterling silver coins with an aggregate value of £500. The firm was preparing for the project by mid-December, and the order was recorded on the twenty-first of the month.

It consisted of 11,886 coins of all denominations: 1,080 ackeys (half-ounce pieces), 2,162 half-ackeys, 2,882 quarters, and 5,762 tackoes, each of the latter weighing one-sixteenth of an ounce. These figures included two proofs of each of the three lower denominations.

Unfortunately, the three larger denominations contained an error in spelling: PARLIMENT for PARLIAMENT. According to Vice, the error was not discovered until the coins had entered circulation on the Gold Coast. A few years later, an opportunity arose to correct the error: in 1801, the African Committee of Merchants requested a second shipment of coinage.

The 1796 date was retained, but the spelling mistake was rectified. On this second occasion, Soho minted 1,200 ackeys, 2,400 halves, 3,200 quarters, and 6,400 eighths, or tackoes. Only the first three coins had the spelling error, so that in the case of the fourth denomination it is impossible to distinguish the issue of 1796 from that of 1801. Combining the 13,200 pieces of the second issue with the 11,886 of the old gives us a total of 25,086 for Matthew Boulton's Gold Coast coinage.

Within a few months of the conclusion of the twelve thousand pieces of the first Gold Coast coinage, Matthew Boulton's presses would be striking that many coins per hour, every hour. For the British copper coinage, whose discussion Boulton had helped initiate, had finally come home to Soho.

It had taken remarkably long to arrive; and when it finally appeared it was far different from anything which might have been anticipated in 1787–8. It would not consist of halfpence, but of pence and a few twopence. It would not feature a raised lettered edge, and it would be struck in a simple, rather than a segmented, collar. Its designs and legends would be arranged differently from those of Boulton's early patterns, and on balance, what would actually emerge from Soho Mint in 1797 would be far less artistic than what had been dreamed of in 1787. But Jean-Pierre Droz would have nothing to do with the new coins, or with the technology which would create them; and he had been at the centre of both considerations a decade previously.

Still, there were points of consistency between the dream and the reality. Boulton had conceived of a steam-struck coinage in 1787, and that is precisely what he presented in 1797. The use of some sort of collar was carried from one era to another; so were low relief and an attempt at artistry for what was, after all, a subsidiary coin of limited value. And above all else, the recipients and the goal of Matthew Boulton's coinage remained unvarying from the 1780s to the 1790s and beyond: those coins would be for the poor and middling classes, and they would be created in a fashion which could not be counterfeited.

We shall probably never know all of the reasons behind the change of mind on the part of Government, leading to the call for a Boulton coinage. Certainly the coiner persistently brought his arguments and claims before anyone who would listen; so did his circle of influential friends, including Sir Joseph Banks. But the beginning of 1796 saw the coiner close to despair ('I remember you askd me if my Mint is employd to which I answer w*th* a Sigh, No except now & then a day for a few provincial ½ pence'[10]).

Then everything happened at once. Boulton received a prestigious if small order for the Gold Coast. He created a far larger one for Madras. And at the beginning of March 1797, the barriers against a copper coinage for Great Britain finally came down.

Vindication: 'Cartwheel' twopence and penny, 1797. (National Numismatic Collection, Smithsonian Institution)

On an official level, the matter was introduced in Parliament during discussion of a proposed curb on small-change notes. That was on 2 March 1797. By the following day, Richard Brinsley Sheridan introduced a motion in the House of Commons requesting a copper coinage from the King, to be minted in the form of pence, twopence, and threepence (the latter concept would soon be dropped, when it became clear that a threepenny copper piece would be too heavy for commerce). Later that day, Lord Liverpool wrote Matthew Boulton with the news, adding that

> There is no Man who can better judge of the Propriety of this Measure, and of the Plan that ought to be adopted, in issuing a Coinage of this Nature, than Yourself; and no one will execute it with more Accuracy, and more Expedition.—[11]

And on the sixth, Matthew Boulton was invited to London to discuss the matter with the Lords of the Committee on Coin. He had won.

But he could not set to work instantly: while the Government may have come to a decision in March, it continued to dither over it for several months, and Boulton would not receive his formal Patent for the work until 9 June. Meanwhile, the industrialist must proceed as if all were well – find copper for the project; consult with designers and officials on details of the reverse (the Lords of the Committee on Coin wanted a number of dates of British victories engraved on the rock upon which Britannia would sit) and obverse (which of Küchler's heads of the King did that monarch prefer?); and get Soho ready for what would certainly be its largest project to date. But copper was obtained (and the first of it was being cut into planchets by the

Proclamation legalizing the 'Cartwheel' copper coinage, 1797. (Author's collection)

By the KING.
A PROCLAMATION,

For giving Currency to a new Coinage of Copper Money of One Penny and Two Penny Pieces.

GEORGE R.

WHEREAS, in confequence of the unanimous Addrefs of Our Commons of *Great Britain*, in Parliament affembled, praying, that We would be gracioufly pleafed to give Directions that Meafures might be taken for an immediate Supply of fuch Copper Coinage as might be beft adapted to the Payment of the Laborious Poor in the prefent Exigency; We have thought fit to order that certain Pieces of Copper fhould be coined, which fhould go and pafs for One Penny and Two Pennies, and that each of fuch Pieces of One Penny fhould weigh One Ounce Avoirdupois, and that each of fuch Two Penny Pieces fhould weigh Two Ounces Avoirdupois; the intrinfic Value of fuch Pieces of One Penny and Two Pennies, Workmanfhip included, correfponding as nearly as poffible with the nominal Value of the fame refpectively; every fuch Piece having on one Side thereof Our Effigies or Portraiture, with Our Name or Title, and on the Reverfe the Figure of *Britannia*, reprefented fitting on a Rock in the Sea, holding a Trident in her Left Hand, and a Branch of Olive in her Right Hand, with the Year of our Lord: And whereas Penny and Two Penny Pieces of Copper, of the Weight and Defcription aforefaid, have been coined, and will be foon ready for Delivery, according to the Orders which We have given for that Purpofe: We have therefore, with the Advice of Our Privy Council, thought fit to iffue this Our Royal Proclamation, and We do hereby ordain, declare, and command, That the faid Pieces of Copper Money, fo coined as aforefaid, fhall be current and lawful Money of Our Kingdom of *Great Britain*, and fhall pafs and be received as current and lawful Money of Our faid Kingdom, that is to fay, fuch Penny Pieces as of the Value of One Penny, and fuch Two Penny Pieces as of the Value of Two Pennies, in all Payments and Tranfactions of Money; provided that no Perfon fhall be obliged to take more of fuch Copper Money in any One Payment, than fhall be of the Value of One Shilling, after the Rate aforefaid.

Given at Our Court at *St. James's*, the Twenty-fixth Day of *July* One thoufand feven hundred and ninety-feven, in the Thirty-feventh Year of Our Reign.

God fave the King.

L O N D O N:
GEORGE EYRE and ANDREW STRAHAN, Printers to the King's moft Excellent Majefty. 1797.

sixth of June), and designs were agreed to, dies cut, machines readied, by the time the Patent arrived.

That document ordered Boulton to strike five hundred tons of pence and twopence, but the precise division between the denominations was left to the discretion of the Lords of the Committee on Coin. The coinage should commence on 26 June 1797, and twenty tons should be struck each week thereafter, made ready for delivery to the Lord High Treasurer. They would be checked for quality by a 'Comptroller' appointed by the Lords – a stipulation which would soon become a point of friction at Soho. The pence would weigh one ounce each, the twopence two ounces. Boulton would receive fourpence per pound, or £37.6.8 per ton, for coining them, plus £4 per ton for shipment. And he would have to find his own copper for the project, receiving £108 for each ton secured. It is apparent that he would not become rich through the workings of this arrangement; but while present, the profit motive was secondary.

The historic 'Cartwheel' coinage actually began on 19 June 1797; the first delivery to Boulton's London agent, the elderly-but-spirited Mrs Charlotte Matthews, took place on 26 July. That same day saw a Proclamation making the new coins legal tender for all transactions up to a shilling; but that summer also saw chaos.

Unofficial competition: counterfeit 'Cartwheel' penny (enlarged; National Numismatic Collection, Smithsonian Institution)

The new pence were an instant success and quickly attracted felonious admirers: despite the coiner's claims (and the threats in an anti-counterfeiting statute, enacted on 19 July 1797), reasonably plausible counterfeits were making their appearance before the end of the summer. There were not enough of them to represent more than a nuisance, but Boulton soon offered a reward of one hundred guineas for information leading to an arrest – which was also a good advertisement for the genuine article. Meanwhile, he scrambled to strike the heavy pieces as quickly as he could at Soho, while Mrs Matthews scrambled to fill orders for them in London. She encountered great difficulties in getting a smooth system of supply in place, and until the Government aided her in doing so, the coins could not be quickly distributed – and the coiner could not be quickly paid for his labours. By the end of the summer, the Government had responded, and a reasonably effective system of disbursement had been established in London. But at Soho, all was not well.

Matthew Boulton found that the heavy coins he was striking were taxing his machinery to the utmost. He would soon be thinking of a better way to connect his presses to the steam engine. But just now, he had no time for devising improvements: the demand for his coin was still too intense, and he had, in addition, to contend with the King's Comptroller, Joseph Sage.

Sage arrived at Soho at the end of June. He and the coiner appear to have taken an instant dislike to each other – perhaps because the latter was simply too busy at the time to pay undivided attention to a bureaucrat, especially one who was also a senior moneyer at the mint in the Tower. Whatever the reason, Boulton had gained a persistently annoying enemy, one who would one day prove a major irritant to operations.

The remainder of the year 1797 saw Boulton producing pence, to the total exclusion of the twopence. But the latter finally got into production in January 1798: appropriately, the first specimens were delivered to Boulton's patron, Sir Joseph Banks. Soho had already shipped more than 2,500 casks of penny pieces to every corner of Britain. And they were soon going abroad as well: on 3 March, Boulton received a request for pence and twopence for Newfoundland, to the amount of £1,000; three months later, his London manager was approached with a much larger order, for Cape Colony. And in April 1799, a second, smaller order was placed for Newfoundland.

By that point, Boulton had long since run through his original agreement for five hundred tons of copper coin. He had been agitating for an extension of the order as early as the end of August 1797, was soon asking as well for the right to strike regal halfpennies and farthings. His contract for the larger coins was indeed renewed – unofficially – on two occasions; but the smaller coins would have to wait.

By the end of July 1798, demand for Boulton's copper pence was beginning to abate. That for the twopence had long since been satisfied, and none of the larger coins had been struck since late April. But production of pence continued through the remainder of 1798 and into 1799 – and it was joined by another coining of twenty tons of twopence at the beginning of 1799. The date when Boulton's first British copper coinage finished cannot be established: extant records tended to speak in terms of *shipments*, which may or may not have coincided with *coinages*. But the industrialist wrote Charles Long of the Treasury on 27 July 1799, advising him that the working dies for the coinage had been destroyed the previous day, under the watchful eye of Mr Sage; and we thus have an ending date of sorts.

By that point, Soho had created some 43,969,204 pence and 722,180 twopence, a total coinage of 44,691,384 pieces. This accomplishment would be considered minor today, when the great mints of the world customarily produce five or even ten *billion* coins within a single year. But we must see Boulton's feat as his contemporaries would have seen it: for most of them, a 1797 'Cartwheel' penny would have been the first time they had ever seen a mass-produced, machine-made article. That heavy, homely piece of metal they now held in their hand presaged a new, industrial age; and their tribute to its creator lay in the fact that they and their children and grandchildren would one day wear it smooth. Or rather, wear smooth the images of the King and the seated lady: even then, the sunken letters of the legends would still have told them whose coin this was.

Agitation began for a second regal coinage even as the first was getting started. You will recall that the centrepiece of the copper coinage reform had always been understood, both by the Committee on Coin and by the industrialist who must obey its wishes, to be the *halfpenny*. This was the coin most widely counterfeited; this was also the coin most currently replicated, in the form of the provincial trade token. So all eyes naturally turned to this lesser monetary entity, and to its subordinate, the farthing.

While conversations between Matthew Boulton and Lord Liverpool over the desirability of a halfpenny and farthing coinage may be traced back to the late summer of 1797, they would bear no fruit until the end of 1799. The coiner must overcome many obstacles before that new opportunity would be his. As he candidly admitted, the 'Cartwheel' venture had taxed Soho Mint to its limits. Prior to another major coinage, basic improvements must be made in the apparatus which would strike the coins, and in the relationships between the component parts of that apparatus. As noted elsewhere, the coiner was reinventing his mint by February 1798, was soon constructing a second Soho Mint to overcome the deficiencies lately discovered at the first.

A second obstacle lay in the rise in the price of copper. This had occasioned the melting down of a good many 'Cartwheel' coins – as well as the Parys Mine penny tokens of Thomas Williams. Anything new struck at Soho would have to be made lighter than the first issue, which might in turn invite counterfeiting.

A final problem lay in the nature of the bureaucracy with which Mr Boulton must contend. He was asked to make a formal proposal for the halfpenny and farthing coinage on 17 August 1798, to which he responded by the twenty-seventh. There now ensued a period of nearly *fifteen months*, during which time Boulton or his London amanuensis, the indefatigable Widow Matthews, wrote, argued, appeared in the halls of the mighty, and generally pestered and prodded the slow-moving authorities to grant the necessary blessing for the commencement of the coinage. Boulton was actually striking the first of the new coins by the beginning of May 1799, and he had minted some twenty tons' worth of halfpence by the twentieth of August. But he would receive no written instructions to proceed until 4 November 1799. During the intervening months, he had had to halt production, throwing many of his people out of work; and he also faced problems in paying for the copper he had already struck but could not yet distribute.

The Government finally responded in the form of an Indenture signed on 4 November. Boulton was to strike 550 tons of new coppers, at a ratio of ten halfpence to each farthing. The designs were stipulated: again, Conrad Heinrich Küchler would create the dies. The new coins were to be struck at thirty-six and seventy-two to the pound, a reflection of the rise in the price of copper since the first coinage. Boulton would receive £47 per ton for striking, packing, and transporting the new money, the Government finding the copper for it; the first delivery of coin was set for 18 November. And a Comptroller would oversee the coining, Boulton only receiving payment for it on this clerk's approval. As in 1797, this precaution would create problems at Soho, and near-distraction for Matthew Boulton.

Let us examine this second copper issue for a moment. Boulton had abandoned the idea of a raised protective rim containing an intaglio legend; the record is silent, but I hazard the guess that that area represented an area of

Great Britain, halfpenny and farthing, 1799. (National Numismatic Collection, Smithsonian Institution)

319

weakness on the dies, one constantly at risk from metal crumbling. Instead, the new issue featured normal legends – but slightly curved fields, so that the legends and the major designs would still wear very well and still be very difficult to counterfeit. And Boulton's concern over forgery led to a final design innovation, one replicated by many coiners over the next half-century: he would mill his planchets with oblique markings, \\\\\\\\\, then strike them in collars as before. He would do so to render sand-casting far more difficult, if not impossible. All of these design details had been decided upon by 15 June 1799, for the coiner mentioned them in a letter written that day.

Coinage finally began about 10 November 1799, and the first shipment of halfpennies left Soho on the twenty-seventh, consigned to Mrs Matthews. It is interesting to note that some of these early coins were consigned to Australia; half a century later, Soho's final products would be remitted to that same destination.

Production of this second order was fraught with difficulty. There were recurrent rumours that the Royal Mint was about to commence a copper coinage of its own; as Boulton saw it, several of the Tower's moneyers, in company with Soho's former Comptroller, Joseph Sage, and its present one, James Morrison, were jealous of him; along with Thomas Williams, they were 'forming a Cabal to rob me of the Coinage, my inventions, my character, and tire me out'.[12] Here, we are probably hearing the voice of an ageing, ailing man; but Morrison, at least, was to prove a perpetual thorn and threat. When Boulton discovered that the latter had been in Soho Mint making sketches of the machinery, he immediately concluded that Morrison was doing so on behalf of his cronies at the Tower.[13] So it went throughout this second copper coinage.

The difficulties created by Morrison were intensified by those from other sources. The halfpence were an immediate success, and Mrs Matthews was besieged by orders she was hard-put to fill even during good weather. Then flooding on the canals between Birmingham and London (and the great majority of Boulton's coins and tokens were sent by water rather than land) made her distributive work still more difficult. There was also opposition in some quarters to the reduction in weight which Boulton had been forced to incorporate into the new coinage.

But difficulties were surmounted or sidestepped, and the coinage of halfpence (and of farthings, which had begun by December), continued through the remainder of the old year and the first half of the new. Production finally concluded in July 1800. Boulton had meanwhile requested an extension of his contract. This was denied him for now, but it would be the germ of a third and final copper coinage some years later.

A Soho memorandum set down the number of casks of coins whose production had just ceased. There had been 3,540 casks of halfpence and 176 of farthings. If we assume an intended count of precisely twelve thousand halfpence, or twenty-four thousand farthings, per cask, we arrive at a total coinage of 42,480,000 halfpence and 4,224,000 farthings, or some 46,704,000 pieces in all.

I have treated these first two coinages together because they are easiest to understand that way. But there were two other coinages being done concurrently with and slightly later than the 'Cartwheel' issue. The first was unrelated to it; the second aped it, by order of the issuer.

We may trace the 1798 coinage for Sumatra back to 3 March 1797. On that date (which Soho would long remember for other reasons) Robert Wissett of the East India Company wrote his old friend Boulton for a set of Sumatran coins of 1786–7; the Chairman had requested them. To Soho, this would have suggested an interest in another issue for Sumatra, and the coins were promptly sent; but larger events soon intervened, and the matter was forgotten. It was revived about a year later. On 23 February 1798, Charlotte Matthews was approached by emissaries of the Company, who requested another fifteen tons of coinage for Sumatra, to be delivered as quickly as possible.

Even in the midst of a major copper coinage for home consumption, Matthew Boulton was able to move quickly on this one for foreign consumption.[14] In less than two months, the issue had been struck and sent off to St Botolph's Wharf – slightly more than fifteen tons of copper, struck into pieces of 150, one hundred, and fifty grains. A total of 639,764 of the largest pieces exited Soho on 27 March, followed by 935,913 of the medium-size on 4 April, and 986,668 of the smallest on 9 April.

These coins were identical in weight and appearance with what had gone before. There was no innovation: the Company did not want it, and Boulton did not have the leisure to supply it. The other of the two coinages also closely copied an earlier model. But the inspiration for the Sumatran coinage was an old coin, while that for the Manx was a new one.

The Isle of Man's monetary history was and is complex. It had long been ruled by its own nobility; as an attribute of their sovereignty, the Lords of the island occasionally had coins struck for Man (and just possibly *on* Man, on one occasion). When the second Duke of Atholl sold the island to the Crown in 1765 for £70,000, coinage might have been expected to cease. But it did not. There was a handsome issue of pence and halfpence from the Tower Mint in 1786; these coins may serve as a bench mark for pre-industrial moneying. But Matthew Boulton would soon appear on the scene, and he would show what could be achieved by a new coining methodology.

He was invited to coin for the Isle of Man by John, Duke of Atholl. Atholl had just seen the first of Boulton's penny pieces; in July 1797 he penned a memorial to George III: since it had already been agreed that Man would be supplied with a copper coinage, let Matthew Boulton rather than the Tower be entrusted with the work.

This was conceded; but the lapse between Atholl's suggestion and Boulton's coining suggests a certain amount of delaying tactics by the Royal Mint, which once again saw an order which should have been filled there being taken over by the pushy Mr Boulton, of Soho, near Birmingham. The latter had to wait until the early months of 1799 to begin the coinage. Considering his other duties, he may have welcomed the delay.

Most of the order was shipped to the Duke on 4 March 1799, with a few hundred stragglers sent along about six weeks later. There was more to this coinage than met the eye. For his obverse, Küchler reproduced his portrait of George III, already seen on the 1797 coins for Great Britain. But he created a new die for the reverse, which featured the traditional Manx emblem, the *triune* or *triskelis*, in place of Britannia, and the Manx motto in place of the British reverse legend and date. (The date would be moved to the obverse of the coin, where it would remain until the ending of traditional Manx coinage

A Manx penny, in proof, 1798. (Reproduced by kind permission of Trustees of the British Museum)

321

in 1839.) All of these changes had to take place within a smaller framework: rather than being struck at sixteen to the pound, Soho's pence for the Isle of Man were struck at twenty-one, its halfpence at forty-two and one-half. The size of the coin must be accordingly reduced, so Küchler's work was nearly as arduous as if he had been starting from scratch.

Some 94,828 pence and 194,376 halfpence, or 289,204 coins in total, were sent to Man in the spring of 1799. Boulton encountered considerable difficulty in receiving payment for them, however, and his polite but insistent letters to a peer of the realm, who must be gently persuaded to pay what he owed (we are speaking of an amount no greater than £640) speaks volumes as to the financial fragility of Matthew Boulton's empire at this time.

But the coiner at length received his due, and his product found a welcome acceptance on the Isle of Man. So popular was the issue that most of it had disappeared from active circulation within a decade of its arrival. In 1812, a petition for a second coinage was received, and Soho Mint prepared a second order of Manx coin.

These were dated 1813, and they were very nearly identical with the coins of 1798. But they were struck fractionally lighter (at twenty-two and forty-four to the pound, respectively). Their dies were probably under the care of John Phillp, for Küchler had died in 1810. And Matthew Robinson rather than Matthew Boulton profited from the order, which went out on 15 June 1813. The second Manx issue consisted of 99,400 pence and 98,308 halfpence; and on this occasion, payment was rendered in a timely fashion.

The grand total for all of Soho's Manx coinage would stand at 486,912 pieces, two-fifths of it pence and the remainder halfpence.

The opening years of the nineteenth century represented a relatively quiet time at Soho Mint. There would soon be large issues for home and abroad – issues, in fact, which would represent the zenith of Matthew Boulton's coining activity. But the months between the summer of 1800 and the spring of 1803 represented a relatively 'dead' time in the Soho story – at least as far as moneying was concerned. And it was during that period, when the industrialist and his friends were agitating for a resumption of regal copper coinage, that Matthew Boulton struck three final groups of copper tokens, substitutes for the coin to come.

None of the issues was large, but each was distinctive in its way. The earliest was a series of halfpenny tokens, struck at fifty-eight to the pound, manufactured for an Irish banker named Woodcock, of Enniscorthy, County Wicklow. The fact that they were intended for Ireland (where thirteen, not twelve, pence made up the shilling) in part explains their light weight. The actual person placing the order was Samuel Baker, a resident of Birmingham – which may explain the absence of correspondence in the Matthew Boulton Papers.

Conrad Heinrich Küchler probably engraved the dies, for he was regularly being paid for such labour during the time when the Enniscorthy token was being prepared. Woodcock must have chosen the designs himself, and they were odd indeed: the reverse depicted Vinegar Hill, scene of the climactic Irish defeat in the Rising of 1798. The pieces were struck with a plain edge; they were so thin that no other alternative existed.

Two orders were shipped in February 1801. The first left Soho on the seventh, consisting of 2,283 papers of fifty-two tokens each (that is, two shillings

Enniscorthy proof halfpenny, dated 1800, struck 1801. (Author's collection)

Davison and Hawksley sixpenny token, dated 1791 but struck in 1802. (Author's collection)

Charleville proof token for 13 pence Irish. (Author's collection)

Irish), or 118,716 pieces. The second order went out on the twenty-seventh, consisting of 10,319 papers, or 536,588 tokens. In all, the Enniscorthy banker received 655,304 halfpenny tokens; and the fact that many of those seen today are very worn suggests that he put them to good use.

Matthew Boulton's next foray into private coinage was unknown until now, and it remains something of an enigma. From the county of Nottinghamshire, rare tokens have been recorded from the Arnold Works, the property of Davison and Hawksley. The pieces are dated 1791, and they exist in denominations of a crown, a halfcrown, a shilling, and a sixpence. It is said that the pieces are rare because a fire in January 1791 destroyed the works, thereby aborting the token issue; but the real story must have been otherwise.

A Mint Day Book for 1801–1805 bore a curious entry on 3 August 1802: payment had just been received from Messrs Davison and Hawksley for tokens struck in four sizes. The order consisted of 173 pounds, ten ounces of pieces struck in 'Mixd Metal' and 404 pounds, ten ounces of pieces struck in silvered copper. There was no description of the numbers or denominations involved, but the reference to a charge 'for Dies of the 4 sizes'[15] gives us a fair idea of what was taking place. Davison and Hawksley were charged £77.15.0 for the work, dies included; unless we are to suppose that Matthew Boulton carried their debt on his books for more than eleven years (admittedly possible but rather unlikely), I think we must view the date on these tokens as commemorative rather than literal. It is a shame that we cannot even determine approximately how many of each denomination were struck.

For Soho's final token for the British Isles, we must return to Ireland. Charles William Bury had become Viscount Charleville and Baron Tullamore in 1800, and his good fortune may have inspired him to emulate Sir George Jackson and issue a copper token for the use of his people. In any case, a gentleman named Frederick Trench made an approach to Matthew Boulton on the new Viscount's behalf in the spring of 1802; the Charleville tokens were the result, struck in 1803 and 1804.

They were interesting pieces from several aspects. First, they reintroduced a designer from the earliest days of Soho Mint, John Gregory Hancock, Sr. Hancock received six guineas in January 1803 for engraving a die for the Charleville token,[16] the final service he performed for Matthew Boulton, and, indeed, his last known work in the token field. Another point of interest lay in the pieces' denomination and size. They were tariffed at thirteen pence Irish, or one shilling English. While they were made of copper, the Viscount wanted them at least to reflect their purported value by means of their size. And they did: with the exception of the five-sol Monnerons and the Anglesey pence of 1792, they were the heaviest tokens Matthew Boulton ever struck. A final point of interest lay in their method of payment. By definition, any token hints at or promises payment in 'real' money: most of the eighteenth-century pieces promised it on demand; Viscount Charleville's thirteenpence pieces promised it on the first Tuesday of each month!

All of the Charleville tokens were dated 1802, but none was struck that year. A first order was sent about the beginning of February 1803, consisting of precisely 4,100 pieces. In late May 1804 Charleville wrote Matthew Boulton for a renewal. He wanted another six thousand or so, and that, in mid-July, was exactly what he got: 6,051 pieces were sent out on the twelfth or thirteenth. Joined with the members of the first order, plus forty-eight specimens in gilt copper and a dozen copper proofs, they brought the number of Charleville pieces to a final figure of 10,211.

Such issues as these must have brought welcome diversion to Matthew Boulton and his designers and coiners; however, they did not bring full employment. Larger coinages were needed for that. A hint of what was to come was received at Soho in the spring of 1802, but a resumption of mass production only began in 1803. And from that year until 1809, the majority of Soho's coining would take place.

The opening act was a coinage for an old client for a new area. As one of the results of the Napoleonic Wars, the East India Company had come into possession of Ceylon in 1796. The new administrators retained the monetary system of the old, and so they began to think about a coinage based on the stuiver and rixdollar of the previous colonizers. Local issues were prepared beginning in 1801; by the following year, Matthew Boulton was being incorporated into the picture.

Ceylon gilt proof 1/48, 1/96, and 1/192 rixdollar, 1802. (National Numismatic Collection, Smithsonian Institution)

Soho's usual contact was the colony's agent, William Huskisson. Huskisson had a friend named Alexander Davison who had had dealings with Matthew Boulton some years previously, when Soho had prepared a commemorative medal for him celebrating Horatio Nelson's victory at the Battle of the Nile. So when Huskisson mentioned a coinage to Davison late in March 1802, the latter knew just where to apply.

Ceylon's Governor North wanted one hundred thousand pounds' worth of coins – eighty thousand pounds of copper struck into stuivers (denominated at forty-eight to the rixdollar), the remaining twenty thousand pounds coined into equal amounts of halves and quarters (tariffed at ninety-six and 192 to the rixdollar, respectively).

Soho began work on the order nearly as soon as it was received. The firm was aided by the simplicity of the coins' designs, which featured an elephant and date on the obverse, the denomination and issuing authority on the reverse. Huskisson inquired about progress on the coinage on 24 May; five days later, the last of it had left Soho for the India Docks, remitted in 256 casks.

The Ceylon coinage consisted of the three denominations listed above, struck at forty-six, ninety-two, and 184 to the pound, respectively. The amount of copper struck would have thus yielded 3,679,212 stivers (the British spelling of the Dutch denomination), 919,989 half-stivers, and 1,840,920 quarter-stivers, for a total of 6,440,121 coins. Boulton's venture into Sri Lankan numismatics proved popular on that island, and Huskisson was soon writing him for another order, a request which could not be honoured due to larger commitments closer to home. But the swift and satisfactory completion of the East India Company's order for one part of its domains may have led to a request for coinage for three others, in very close succession.

The first would be for the Presidency of Madras. Robert Wissett had been inquiring about the possibility of such a coinage since the beginning of 1800; Boulton had put him off, pleading the exigencies of his second copper coinage for Great Britain. But the Company was persistent, and by the summer of 1802 a very large order for Madras was in view.

It would consist of around thirty-five million coins, struck in four denominations, ranging downward from a twenty-cash piece (at thirty-six to the pound) to a ten-cash (at seventy-two pieces to the pound), a five-cash (at

The large and small of it: 20 cash, 1808 and cash, 1803, both for Madras and actual size. (National Numismatic Collection, Smithsonian Institution)

144), and a cash. The latter would be so tiny (it would require 720 of these coins to equal a single pound of metal) that Boulton would have to invent special tools to strike it.

A discussion on designs ensued. The Persian inscriptions gave particular difficulty, and designer John Phillp was sent to London to confer with the Company's resident philologist, Dr Charles Wilkins, as to the correctness of the lettering and designs. Wilkins proved a stickler for detail on this and later occasions – and Phillp also had to contend with an irate Conrad Heinrich Küchler, who felt it his right to take over the work from the younger artist. But Phillp endured the pedagogy of Dr Wilkins (and avoided Herr Küchler as much as possible); he returned home with his perfected dies about the beginning of October, and coining began soon thereafter.

Boulton's people undertook the larger coins first, as their master fretted over how to strike the smallest. He finally perfected a means of doing so (featuring special weights and layers-on for the purpose) by the beginning of January 1803 – only to receive word from Robert Wissett that, since no additional cash pieces were in contemplation, he need not have bothered.

The first of the coins reached London in early November 1802. This shipment consisted of the three largest denominations, and their delivery continued until 23 May 1803. By then, some 1,323,360 twenty-cash coins, 6,304,560 tens, and 12,304,416 fives had been sent. The tiny cash brought up the rear, and they remained a problem even after Boulton had devised a viable way of striking them. The first were sent on 21 March 1803, and they were packed loose instead of in rouleaus because they were too small to wrap. Several of the casks which carried them split, and some fourteen pounds' worth were lost as thousands of the tiny coins went rolling and skipping across the East India Docks, avidly pursued by anyone in the vicinity. Two additional shipments took place in May, by which time 17,994,240 cash pieces had been safely delivered and consigned for Madras. Their output very nearly equalled all of the other denominations combined, and the total for this 1803 order amounted to no fewer than 37,926,576 coins. They would soon be joined by twenty-two million coppers for Bombay and Sumatra.

The Bombay order arose from the local inability to provide an adequate copper coinage, which had become obvious by late 1802. Boulton, Watt & Company did not come into the equation for another year, and the Bombay copper coinage was initially discussed as part of a much larger plan, one of several to provide a Soho Indian coinage of copper and *silver*. The silver idea was soon abandoned, but an order to strike copper was indeed given, and it was very quickly honoured. The Matthew Boulton Papers suggest that the Bombay coinage was prepared in two batches, coined along with another order for Sumatra, to be discussed in a moment. The first portion of the Bombay coin was finished and shipped between 3 and 31 January, the second between 6 March and 28 April – a time-frame exactly adhered to for the Sumatran order as well. As usual for Bombay, pieces weighing fifty, one hundred, and two hundred grains were struck, corresponding to the half-pice, pice, and double-pice. Some 6,991,600 of the small, 3,505,180 of the medium, and 1,743,770 of the large size were minted, for a total of 12,240,550 coins.

The order for Sumatra or Bencoolen closely resembled the Bombay coinage as to design; it was identical as to the sizes of the coins struck – pieces of fifty, one hundred, and two hundred grains, but denominated one, two, and four kepings. The Bencoolen coins were prepared at Soho during the same months which saw the elaboration of the Bombay order, but they were minted in somewhat smaller numbers – 5,567,800 kepings, 2,817,340 double-kepings, and 1,389,885 four-kepings, for a total of 9,775,025 coins. These 1804-dated pieces should not be confused with a lighter series bearing the same date. Soho manufactured them too, but much later and for an interesting reason.

Even as he was alleviating a shortage of decent small change abroad, Matthew Boulton had made sincere efforts to attack the problem at home. His efforts were impressive as far as they went. But they were necessarily conditioned upon the decisions of Government, the rise or fall in the value of copper, and a number of other factors over which the coiner had little or no control. By the time he was finishing the coinages for Bombay and Sumatra, events at home were about to propel him and his mint into a new, expanded, and more intense employment as coiner to the British Isles. For the first time, Boulton would provide them with a *silver* coinage – and here was the boldest admission yet of the Royal Mint's incapacity. And there would be another such admission: the Tower Mint had been the traditional provider of Irish copper coinage; now, Matthew Boulton would step into that role too. To cap off everything, there would be a final, very large copper coinage for Great Britain. But while it would begin brilliantly, it would end in failure and hard feelings. Soho would forever see these few years as its apogee; but they also contained the seeds of its dramatic decline.

Elsewhere, I have related the story of the Royal Mint's two abortive attempts to countermark Spanish-American Pieces of Eight for the Bank of England. The coins were widely counterfeited, as were the official counter-marks applied to them; the second of the two attempts had come to an inglorious end early in 1804. By then, Matthew Boulton was actively considering the problem, and he soon came up with an obvious solution, obvious at least to him: create a countermark as large as the host coin itself, and strike the old coin with the new countermark in a one-piece collar. Thus was born what Boulton always called the 'regenerated dollars' of 1804.

We do not know when he devised this answer to the country's silver plight. He may have thought of it late in 1803; he was certainly experimenting with it by the beginning of 1804. Encouraged by such good friends as Sir Joseph Banks, the idea was soon put forward to the Government and the Directors of the Bank of England, and it was agreed to on principle in early March.

It appealed to Matthew Boulton for several reasons. First, it would allow him to demonstrate the virtues of his new technology in a most dramatic fashion: anyone who compared his new coins with the crude Spanish-American originals (with or without the equally crude stamp applied to them at the Tower) would *have* to draw the correct conclusion. And the new coins would be the best advertisement for a new silver coinage at a new Royal Mint – with a new apparatus, built by Boulton, Watt & Company.

But there were several other attractions to the recycling plan. It would make possible a rapid gratification of the country's needs: since Boulton would be striking the silver *as it was*, not needing to alloy, roll, or blank it, many of the slower steps in all coining processes including his own would be unnecessary. That procedure would also mean that he would not have to assay the silver and guarantee its purity – and the recent experiences with the meddlesome Messrs Sage and Morrison were still very much in view. And finally, the whole process could be done very cheaply, at a small fraction of the cost of a normal coinage. Boulton could in fact do the work for £1 per thousand coins – and while he made no profit, he incurred no loss.

The late winter and early spring of 1804 saw furious activity in London and at Soho. Worried Bank Directors wondered whether Boulton's recoining could obliterate the original types *and* the British countermarks; a unique specimen in the British Museum illustrates Boulton's response, at a time when he was unable completely to do so.[17] Even as they were approving the recoinage, they must also devise ways of safely transmitting wagon-loads of silver from London to Soho and back again. The last of the copper orders for Bombay and Sumatra were hurriedly finished and pushed out the door, Soho Mint cleaned and made ready for the new coinage. And ideas for designs went back and forth between Matthew Boulton, Sir Joseph Banks, and a number of others at Soho and in the capital. All was in readiness by the last days of April 1804, and on the twenty-eighth day of that month, Boulton's London agent John Woodward was able to report that the first of the Spanish-American dollars had just left the Bank of England for their appointment at Soho. The first step in the recoinage had been taken.

At Soho, work on the Bank of England pieces began around 10 May, and Boulton delivered the first of the regenerated dollars to the carriers two days later. He was striking forty-two thousand a day, a rate which could have been doubled, were it not for all of the intricate cleaning processes which the frequently filthy dollars had to undergo prior to coining. By 27 June 1804, Boulton had received, recoined, and remitted some 1,005,523 overstruck Bank of England dollars. He had also made 1,420 proof or specimen pieces from new silver, intended for presentation to the influential and possible sale to collectors. In all, therefore, 1,006,943 Bank of England dollars dated 1804 were actually struck during that year.

An early 'regenerated' dollar for the Bank of England: Boulton managed to obliterate the Spanish-American undertype, but the octagonal Bank of England countermark still showed through. (Reproduced by kind permission of the Trustees of the British Museum)

Bank of England dollar, struck over a Mexican peso dated 1797 (left; portions of the earlier date may be faintly seen between the mural crown and the E of ENGLAND); an original (and unregenerated) Mexican peso of 1797 (right). (National Numismatic Collection, Smithsonian Institution)

A similar coinage for the Bank of Ireland had been requested and agreed to at about the same time. A reflection of the differing values of the monies of the two islands, while the Bank of England tokens (and we do well to remember that these pieces were deliberately referred to as *tokens* throughout; they were *not* placed on the same lofty footing as actual coins) were denominated at five shillings, those struck for Ireland were tariffed at six. Work on the Irish dollars commenced in a small way on 16 May, but it only became significant as the order for the Bank of England was winding down. All of the regular coinage was shipped at once, on 19 June 1804. There were 790,509 of them. Again, Boulton had struck specimens from silver which he

Bank of Ireland proof dollar, 1804. (National Numismatic Collection, Smithsonian Institution)

had rolled at his mint – 1,052 of them. All Irish bank dollars therefore totalled 791,561 pieces.

There would only be a single dollar issue for the Bank of Ireland. But there would be several more issues for the Bank of England, occasioned as before by the failure of the Royal Mint to provide a viable regal alternative (although one must be fair and add that that establishment was scarcely in a condition to do so at the time of the first request; it was in the process of being dismantled to make way for Matthew Boulton's new machinery and was not fully operable).

Henry Hase of the Bank first approached Matthew Boulton on 21 July 1809: the Bank needed another four hundred thousand recoined dollars. Boulton's son responded quickly, and the Bank received its new money in two batches on 4 and 14 September 1809 – some 397,780 dollars.

More coins were sent before the end of 1809 and throughout most of 1810. By 3 September of the latter year, another 2,233,955 dollars had been recoined and shipped to the Bank. And there would be a final issue embracing the five months between mid-November 1810 and mid-April 1811, wherein another 857,514 Pieces of Eight would come to Soho, be regenerated, and travel back to the Bank, the first leg of their lengthy journey along the channels of nineteenth-century British commerce. In all, some 4,496,192 Bank of England dollars were struck at Matthew Boulton's mint. All of them were clearly dated 1804 – although a few lucky collectors have found coins with a genuine, *later* date, put there by the minters of Mexico and Perú some years after the purported one put there by Matthew Boulton.

A year or so after Ireland received her silver dollars from Matthew Boulton, she began receiving the first deliveries of a copper coinage, one completely created at Soho Mint. Its owner had already minted several copper tokens specifically for that island; but now he would provide it with official pence, halfpence and farthings.

This Irish issue generally paralleled Soho's third and final copper coinage for Great Britain. The same artist, Küchler, was responsible for its designs, and it was manufactured by the same people and on the same machinery as those employed on behalf of its sister realm. But there were some differences.

It began prior to the British issue, and it concluded sooner as well. It appears to have given all parties less trouble than its British counterpart. Its designs were unique: there was little opposition to a simple Irish harp rather than a seated female figure for the reverse, while the bust of King George was carried over from the British copper coinage of 1799; when Soho next struck for Great Britain, Küchler would create a completely new portrait. Finally, the

Ireland, halfpenny (1805) and farthing (1806). (National Numismatic Collection, Smithsonian Institution)

Irish coinage differed in weight, a reflection of the lower value of the Irish penny compared the British.

Talk about an Irish copper coinage went back to April 1804, but Boulton would only be given orders to proceed with it early in the following year, in the form of an indenture for coinage for Ireland and Great Britain signed on 26 March. Küchler had been working on the dies for the project all along, so that Boulton was able to start striking by the beginning of April 1805.

Penny pieces, struck at twenty-six to the pound, were the first coins to be minted and shipped. Throughout the production period, Boulton's Irish coins were sent to Liverpool by canal, transferred there, and carried on to Dublin, remitted to the care of a banking house called Puget & Bainbridge in such vessels as the *Elizabeth*, the *Shaw*, and the *Sarah*. The first penny coins sent across the Irish Sea arrived in Dublin at the end of June. Halfpennies began following on 9 July, and this denomination would be the only one shipped through the remainder of 1805; the final cargo left on 24 February 1806. That same day saw the remittance of a single batch of farthings, all dated 1806. (The two larger denominations were dated 1805.) This shipment had trouble reaching Liverpool in the wintry weather, but it was finally tran-shipped from that port on 6 March, on board the *Irene*, G. C. Norris, Master.

In all, Soho Mint sent 8,788,416 pence, 49,795,200 halfpence, and 4,996,992 farthings to Ireland, a total of 63,580,608 coins. It had also struck a number of proofs in all three denominations (and in the case of the far-things, with dates of 1805 *and* 1806) – but the Matthew Boulton Papers were silent as to precise numbers, and I have not included the proofs in the figures just given. This was an impressive number of coins; but it would soon be dwarfed by Boulton's last British copper issue and the final coinages for India.

These two projects were gigantic, and they would occupy most of the remaining days of Soho Mint's most prolific period. But that time saw a much smaller project too, sandwiched neatly between the Irish and British copper coinages. This was for the Bahamas, and it may serve as another example of Matthew Boulton's tendency to re-use old elements in the creation of new coinages.

The provision of copper money for this small colony off Spanish Florida was first discussed in 1802. On 14 April, the local House of Assembly passed an Act to get such a coinage made in Great Britain, and Governor Halkett's assent to the measure was secured six days later. But the project languished for the next two years, only reviving in the summer of 1804, when the islands' agent George Chalmers approached Soho's man in London, John Mosley, upon their behalf. Mosley mistakenly thought that Chalmers wanted a coinage for *Bermuda*; by the time this geographical misapprehension had been cleared up, another year had passed.

On 15 August 1805, Matthew Boulton received word from Chalmers that Soho had been chosen to coin the Bahamas pieces; but the Board of Trade took another ten and a half months to grant its sanction (which must be obtained before the project could proceed). By the time assent was received, the third and final copper coinage for Great Britain was getting under way, and the Boultons were hard-pressed to meet this small but prestigious order at the same time as the far larger and even more prestigious one for home.

Bahamas penny, 1806. (National Numismatic Collection, Smithsonian Institution)

329

This probably explains what happened next. A new reverse die, adapted from the colony's seal, was created by Conrad Heinrich Küchler. But for the obverse, Soho simply commandeered the dies it was already using for the British *halfpenny*, recycling them for the Bahamian *penny*.

The new coins would be struck at forty-eight to the pound, the same weight as the new halfpenny – which of course was why one die could be pressed into service for two places. The islands' authorities had wanted 120,000 pennies, and that was very nearly what they got: on 11 November 1806, Soho forwarded 2,506 rouleaus of forty-eight pieces each, plus twenty-nine loose coins, for a total mintage of 120,317. A small number of proofs and restrikes are known, but there is no way of determining their exact number or the time when they were made.

The Bahamas provided for, let us turn to Soho Mint's primary concerns during these years, copper coinage for Britain, and for India.

Conversations about a new copper issue for Great Britain began in the spring of 1804. The dollar coinage took precedence, however, for the shortage of silver coin was even worse (and considerably more visible) than that of copper. Discussions continued throughout the year. Matthew Boulton was asked to put forward a coining proposal on 20 November and had done so by the twenty-sixth (for pence, halfpence, and farthings numbering twenty-four, forty-eight, and ninety-six to the pound: the reduced weights reflected the rise in the price of copper since the coinage of 1799). His offer was agreed to on 19 December 1804.

But production would not commence for many months. This was partly a reflection of the order for Irish copper coinage, which was given precedence over that for Britain. It was also a reflection of inconsistency on the part of the authorities: on 14 March 1806, an irate Matthew Boulton observed that the Lords of the Committee on Coin had ordered him to begin the coinage with the pennies, then had suddenly changed their minds, leaving him with 150 tons of penny blanks, dead stock which could not be conveniently used for anything else.[18] Such veering of policy annoyed the coiner; it also held back the coinage.

Soho received permission to begin on 20 March 1806, and it initiated production with the smallest and least-demanded denomination of the new coinage, the farthing. Some 150 casks were completed on 31 March, and they would constitute the sole coinage of that denomination for that year, 4,833,768 pieces.

The pence followed in quick succession, coining having begun on 28 April, the first delivery taking place on 7 May – to Boulton's people in London, who received them along with the farthings. From the capital, they would be distributed across the kingdom, under the same general arrangement as that adopted during the previous coinages. In all, some 19,355,480 pennies of 1806 would swell the nation's money supply; but the coinage of halfpence would swell it even more. That coin was always intended as the linchpin of the copper system, and the coinage figures for 1806 confirmed its importance: with a first delivery on 28 June, no fewer than 87,893,526 halfpennies of 1806 were struck and sent into circulation.

Coinage of all three denominations continued during 1807, with halfpence still predominating. Some 41,394,384 of them were struck in 1807, joined by another 11,290,168 pence and 1,075,200 farthings. Distribution of these coins

Great Britain penny, halfpenny, and farthing, 1806. (National Numismatic Collection, Smithsonian Institution)

went on through 1807, 1808, and the first three months of 1809. Matthew Robinson Boulton asked for permission to resume the coinage on 27 July of that year; four weeks later, permission was refused.

The Boulton Mint had struck a total of 165,842,526 pence, halfpence, and farthings during this third coinage. By early 1808, complaints were coming in from brewers, distillers, and other merchants that they were experiencing a glut of copper coin: apparently, poor workers were receiving their entire wages in Soho's new money, then tendering them to tavern-owners and others in exchange for drinks, meals, cheap clothing and lodging – and the other commodities upon which the poor spent their limited wages. This agitation grew, even as the Boultons continued to remit their coins to anyone who wanted them, and it was one of the reasons for the rejection of Matthew Robinson Boulton's petition to coin still more coppers.

There was another reason, however: Matthew Boulton had always assumed (and he had been guided to the assumption by hints thrown out by the Government) that once the Royal Mint had been refurbished with his new machinery, a division of coining labour would ensue. *He* and his successors would continue to enjoy the right to provide copper coinage for Great Britain and its possessions. The *Royal Mint* would enjoy the right to strike all silver and gold. This division was a reasonable one in Boulton's eyes: he knew more about coining copper than any man living, and if the Royal Mint coined silver and gold, it, and not Soho, would have to perform the tedious and delicate tasks of assaying, cupellation, and precise rolling. Let each party perform that labour for which it was most fitted; there was certainly enough work for everyone.

The Government did not see things that way. It reserved the right to use Soho Mint as it chose – or did not choose. And just now, it did not choose to do so. Problems with the just-completed coinage for Madras would have contributed to this decision, and by 1809, the Government was coming to a momentous conclusion: in future, it would likely provide *all* British coinage, copper as well as silver. It might do so for subordinate organizations such as the East India Company as well. And in fact it would do so within half a year's time: the first coinage struck at the new Royal Mint, Matthew Boulton's Royal Mint, was an issue of copper for the Company's holdings at Penang.

Matthew Robinson Boulton was becoming aware of the drift of events by early 1809, and he directed a shrill protest to the Lords of the Committee on Coin on 14 April. He dwelled on Soho's understanding with Government, only to learn that an understanding requires two parties. He continued his protests throughout that summer but to no avail: relations between the private firm and the public authority, which had been marked by mutual unease since the very beginning, now suffered a permanent deterioration. In future, Boulton, Watt & Company might provide tools to the Royal Mint; it might help train skilled personnel; it might strike silver coinage for the Bank of England (and even be solicited for another copper coinage in 1811, a project which went nowhere); but the relationship had diminished.

Part of the mutual estrangement originated in the second of Soho's major coinages at this time, prepared for the East India Company's Madras Presidency. This project was dogged by ill fortune from the beginning: first discussed in September 1807, conversations immediately dissolved into a squabble as to whether the coiners or the Company should procure the copper, how much should be procured, from where, and at what price. Coining must have begun at the end of the year, for some forty tons of twenty-cash pieces had been struck by mid-January 1808. By early February, some 4,300,000 of the twenties had been joined by nearly three million of the tens. Coinage then ceased for a few months, to be resumed in June and July, when another eleven million twenty-cash and two million tens were created. There would be a final coinage between the end of 1808 and the middle of 1809: by 2 June 1809, Soho had struck 33,590,406 twenty-cash pieces and 52,924,938 tens, for a total output of 86,515,344 coins. This was the second-largest issue ever created at Soho Mint, exceeded only by its recent copper coinage for the home islands.

But as mentioned, the Madras coinage was dogged by misfortune and controversy. Early in 1809, the *Admiral Gardner* went down on the Goodwin Sands; it carried a heavy cargo of ten-cash pieces, the more popular of the two denominations struck for Madras. At the same time, Soho had shamefacedly to announce that it had accidentally struck twenty-two more tons (that is, nearly 2.4 million coins) of twenty-cash pieces than had been ordered. Typically, Matthew Robinson Boulton blamed it on someone else – the Mint Manager, William D. Brown. He begged the Company to accept the coins anyway; but having just learned there would be fewer ten cash than expected, East India House was somewhat miffed. To close this unhappy period, a projected coinage for Bengal (which might have been even larger than that just completed for Madras) dissolved into thin air, a victim of rising copper prices, ill-feeling, the illness of one designer (John Phillp) and the consequent overwork of the other (Conrad Heinrich Küchler), and the pedantry of Dr Wilkins, the perfectionist to whom the creation of the three native languages spelling out the denomination had been entrusted. The mistake over the Madras twenty-cash coinage was the final blow, from which the Bengal coinage never recovered. A few pattern pice and half-pice survive, to show what might have been; by the following year, Soho had a new competitor for the Indian coinage, one it had created itself.

The decade between 1811 and 1821 represented the nadir of Soho's coining story. With the exception of a small issue for the Isle of Man, the mint struck no coins during those years. And the Manx order of 1813 was a direct result of the earlier coinage of 1798; Soho received few invitations to coin, and the records indicate that it sought very few. These were not uneventful years in other branches of the Boulton concern: copper planchets were produced for the United States and Brazil, while a mint was sent to the latter place, even if it lay dormant there for many years. But Matthew Robinson Boulton appears to have considered his mint's coining days to have ended. As related elsewhere, he attempted to sell it toward the end of that decade, and he actually succeeded in doing so in the middle of the next – only to find that he was wanted in the coining field after all.

There were signs pointing in that direction by the beginning of 1821. That March, a copper coinage for St Helena was in contemplation by the East India Company. This did not look as odd then as it appears now: David Vice reminds us that Napoleon Bonaparte was still resident on the island, and anywhere the erstwhile Emperor of the French resided was also likely to see a heavy concentration of British troops. Soldiers need money; soldiers receiving the low wages paid in those days needed small money. And Soho would be called upon to provide it.

A pice pattern from the abortive Bengal project, 1809. (Courtesy Birmingham Museums and Art Gallery)

By this time, the elder Boulton and Watt had long departed the scene. Their sons held their places, Matthew Robinson Boulton at Soho (or more generally at his estate in Oxfordshire), James Watt, Jr. in London. The younger Watt had keen antennae: most of the business opportunities which Soho received in the twenties and thirties resulted from hints picked up by Watt and carried to Boulton.

Such was the progression in the case of St Helena. Watt was approached by Lieutenant Forbes, acting on behalf of the East India Company. Forbes would go on to erect a Boulton mint at Calcutta; for now, his mission was less lofty. The Company wanted £1,000 worth of halfpence struck for St Helena as quickly as possible; to speed things up, Soho could use the same obverse die it had employed for Penang back in 1810! The Company was eventually set straight on the origins of the Penang coinage (a point which still rankled, eleven years after the fact); and Boulton agreed to do the new order, creating new dies for the purpose. On the following 5 June, forty-four casks of coppers left Soho, beginning their trip half-way around the globe to St Helena. They were struck at forty-eight to the pound, and exactly 702,745 of them were shipped.

Napoleon had inconsiderately died by the time they arrived, and most of the garrison had been or was about to be sent away. The presence of seven hundred thousand coppers on an island with a population reduced to a few hundred was deemed overly generous, and the Company resolved to ship back most of the coinage, so that it could be melted down and used for other purposes. Some thirty-five of the forty-four casks were therefore returned to Soho at the end of June 1831; if we assume that they had never been opened in the first place (which appears probable to me: they could not have been needed by the time they were received), then we must subtract that many coins, 564,480, from our original total. The number of likely survivors from the St Helena coinage would thus stand at 138,265 – plenty still for the modest number of nineteenth-century inhabitants and the modest number of twentieth-century collectors.

Oddly enough, something similar awaited the next coinage which Soho created. This was for the Province of Buenos Aires, and it represented the first time Boulton, Watt – or indeed any British coiner – ventured into that part of South America.

The order represented a logical extension to British penetration of South America after the eclipse of Spanish control, which collapse had in fact been abetted by England's official and not-so-official assistance and sympathy. Mindful of the recent and current importance of Great Britain in the region, we should not be surprised to learn that Boulton, Watt would never deal directly with the authorities of this or any of the other new Latin American entities, but rather with their British intermediaries – in this case, Hullett Brothers & Company, of London.

The Hulletts contacted Matthew Robinson Boulton with a request for Buenos Aires coinage at the beginning of March 1822. He responded on the seventh, tendering terms for two sizes of copper coins, worth one-fifth and one-tenth of the silver real. Patterns exist of the larger piece, but only the smaller, called a décimo, was ever struck for circulation. The first trial impressions were being prepared by the end of 1822, and the first of two shipments, consisting of precisely four million coppers, went out in several stages during April 1823.

The Argentine fifth-real never got beyond the pattern stage, but Soho struck eight million tenth-reals in 1823–4. (Reproduced by kind permission of the Trustees of the British Museum)

The authorities at Buenos Aires liked what they received; by our standards the coins were rather plain-looking, but by their standards they were immensely superior to anything previously seen at Buenos Aires. They asked for a second order, Hullett Brothers conveyed their request to Matthew Robinson Boulton on 7 August 1824, and the latter (after pleading the difficulties involved in striking a coinage when he was still building the new Soho Mint), reluctantly agreed to the order on the twenty-eighth.

This second batch of four million décimos was the first coinage struck at Matthew Robinson Boulton's new facility. The coinage was prepared during the autumn of 1824,[19] and it was shipped from Soho between December 1824 and February 1825. The grand total for Boulton's Argentine coinage now stood at eight million.

Unfortunately, much of it enjoyed a very brief commercial life. As at St Helena (and in Great Britain), local authorities found that they must deal with rather more of the Boulton coinage than they wished. At St Helena, they sent it back for melting. In Great Britain, they kept it, but put no more in circulation for a decade. In Argentina, they retired it, then recoined and reissued it.

Buenos Aires called it in in 1827, then immediately restruck it with new dies, issuing it in the name of President Rivadavia's new *Banco Nacional*. It took the coiners until 1831 to finish the job, by which time the dynamic Rivadavia had been deposed in favour of the less dynamic but altogether more durable Juan Manuel de Rosas. The recoiners frequently did a poor job, and we can often see Boulton's original coin just beneath the surface. But Rivadavia and his party were making a point: they were attempting to give notice that a national entity rather than a provincial authority would be responsible for the nation's money; and a sloppy restrike would be an excellent advertisement of their intentions.

There is no way of knowing how many of Boulton's coins were restruck, how many survived unscathed. Based on a completely unscientific series of sightings over the years, I would guess that about half were overstruck, half not. Matthew Robinson Boulton's next and final South American coinage would have a happier fate; but we must discuss a few other coinages before turning to it.

The first of these occupied the months between the two Argentine orders; it was the final Soho coinage for the place which had begun it all, Sumatra. Discussed as early as the summer of 1822, a year would elapse before the first of it left Soho. That initial batch consisted of four-, two-, and one-keping coins, all dated 1804. But they were struck at fifty-three, 106, and 212 pieces to the pound, for the rise in the price of copper had made the weights used for earlier issues impractical. Some 1,614,788 fours, 4,699,760 twos, and 6,061,933 ones, packed into 308 casks, left Soho Mint on 7 August 1823. There would be a second shipment of four-keping pieces, some 1,184,051 coins, on 24 February 1824. This batch was intended as a teaching aid and a guarantee to the East India Company that the Soho Mint was in good working order, would serve well in its upcoming assignment at Bombay. The 1823–4 Sumatran coinage totalled 13,560,532 pieces. It would be the last time Soho struck money for the East India Company. But it would emphatically *not* be the last time Soho struck money for the East Indies.

Between 1831 and 1847, the Boulton mint would strike many millions of keping tokens for Singapore. But it would first turn its attentions to a final

One of Soho's Argentine tenth-reals, recycled into a local product; the crossed sprays of the wreath on the original may be clearly seen at the top of the new coin. (National Numismatic Collection, Smithsonian Institution)

coinage much closer to home: in the summer of 1830, it shipped its first coins to Guernsey, one of the Channel Islands.

The history of Guernsey, Jersey, Sark, and the other members of the group has always been conditioned by their possession by England but their proximity to France. So it was that, when Daniel de Lisle Brock, Bailiff and Chief Magistrate of the Isle of Guernsey requested a coinage on 10 November 1829, he was thinking of something which would closely resemble British coinage but simultaneously adhere to local, French-steeped tradition.

Thus was born a Soho copper coinage of three denominations, two of them reasonably close to pieces in use in Great Britain; but the coins would have odd-sounding names. The coinage unit would be the double (from an old French coin called the double tournois). An eight-double piece would be the rough equivalent of the English penny, for twenty-two of these coins would equal a pound of copper. And the four-double coin would roughly correspond to the ordinary halfpenny, being struck at forty-five to the pound. In time there would be a two-double piece, resembling a farthing; but it would only appear in 1858, and Boulton, Watt would have no role in its creation. At the bottom of the scale would be a one-double coin, a tiny piece struck at 184 to the pound. There was no comparable coin in Great Britain; perhaps for that reason, this was the piece which Soho was first asked to strike.

Guernsey, 8 doubles, 1834. (National Numismatic Collection, Smithsonian Institution)

It sent a single order in mid-July 1830, following it with the more popular, larger denominations. Its first fours were sent in early November 1830,[20] succeeded by remittances in 1831, 1836, 1837, and 1839; all bore the date 1830. Its first eight-double pieces did not see shipment until September 1834 (and all of Soho's strikings would bear that date). Later remittances took place at the same time as the fours. In all, Soho sent 1,648,640 doubles, 652,200 four-doubles, and 221,760 eights, a total of 2,522,600 coins.

For Singapore, Soho created copper tokens. These were mostly kepings, and they were incredibly light pieces, made for unofficial mercantile use in this dynamic new settlement and its surrounding areas. There was little attempt in the Matthew Boulton Papers to describe the devices placed on these coppers, and even the dates placed on them tended to go unrecorded. I can only say that the first of these tokens were created for a Scotsman named John Colville and were sent from Soho on 23 July 1831; and between then and late September 1847, there would be no fewer than sixteen orders filled for a number of different individuals or houses, a total number of 45,286,990 kepings. When we add the 6,648,320 double-kepings sent by the beginning of 1835, we reach a total for the Singapore coinage of 51,935,310 pieces.

To anyone investigating the later coining activities of Boulton, Watt & Company, an artistic decline becomes apparent after the elder Boulton's death in 1809. The coinages became less beautiful, more predictable, far more purely utilitarian. But this is not to say that they were not solid, useful articles for commerce: Soho always gave good value for money, and the next coinage with which it was involved is a case in point.

This was the first copper coinage for Chile, which came the firm's way through the ministrations of Alexander Caldcleugh, the British Consul General at Valparaíso. Chilean authorities approached this functionary for a British-made coinage of centavos and their halves in May 1835; Caldcleugh notified his associates at home, and they in turn wrote to Boulton, Watt & Company.

Original drawing for the Chilean centavo, and one of the Soho coins it inspired. (Drawing courtesy Birmingham City Archives, Birmingham Central Library; coin from National Numismatic Collection, Smithsonian Institution)

The result was a fairly extensive coinage, sent sporadically between January and September 1836. A drawing of the centavo has survived in the Matthew Boulton Papers, sent from Chile with Caldcleugh's letter; it is reproduced here and suggests that the idea for a pedestrian design for once originated elsewhere than at Soho. In all, some 2,559,838 half-centavos and 1,279,666 centavos were sent, for a total production for circulation of 3,839,504 coins. A small, unspecified number of proofs was also struck at the beginning of 1836.

The coins proved popular in Chile, and they would be copied by local authorities in the years to come. The latter would be able to do so because Soho sent along a pair of master dies for each of the two denominations: in a very minor way, here is another example of Boulton, Watt's role in the spread of a modern coining technology.

I have recently published an article of the firm's activities in Canada, to which the reader is referred.[21] What I said there I would repeat here: the tokens which Boulton, Watt & Company produced for four banks in Lower Canada and the series of quasi-official coins for the Province of New Brunswick represented a final flowering of artistry and excellence at the venerable firm, which would be out of business within a few years of the final shipment. Here, we are primarily concerned with the numbers of tokens and coins struck.

In 1838, Soho carried out orders of tokens for four Lower Canada banks, the Bank of Montreal, the City Bank, the Quebec Bank, and the Banque du Peuple. Halfpenny and penny tokens dated 1837 were struck, handsome pieces with the figure of a *habitant* (which some said was meant to represent Louis Joseph Papineau, leader of a recently-failed rebellion in Quebec; this rumour was unfounded) on the obverse, the arms of Montreal on the reverse, with the name of the issuing bank on a ribbon, put there in intaglio. The Bank of Montreal received the largest number of tokens, followed in order by the City Bank, the Quebec Bank, and the Banque du Peuple. The Bank of Montreal requested and received additional orders dated 1842 and 1844, a rendition of the bank building now being substituted for the offending habitant. This was the only one of the four banks to issue tokens dated other than 1837. Soho's production, then, stood as follows:

Year	Bank	Pence	Halfpence
1837	Bank of Montreal	154,560	309,120
	Quebec Bank	356,160	712,320
	Banque du Peuple	154,560	309,120
	City Bank	612,864	1,223,040
1842	Bank of Montreal	388,020	750,840
1844	Bank of Montreal	–	2,644,992

Total Lower Canada Bank tokens, 7,615,596

If we add the coins ordered for New Brunswick in January 1843 and sent out two months later (498,576 pence, struck at twenty-six to the pound, and 710,112 halfpence, struck at fifty-two), we reach a total for Canadian coins and tokens of 8,824,284 pieces. This figure is impressive, both in terms of size and in terms of artistic quality – and as a suggestion, in the case of the New Brunswick coinage, that Boulton, Watt & Company could still move very quickly and effectively when it so desired.

Boulton, Watt's Canadian adventure: penny tokens for the Bank of Montreal (1842) and the Province of New Brunswick (1843). (National Numismatic Collection, Smithsonian Institution)

But the desire had largely left it by this time: the remainder of the 1840s saw an unhappy situation at the world's first industrialized mint, as the grandson of the founder gradually came to the conclusion that he would prefer a life of leisure to a life of coining, and a devoted body of retainers attempted to drum up business to persuade him otherwise. The outcome was inevitable, and it would not be long in coming. But before the demise of the firm, there would be one final, curious episode.

Just as Matthew Boulton was building the first Soho Mint, British settlement of Australia was getting under way. And immediately prior to the closing of the doors at the third Soho Mint, an enterprising firm of 'family grocers', Annand Smith & Company of Melbourne (which had only been founded in 1835, decades after Soho's palmy days) wrote home for an issue of penny tokens. Thomas Elwell & Sons of Wolverhampton passed the order on to Boulton, Watt. The latter was caught off-guard, for it had already been determined to wind up the concern. But someone at the mint was still game: a simple obverse die was hastily sunk, married to a penny die left over from the regal copper issues made some forty years before – and some 15,400 penny tokens were remitted to Messrs Elwell on 23 May 1849. The Elwells liked what they received, and they placed two more orders of similar size, which were filled and sent off on 12 October 1849 and 15 January 1850. In all, some 45,503 tokens for Annand Smith & Company were created, the last work Soho ever did.

It is difficult to conceive of the conditions under which those final pieces must have been struck: a lonely press running in one corner of the mint, while workmen were busily dismantling machinery in another. But the Annand Smith tokens enjoyed a linear descent from and a consistency with all that had gone before, from the first, halting efforts of the first Matthew Boulton. Like those distant predecessors, they were useful. They gave good value. And they eased and made possible the transition into the industrial age.

SOURCES

The writing of this chapter involved work with virtually everything pertaining to coining in the Matthew Boulton Papers – and use of a goodly number of other sources besides. A few general guidelines may be of help to the reader.

The actual records of coinage output may usually be found in a broken sequence of Mint Books, starting with MBP29 and ending with MBP81. The

End of the line: the Annand Smith & Company penny token, 1849. (National Numismatic Collection, Smithsonian Institution)

beginnings of Matthew Boulton's coining venture – the pieces for Sumatra, Cronebane, Roe & Company, and the earliest Parys Mine tokens form the largest exception to this rule. For these early coinages, resort must be made to a series of letter books from the late 1780s and early 1790s (particularly MBP148, 149, 150, and 151, Letter Books O–R) Later letter books may be of help for later coinages – for example, MBP86, covering the years 1840–1845, for the coinage of New Brunswick.

Boxes pertaining to individuals were also essential to the creation of this chapter – especially MBP272, 295, 354–6, 367, and 368, the respective correspondence boxes of the Banks family, William D. Brown, James Watt, Jr., the Wilkinson family, and Thomas Williams.

A goodly percentage of the Matthew Boulton Papers reposes in boxes dealing with specific countries or groups of countries, and frequent recourse was also had to these sources in the preparation of this chapter. MBP406 (British Coinage) is a prime example; but MBP405 (Brazil, Haiti, Argentine, USA and San Salvador mints) holds many important documents, as does MBP411 (East India Company coinage).

I have also utilized more modern materials in the preparation of this section. The contributions of Richard Margolis, David Vice, and Brian Gould have already been mentioned, but a privately-published, two-part monograph on the Manx coinage also deserves citation. John F. Rainey brought it to my attention some years ago, 'The Atholl Papers – Currency of the Isle of Man' (1986), by Alan E. Kelly, and I found it very useful in fleshing out the Manx story.

NOTES

1 MBP148, [Private] Letter Book O: Matthew Boulton to John Motteux, 19 April 1787. Anyone interested in a published perusal of surviving correspondence concerning Boulton's maiden attempt to coin should consult B. M. Gould, 'Matthew Boulton's East India Mint in London, 1786–88', *Seaby's Coin and Medal Bulletin* 612 (August 1969), pp. 270–7.
2 It is more likely to have been finished in April or May 1788.
3 MBP145, Letter Book L: Matthew Boulton to Thomas Williams, 3 July 1788.
4 MBP261, Letter Box W2: Matthew Boulton to Roe & Company, 30 May 1789.
5 MBP385, 'A.W.' box: Matthew Boulton to James Watt, 6 July 1789.
6 While peak productivity at Parys was in decline by the end of the 1780s, Thomas Williams had many other sources of copper supply, and he continued to be a major irritant to Matthew Boulton's activities until his death in 1802.
7 MBP150, [Private] Letter Book Q: Matthew Boulton to John Motteux, 11 December 1791.
8 MBP230, Letter Box E1: Daniel Eccleston to Matthew Robinson Boulton, 16 August 1804.
9 MBP227, Letter Box C3: George Cotton to Matthew Boulton, 20 June 1795.
10 MBP411, East India Company coinage: Matthew Boulton to Robert Wissett, 18 February 1796; spelling in original.
11 MBP243, Letter Box L2: Lord Liverpool to Matthew Boulton, 3 March 1797.
12 MBP362, Weston, Ambrose, 1792–99 (box 1): Matthew Boulton to Ambrose Weston, 2 December 1799.
13 It was activity such as this which led Boulton to a logical if regrettable decision in late May 1802: henceforth, visitors would be banned from the premises of Soho Mint.
14 Boulton moved somewhat *too* quickly. While the coins should have been denominated by the Arabic equivalents of '1', '2', and '3', his designer inadvertently placed the same figure, '3', on all three denominations! The East India Company allowed the slip to stand, for Sumatra's need was great.
15 MBP46, Mint Day Book, 1801–1805, p 212.
16 This raises a minor mystery: Hancock received payment for *a* die (and the fee sounds correct for the work involved). But *four* distinct varieties of the Charleville token exist. Most of

the variations, however, occur on the reverse, which might have been created by someone else, possibly John Phillp. And the differences between the two obverse dies are such that they could be explained by minor recutting of a single die. We should probably take this entry (from MBP46, p. 121, under date of 22 January 1803) literally: Hancock engraved *a* die, an obverse die.

17 There has long been a lively debate on whether Boulton's dollars for the Banks of England and Ireland show traces of the original coins through deliberate action or unavoidable limitation. Boulton made a virtue of these traces, for they showed the public that there was a good old coin underneath the new. As he appears to have come up with this argument *before* experience had taught him its inevitability, I shall give him the benefit of the doubt. And he probably could have completed the obliteration with a second strike (using blank dies for the first), had there been time. But the authorities recognized a crisis when they saw one, and Boulton was forced to coin in a hurry.

18 This story had a happy ending. The Lords relented on the following day, and Boulton was allowed to coin pence prior to halfpence.

19 Just how it was coined remains a mystery. Boulton's new Soho Mint would not be operable by steam for several years – although it would have been possible to work its presses by hand, especially if the coinage being created was not too demanding. The Argentine décimos were relatively small, and it would not have been an inhuman task to create four million of them on manually-operated presses over a period of several months.

20 All of the one-double and the first four-double coins must have been struck by hand; Soho's presses were only connected to their steam engine in July 1831.

21 'Boulton, Watt and the Canadian Adventure', in *Canada* (Proceedings of the Eighth Coinage of the Americas Conference, New York, 7 November 1992 [New York, 1994]), pp. 37–48.

AFTERWORD:

Soho's Legacy

As I write, my museum is actively considering an exhibit on modern money – credit cards, debit cards, electronic banking, innovative coins and notes. Central to this exhibit will be the question of *trust* – our faith that the money we employ is safe, is as immutable as these uncertain times permit. It seems appropriate to linger for a moment on the fortunes of one of the pioneers in modern coinage, and the modern mint. For Matthew Boulton and those who worked with and after him were also dealing, at least in part, with the problem of public trust in the money supply. Their responses to the problem have shaped the contents of this book.

Those responses were enunciated in two phases. During the first, Soho would provide the public with a new type of money, a coin with a distinctive appearance. This coin would be struck in such a way as to be instantly recognizable as a product which only Soho made, which only it *could* make. And that led to the second phase: the Boultons would sell their skills and secrets to legitimate coiners at home and abroad, so that the manufacture of the new money could be extended, while control over it could remain as tight as before. In the founder's eyes, the two-step process, new coins, from new mints, would redress and negate the evils of counterfeiting, save many from the gallows – and prove to the world that the skill and enterprise which had made Birmingham the centre of forgery could be turned to better uses, could eradicate the problems once created.

The timing of Matthew Boulton and his people could scarcely have been better, for the Industrial Revolution was creating the largest wage economy yet seen, with the greatest need for trustworthy, low-denomination coins yet seen. He and his partner Watt were deeply involved with the new economic and technological movement and therefore shared a measure of responsibility for the payment problem it created. Boulton's triumph was to turn the problem into a solution: he would build a money factory, and it would supply the wages needed by the other factories now springing up. The concept of using a motive force to solve the very problem it engendered strikes me as one of the most elegant ideas in the entire history of technology.

But a larger question must be posed. In the long run, how successful was Soho? What were its enduring accomplishments? The answer varies from object to object, and from place to place.

We can certainly say that Soho was successful in introducing a new, universally-accepted definition of the modern coin. It must be mass-produced. It must feature shallow relief, unvarying diameter, perfect roundness, absolutely flat edges. Each coin must be identical with every other coin. We cannot conceive of any other characteristics for our modern coins; and for that we must thank Matthew Boulton. His methods of manufacture would eventually fall from favour, but his idea of the correct nature of the coin is likely to be with us until the end of coinage itself.

We can add that Boulton solved his most immediate problem, the provision of large numbers of safe coins to his audience, whether in England or in India. Those who came after him successfully met this same, most basic criterion of a coiner – the satisfaction of a monetary demand. But we also remember that Soho approached moneying in two phases – first providing acceptable coins, then providing acceptable mints. How successful was the firm in this second phase?

We must say that it was rather less successful; and if we theorize that what Soho ultimately wanted was a purchaser who would follow its advice in all matters, do things its way forever (and gratefully render payment on time) – then we must say that it was a failure everywhere.

Matthew Boulton would surely observe that that judgement was too harsh, that success in his day was no more absolute than it is in ours. And he would have a point, of course; but a glance at the record raises questions nonetheless.

The firm's most unqualified success abroad was probably the Danish mint, which was constructed under trying circumstances but came on line in a timely fashion and did what its makers intended, to the satisfaction of the customer. But the customer in question took a decade to render payment.

Another customer used its new mint to undercut the Boulton coining operation. This was the Royal Mint, and what the Boultons saw as official perfidy poisoned relations between Britain's public and private coiner for decades.

In Russia, a Boulton mint was misused – at least in the eyes of the man who sent it to St Petersburg. He thought it would serve to strike copper coinage for Russia's toiling millions. But the Tsar thought it would serve to proclaim his modernity; the toiling millions would receive whatever copper coinage he chose to supply, and be grateful for it.

In Brazil, a mint was lost.

In the United States, opportunities were lost.

And in Mexico and India, the cutting edge of industrial technology was blunted by contact with reality; the blade must be rehoned, and it would assume a slightly different shape in the process.

So success was incomplete. But with that said, the Soho story still fills me with amazement. The vision and persistence of Matthew Boulton, who dragged moneying into the modern age by sheer force of will; the dedication and enterprise of those craftsmen he and his son sent to distant places, entrusted with creating copies of the new industrial dispensation (men who might not know how to write proper English but were among the most gifted representatives of the new industrial age); images and sounds: of wooden ships and iron machinery, of bright new coins, coming from the presses (recompense for labour and its cause); all this remains with me, all stands as the Soho legacy.

And a splendid legacy it is.

Index
